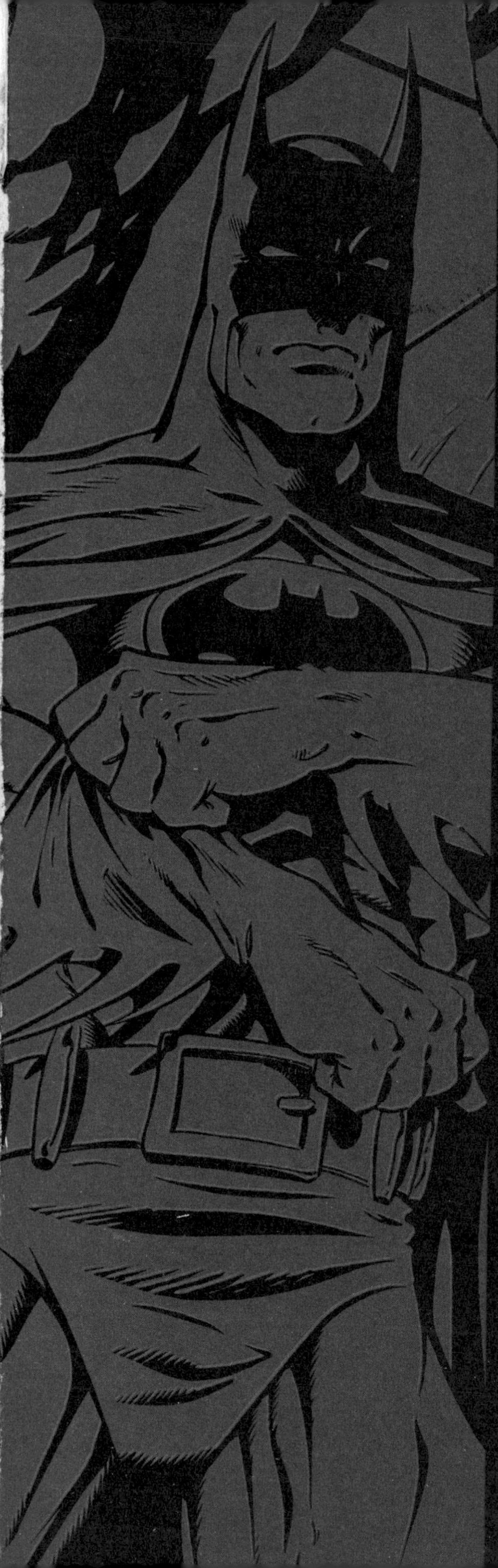

BATMAN
KNIGHTFALL
PART THREE:
KNIGHTSEND

BATMAN

KNIGHTFALL

PART THREE: KNIGHTSEND

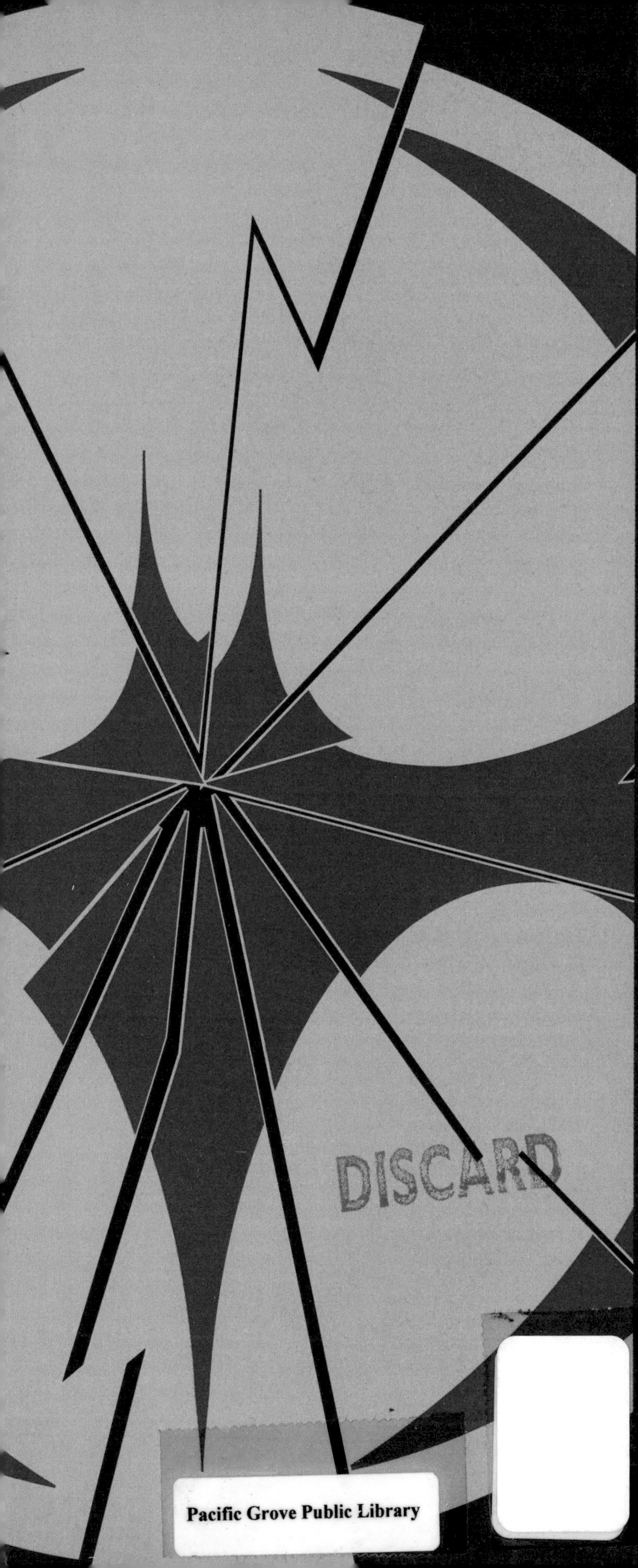

CHUCK DIXON
ALAN GRANT
JO DUFFY
DOUG MOENCH
DENNIS O'NEIL
WRITERS

GRAHAM NOLAN
BRET BLEVINS
MIKE MANLEY
TOM GRUMMETT
RON WAGNER
JIM BALENT
BARRY KITSON
PENCILLERS

SCOTT HANNA
RAY KRYSSING
DICK GIORDANO
BOB SMITH
RON McCAIN
RICK BURCHETT
JOSEF RUBINSTEIN
BRET BLEVINS
INKERS

ADRIENNE ROY
DIGITAL CHAMELEON
BUZZ SETZER
COLORISTS

KEN BRUZENAK
TODD KLEIN
JOHN COSTANZA
WILLIE SCHUBERT
ALBERT DeGUZMAN
BOB PINAHA
LETTERERS

BATMAN CREATED BY
BOB KANE

BATMAN: KNIGHTFALL PART THREE: KNIGHTSEND
Published by DC Comics. Cover and design pages © 2000.
Compilation copyright © 1995 DC Comics. All Rights Reserved.
Originally published in single magazine form as BATMAN 509-510,
BATMAN: SHADOW OF THE BAT 29-30, DETECTIVE COMICS 676-677,
BATMAN: LEGENDS OF THE DARK KNIGHT 62-63 and CATWOMAN 12.
Copyright © 1994 DC Comics. All Rights Reserved. All characters, the
distinctive likenesses thereof and related elements featured in this
publication are trademarks of DC Comics. The stories, characters,
and incidents featured in this publication are entirely fictional.
DC Comics does not read or accept unsolicited submissions of ideas,
stories or artwork.

DC Comics, 1700 Broadway, New York, NY 10019
A Warner Bros. Entertainment Company
Printed in Canada. Fifth Printing.
ISBN: 1-56389-191-3.
Cover illustration by Mike Deodato.
Cover color by Lee Loughridge.
Publication design by Louis Prandi.

The Story So Far...

After a mass breakout at Arkham Asylum, Batman was forced to confront nearly every one of Gotham City's major villains, from the Joker to Poison Ivy. One by one, he battled them all before ultimately facing the mastermind who engineered their escape — a mysterious man-mountain named Bane.

Battered and exhausted from fighting a seemingly endless string of his toughest foes, Batman was no match for the Venom-enhanced Bane. After a brief but bloody battle within the very walls of Wayne Manor, Bane did the unthinkable — breaking the back of the Darknight Detective. But Bruce Wayne's campaign against crime and terror was not abated by his injury. He summoned a new hero to fill his boots — Jean Paul Valley, known to the world as Azrael. A brilliant student who had been programmed by the mysterious Order of St. Dumas to become an unstoppable assassin, Valley struggled to find his own identity as a hero. As the new Batman, however, he returned to the unrestrained vehemence of his past. And while Bruce Wayne painstakingly battled the effects of his injuries to reach his former state of physical prowess, Valley descended into an abyss of madness and violence.

Now, after several months of recuperation, Bruce Wayne stands ready to reclaim the mantle of the Bat.

Only one man stands in his way...

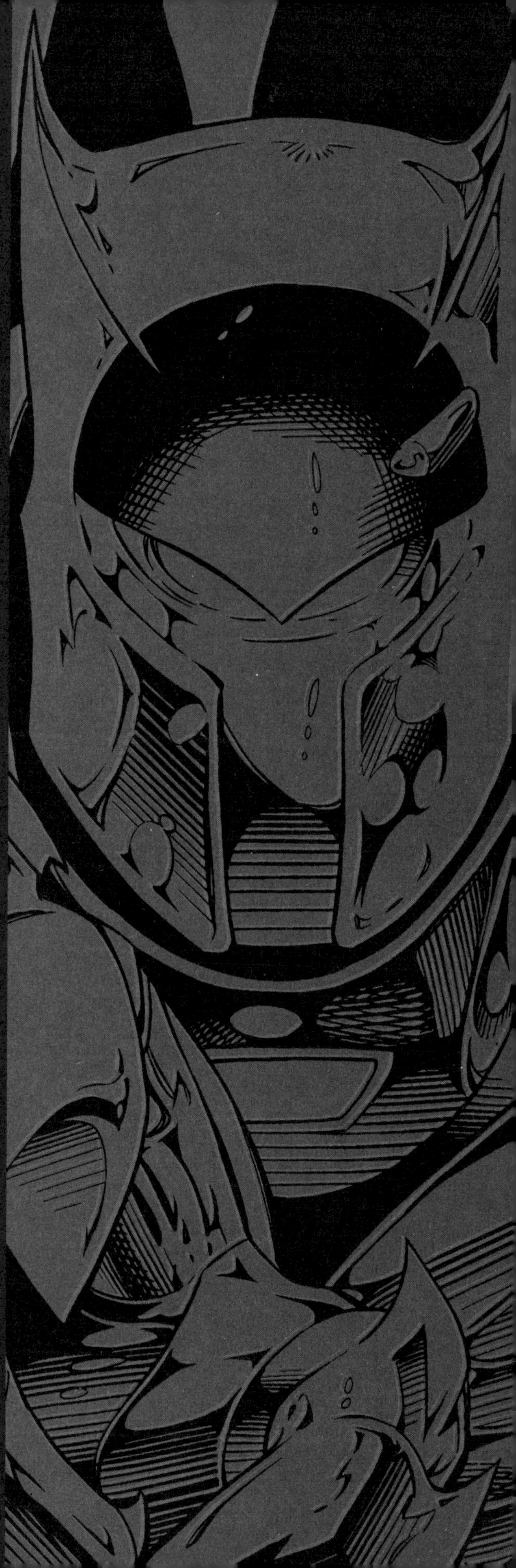

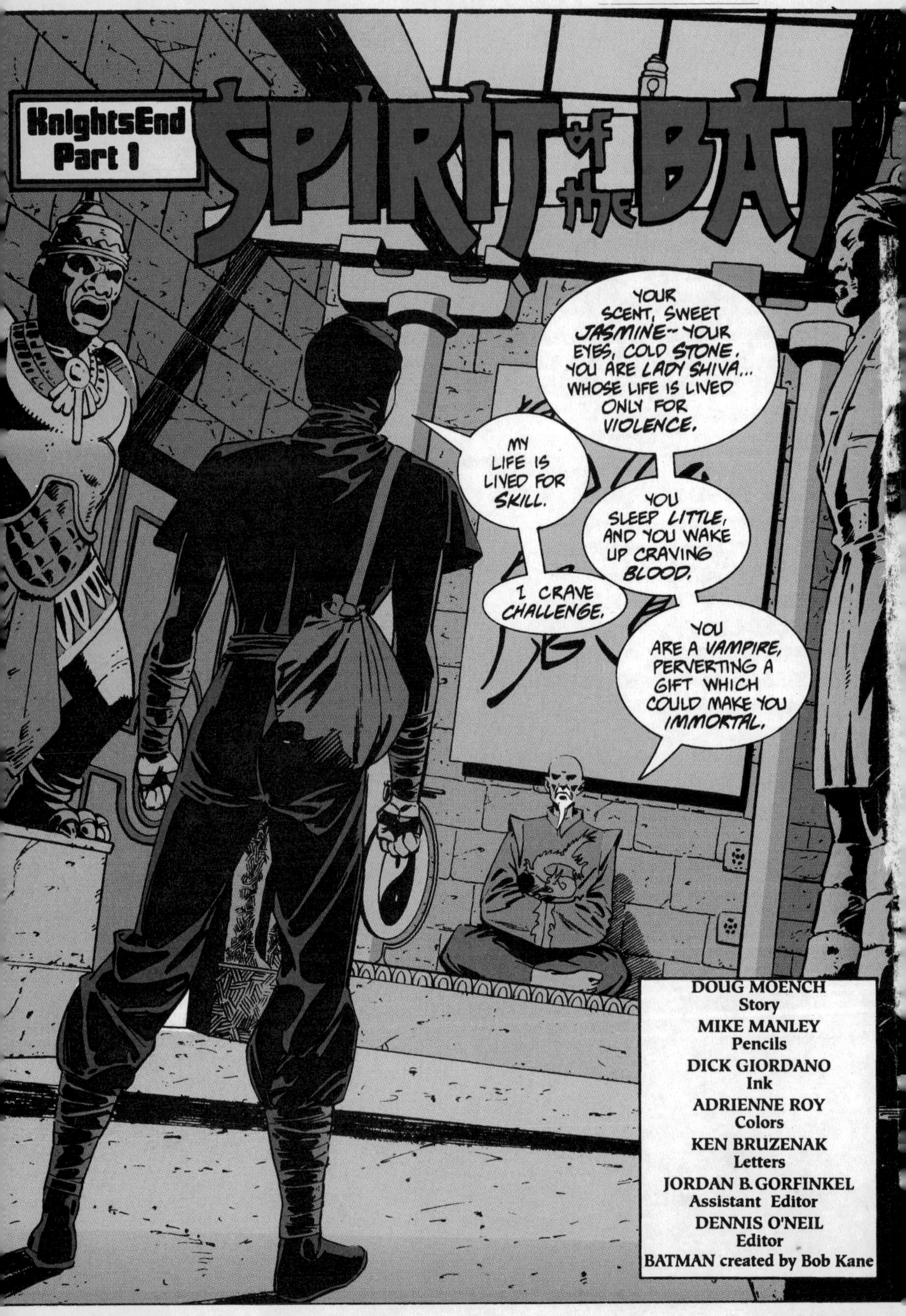
KnightsEnd
Part 1
SPIRIT of the BAT
YOUR SCENT, SWEET JASMINE-- YOUR EYES, COLD STONE. YOU ARE LADY SHIVA... WHOSE LIFE IS LIVED ONLY FOR VIOLENCE.
MY LIFE IS LIVED FOR SKILL.
YOU SLEEP LITTLE, AND YOU WAKE UP CRAVING BLOOD.
I CRAVE CHALLENGE.
YOU ARE A VAMPIRE, PERVERTING A GIFT WHICH COULD MAKE YOU IMMORTAL.
DOUG MOENCH Story
MIKE MANLEY Pencils
DICK GIORDANO Ink
ADRIENNE ROY Colors
KEN BRUZENAK Letters
JORDAN B.GORFINKEL Assistant Editor
DENNIS O'NEIL Editor
BATMAN created by Bob Kane

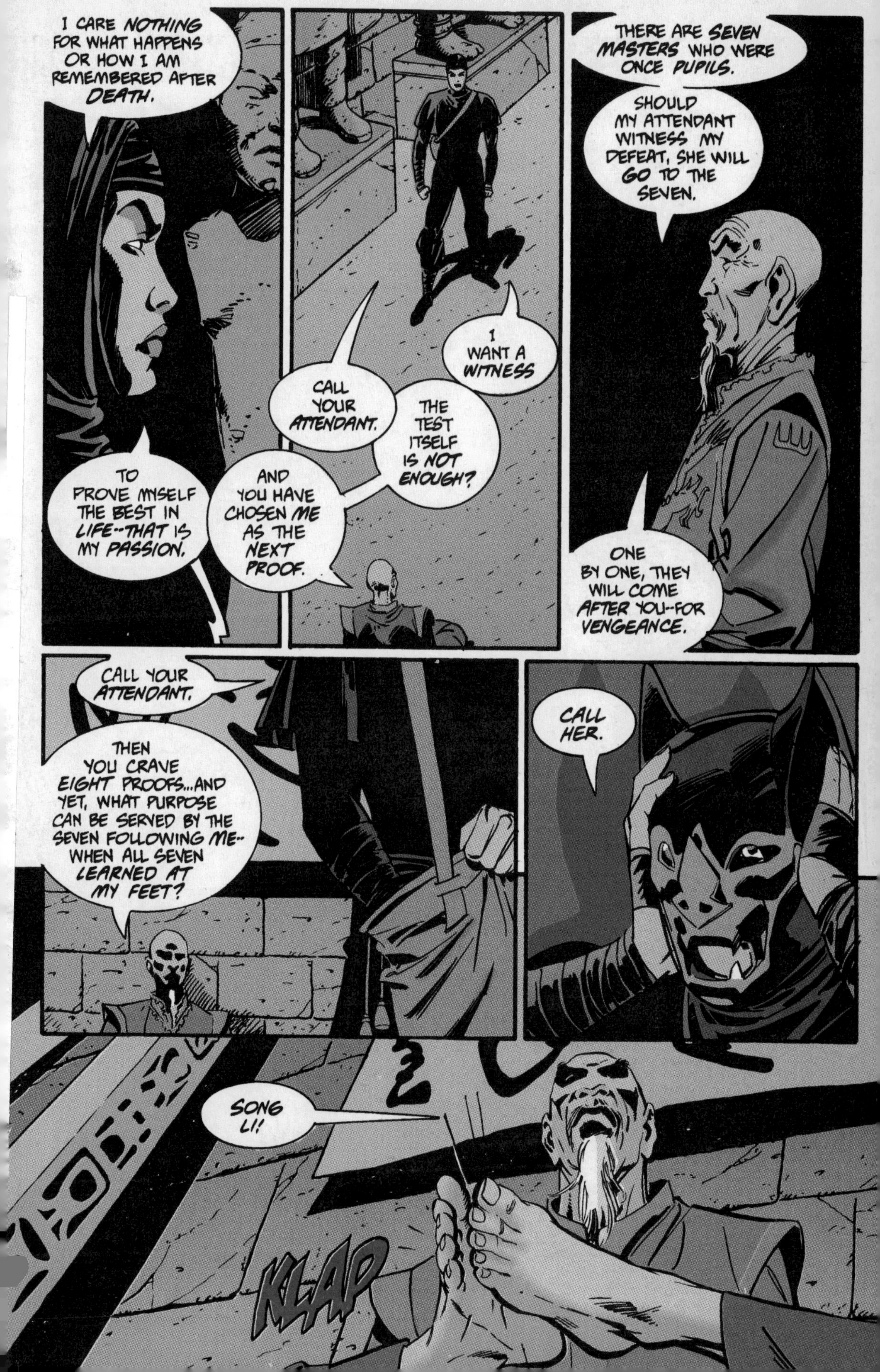
I CARE NOTHING FOR WHAT HAPPENS OR HOW I AM REMEMBERED AFTER DEATH.
TO PROVE MYSELF THE BEST IN LIFE--THAT IS MY PASSION.
I WANT A WITNESS
CALL YOUR ATTENDANT.
THE TEST ITSELF IS NOT ENOUGH?
AND YOU HAVE CHOSEN ME AS THE NEXT PROOF.
THERE ARE SEVEN MASTERS WHO WERE ONCE PUPILS.
SHOULD MY ATTENDANT WITNESS MY DEFEAT, SHE WILL GO TO THE SEVEN.
ONE BY ONE, THEY WILL COME AFTER YOU--FOR VENGEANCE.
CALL YOUR ATTENDANT.
THEN YOU CRAVE EIGHT PROOFS...AND YET, WHAT PURPOSE CAN BE SERVED BY THE SEVEN FOLLOWING ME-- WHEN ALL SEVEN LEARNED AT MY FEET?
CALL HER.
SONG LI!
KLAP

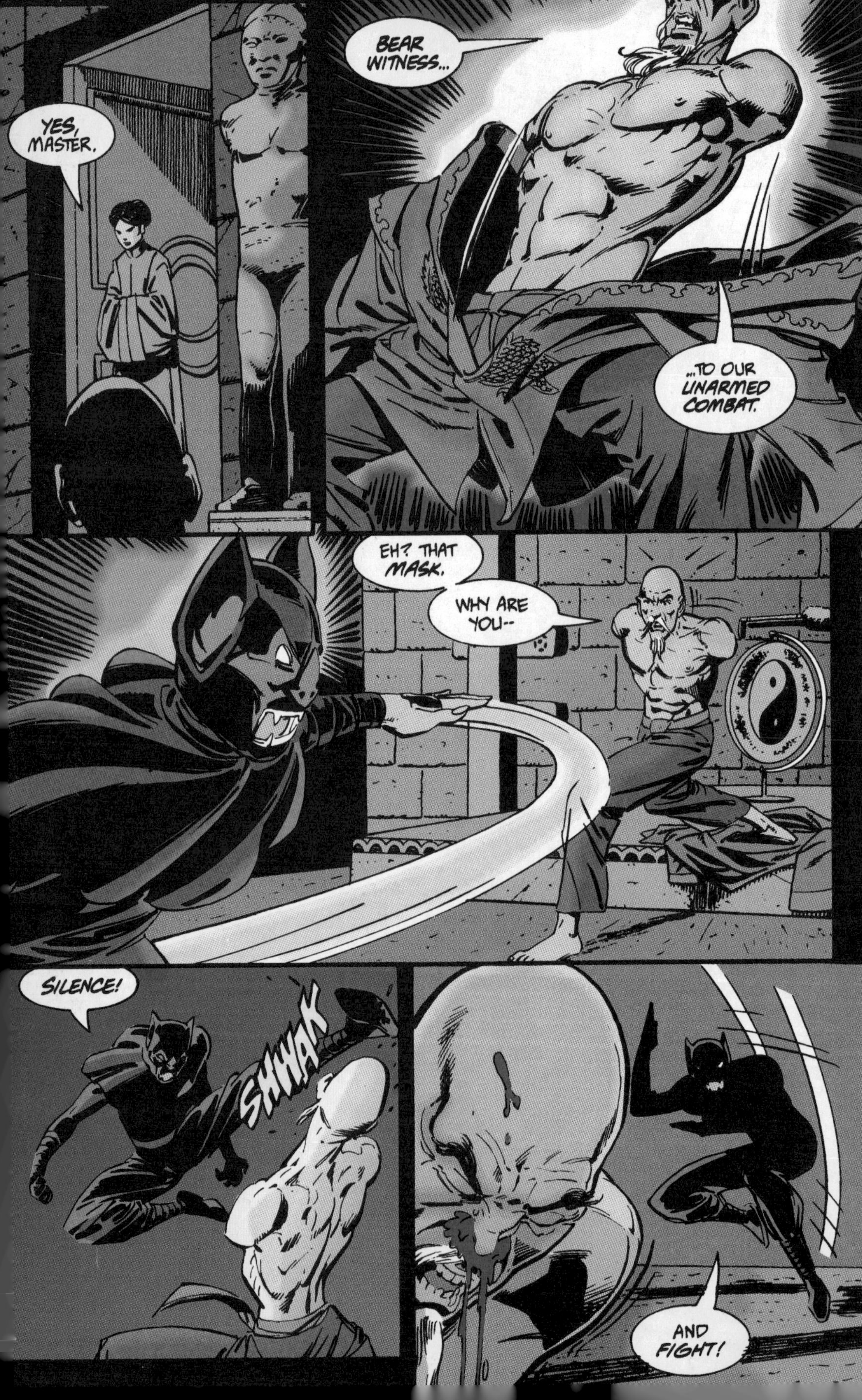
YES, MASTER.
BEAR WITNESS...
...TO OUR UNARMED COMBAT.
EH? THAT MASK.
WHY ARE YOU--
SILENCE!
SHWAK
AND FIGHT!

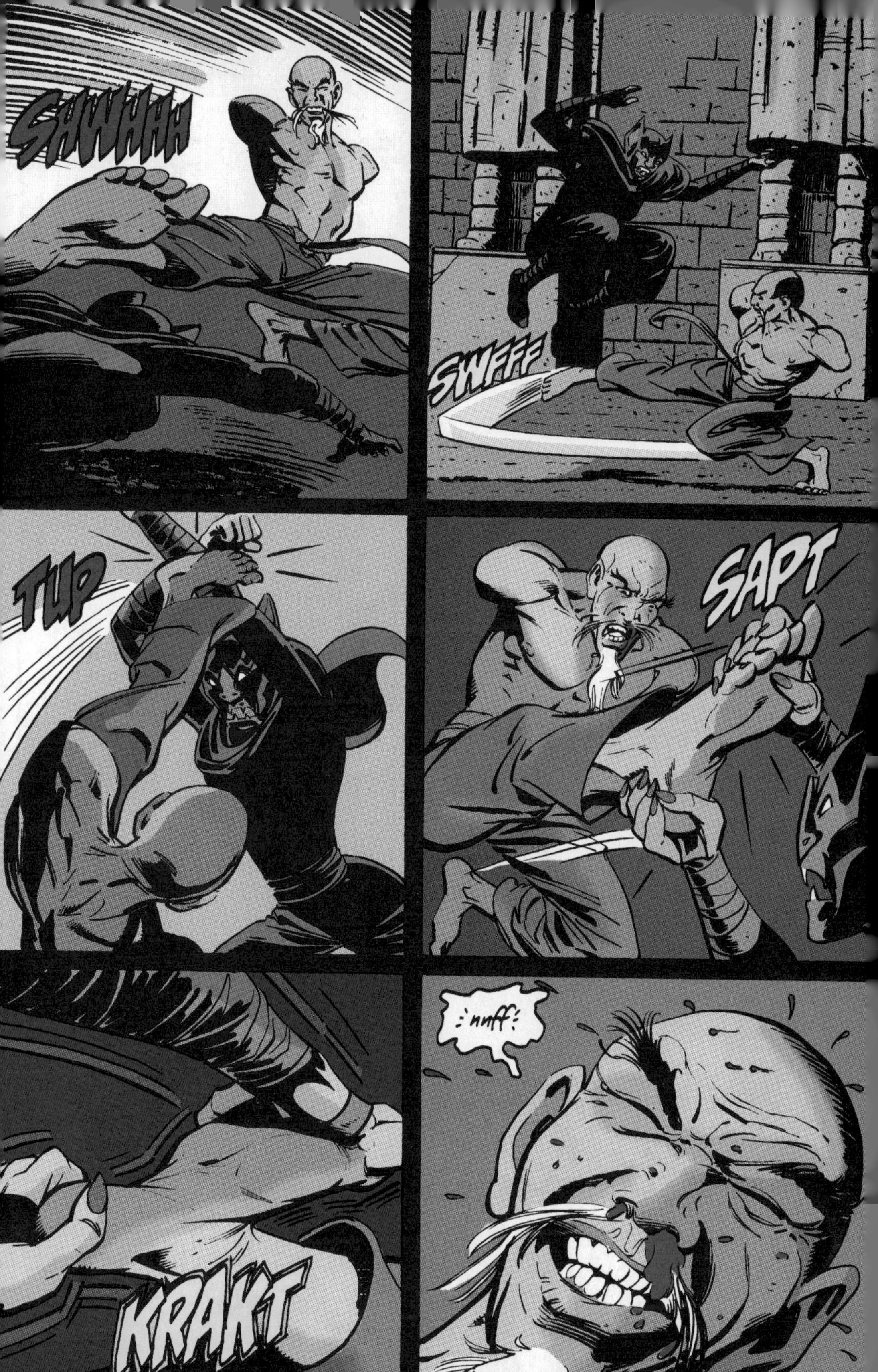
SHWHHH
SWFFF
TUP
SAPT
KRAKT
nnff

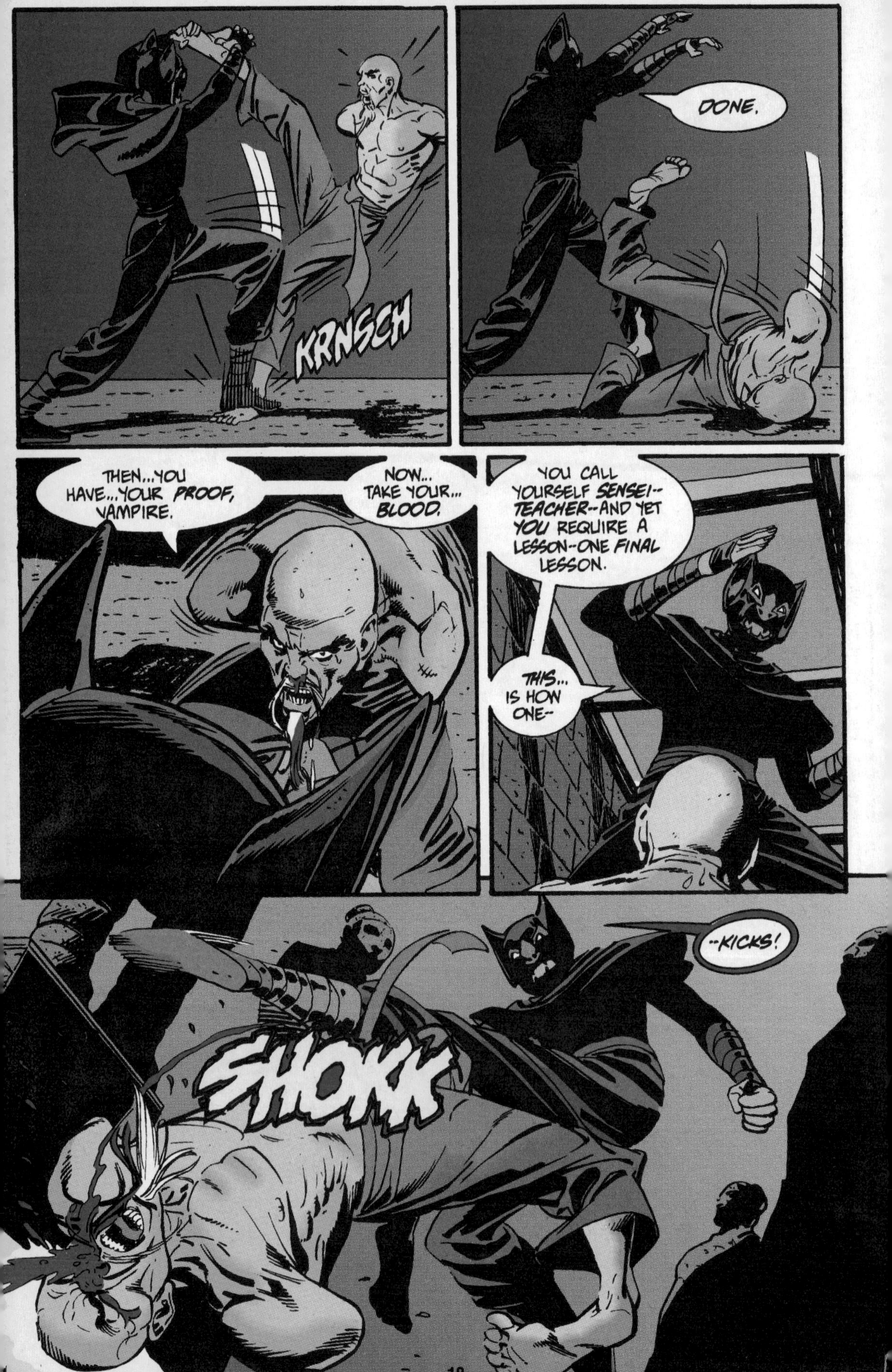
KRNSCH
DONE.
THEN...YOU HAVE...YOUR PROOF, VAMPIRE.
NOW... TAKE YOUR... BLOOD.
YOU CALL YOURSELF SENSEI--TEACHER--AND YET YOU REQUIRE A LESSON--ONE FINAL LESSON.
THIS... IS HOW ONE--
--KICKS!
SHOKK

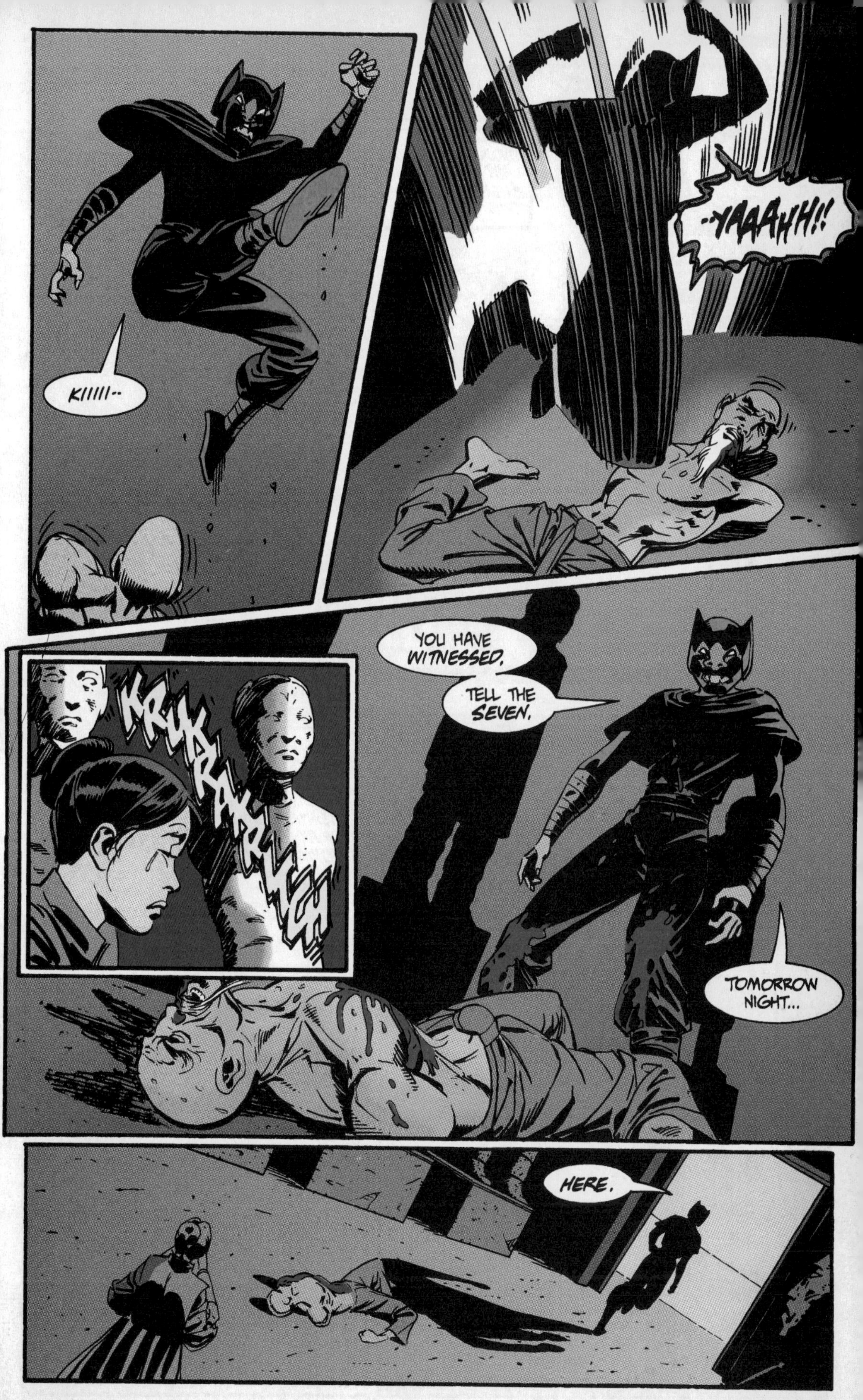
KIIIII--
-YAAAHH!!
KRUKRAKRUCH
YOU HAVE WITNESSED.
TELL THE SEVEN.
TOMORROW NIGHT...
HERE.

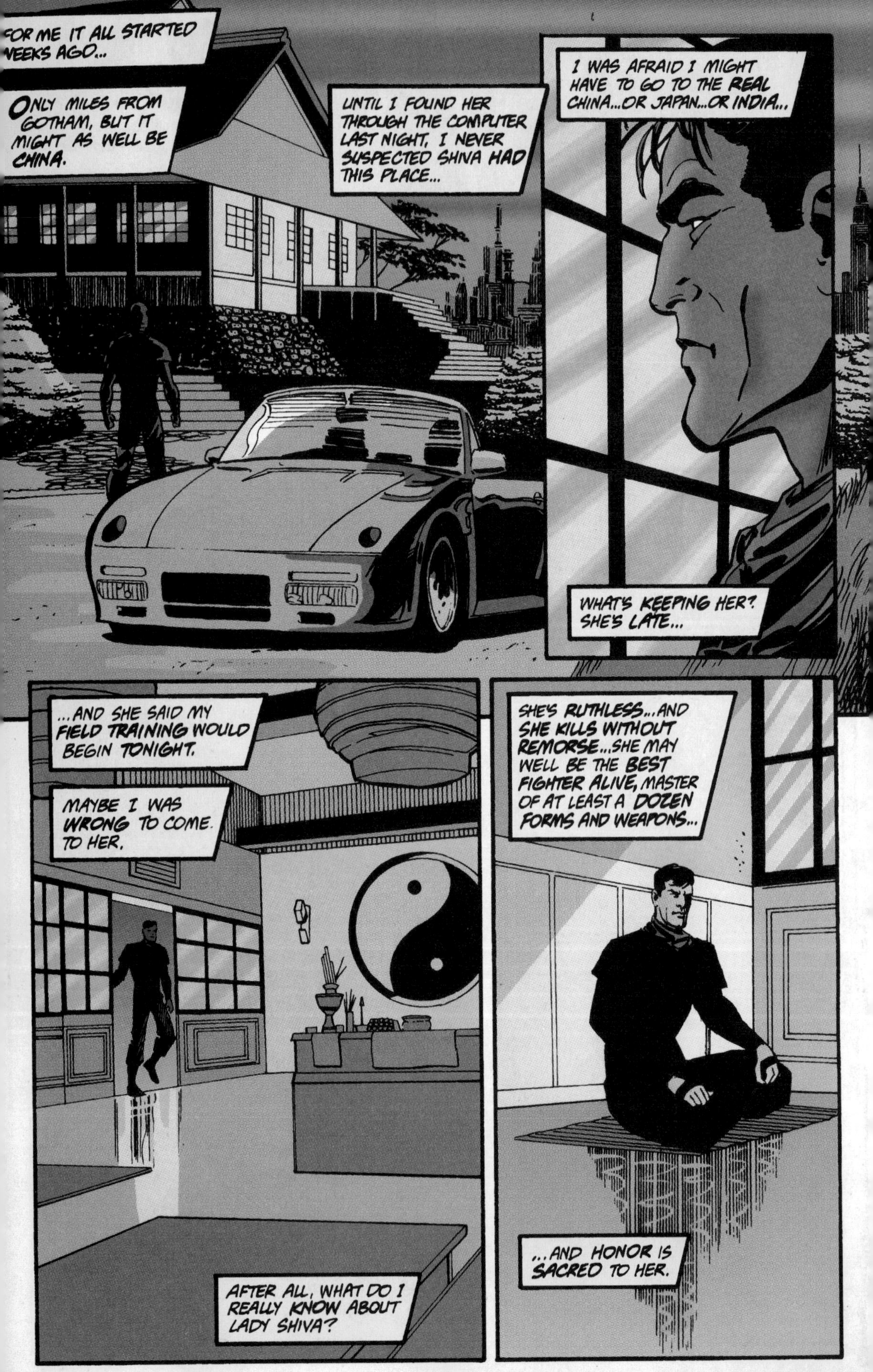
FOR ME IT ALL STARTED WEEKS AGO...
ONLY MILES FROM GOTHAM, BUT IT MIGHT AS WELL BE CHINA.
UNTIL I FOUND HER THROUGH THE COMPUTER LAST NIGHT, I NEVER SUSPECTED SHIVA HAD THIS PLACE...
I WAS AFRAID I MIGHT HAVE TO GO TO THE REAL CHINA...OR JAPAN...OR INDIA...
WHAT'S KEEPING HER? SHE'S LATE...
...AND SHE SAID MY FIELD TRAINING WOULD BEGIN TONIGHT.
MAYBE I WAS WRONG TO COME TO HER.
AFTER ALL, WHAT DO I REALLY KNOW ABOUT LADY SHIVA?
SHE'S RUTHLESS...AND SHE KILLS WITHOUT REMORSE...SHE MAY WELL BE THE BEST FIGHTER ALIVE, MASTER OF AT LEAST A DOZEN FORMS AND WEAPONS...
...AND HONOR IS SACRED TO HER.

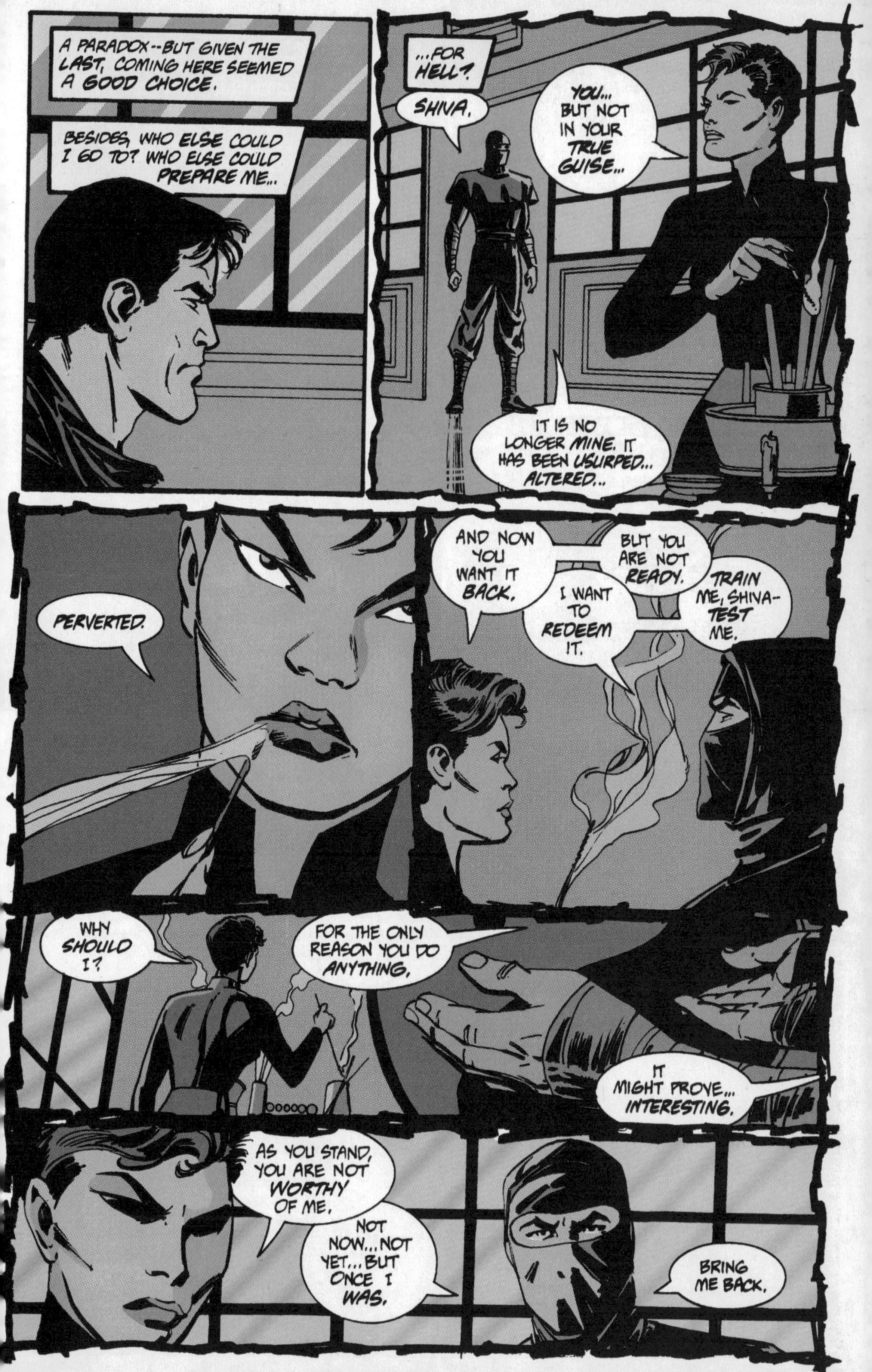
A PARADOX--BUT GIVEN THE LAST, COMING HERE SEEMED A GOOD CHOICE.
BESIDES, WHO ELSE COULD I GO TO? WHO ELSE COULD PREPARE ME...
...FOR HELL?
SHIVA.
YOU... BUT NOT IN YOUR TRUE GUISE...
IT IS NO LONGER MINE. IT HAS BEEN USURPED... ALTERED...
PERVERTED.
AND NOW YOU WANT IT BACK.
I WANT TO REDEEM IT.
BUT YOU ARE NOT READY.
TRAIN ME, SHIVA-- TEST ME.
WHY SHOULD I?
FOR THE ONLY REASON YOU DO ANYTHING.
IT MIGHT PROVE... INTERESTING.
AS YOU STAND, YOU ARE NOT WORTHY OF ME.
NOT NOW... NOT YET... BUT ONCE I WAS.
BRING ME BACK.

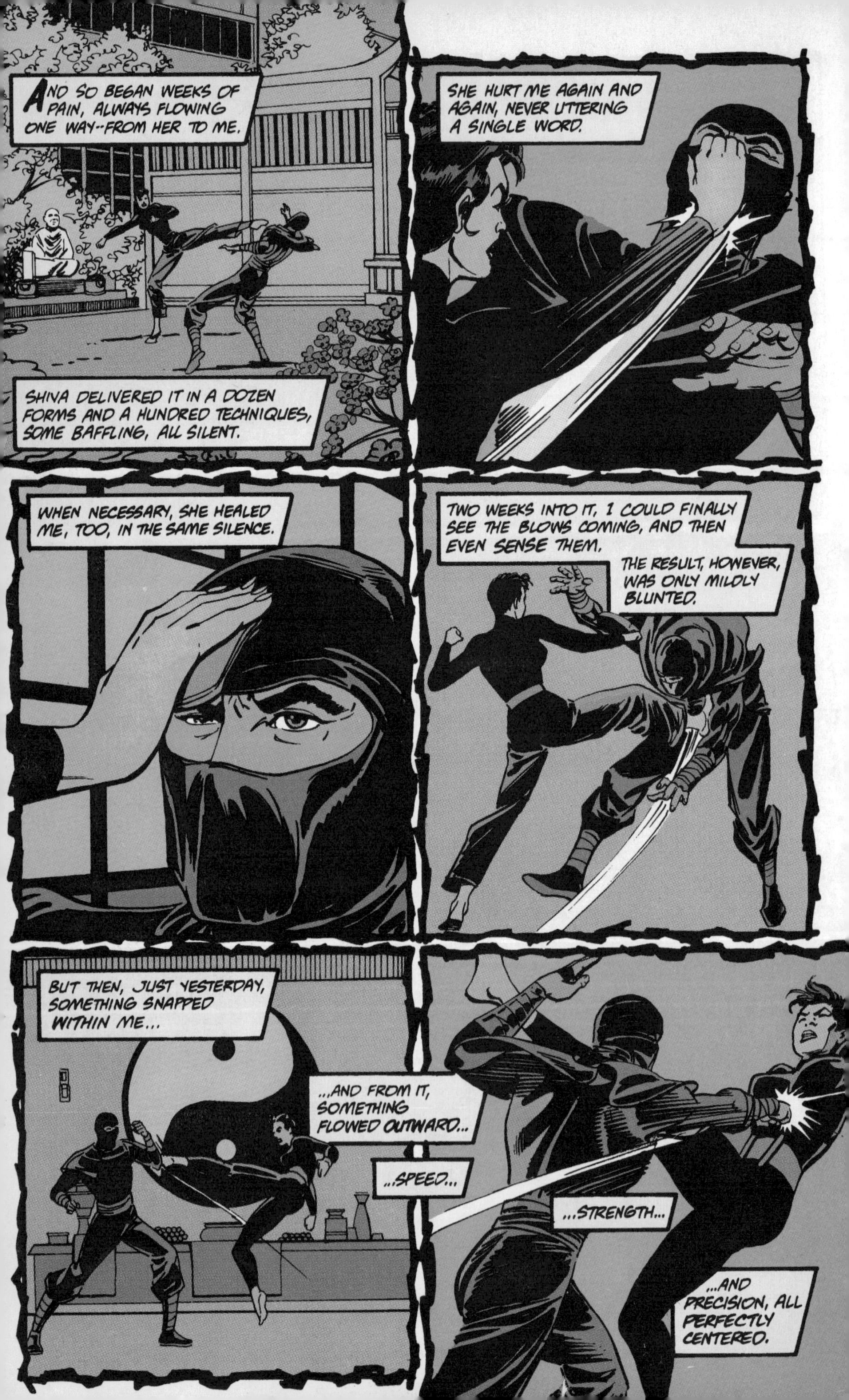
AND SO BEGAN WEEKS OF PAIN, ALWAYS FLOWING ONE WAY--FROM HER TO ME.
SHIVA DELIVERED IT IN A DOZEN FORMS AND A HUNDRED TECHNIQUES, SOME BAFFLING, ALL SILENT.
SHE HURT ME AGAIN AND AGAIN, NEVER UTTERING A SINGLE WORD.
WHEN NECESSARY, SHE HEALED ME, TOO, IN THE SAME SILENCE.
TWO WEEKS INTO IT, I COULD FINALLY SEE THE BLOWS COMING, AND THEN EVEN SENSE THEM.
THE RESULT, HOWEVER, WAS ONLY MILDLY BLUNTED.
BUT THEN, JUST YESTERDAY, SOMETHING SNAPPED WITHIN ME...
...AND FROM IT, SOMETHING FLOWED OUTWARD...
...SPEED...
...STRENGTH...
...AND PRECISION, ALL PERFECTLY CENTERED.

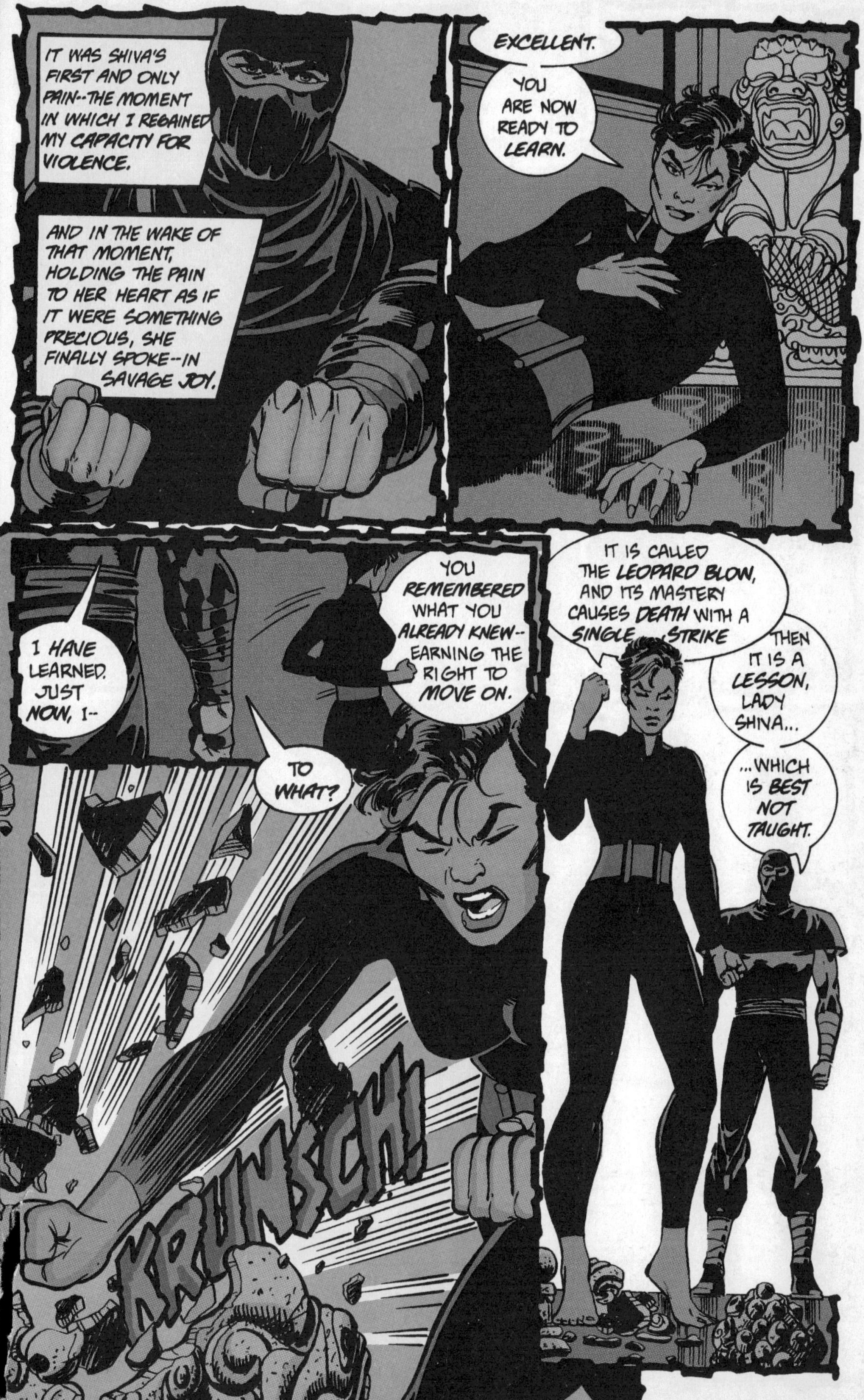
IT WAS SHIVA'S FIRST AND ONLY PAIN--THE MOMENT IN WHICH I REGAINED MY CAPACITY FOR VIOLENCE.
AND IN THE WAKE OF THAT MOMENT, HOLDING THE PAIN TO HER HEART AS IF IT WERE SOMETHING PRECIOUS, SHE FINALLY SPOKE--IN SAVAGE JOY.
EXCELLENT.
YOU ARE NOW READY TO LEARN.
I HAVE LEARNED. JUST NOW, I--
YOU REMEMBERED WHAT YOU ALREADY KNEW--EARNING THE RIGHT TO MOVE ON.
TO WHAT?
KRUNSCH!!
IT IS CALLED THE LEOPARD BLOW, AND ITS MASTERY CAUSES DEATH WITH A SINGLE... STRIKE
THEN IT IS A LESSON, LADY SHIVA...
...WHICH IS BEST NOT TAUGHT.

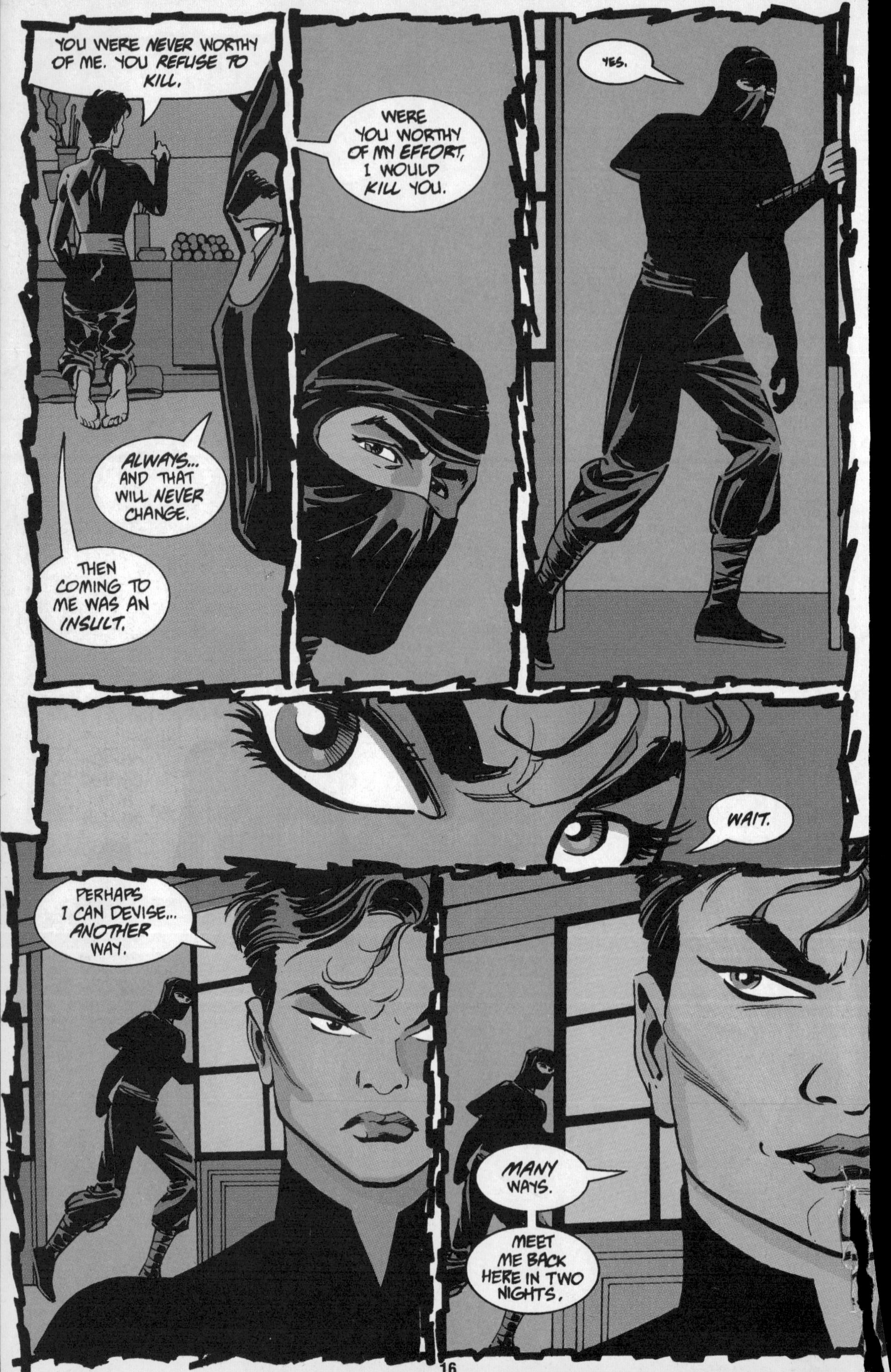
YOU WERE NEVER WORTHY OF ME. YOU REFUSE TO KILL.
ALWAYS... AND THAT WILL NEVER CHANGE.
THEN COMING TO ME WAS AN INSULT.
WERE YOU WORTHY OF MY EFFORT, I WOULD KILL YOU.
YES.
WAIT.
PERHAPS I CAN DEVISE... ANOTHER WAY.
MANY WAYS.
MEET ME BACK HERE IN TWO NIGHTS.

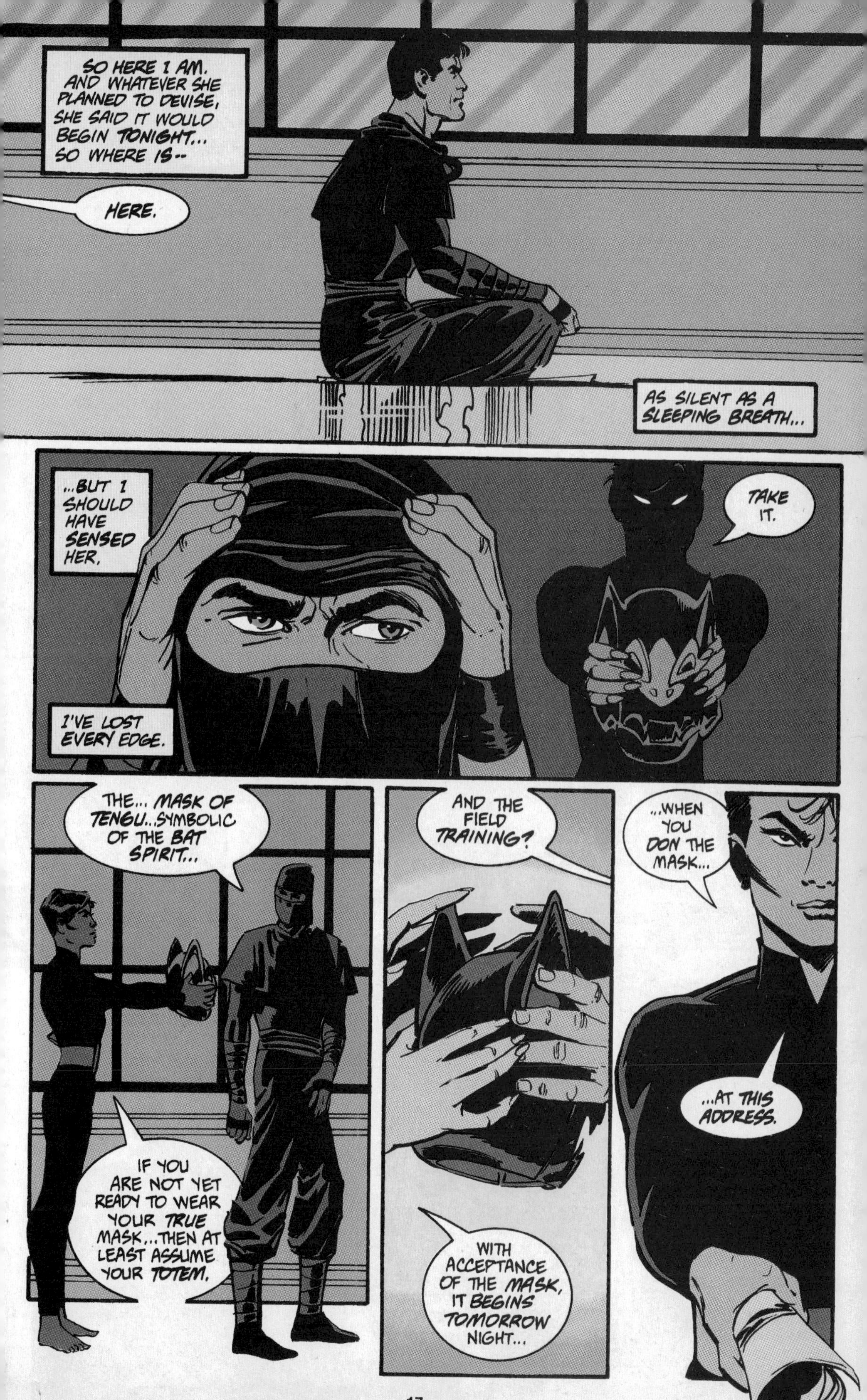
SO HERE I AM. AND WHATEVER SHE PLANNED TO DEVISE, SHE SAID IT WOULD BEGIN TONIGHT... SO WHERE IS--
HERE.
AS SILENT AS A SLEEPING BREATH...
...BUT I SHOULD HAVE SENSED HER.
TAKE IT.
I'VE LOST EVERY EDGE.
THE... MASK OF TENGU...SYMBOLIC OF THE BAT SPIRIT...
IF YOU ARE NOT YET READY TO WEAR YOUR TRUE MASK...THEN AT LEAST ASSUME YOUR TOTEM.
AND THE FIELD TRAINING?
WITH ACCEPTANCE OF THE MASK, IT BEGINS TOMORROW NIGHT...
...WHEN YOU DON THE MASK...
...AT THIS ADDRESS.

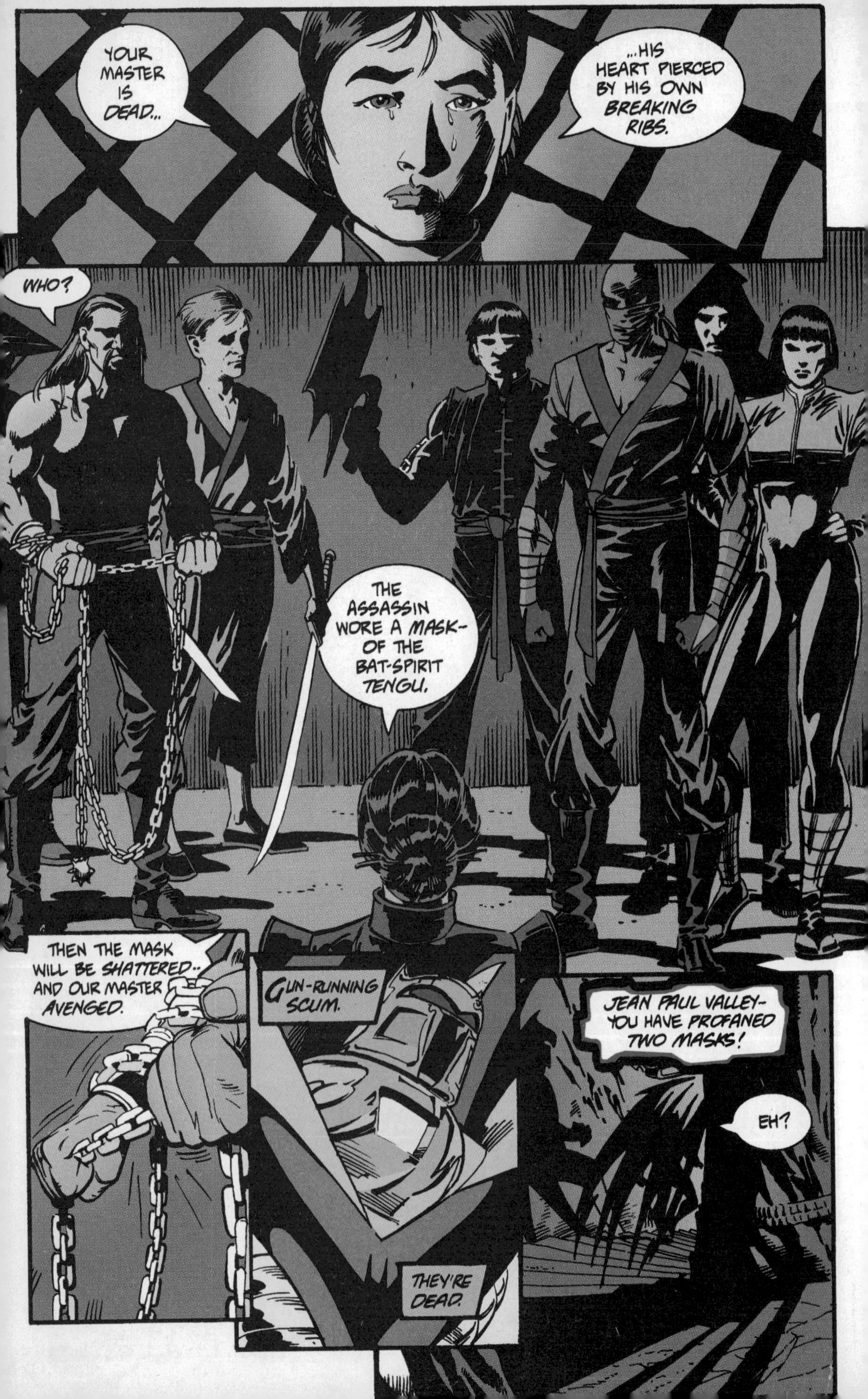
YOUR MASTER IS DEAD...
...HIS HEART PIERCED BY HIS OWN BREAKING RIBS.
WHO?
THE ASSASSIN WORE A MASK- OF THE BAT-SPIRIT TENGU.
THEN THE MASK WILL BE SHATTERED... AND OUR MASTER AVENGED.
GUN-RUNNING SCUM.
THEY'RE DEAD.
JEAN PAUL VALLEY- YOU HAVE PROFANED TWO MASKS!
EH?

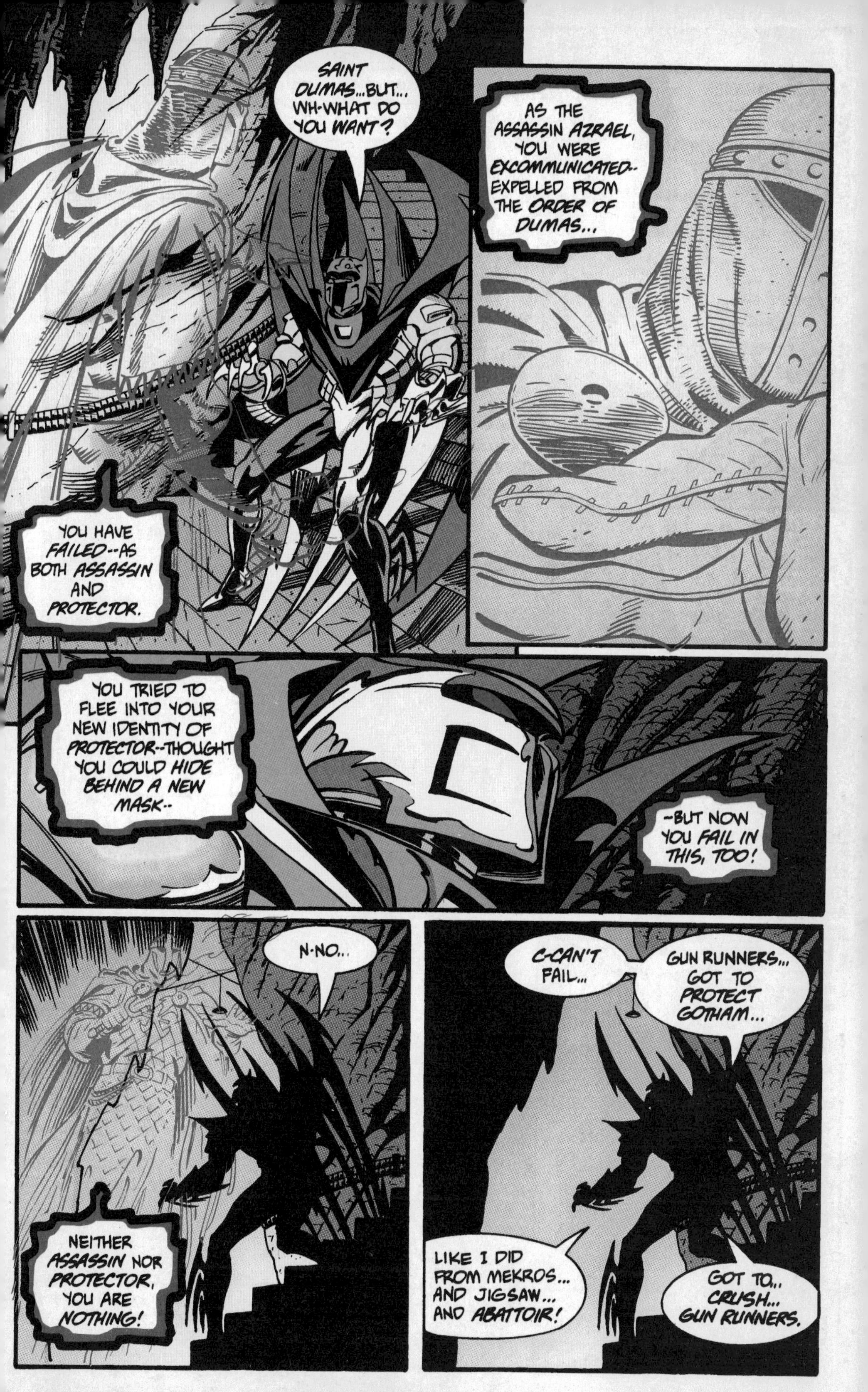
SAINT DUMAS...BUT... WH-WHAT DO YOU WANT?
AS THE ASSASSIN AZRAEL, YOU WERE EXCOMMUNICATED-- EXPELLED FROM THE ORDER OF DUMAS...
YOU HAVE FAILED--AS BOTH ASSASSIN AND PROTECTOR.
YOU TRIED TO FLEE INTO YOUR NEW IDENTITY OF PROTECTOR--THOUGHT YOU COULD HIDE BEHIND A NEW MASK--
--BUT NOW YOU FAIL IN THIS, TOO!
N-NO...
NEITHER ASSASSIN NOR PROTECTOR, YOU ARE NOTHING!
C-CAN'T FAIL...
GUN RUNNERS... GOT TO PROTECT GOTHAM...
LIKE I DID FROM MEKROS... AND JIGSAW... AND ABATTOIR!
GOT TO... CRUSH... GUN RUNNERS.

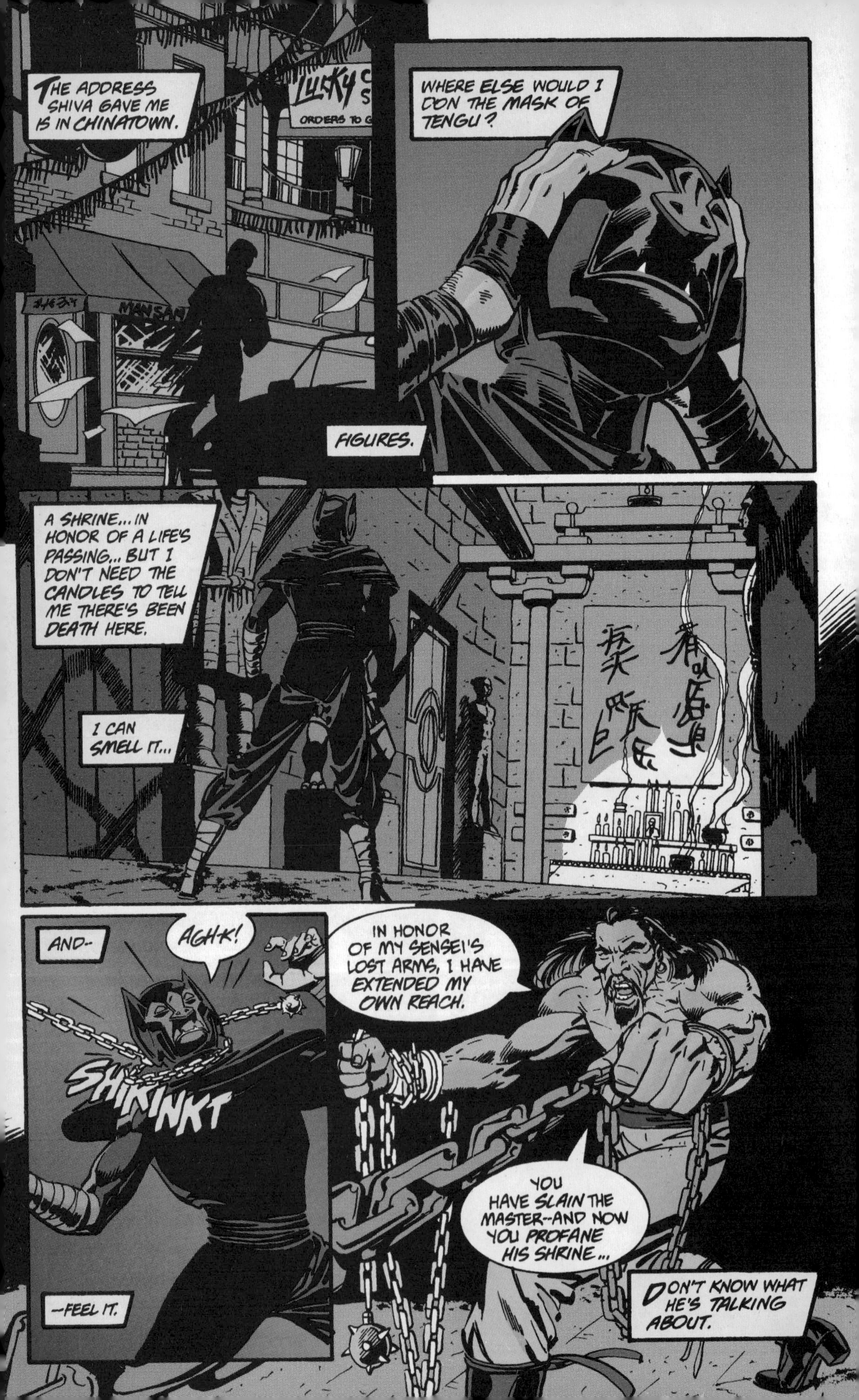
THE ADDRESS SHIVA GAVE ME IS IN CHINATOWN.
LUCKY
ORDERS TO G
WHERE ELSE WOULD I DON THE MASK OF TENGU?
FIGURES.
A SHRINE... IN HONOR OF A LIFE'S PASSING... BUT I DON'T NEED THE CANDLES TO TELL ME THERE'S BEEN DEATH HERE.
I CAN SMELL IT...
AND-
AGHK!
SHKINKT
--FEEL IT.
IN HONOR OF MY SENSEI'S LOST ARMS, I HAVE EXTENDED MY OWN REACH.
YOU HAVE SLAIN THE MASTER--AND NOW YOU PROFANE HIS SHRINE...
DON'T KNOW WHAT HE'S TALKING ABOUT.

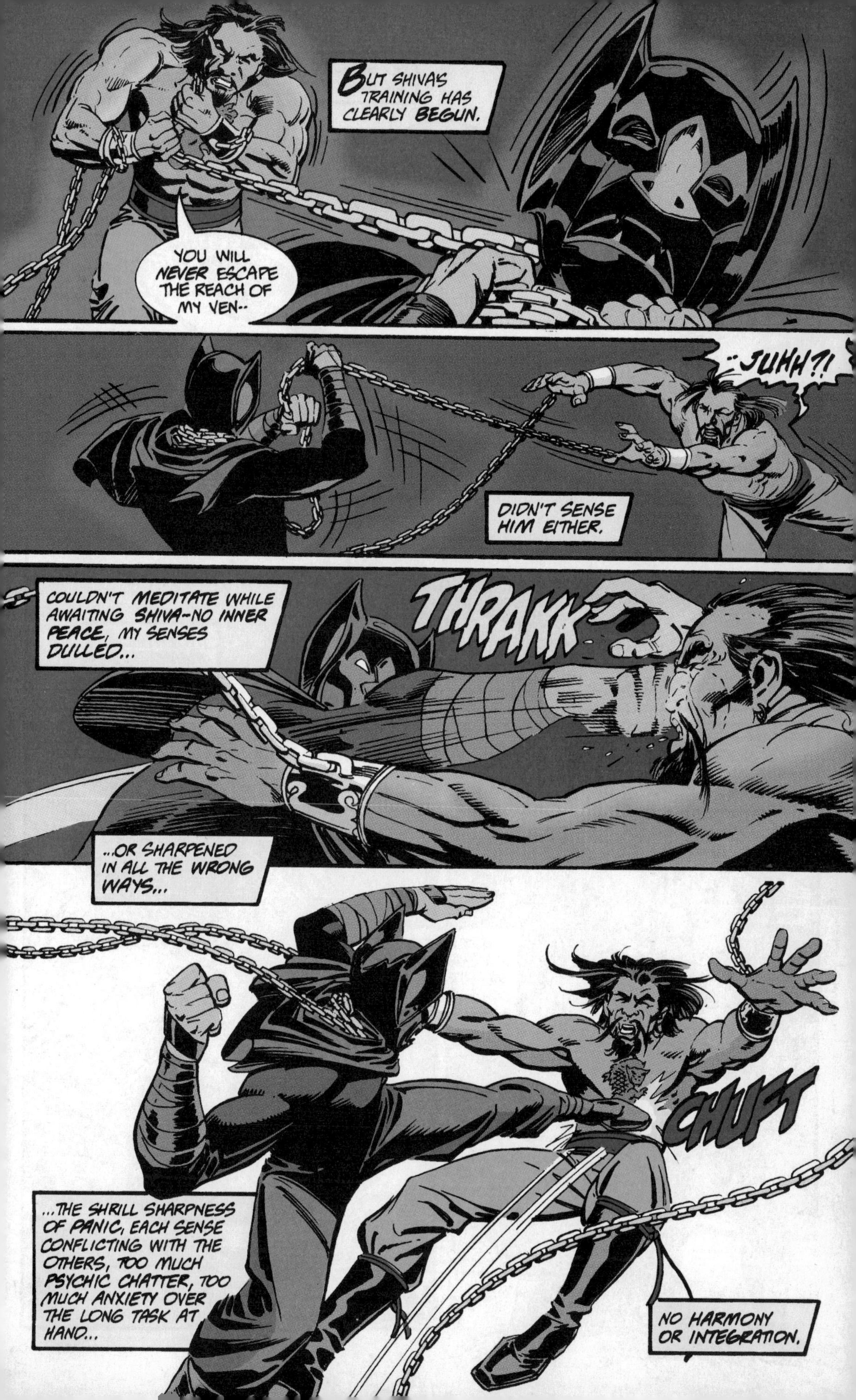
BUT SHIVA'S TRAINING HAS CLEARLY BEGUN.
YOU WILL NEVER ESCAPE THE REACH OF MY VEN--
..JUHH?!
DIDN'T SENSE HIM EITHER.
COULDN'T MEDITATE WHILE AWAITING SHIVA--NO INNER PEACE, MY SENSES DULLED...
THRAKK
...OR SHARPENED IN ALL THE WRONG WAYS...
CHUFT
...THE SHRILL SHARPNESS OF PANIC, EACH SENSE CONFLICTING WITH THE OTHERS, TOO MUCH PSYCHIC CHATTER, TOO MUCH ANXIETY OVER THE LONG TASK AT HAND...
NO HARMONY OR INTEGRATION.

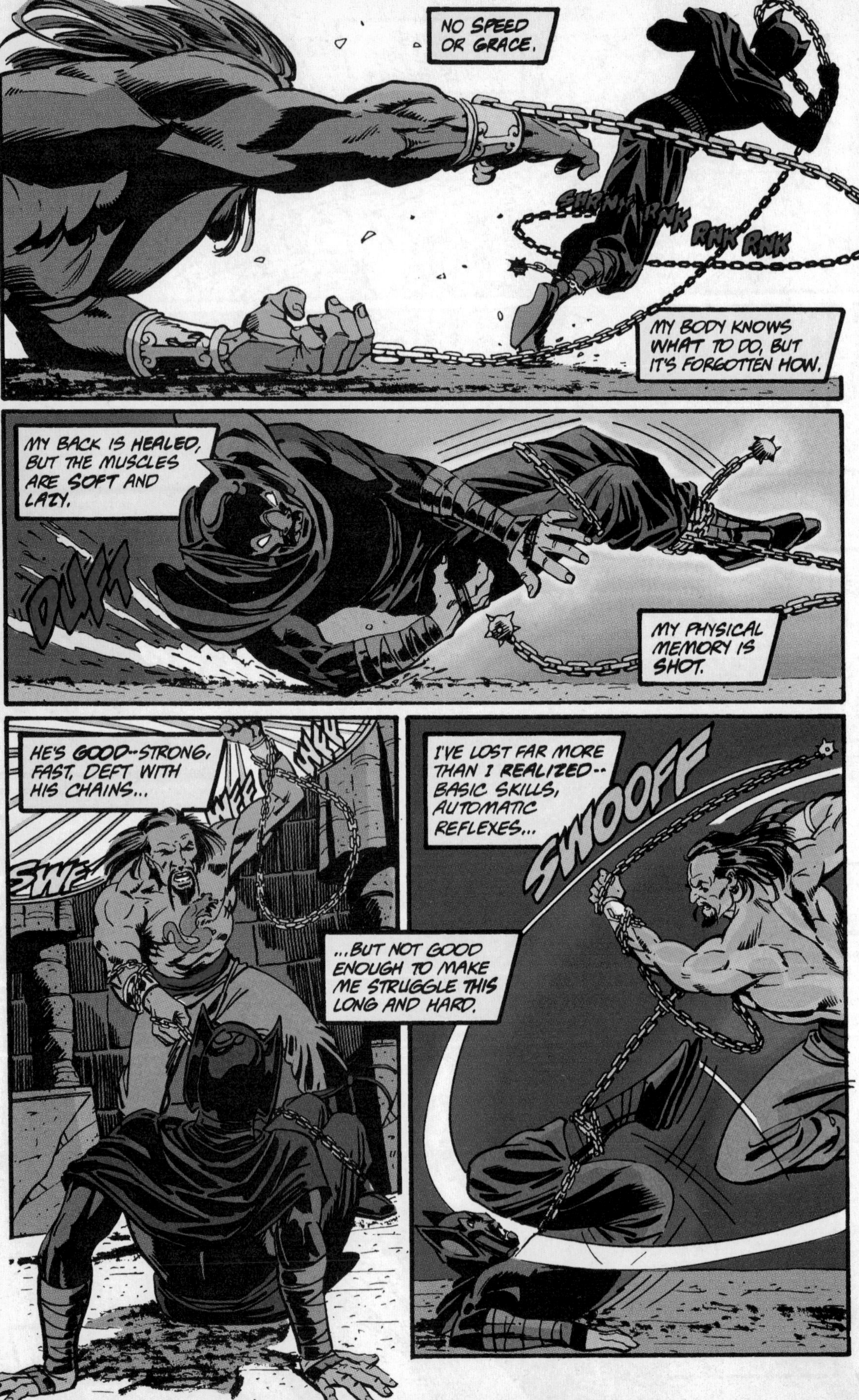
NO SPEED OR GRACE.
RNK RNK RNK
MY BODY KNOWS WHAT TO DO, BUT IT'S FORGOTTEN HOW.
MY BACK IS HEALED, BUT THE MUSCLES ARE SOFT AND LAZY.
MY PHYSICAL MEMORY IS SHOT.
HE'S GOOD--STRONG, FAST, DEFT WITH HIS CHAINS...
...BUT NOT GOOD ENOUGH TO MAKE ME STRUGGLE THIS LONG AND HARD.
I'VE LOST FAR MORE THAN I REALIZED--BASIC SKILLS, AUTOMATIC REFLEXES...
SWOOFF

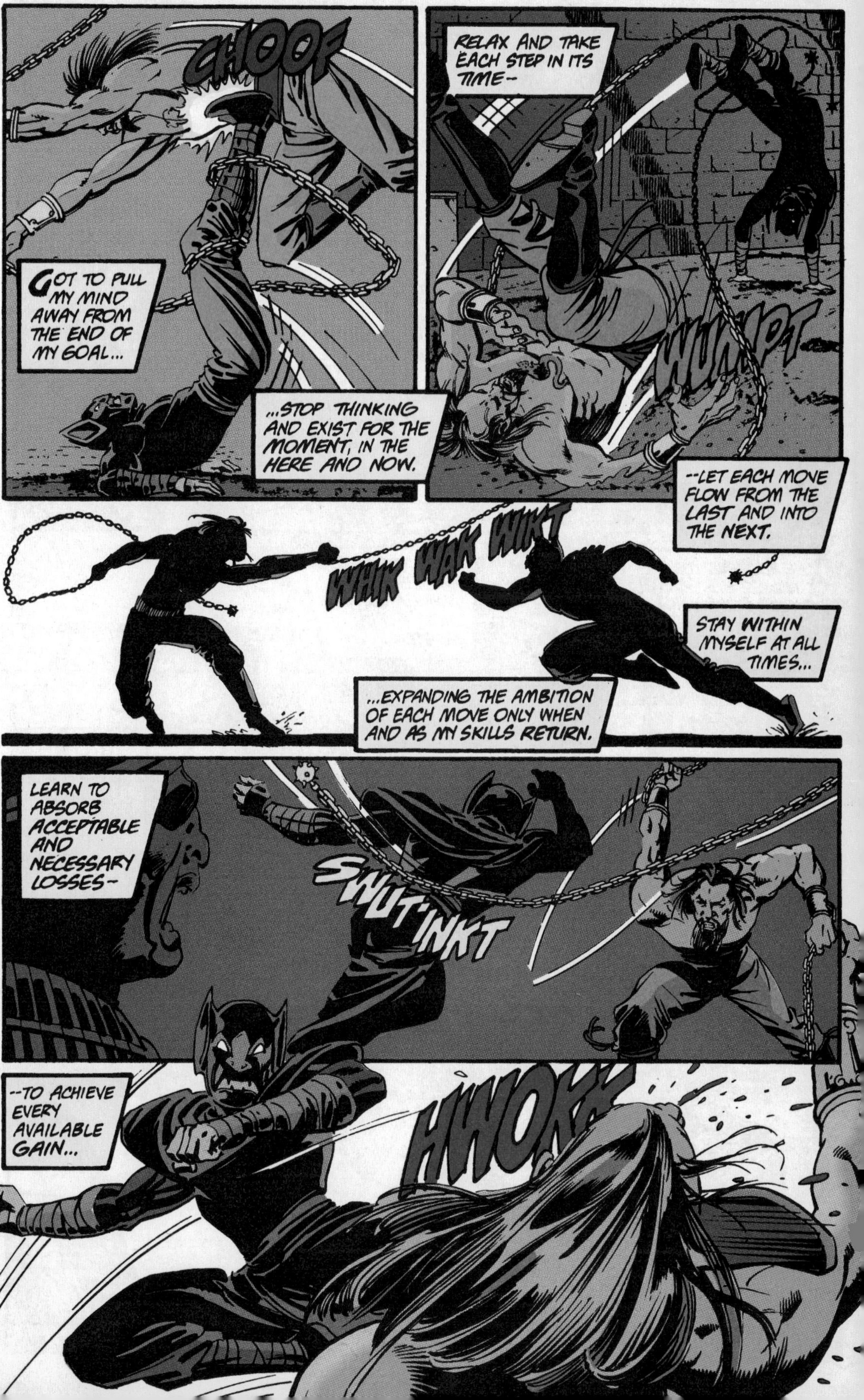

CHOOF
GOT TO PULL MY MIND AWAY FROM THE END OF MY GOAL...
...STOP THINKING AND EXIST FOR THE MOMENT, IN THE HERE AND NOW.
RELAX AND TAKE EACH STEP IN ITS TIME--
WUMPT
--LET EACH MOVE FLOW FROM THE LAST AND INTO THE NEXT.
WHIK WAK WIKT
STAY WITHIN MYSELF AT ALL TIMES...
...EXPANDING THE AMBITION OF EACH MOVE ONLY WHEN AND AS MY SKILLS RETURN.
LEARN TO ABSORB ACCEPTABLE AND NECESSARY LOSSES-
SWUT'INKT
--TO ACHIEVE EVERY AVAILABLE GAIN...

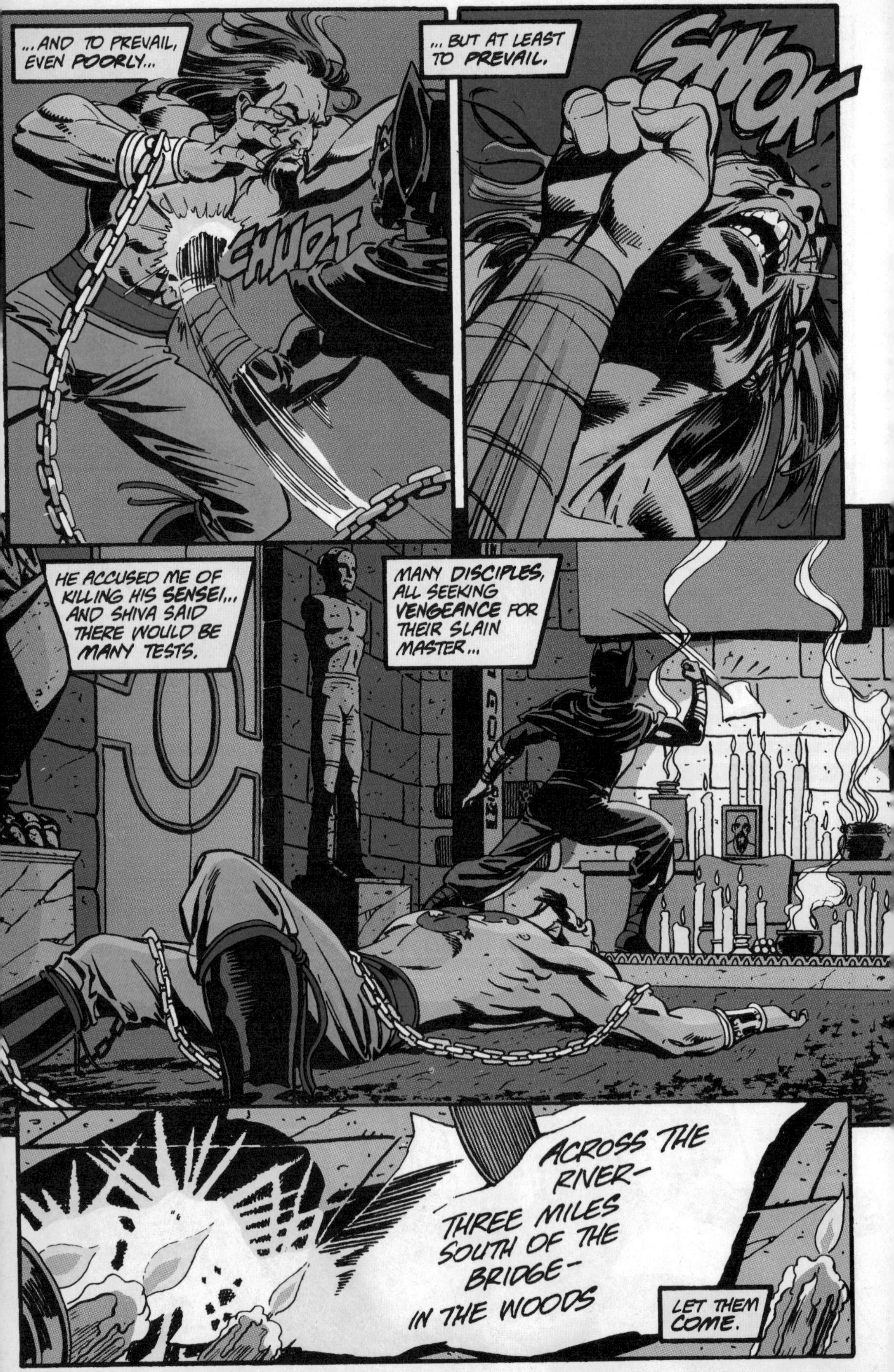
...AND TO PREVAIL, EVEN POORLY...
CHUDT
...BUT AT LEAST TO PREVAIL.
SHOK
HE ACCUSED ME OF KILLING HIS SENSEI... AND SHIVA SAID THERE WOULD BE MANY TESTS.
MANY DISCIPLES, ALL SEEKING VENGEANCE FOR THEIR SLAIN MASTER...
ACROSS THE RIVER-
THREE MILES SOUTH OF THE BRIDGE-
IN THE WOODS
LET THEM COME.

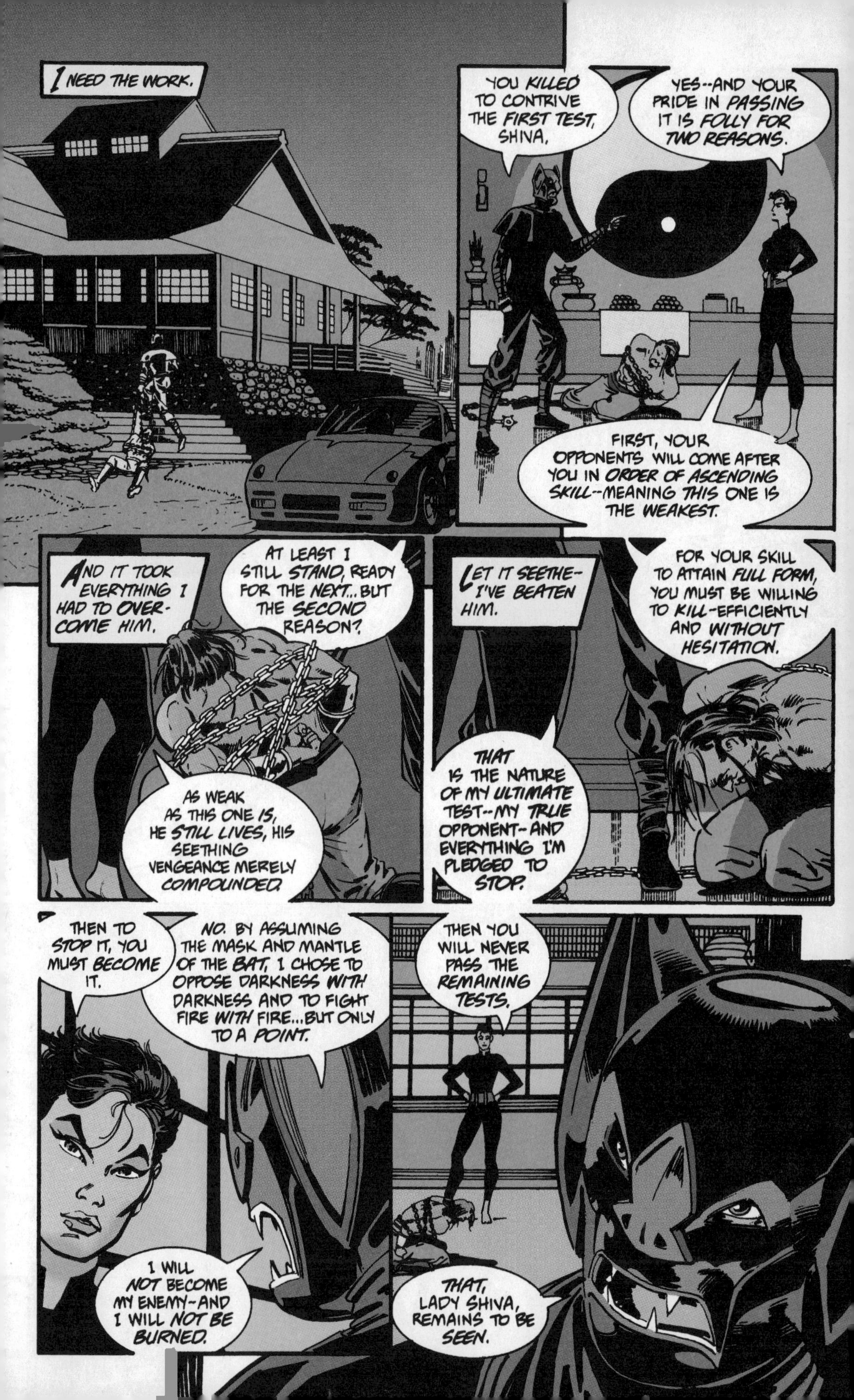
I NEED THE WORK.
YOU KILLED TO CONTRIVE THE FIRST TEST, SHIVA.
YES--AND YOUR PRIDE IN PASSING IT IS FOLLY FOR TWO REASONS.
FIRST, YOUR OPPONENTS WILL COME AFTER YOU IN ORDER OF ASCENDING SKILL--MEANING THIS ONE IS THE WEAKEST.
AND IT TOOK EVERYTHING I HAD TO OVERCOME HIM.
AT LEAST I STILL STAND, READY FOR THE NEXT... BUT THE SECOND REASON?
AS WEAK AS THIS ONE IS, HE STILL LIVES, HIS SEETHING VENGEANCE MERELY COMPOUNDED.
LET IT SEETHE-- I'VE BEATEN HIM.
FOR YOUR SKILL TO ATTAIN FULL FORM, YOU MUST BE WILLING TO KILL--EFFICIENTLY AND WITHOUT HESITATION.
THAT IS THE NATURE OF MY ULTIMATE TEST--MY TRUE OPPONENT--AND EVERYTHING I'M PLEDGED TO STOP.
THEN TO STOP IT, YOU MUST BECOME IT.
NO. BY ASSUMING THE MASK AND MANTLE OF THE BAT, I CHOSE TO OPPOSE DARKNESS WITH DARKNESS AND TO FIGHT FIRE WITH FIRE... BUT ONLY TO A POINT.
I WILL NOT BECOME MY ENEMY--AND I WILL NOT BE BURNED.
THEN YOU WILL NEVER PASS THE REMAINING TESTS.
THAT, LADY SHIVA, REMAINS TO BE SEEN.

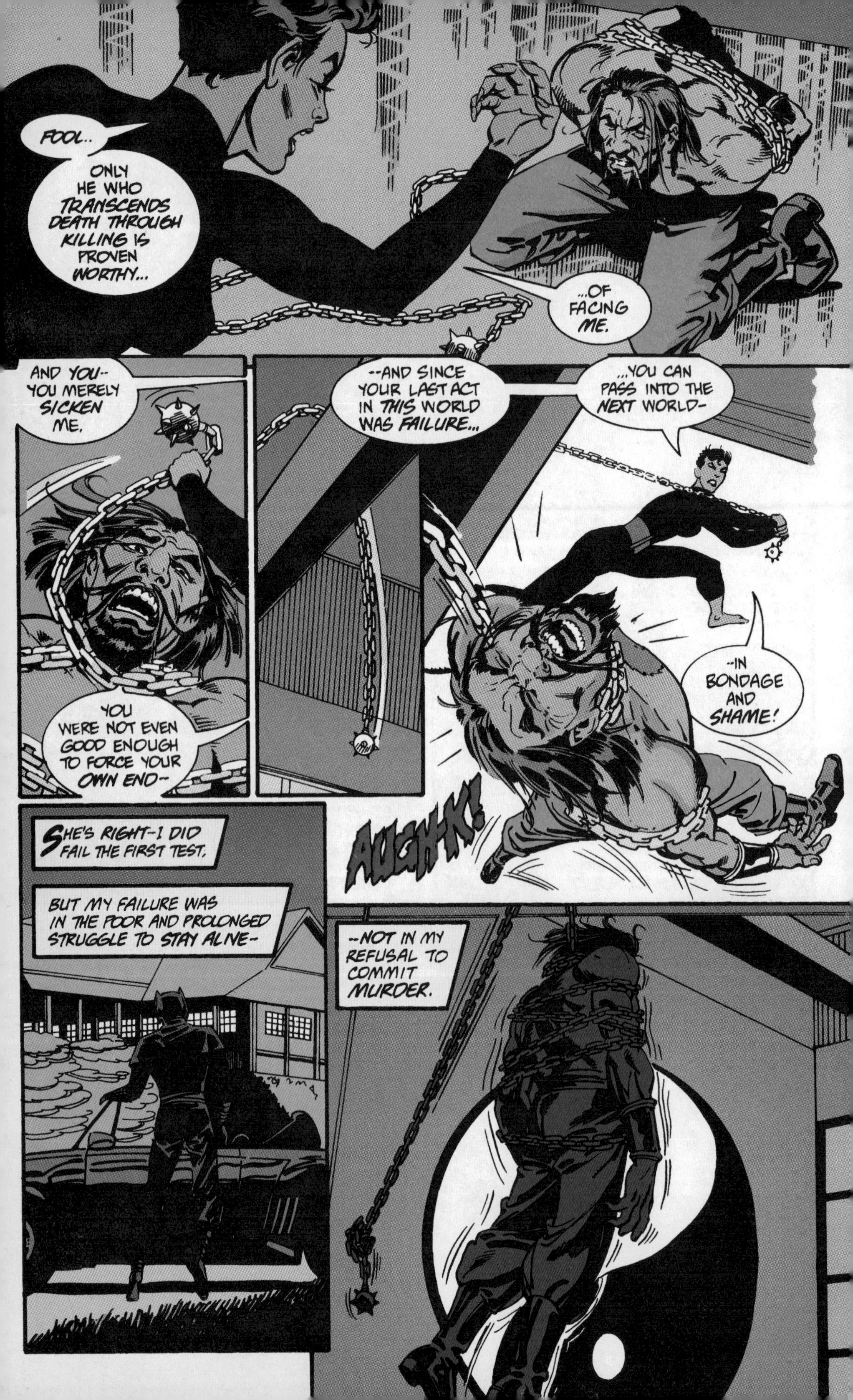
FOOL..
ONLY HE WHO TRANSCENDS DEATH THROUGH KILLING IS PROVEN WORTHY...
...OF FACING ME.
AND YOU-- YOU MERELY SICKEN ME.
YOU WERE NOT EVEN GOOD ENOUGH TO FORCE YOUR OWN END--
--AND SINCE YOUR LAST ACT IN THIS WORLD WAS FAILURE...
...YOU CAN PASS INTO THE NEXT WORLD-
--IN BONDAGE AND SHAME!
AUGHHK!
SHE'S RIGHT--I DID FAIL THE FIRST TEST.
BUT MY FAILURE WAS IN THE POOR AND PROLONGED STRUGGLE TO STAY ALIVE--
--NOT IN MY REFUSAL TO COMMIT MURDER.

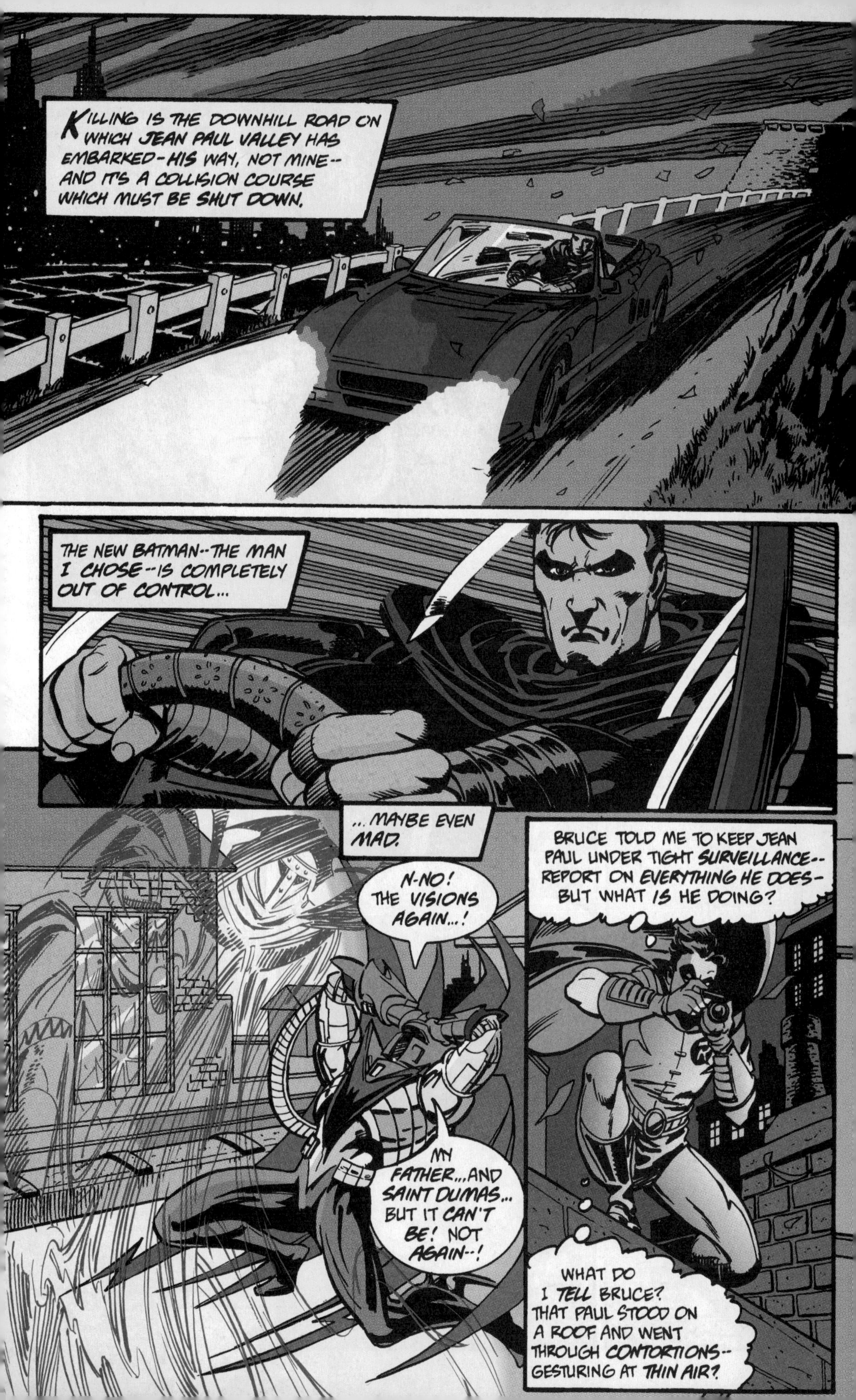
KILLING IS THE DOWNHILL ROAD ON WHICH JEAN PAUL VALLEY HAS EMBARKED--HIS WAY, NOT MINE--AND IT'S A COLLISION COURSE WHICH MUST BE SHUT DOWN.
THE NEW BATMAN--THE MAN I CHOSE--IS COMPLETELY OUT OF CONTROL...
...MAYBE EVEN MAD.
N-NO! THE VISIONS AGAIN...!
MY FATHER...AND SAINT DUMAS... BUT IT CAN'T BE! NOT AGAIN--!
BRUCE TOLD ME TO KEEP JEAN PAUL UNDER TIGHT SURVEILLANCE--REPORT ON EVERYTHING HE DOES-BUT WHAT IS HE DOING?
WHAT DO I TELL BRUCE? THAT PAUL STOOD ON A ROOF AND WENT THROUGH CONTORTIONS--GESTURING AT THIN AIR?

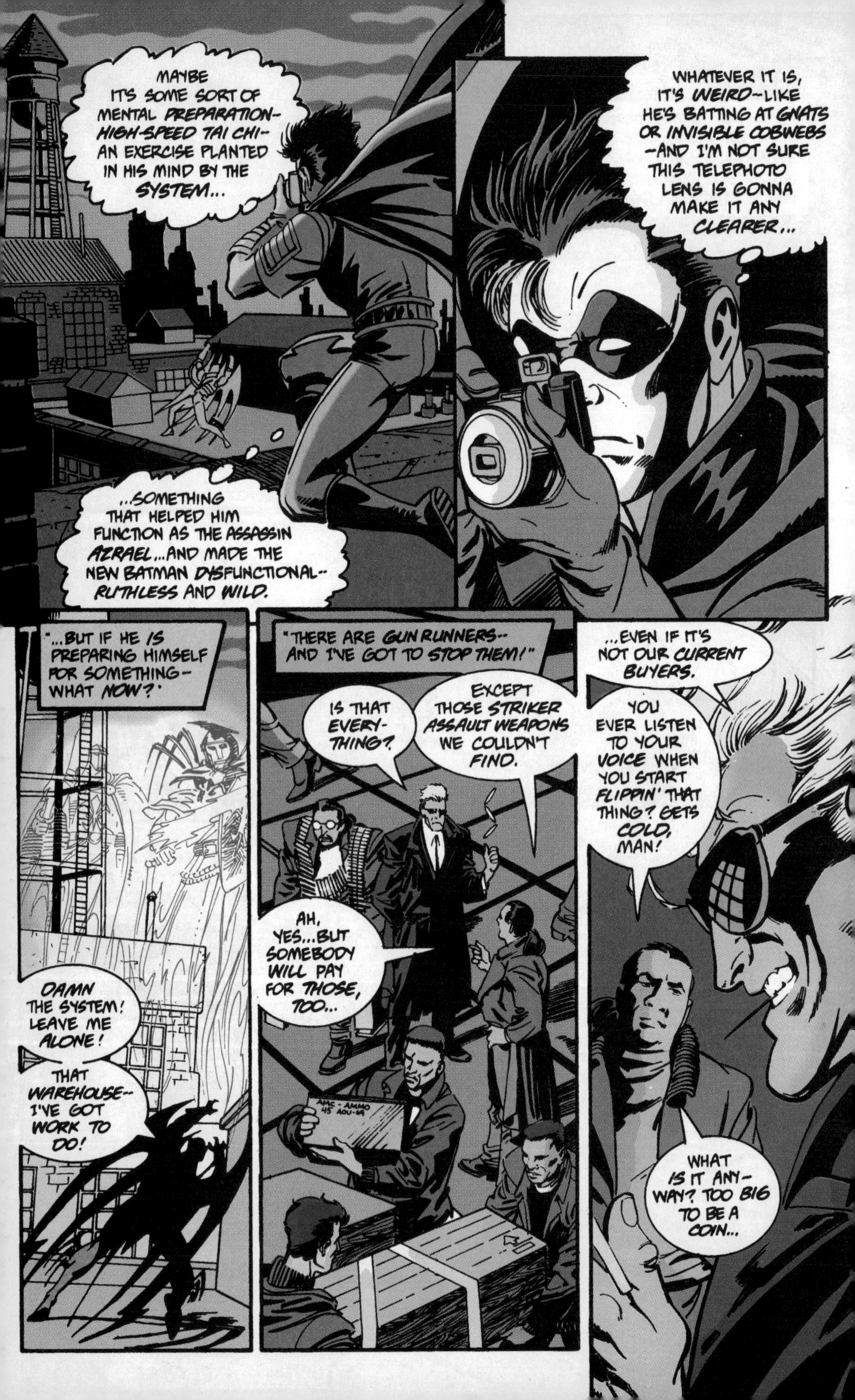
MAYBE IT'S SOME SORT OF MENTAL PREPARATION-HIGH-SPEED TAI CHI-AN EXERCISE PLANTED IN HIS MIND BY THE SYSTEM...
...SOMETHING THAT HELPED HIM FUNCTION AS THE ASSASSIN AZRAEL...AND MADE THE NEW BATMAN DYSFUNCTIONAL-RUTHLESS AND WILD.
WHATEVER IT IS, IT'S WEIRD--LIKE HE'S BATTING AT GNATS OR INVISIBLE COBWEBS-AND I'M NOT SURE THIS TELEPHOTO LENS IS GONNA MAKE IT ANY CLEARER...
"...BUT IF HE IS PREPARING HIMSELF FOR SOMETHING-WHAT NOW?"
DAMN THE SYSTEM! LEAVE ME ALONE!
THAT WAREHOUSE--I'VE GOT WORK TO DO!
"THERE ARE GUN RUNNERS--AND I'VE GOT TO STOP THEM!"
IS THAT EVERY-THING?
EXCEPT THOSE STRIKER ASSAULT WEAPONS WE COULDN'T FIND.
AH, YES...BUT SOMEBODY WILL PAY FOR THOSE, TOO...
...EVEN IF IT'S NOT OUR CURRENT BUYERS.
YOU EVER LISTEN TO YOUR VOICE WHEN YOU START FLIPPIN' THAT THING? GETS COLD, MAN!
WHAT IS IT ANY-WAY? TOO BIG TO BE A COIN...

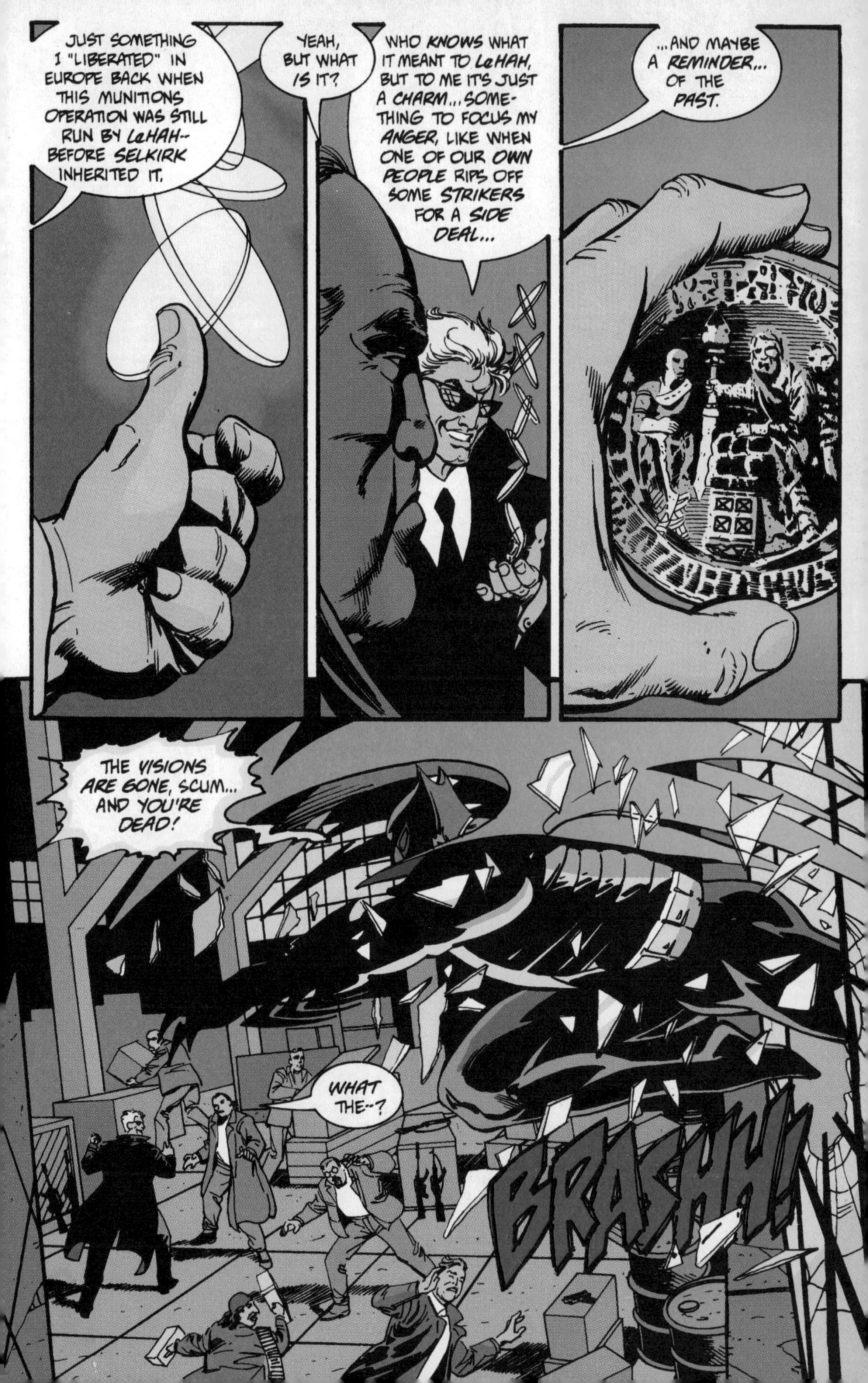
JUST SOMETHING I "LIBERATED" IN EUROPE BACK WHEN THIS MUNITIONS OPERATION WAS STILL RUN BY LeHAH-- BEFORE SELKIRK INHERITED IT.
YEAH, BUT WHAT IS IT?
WHO KNOWS WHAT IT MEANT TO LeHAH, BUT TO ME IT'S JUST A CHARM... SOME-THING TO FOCUS MY ANGER, LIKE WHEN ONE OF OUR OWN PEOPLE RIPS OFF SOME STRIKERS FOR A SIDE DEAL...
...AND MAYBE A REMINDER... OF THE PAST.
THE VISIONS ARE GONE, SCUM... AND YOU'RE DEAD!
WHAT THE--?
BRASHH!

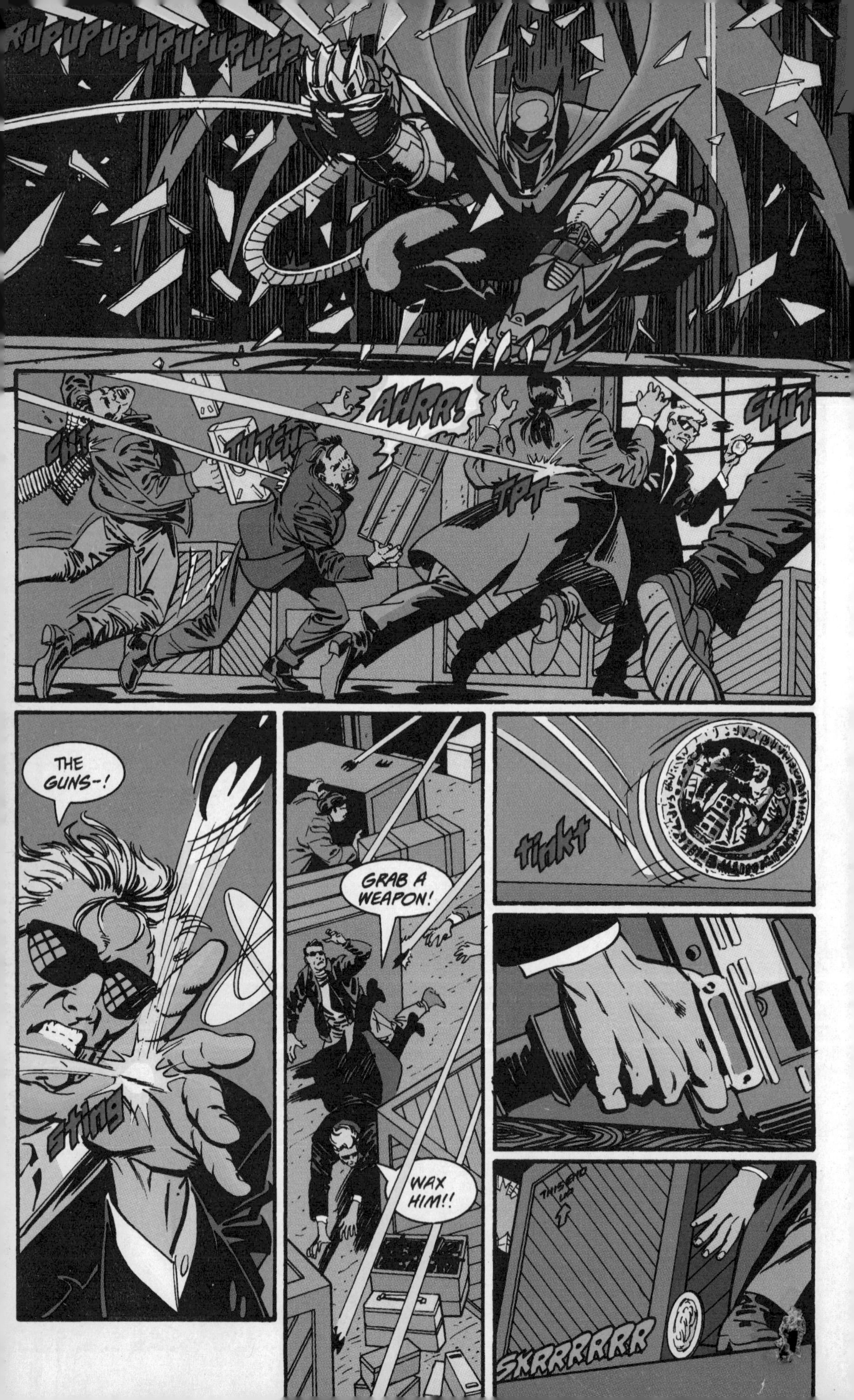
RUPUP UP UPUPUPUPP
AHRR!
TITCH
TPT
THE GUNS-!
sting
GRAB A WEAPON!
WAX HIM!!
tink
SKRRRRRRR

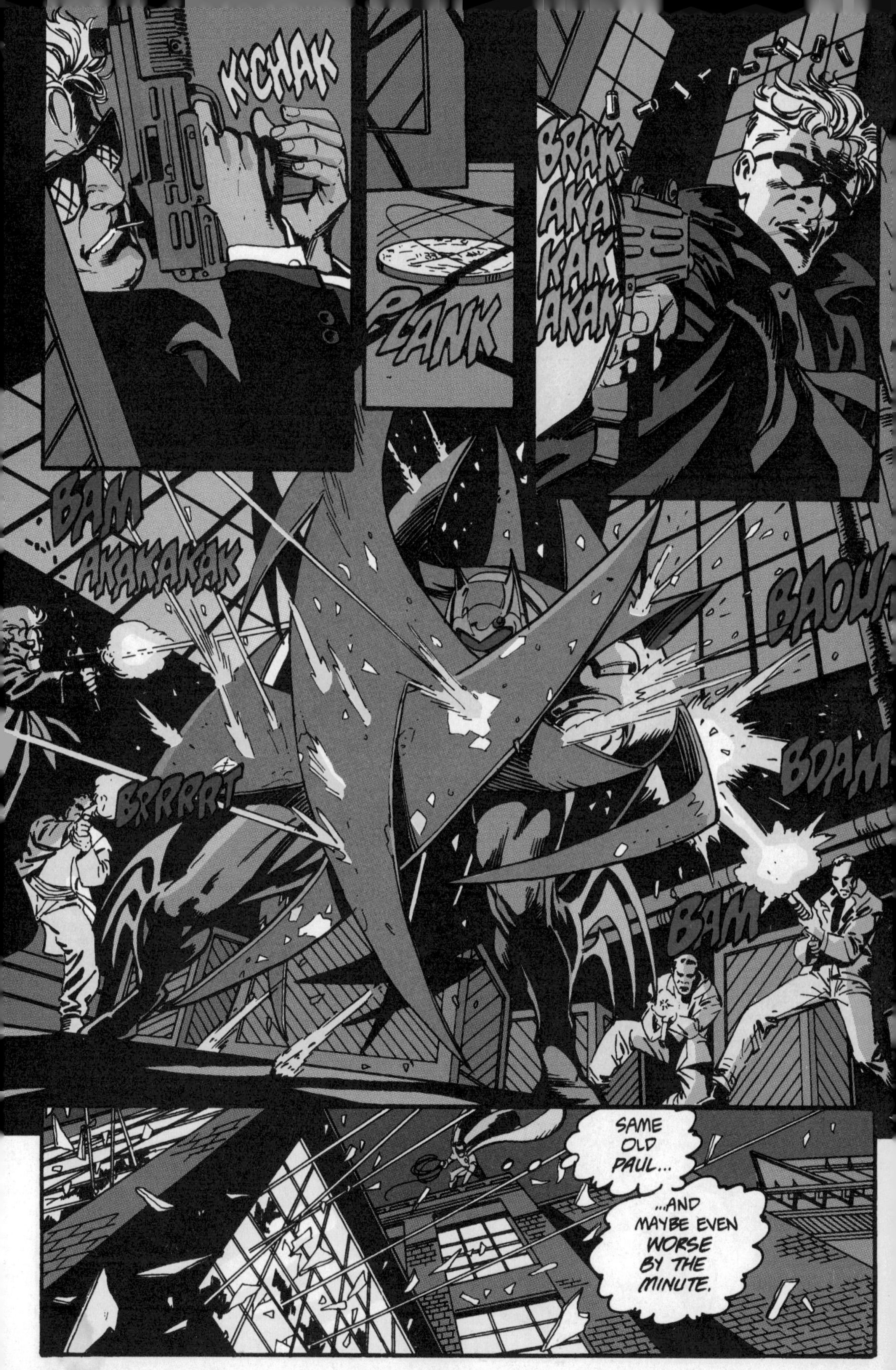
K'CHAK
PLANK
BRAKAKAKAKAKAK
BAM AKAKAKAK
BAOU
BRRRRT
BDAM
BAM
SAME OLD PAUL...
...AND MAYBE EVEN WORSE BY THE MINUTE.

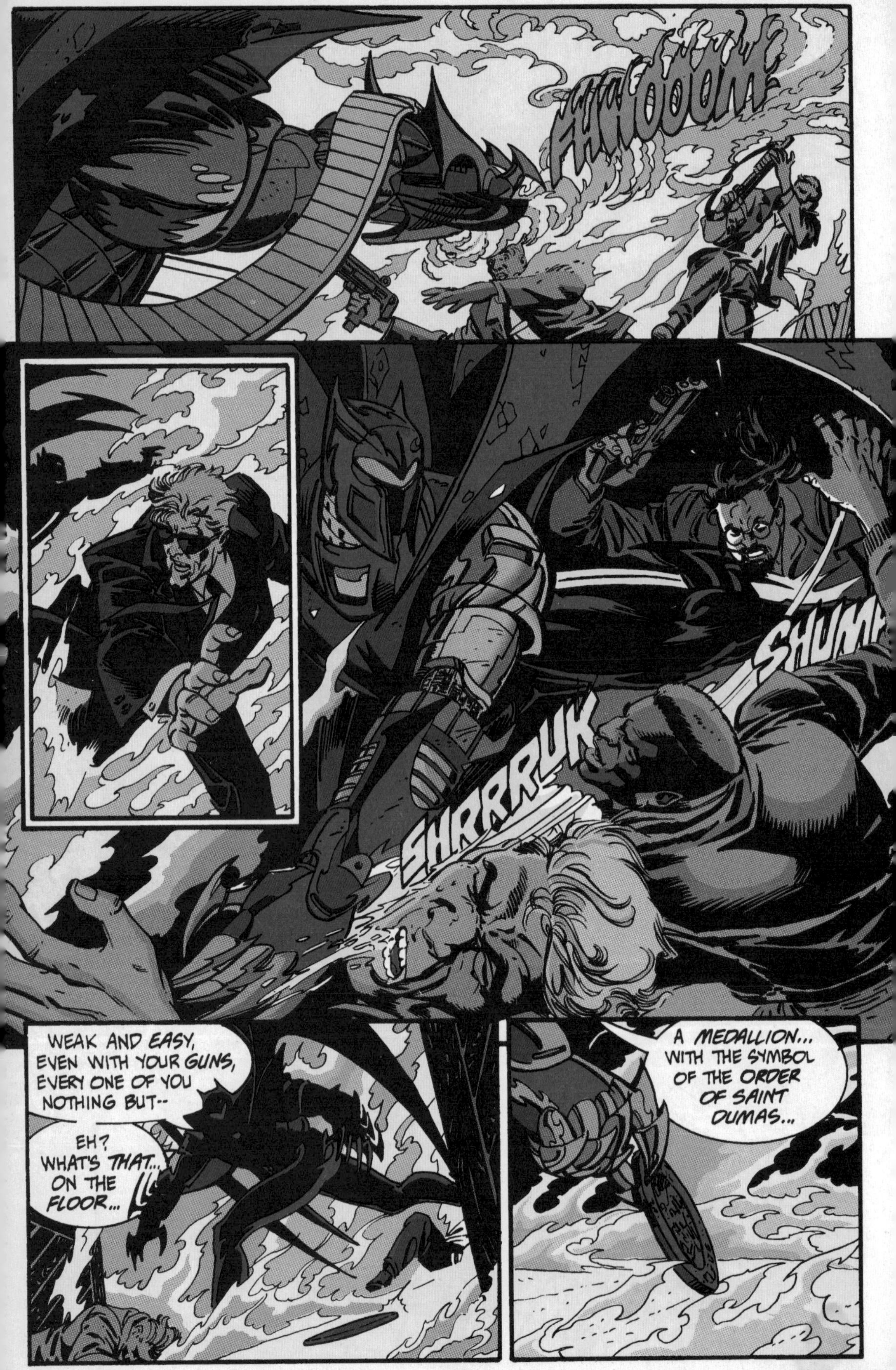
FWHOOOM!
SHUMP
SHRRRUK
WEAK AND EASY, EVEN WITH YOUR GUNS, EVERY ONE OF YOU NOTHING BUT--
EH? WHAT'S THAT... ON THE FLOOR...
A MEDALLION... WITH THE SYMBOL OF THE ORDER OF SAINT DUMAS...

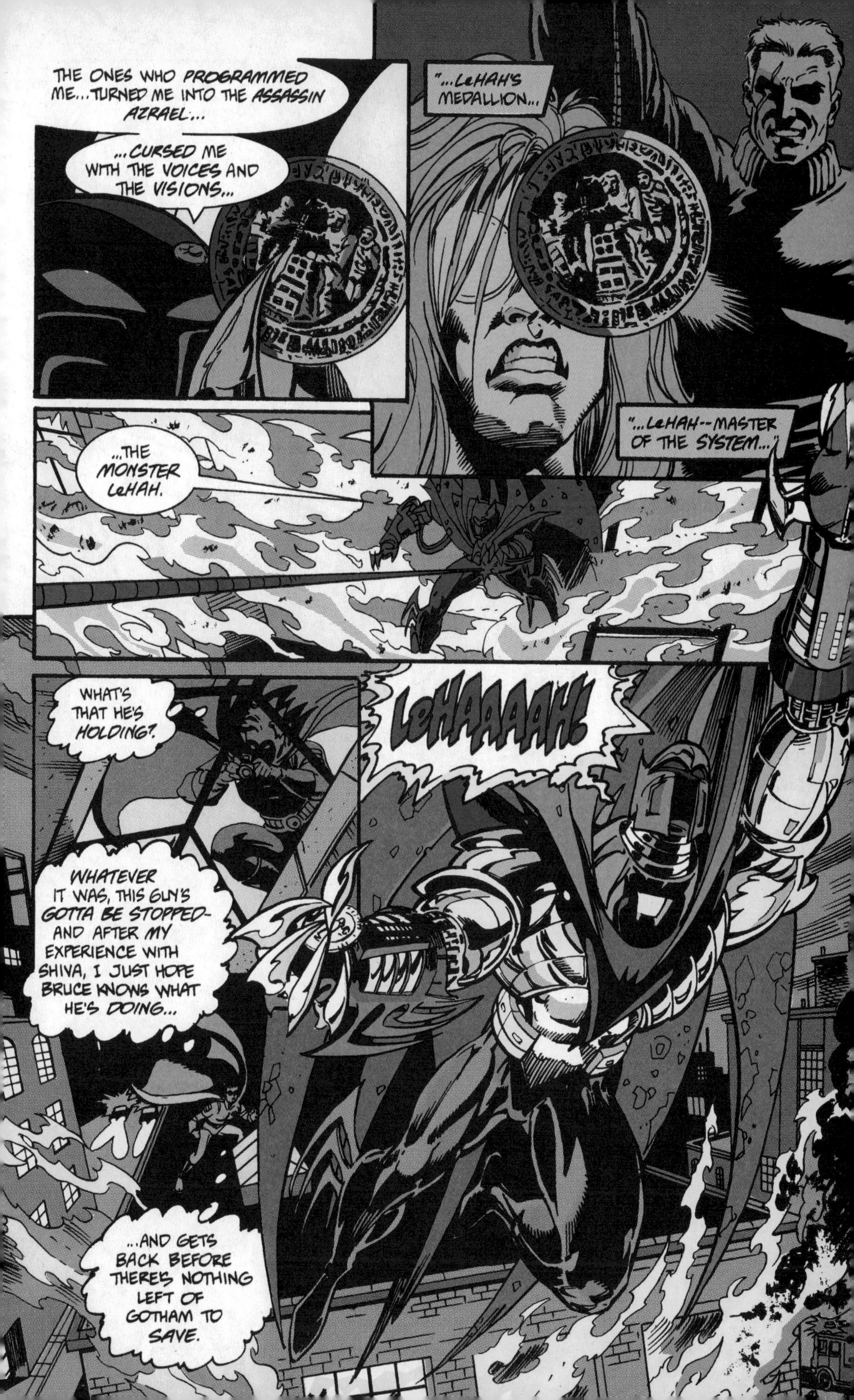
THE ONES WHO PROGRAMMED ME...TURNED ME INTO THE ASSASSIN AZRAEL...
...CURSED ME WITH THE VOICES AND THE VISIONS...
"...LeHAH'S MEDALLION...
"...LeHAH--MASTER OF THE SYSTEM..."
...THE MONSTER LeHAH.
WHAT'S THAT HE'S HOLDING?
LeHAAAAH!
WHATEVER IT WAS, THIS GUY'S GOTTA BE STOPPED- AND AFTER MY EXPERIENCE WITH SHIVA, I JUST HOPE BRUCE KNOWS WHAT HE'S DOING...
...AND GETS BACK BEFORE THERE'S NOTHING LEFT OF GOTHAM TO SAVE.

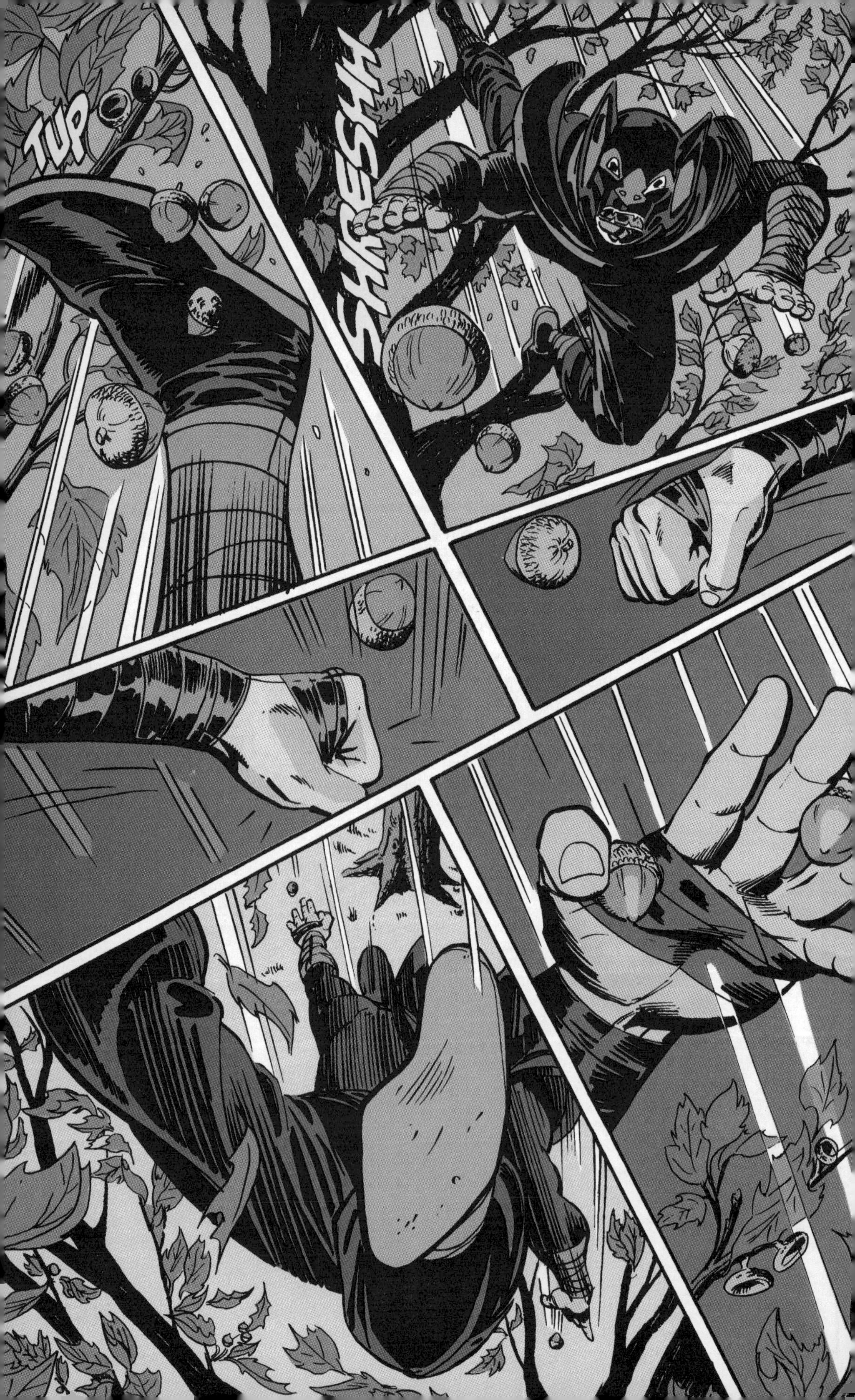
TUP

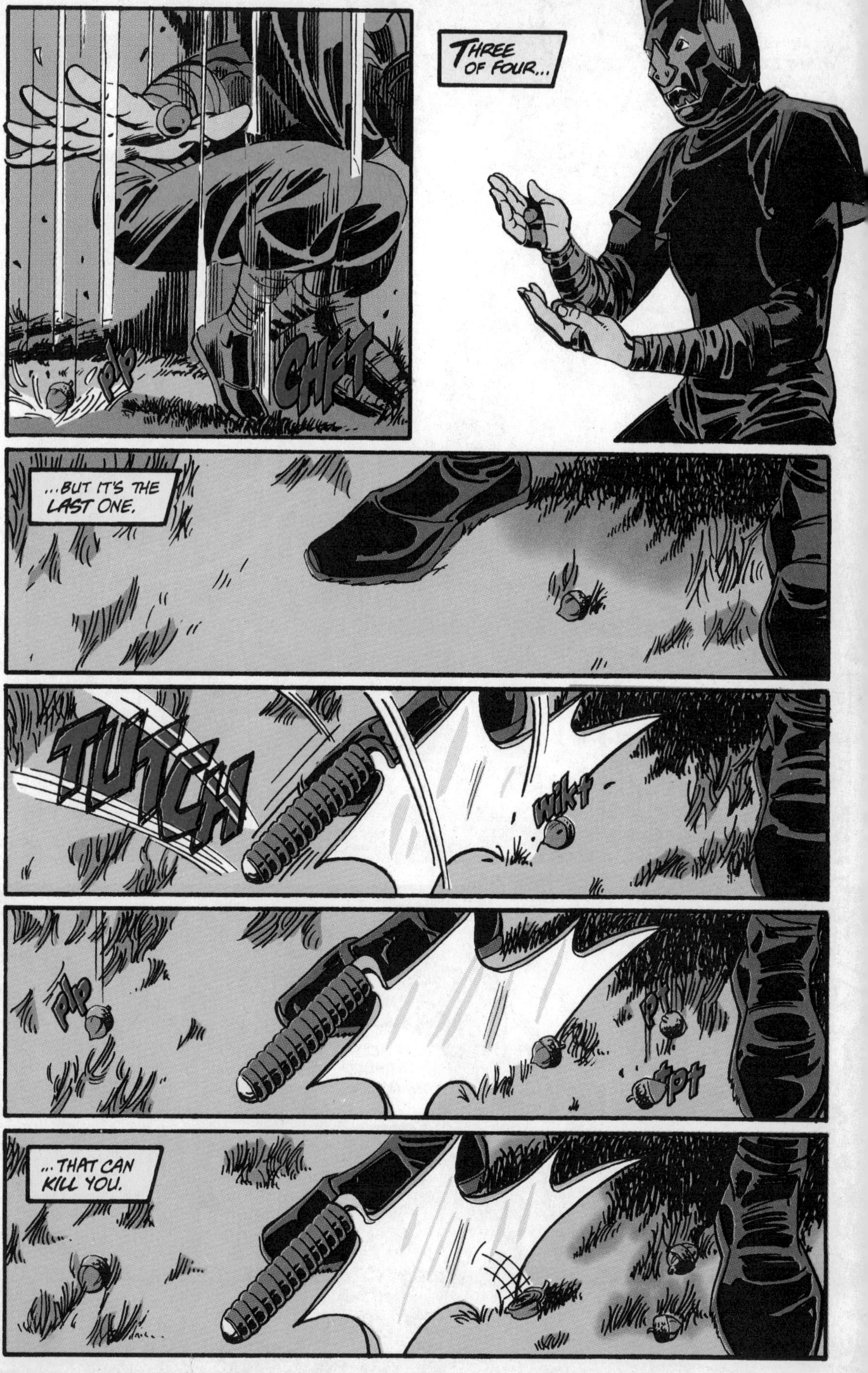
THREE OF FOUR...
plp
CHFT
...BUT IT'S THE LAST ONE.
TUTCH
wikt
plp
pt
pt
...THAT CAN KILL YOU.

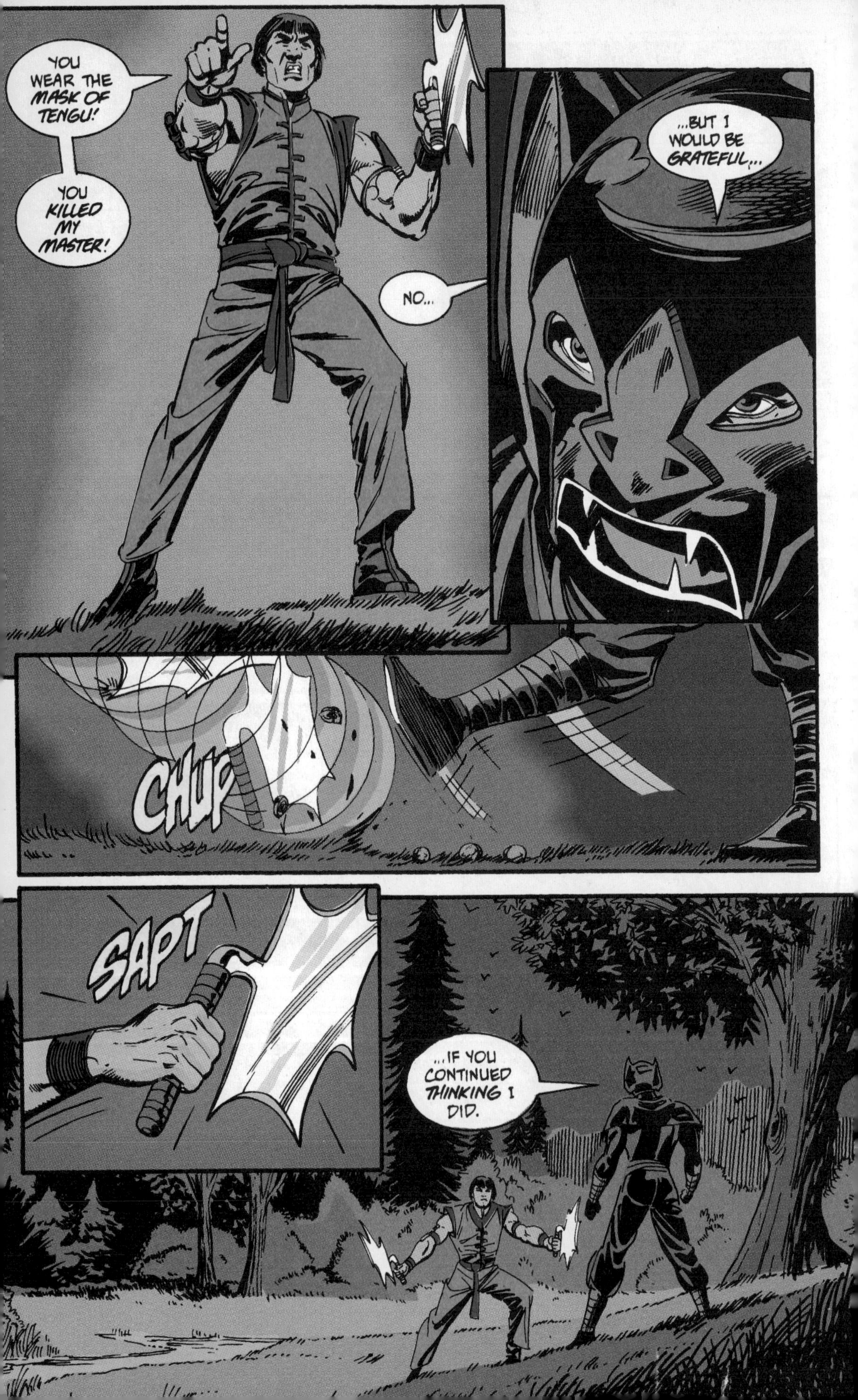
YOU WEAR THE MASK OF TENGU!
YOU KILLED MY MASTER!
NO...
...BUT I WOULD BE GRATEFUL...
CHUP
SAPT
...IF YOU CONTINUED THINKING I DID.

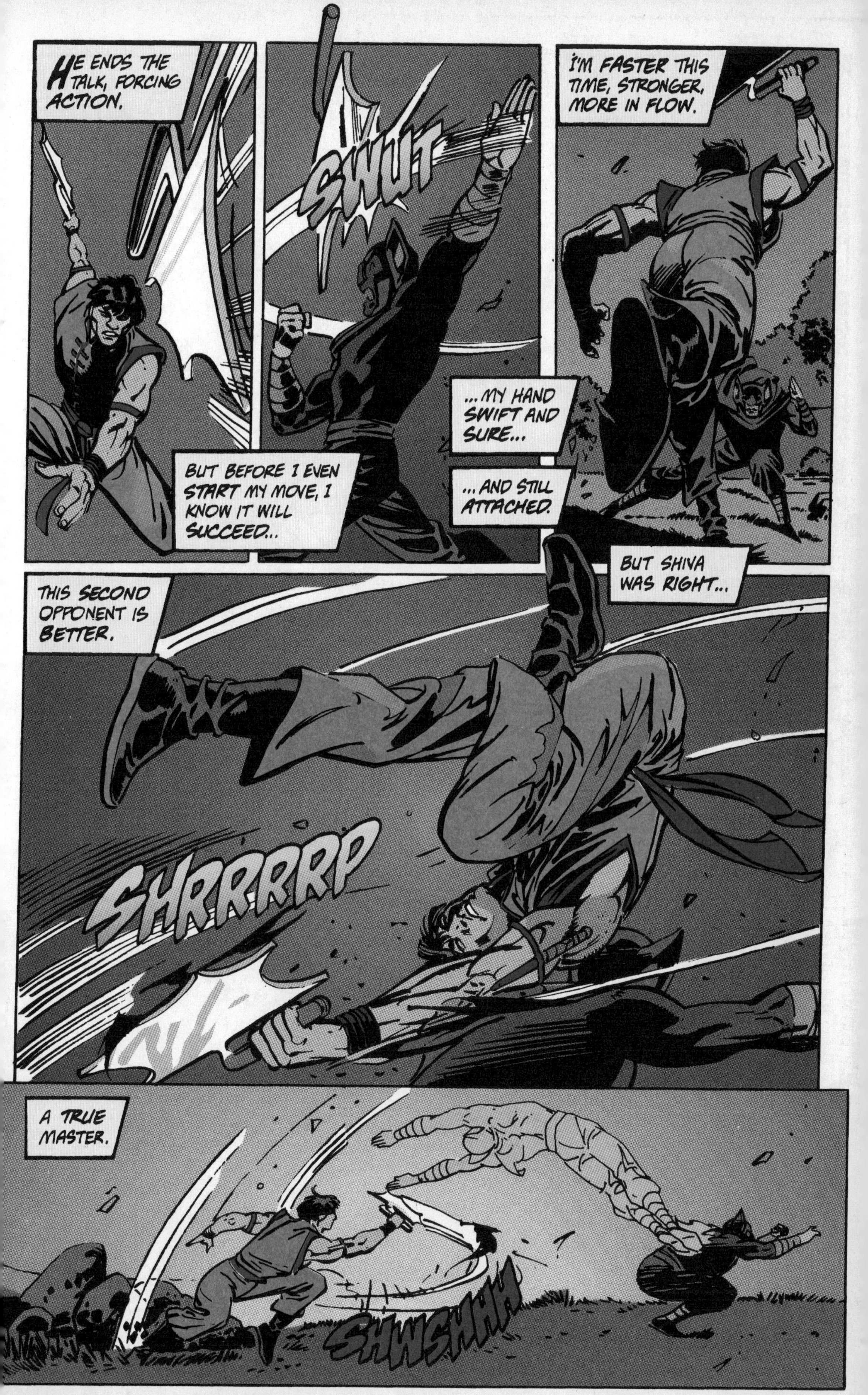
HE ENDS THE TALK, FORCING ACTION.
SWUT
BUT BEFORE I EVEN START MY MOVE, I KNOW IT WILL SUCCEED...
...MY HAND SWIFT AND SURE...
...AND STILL ATTACHED.
I'M FASTER THIS TIME, STRONGER, MORE IN FLOW.
THIS SECOND OPPONENT IS BETTER.
BUT SHIVA WAS RIGHT...
SHRRRRP
A TRUE MASTER.
SHWSHHH

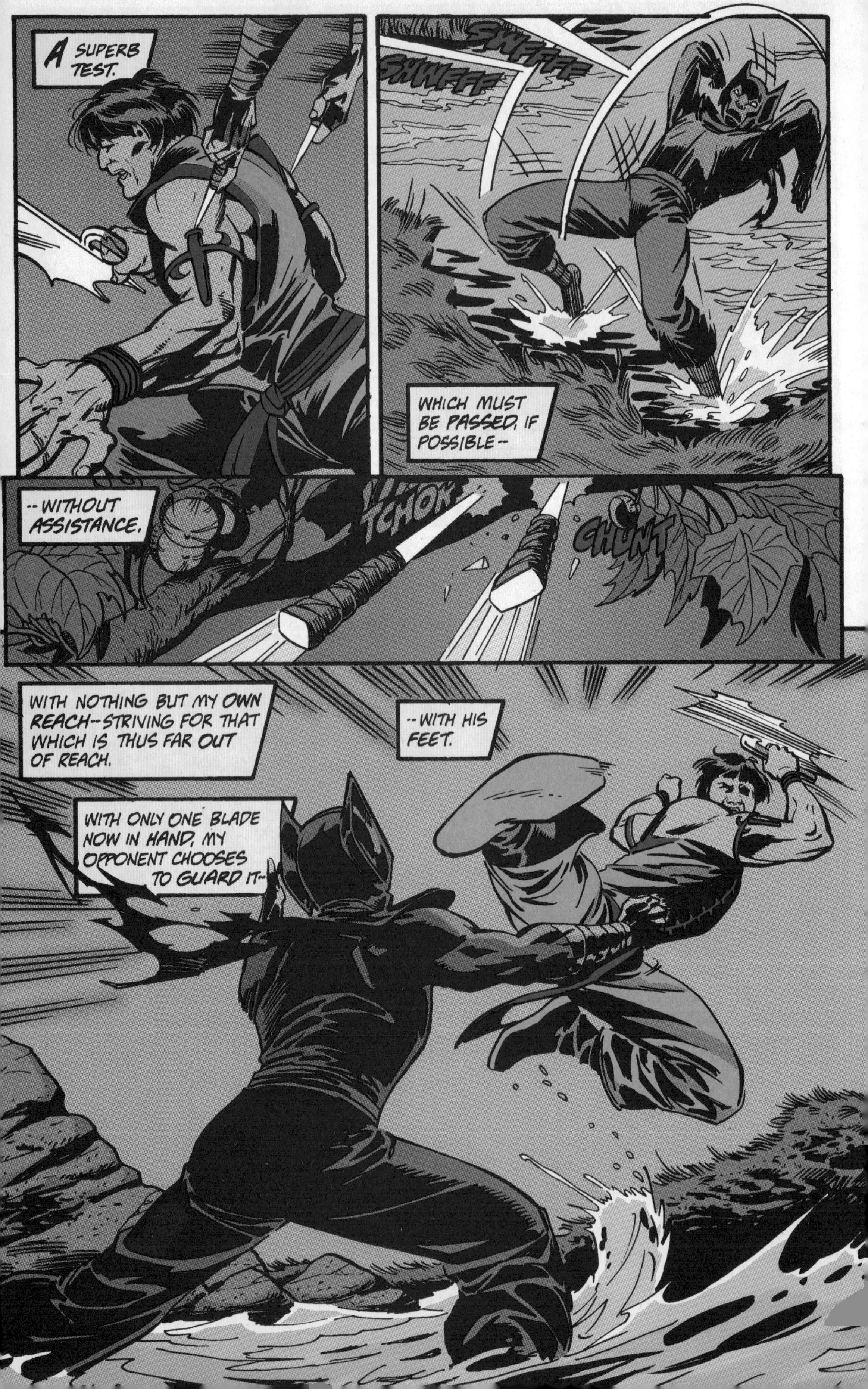
A SUPERB TEST.
SHWIFFF
SHWFFFFF
WHICH MUST BE PASSED, IF POSSIBLE--
--WITHOUT ASSISTANCE.
TCHOK
CHUNT
WITH NOTHING BUT MY OWN REACH--STRIVING FOR THAT WHICH IS THUS FAR OUT OF REACH.
--WITH HIS FEET.
WITH ONLY ONE BLADE NOW IN HAND, MY OPPONENT CHOOSES TO GUARD IT--

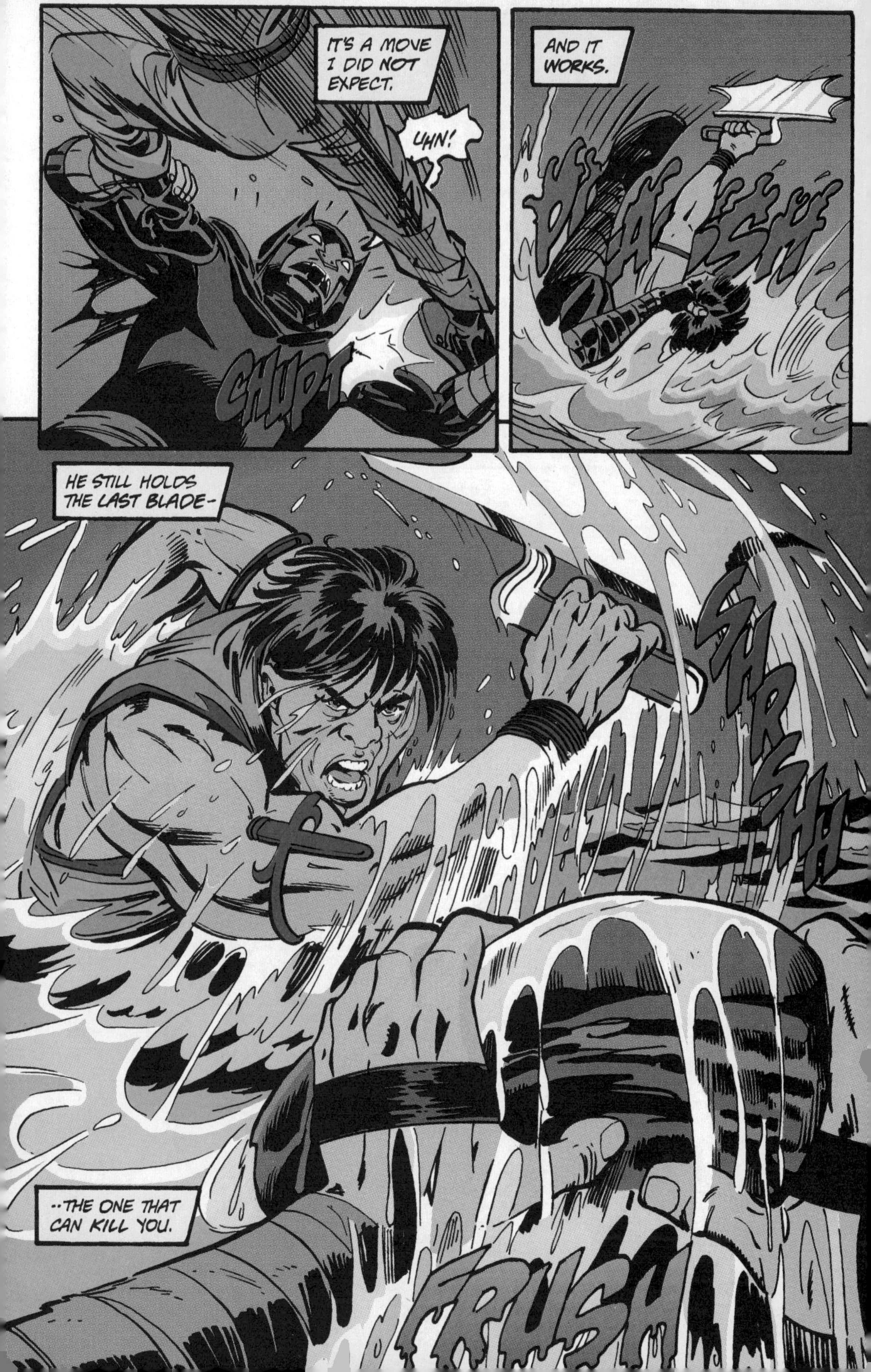
IT'S A MOVE I DID NOT EXPECT.
UHN!
CHUPT
AND IT WORKS.
HE STILL HOLDS THE LAST BLADE-
SHRSHH
..THE ONE THAT CAN KILL YOU.

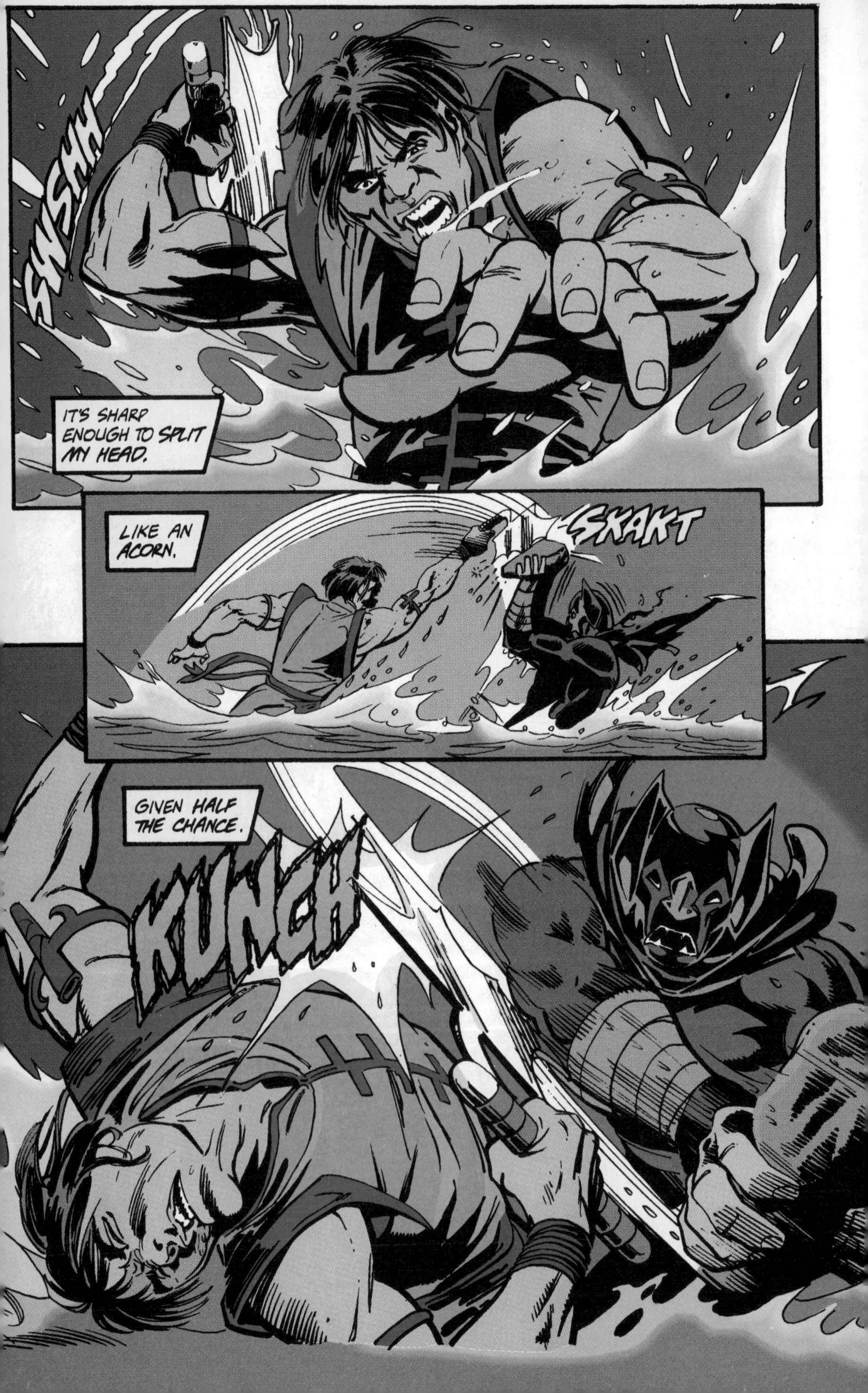
SHSHH
IT'S SHARP ENOUGH TO SPLIT MY HEAD.
LIKE AN ACORN.
SKAKT
GIVEN HALF THE CHANCE.
KUNCH

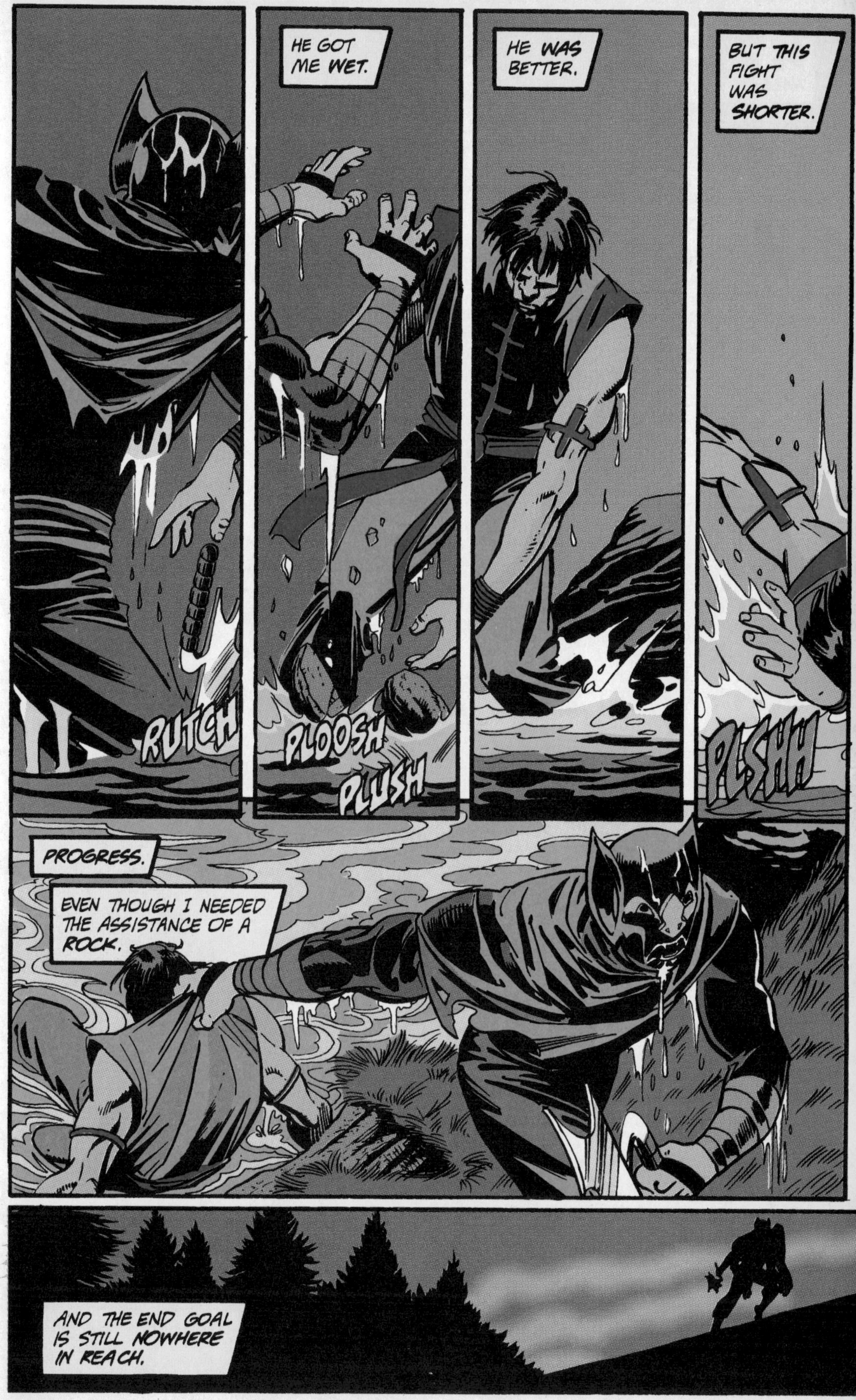
HE GOT ME WET.
HE WAS BETTER.
BUT THIS FIGHT WAS SHORTER.
RUTCH
PLOOSH
PLUSH
PLSHH
PROGRESS.
EVEN THOUGH I NEEDED THE ASSISTANCE OF A ROCK.
AND THE END GOAL IS STILL NOWHERE IN REACH.

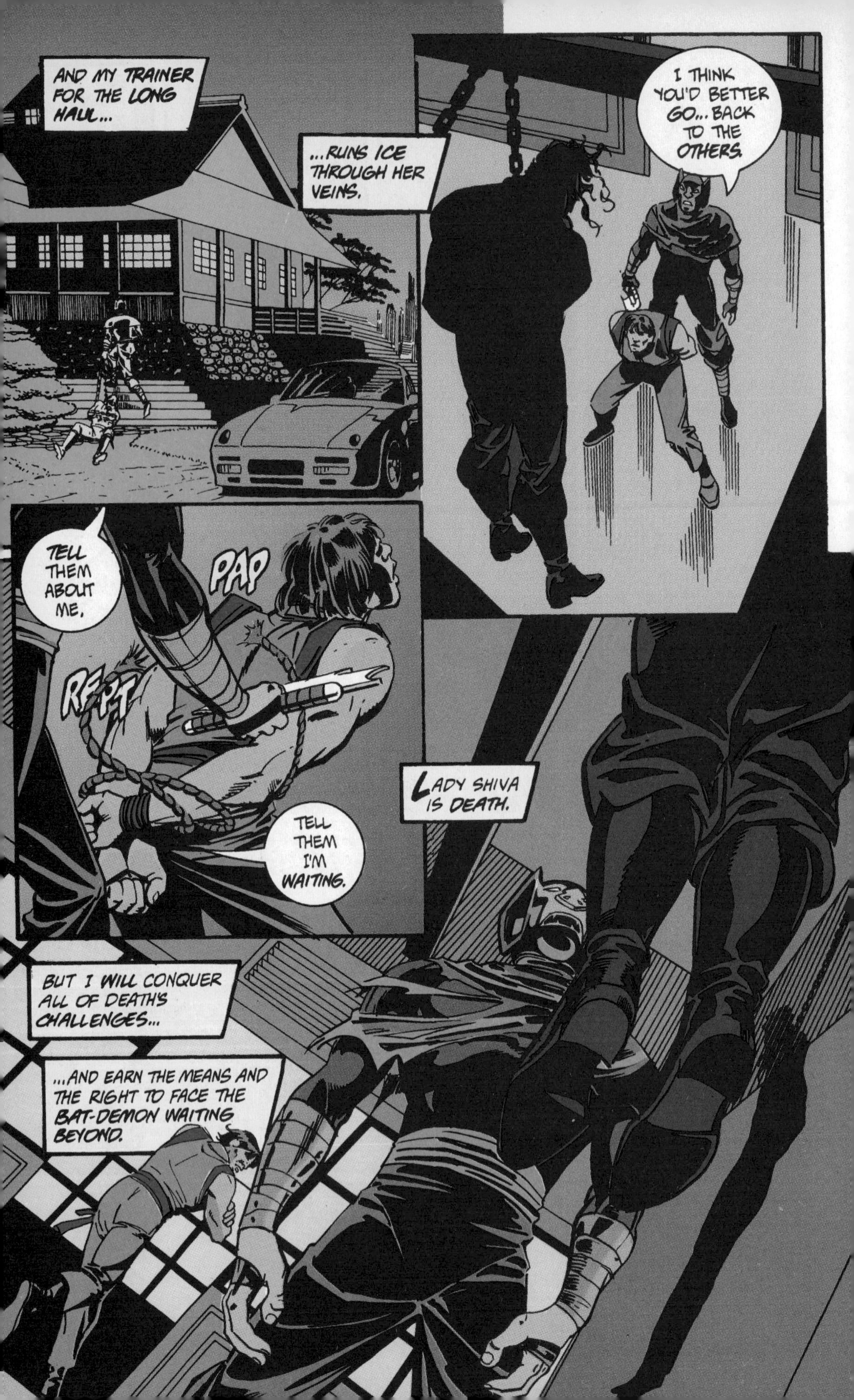
AND MY TRAINER FOR THE LONG HAUL...
...RUNS ICE THROUGH HER VEINS.
I THINK YOU'D BETTER GO... BACK TO THE OTHERS.
TELL THEM ABOUT ME.
PAP
REPT
TELL THEM I'M WAITING.
LADY SHIVA IS DEATH.
BUT I WILL CONQUER ALL OF DEATH'S CHALLENGES...
...AND EARN THE MEANS AND THE RIGHT TO FACE THE BAT-DEMON WAITING BEYOND.

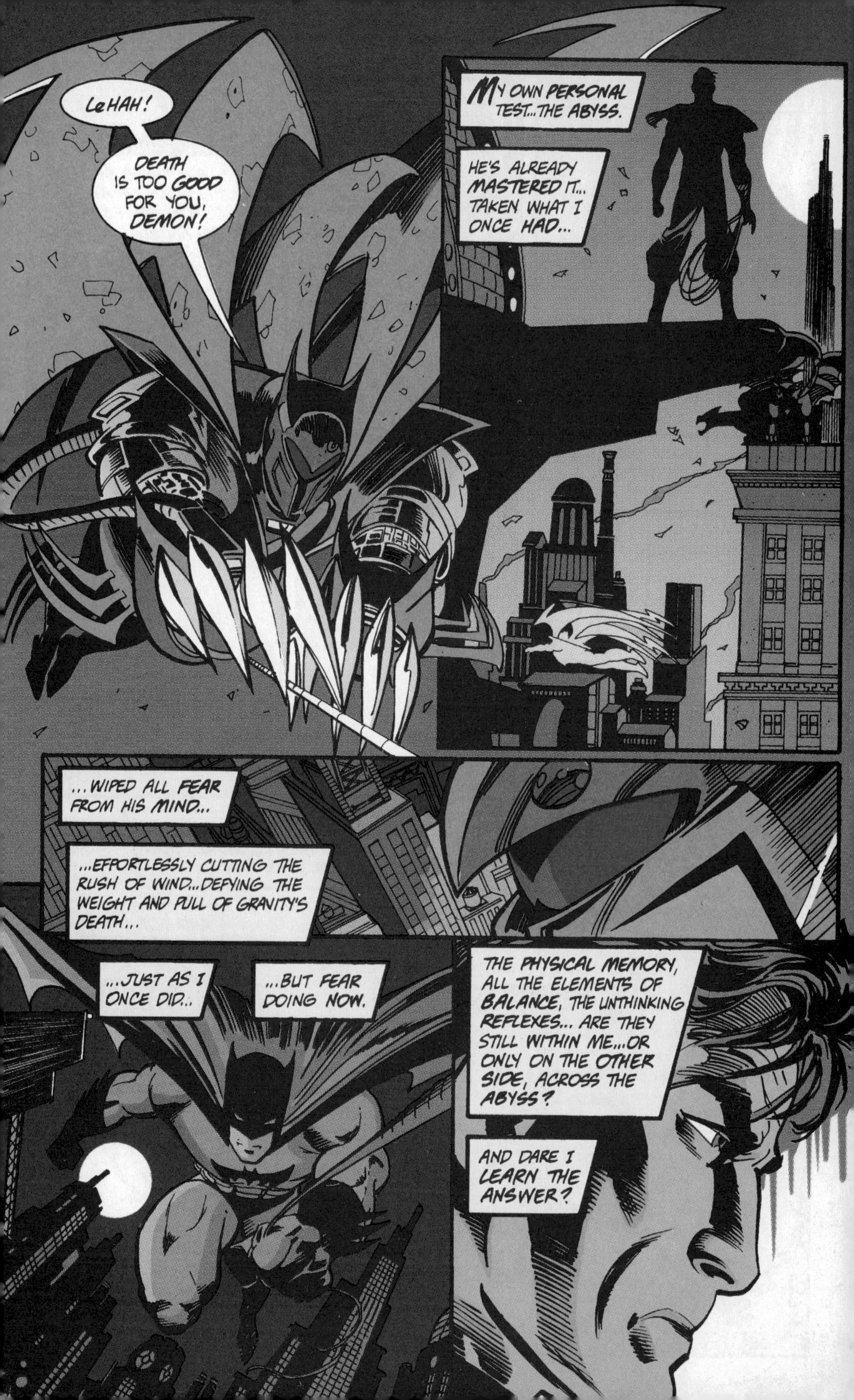
LeHAH!
DEATH IS TOO GOOD FOR YOU, DEMON!
MY OWN PERSONAL TEST...THE ABYSS.
HE'S ALREADY MASTERED IT... TAKEN WHAT I ONCE HAD...
...WIPED ALL FEAR FROM HIS MIND...
...EFFORTLESSLY CUTTING THE RUSH OF WIND...DEFYING THE WEIGHT AND PULL OF GRAVITY'S DEATH...
...JUST AS I ONCE DID...
...BUT FEAR DOING NOW.
THE PHYSICAL MEMORY, ALL THE ELEMENTS OF BALANCE, THE UNTHINKING REFLEXES... ARE THEY STILL WITHIN ME...OR ONLY ON THE OTHER SIDE, ACROSS THE ABYSS?
AND DARE I LEARN THE ANSWER?

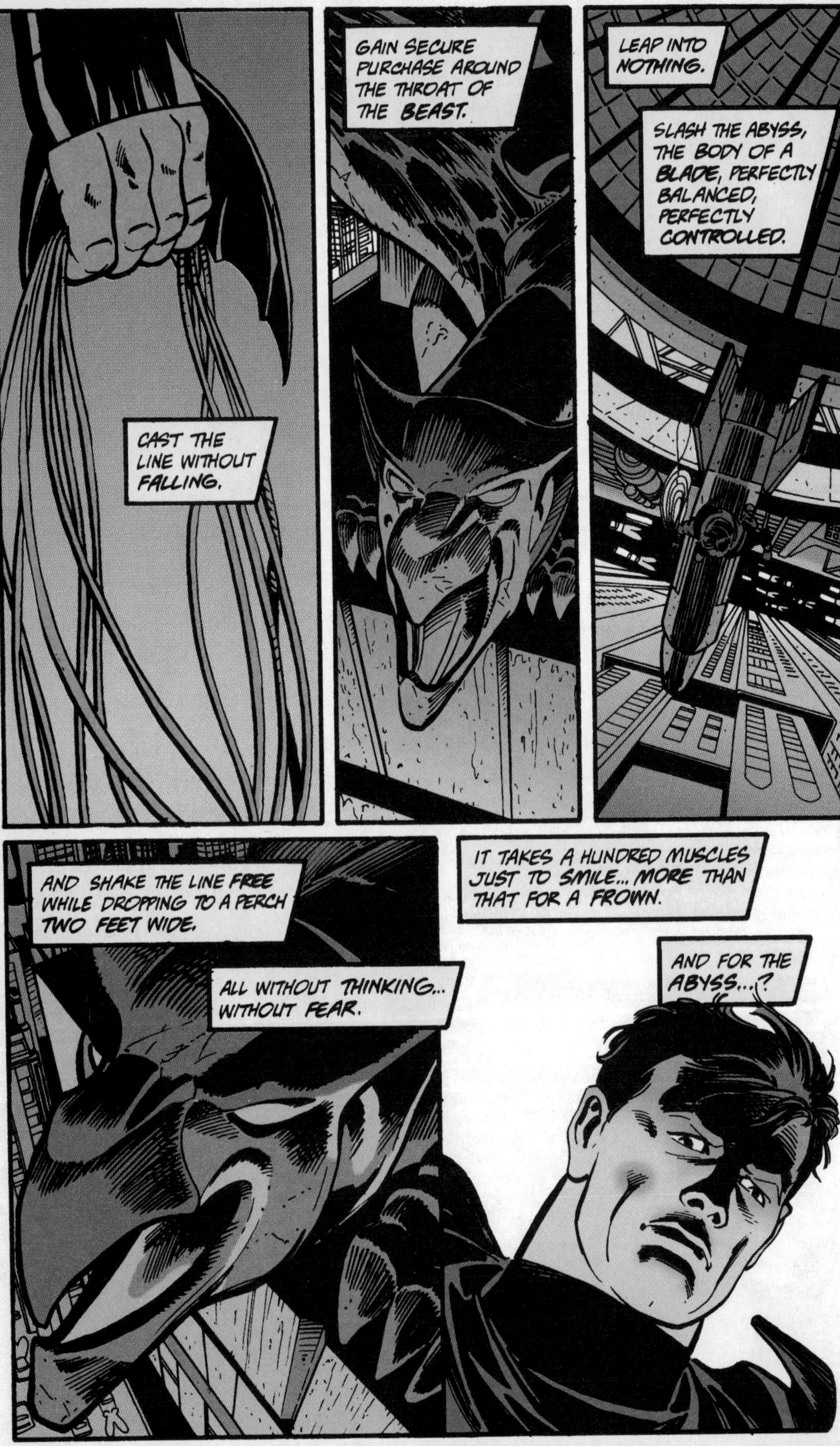
GAIN SECURE PURCHASE AROUND THE THROAT OF THE BEAST.
LEAP INTO NOTHING.
SLASH THE ABYSS, THE BODY OF A BLADE, PERFECTLY BALANCED, PERFECTLY CONTROLLED.
CAST THE LINE WITHOUT FALLING.
AND SHAKE THE LINE FREE WHILE DROPPING TO A PERCH TWO FEET WIDE.
ALL WITHOUT THINKING... WITHOUT FEAR.
IT TAKES A HUNDRED MUSCLES JUST TO SMILE... MORE THAN THAT FOR A FROWN.
AND FOR THE ABYSS...?

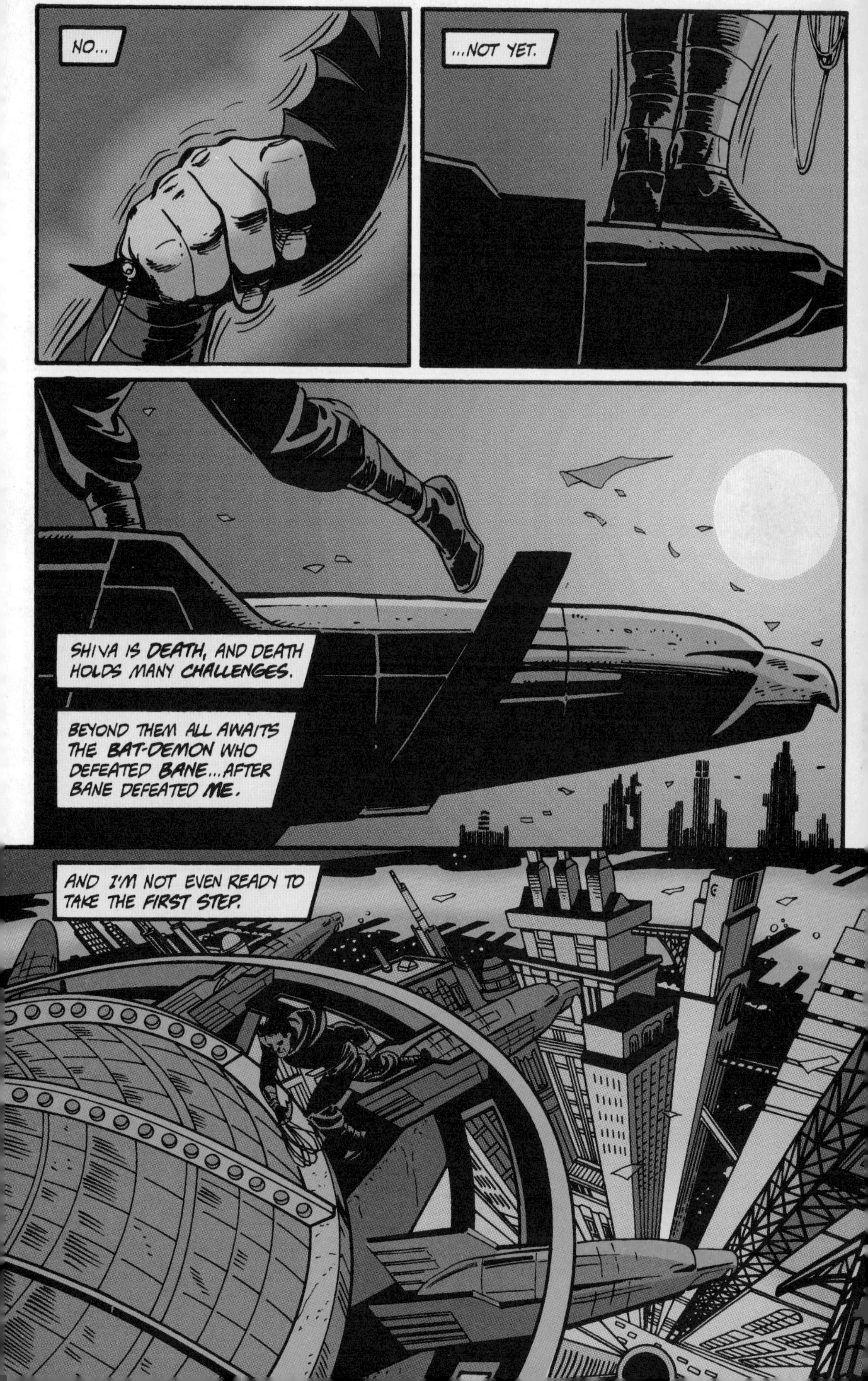
NO...
...NOT YET.
SHIVA IS DEATH, AND DEATH HOLDS MANY CHALLENGES.
BEYOND THEM ALL AWAITS THE BAT-DEMON WHO DEFEATED BANE...AFTER BANE DEFEATED ME.
AND I'M NOT EVEN READY TO TAKE THE FIRST STEP.

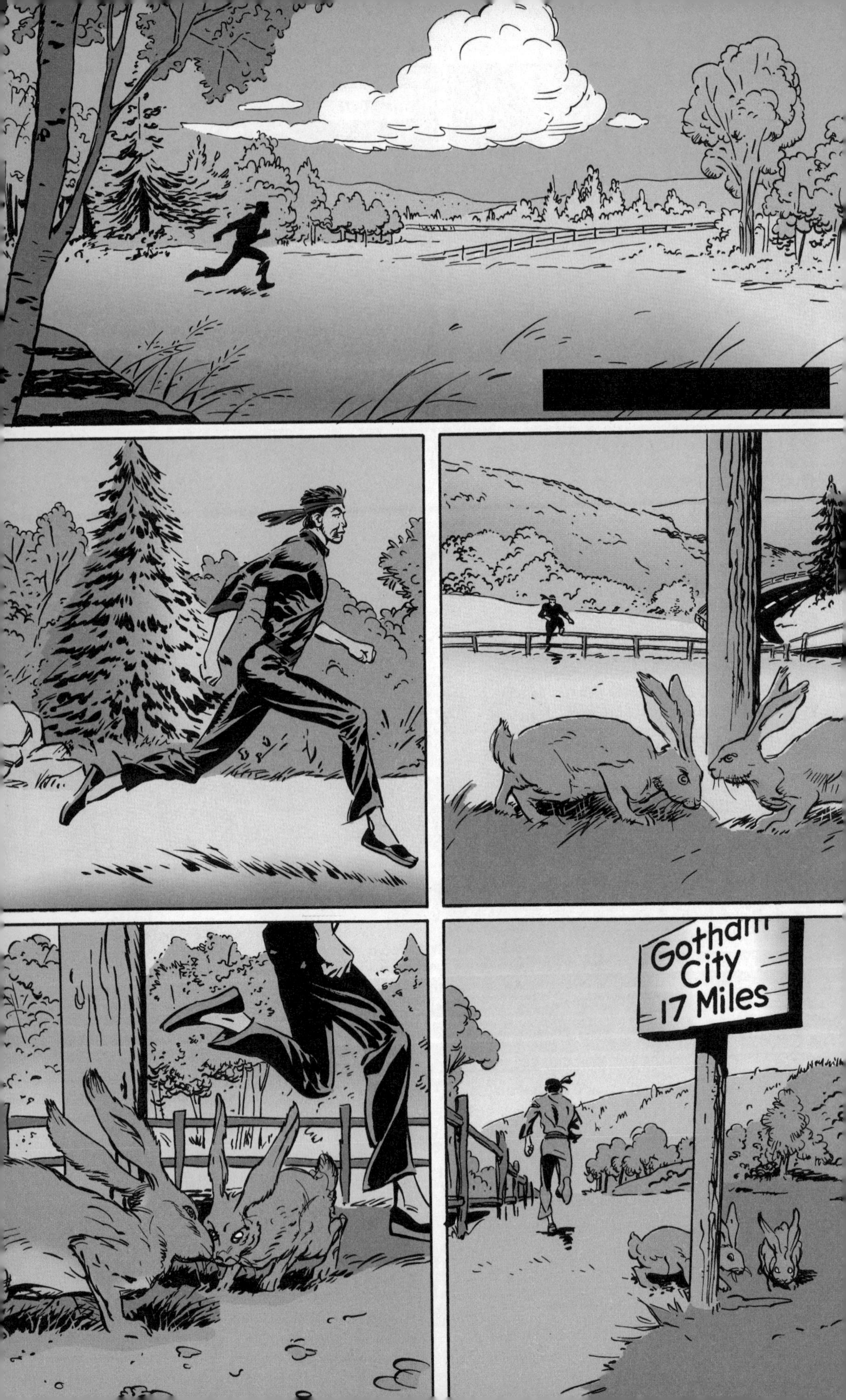
[redacted]
Gotham City 17 Miles

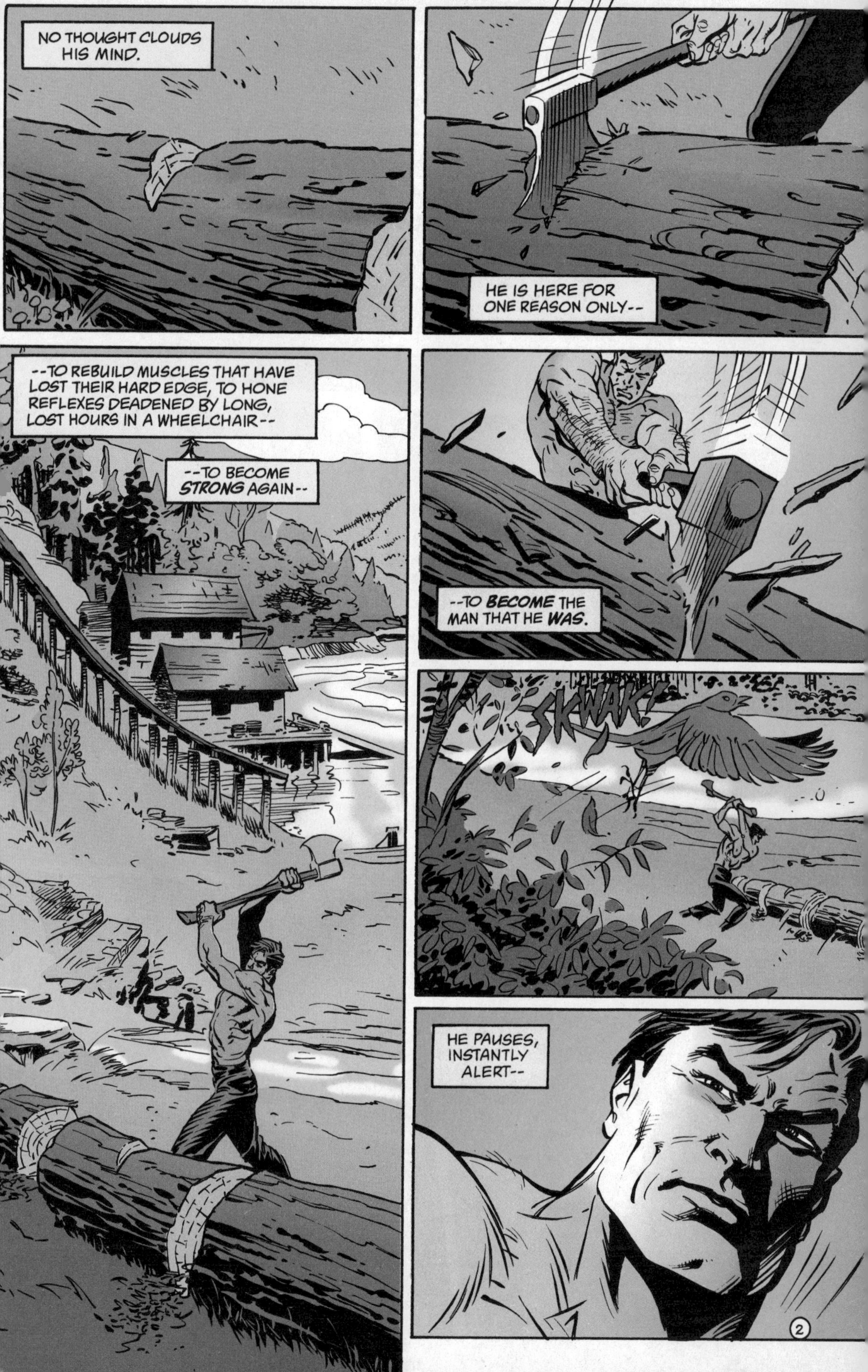

NO THOUGHT CLOUDS HIS MIND.
HE IS HERE FOR ONE REASON ONLY--
--TO REBUILD MUSCLES THAT HAVE LOST THEIR HARD EDGE, TO HONE REFLEXES DEADENED BY LONG, LOST HOURS IN A WHEELCHAIR--
--TO BECOME STRONG AGAIN--
--TO BECOME THE MAN THAT HE WAS.
SKWAK!
HE PAUSES, INSTANTLY ALERT--

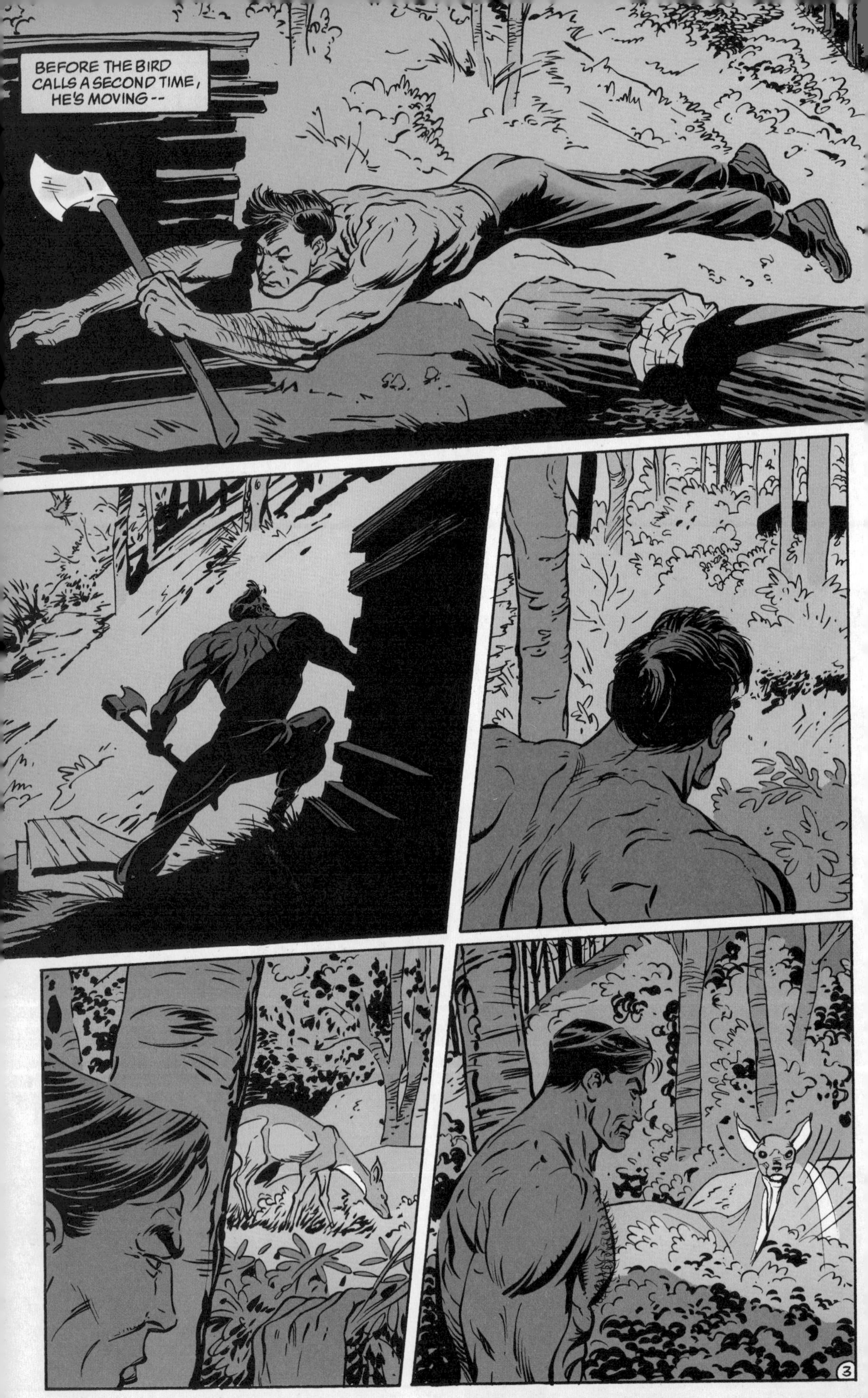
BEFORE THE BIRD CALLS A SECOND TIME, HE'S MOVING --
3

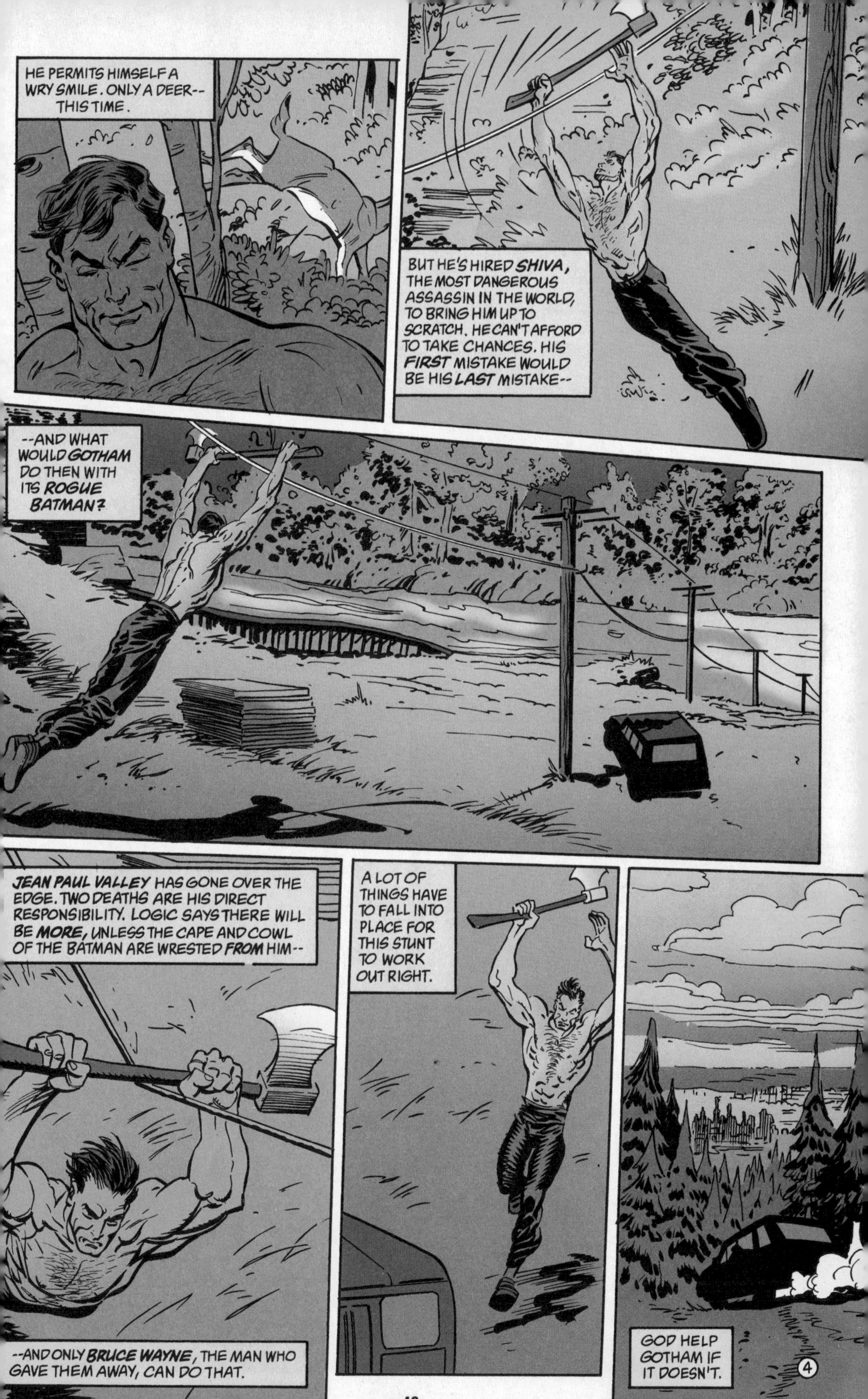

HE PERMITS HIMSELF A WRY SMILE. ONLY A DEER-- THIS TIME.
BUT HE'S HIRED SHIVA, THE MOST DANGEROUS ASSASSIN IN THE WORLD, TO BRING HIM UP TO SCRATCH. HE CAN'T AFFORD TO TAKE CHANCES. HIS FIRST MISTAKE WOULD BE HIS LAST MISTAKE--
--AND WHAT WOULD GOTHAM DO THEN WITH ITS ROGUE BATMAN?
JEAN PAUL VALLEY HAS GONE OVER THE EDGE. TWO DEATHS ARE HIS DIRECT RESPONSIBILITY. LOGIC SAYS THERE WILL BE MORE, UNLESS THE CAPE AND COWL OF THE BATMAN ARE WRESTED FROM HIM--
--AND ONLY BRUCE WAYNE, THE MAN WHO GAVE THEM AWAY, CAN DO THAT.
A LOT OF THINGS HAVE TO FALL INTO PLACE FOR THIS STUNT TO WORK OUT RIGHT.
GOD HELP GOTHAM IF IT DOESN'T.
4

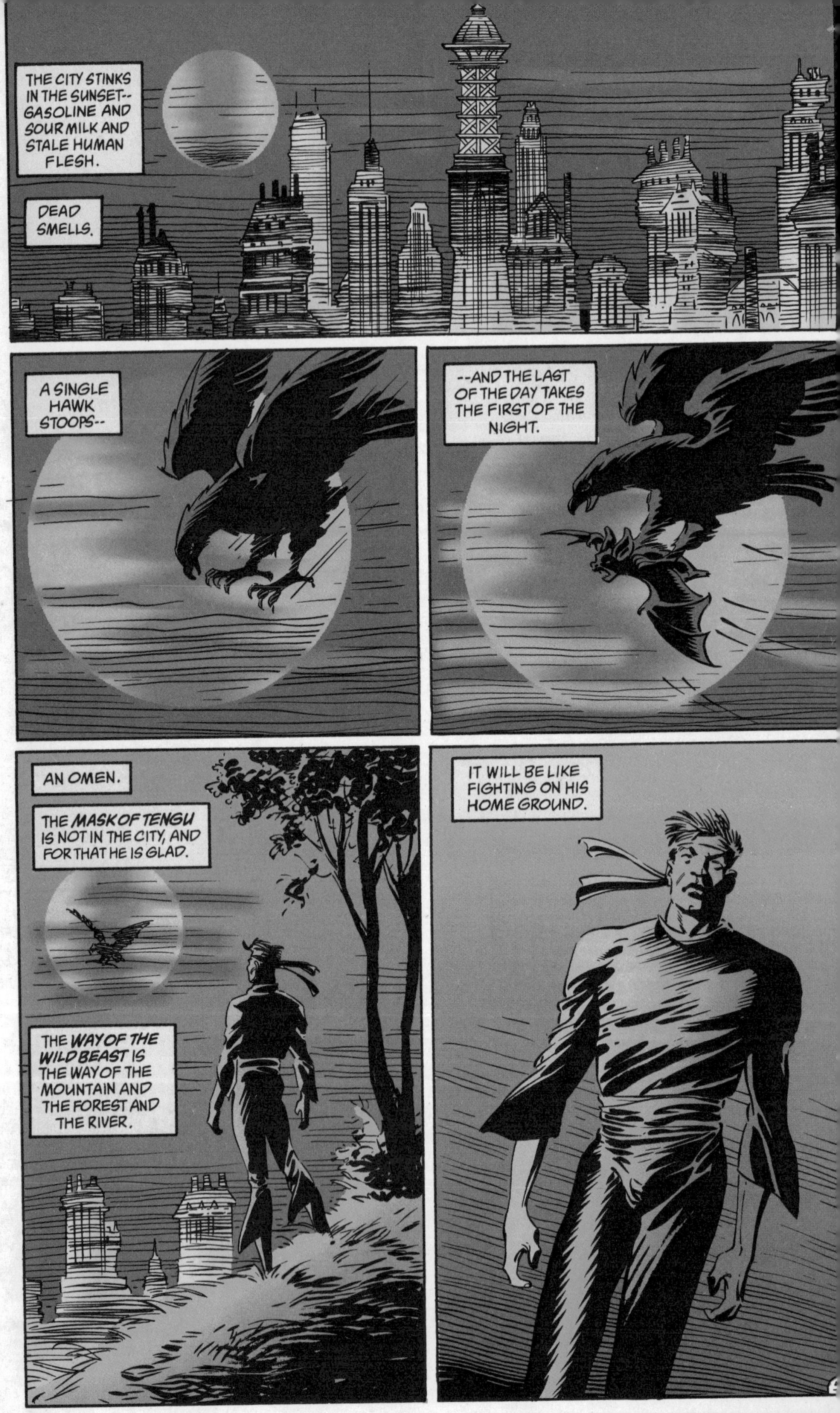
THE CITY STINKS IN THE SUNSET-- GASOLINE AND SOUR MILK AND STALE HUMAN FLESH.
DEAD SMELLS.
A SINGLE HAWK STOOPS--
--AND THE LAST OF THE DAY TAKES THE FIRST OF THE NIGHT.
AN OMEN.
THE *MASK OF TENGU* IS NOT IN THE CITY, AND FOR THAT HE IS GLAD.
THE *WAY OF THE WILD BEAST* IS THE WAY OF THE MOUNTAIN AND THE FOREST AND THE RIVER.
IT WILL BE LIKE FIGHTING ON HIS HOME GROUND.

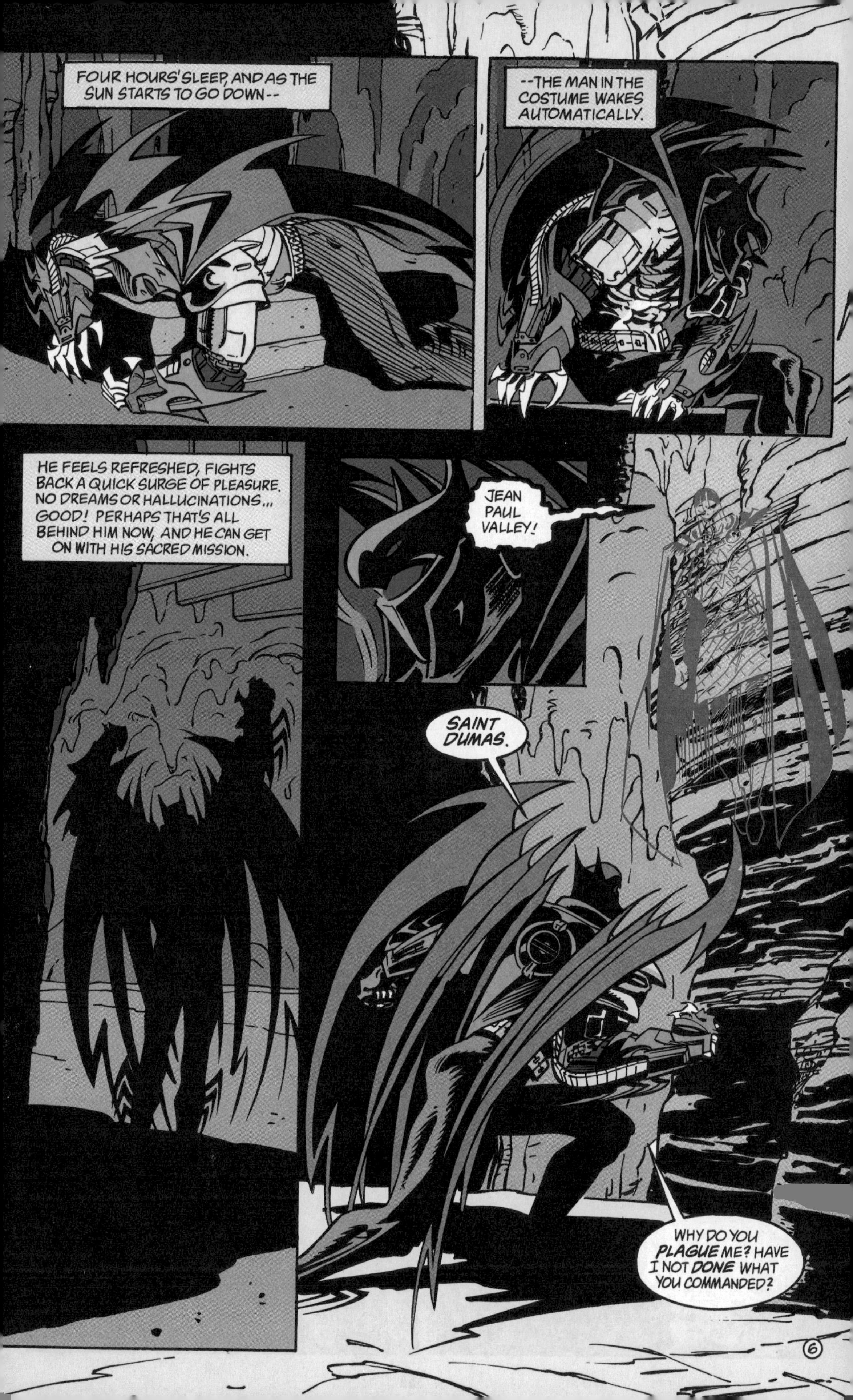

FOUR HOURS' SLEEP, AND AS THE SUN STARTS TO GO DOWN--
--THE MAN IN THE COSTUME WAKES AUTOMATICALLY.
HE FEELS REFRESHED, FIGHTS BACK A QUICK SURGE OF PLEASURE. NO DREAMS OR HALLUCINATIONS... GOOD! PERHAPS THAT'S ALL BEHIND HIM NOW, AND HE CAN GET ON WITH HIS SACRED MISSION.
JEAN PAUL VALLEY!
SAINT DUMAS.
WHY DO YOU PLAGUE ME? HAVE I NOT DONE WHAT YOU COMMANDED?
6

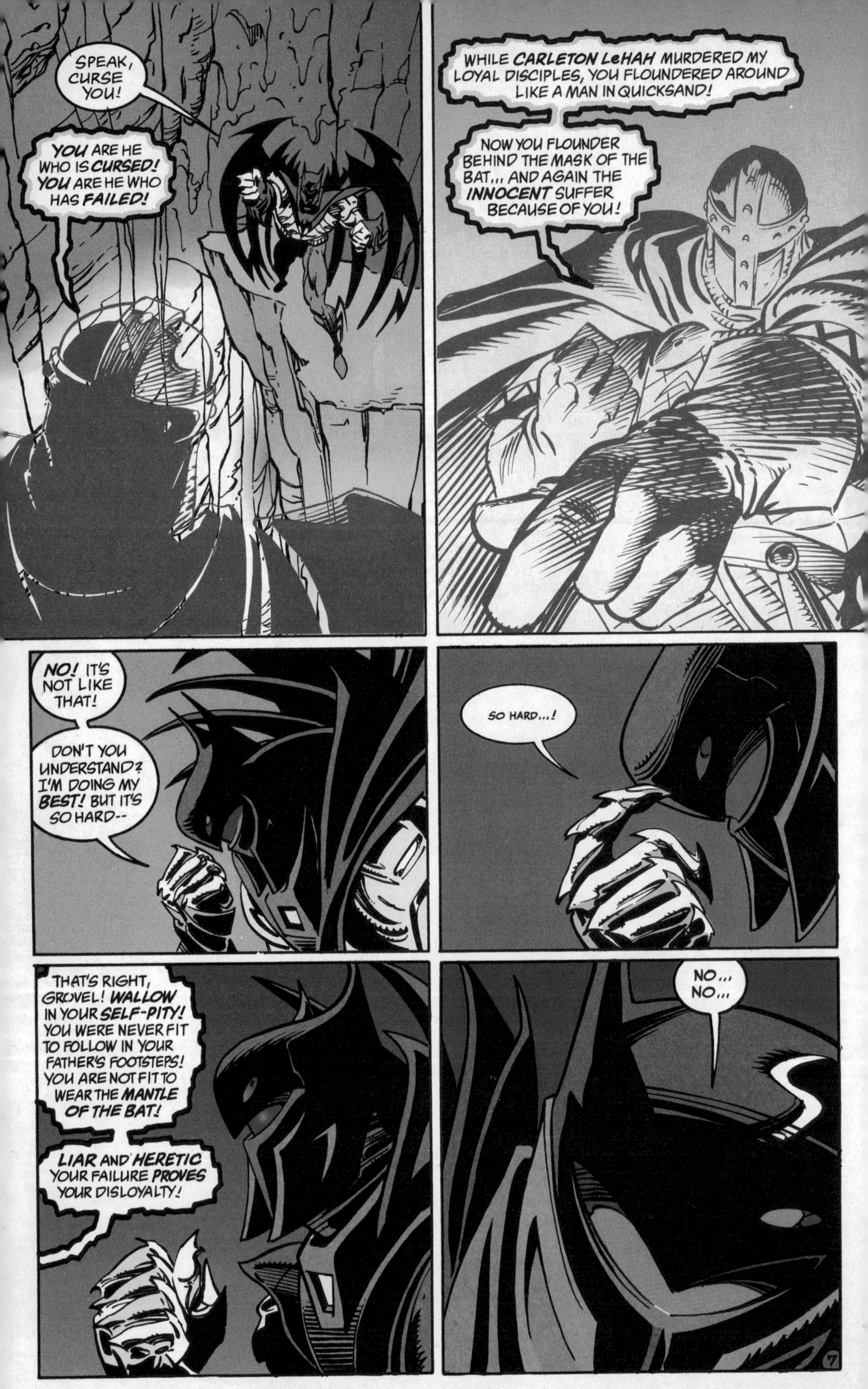
SPEAK, CURSE YOU!
YOU ARE HE WHO IS CURSED! YOU ARE HE WHO HAS FAILED!
WHILE CARLETON LeHAH MURDERED MY LOYAL DISCIPLES, YOU FLOUNDERED AROUND LIKE A MAN IN QUICKSAND!
NOW YOU FLOUNDER BEHIND THE MASK OF THE BAT... AND AGAIN THE INNOCENT SUFFER BECAUSE OF YOU!
NO! IT'S NOT LIKE THAT!
DON'T YOU UNDERSTAND? I'M DOING MY BEST! BUT IT'S SO HARD--
SO HARD...!
THAT'S RIGHT, GROVEL! WALLOW IN YOUR SELF-PITY! YOU WERE NEVER FIT TO FOLLOW IN YOUR FATHER'S FOOTSTEPS! YOU ARE NOT FIT TO WEAR THE MANTLE OF THE BAT!
LIAR AND HERETIC YOUR FAILURE PROVES YOUR DISLOYALTY!
NO... NO...
7

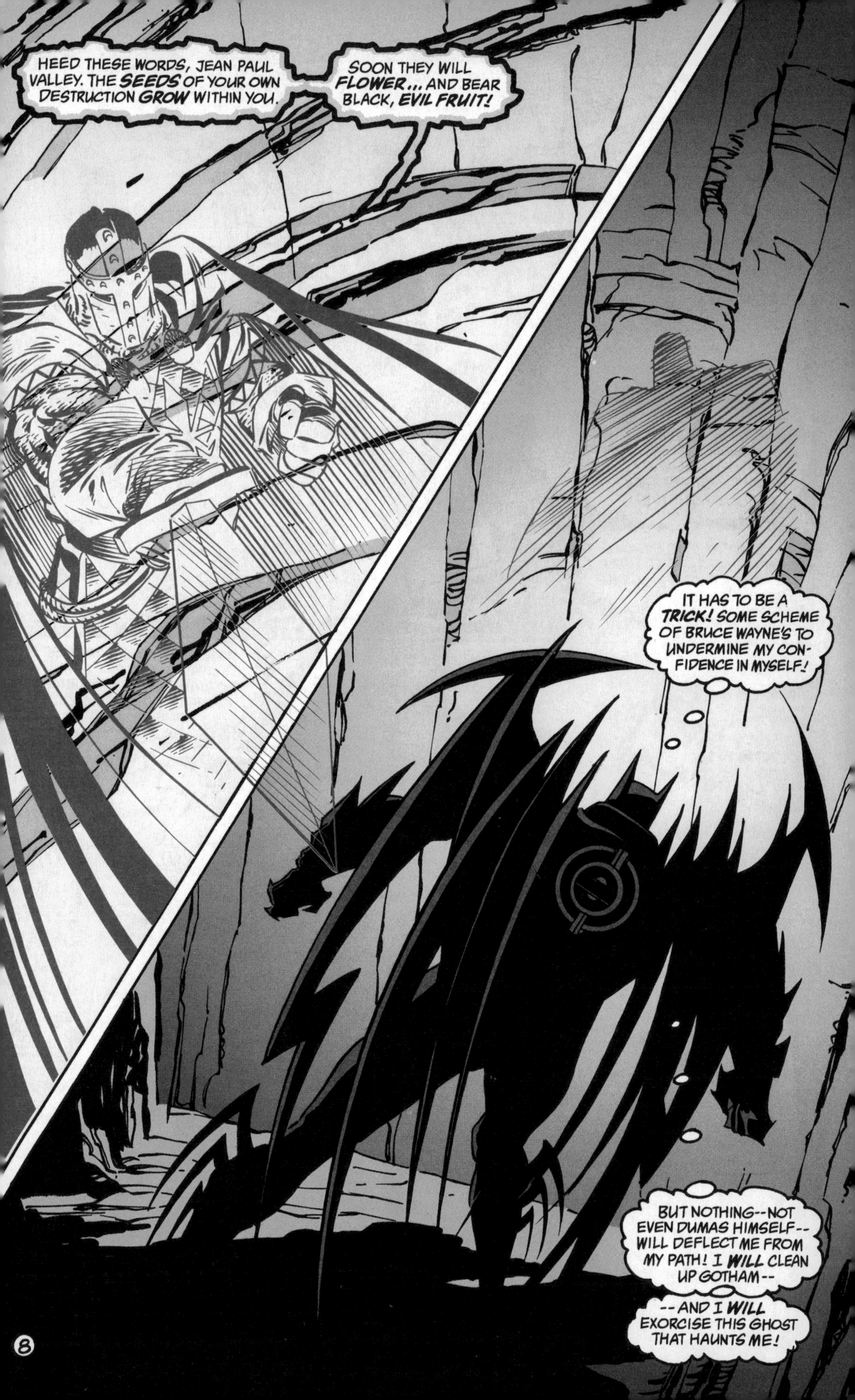
HEED THESE WORDS, JEAN PAUL VALLEY. THE SEEDS OF YOUR OWN DESTRUCTION GROW WITHIN YOU.
SOON THEY WILL FLOWER... AND BEAR BLACK, EVIL FRUIT!
IT HAS TO BE A TRICK! SOME SCHEME OF BRUCE WAYNE'S TO UNDERMINE MY CON-FIDENCE IN MYSELF!
BUT NOTHING--NOT EVEN DUMAS HIMSELF--WILL DEFLECT ME FROM MY PATH! I WILL CLEAN UP GOTHAM--
--AND I WILL EXORCISE THIS GHOST THAT HAUNTS ME!

--HAS TO MEAN *SOMETHING!*

TOLTEC--ANCIENT ROMAN-- MAORI...I'VE DREDGED THE CRAYS' DATA-BANKS FOR EVERY MAJOR CULTURE IN HISTORY--

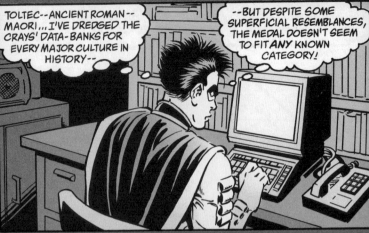

--BUT DESPITE SOME SUPERFICIAL RESEMBLANCES, THE MEDAL DOESN'T SEEM TO FIT *ANY* KNOWN CATEGORY!

I TOOK THE PHOTO LAST NIGHT, WHEN *PAUL* FOUND THE MEDAL DURING THAT ARMS DEAL BUST. HE SEEMED TO KNOW WHAT IT WAS ALL ABOUT-- WHICH SUGGESTS I SHOULD FIND OUT *FAST!*

I'LL FAX IT TO BRUCE'S APARTMENT-- GIVE HIM A HEAD START AT FIGURING IT OUT.

PAUL SEEMS TO BE GOING CRAZY, SPINNING OUT OF ALL CONTROL.

HOW MANY MORE *CORPSES* WILL WE HAVE TO PICK OFF GOTHAM'S STREETS, COURTESY OF ITS ONE-TIME PROTECTOR-- THE *BATMAN?*

I'VE GOT A GUT FEELING THAT THE QUICKER WE SOLVE THIS ONE, THE BETTER! BUT I'M GETTING NO—WHERE FAST.

MAYBE A *WISER* HEAD THAN MINE'LL KNOW....!

... ONE NINETY-THREE...

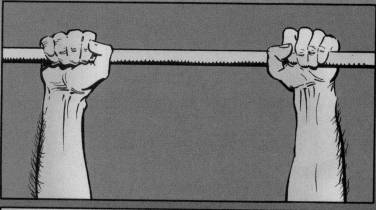

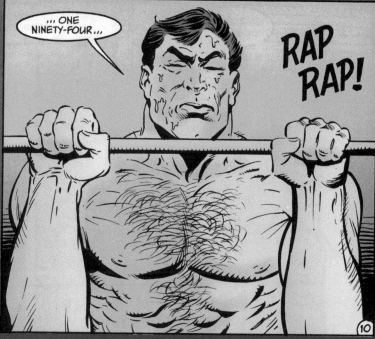

... ONE NINETY-FOUR...

RAP RAP!

10

EXPECTING TROUBLE?

ALWAYS -- AT LEAST, WHEN *SHIVA'S* IN THE GAME!

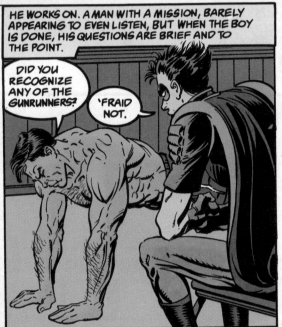

HE WORKS ON. A MAN WITH A MISSION, BARELY APPEARING TO EVEN LISTEN, BUT WHEN THE BOY IS DONE, HIS QUESTIONS ARE BRIEF AND TO THE POINT.

DID YOU RECOGNIZE ANY OF THE GUNRUNNERS?

'FRAID NOT.

CARLETON LeHAH?

I THOUGHT HE WAS *DEAD...?*

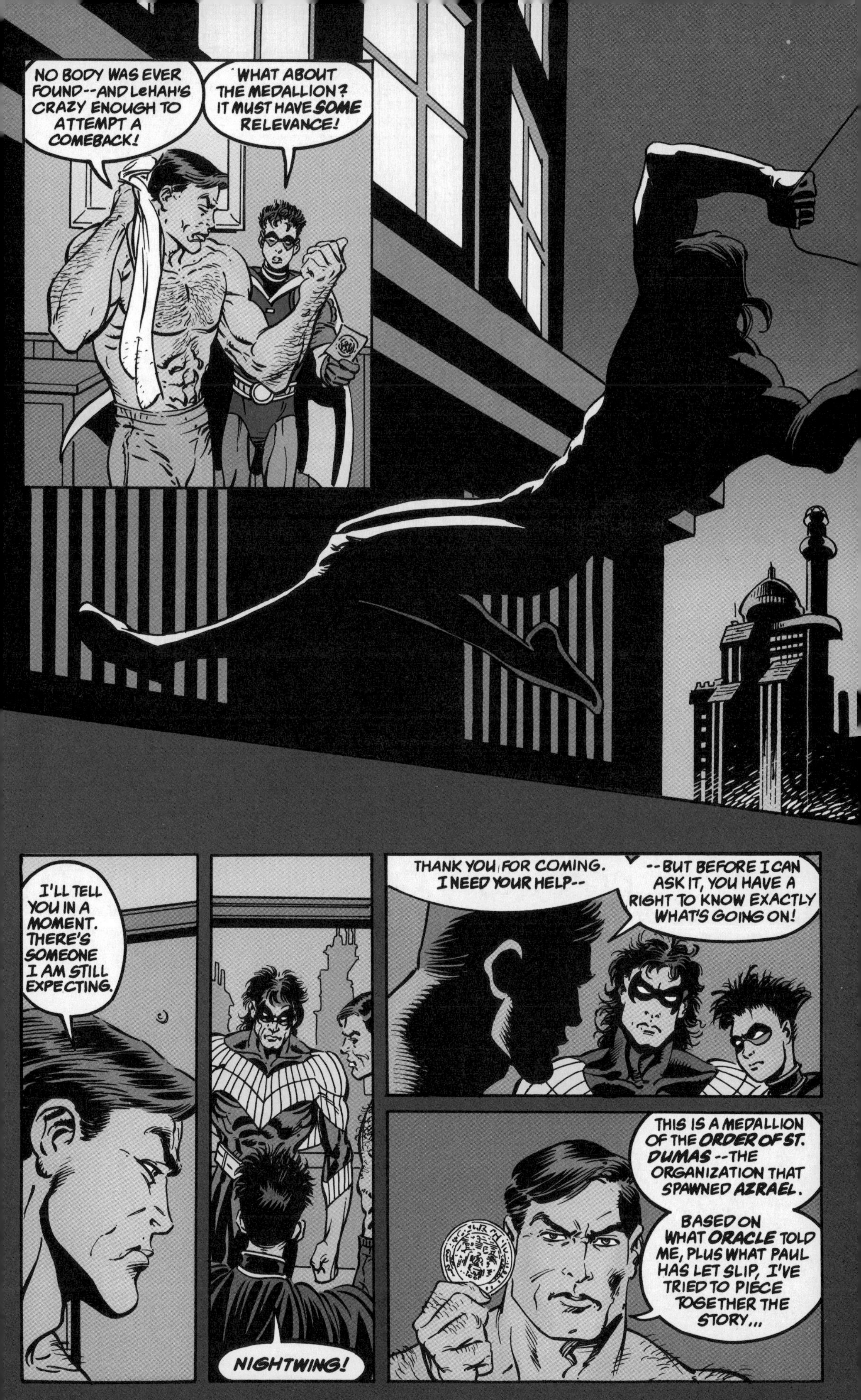
NO BODY WAS EVER FOUND--AND LeHAH'S CRAZY ENOUGH TO ATTEMPT A COMEBACK!
WHAT ABOUT THE MEDALLION? IT MUST HAVE SOME RELEVANCE!
I'LL TELL YOU IN A MOMENT. THERE'S SOMEONE I AM STILL EXPECTING.
NIGHTWING!
THANK YOU FOR COMING. I NEED YOUR HELP--
--BUT BEFORE I CAN ASK IT, YOU HAVE A RIGHT TO KNOW EXACTLY WHAT'S GOING ON!
THIS IS A MEDALLION OF THE ORDER OF ST. DUMAS--THE ORGANIZATION THAT SPAWNED AZRAEL.
BASED ON WHAT ORACLE TOLD ME, PLUS WHAT PAUL HAS LET SLIP, I'VE TRIED TO PIECE TOGETHER THE STORY...

A CERTAIN SECT BROKE AWAY FROM THE **KNIGHTS TEMPLAR** BACK IN THE FOURTEENTH CENTURY, CLAIMING TO FOLLOW **DUMAS**-- A "SAINT" WHO SEEMS NEVER TO HAVE EXISTED!

"THERE ARE FEW HISTORIC RECORDS, BUT IT APPEARS THEY PROSPERED OVER THE CENTURIES AND AMASSED FANTASTIC WEALTH AND POWER AMONG THEIR RELATIVELY FEW MEMBERS.

"THEY DEVELOPED A WHOLE THEOLOGY AROUND THIS MYSTERIOUS DUMAS AND HIS FOE, THE DEMON **BIIS**. AND TO MAKE SURE THE ORDER'S STRICT RULES WERE KEPT, THEY CAME UP WITH THEIR VERY OWN VERSION OF A COP--

"--AZRAEL, THE SO-CALLED AVENGING ANGEL!

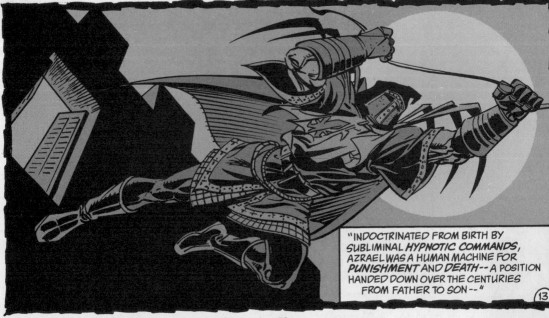

"INDOCTRINATED FROM BIRTH BY SUBLIMINAL **HYPNOTIC COMMANDS**, AZRAEL WAS A HUMAN MACHINE FOR **PUNISHMENT** AND **DEATH**-- A POSITION HANDED DOWN OVER THE CENTURIES FROM FATHER TO SON--"

⑬

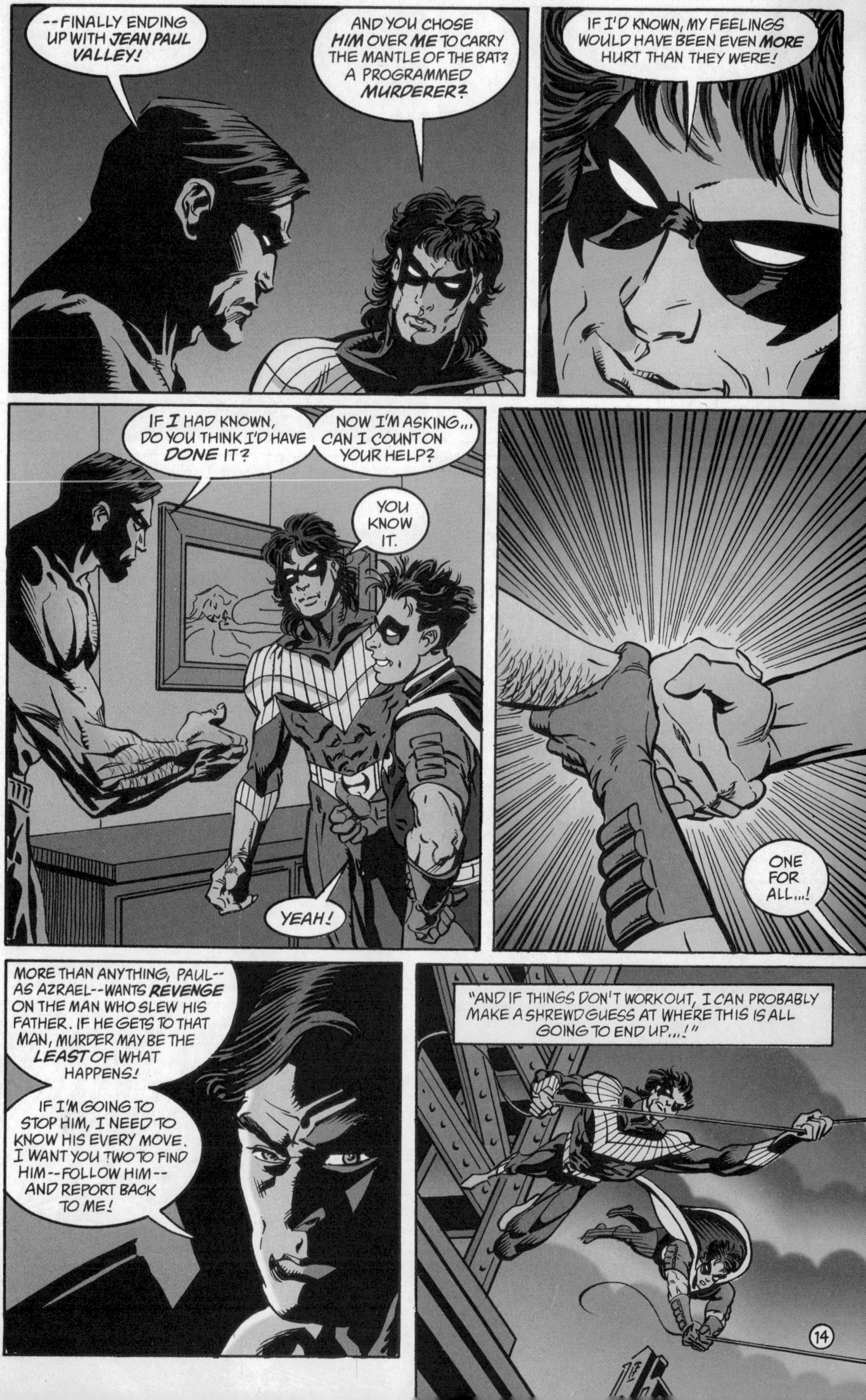
--FINALLY ENDING UP WITH JEAN PAUL VALLEY!
AND YOU CHOSE HIM OVER ME TO CARRY THE MANTLE OF THE BAT? A PROGRAMMED MURDERER?
IF I'D KNOWN, MY FEELINGS WOULD HAVE BEEN EVEN MORE HURT THAN THEY WERE!
IF I HAD KNOWN, DO YOU THINK I'D HAVE DONE IT?
NOW I'M ASKING... CAN I COUNT ON YOUR HELP?
YOU KNOW IT.
YEAH!
ONE FOR ALL...!
MORE THAN ANYTHING, PAUL--AS AZRAEL--WANTS REVENGE ON THE MAN WHO SLEW HIS FATHER. IF HE GETS TO THAT MAN, MURDER MAY BE THE LEAST OF WHAT HAPPENS!
IF I'M GOING TO STOP HIM, I NEED TO KNOW HIS EVERY MOVE. I WANT YOU TWO TO FIND HIM--FOLLOW HIM--AND REPORT BACK TO ME!
"AND IF THINGS DON'T WORK OUT, I CAN PROBABLY MAKE A SHREWD GUESS AT WHERE THIS IS ALL GOING TO END UP...!"
14

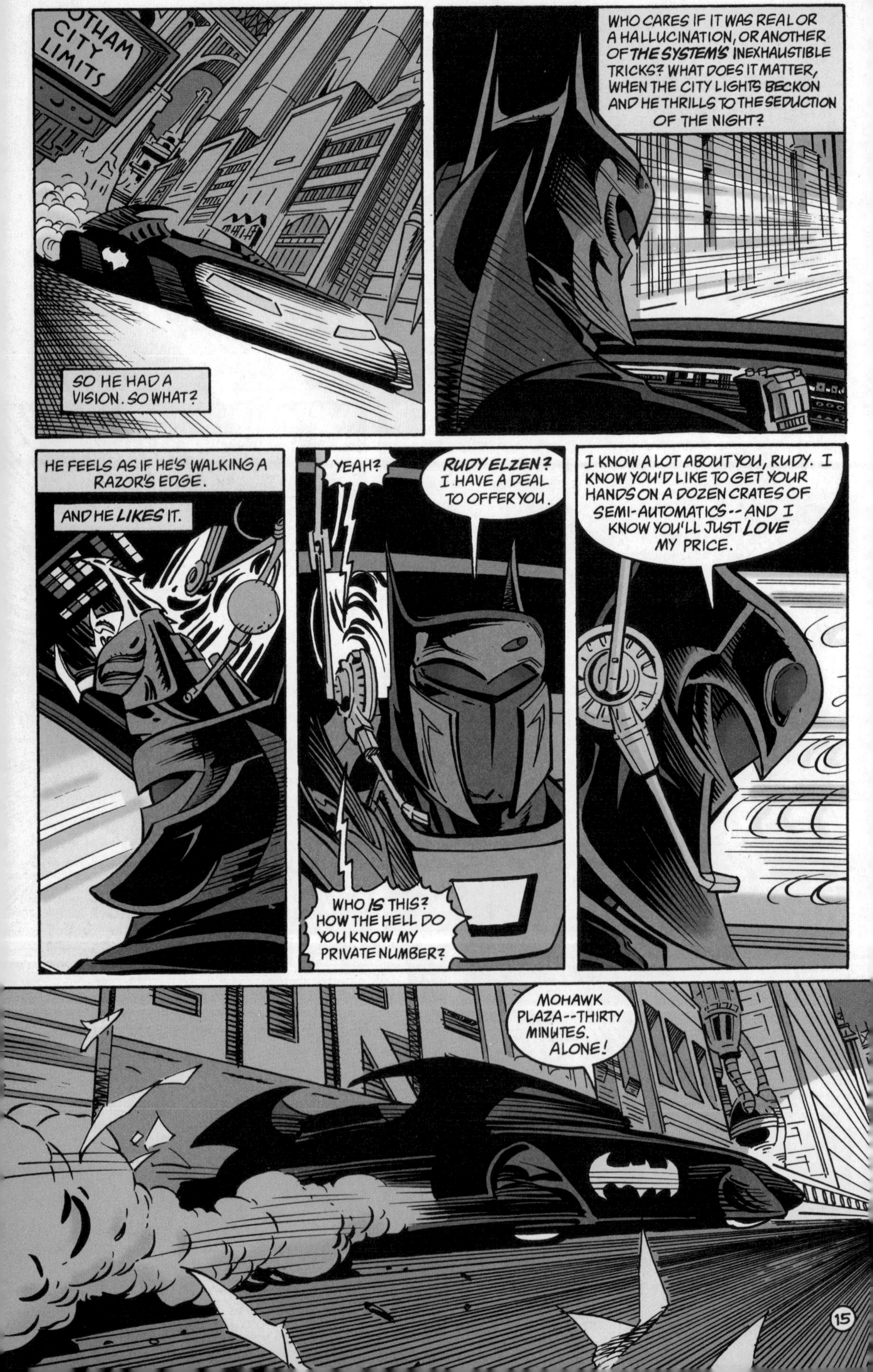
OTHAM CITY LIMITS
SO HE HAD A VISION. SO WHAT?
WHO CARES IF IT WAS REAL OR A HALLUCINATION, OR ANOTHER OF THE SYSTEM'S INEXHAUSTIBLE TRICKS? WHAT DOES IT MATTER, WHEN THE CITY LIGHTS BECKON AND HE THRILLS TO THE SEDUCTION OF THE NIGHT?
HE FEELS AS IF HE'S WALKING A RAZOR'S EDGE.
AND HE LIKES IT.
YEAH?
RUDY ELZEN? I HAVE A DEAL TO OFFER YOU.
WHO IS THIS? HOW THE HELL DO YOU KNOW MY PRIVATE NUMBER?
I KNOW A LOT ABOUT YOU, RUDY. I KNOW YOU'D LIKE TO GET YOUR HANDS ON A DOZEN CRATES OF SEMI-AUTOMATICS--AND I KNOW YOU'LL JUST LOVE MY PRICE.
MOHAWK PLAZA--THIRTY MINUTES. ALONE!
15

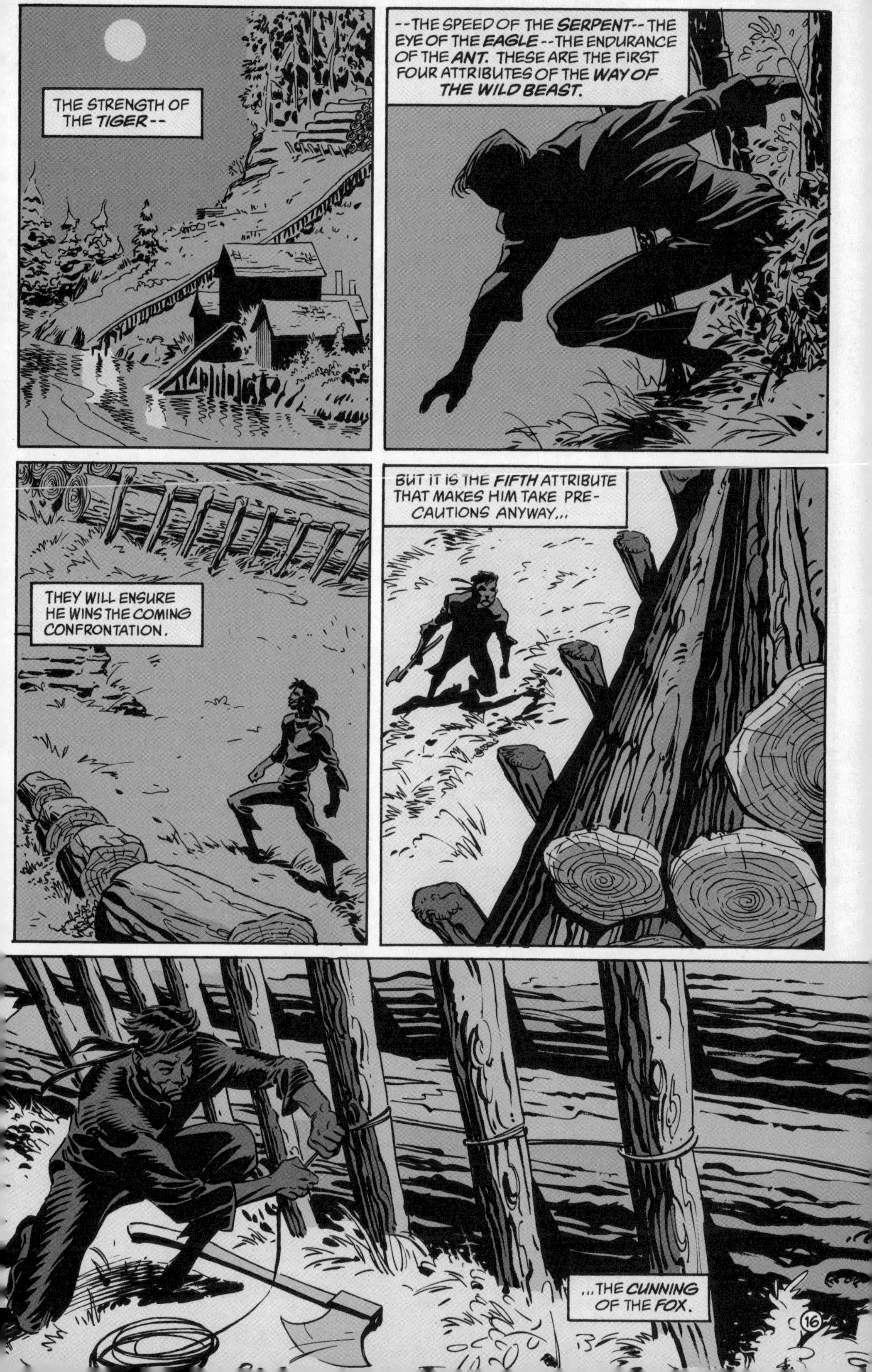
THE STRENGTH OF THE TIGER--
--THE SPEED OF THE SERPENT--THE EYE OF THE EAGLE--THE ENDURANCE OF THE ANT. THESE ARE THE FIRST FOUR ATTRIBUTES OF THE WAY OF THE WILD BEAST.
THEY WILL ENSURE HE WINS THE COMING CONFRONTATION.
BUT IT IS THE FIFTH ATTRIBUTE THAT MAKES HIM TAKE PRE-CAUTIONS ANYWAY...
...THE CUNNING OF THE FOX.

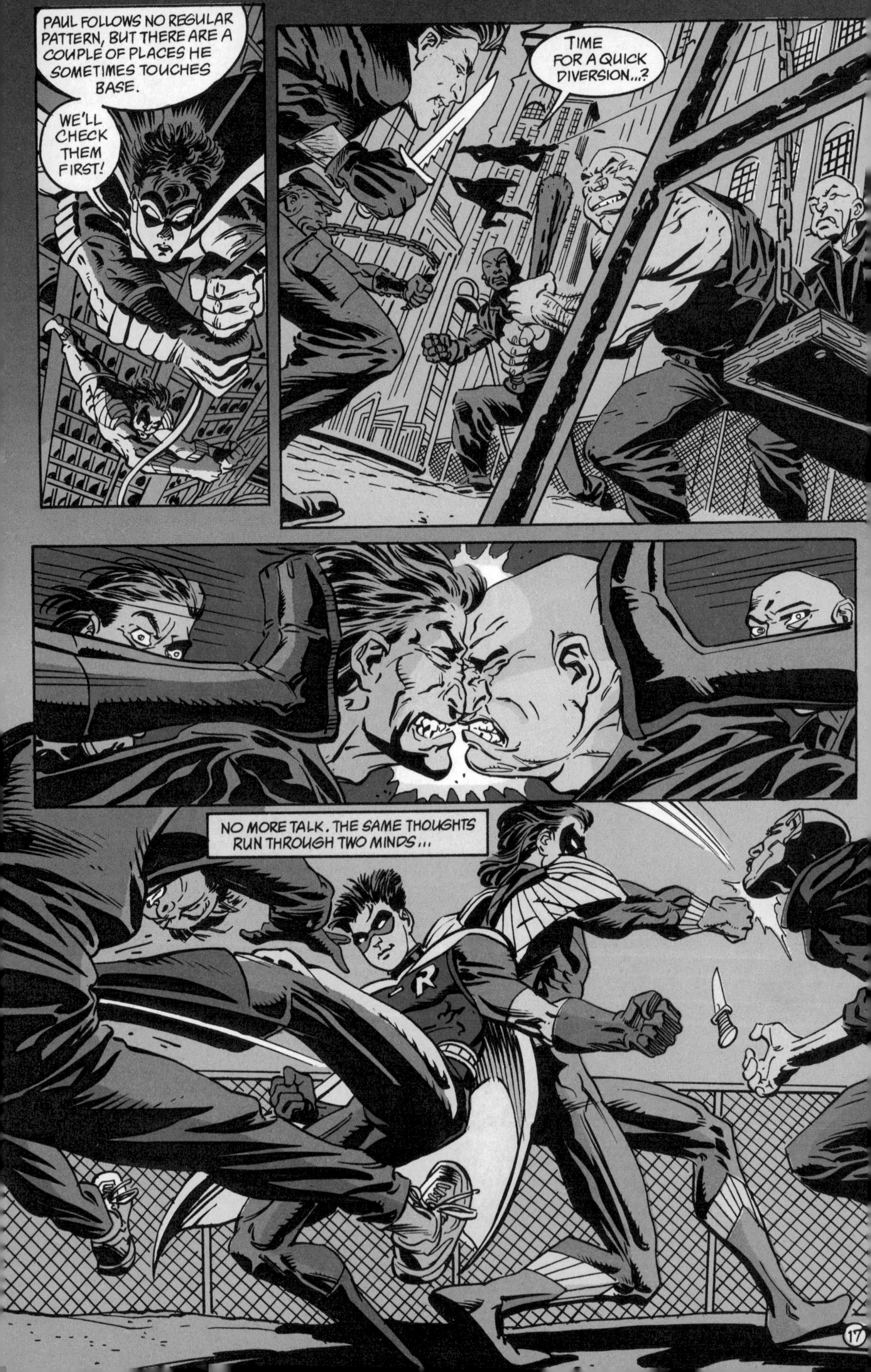
PAUL FOLLOWS NO REGULAR PATTERN, BUT THERE ARE A COUPLE OF PLACES HE SOMETIMES TOUCHES BASE.
WE'LL CHECK THEM FIRST!
TIME FOR A QUICK DIVERSION...?
NO MORE TALK. THE SAME THOUGHTS RUN THROUGH TWO MINDS...

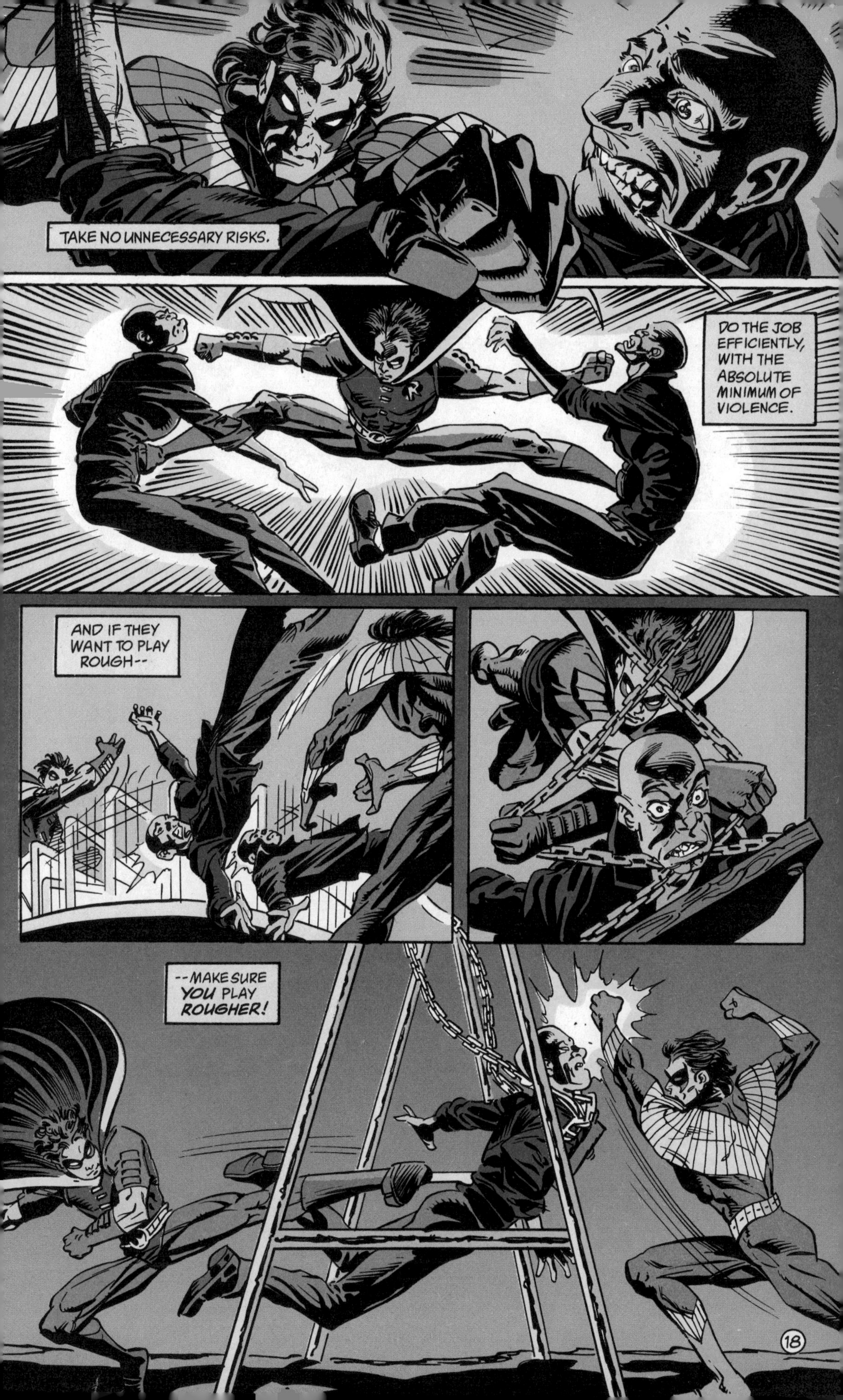
TAKE NO UNNECESSARY RISKS.
DO THE JOB EFFICIENTLY, WITH THE ABSOLUTE MINIMUM OF VIOLENCE.
AND IF THEY WANT TO PLAY ROUGH--
--MAKE SURE YOU PLAY ROUGHER!
18

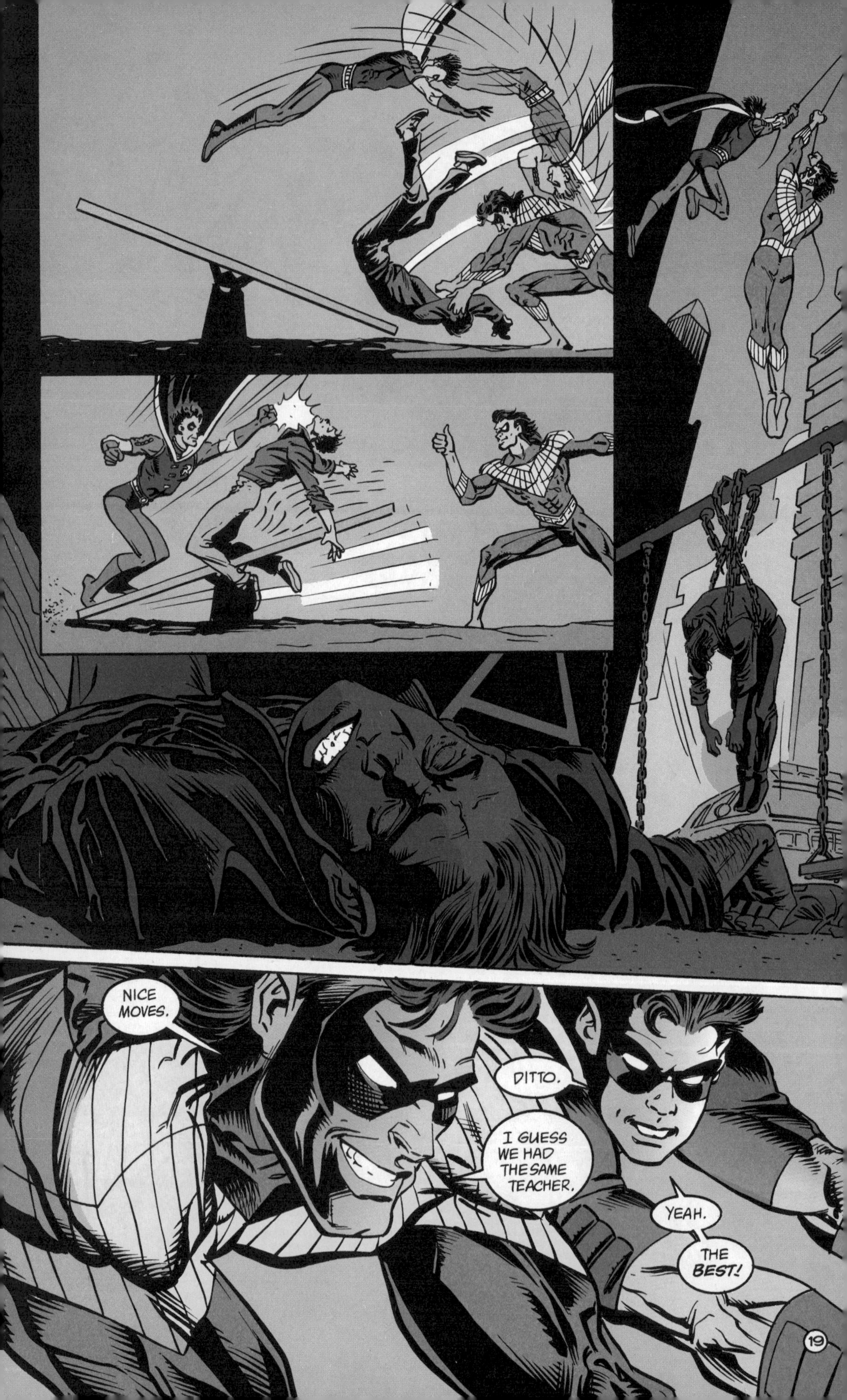
NICE MOVES.
DITTO.
I GUESS WE HAD THE SAME TEACHER.
YEAH.
THE BEST!

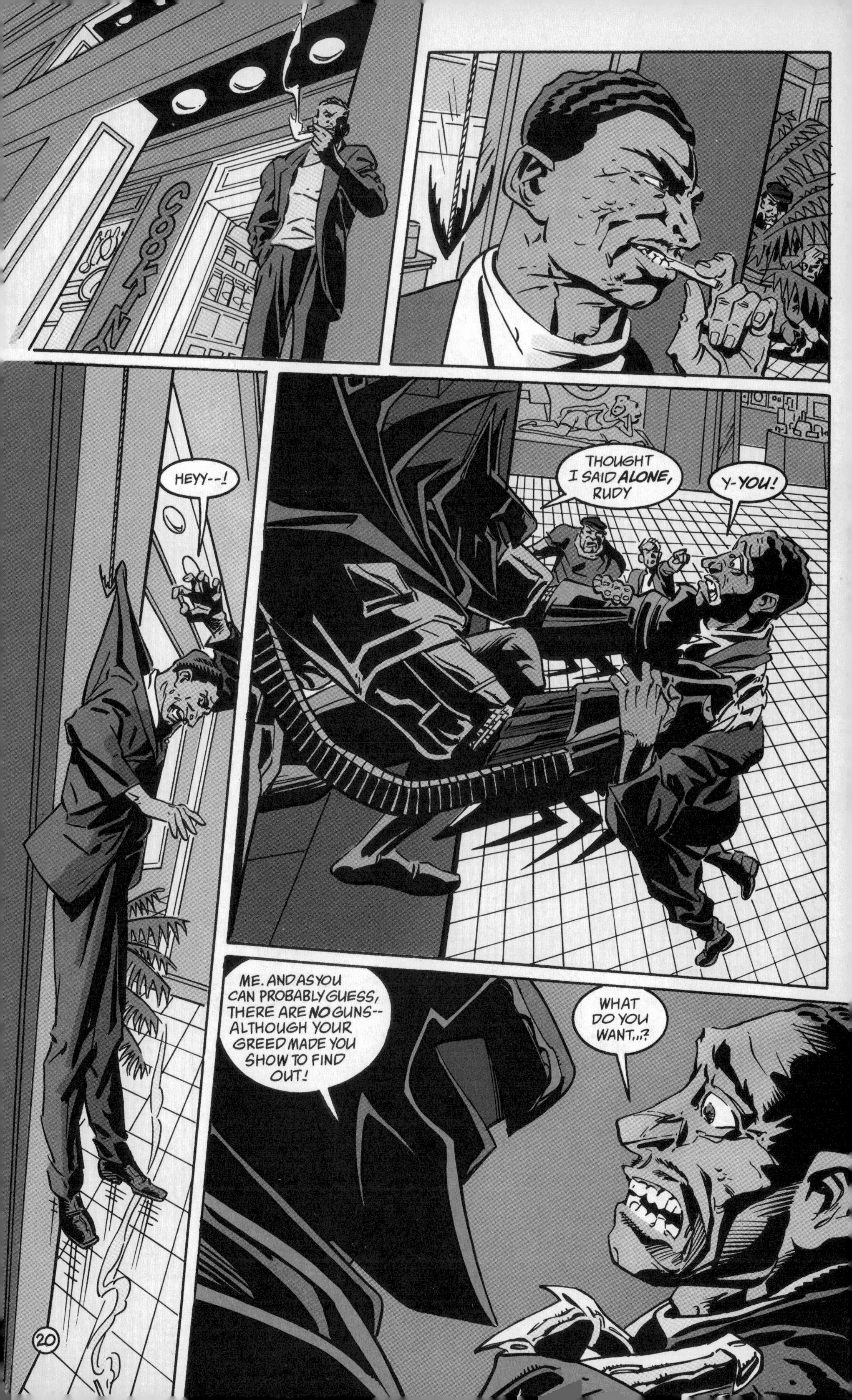
COOK
HEYY--!
THOUGHT I SAID ALONE, RUDY
Y-YOU!
ME. AND AS YOU CAN PROBABLY GUESS, THERE ARE NO GUNS-- ALTHOUGH YOUR GREED MADE YOU SHOW TO FIND OUT!
WHAT DO YOU WANT...?

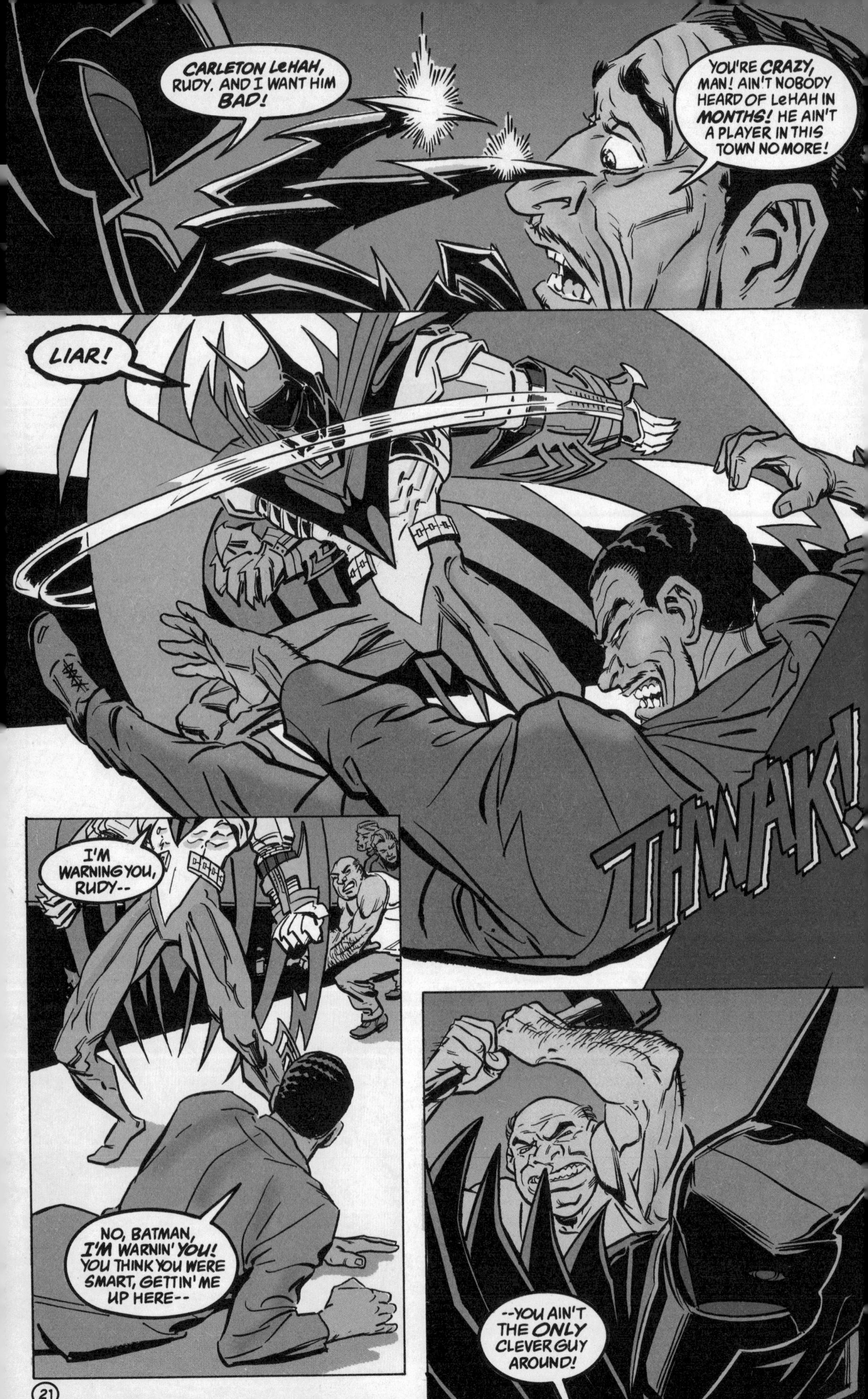

CARLETON LeHAH, RUDY. AND I WANT HIM BAD!
YOU'RE CRAZY, MAN! AIN'T NOBODY HEARD OF LeHAH IN MONTHS! HE AIN'T A PLAYER IN THIS TOWN NO MORE!
LIAR!
THWAK!
I'M WARNING YOU, RUDY--
NO, BATMAN, I'M WARNIN' YOU! YOU THINK YOU WERE SMART, GETTIN' ME UP HERE--
--YOU AIN'T THE ONLY CLEVER GUY AROUND!

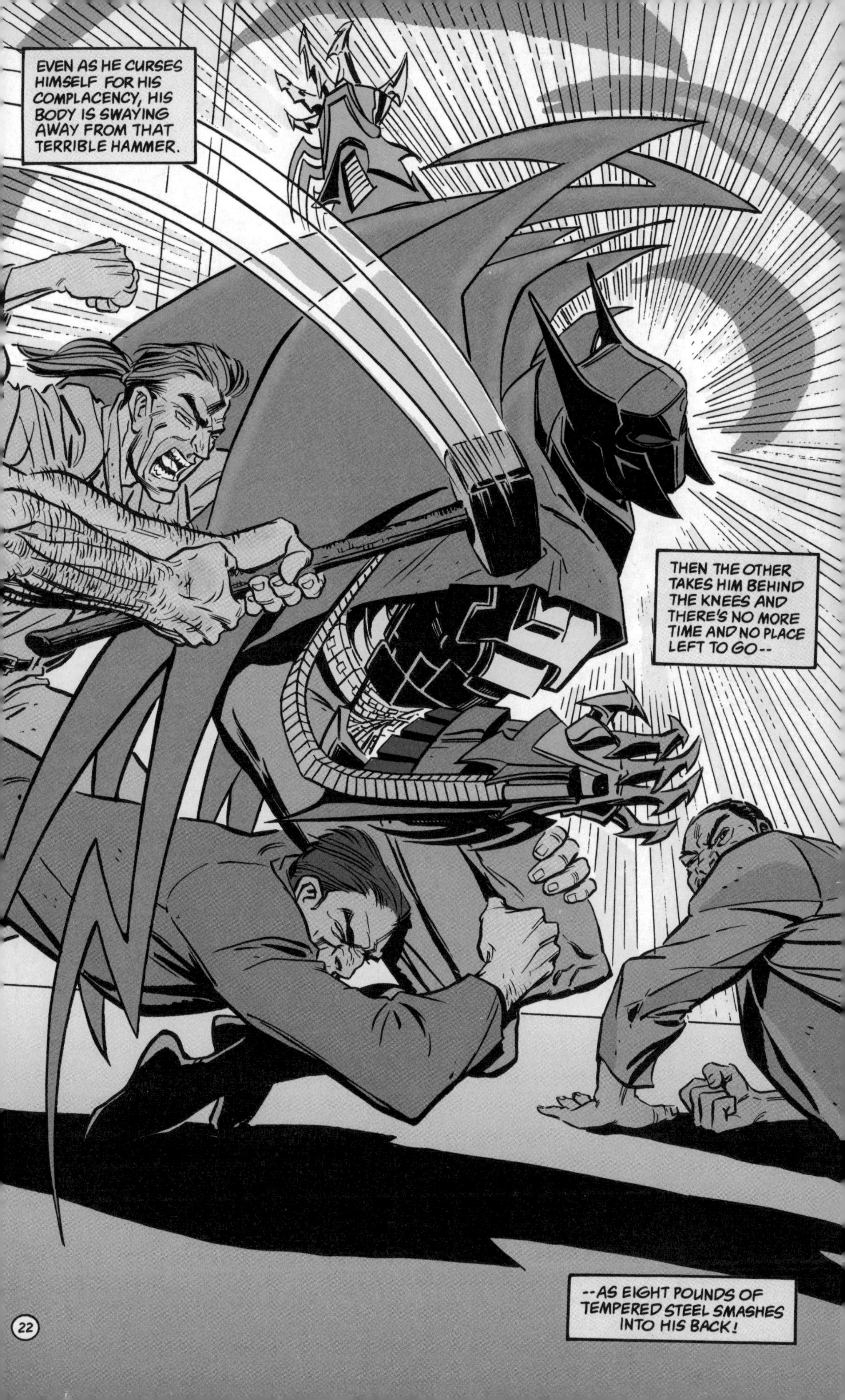
EVEN AS HE CURSES HIMSELF FOR HIS COMPLACENCY, HIS BODY IS SWAYING AWAY FROM THAT TERRIBLE HAMMER.
THEN THE OTHER TAKES HIM BEHIND THE KNEES AND THERE'S NO MORE TIME AND NO PLACE LEFT TO GO--
--AS EIGHT POUNDS OF TEMPERED STEEL SMASHES INTO HIS BACK!

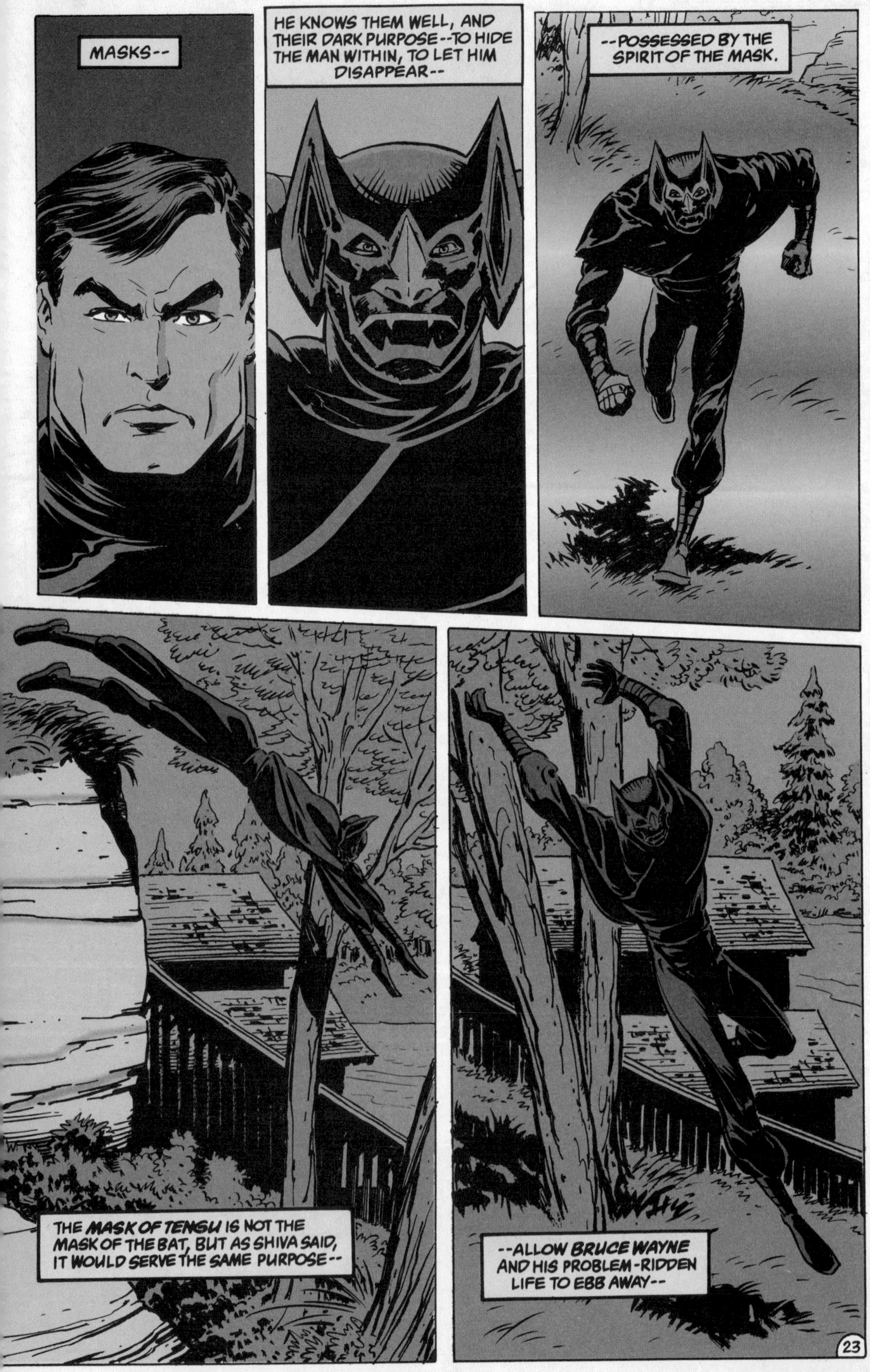
MASKS--
HE KNOWS THEM WELL, AND THEIR DARK PURPOSE--TO HIDE THE MAN WITHIN, TO LET HIM DISAPPEAR--
--POSSESSED BY THE SPIRIT OF THE MASK.
THE MASK OF TENGU IS NOT THE MASK OF THE BAT, BUT AS SHIVA SAID, IT WOULD SERVE THE SAME PURPOSE--
--ALLOW BRUCE WAYNE AND HIS PROBLEM-RIDDEN LIFE TO EBB AWAY--
23

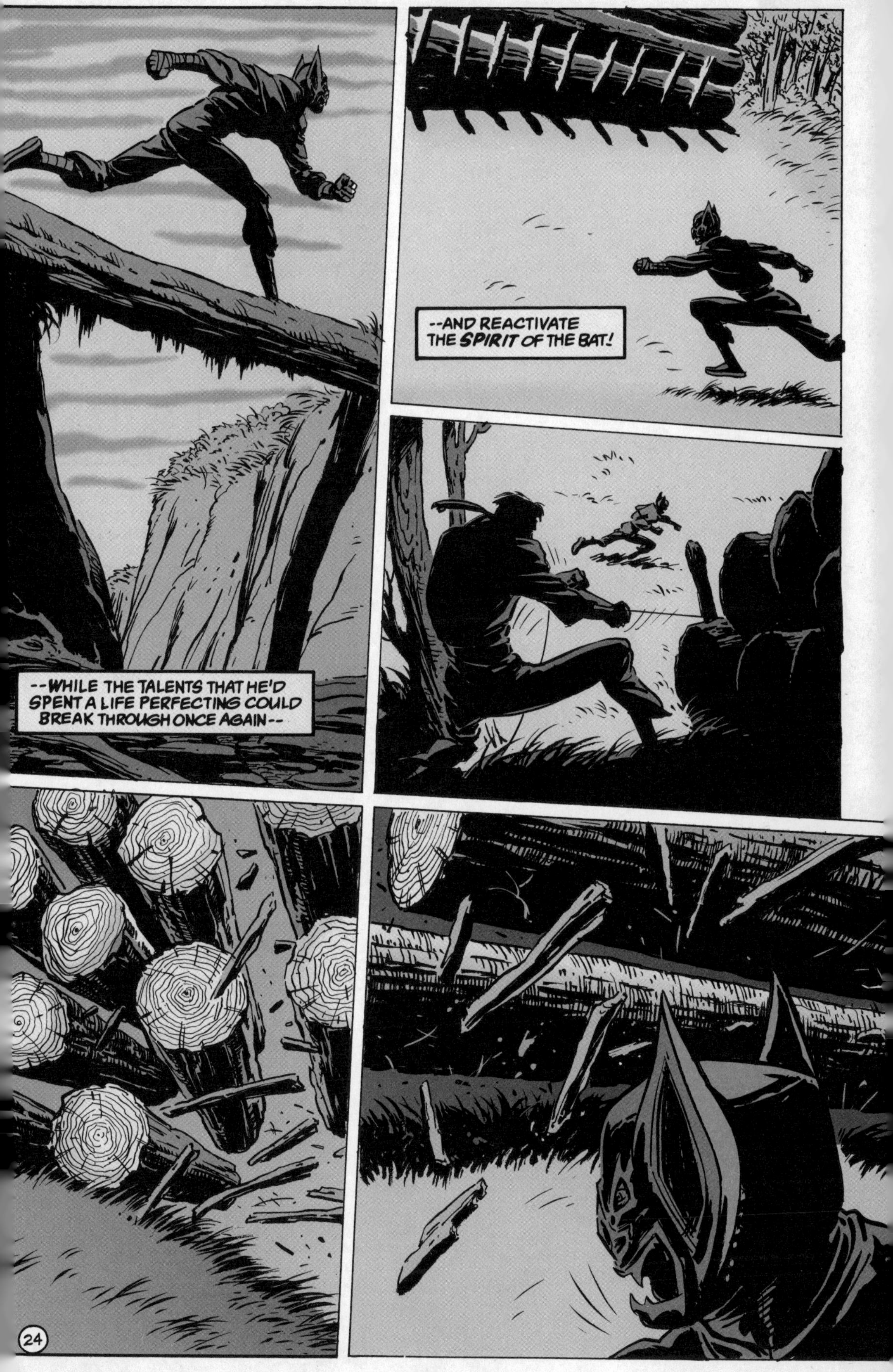
--WHILE THE TALENTS THAT HE'D SPENT A LIFE PERFECTING COULD BREAK THROUGH ONCE AGAIN--
--AND REACTIVATE THE SPIRIT OF THE BAT!
24

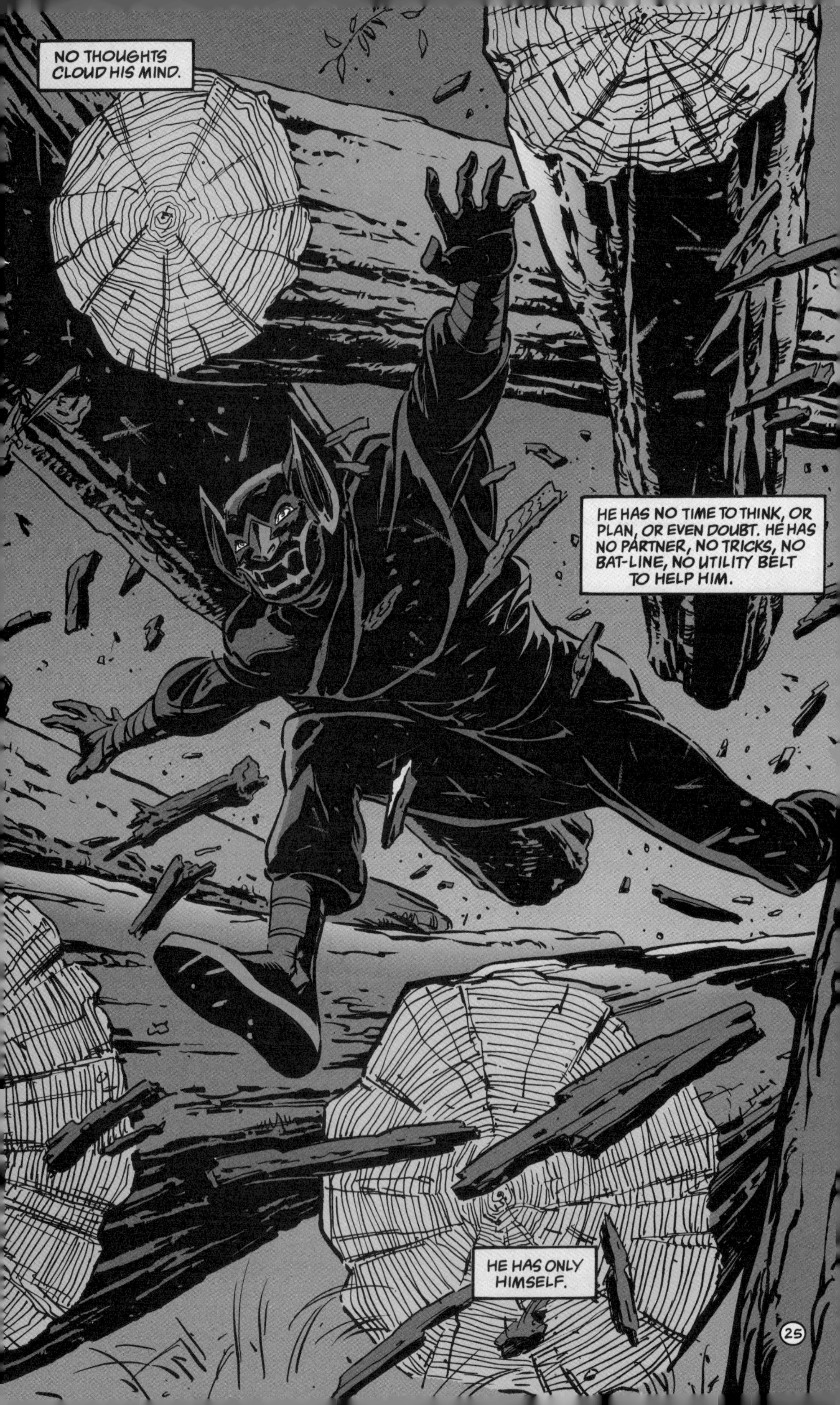
NO THOUGHTS CLOUD HIS MIND.
HE HAS NO TIME TO THINK, OR PLAN, OR EVEN DOUBT. HE HAS NO PARTNER, NO TRICKS, NO BAT-LINE, NO UTILITY BELT TO HELP HIM.
HE HAS ONLY HIMSELF.

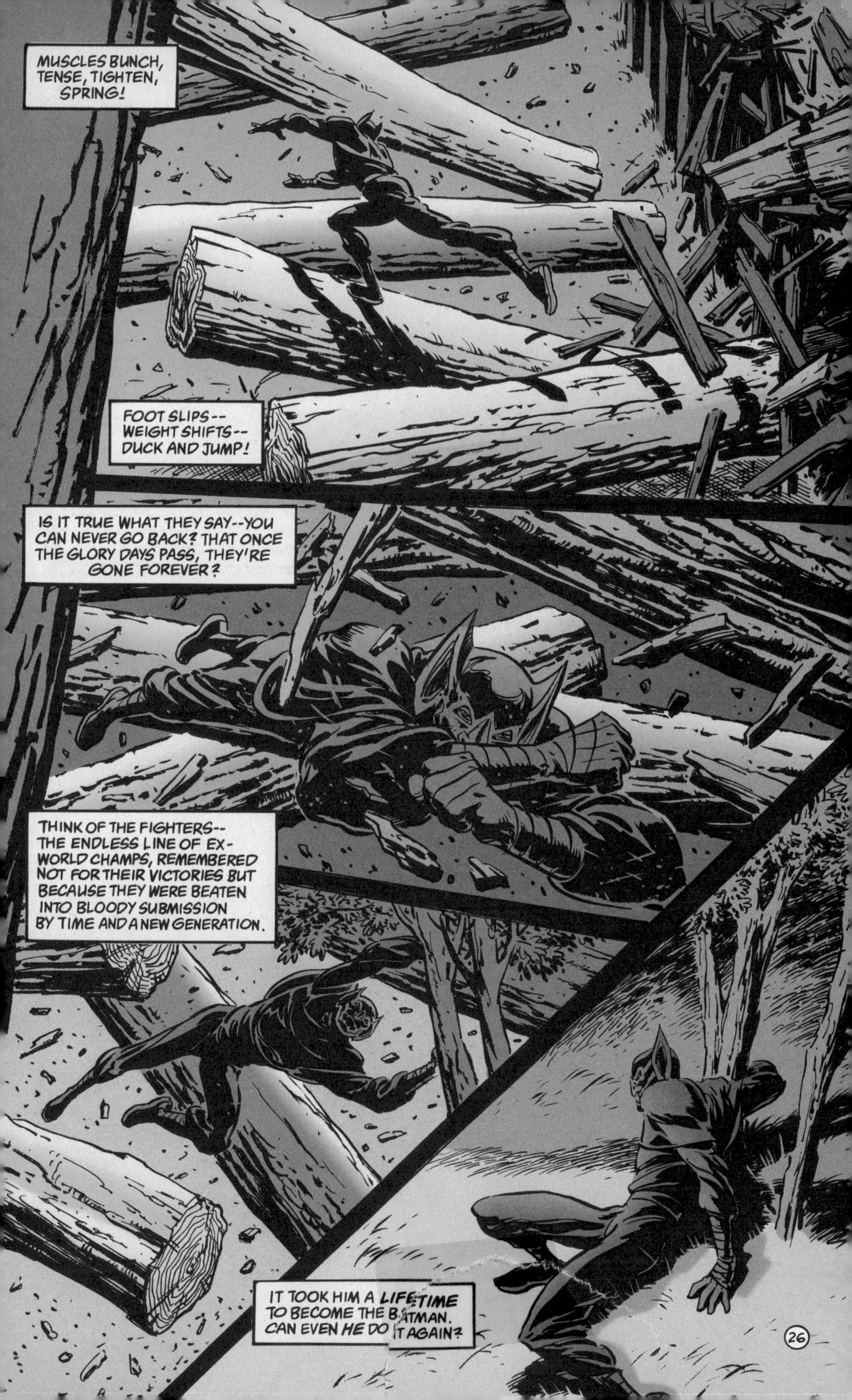
MUSCLES BUNCH, TENSE, TIGHTEN, SPRING!
FOOT SLIPS-- WEIGHT SHIFTS-- DUCK AND JUMP!
IS IT TRUE WHAT THEY SAY--YOU CAN NEVER GO BACK? THAT ONCE THE GLORY DAYS PASS, THEY'RE GONE FOREVER?
THINK OF THE FIGHTERS-- THE ENDLESS LINE OF EX-WORLD CHAMPS, REMEMBERED NOT FOR THEIR VICTORIES BUT BECAUSE THEY WERE BEATEN INTO BLOODY SUBMISSION BY TIME AND A NEW GENERATION.
IT TOOK HIM A LIFETIME TO BECOME THE BATMAN. CAN EVEN HE DO IT AGAIN?

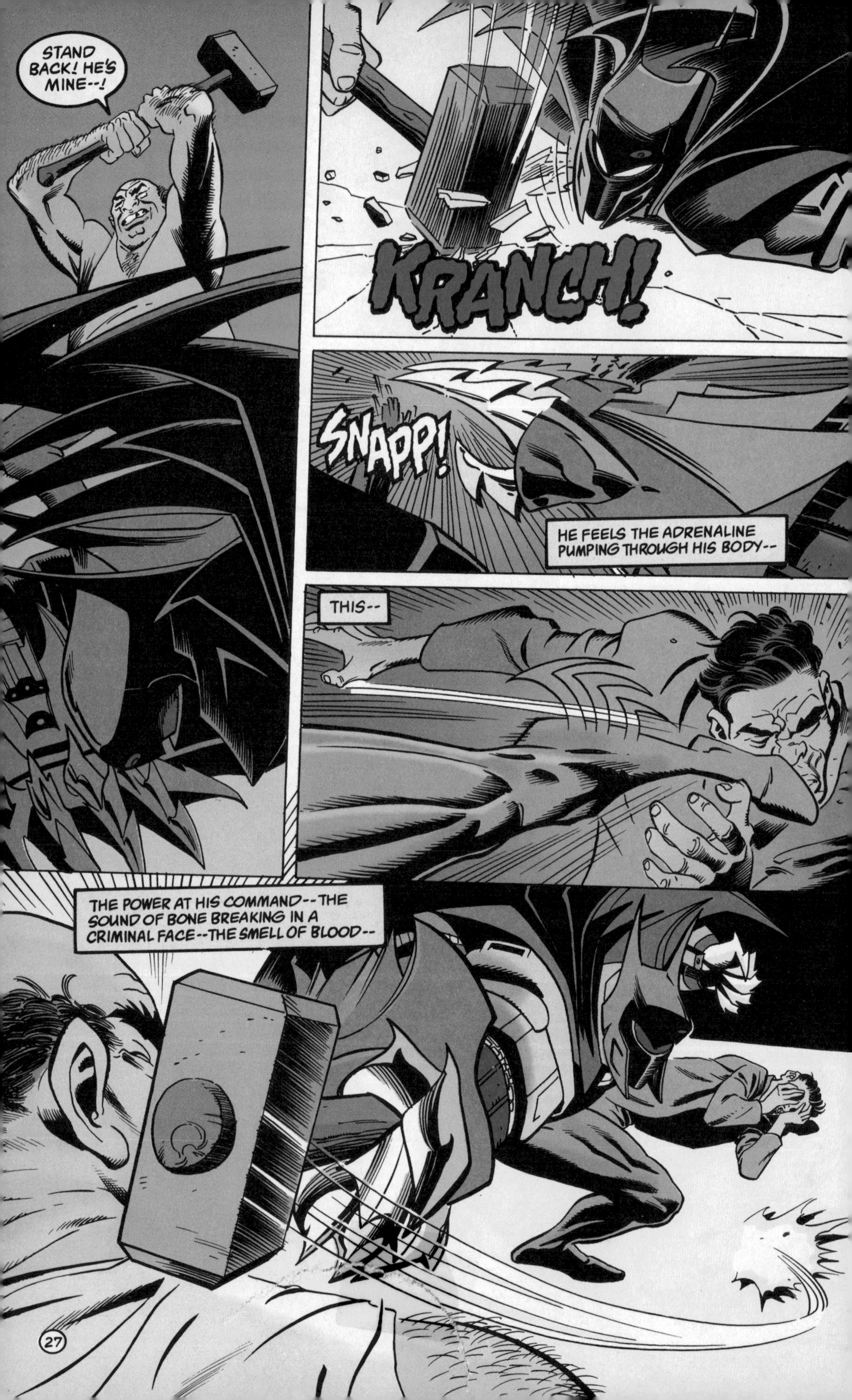
STAND BACK! HE'S MINE--!
KRANCH!
SNAPP!
HE FEELS THE ADRENALINE PUMPING THROUGH HIS BODY--
THIS--
THE POWER AT HIS COMMAND--THE SOUND OF BONE BREAKING IN A CRIMINAL FACE--THE SMELL OF BLOOD--

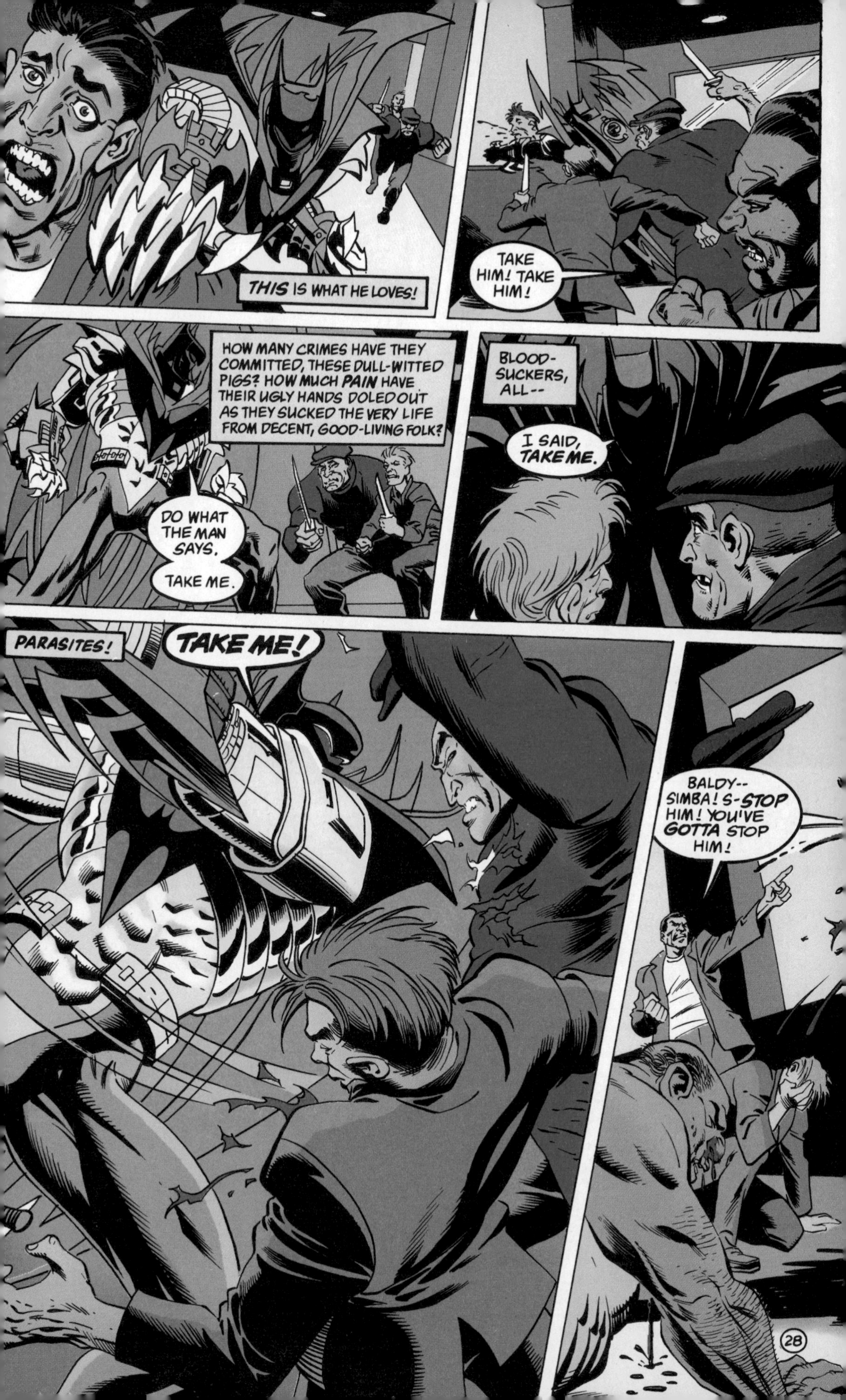
THIS IS WHAT HE LOVES!
TAKE HIM! TAKE HIM!
HOW MANY CRIMES HAVE THEY COMMITTED, THESE DULL-WITTED PIGS? HOW MUCH PAIN HAVE THEIR UGLY HANDS DOLED OUT AS THEY SUCKED THE VERY LIFE FROM DECENT, GOOD-LIVING FOLK?
DO WHAT THE MAN SAYS.
TAKE ME.
BLOOD-SUCKERS, ALL--
I SAID, TAKE ME.
PARASITES!
TAKE ME!
BALDY-- SIMBA! S-STOP HIM! YOU'VE GOTTA STOP HIM!
28

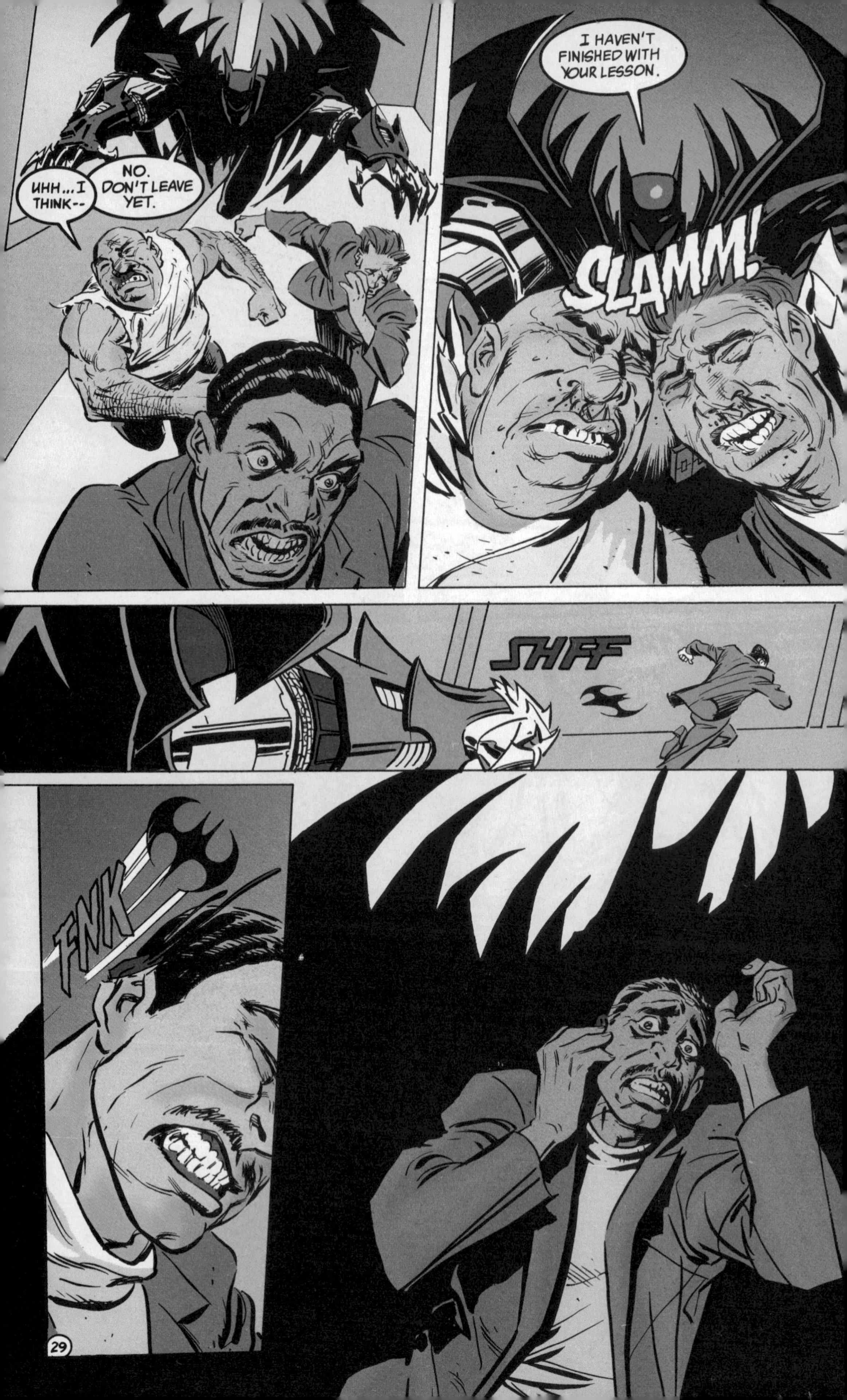
UHH... I THINK--
NO. DON'T LEAVE YET.
I HAVEN'T FINISHED WITH YOUR LESSON.
SLAMM!
SHFF
FNK

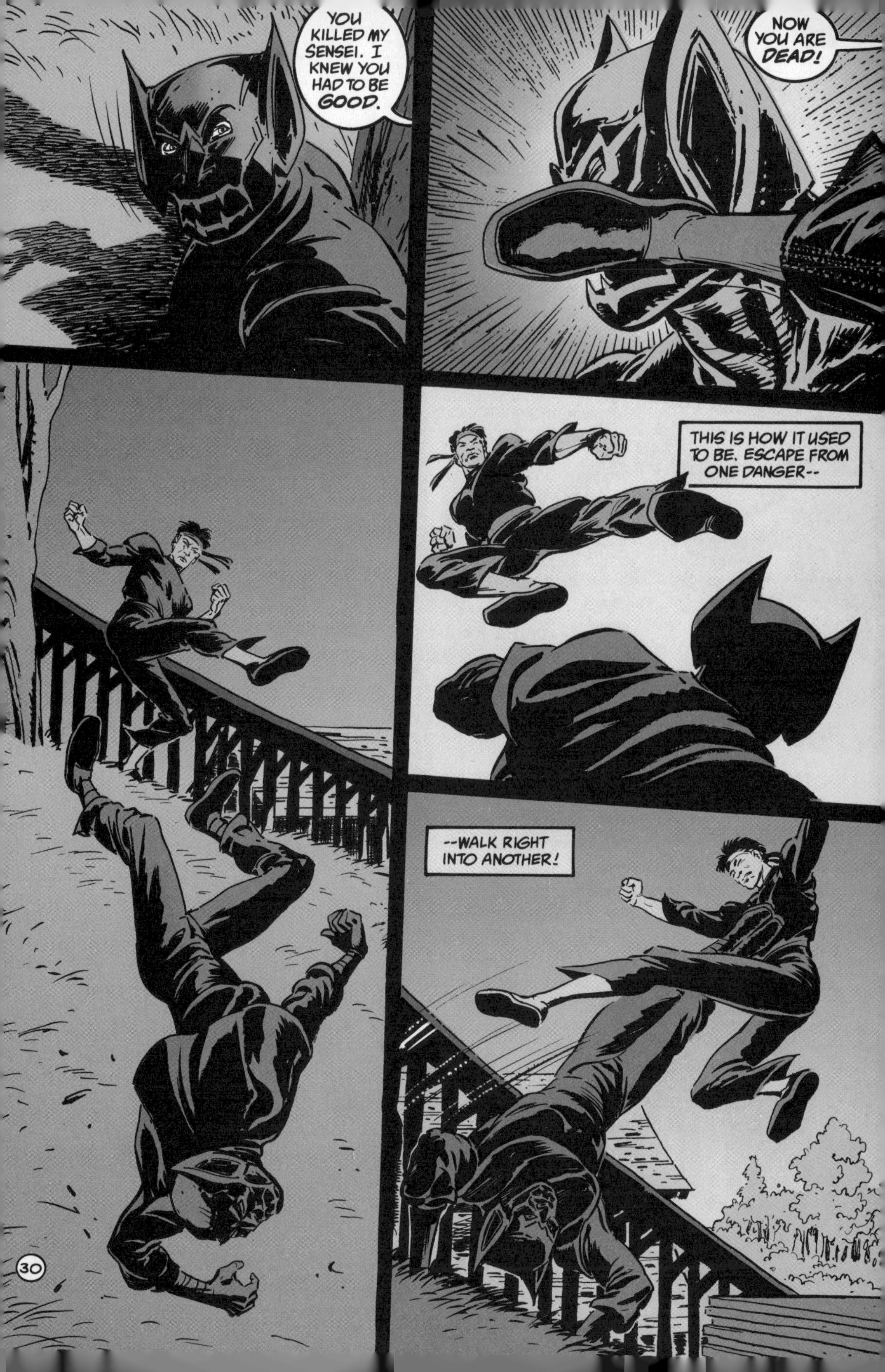
YOU KILLED MY SENSEI. I KNEW YOU HAD TO BE GOOD.
NOW YOU ARE DEAD!
THIS IS HOW IT USED TO BE. ESCAPE FROM ONE DANGER--
--WALK RIGHT INTO ANOTHER!
30

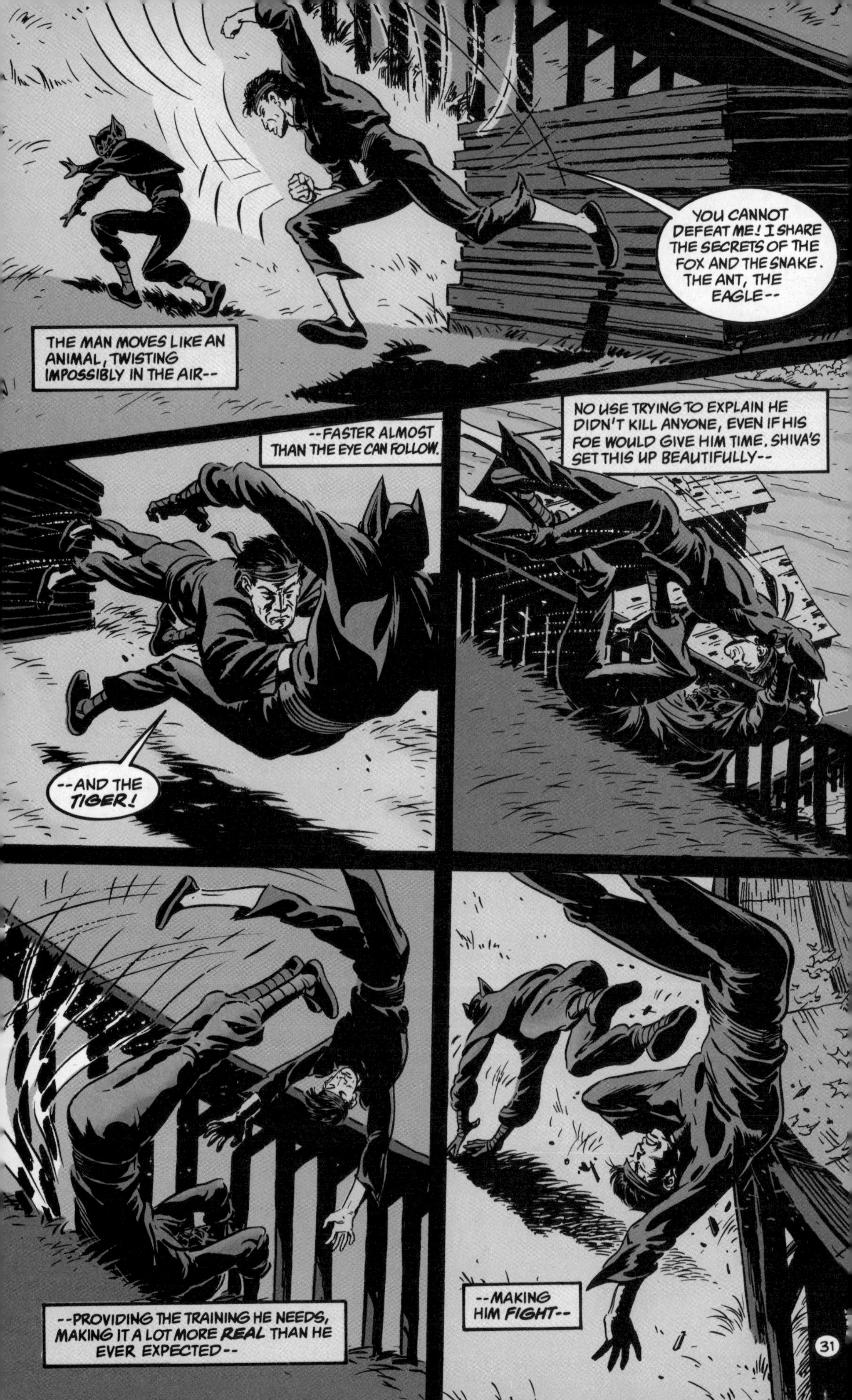
YOU CANNOT DEFEAT ME! I SHARE THE SECRETS OF THE FOX AND THE SNAKE. THE ANT, THE EAGLE--
THE MAN MOVES LIKE AN ANIMAL, TWISTING IMPOSSIBLY IN THE AIR--
--FASTER ALMOST THAN THE EYE CAN FOLLOW.
--AND THE TIGER!
NO USE TRYING TO EXPLAIN HE DIDN'T KILL ANYONE, EVEN IF HIS FOE WOULD GIVE HIM TIME. SHIVA'S SET THIS UP BEAUTIFULLY--
--PROVIDING THE TRAINING HE NEEDS, MAKING IT A LOT MORE REAL THAN HE EVER EXPECTED--
--MAKING HIM FIGHT--

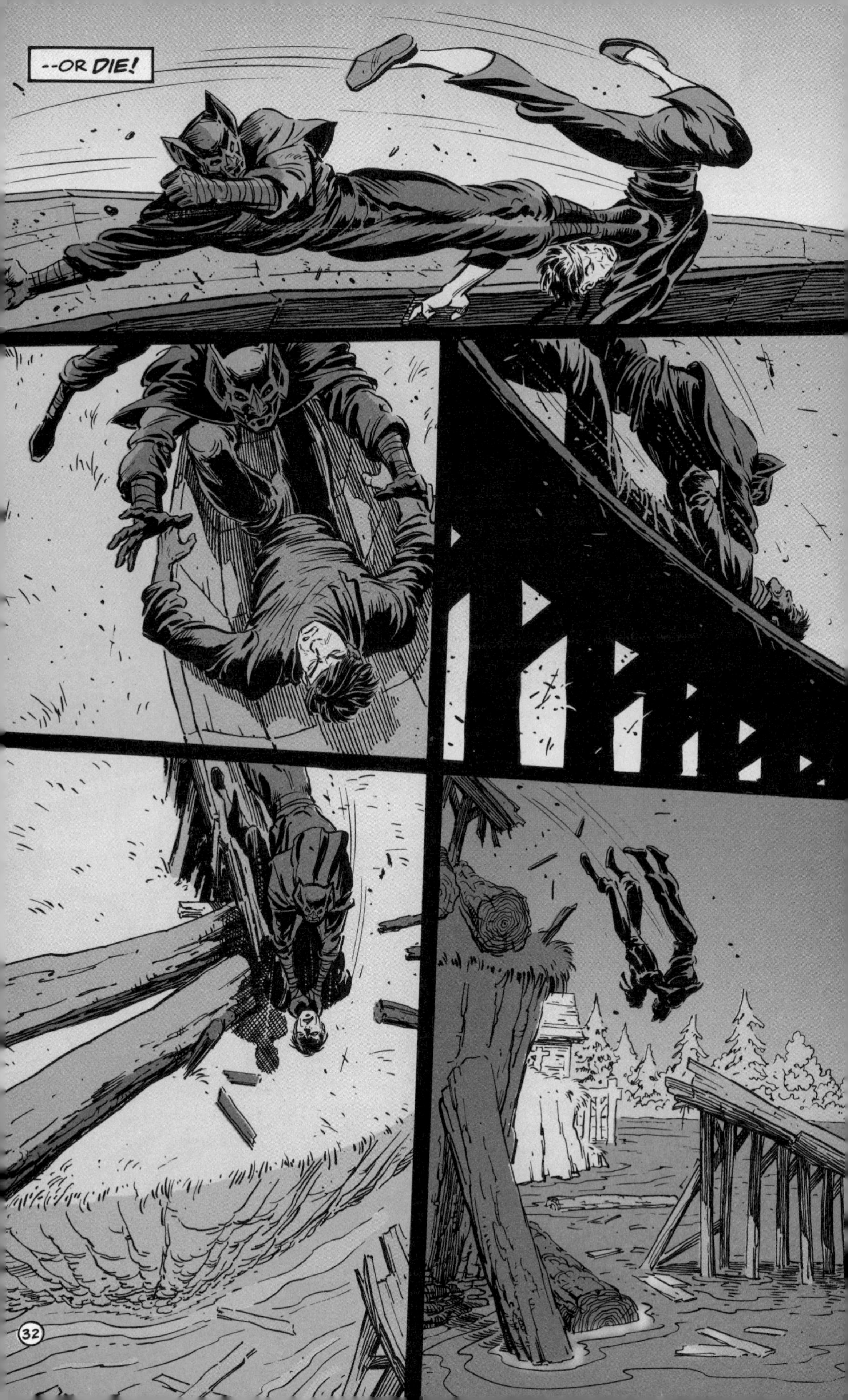
--OR DIE!

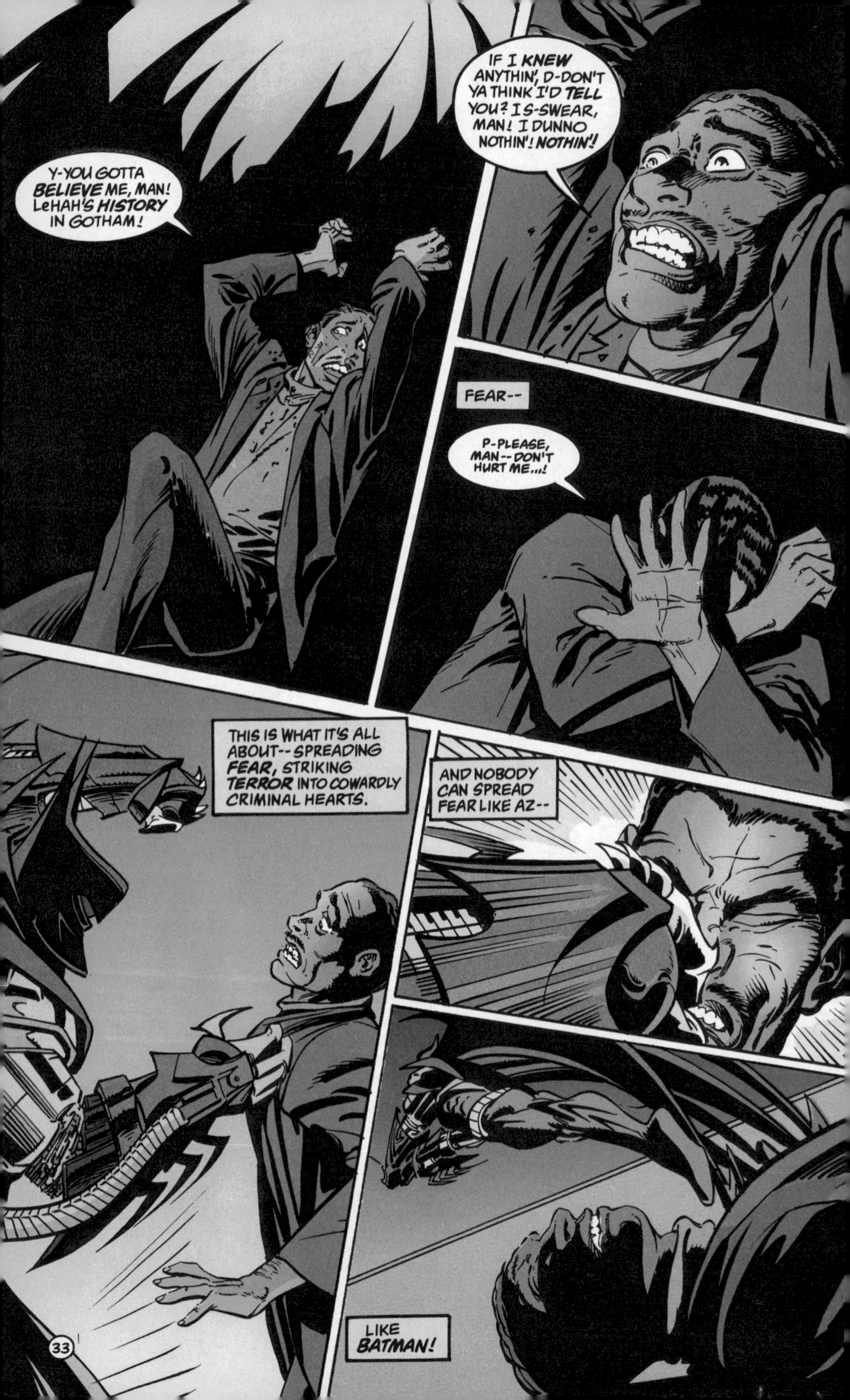

Y-YOU GOTTA BELIEVE ME, MAN! LeHAH'S HISTORY IN GOTHAM!
IF I KNEW ANYTHIN', D-DON'T YA THINK I'D TELL YOU? I S-SWEAR, MAN! I DUNNO NOTHIN'! NOTHIN'!
FEAR--
P-PLEASE, MAN--DON'T HURT ME...!
THIS IS WHAT IT'S ALL ABOUT--SPREADING FEAR, STRIKING TERROR INTO COWARDLY CRIMINAL HEARTS.
AND NOBODY CAN SPREAD FEAR LIKE AZ--
LIKE BATMAN!
33

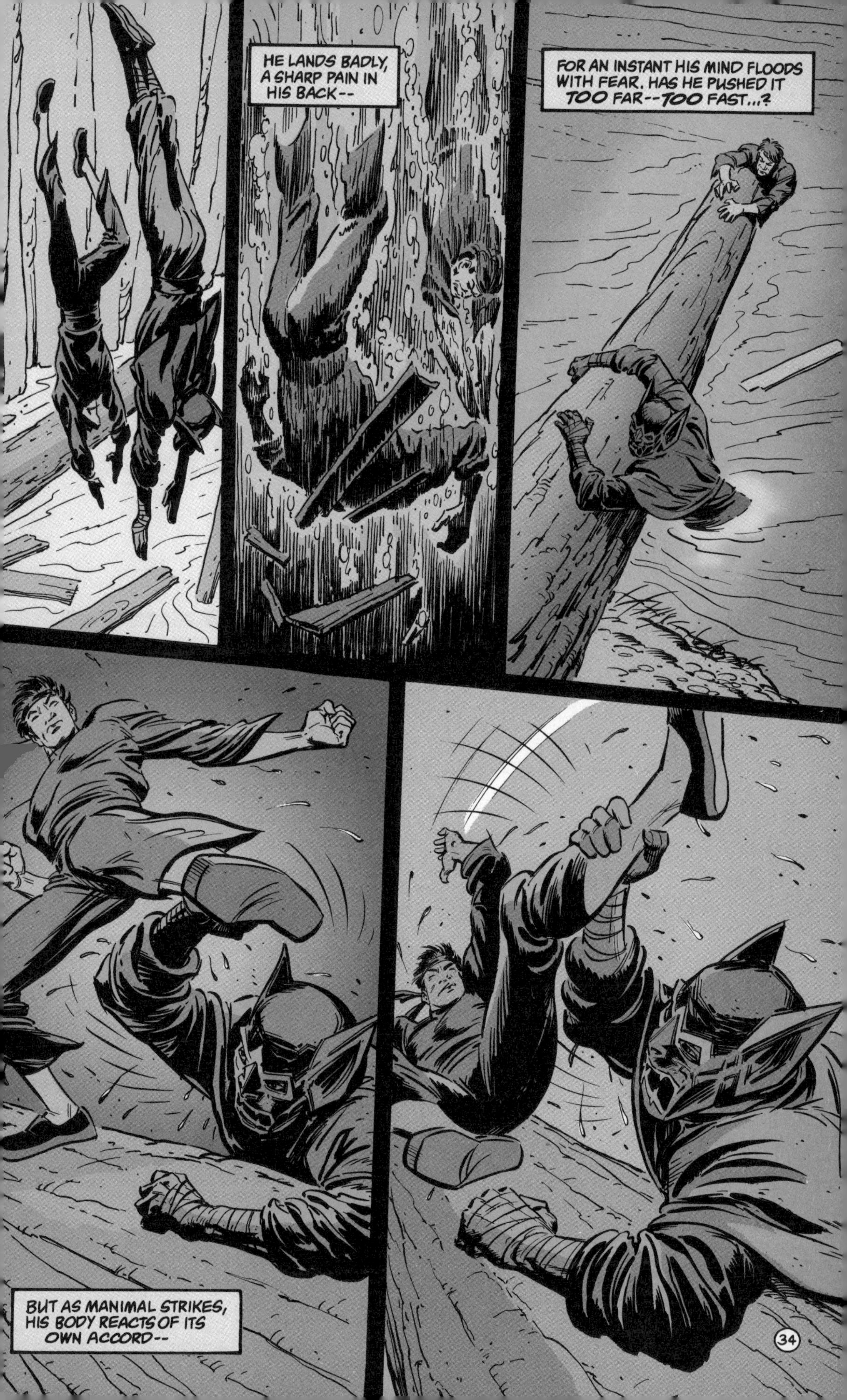
HE LANDS BADLY, A SHARP PAIN IN HIS BACK--
FOR AN INSTANT HIS MIND FLOODS WITH FEAR. HAS HE PUSHED IT TOO FAR--TOO FAST...?
BUT AS MANIMAL STRIKES, HIS BODY REACTS OF ITS OWN ACCORD--
34

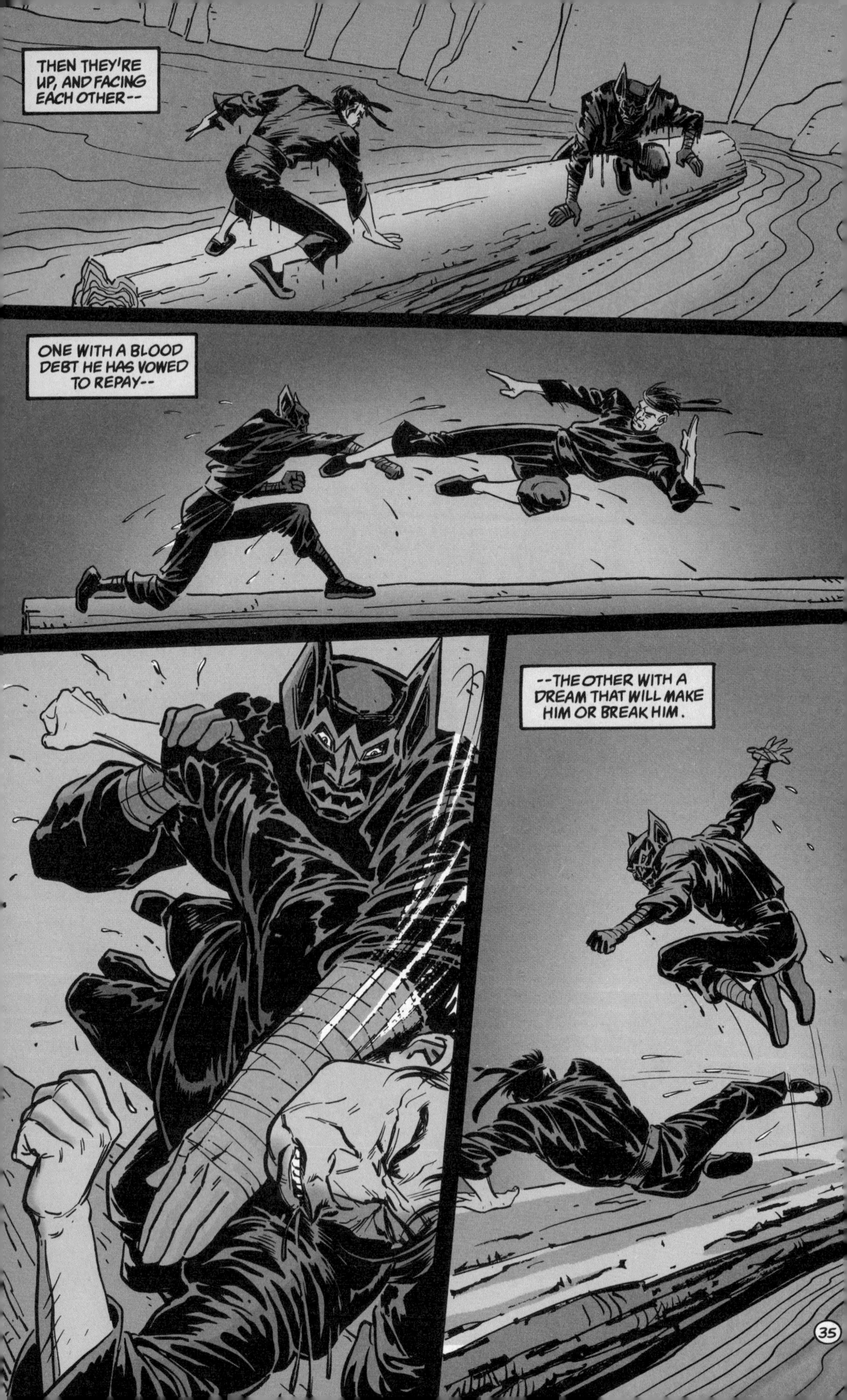
THEN THEY'RE UP, AND FACING EACH OTHER--
ONE WITH A BLOOD DEBT HE HAS VOWED TO REPAY--
--THE OTHER WITH A DREAM THAT WILL MAKE HIM OR BREAK HIM.

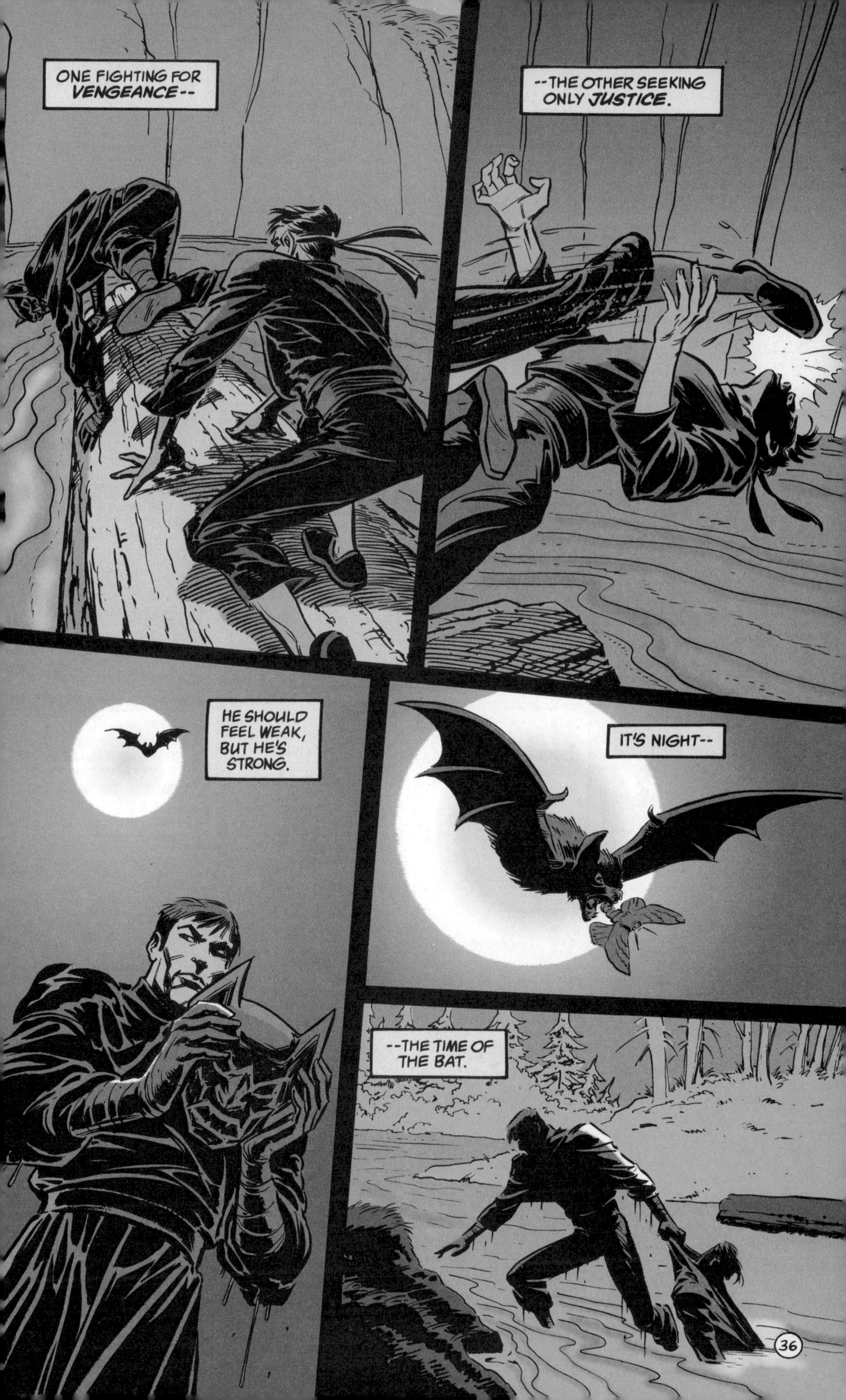
ONE FIGHTING FOR VENGEANCE--
--THE OTHER SEEKING ONLY JUSTICE.
HE SHOULD FEEL WEAK, BUT HE'S STRONG.
IT'S NIGHT--
--THE TIME OF THE BAT.

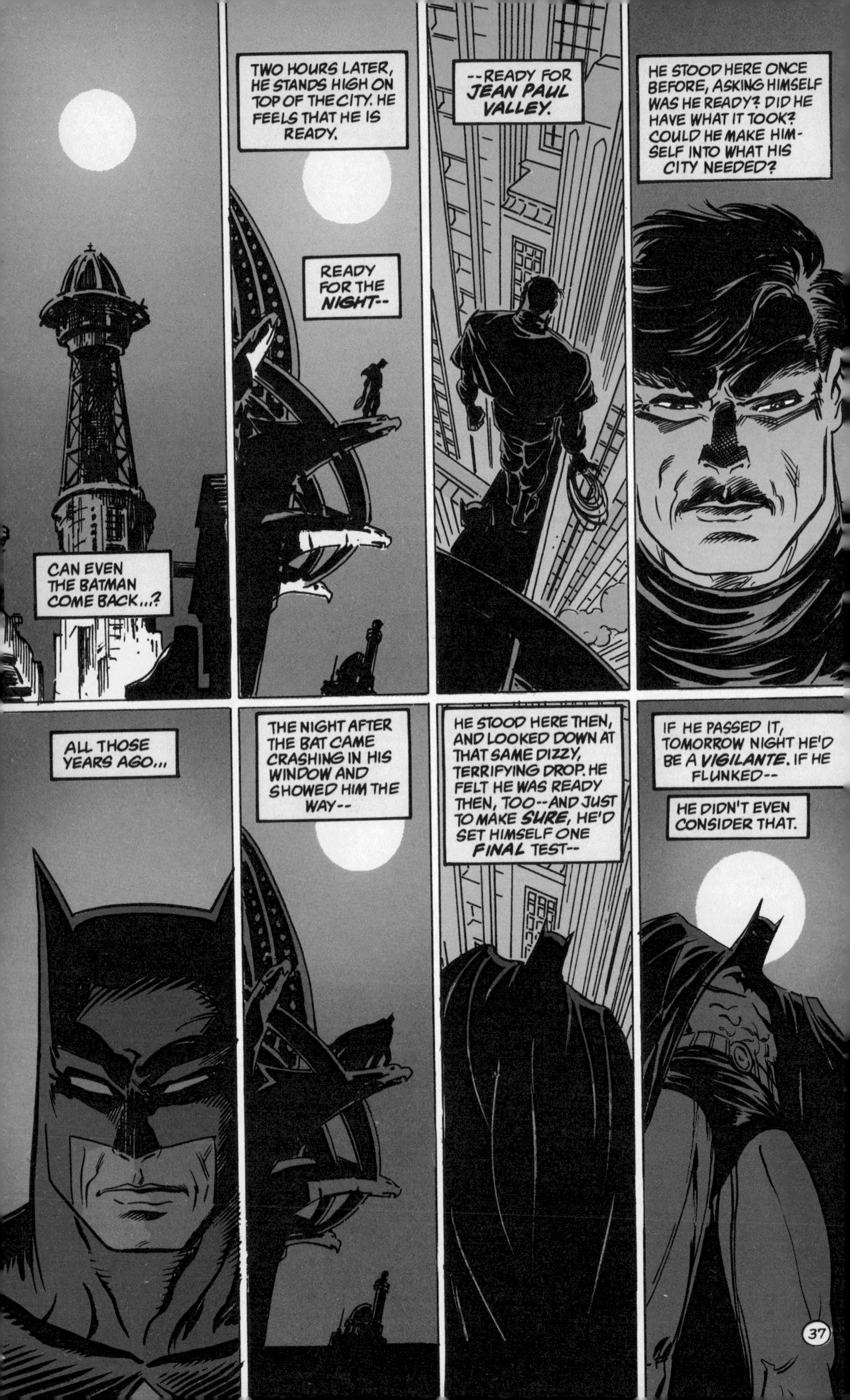
CAN EVEN THE BATMAN COME BACK...?
TWO HOURS LATER, HE STANDS HIGH ON TOP OF THE CITY. HE FEELS THAT HE IS READY.
READY FOR THE NIGHT--
--READY FOR JEAN PAUL VALLEY.
HE STOOD HERE ONCE BEFORE, ASKING HIMSELF WAS HE READY? DID HE HAVE WHAT IT TOOK? COULD HE MAKE HIMSELF INTO WHAT HIS CITY NEEDED?
ALL THOSE YEARS AGO...
THE NIGHT AFTER THE BAT CAME CRASHING IN HIS WINDOW AND SHOWED HIM THE WAY--
HE STOOD HERE THEN, AND LOOKED DOWN AT THAT SAME DIZZY, TERRIFYING DROP. HE FELT HE WAS READY THEN, TOO--AND JUST TO MAKE SURE, HE'D SET HIMSELF ONE FINAL TEST--
IF HE PASSED IT, TOMORROW NIGHT HE'D BE A VIGILANTE. IF HE FLUNKED--
HE DIDN'T EVEN CONSIDER THAT.

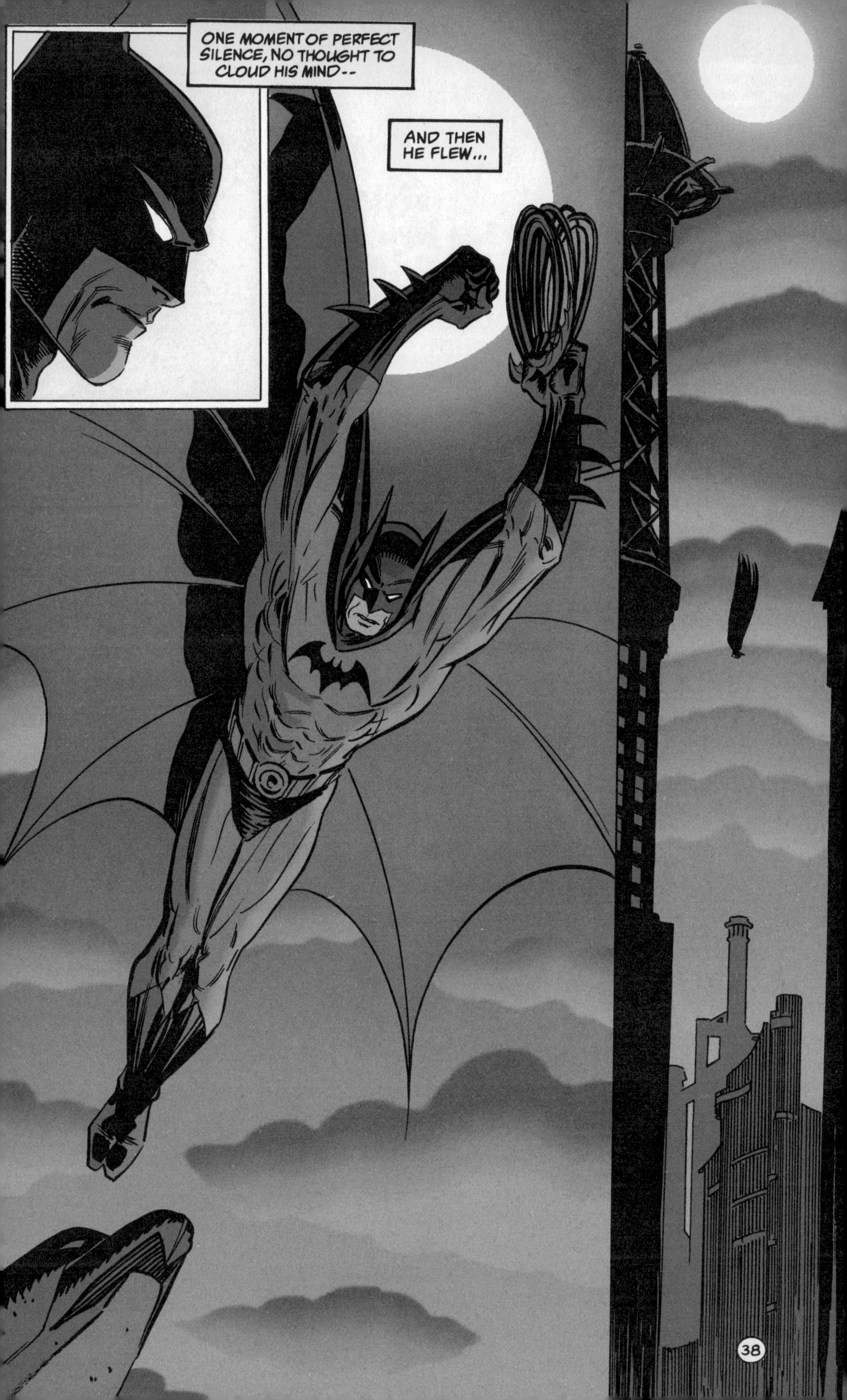
ONE MOMENT OF PERFECT SILENCE, NO THOUGHT TO CLOUD HIS MIND--
AND THEN HE FLEW...

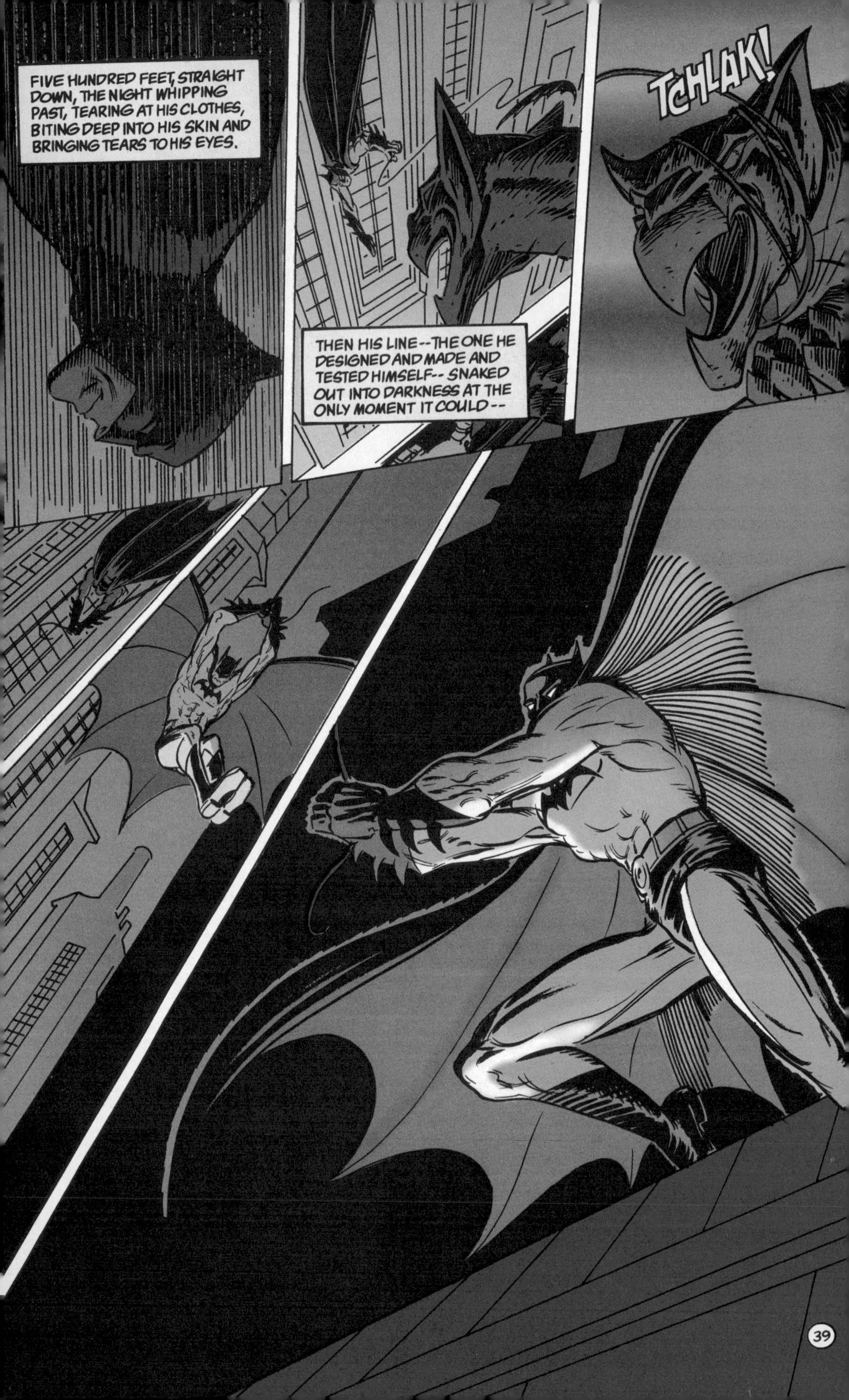
FIVE HUNDRED FEET, STRAIGHT DOWN, THE NIGHT WHIPPING PAST, TEARING AT HIS CLOTHES, BITING DEEP INTO HIS SKIN AND BRINGING TEARS TO HIS EYES.
THEN HIS LINE--THE ONE HE DESIGNED AND MADE AND TESTED HIMSELF-- SNAKED OUT INTO DARKNESS AT THE ONLY MOMENT IT COULD--
TCHLAK!

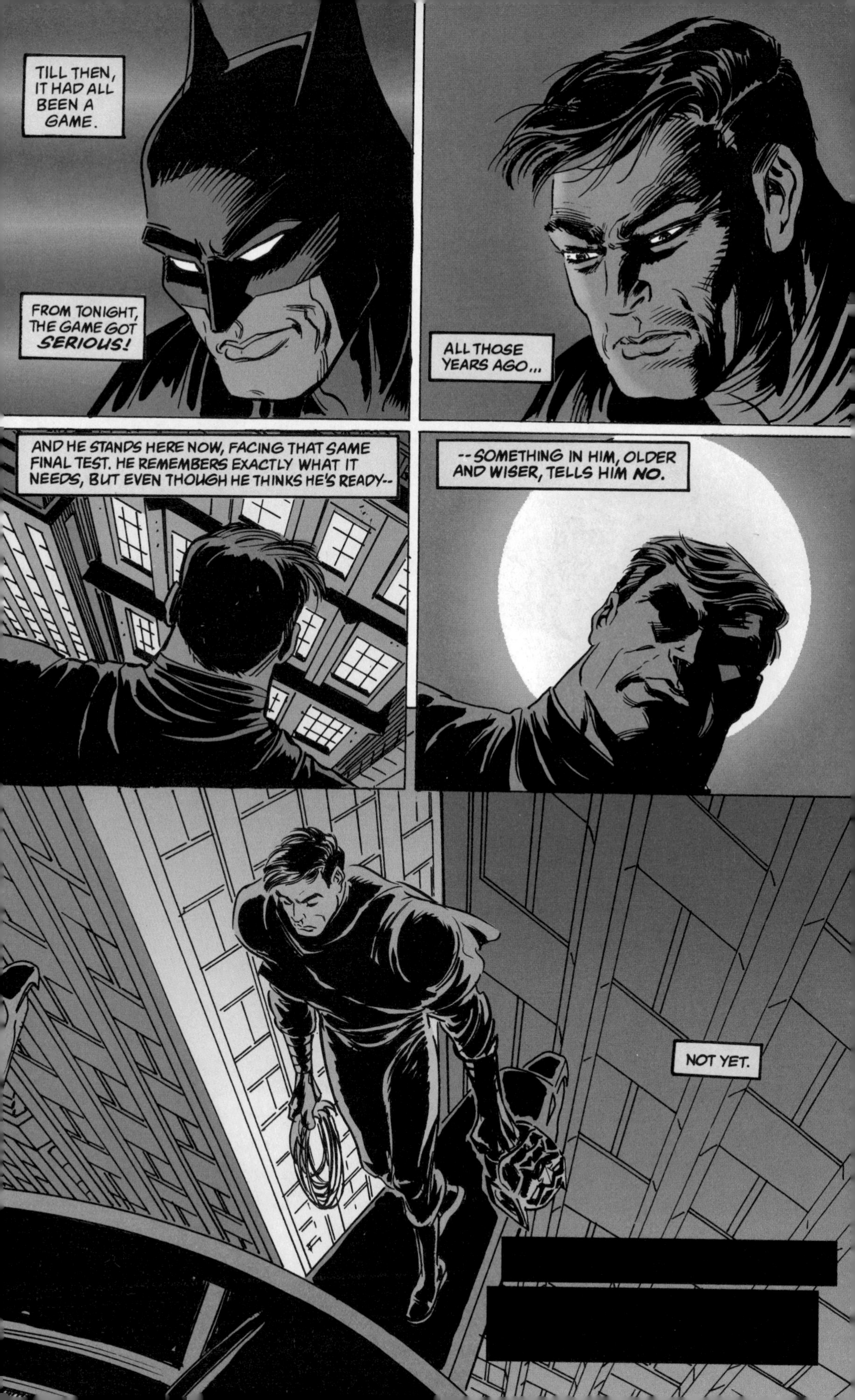
TILL THEN, IT HAD ALL BEEN A GAME.
FROM TONIGHT, THE GAME GOT SERIOUS!
ALL THOSE YEARS AGO...
AND HE STANDS HERE NOW, FACING THAT SAME FINAL TEST. HE REMEMBERS EXACTLY WHAT IT NEEDS, BUT EVEN THOUGH HE THINKS HE'S READY--
--SOMETHING IN HIM, OLDER AND WISER, TELLS HIM NO.
NOT YET.
[redacted]

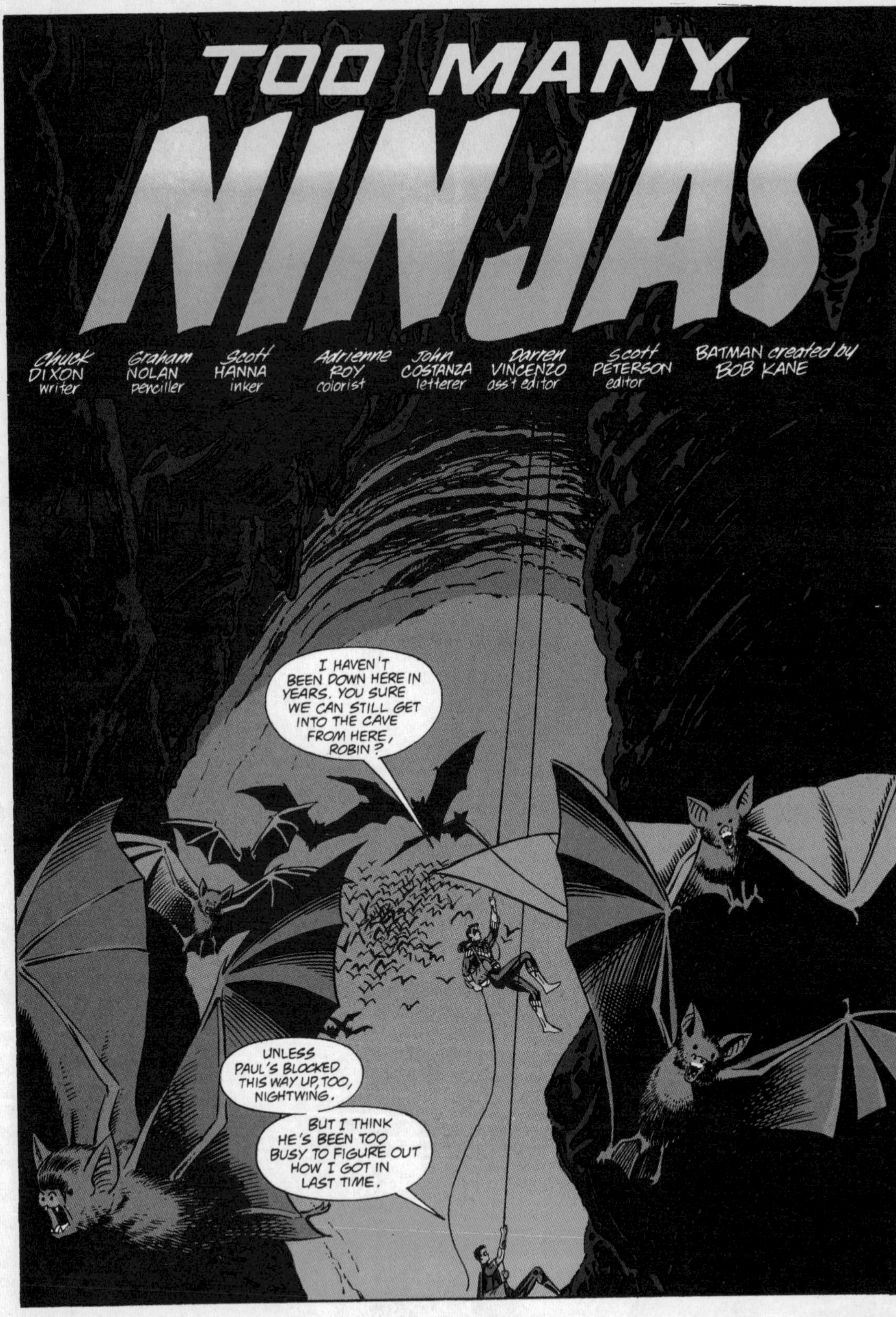
TOO MANY
NINJAS
Chuck DIXON writer
Graham NOLAN penciller
Scott HANNA inker
Adrienne ROY colorist
John COSTANZA letterer
Darren VINCENZO ass't editor
Scott PETERSON editor
BATMAN created by BOB KANE
I HAVEN'T BEEN DOWN HERE IN YEARS. YOU SURE WE CAN STILL GET INTO THE CAVE FROM HERE, ROBIN?
UNLESS PAUL'S BLOCKED THIS WAY UP, TOO, NIGHTWING.
BUT I THINK HE'S BEEN TOO BUSY TO FIGURE OUT HOW I GOT IN LAST TIME.

YOU SAID HE HAS THE CAVE RIGGED WITH ALARMS.

NOTHING I COULDN'T BOLLIX THROUGH THE COMPUTER. SONICS AND LOW SPECTRUMS ARE OFF. I DON'T THINK HE KNOWS I CAN ACCESS THE MIGHTY CRAYS.

IF YOU SAY SO. COMPUTERS ARE *YOUR* THING.

THE BATMOBILE'S GONE. BUT THAT DOESN'T MEAN WE CAN RELAX.

HE'S GOT ANOTHER WAY OF GETTING AROUND THAT I HAVEN'T BEEN ABLE TO FIGURE OUT YET.

SO HE *COULD* STILL BE HERE.

CASE OF THE PROPHETIC PICTURES

MASK OF THE DRUMA DAVE

HOOD OF THE MONK

GAVEL OF JUDGE CLAY

YEAH. AND *THAT* WOULD BE BAD.

I SEE WHAT YOU MEAN.

THE SOONER WE CAN GET THESE SURVEILLANCE DEVICES PLACED AND GET OUT OF HERE, THE HAPPIER *I'LL* BE.

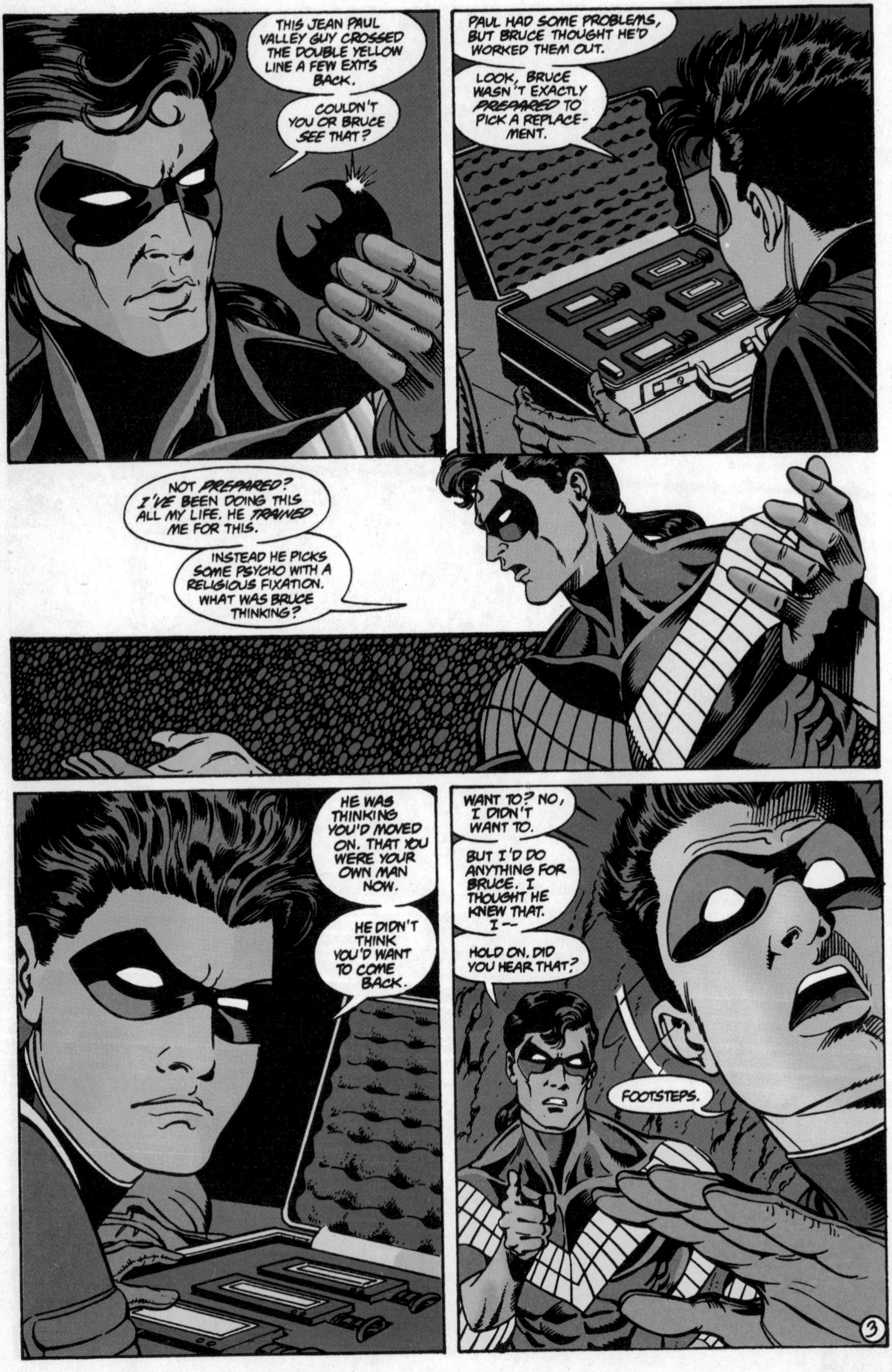
THIS JEAN PAUL VALLEY GUY CROSSED THE DOUBLE YELLOW LINE A FEW EXITS BACK.
COULDN'T YOU OR BRUCE SEE THAT?
PAUL HAD SOME PROBLEMS, BUT BRUCE THOUGHT HE'D WORKED THEM OUT.
LOOK, BRUCE WASN'T EXACTLY PREPARED TO PICK A REPLACE-MENT.
NOT PREPARED? I'VE BEEN DOING THIS ALL MY LIFE. HE TRAINED ME FOR THIS.
INSTEAD HE PICKS SOME PSYCHO WITH A RELIGIOUS FIXATION. WHAT WAS BRUCE THINKING?
HE WAS THINKING YOU'D MOVED ON. THAT YOU WERE YOUR OWN MAN NOW.
HE DIDN'T THINK YOU'D WANT TO COME BACK.
WANT TO? NO, I DIDN'T WANT TO.
BUT I'D DO ANYTHING FOR BRUCE. I THOUGHT HE KNEW THAT. I--
HOLD ON. DID YOU HEAR THAT?
FOOTSTEPS.
3

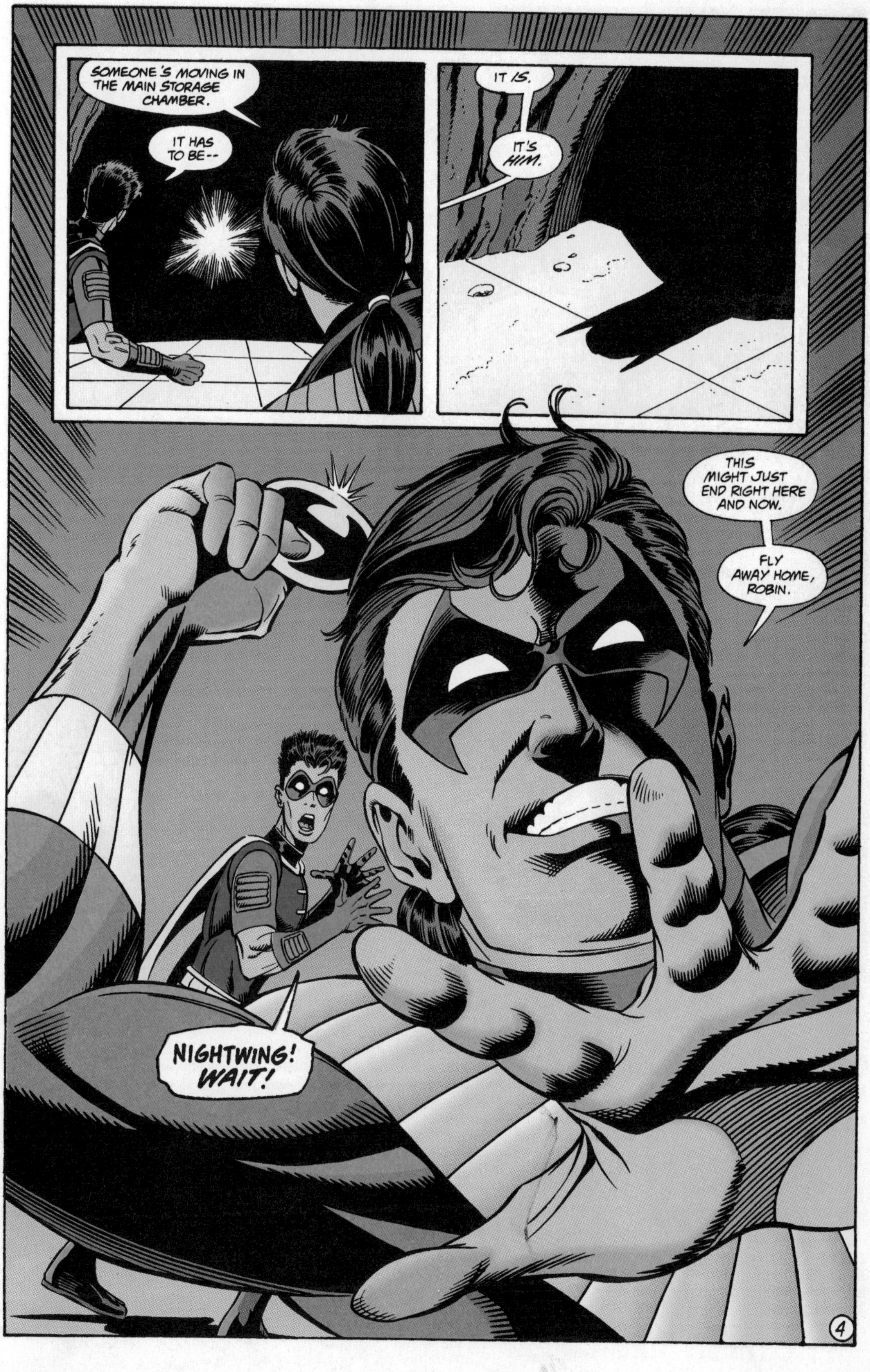
SOMEONE'S MOVING IN THE MAIN STORAGE CHAMBER.
IT HAS TO BE--
IT IS.
IT'S HIM.
THIS MIGHT JUST END RIGHT HERE AND NOW.
FLY AWAY HOME, ROBIN.
NIGHTWING! WAIT!
4

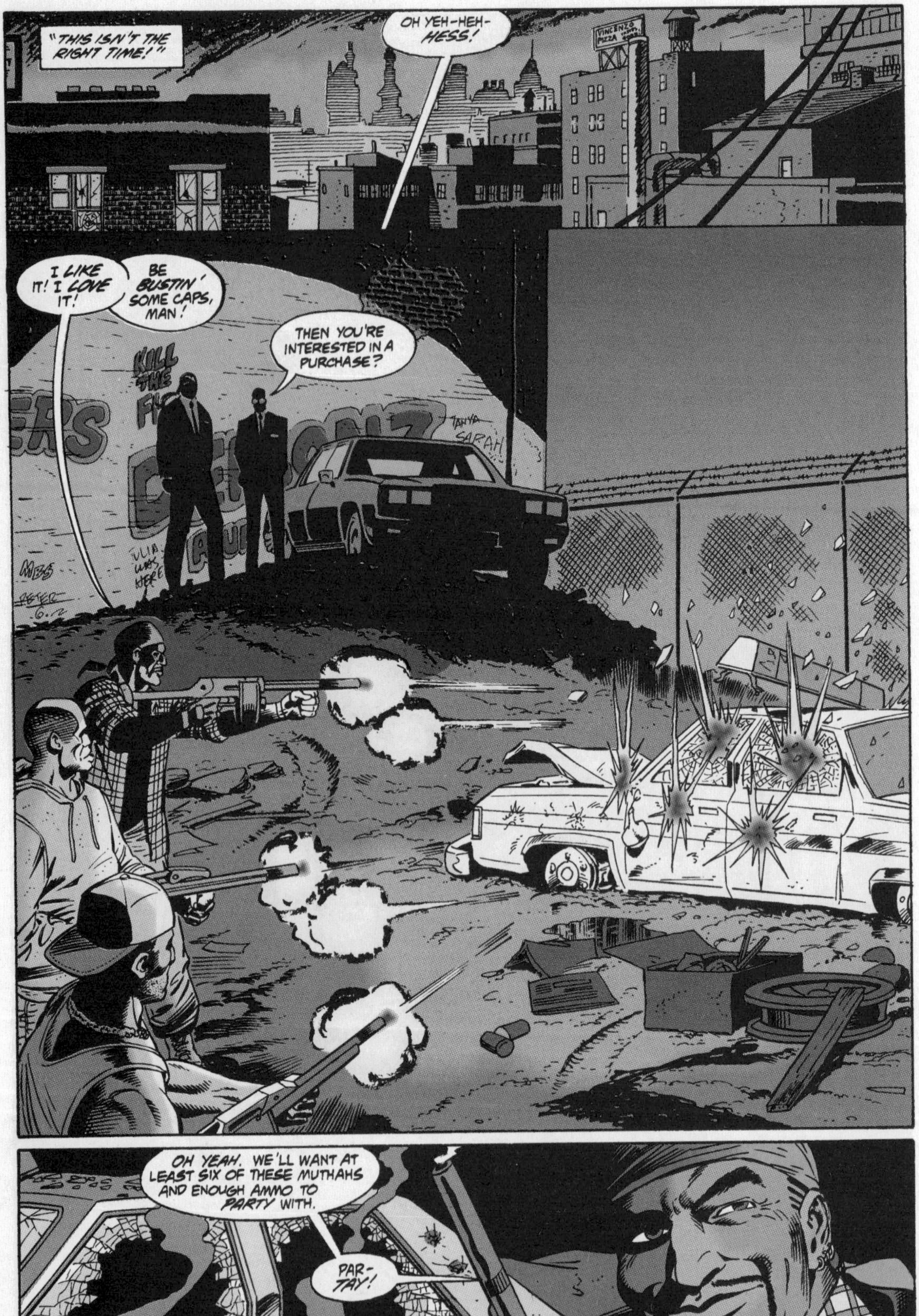
"THIS ISN'T THE RIGHT TIME!"
OH YEH-HEH-HESS!
I LIKE IT! I LOVE IT!
BE BUSTIN' SOME CAPS, MAN!
THEN YOU'RE INTERESTED IN A PURCHASE?

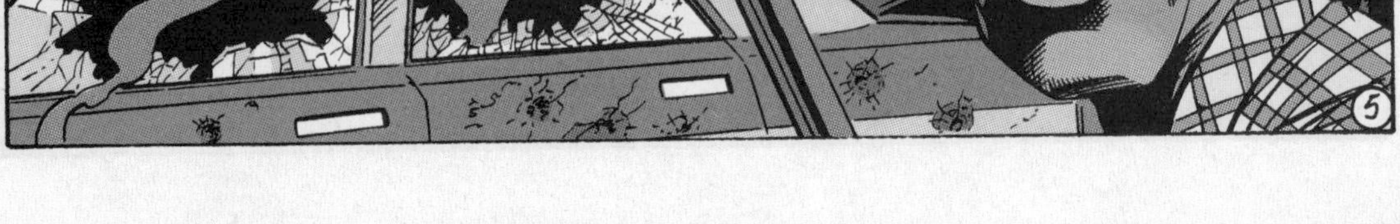
OH YEAH. WE'LL WANT AT LEAST SIX OF THESE MUTHAHS AND ENOUGH AMMO TO PARTY WITH.
PAR-TAY!
5

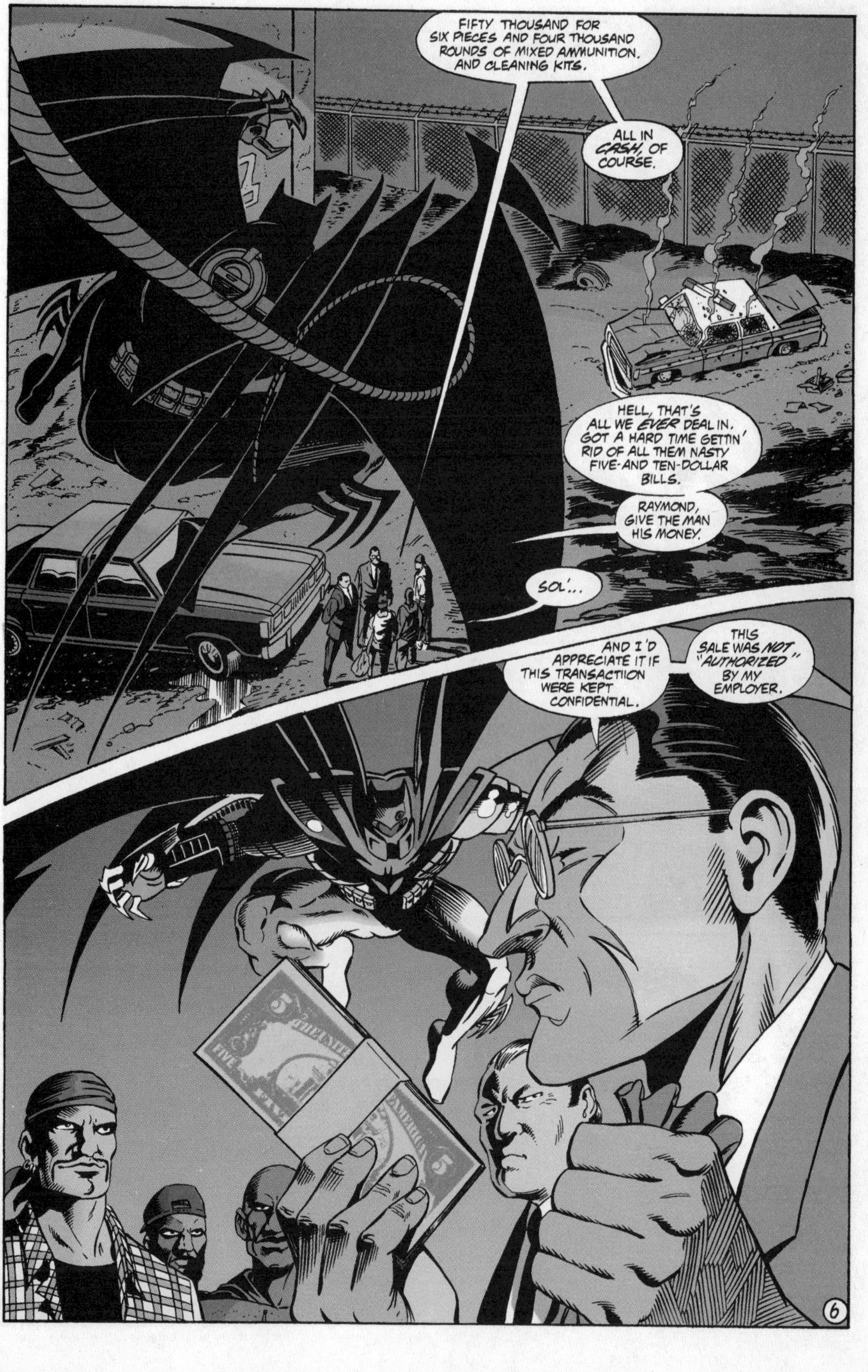

FIFTY THOUSAND FOR SIX PIECES AND FOUR THOUSAND ROUNDS OF MIXED AMMUNITION. AND CLEANING KITS.
ALL IN CASH, OF COURSE.
HELL, THAT'S ALL WE EVER DEAL IN. GOT A HARD TIME GETTIN' RID OF ALL THEM NASTY FIVE-AND TEN-DOLLAR BILLS.
RAYMOND, GIVE THE MAN HIS MONEY.
SOL'...
THIS SALE WAS NOT "AUTHORIZED" BY MY EMPLOYER.
AND I'D APPRECIATE IT IF THIS TRANSACTIION WERE KEPT CONFIDENTIAL.
6

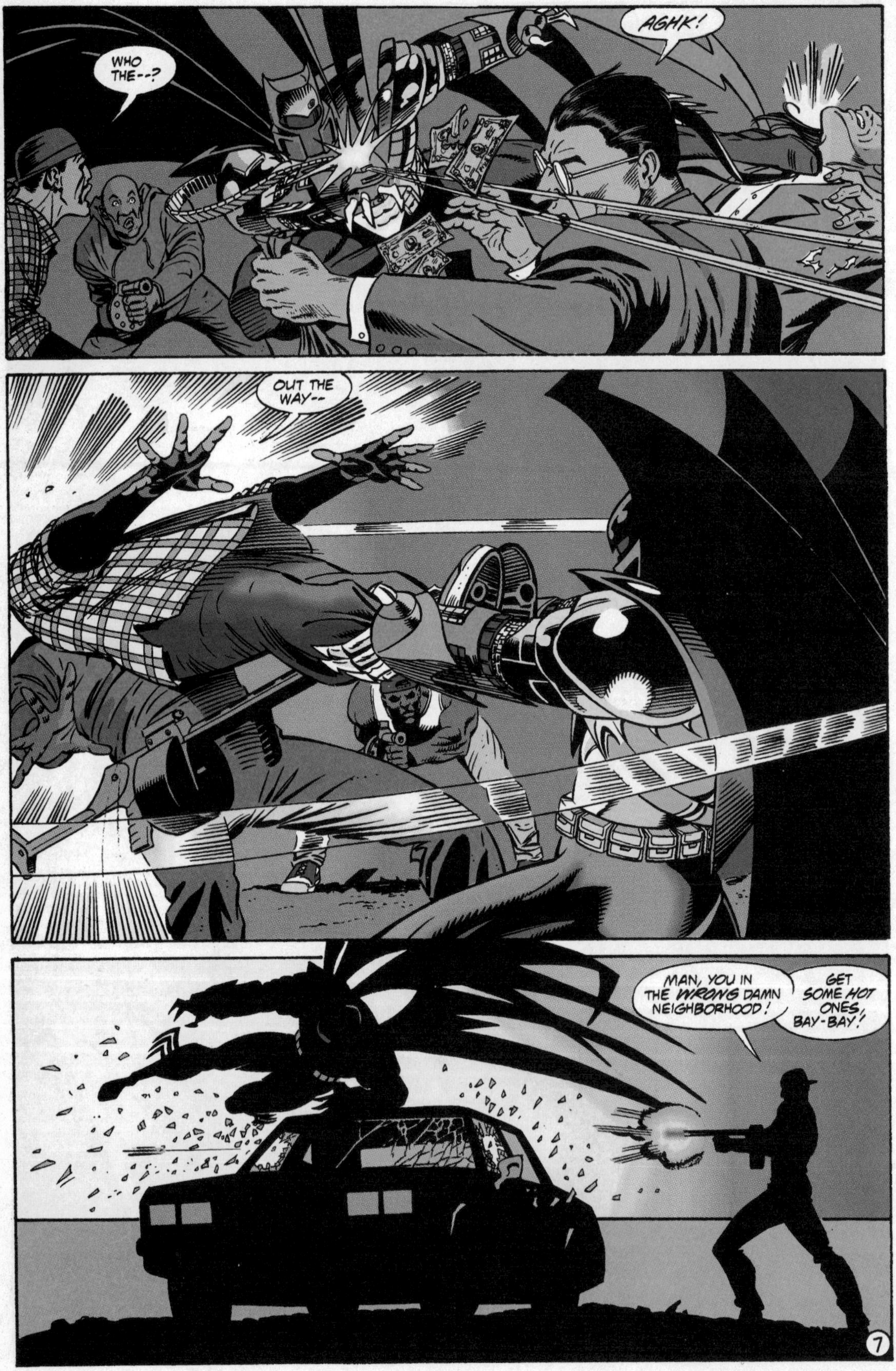
WHO THE--?
AGHK!
OUT THE WAY--
MAN, YOU IN THE WRONG DAMN NEIGHBORHOOD!
GET SOME HOT ONES, BAY-BAY!
7

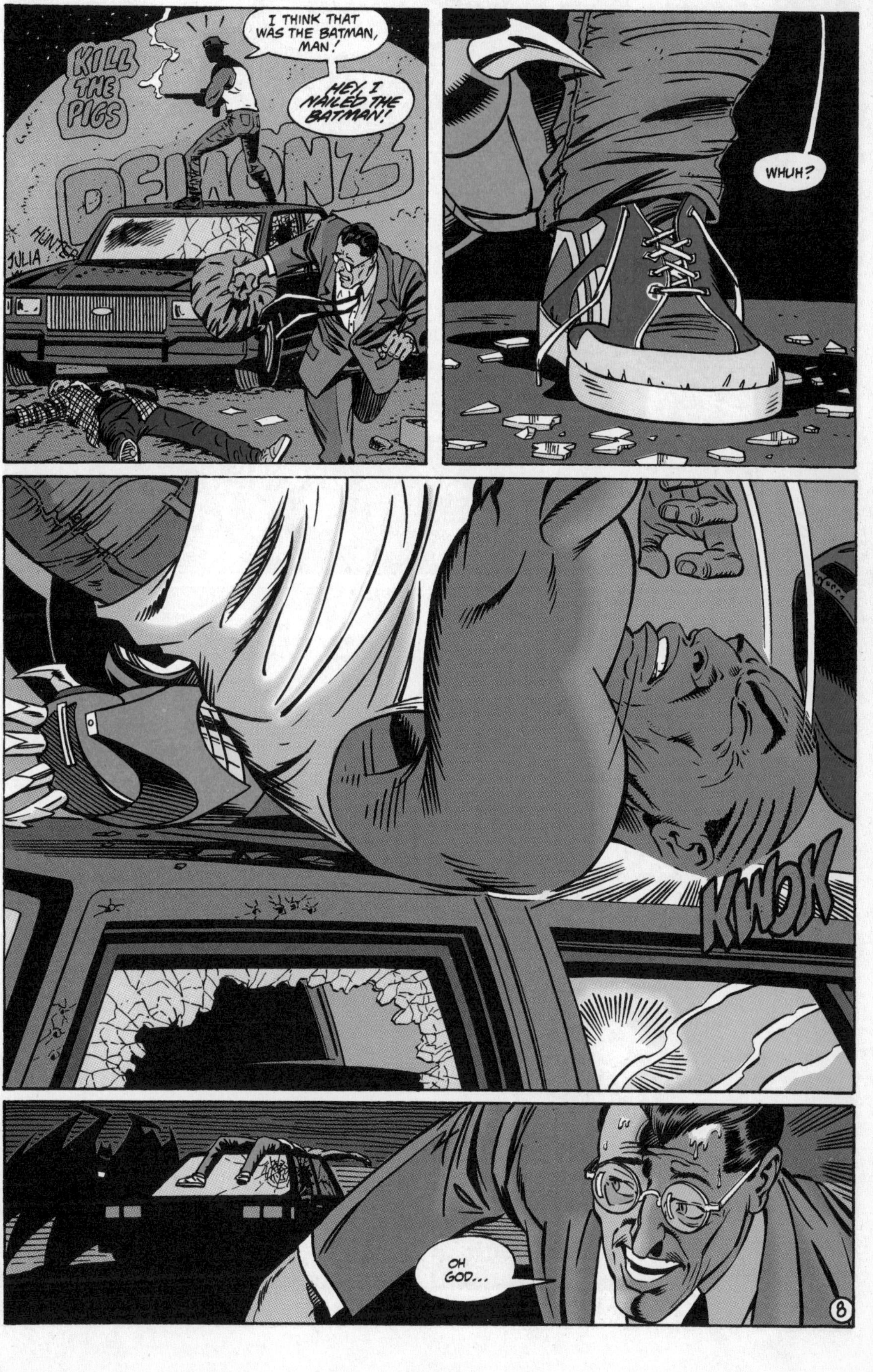
I THINK THAT WAS THE BATMAN, MAN!
HEY, I NAILED THE BATMAN!
KILL THE PIGS
DEMONZ
HUNTER
JULIA
WHUH?
KWOK
OH GOD...
8

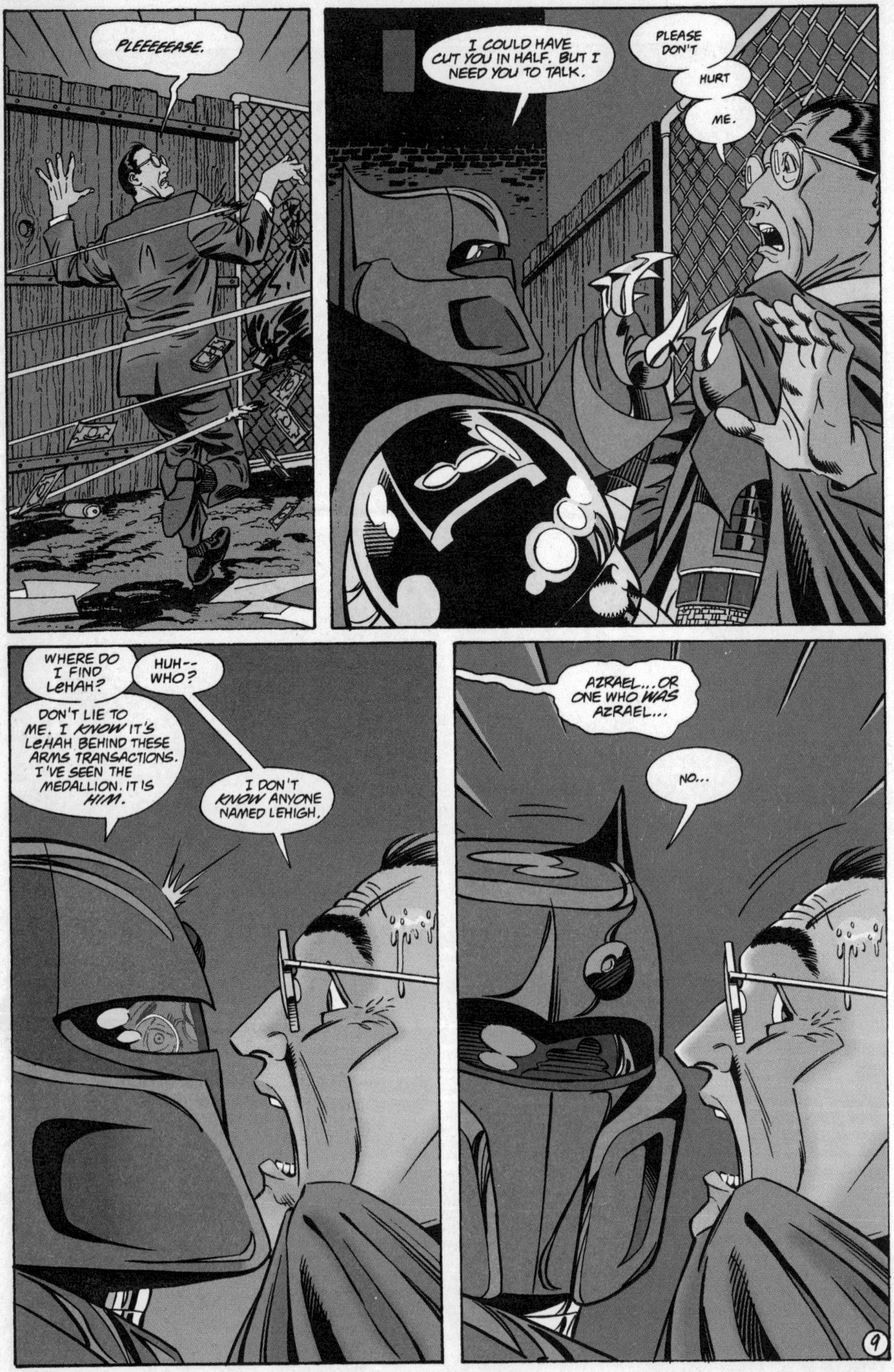
PLEEEEEASE.
I COULD HAVE CUT YOU IN HALF. BUT I NEED YOU TO TALK.
PLEASE DON'T
HURT
ME.
WHERE DO I FIND LeHAH?
HUH-- WHO?
DON'T LIE TO ME. I KNOW IT'S LeHAH BEHIND THESE ARMS TRANSACTIONS. I'VE SEEN THE MEDALLION. IT IS HIM.
I DON'T KNOW ANYONE NAMED LEHIGH.
AZRAEL... OR ONE WHO WAS AZRAEL...
NO...
9

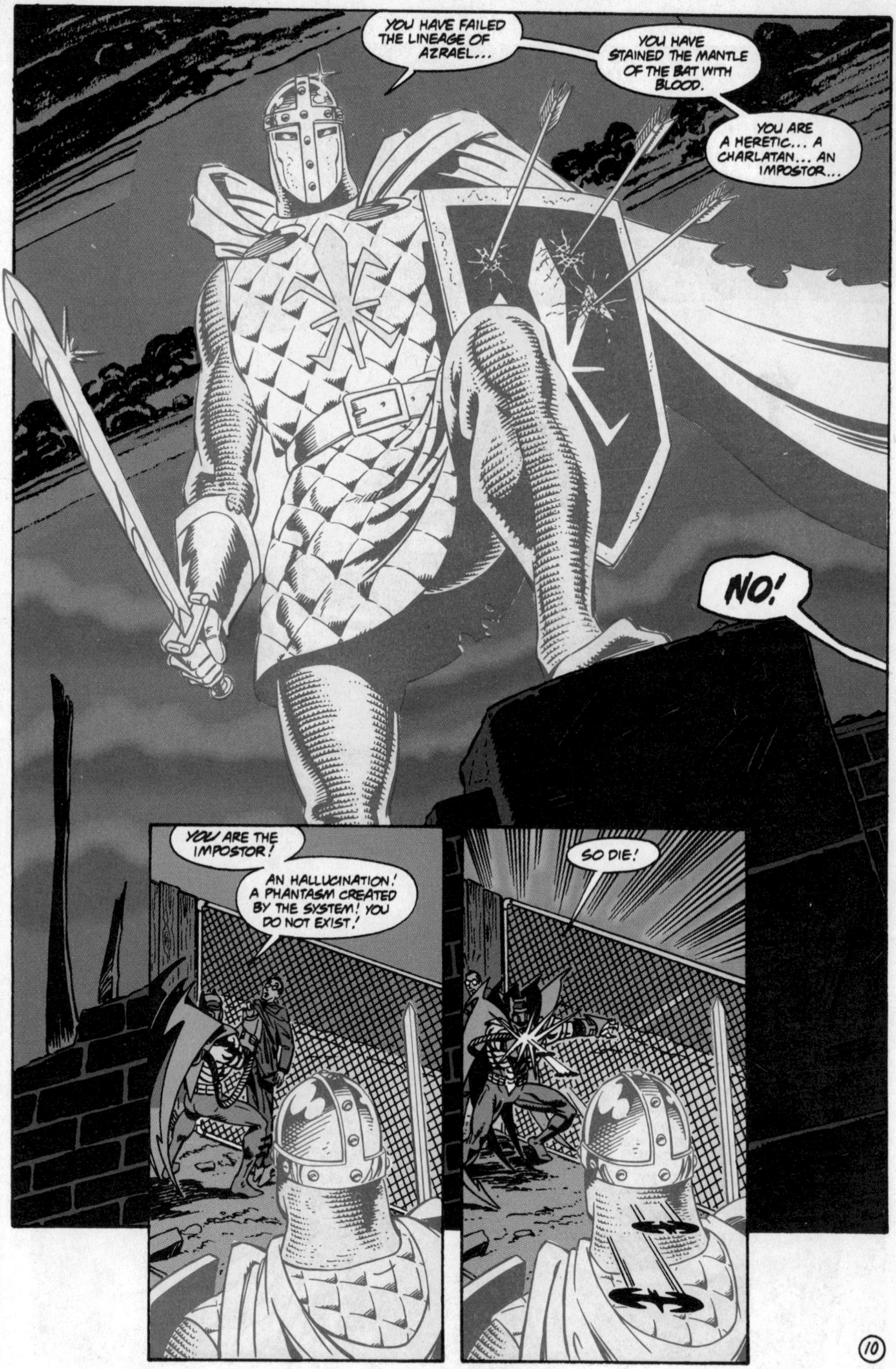
YOU HAVE FAILED THE LINEAGE OF AZRAEL...
YOU HAVE STAINED THE MANTLE OF THE BAT WITH BLOOD.
YOU ARE A HERETIC... A CHARLATAN... AN IMPOSTOR...
NO!
YOU ARE THE IMPOSTOR!
AN HALLUCINATION! A PHANTASM CREATED BY THE SYSTEM! YOU DO NOT EXIST!
SO DIE!
10

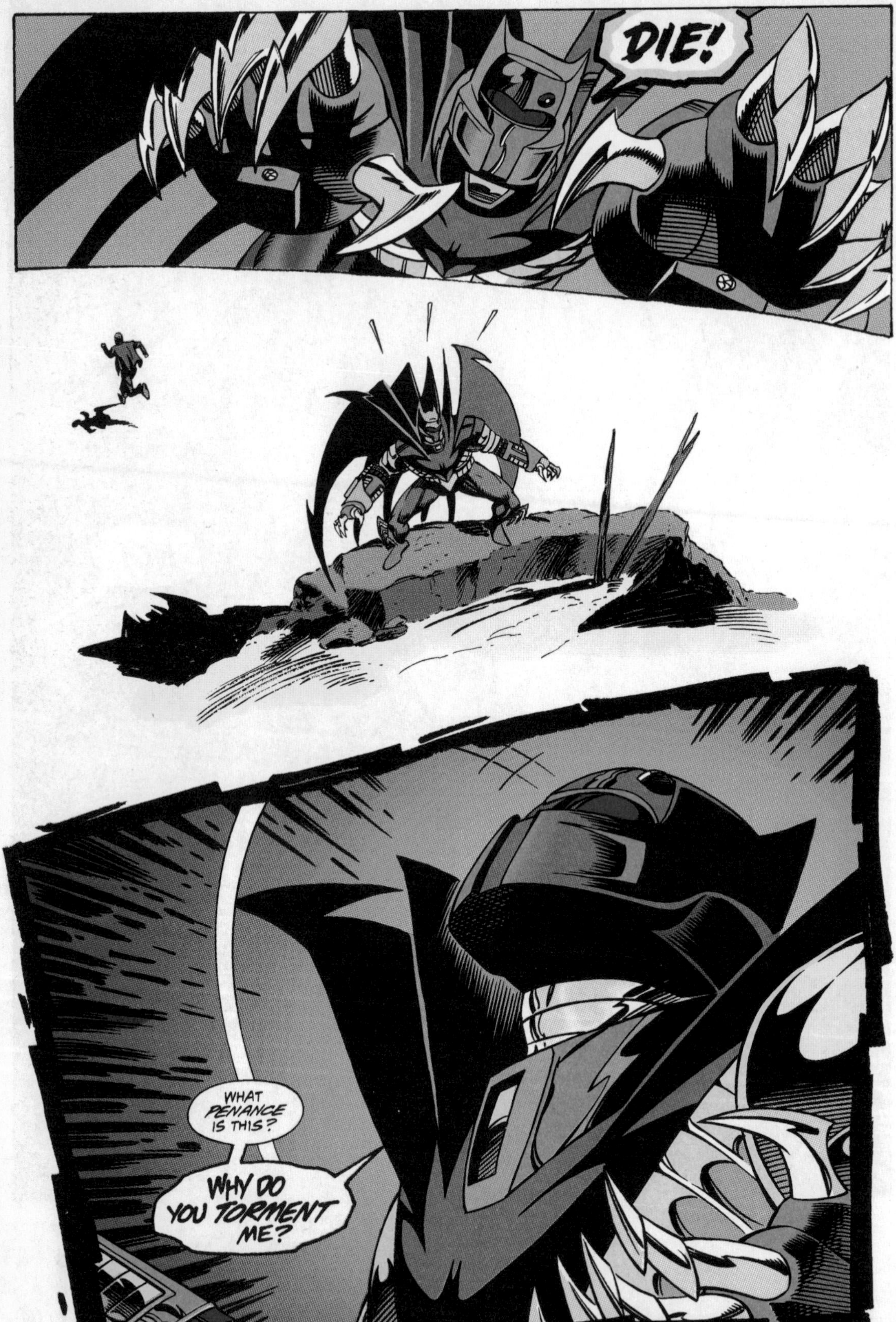
DIE!
WHAT PENANCE IS THIS?
WHY DO YOU TORMENT ME?

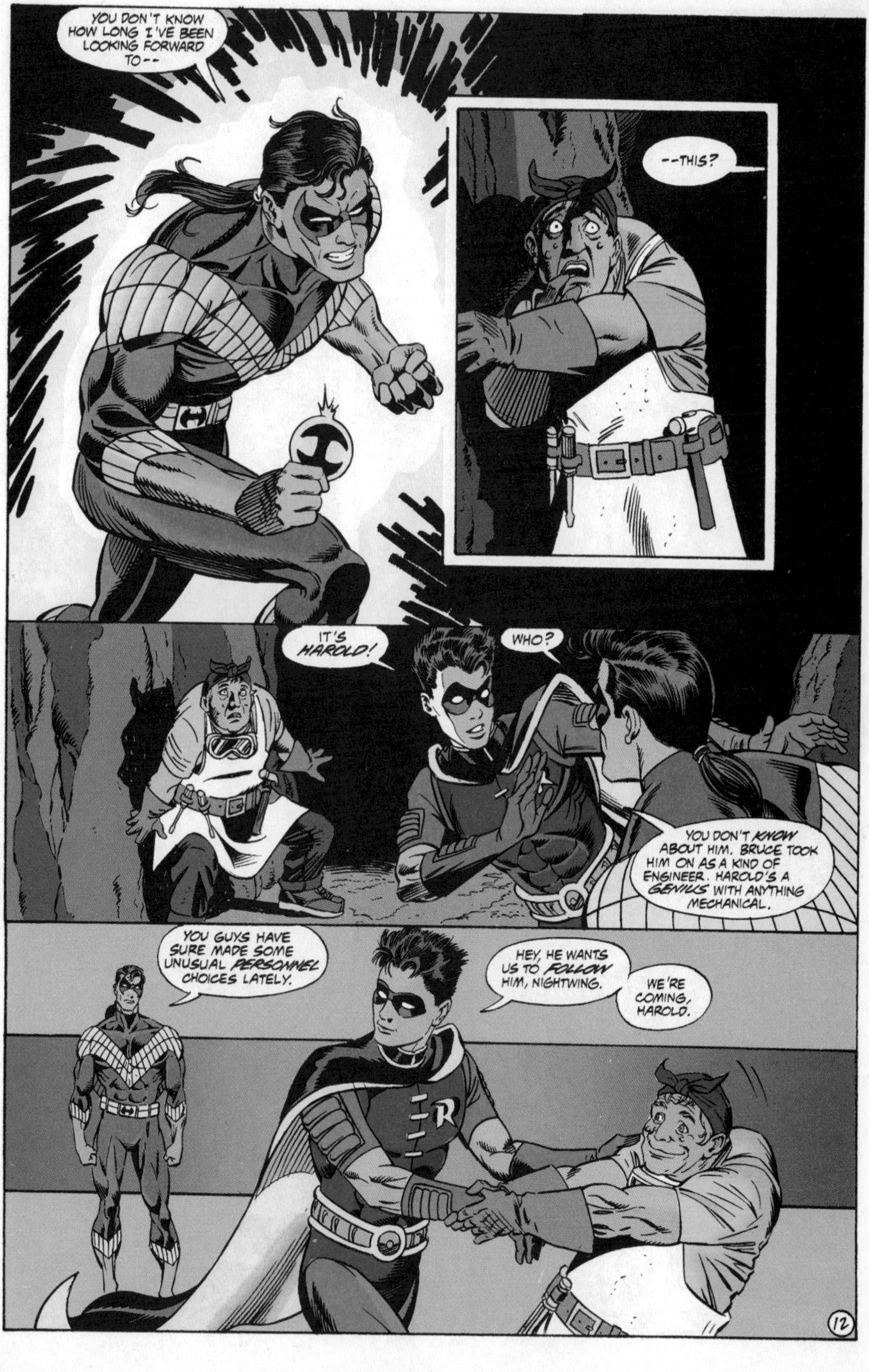

YOU DON'T KNOW HOW LONG I'VE BEEN LOOKING FORWARD TO--
--THIS?
IT'S HAROLD!
WHO?
YOU DON'T KNOW ABOUT HIM. BRUCE TOOK HIM ON AS A KIND OF ENGINEER. HAROLD'S A GENIUS WITH ANYTHING MECHANICAL.
YOU GUYS HAVE SURE MADE SOME UNUSUAL PERSONNEL CHOICES LATELY.
HEY, HE WANTS US TO FOLLOW HIM, NIGHTWING.
WE'RE COMING, HAROLD.
12

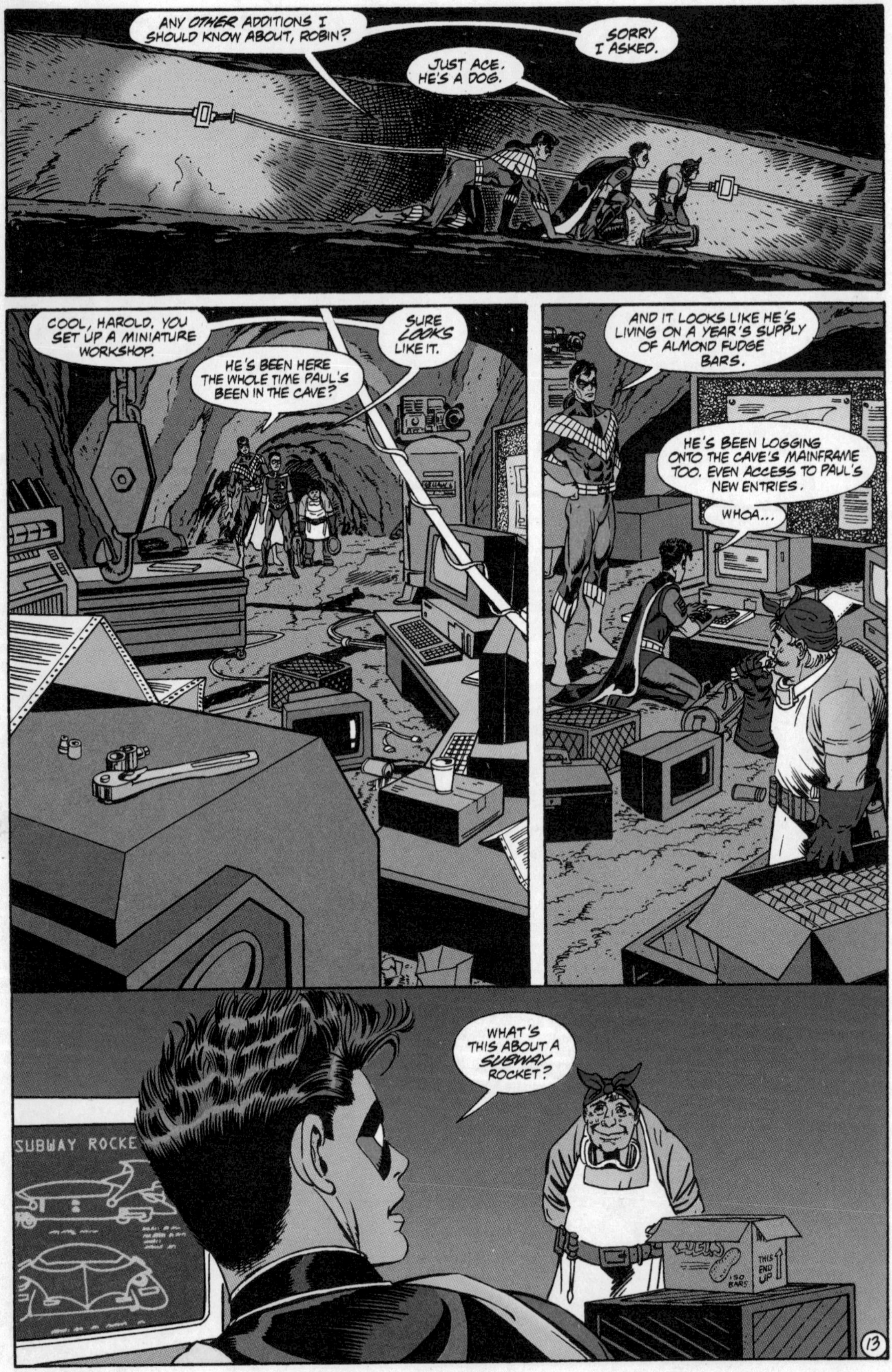
ANY OTHER ADDITIONS I SHOULD KNOW ABOUT, ROBIN?
JUST ACE. HE'S A DOG.
SORRY I ASKED.
COOL, HAROLD. YOU SET UP A MINIATURE WORKSHOP.
HE'S BEEN HERE THE WHOLE TIME PAUL'S BEEN IN THE CAVE?
SURE LOOKS LIKE IT.
AND IT LOOKS LIKE HE'S LIVING ON A YEAR'S SUPPLY OF ALMOND FUDGE BARS.
HE'S BEEN LOGGING ONTO THE CAVE'S MAINFRAME TOO. EVEN ACCESS TO PAUL'S NEW ENTRIES.
WHOA...
WHAT'S THIS ABOUT A SUBWAY ROCKET?
SUBWAY ROCKE
150 BARS
THIS END UP
13

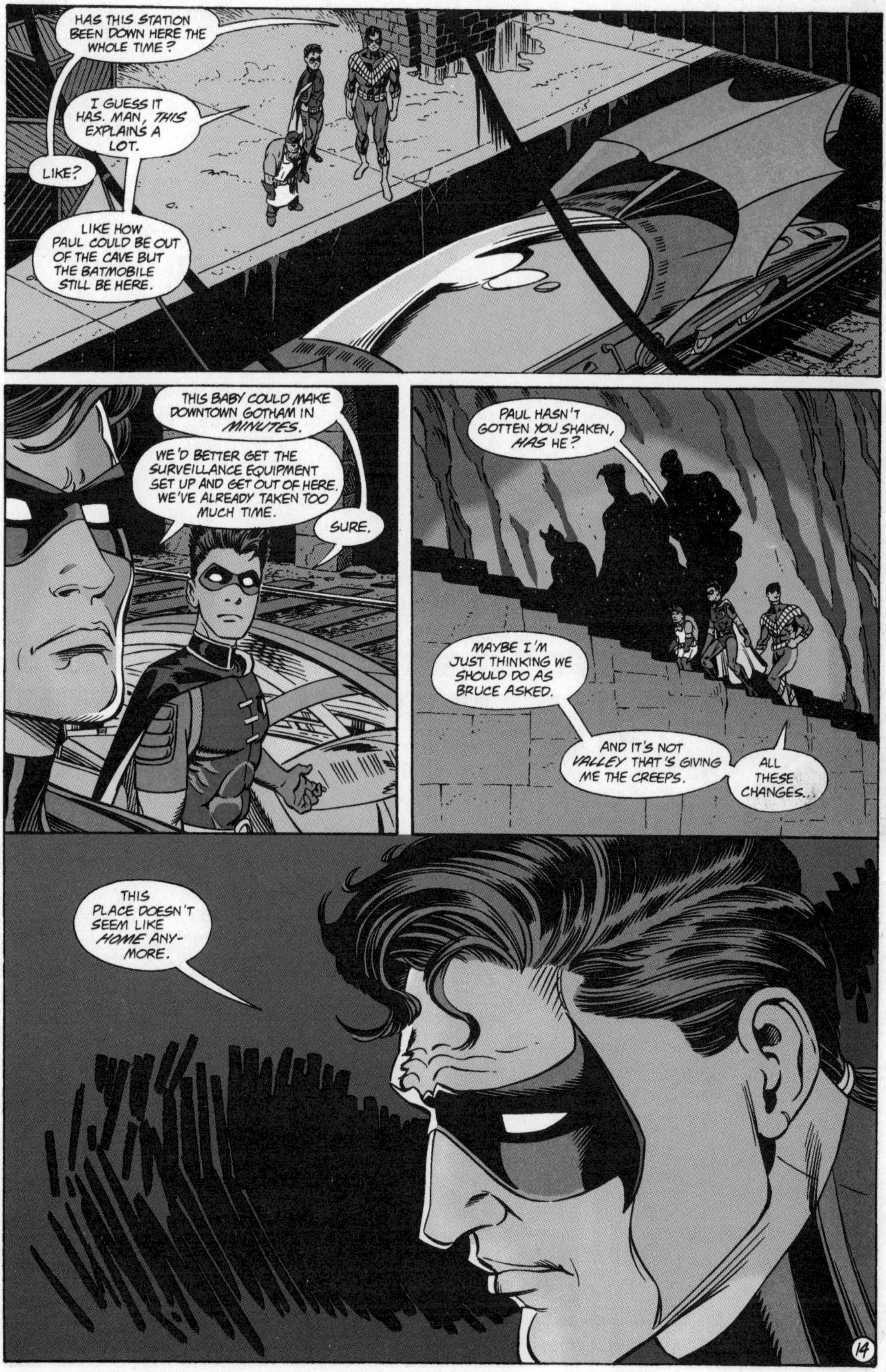
HAS THIS STATION BEEN DOWN HERE THE WHOLE TIME?
I GUESS IT HAS. MAN, THIS EXPLAINS A LOT.
LIKE?
LIKE HOW PAUL COULD BE OUT OF THE CAVE BUT THE BATMOBILE STILL BE HERE.
THIS BABY COULD MAKE DOWNTOWN GOTHAM IN MINUTES.
WE'D BETTER GET THE SURVEILLANCE EQUIPMENT SET UP AND GET OUT OF HERE. WE'VE ALREADY TAKEN TOO MUCH TIME.
SURE.
PAUL HASN'T GOTTEN YOU SHAKEN, HAS HE?
MAYBE I'M JUST THINKING WE SHOULD DO AS BRUCE ASKED.
AND IT'S NOT VALLEY THAT'S GIVING ME THE CREEPS.
ALL THESE CHANGES...
THIS PLACE DOESN'T SEEM LIKE HOME ANY-MORE.
14

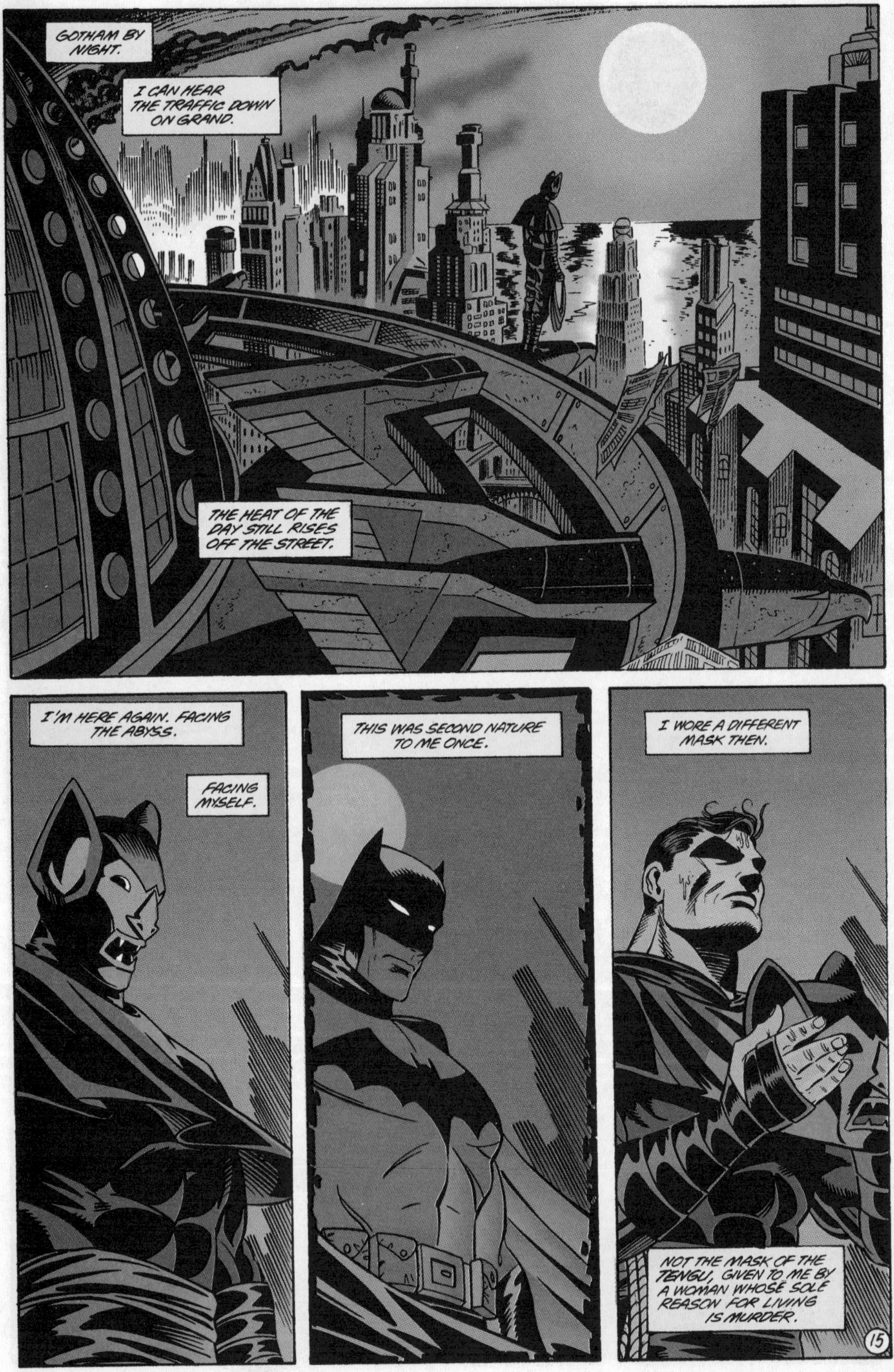
GOTHAM BY NIGHT.
I CAN HEAR THE TRAFFIC DOWN ON GRAND.
THE HEAT OF THE DAY STILL RISES OFF THE STREET.
I'M HERE AGAIN. FACING THE ABYSS.
FACING MYSELF.
THIS WAS SECOND NATURE TO ME ONCE.
I WORE A DIFFERENT MASK THEN.
NOT THE MASK OF THE TENGU, GIVEN TO ME BY A WOMAN WHOSE SOLE REASON FOR LIVING IS MURDER.
15

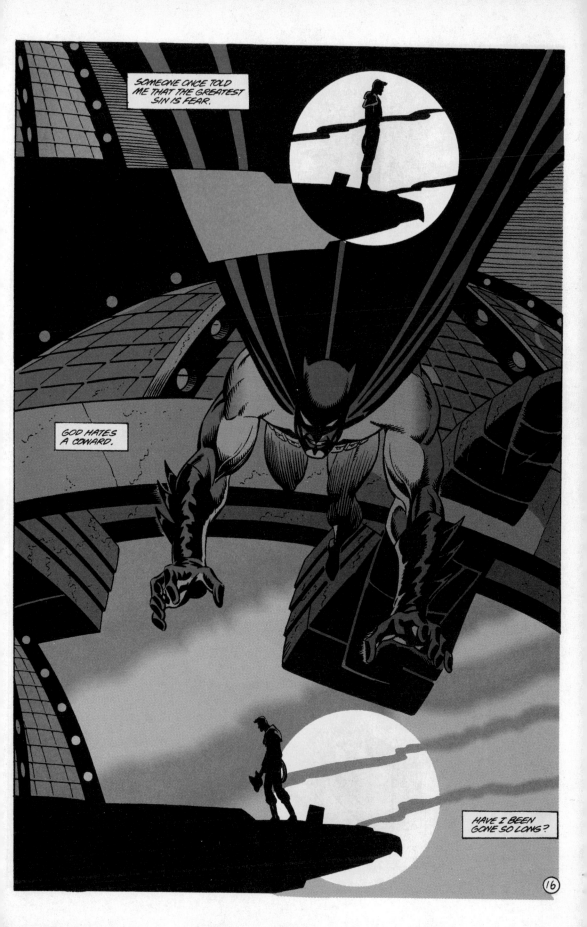

SOMEONE ONCE TOLD ME THAT THE GREATEST SIN IS FEAR.

GOD HATES A COWARD.

HAVE I BEEN GONE SO LONG?

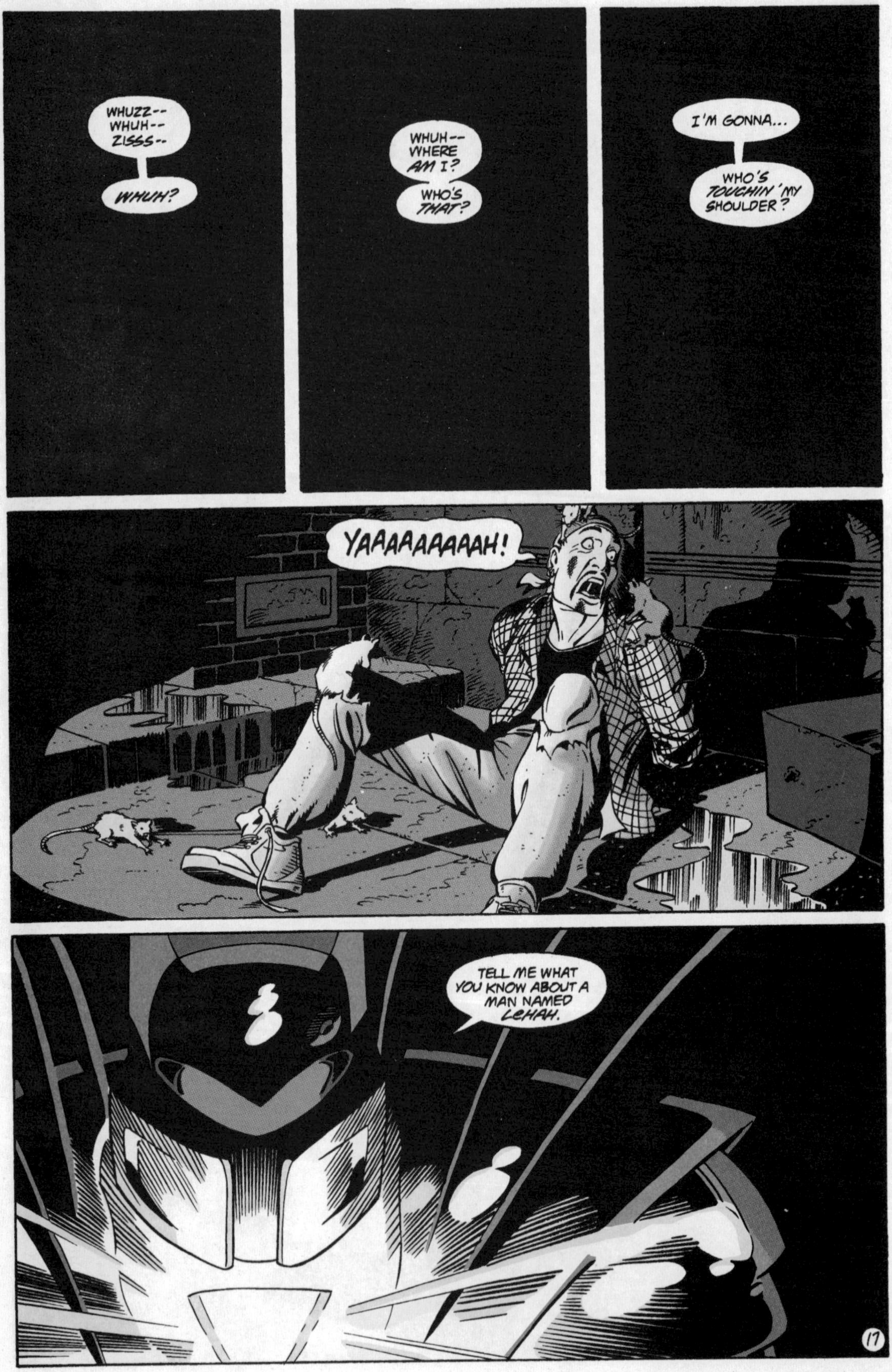
WHUZZ--
WHUH--
ZISSS--
WHUH?
WHUH--
WHERE
AM I?
WHO'S
THAT?
I'M GONNA...
WHO'S
TOUCHIN' MY
SHOULDER?
YAAAAAAAAAH!
TELL ME WHAT
YOU KNOW ABOUT A
MAN NAMED
LEHAH.
17

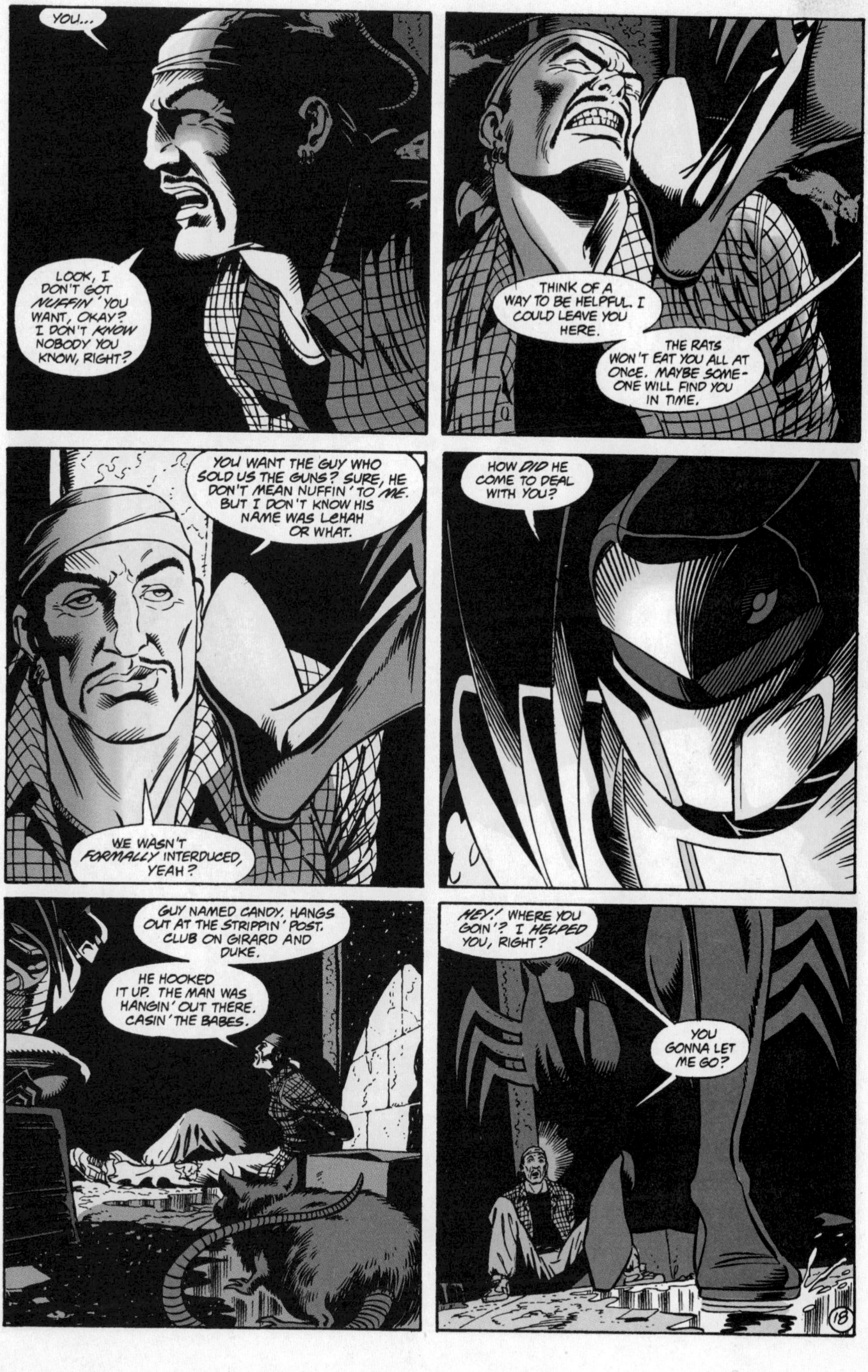
YOU...
LOOK, I DON'T GOT NUFFIN' YOU WANT, OKAY? I DON'T KNOW NOBODY YOU KNOW, RIGHT?
THINK OF A WAY TO BE HELPFUL. I COULD LEAVE YOU HERE.
THE RATS WON'T EAT YOU ALL AT ONCE. MAYBE SOME-ONE WILL FIND YOU IN TIME.
YOU WANT THE GUY WHO SOLD US THE GUNS? SURE, HE DON'T MEAN NUFFIN' TO ME. BUT I DON'T KNOW HIS NAME WAS LEHAH OR WHAT.
WE WASN'T FORMALLY INTERDUCED, YEAH?
HOW DID HE COME TO DEAL WITH YOU?
GUY NAMED CANDY. HANGS OUT AT THE STRIPPIN' POST. CLUB ON GIRARD AND DUKE.
HE HOOKED IT UP. THE MAN WAS HANGIN' OUT THERE. CASIN' THE BABES.
HEY! WHERE YOU GOIN'? I HELPED YOU, RIGHT?
YOU GONNA LET ME GO?
18

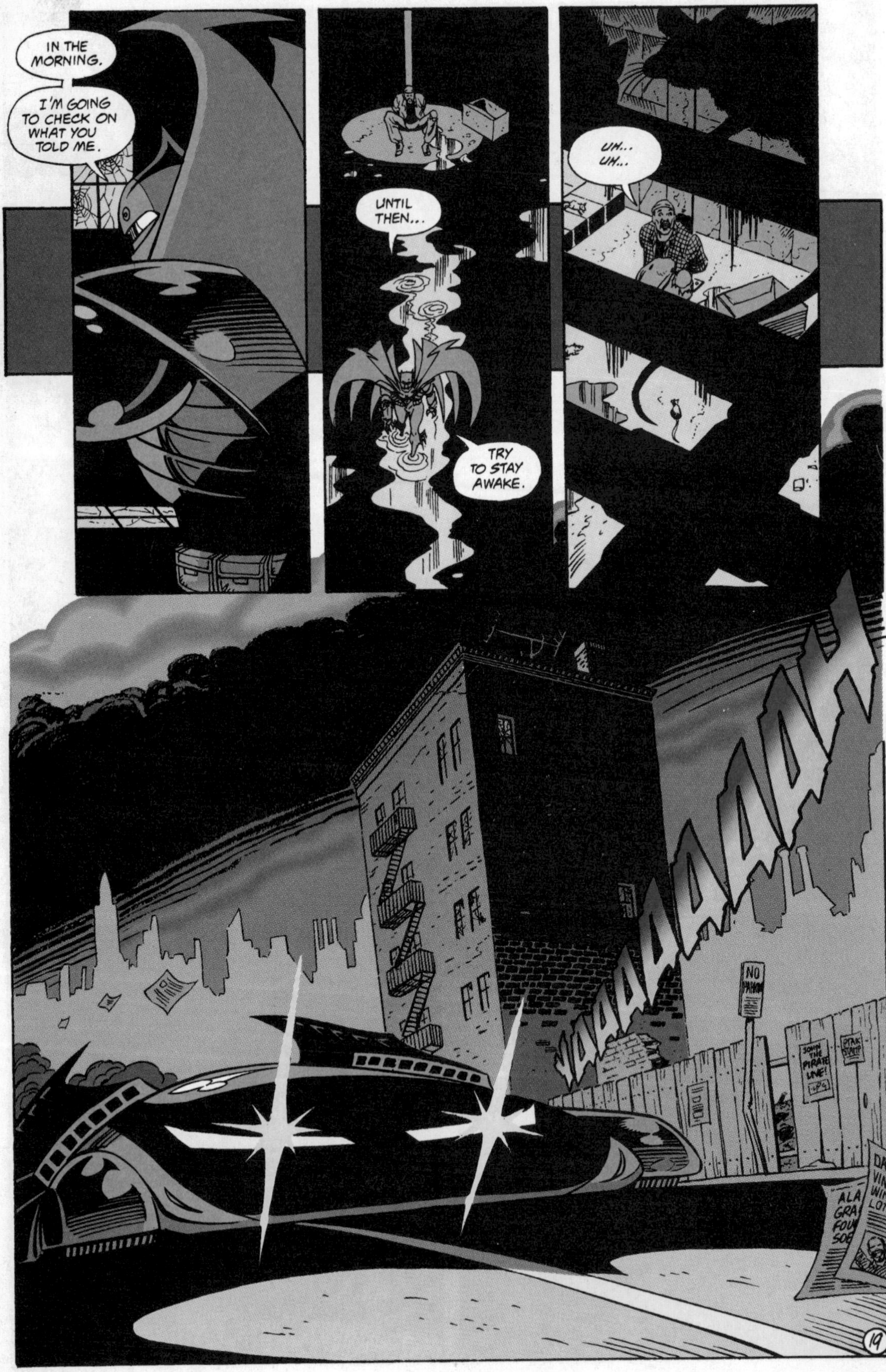
IN THE MORNING.
I'M GOING TO CHECK ON WHAT YOU TOLD ME.
UNTIL THEN...
TRY TO STAY AWAKE.
UH... UH...
NO
JOHN THE PIRATE LIVE!
19

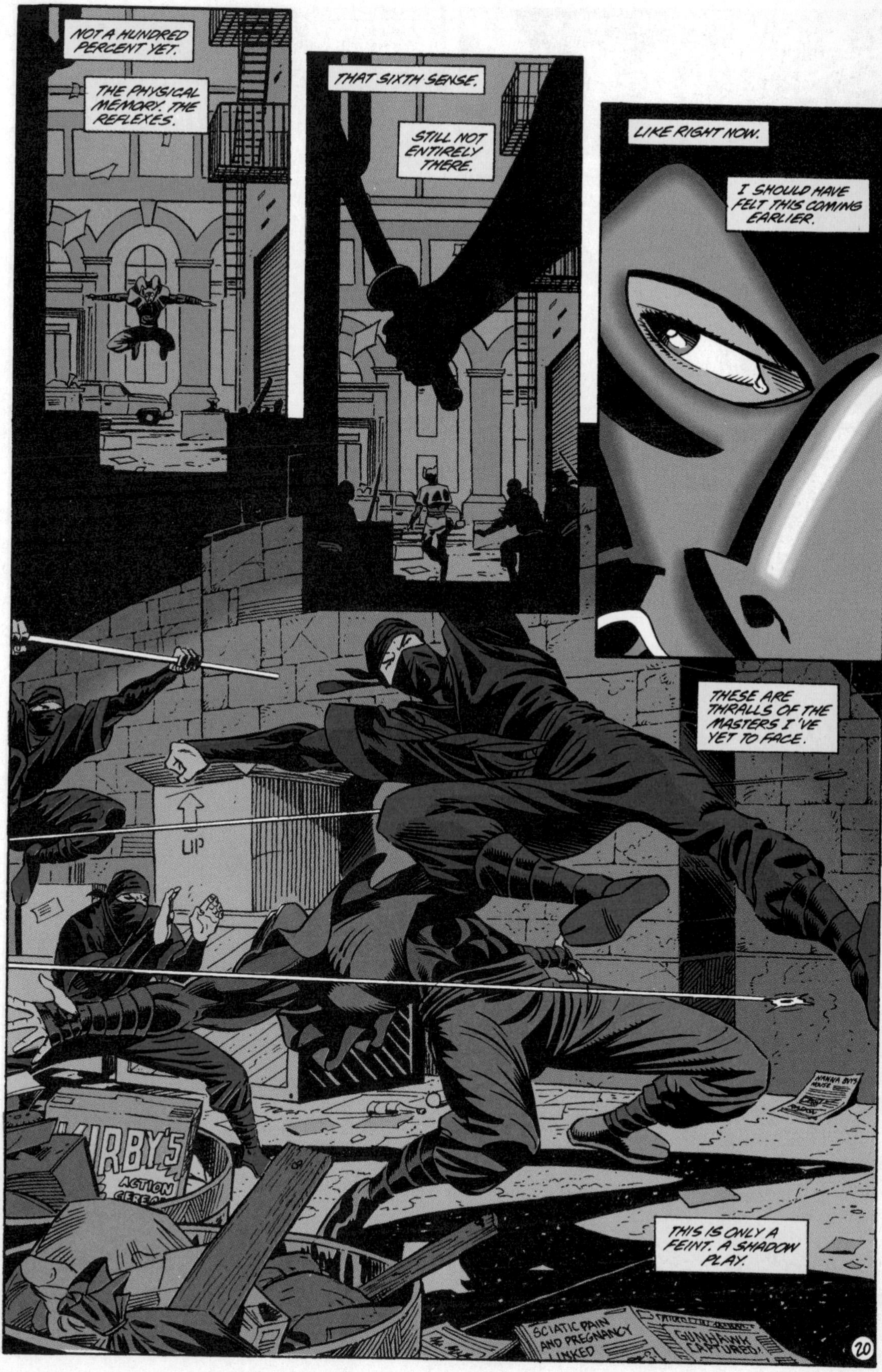
NOT A HUNDRED PERCENT YET.
THE PHYSICAL MEMORY. THE REFLEXES.
THAT SIXTH SENSE.
STILL NOT ENTIRELY THERE.
LIKE RIGHT NOW.
I SHOULD HAVE FELT THIS COMING EARLIER.
THESE ARE THRALLS OF THE MASTERS I'VE YET TO FACE.
UP
THIS IS ONLY A FEINT. A SHADOW PLAY.
KIRBY'S ACTION
SCIATIC PAIN AND PREGNANCY LINKED
GUNHAWK CAPTURED!
20

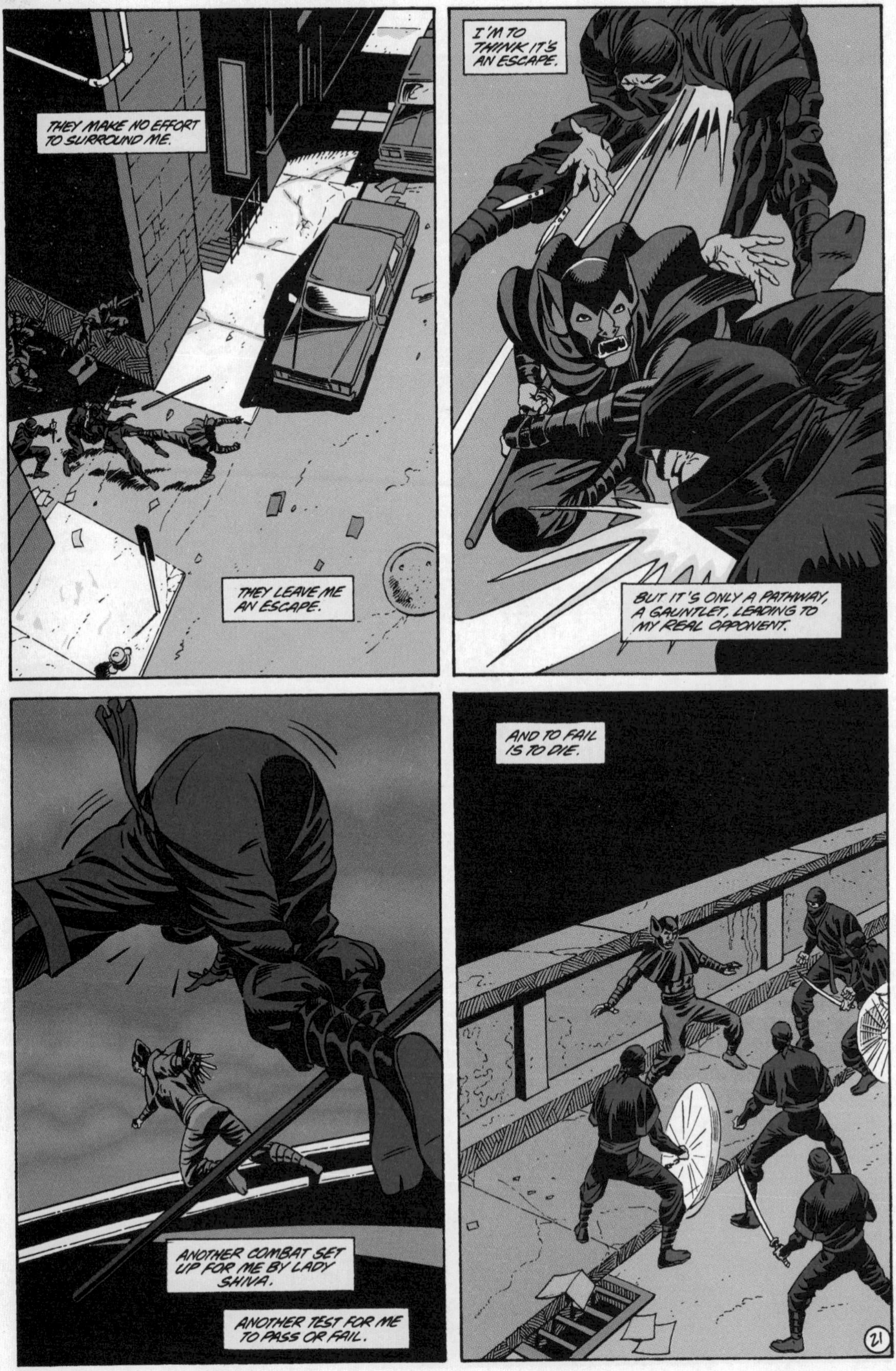
THEY MAKE NO EFFORT TO SURROUND ME.
THEY LEAVE ME AN ESCAPE.
I'M TO THINK IT'S AN ESCAPE.
BUT IT'S ONLY A PATHWAY, A GAUNTLET, LEADING TO MY REAL OPPONENT.
ANOTHER COMBAT SET UP FOR ME BY LADY SHIVA.
ANOTHER TEST FOR ME TO PASS OR FAIL.
AND TO FAIL IS TO DIE.
21

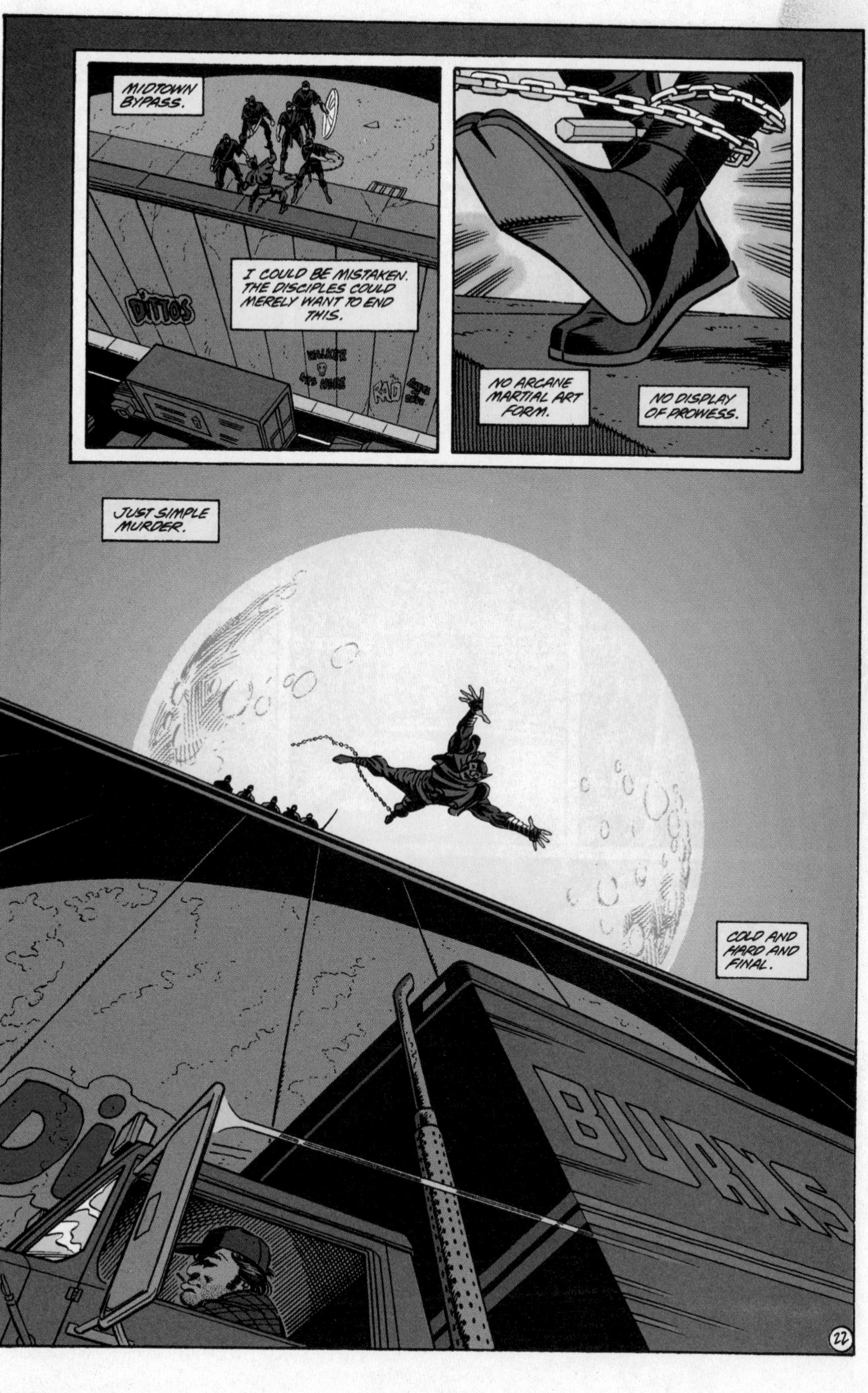
MIDTOWN BYPASS.
I COULD BE MISTAKEN. THE DISCIPLES COULD MERELY WANT TO END THIS.
DITTOS
RAD
NO ARCANE MARTIAL ART FORM.
NO DISPLAY OF PROWESS.
JUST SIMPLE MURDER.
COLD AND HARD AND FINAL.
22

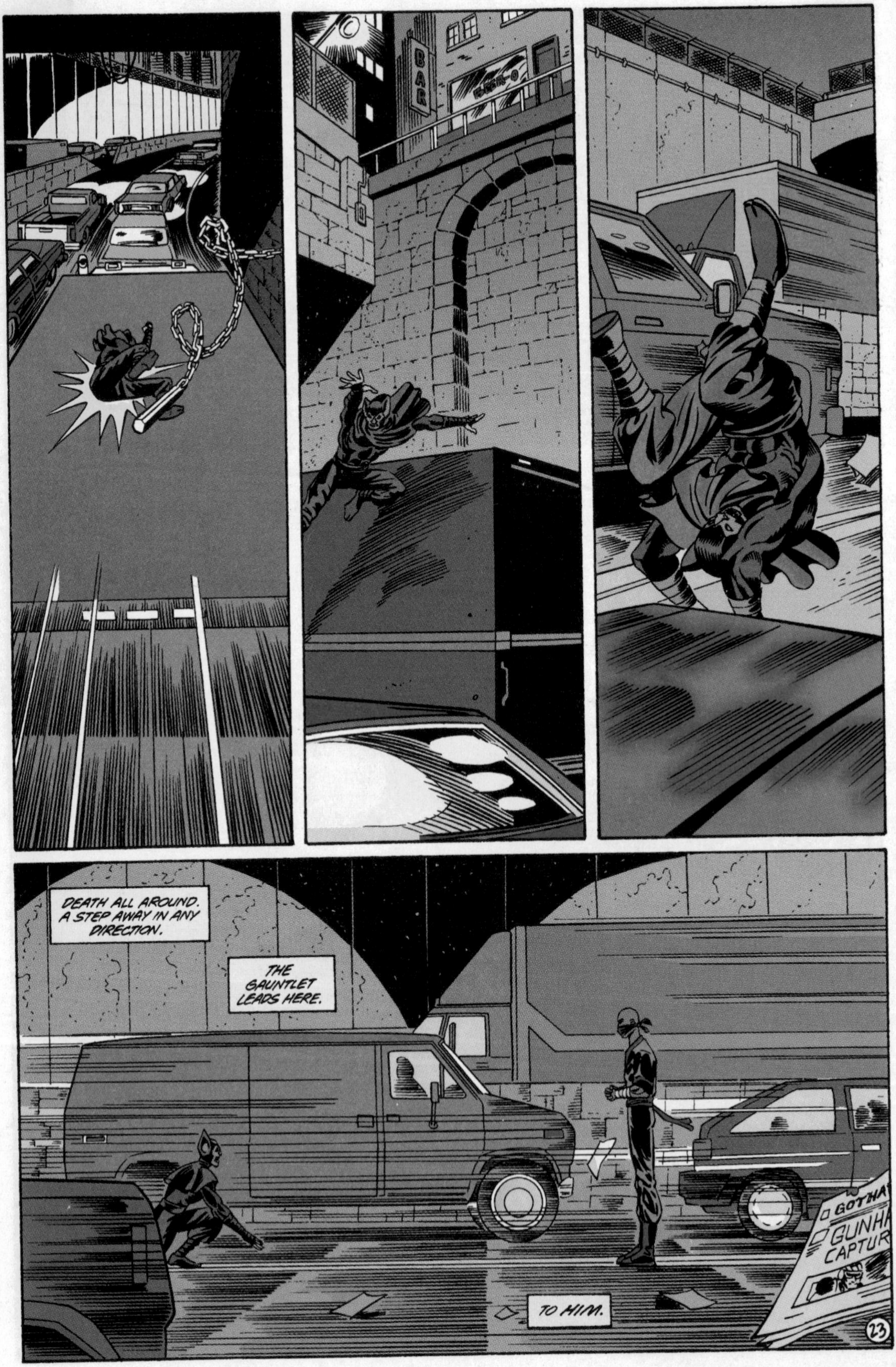
BAR
DEATH ALL AROUND. A STEP AWAY IN ANY DIRECTION.
THE GAUNTLET LEADS HERE.
TO HIM.
23

LIKE I *NEED* THIS AGGRAVATION. I GOT DEALS GOIN'. STUFF HANGIN' FIRE.

STRIPPIN' POST

GIRLS

NICKY JUST SAID HE'S IN TROUBLE. GETTIN' SOME HEAT FROM THE BULLS.

I'M SORRY YA EVER GOT A PORTABLE PHONE, MIKEY.

WHICH ONE OF YOU IS CANDY?

JEEZE!

LET ME GUESS...

YOU *LOOK* LIKE A CANDY.

OWW!

24

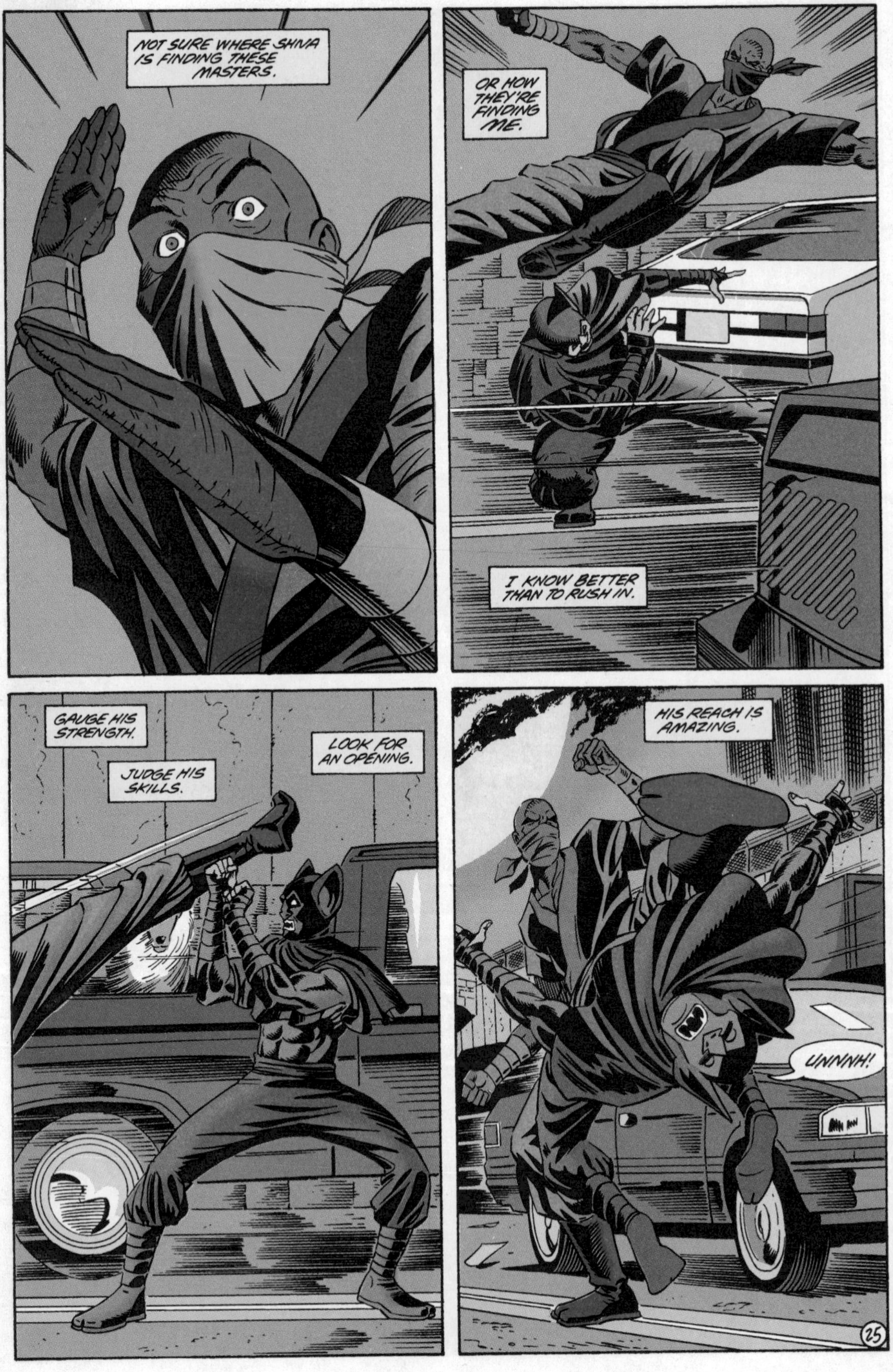
NOT SURE WHERE SHIVA IS FINDING THESE MASTERS.
OR HOW THEY'RE FINDING ME.
I KNOW BETTER THAN TO RUSH IN.
GAUGE HIS STRENGTH.
JUDGE HIS SKILLS.
LOOK FOR AN OPENING.
HIS REACH IS AMAZING.
UNNNH!
25

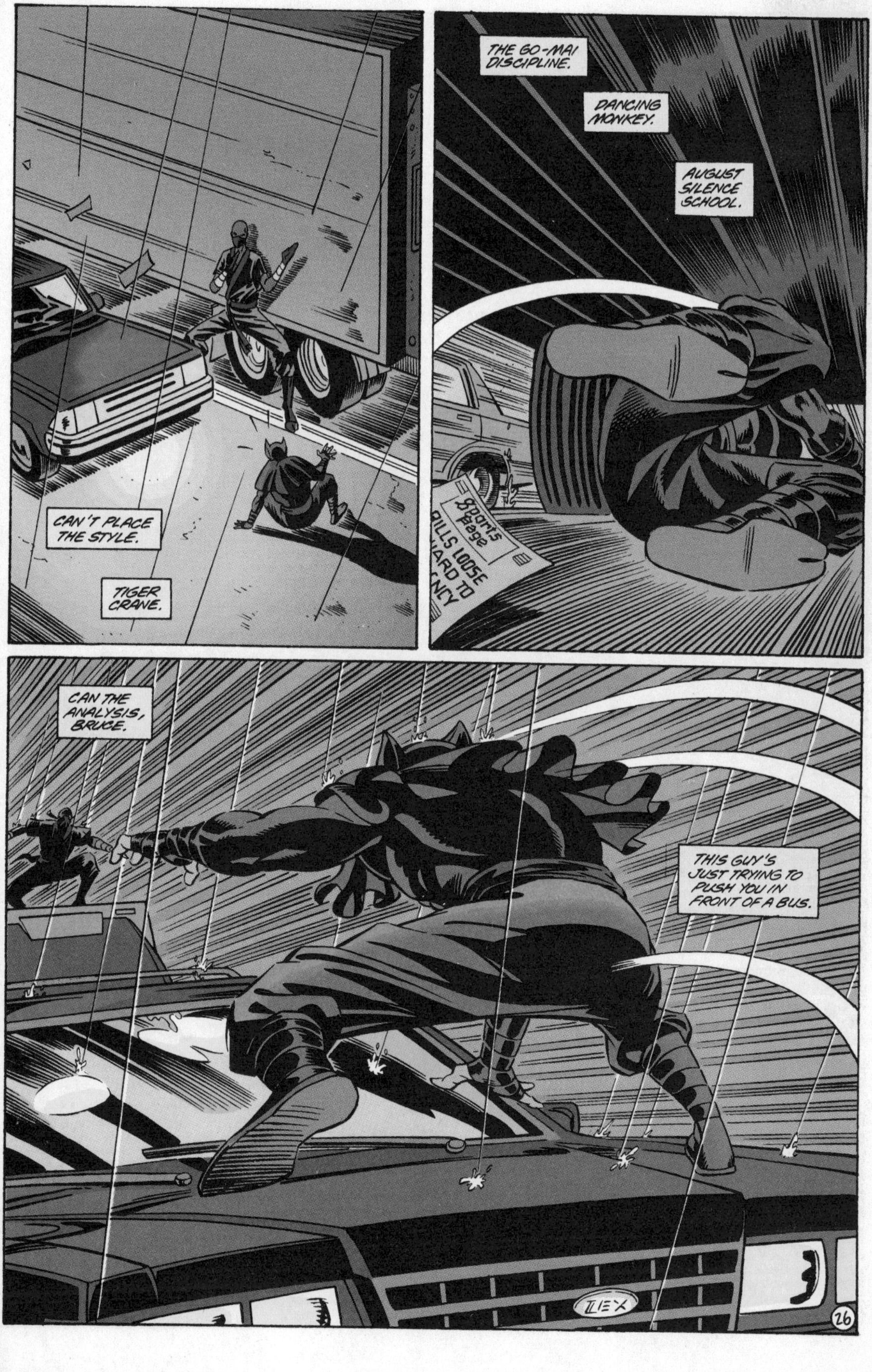
CAN'T PLACE THE STYLE.
TIGER CRANE.
THE GO-MAI DISCIPLINE.
DANCING MONKEY.
AUGUST SILENCE SCHOOL.
Sports Page
BILLS LOOSE
CAN THE ANALYSIS, BRUCE.
THIS GUY'S JUST TRYING TO PUSH YOU IN FRONT OF A BUS.
26

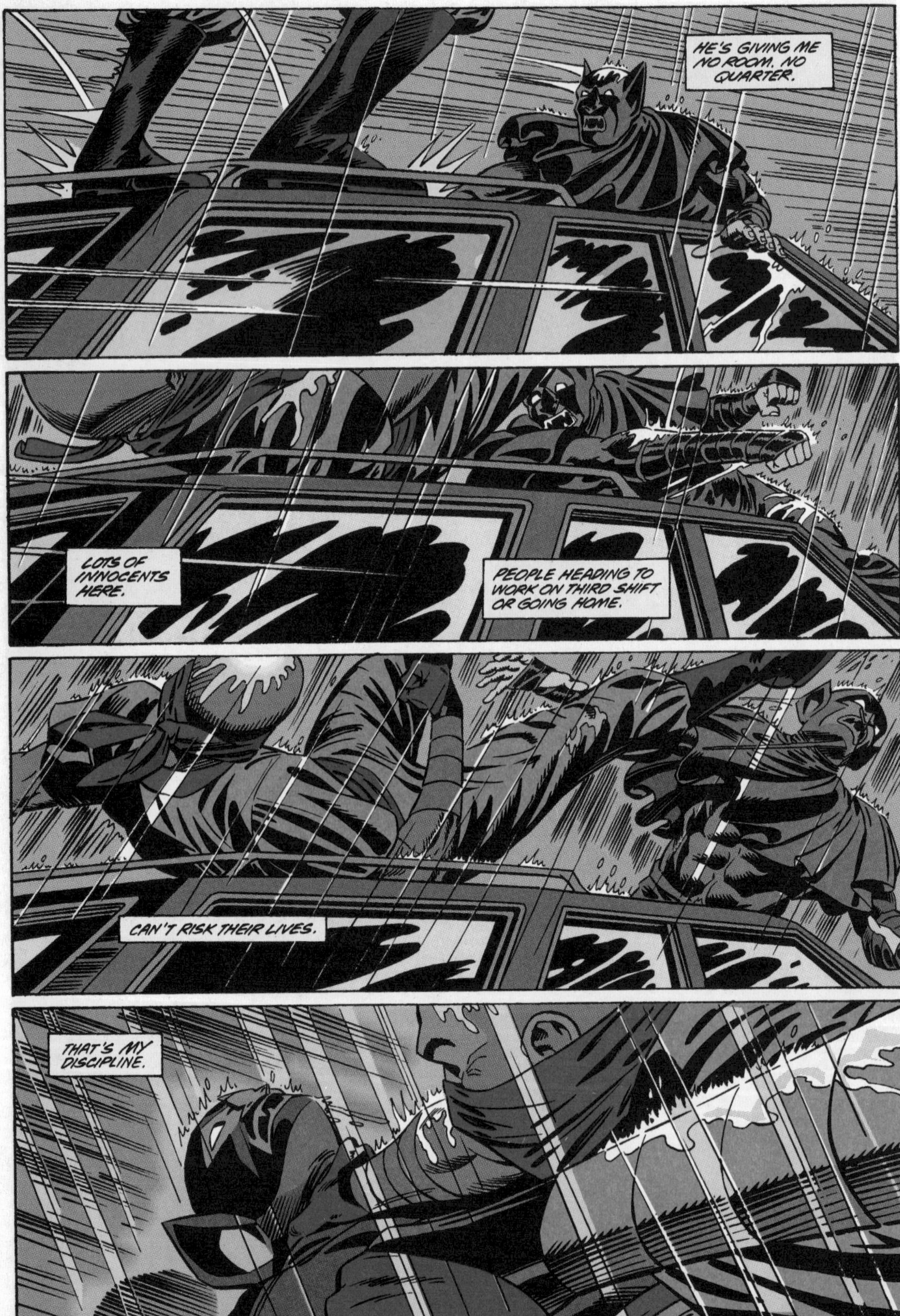
HE'S GIVING ME NO ROOM. NO QUARTER.
LOTS OF INNOCENTS HERE.
PEOPLE HEADING TO WORK ON THIRD SHIFT OR GOING HOME.
CAN'T RISK THEIR LIVES.
THAT'S MY DISCIPLINE.
27

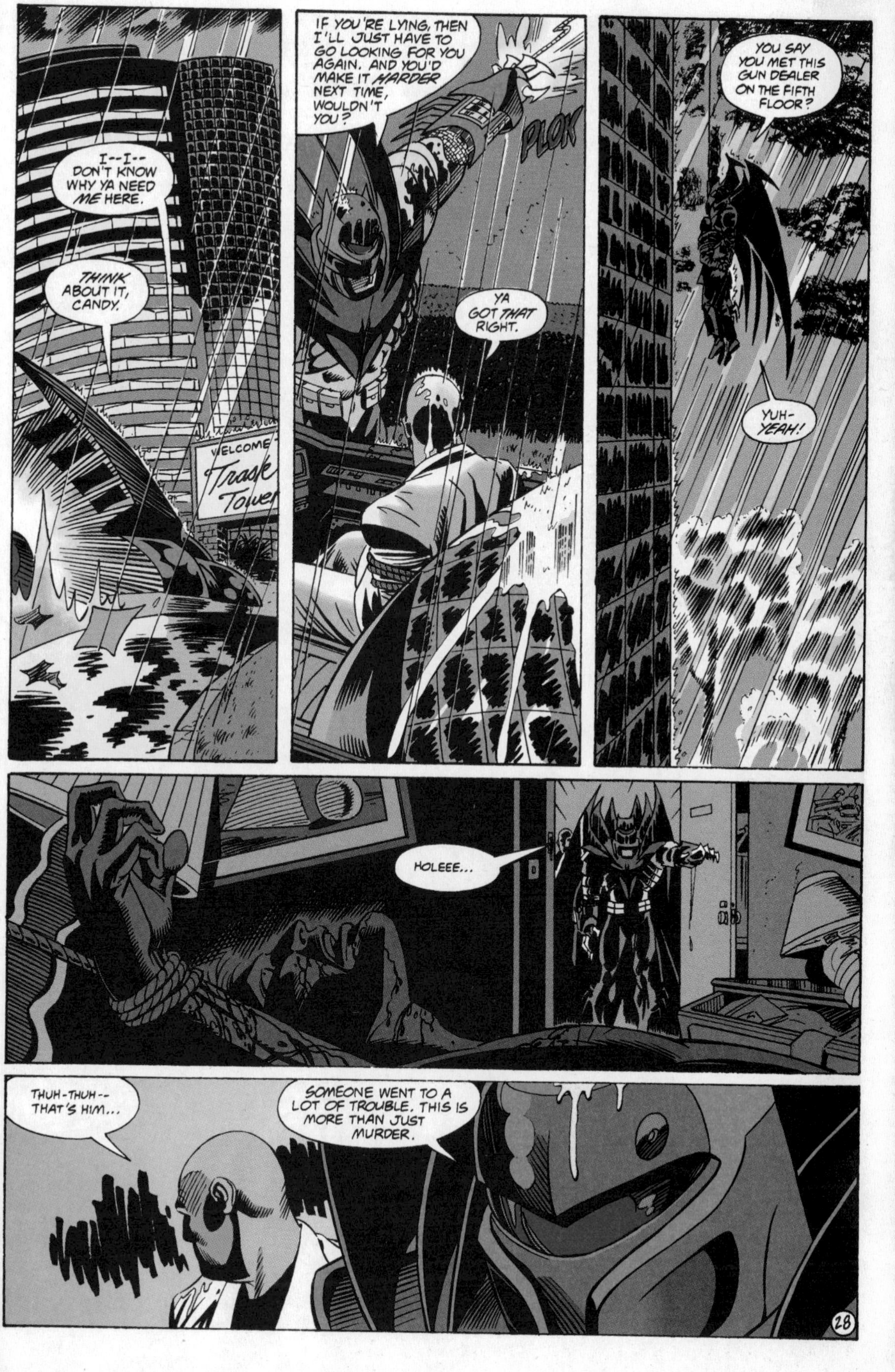
I--I--
DON'T KNOW
WHY YA NEED
ME HERE.
THINK
ABOUT IT,
CANDY.
WELCOME
Trask
Tower
IF YOU'RE LYING, THEN
I'LL JUST HAVE TO
GO LOOKING FOR YOU
AGAIN. AND YOU'D
MAKE IT HARDER
NEXT TIME,
WOULDN'T
YOU?
PLOK
YA
GOT THAT
RIGHT.
YOU SAY
YOU MET THIS
GUN DEALER
ON THE FIFTH
FLOOR?
YUH-
YEAH!
HOLEEE...
THUH-THUH--
THAT'S HIM...
SOMEONE WENT TO A
LOT OF TROUBLE. THIS IS
MORE THAN JUST
MURDER.
28

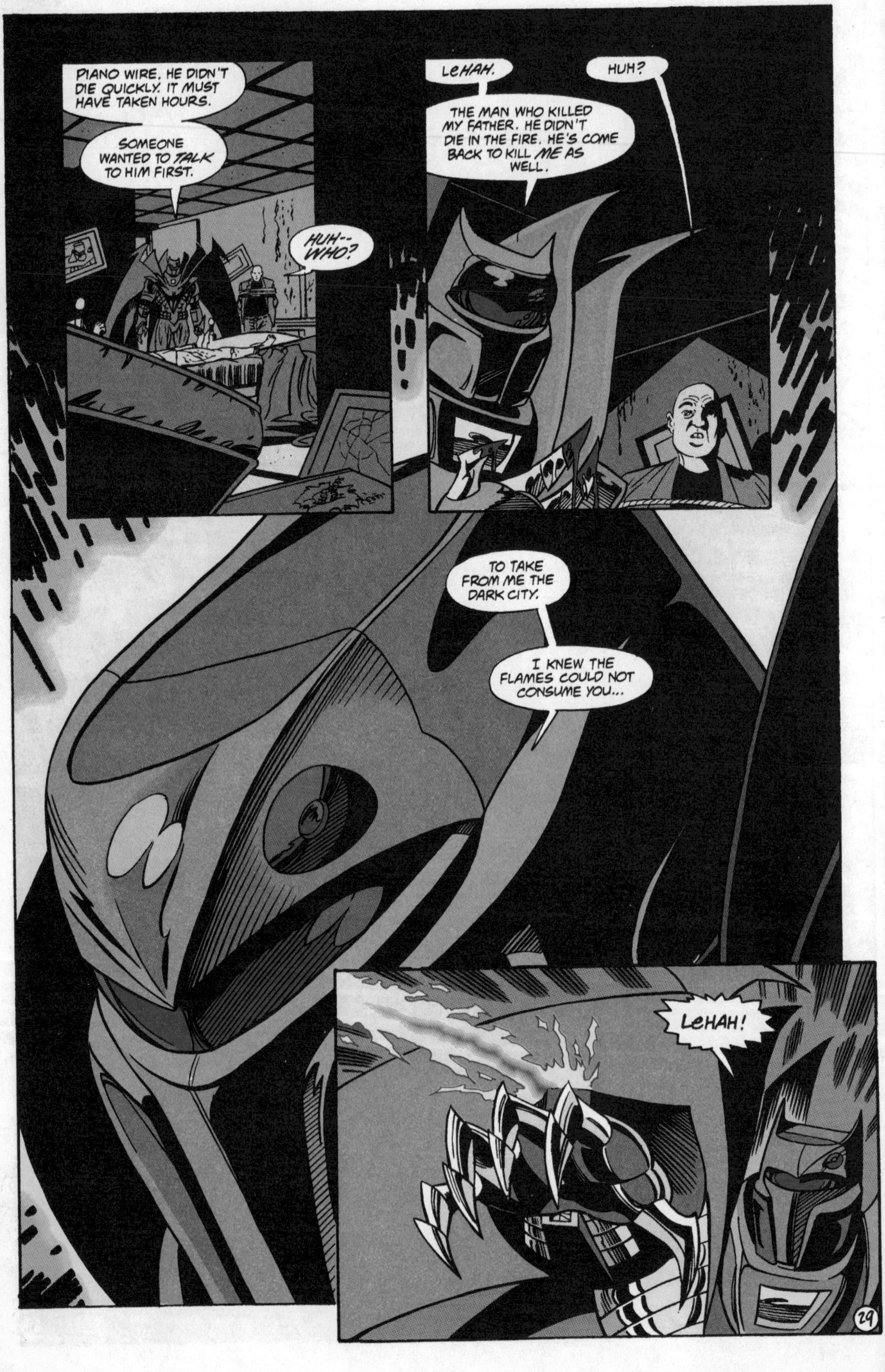
PIANO WIRE. HE DIDN'T DIE QUICKLY. IT MUST HAVE TAKEN HOURS.
SOMEONE WANTED TO TALK TO HIM FIRST.
HUH-- WHO?
LeHAH.
HUH?
THE MAN WHO KILLED MY FATHER. HE DIDN'T DIE IN THE FIRE. HE'S COME BACK TO KILL ME AS WELL.
TO TAKE FROM ME THE DARK CITY.
I KNEW THE FLAMES COULD NOT CONSUME YOU...
LeHAH!
29

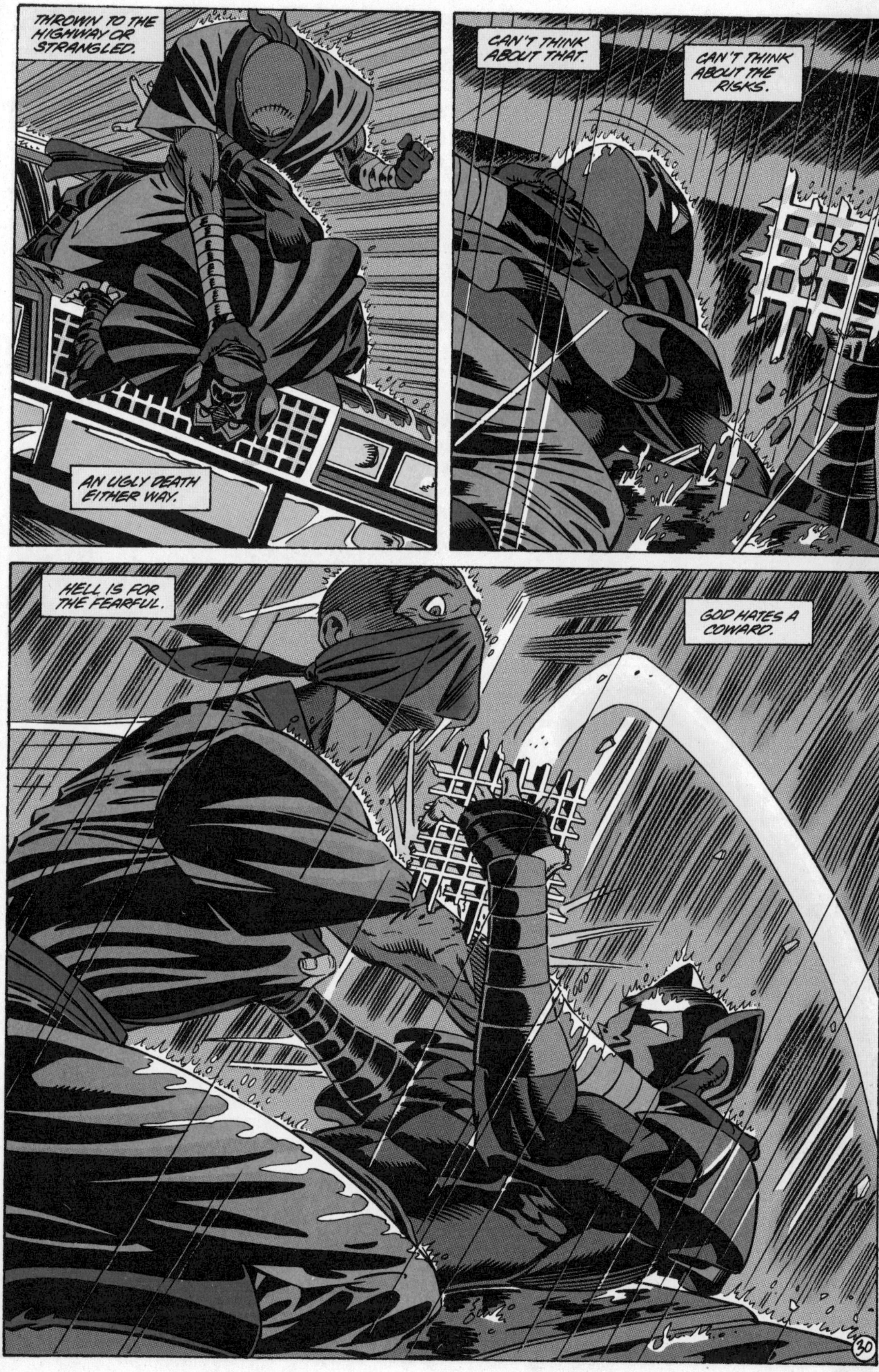
THROWN TO THE HIGHWAY OR STRANGLED.
AN UGLY DEATH EITHER WAY.
CAN'T THINK ABOUT THAT.
CAN'T THINK ABOUT THE RISKS.
HELL IS FOR THE FEARFUL.
GOD HATES A COWARD.
30

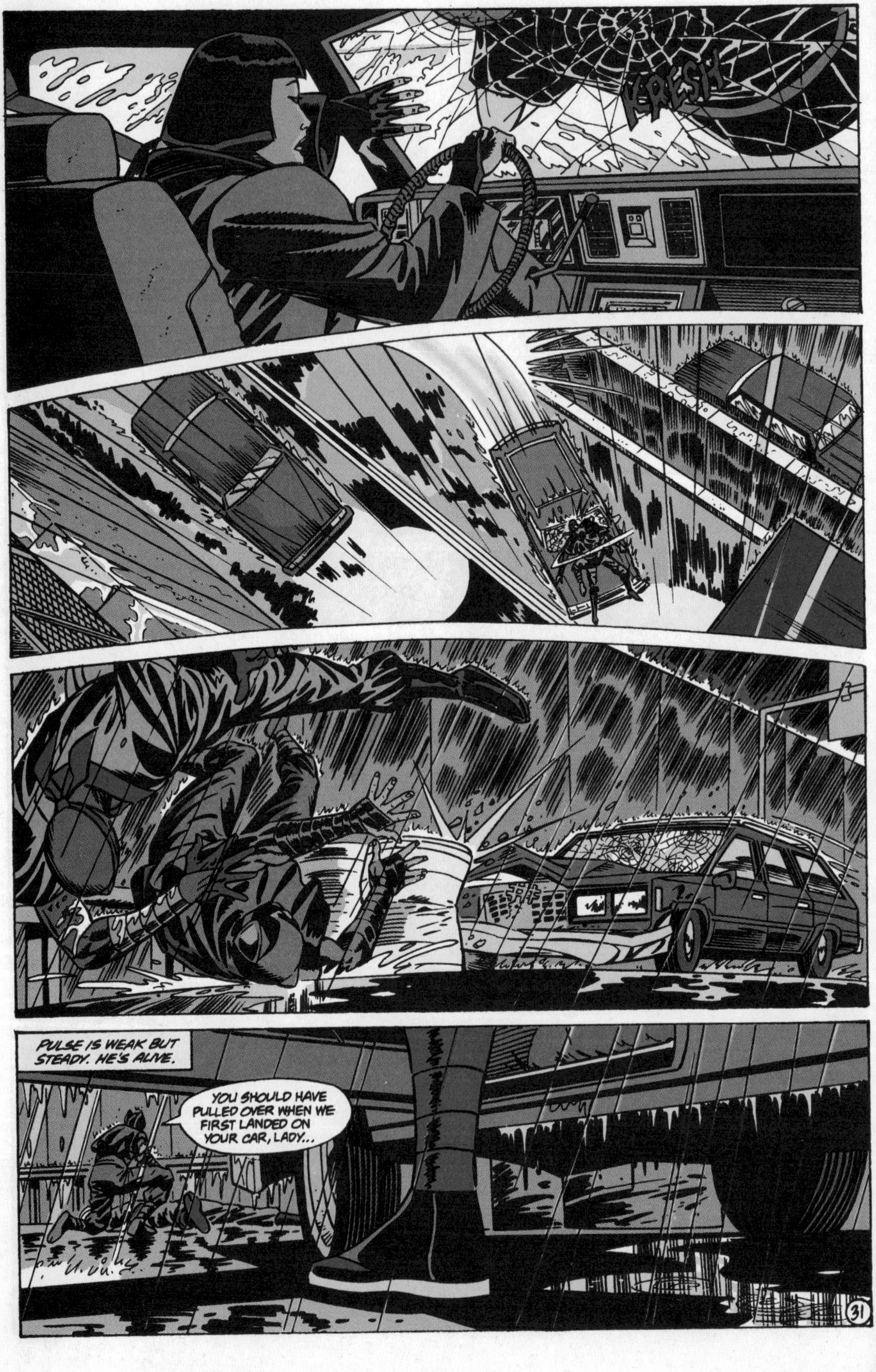
KRESH
PULSE IS WEAK BUT STEADY. HE'S ALIVE.
YOU SHOULD HAVE PULLED OVER WHEN WE FIRST LANDED ON YOUR CAR, LADY...
31

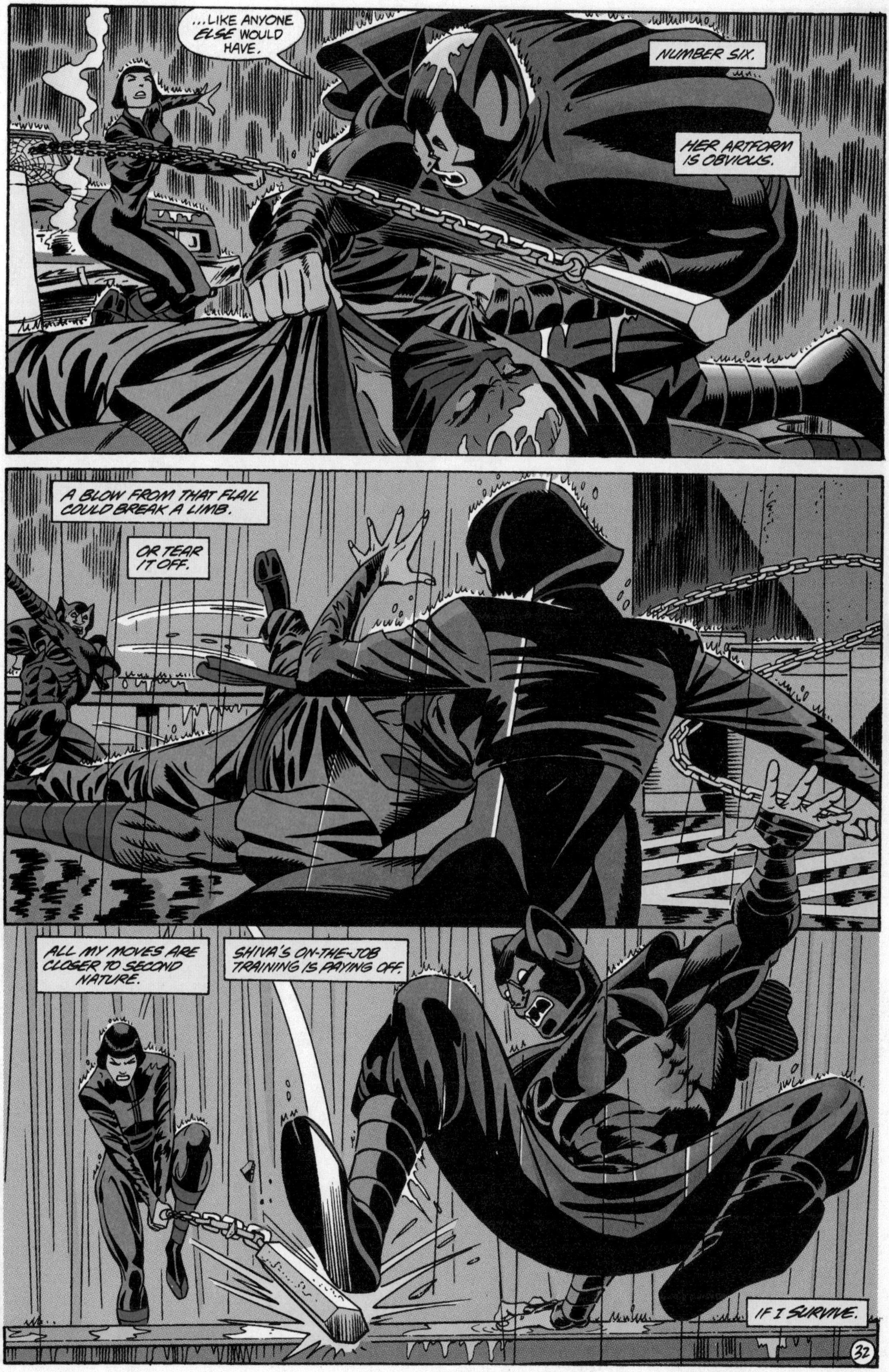
...LIKE ANYONE ELSE WOULD HAVE.
NUMBER SIX.
HER ARTFORM IS OBVIOUS.
A BLOW FROM THAT FLAIL COULD BREAK A LIMB.
OR TEAR IT OFF.
ALL MY MOVES ARE CLOSER TO SECOND NATURE.
SHIVA'S ON-THE-JOB TRAINING IS PAYING OFF.
IF I SURVIVE.
32

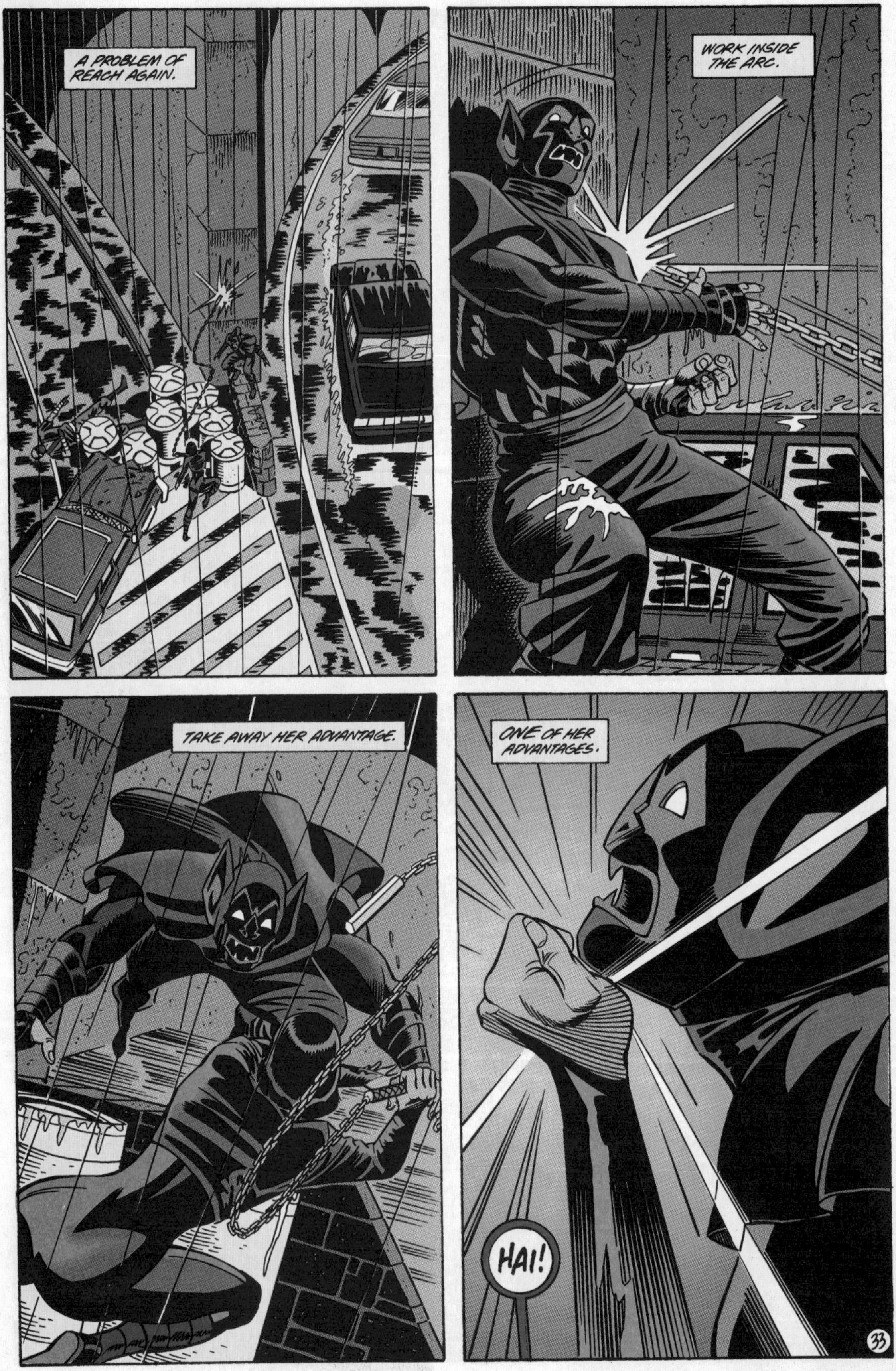
A PROBLEM OF REACH AGAIN.
WORK INSIDE THE ARC.
TAKE AWAY HER ADVANTAGE.
ONE OF HER ADVANTAGES.
HAI!
33

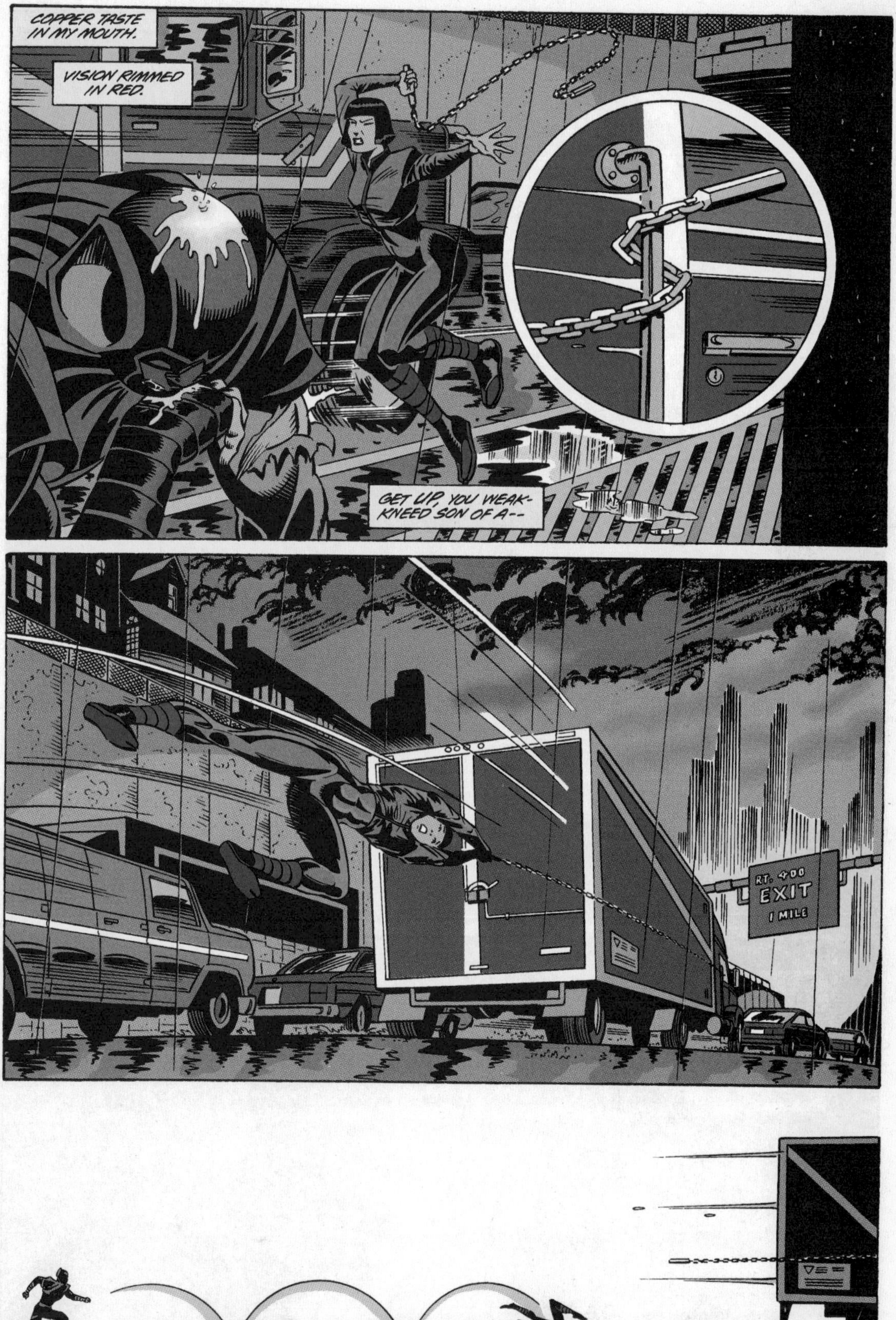
COPPER TASTE IN MY MOUTH.
VISION RIMMED IN RED.
GET UP, YOU WEAK-KNEED SON OF A--
RT. 400
EXIT
1 MILE
34

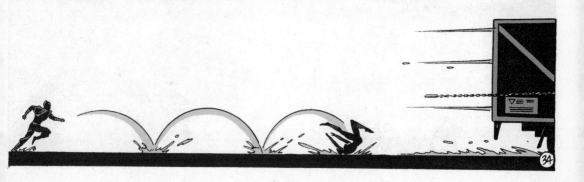

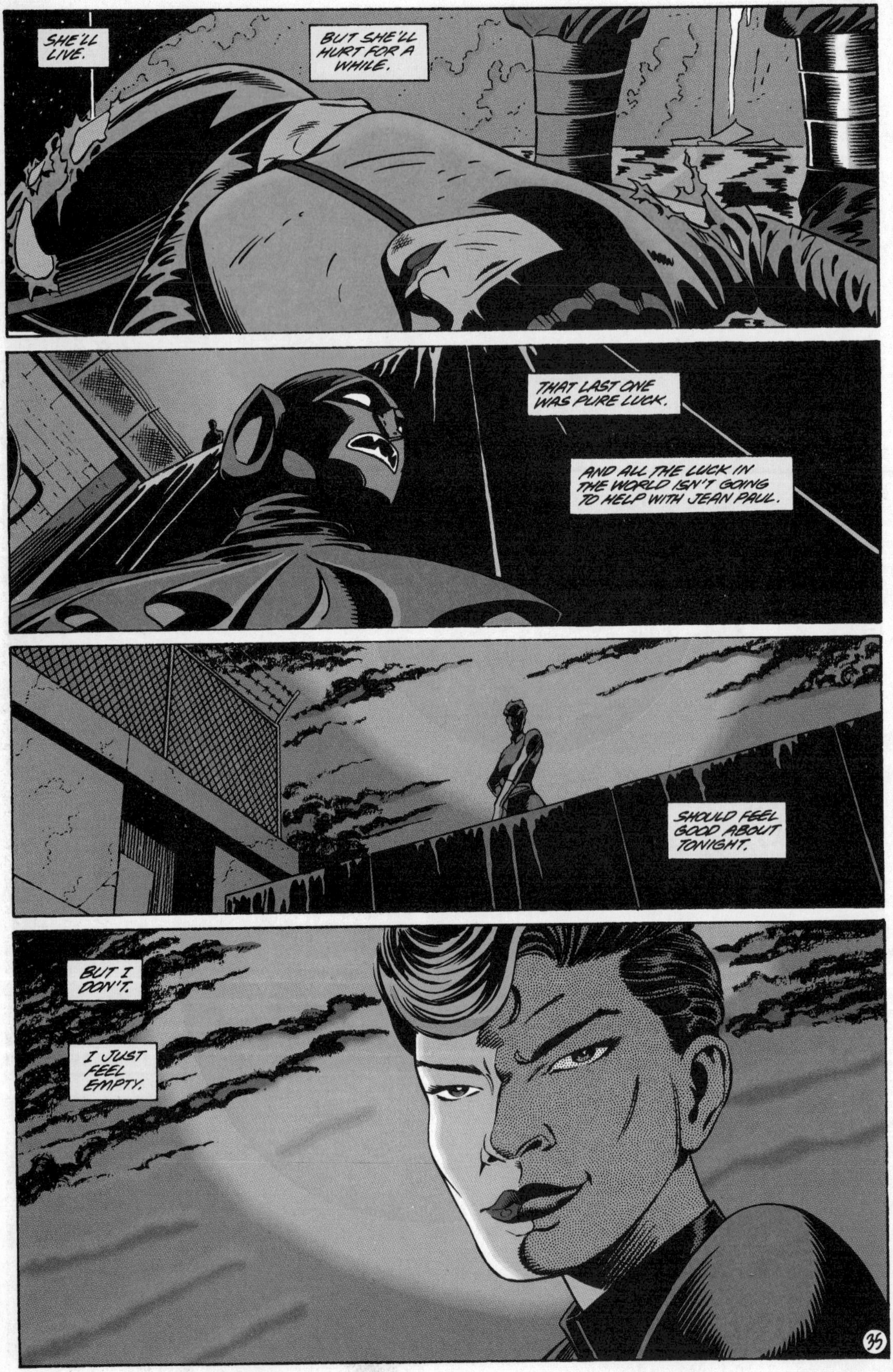

SHE'LL LIVE.
BUT SHE'LL HURT FOR A WHILE.
THAT LAST ONE WAS PURE LUCK.
AND ALL THE LUCK IN THE WORLD ISN'T GOING TO HELP WITH JEAN PAUL.
SHOULD FEEL GOOD ABOUT TONIGHT.
BUT I DON'T.
I JUST FEEL EMPTY.
35

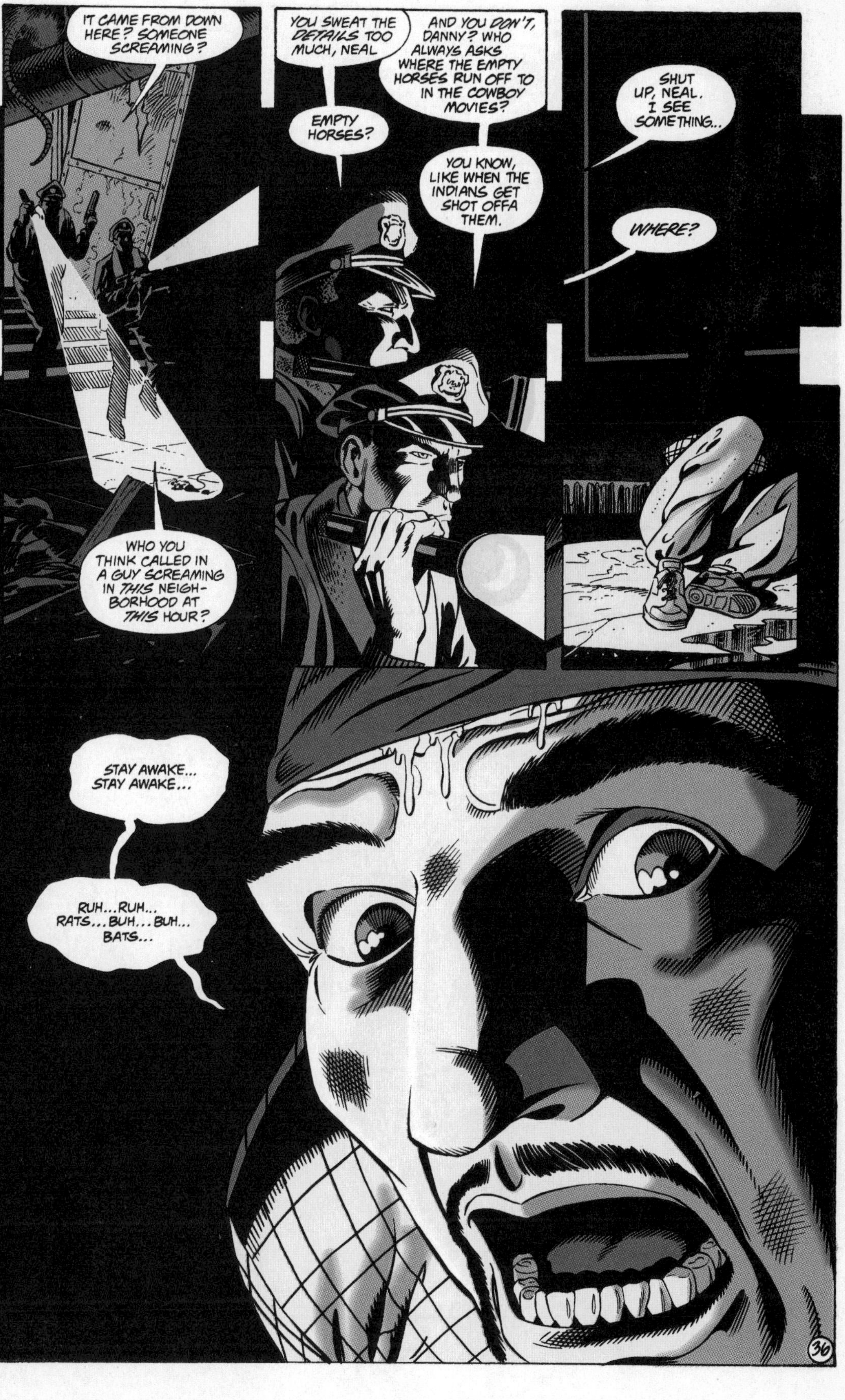
IT CAME FROM DOWN HERE? SOMEONE SCREAMING?
WHO YOU THINK CALLED IN A GUY SCREAMING IN THIS NEIGHBORHOOD AT THIS HOUR?
YOU SWEAT THE DETAILS TOO MUCH, NEAL
AND YOU DON'T, DANNY? WHO ALWAYS ASKS WHERE THE EMPTY HORSES RUN OFF TO IN THE COWBOY MOVIES?
EMPTY HORSES?
YOU KNOW, LIKE WHEN THE INDIANS GET SHOT OFFA THEM.
SHUT UP, NEAL. I SEE SOMETHING...
WHERE?
STAY AWAKE... STAY AWAKE...
RUH... RUH... RATS... BUH... BUH... BATS...
36

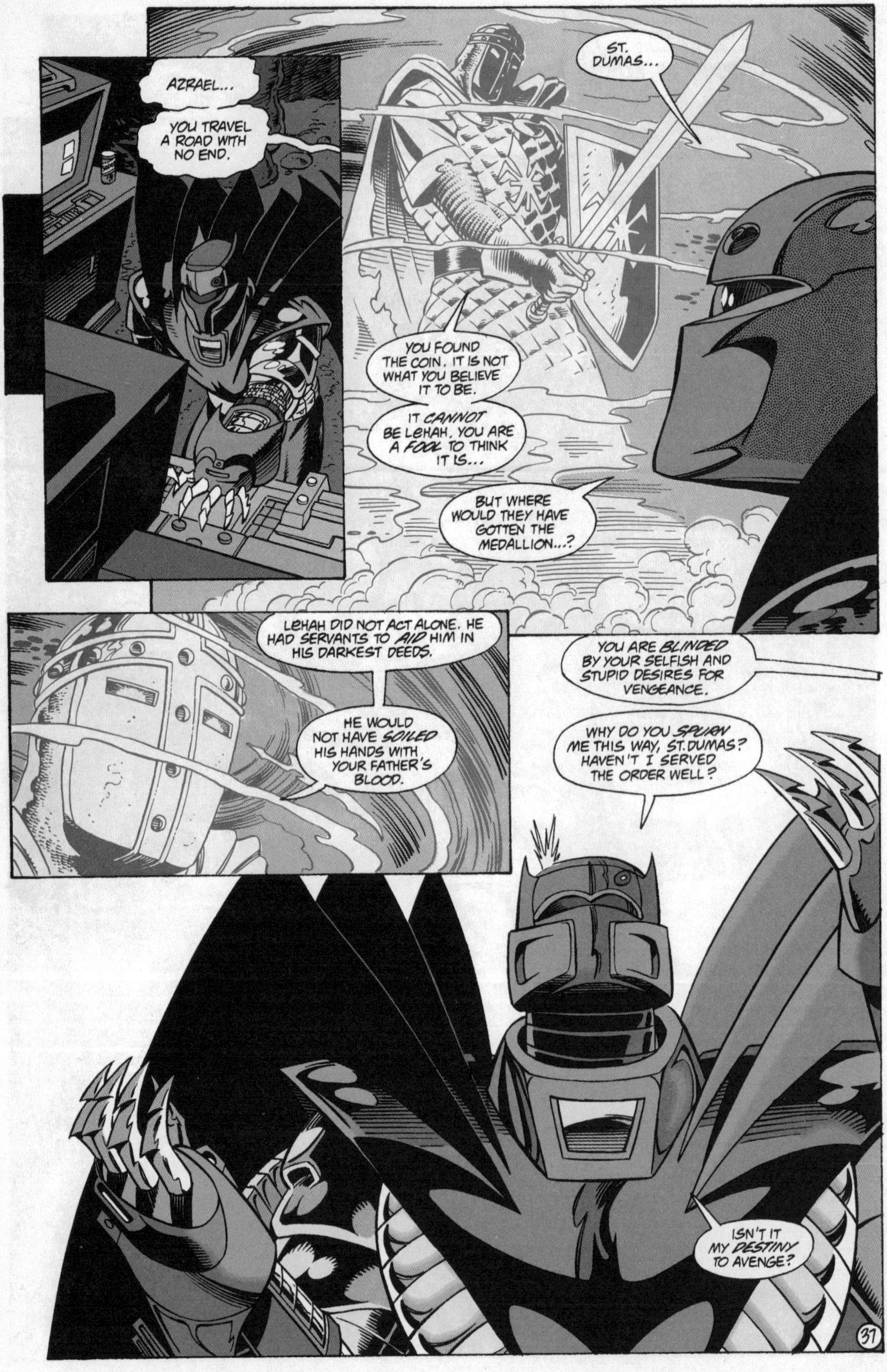
AZRAEL...
YOU TRAVEL A ROAD WITH NO END.
ST. DUMAS...
YOU FOUND THE COIN. IT IS NOT WHAT YOU BELIEVE IT TO BE.
IT CANNOT BE LEHAH. YOU ARE A FOOL TO THINK IT IS...
BUT WHERE WOULD THEY HAVE GOTTEN THE MEDALLION...?
LEHAH DID NOT ACT ALONE. HE HAD SERVANTS TO AID HIM IN HIS DARKEST DEEDS.
HE WOULD NOT HAVE SOILED HIS HANDS WITH YOUR FATHER'S BLOOD.
YOU ARE BLINDED BY YOUR SELFISH AND STUPID DESIRES FOR VENGEANCE.
WHY DO YOU SPURN ME THIS WAY, ST. DUMAS? HAVEN'T I SERVED THE ORDER WELL?
ISN'T IT MY DESTINY TO AVENGE?
37

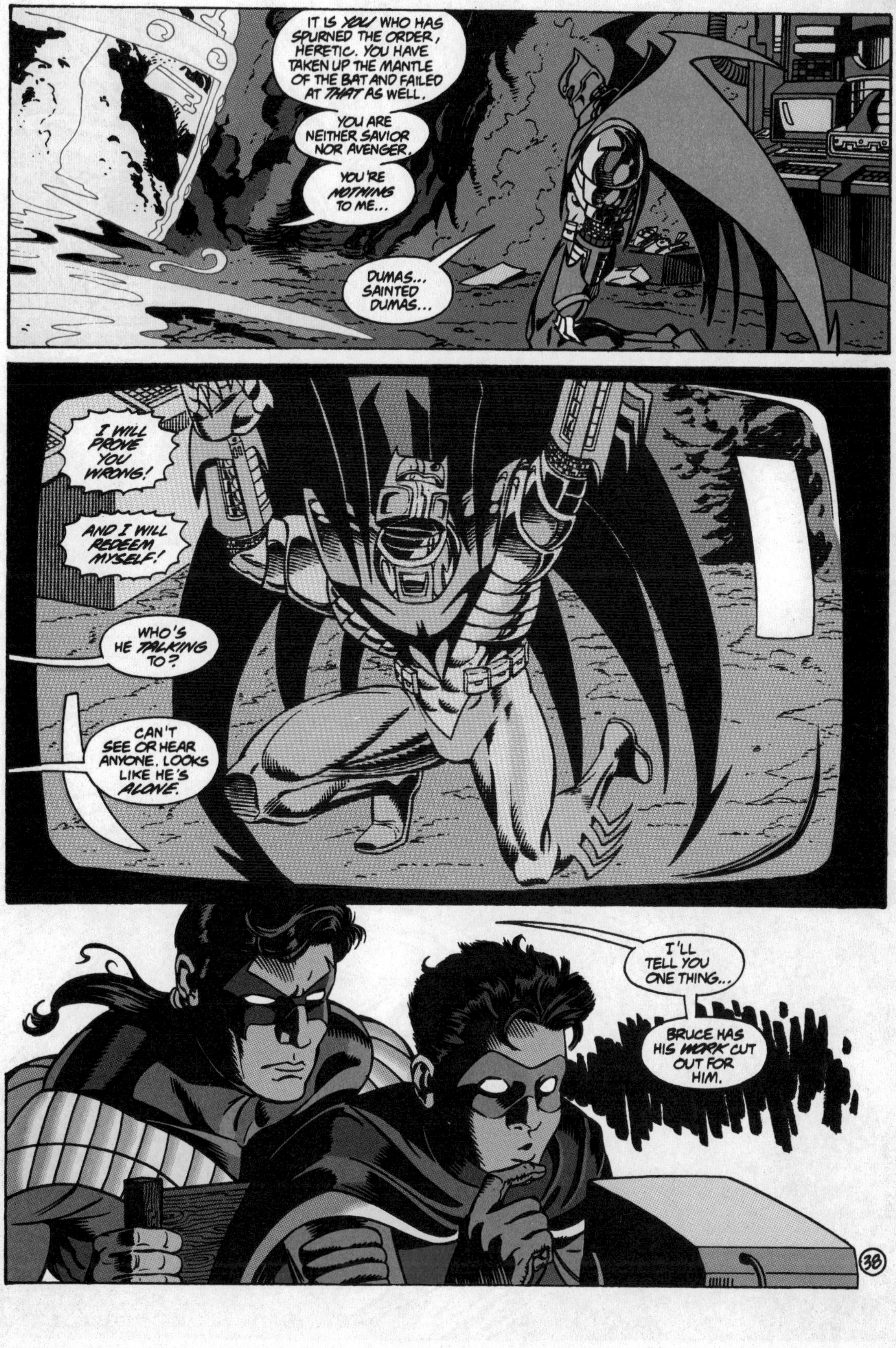
IT IS YOU! WHO HAS SPURNED THE ORDER, HERETIC. YOU HAVE TAKEN UP THE MANTLE OF THE BAT AND FAILED AT THAT AS WELL.
YOU ARE NEITHER SAVIOR NOR AVENGER.
YOU'RE NOTHING TO ME...
DUMAS... SAINTED DUMAS...
I WILL PROVE YOU WRONG!
AND I WILL REDEEM MYSELF!
WHO'S HE TALKING TO?
CAN'T SEE OR HEAR ANYONE. LOOKS LIKE HE'S ALONE.
I'LL TELL YOU ONE THING...
BRUCE HAS HIS WORK CUT OUT FOR HIM.
38

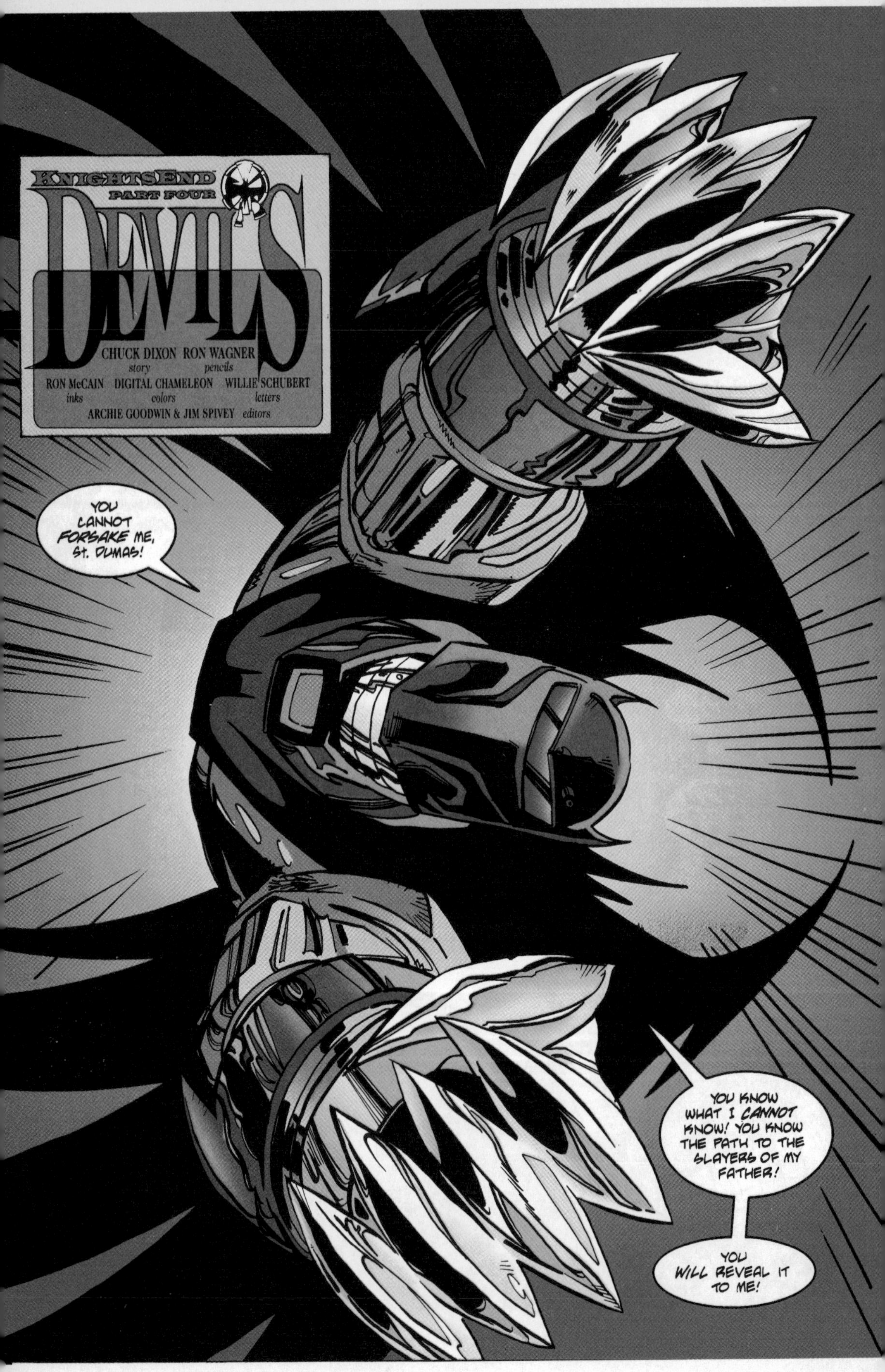
KNIGHTSEND
PART FOUR
DEVILS
CHUCK DIXON story
RON WAGNER pencils
RON McCAIN inks
DIGITAL CHAMELEON colors
WILLIE SCHUBERT letters
ARCHIE GOODWIN & JIM SPIVEY editors
YOU CANNOT FORSAKE ME, St. DUMAS!
YOU KNOW WHAT I CANNOT KNOW! YOU KNOW THE PATH TO THE SLAYERS OF MY FATHER!
YOU WILL REVEAL IT TO ME!

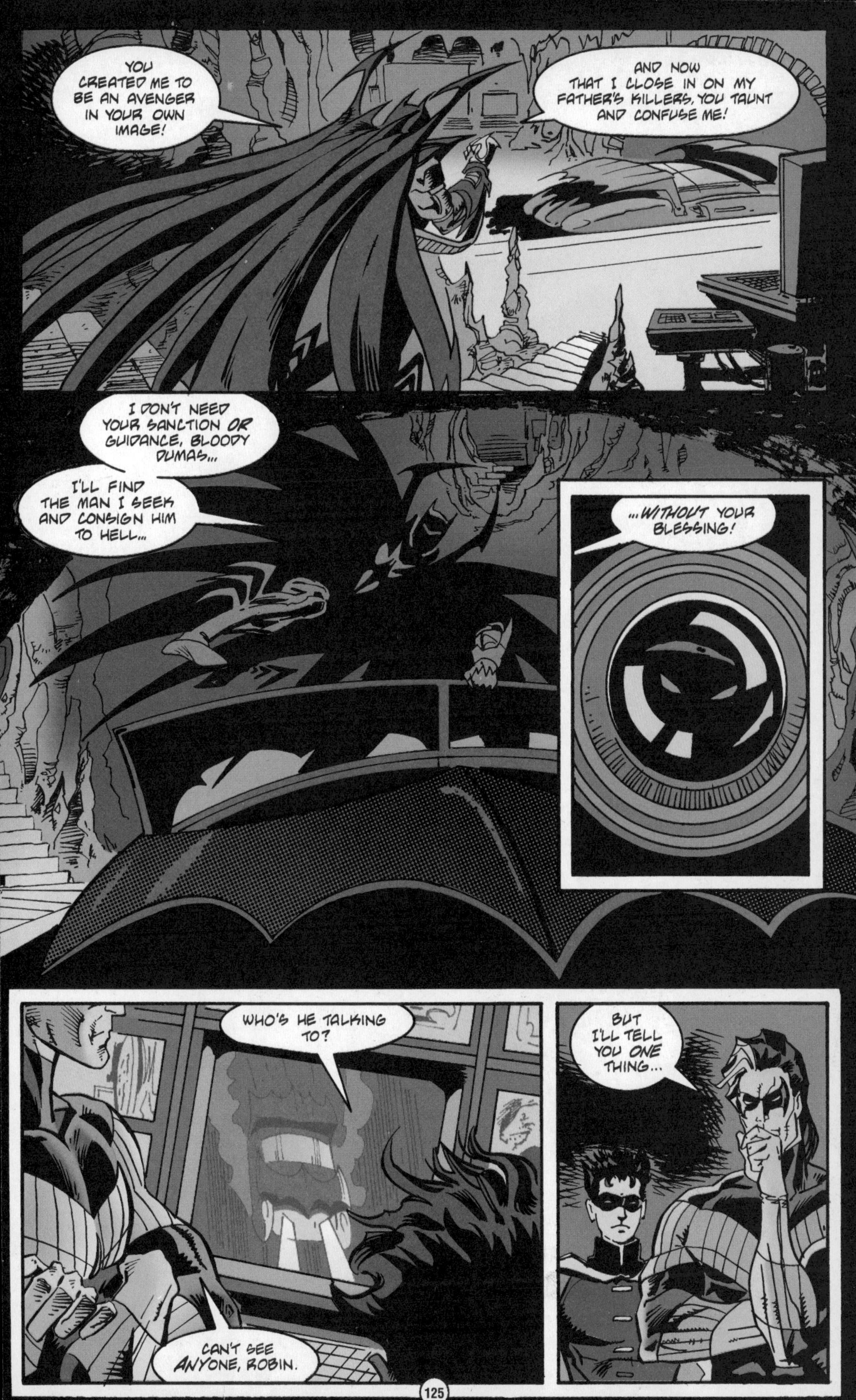
YOU CREATED ME TO BE AN AVENGER IN YOUR OWN IMAGE!
AND NOW THAT I CLOSE IN ON MY FATHER'S KILLERS, YOU TAUNT AND CONFUSE ME!
I DON'T NEED YOUR SANCTION OR GUIDANCE, BLOODY DUMAS...
I'LL FIND THE MAN I SEEK AND CONSIGN HIM TO HELL...
...WITHOUT YOUR BLESSING!
WHO'S HE TALKING TO?
CAN'T SEE ANYONE, ROBIN.
BUT I'LL TELL YOU ONE THING...

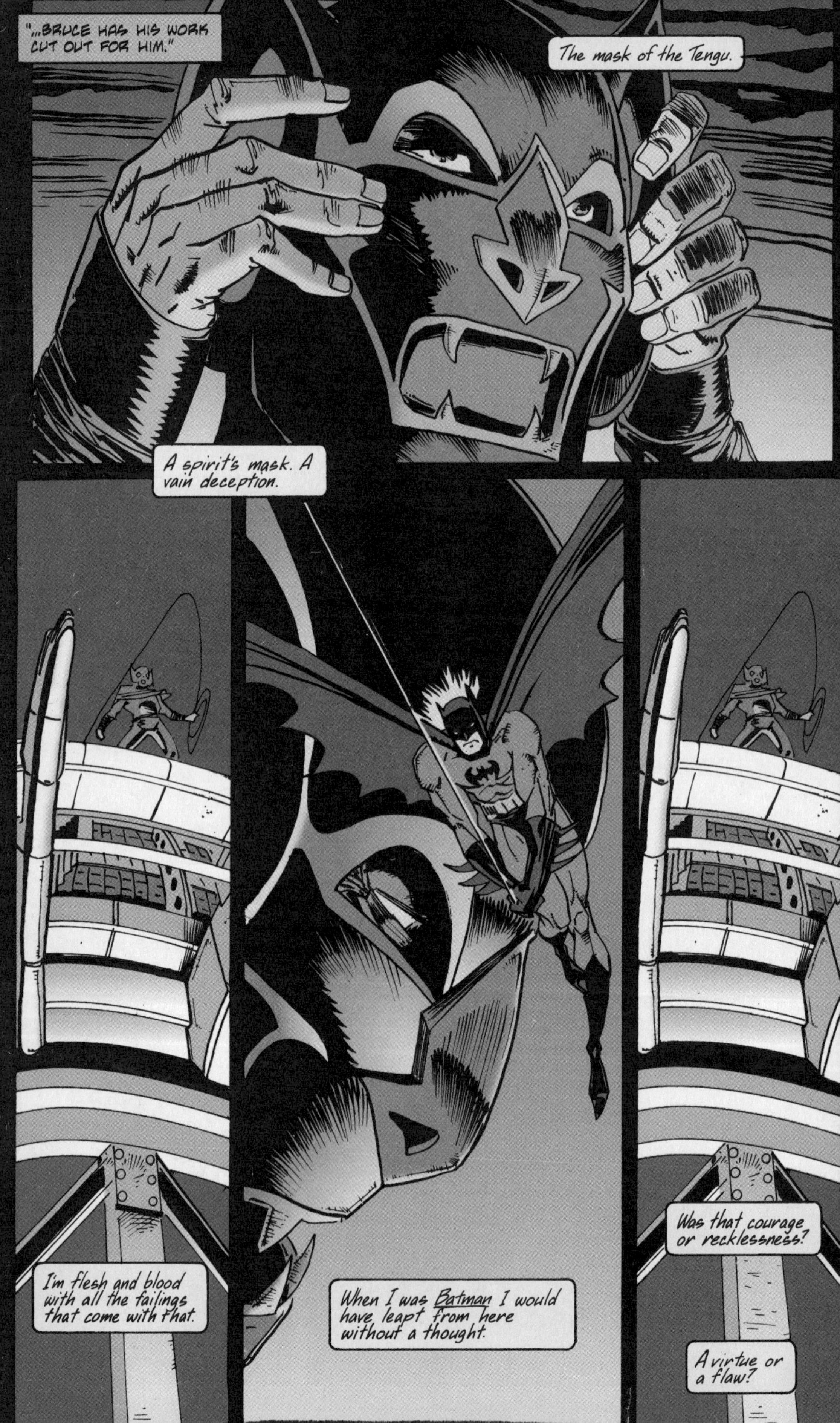
"...BRUCE HAS HIS WORK CUT OUT FOR HIM."
The mask of the Tengu.
A spirit's mask. A vain deception.
I'm flesh and blood with all the failings that come with that.
When I was Batman I would have leapt from here without a thought.
Was that courage or recklessness?
A virtue or a flaw?

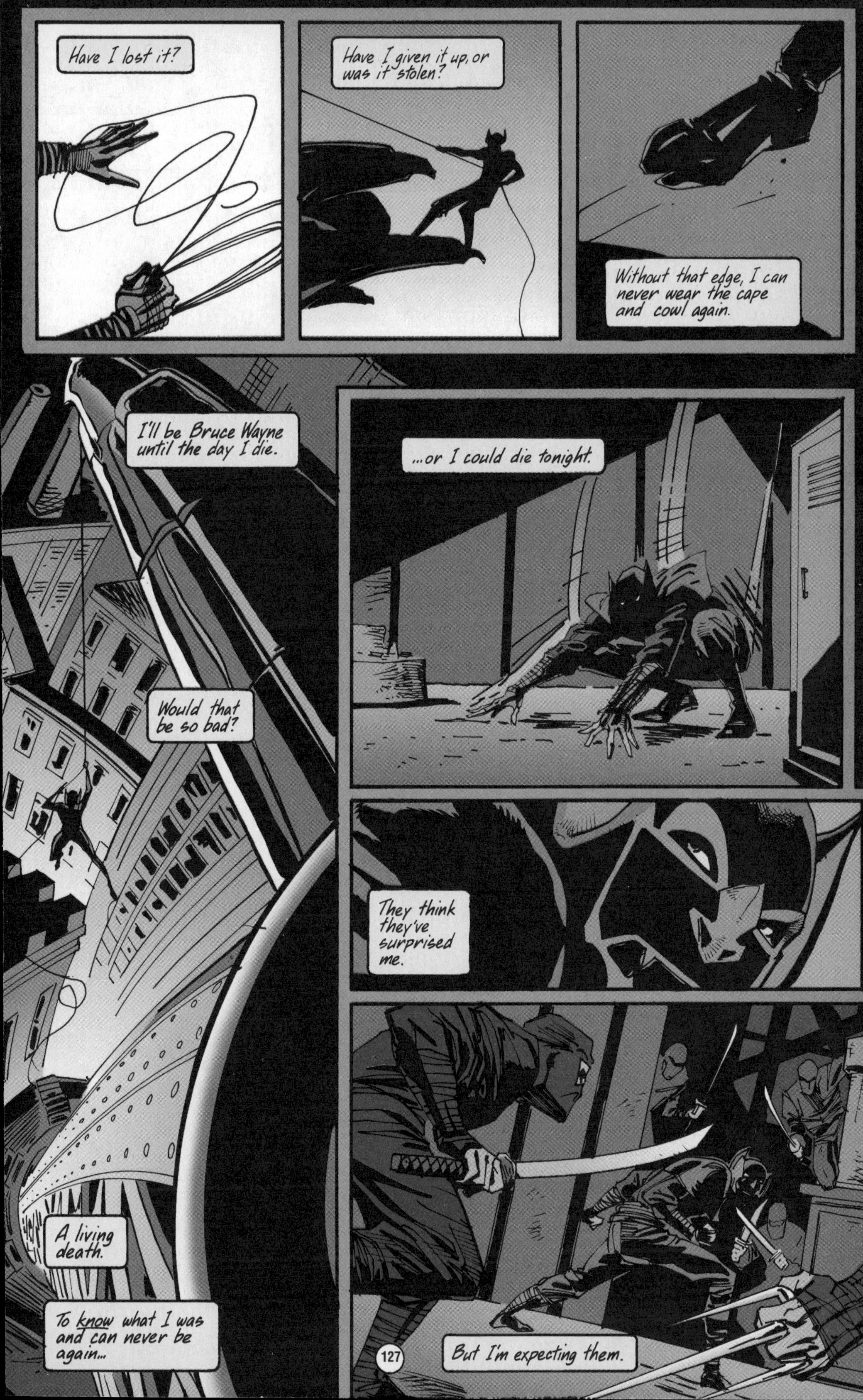

Have I lost it?
Have I given it up, or was it stolen?
Without that edge, I can never wear the cape and cowl again.
I'll be Bruce Wayne until the day I die.
Would that be so bad?
A living death.
To know what I was and can never be again...
...or I could die tonight.
They think they've surprised me.
But I'm expecting them.

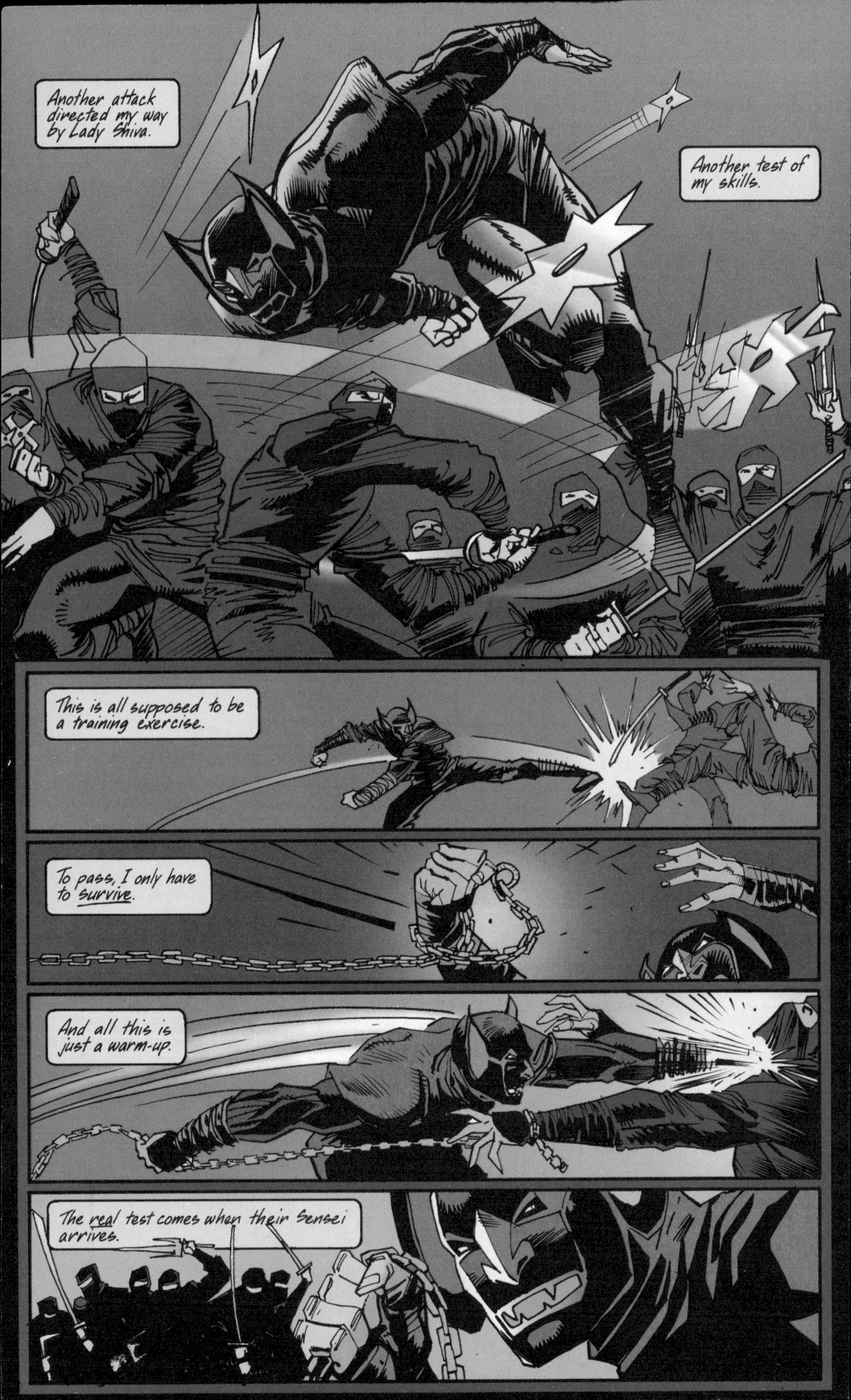

Another attack directed my way by Lady Shiva.
Another test of my skills.
This is all supposed to be a training exercise.
To pass, I only have to survive.
And all this is just a warm-up.
The real test comes when their Sensei arrives.

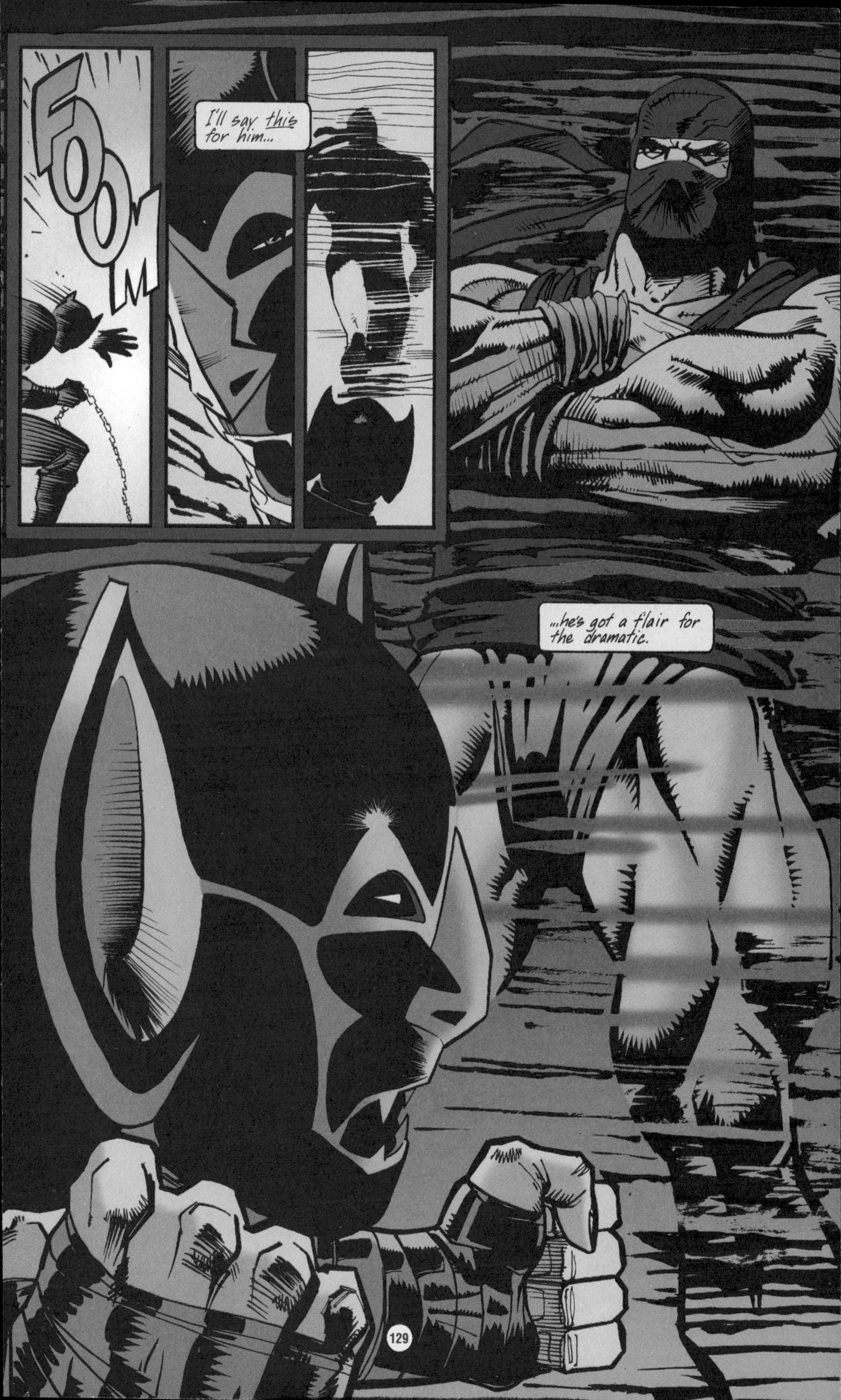
FOOOM
I'll say this for him...
...he's got a flair for the dramatic.

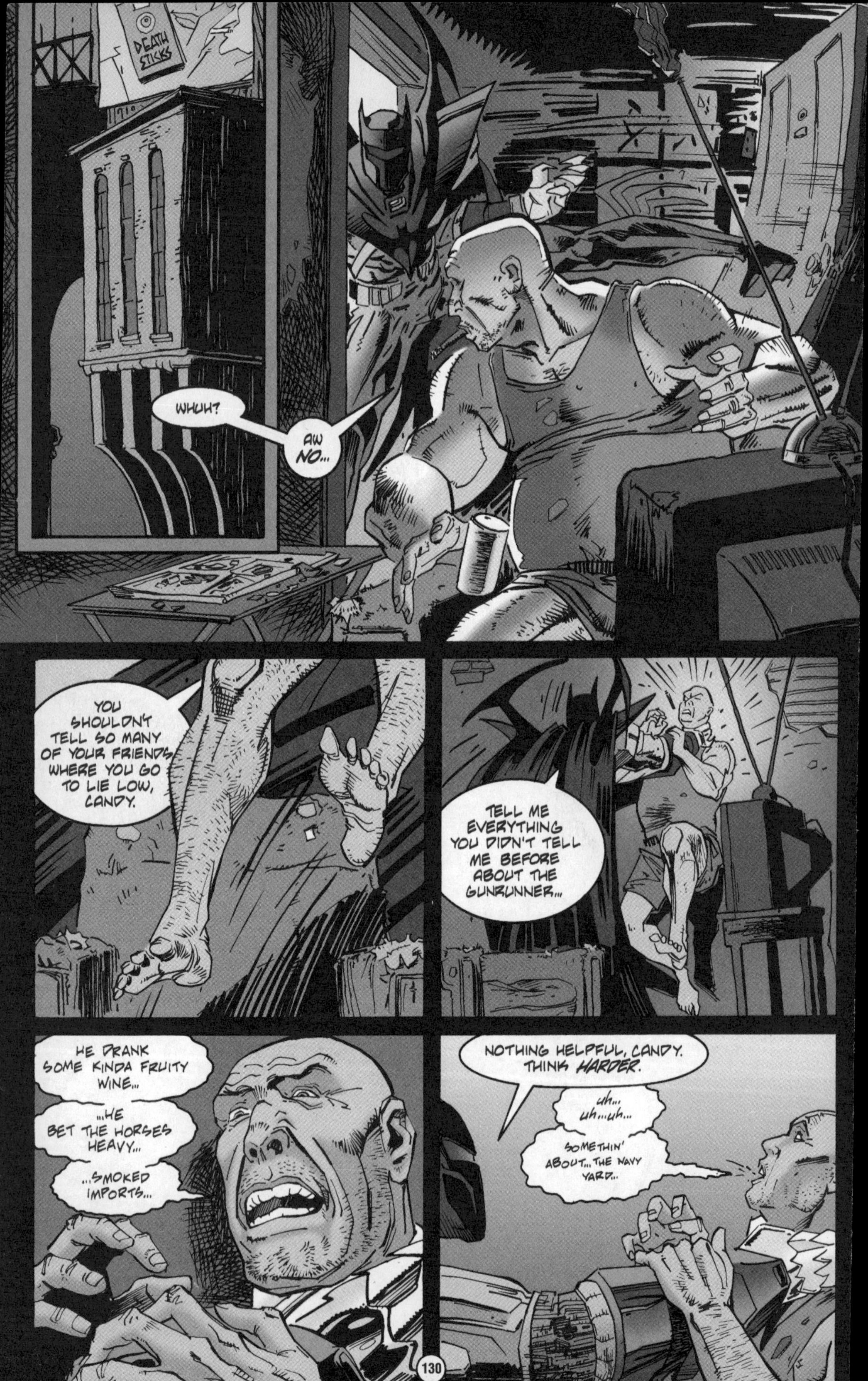
DEATH STICKS
WHUH?
AW NO...
YOU SHOULDN'T TELL SO MANY OF YOUR FRIENDS WHERE YOU GO TO LIE LOW, CANDY.
TELL ME EVERYTHING YOU DIDN'T TELL ME BEFORE ABOUT THE GUNRUNNER...
HE DRANK SOME KINDA FRUITY WINE...
...HE BET THE HORSES HEAVY...
...SMOKED IMPORTS...
NOTHING HELPFUL, CANDY. THINK HARDER.
uh... uh...uh...
SOMETHIN' ABOUT... THE NAVY YARD...

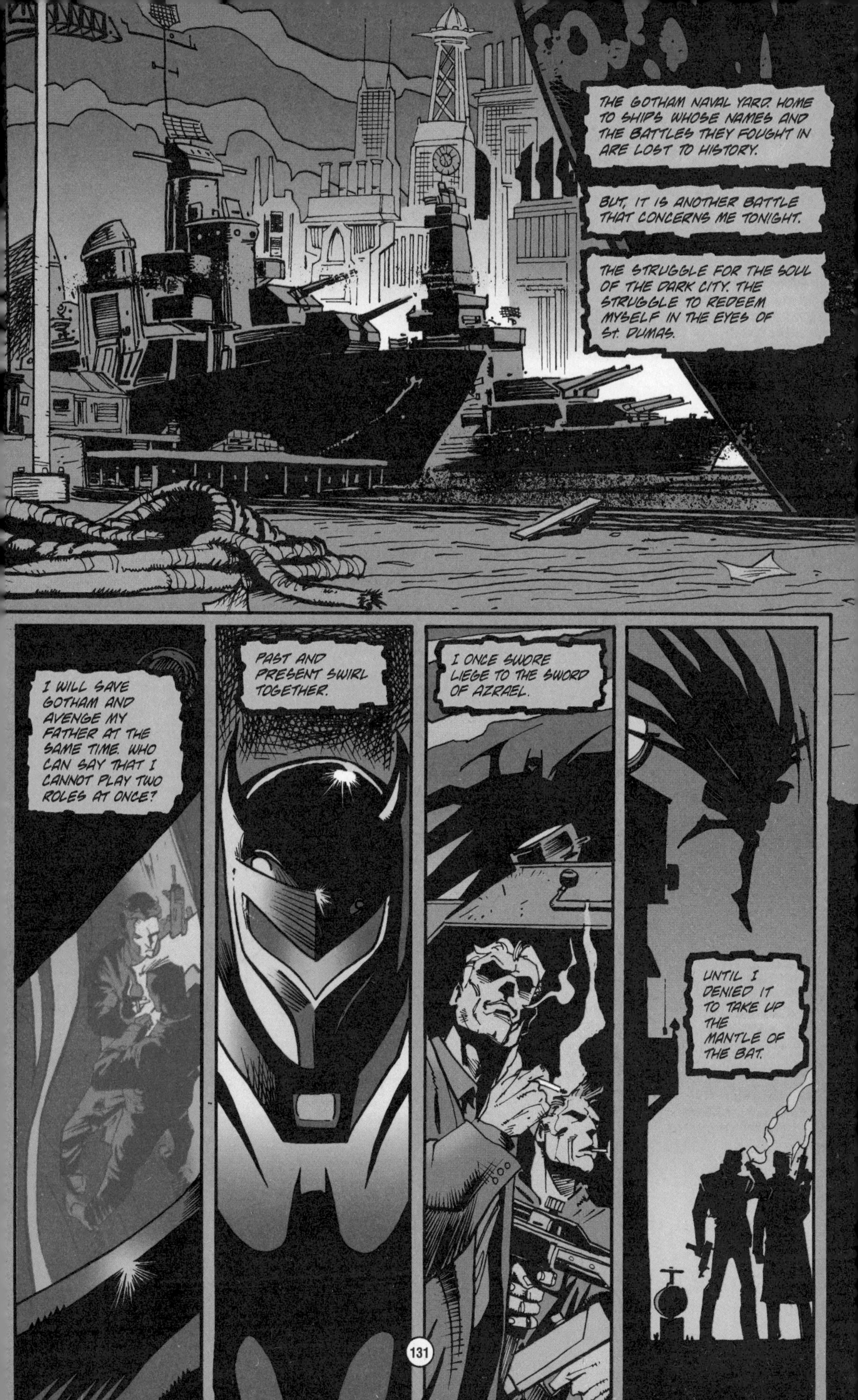
THE GOTHAM NAVAL YARD. HOME TO SHIPS WHOSE NAMES AND THE BATTLES THEY FOUGHT IN ARE LOST TO HISTORY.
BUT, IT IS ANOTHER BATTLE THAT CONCERNS ME TONIGHT.
THE STRUGGLE FOR THE SOUL OF THE DARK CITY. THE STRUGGLE TO REDEEM MYSELF IN THE EYES OF St. DUMAS.
I WILL SAVE GOTHAM AND AVENGE MY FATHER AT THE SAME TIME. WHO CAN SAY THAT I CANNOT PLAY TWO ROLES AT ONCE?
PAST AND PRESENT SWIRL TOGETHER.
I ONCE SWORE LIEGE TO THE SWORD OF AZRAEL.
UNTIL I DENIED IT TO TAKE UP THE MANTLE OF THE BAT.

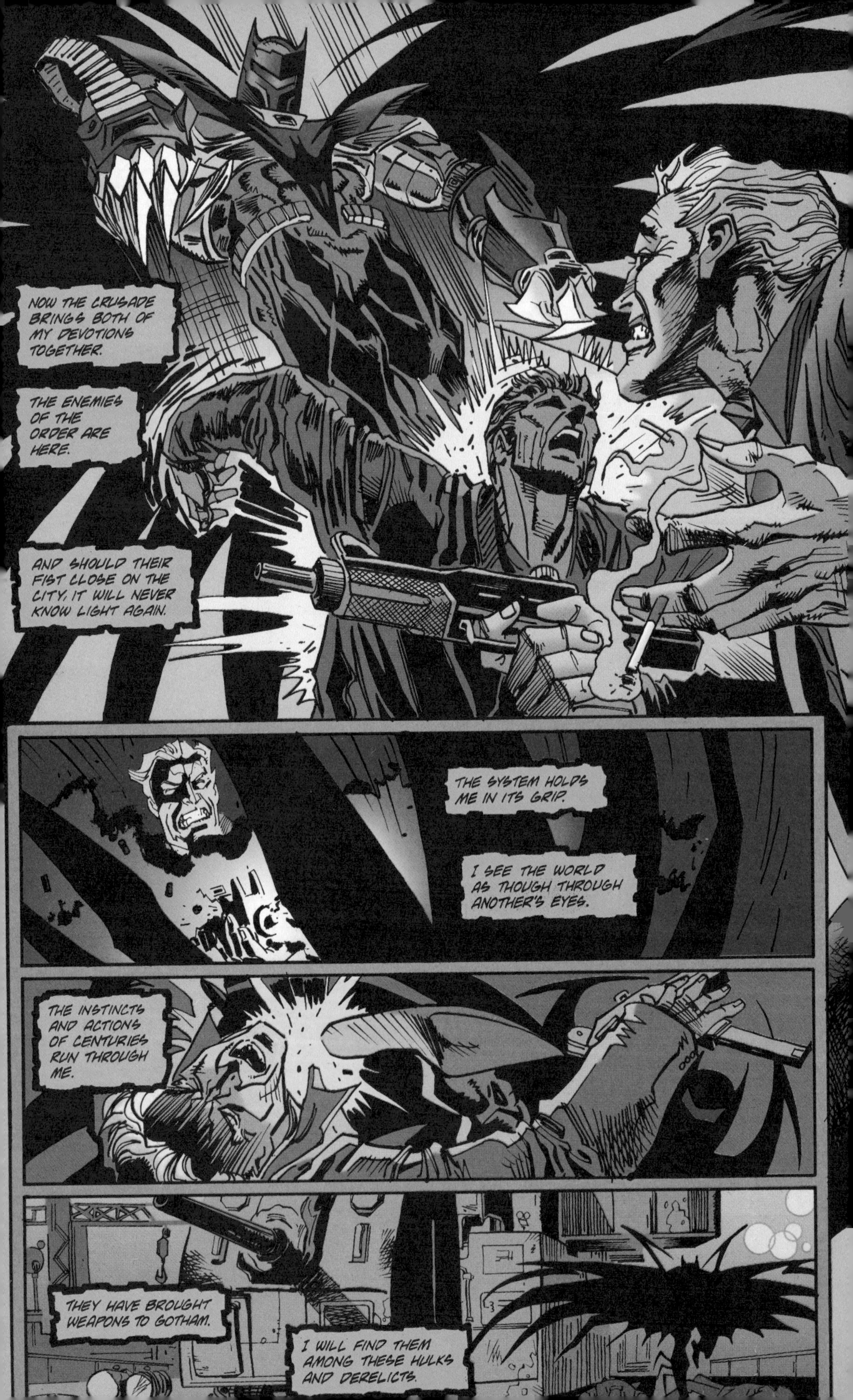
NOW THE CRUSADE BRINGS BOTH OF MY DEVOTIONS TOGETHER.
THE ENEMIES OF THE ORDER ARE HERE.
AND SHOULD THEIR FIST CLOSE ON THE CITY, IT WILL NEVER KNOW LIGHT AGAIN.
THE SYSTEM HOLDS ME IN ITS GRIP.
I SEE THE WORLD AS THOUGH THROUGH ANOTHER'S EYES.
THE INSTINCTS AND ACTIONS OF CENTURIES RUN THROUGH ME.
THEY HAVE BROUGHT WEAPONS TO GOTHAM.
I WILL FIND THEM AMONG THESE HULKS AND DERELICTS.

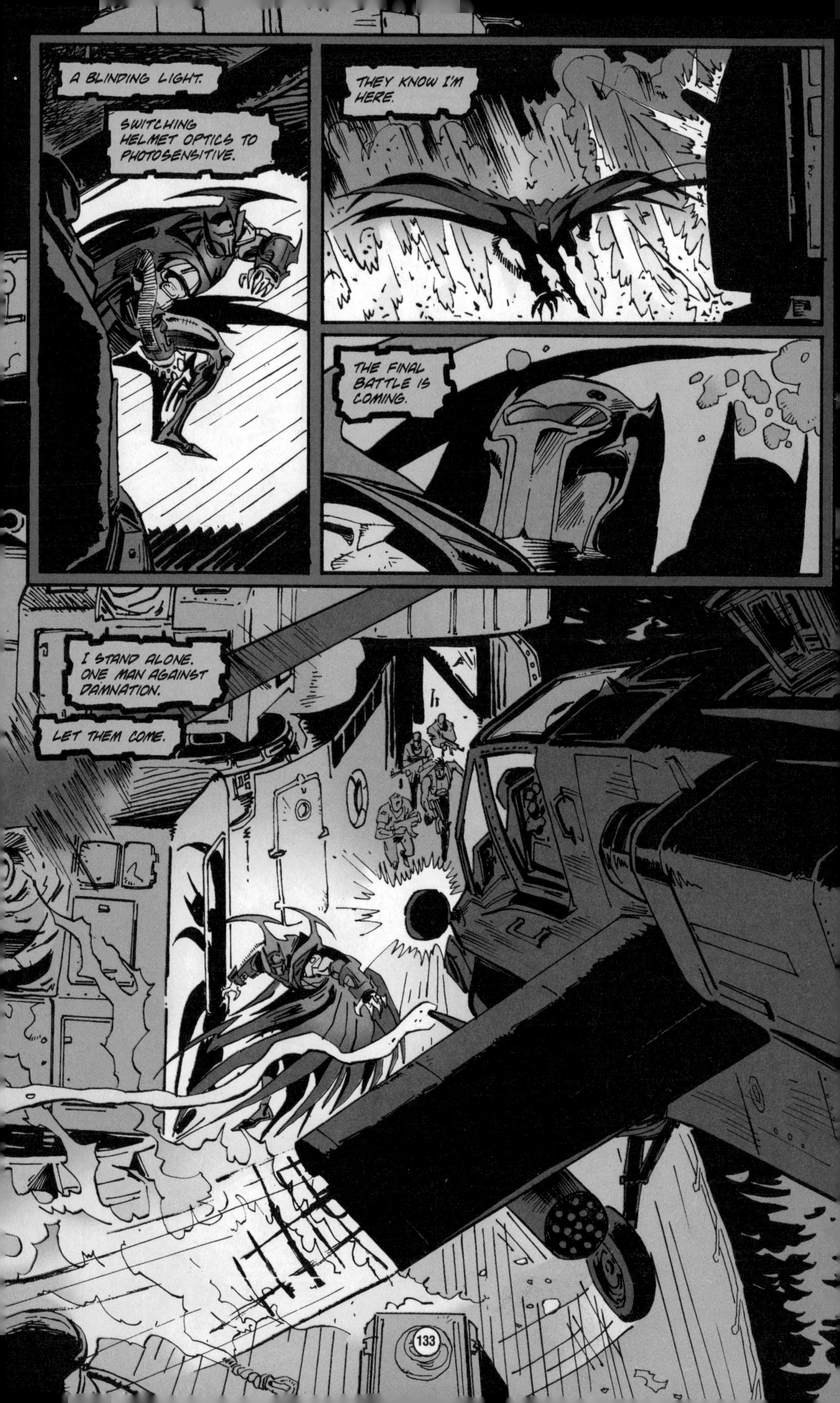
A BLINDING LIGHT.
SWITCHING HELMET OPTICS TO PHOTOSENSITIVE.
THEY KNOW I'M HERE.
THE FINAL BATTLE IS COMING.
I STAND ALONE. ONE MAN AGAINST DAMNATION.
LET THEM COME.

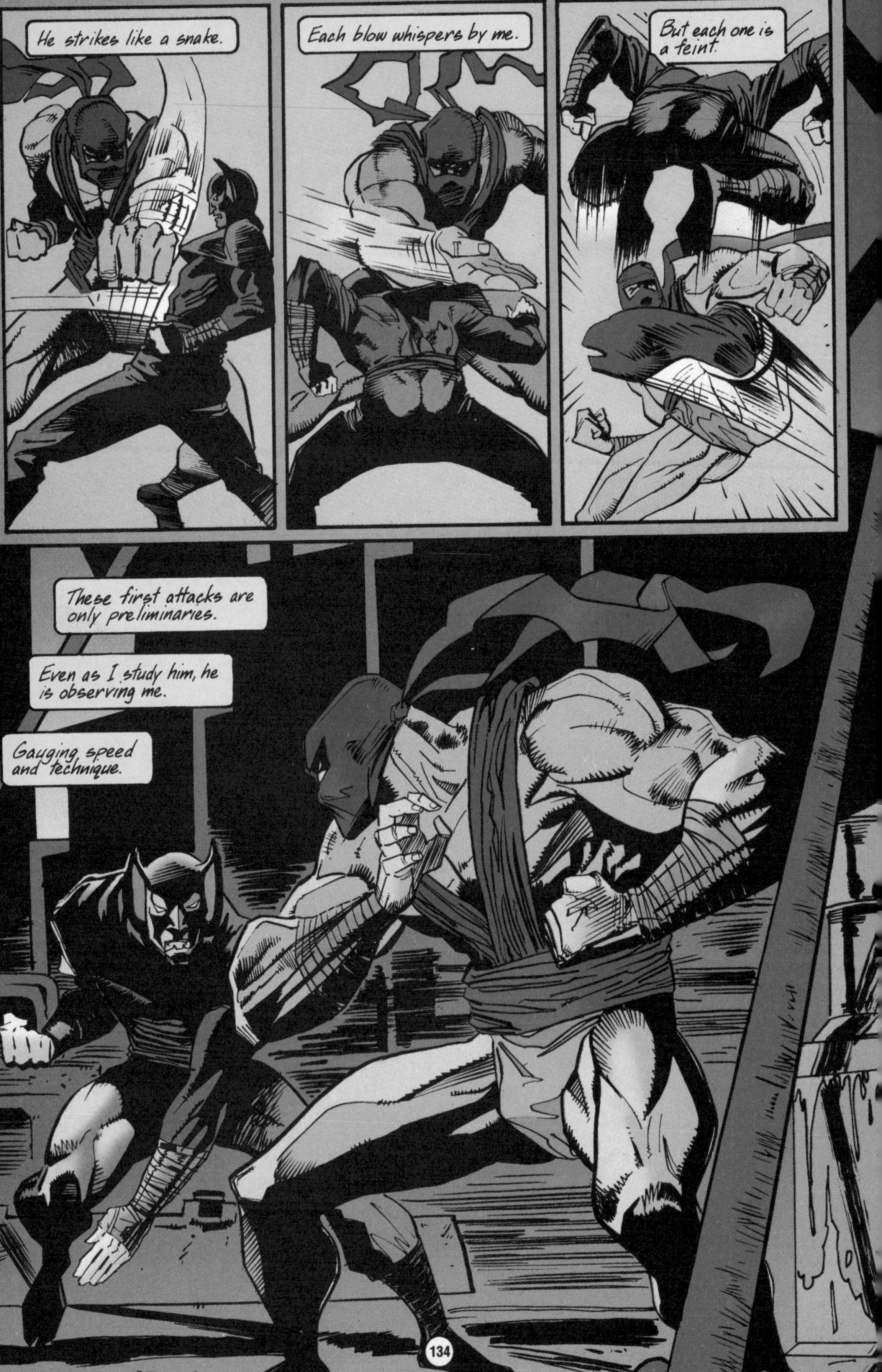
He strikes like a snake.
Each blow whispers by me.
But each one is a feint.
These first attacks are only preliminaries.
Even as I study him, he is observing me.
Gauging speed and technique.

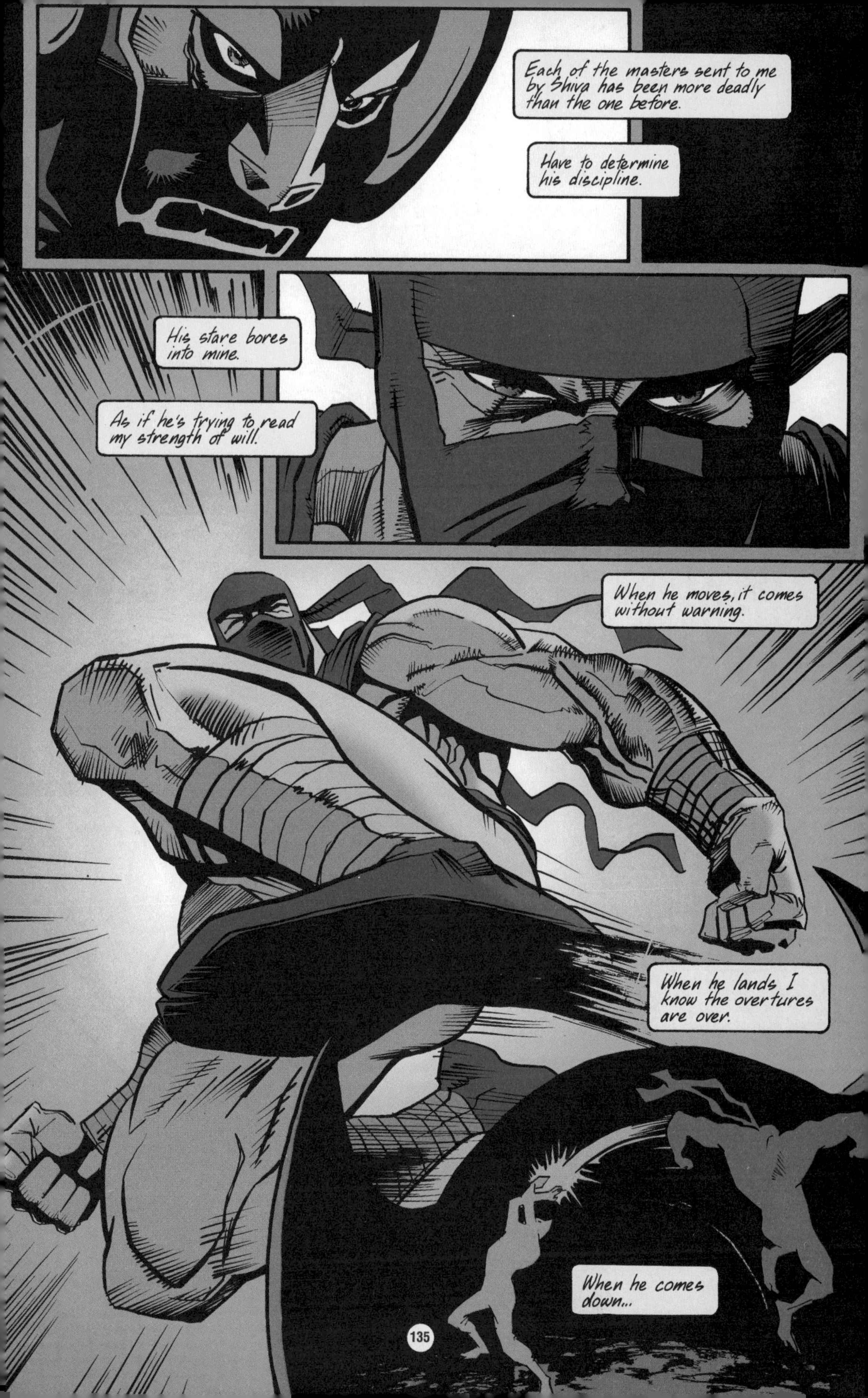
Each of the masters sent to me by Shiva has been more deadly than the one before.
Have to determine his discipline.
His stare bores into mine.
As if he's trying to read my strength of will.
When he moves, it comes without warning.
When he lands I know the overtures are over.
When he comes down...

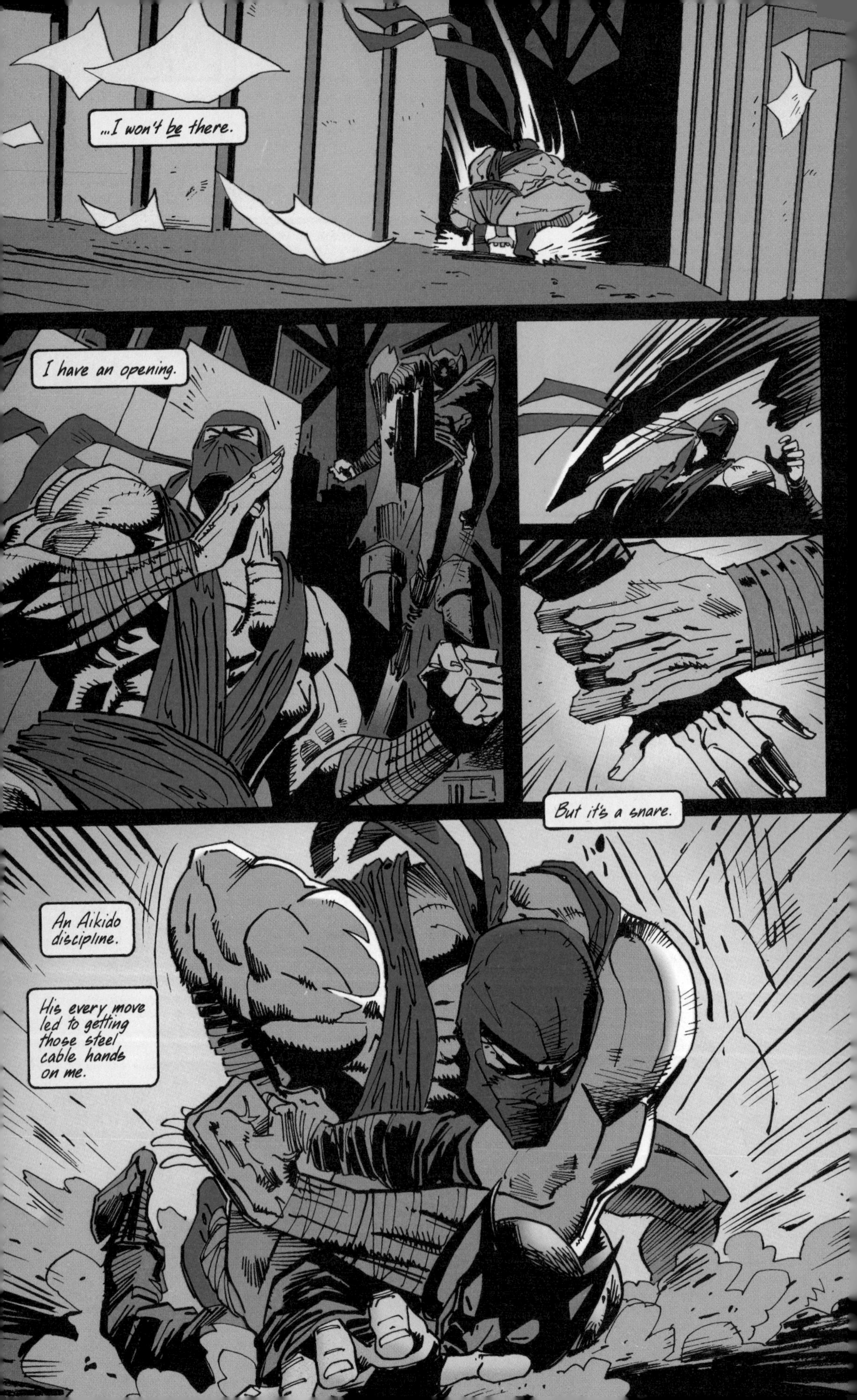
...I won't be there.
I have an opening.
But it's a snare.
An Aikido discipline.
His every move led to getting those steel cable hands on me.

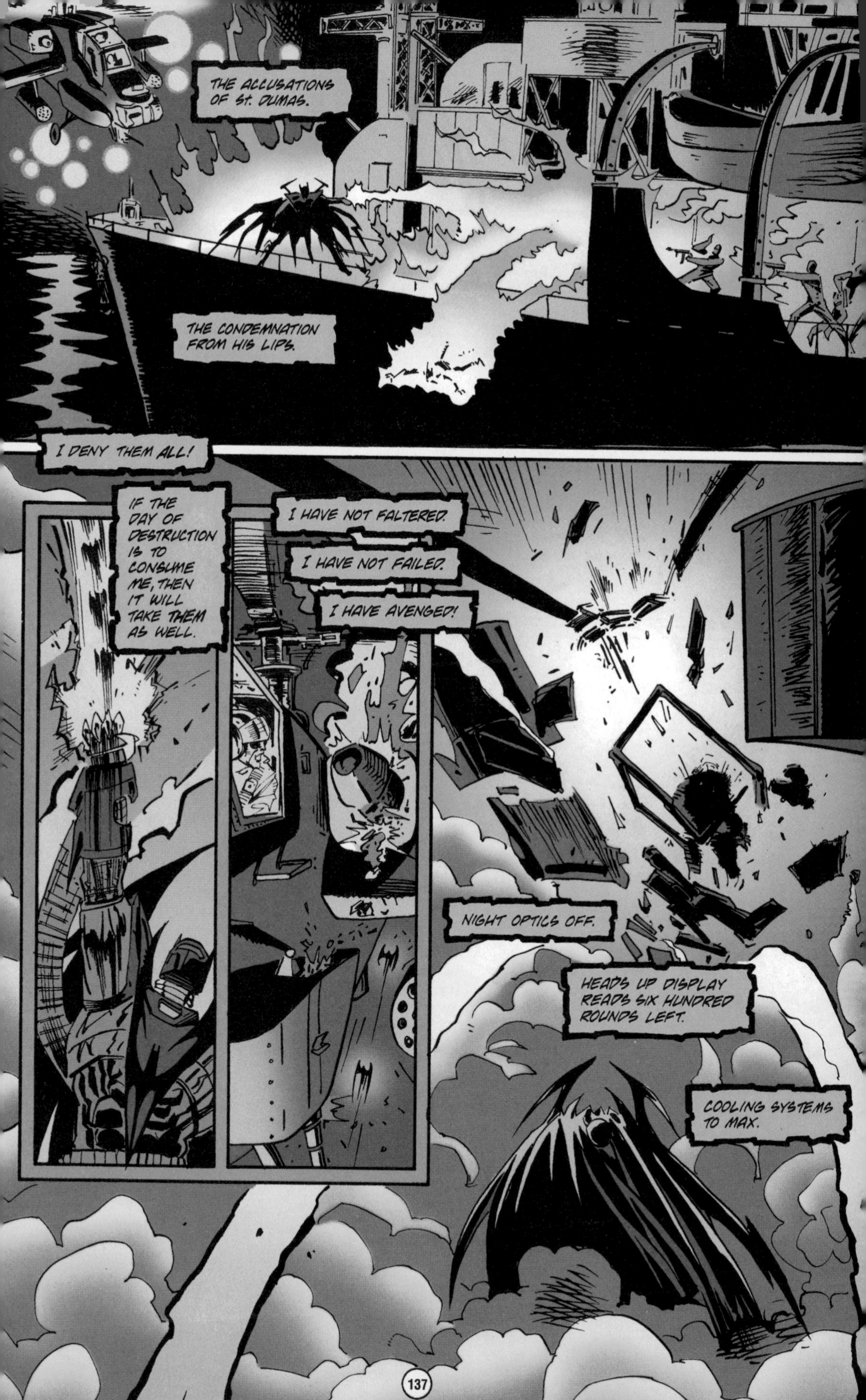

THE ACCUSATIONS OF St. DUMAS.
THE CONDEMNATION FROM HIS LIPS.
I DENY THEM ALL!
IF THE DAY OF DESTRUCTION IS TO CONSUME ME, THEN IT WILL TAKE THEM AS WELL.
I HAVE NOT FALTERED.
I HAVE NOT FAILED.
I HAVE AVENGED!
NIGHT OPTICS OFF.
HEADS UP DISPLAY READS SIX HUNDRED ROUNDS LEFT.
COOLING SYSTEMS TO MAX.

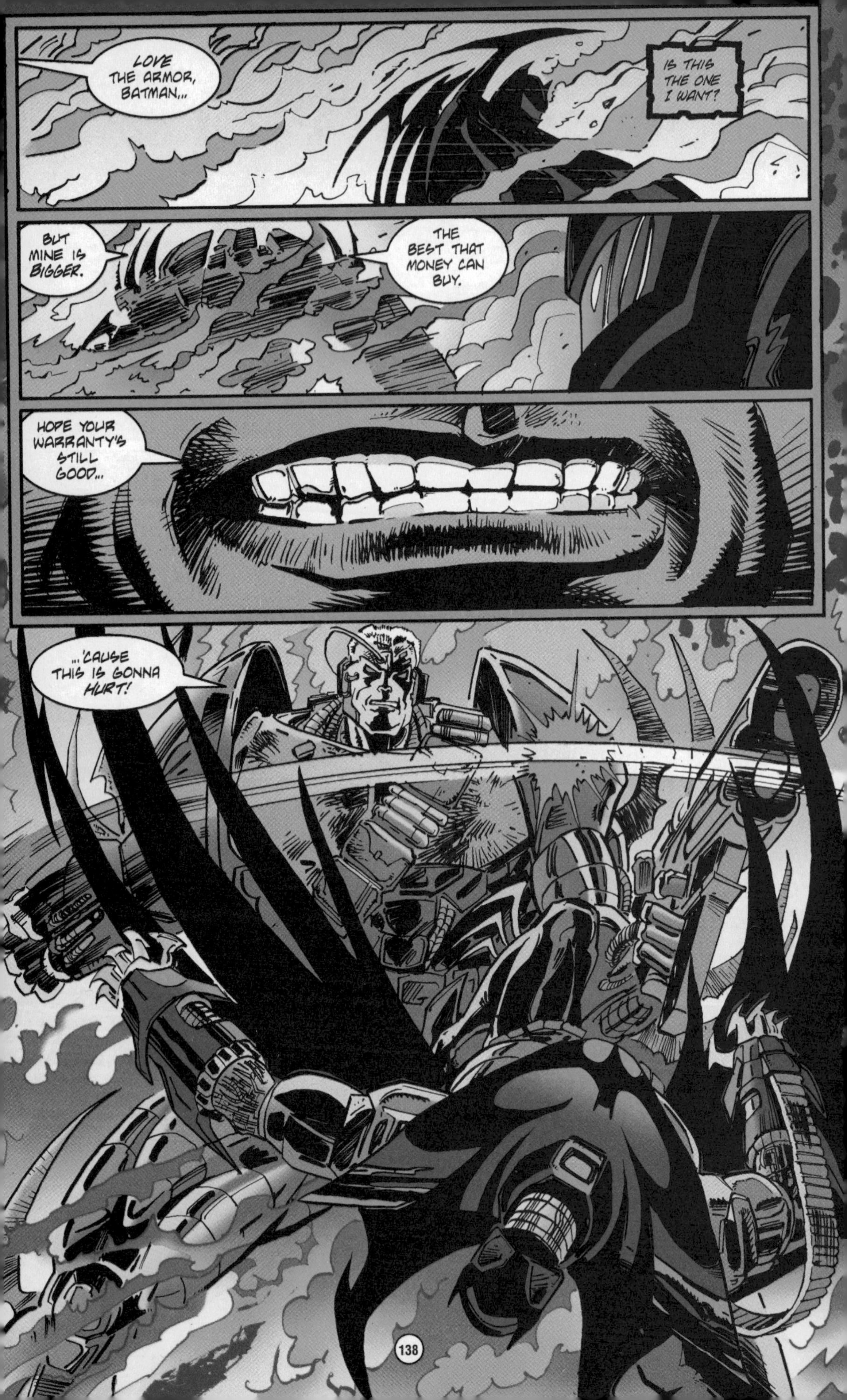
LOVE THE ARMOR, BATMAN...
IS THIS THE ONE I WANT?
BUT MINE IS BIGGER.
THE BEST THAT MONEY CAN BUY.
HOPE YOUR WARRANTY'S STILL GOOD...
...'CAUSE THIS IS GONNA HURT!

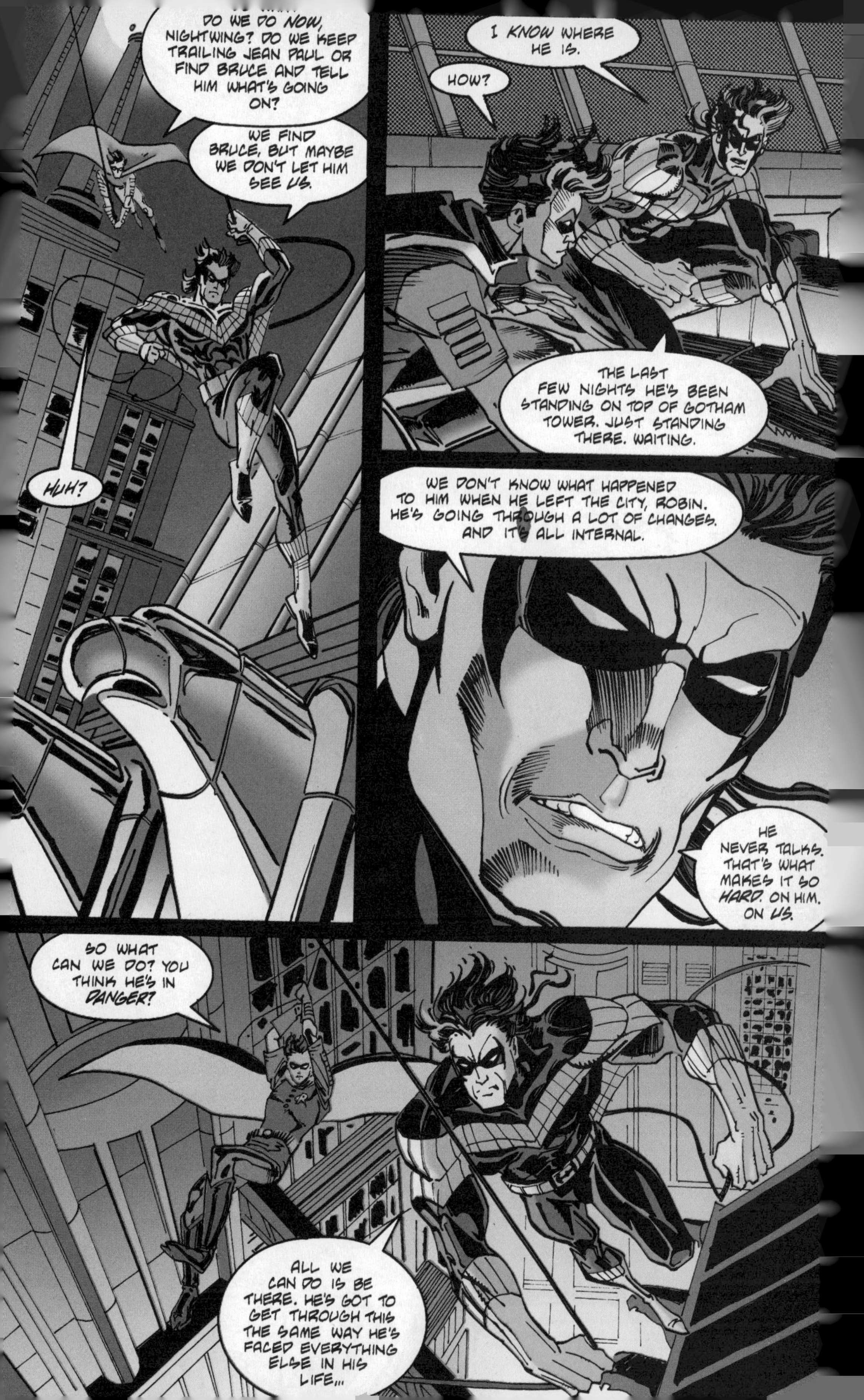
DO WE DO NOW, NIGHTWING? DO WE KEEP TRAILING JEAN PAUL OR FIND BRUCE AND TELL HIM WHAT'S GOING ON?
WE FIND BRUCE, BUT MAYBE WE DON'T LET HIM SEE US.
HUH?
I KNOW WHERE HE IS.
HOW?
THE LAST FEW NIGHTS HE'S BEEN STANDING ON TOP OF GOTHAM TOWER. JUST STANDING THERE. WAITING.
WE DON'T KNOW WHAT HAPPENED TO HIM WHEN HE LEFT THE CITY, ROBIN. HE'S GOING THROUGH A LOT OF CHANGES. AND IT'S ALL INTERNAL.
HE NEVER TALKS. THAT'S WHAT MAKES IT SO HARD. ON HIM. ON US.
SO WHAT CAN WE DO? YOU THINK HE'S IN DANGER?
ALL WE CAN DO IS BE THERE. HE'S GOT TO GET THROUGH THIS THE SAME WAY HE'S FACED EVERYTHING ELSE IN HIS LIFE...

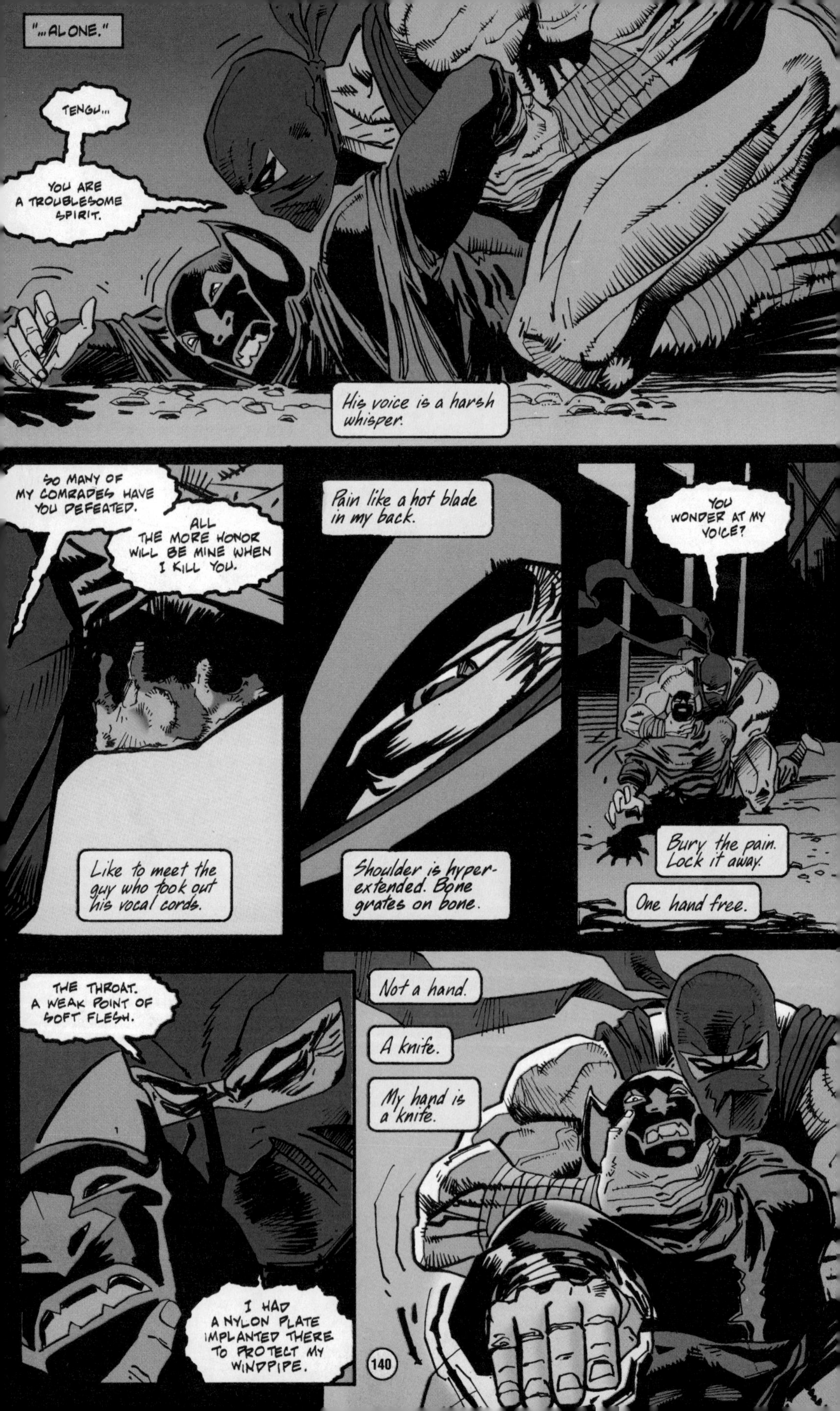

"...ALONE."
TENGU...
YOU ARE A TROUBLESOME SPIRIT.
His voice is a harsh whisper.
SO MANY OF MY COMRADES HAVE YOU DEFEATED.
ALL THE MORE HONOR WILL BE MINE WHEN I KILL YOU.
Like to meet the guy who took out his vocal cords.
Pain like a hot blade in my back.
Shoulder is hyper-extended. Bone grates on bone.
YOU WONDER AT MY VOICE?
Bury the pain. Lock it away.
One hand free.
THE THROAT. A WEAK POINT OF SOFT FLESH.
I HAD A NYLON PLATE IMPLANTED THERE TO PROTECT MY WINDPIPE.
Not a hand.
A knife.
My hand is a knife.

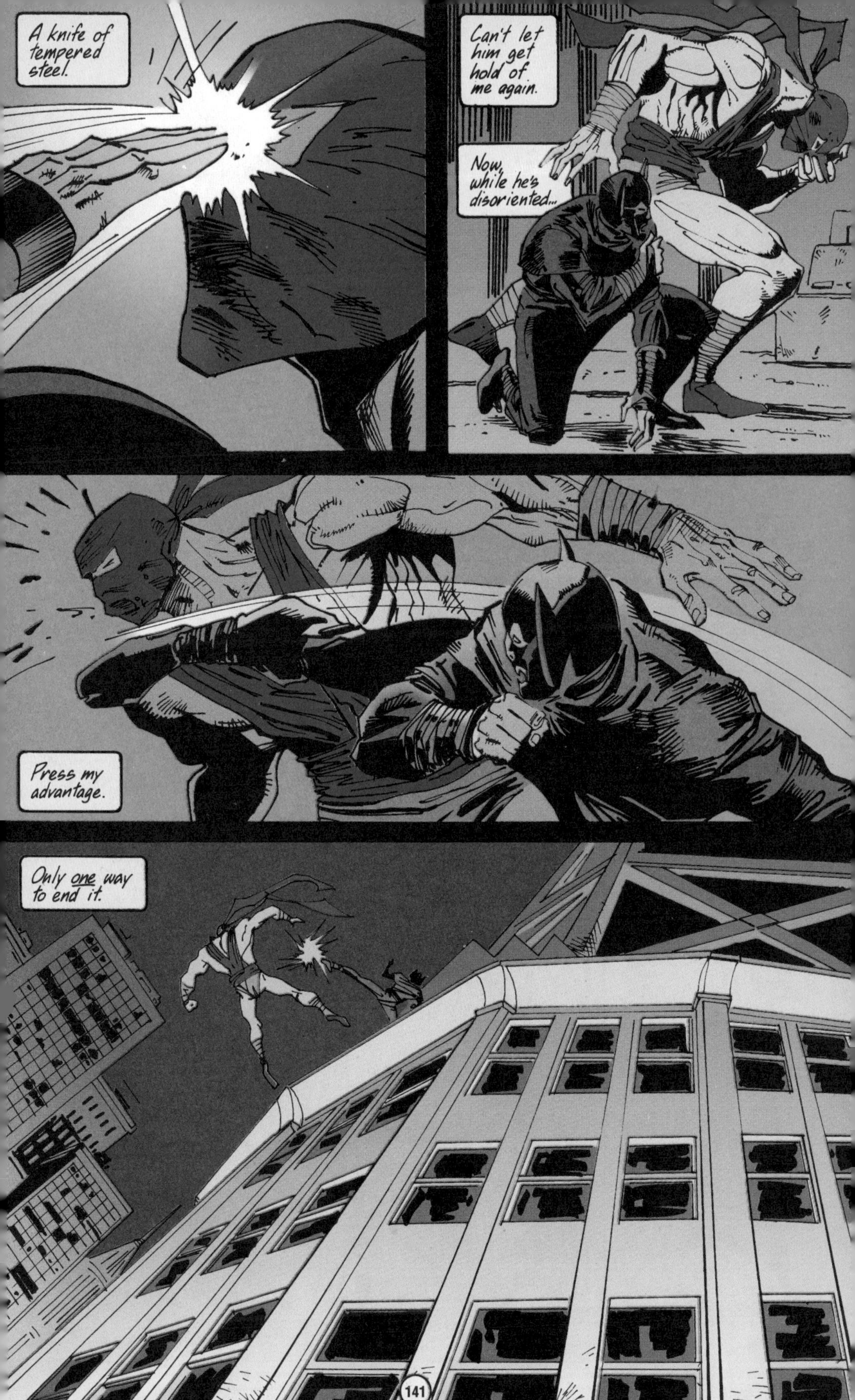
A knife of tempered steel.
Can't let him get hold of me again.
Now, while he's disoriented...
Press my advantage.
Only one way to end it.

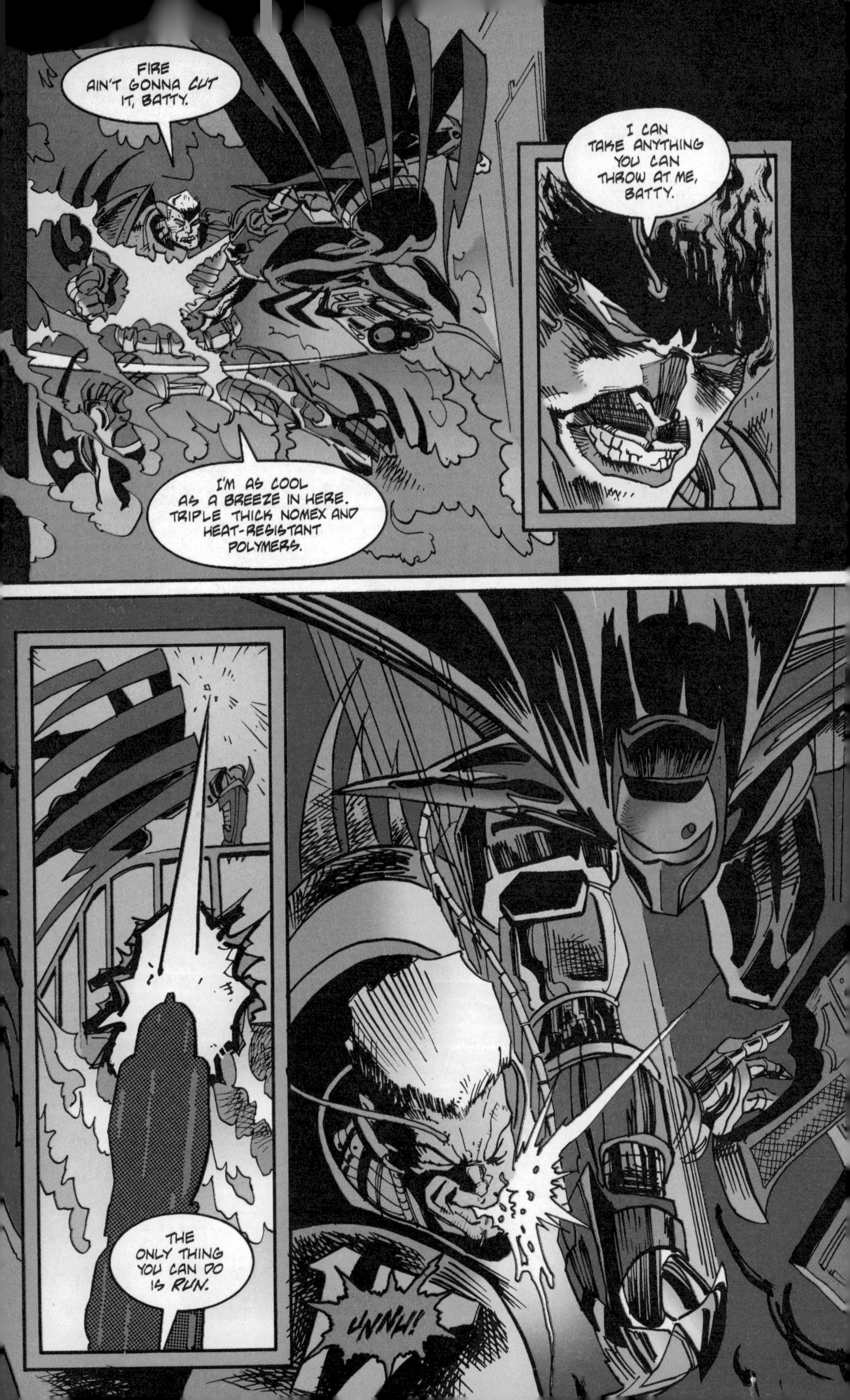
FIRE AIN'T GONNA CUT IT, BATTY.
I'M AS COOL AS A BREEZE IN HERE. TRIPLE THICK NOMEX AND HEAT-RESISTANT POLYMERS.
I CAN TAKE ANYTHING YOU CAN THROW AT ME, BATTY.
THE ONLY THING YOU CAN DO IS RUN.
UNNH!

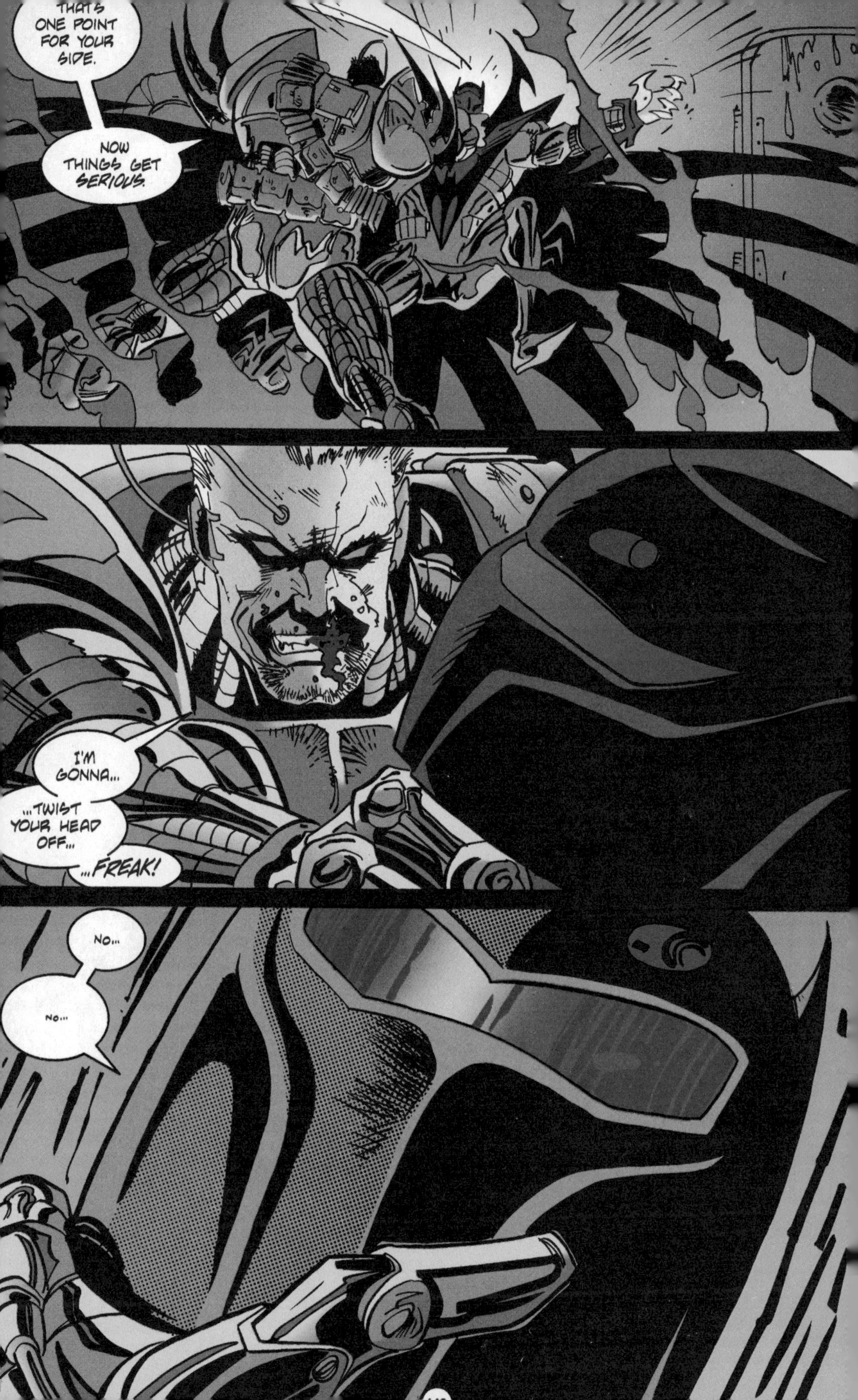
THAT'S ONE POINT FOR YOUR SIDE.
NOW THINGS GET SERIOUS.
I'M GONNA...
...TWIST YOUR HEAD OFF...
...FREAK!
NO...
NO...

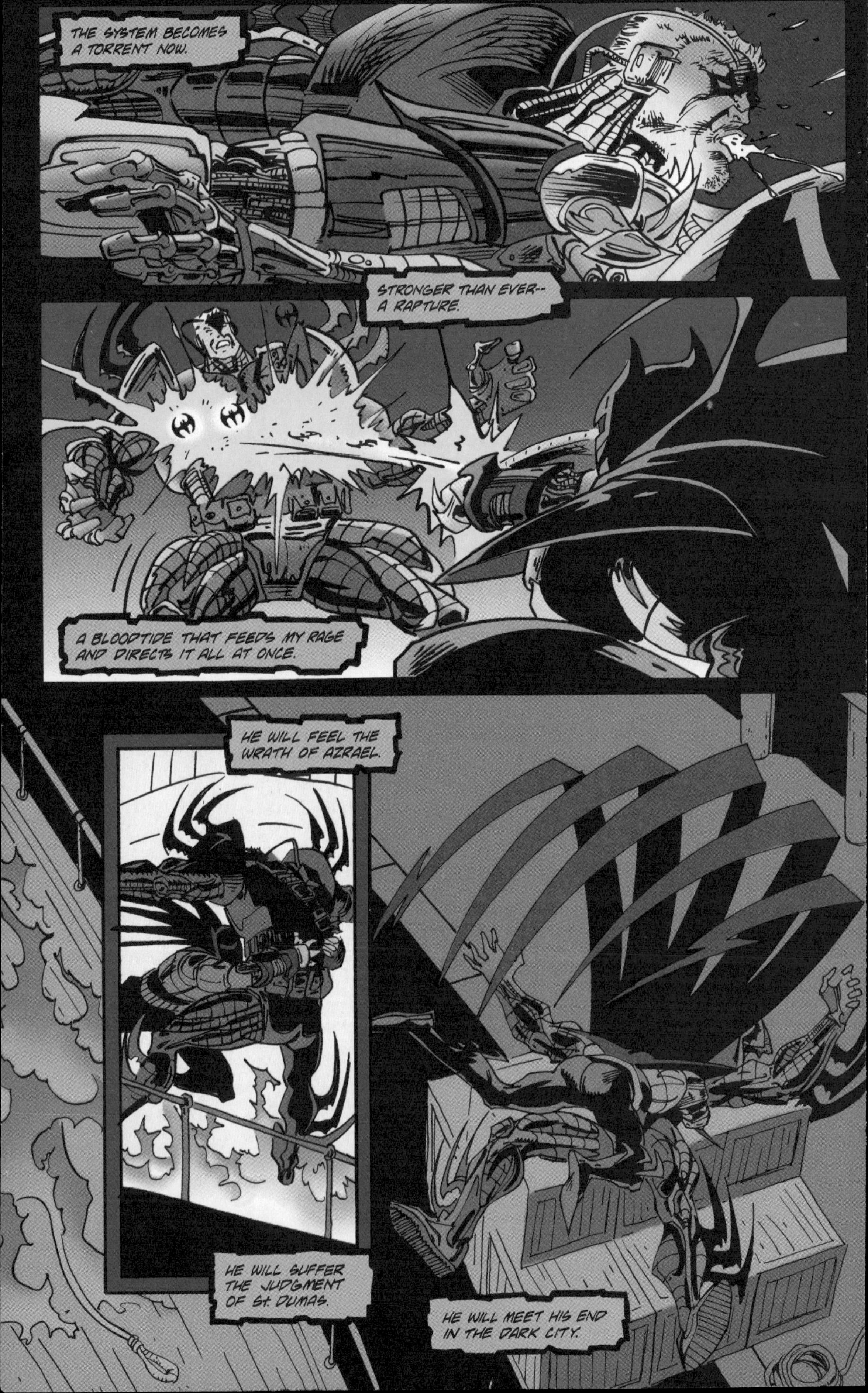
THE SYSTEM BECOMES A TORRENT NOW.
STRONGER THAN EVER-- A RAPTURE.
A BLOODTIDE THAT FEEDS MY RAGE AND DIRECTS IT ALL AT ONCE.
HE WILL FEEL THE WRATH OF AZRAEL.
HE WILL SUFFER THE JUDGMENT OF St. DUMAS.
HE WILL MEET HIS END IN THE DARK CITY.

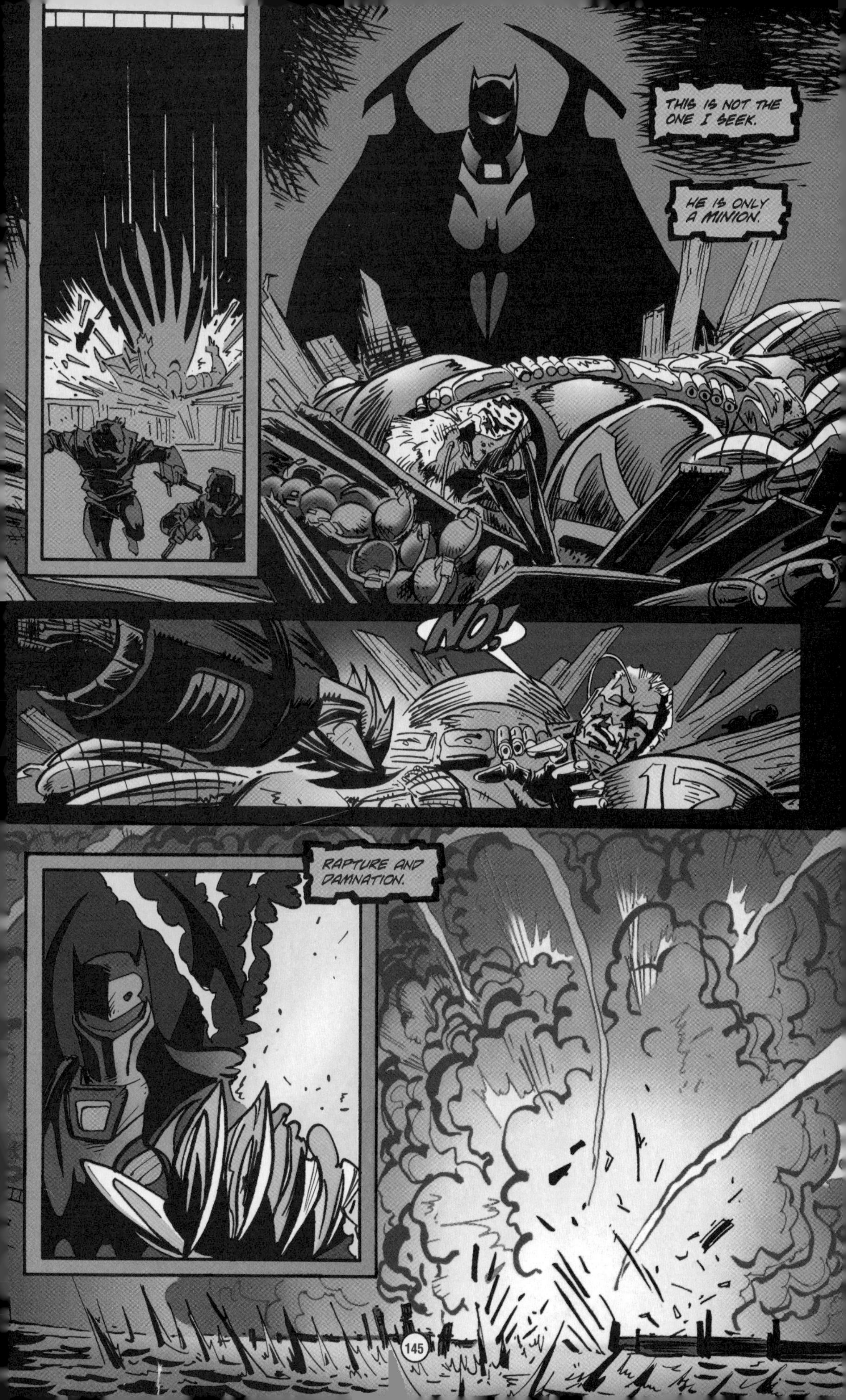
THIS IS NOT THE ONE I SEEK.
HE IS ONLY A MINION.
NO!
RAPTURE AND DAMNATION.

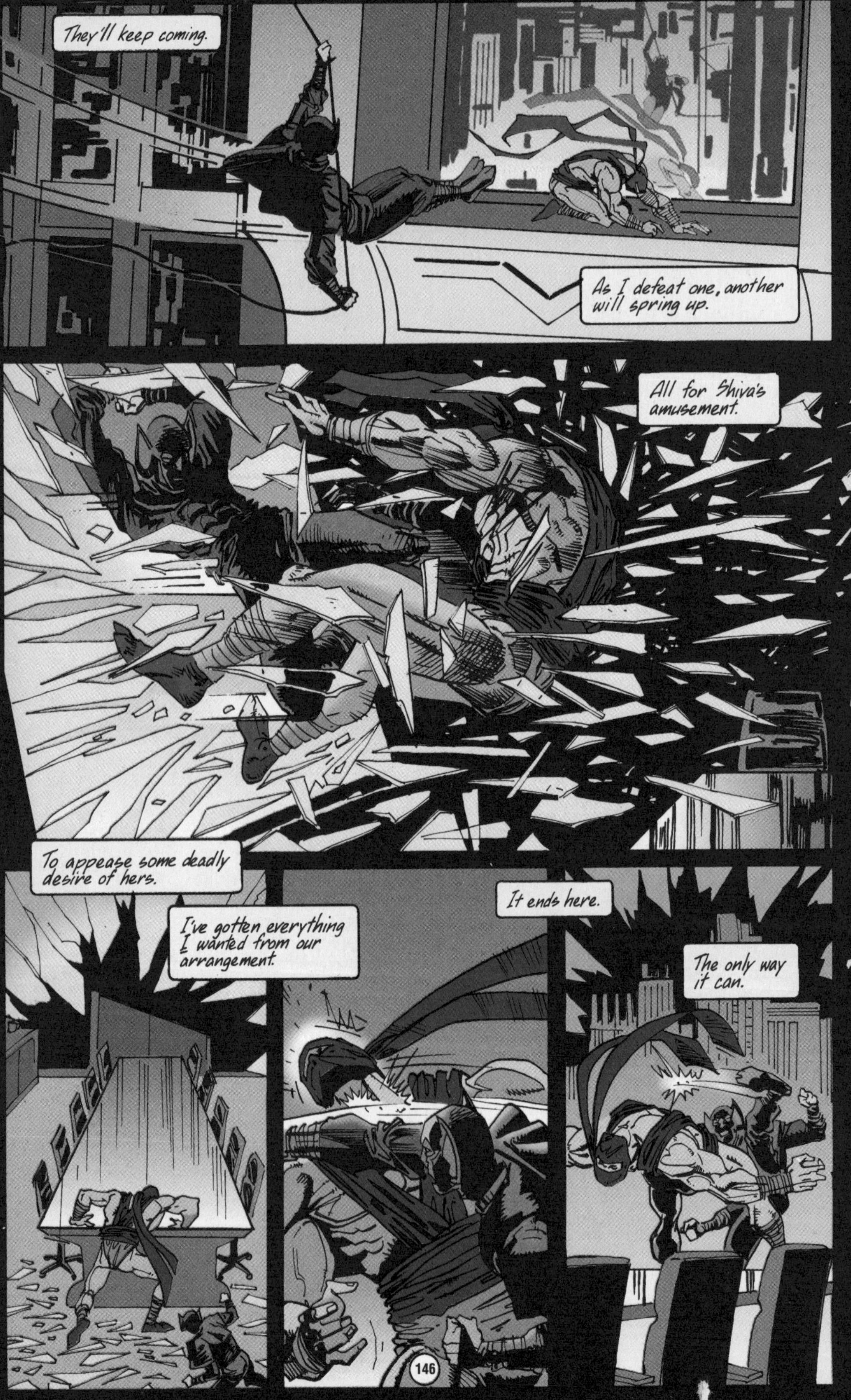
They'll keep coming.
As I defeat one, another will spring up.
All for Shiva's amusement.
To appease some deadly desire of hers.
I've gotten everything I wanted from our arrangement.
It ends here.
The only way it can.

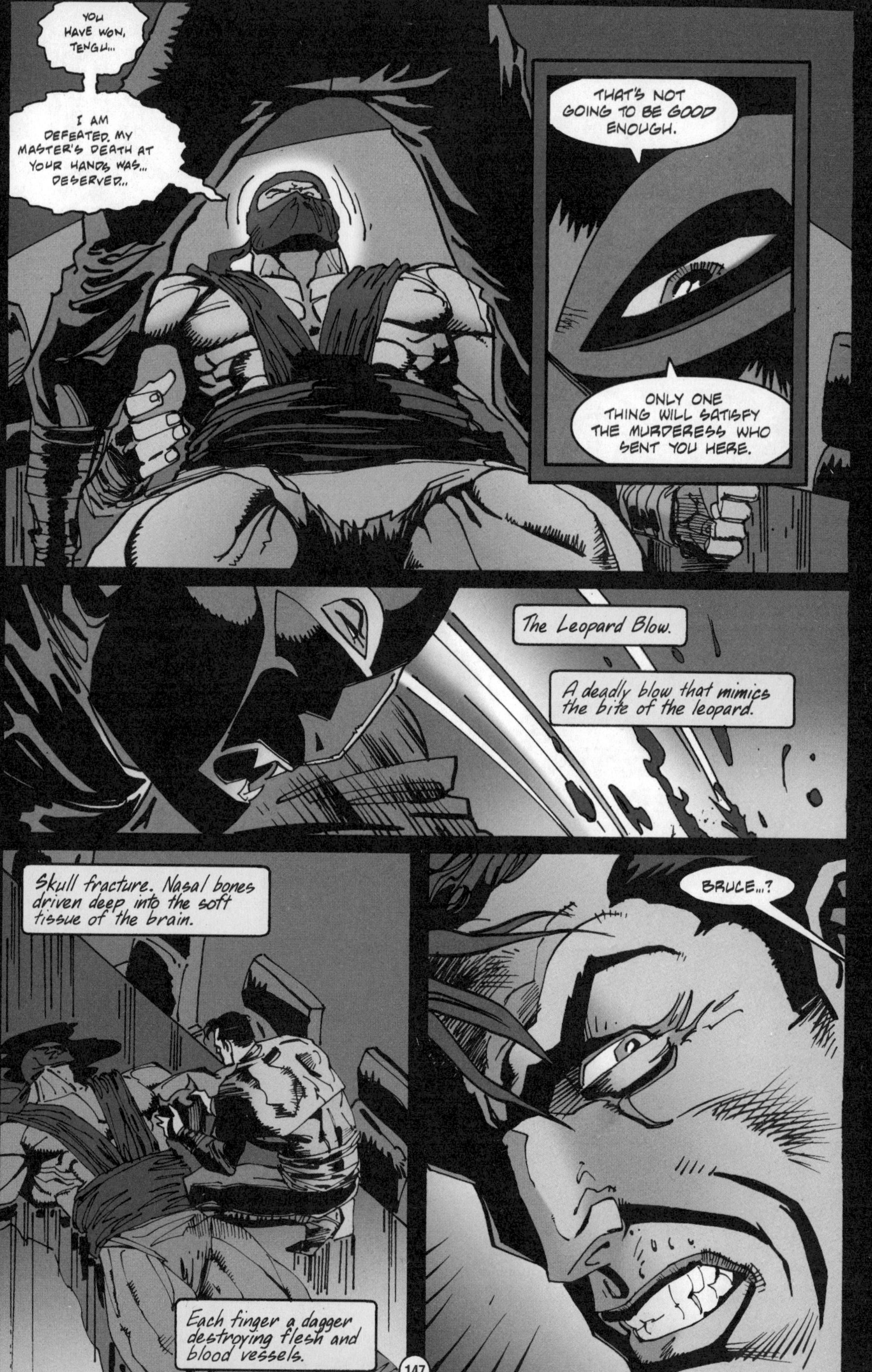
YOU HAVE WON, TENGU...
I AM DEFEATED. MY MASTER'S DEATH AT YOUR HANDS WAS... DESERVED...
THAT'S NOT GOING TO BE GOOD ENOUGH.
ONLY ONE THING WILL SATISFY THE MURDERESS WHO SENT YOU HERE.
The Leopard Blow.
A deadly blow that mimics the bite of the leopard.
Skull fracture. Nasal bones driven deep into the soft tissue of the brain.
Each finger a dagger destroying flesh and blood vessels.
BRUCE...?

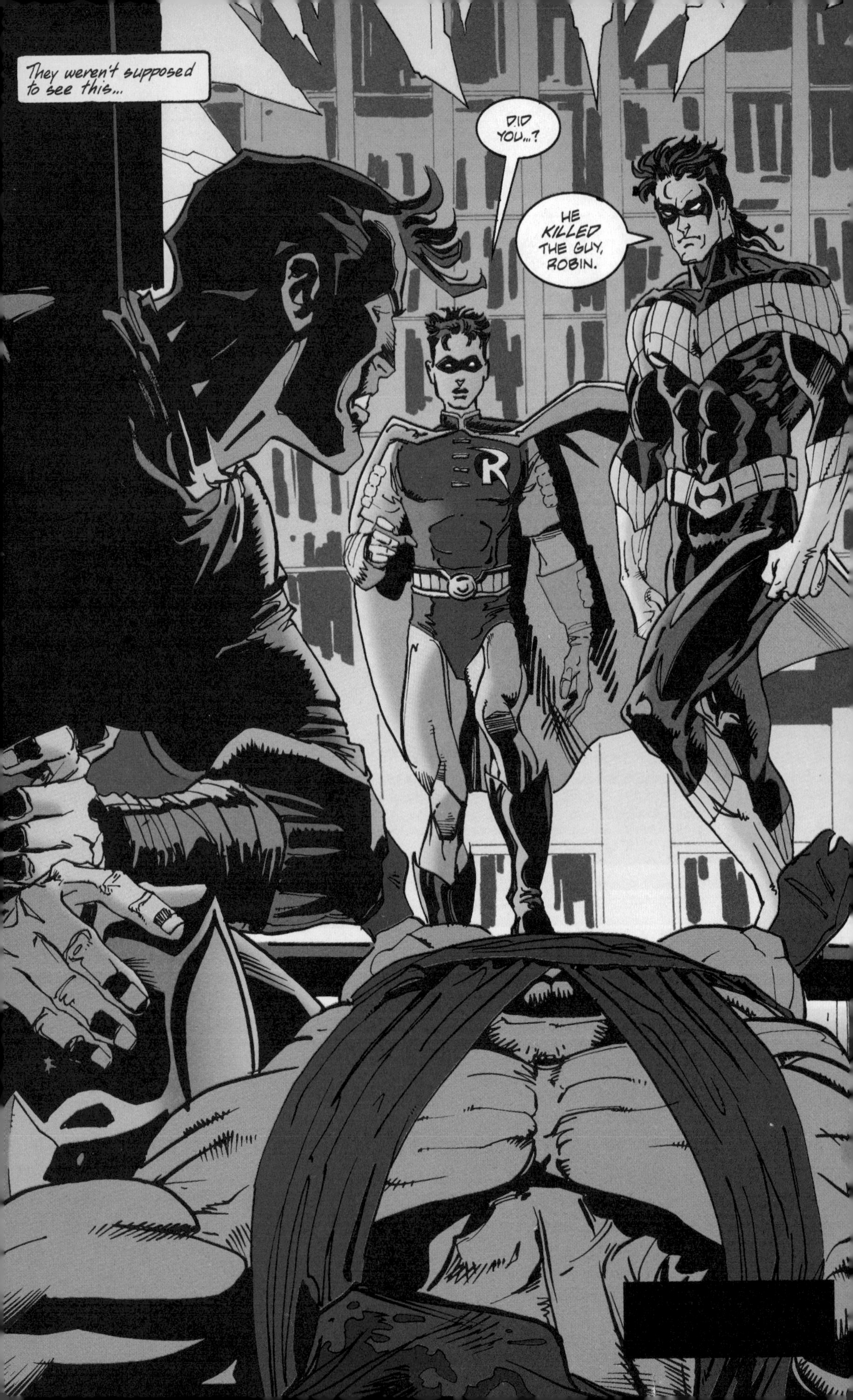
They weren't supposed to see this...
DID YOU...?
HE KILLED THE GUY, ROBIN.
[redacted]

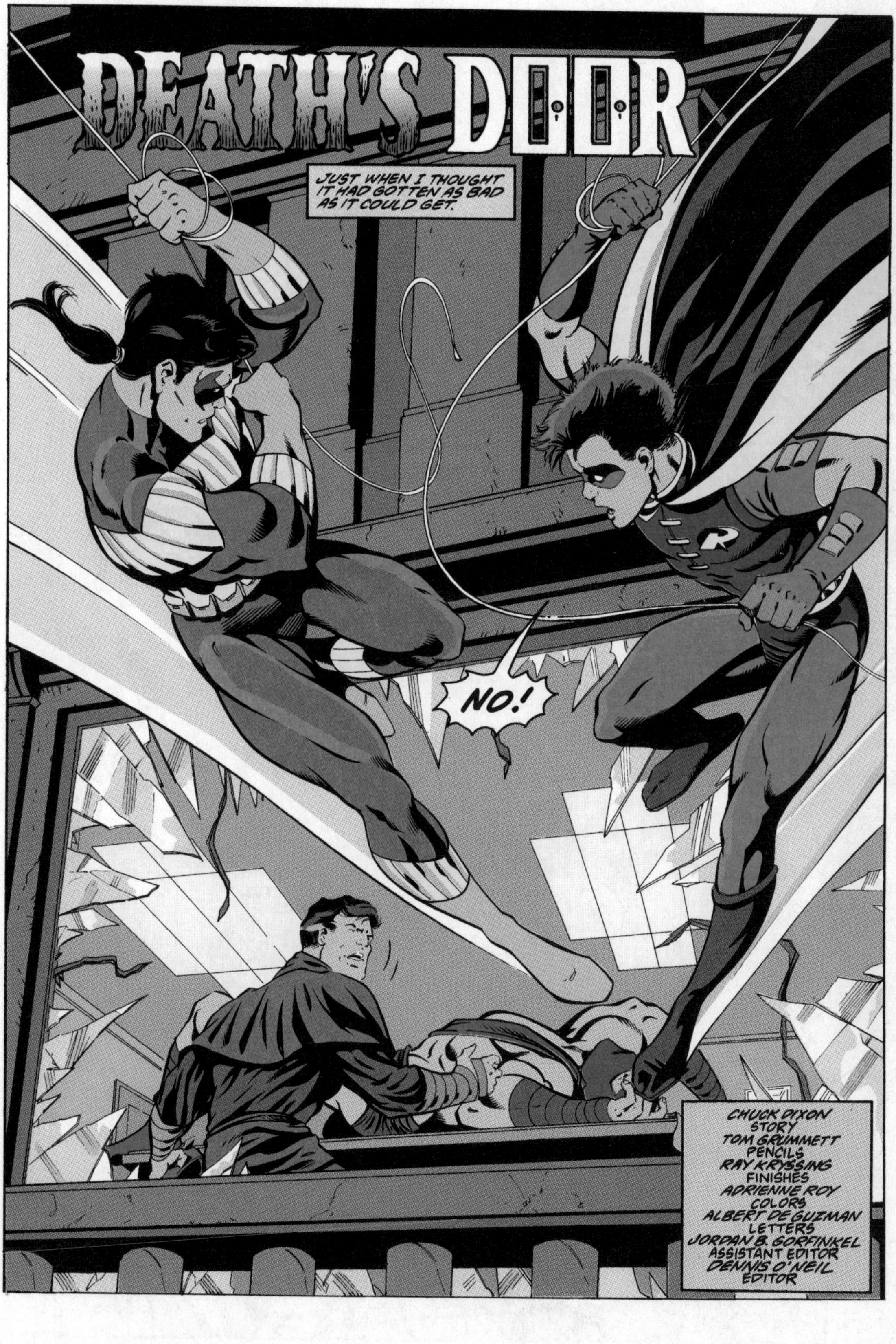
DEATH'S DOOR
JUST WHEN I THOUGHT IT HAD GOTTEN AS BAD AS IT COULD GET.
NO!
CHUCK DIXON STORY
TOM GRUMMETT PENCILS
RAY KRYSSING FINISHES
ADRIENNE ROY COLORS
ALBERT DE GUZMAN LETTERS
JORDAN B. GORFINKEL ASSISTANT EDITOR
DENNIS O'NEIL EDITOR

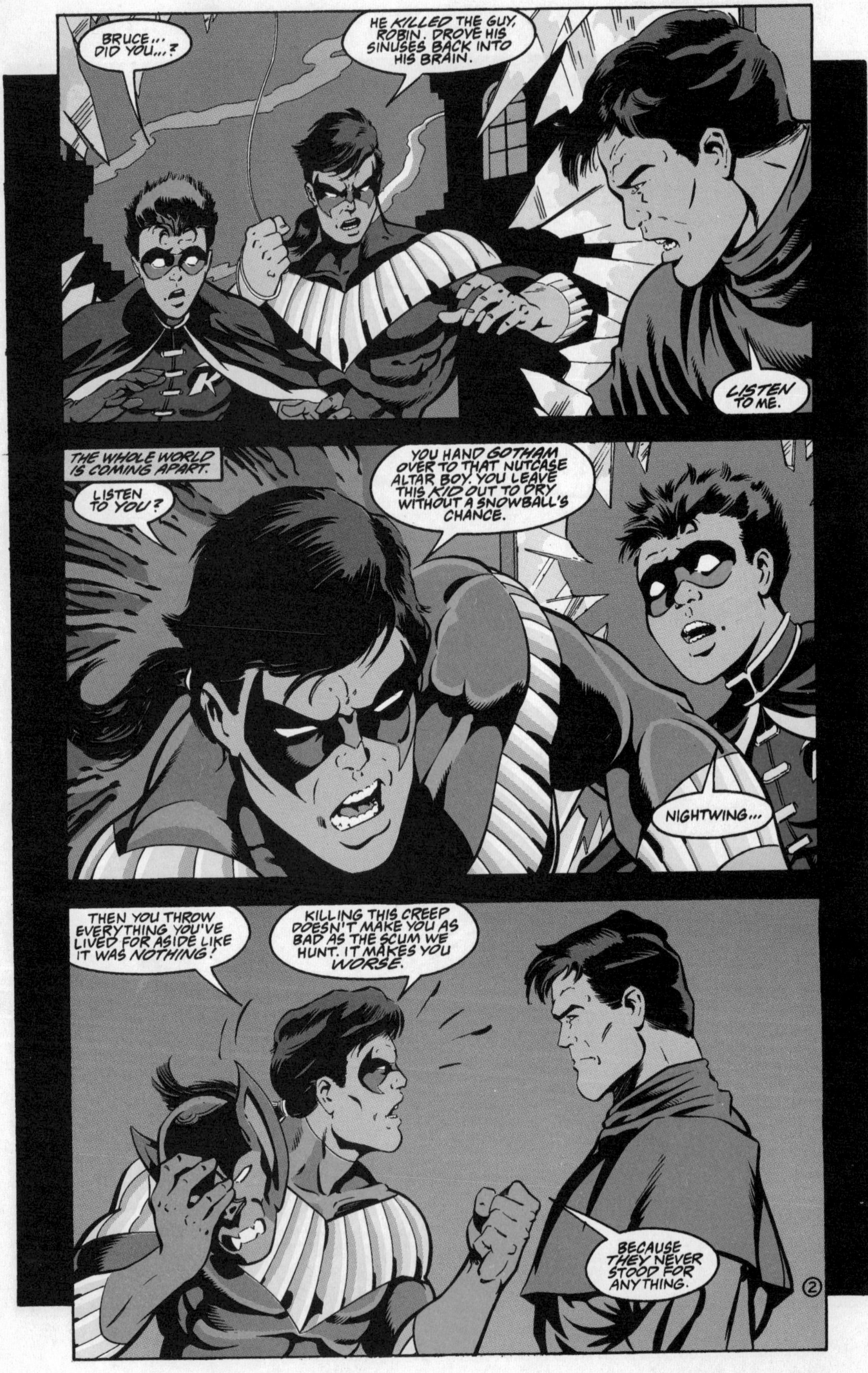
BRUCE... DID YOU...?
HE KILLED THE GUY, ROBIN. DROVE HIS SINUSES BACK INTO HIS BRAIN.
LISTEN TO ME.
THE WHOLE WORLD IS COMING APART.
LISTEN TO YOU?
YOU HAND GOTHAM OVER TO THAT NUTCASE ALTAR BOY. YOU LEAVE THIS KID OUT TO DRY WITHOUT A SNOWBALL'S CHANCE.
NIGHTWING...
THEN YOU THROW EVERYTHING YOU'VE LIVED FOR ASIDE LIKE IT WAS NOTHING!
KILLING THIS CREEP DOESN'T MAKE YOU AS BAD AS THE SCUM WE HUNT. IT MAKES YOU WORSE.
BECAUSE THEY NEVER STOOD FOR ANYTHING.
2

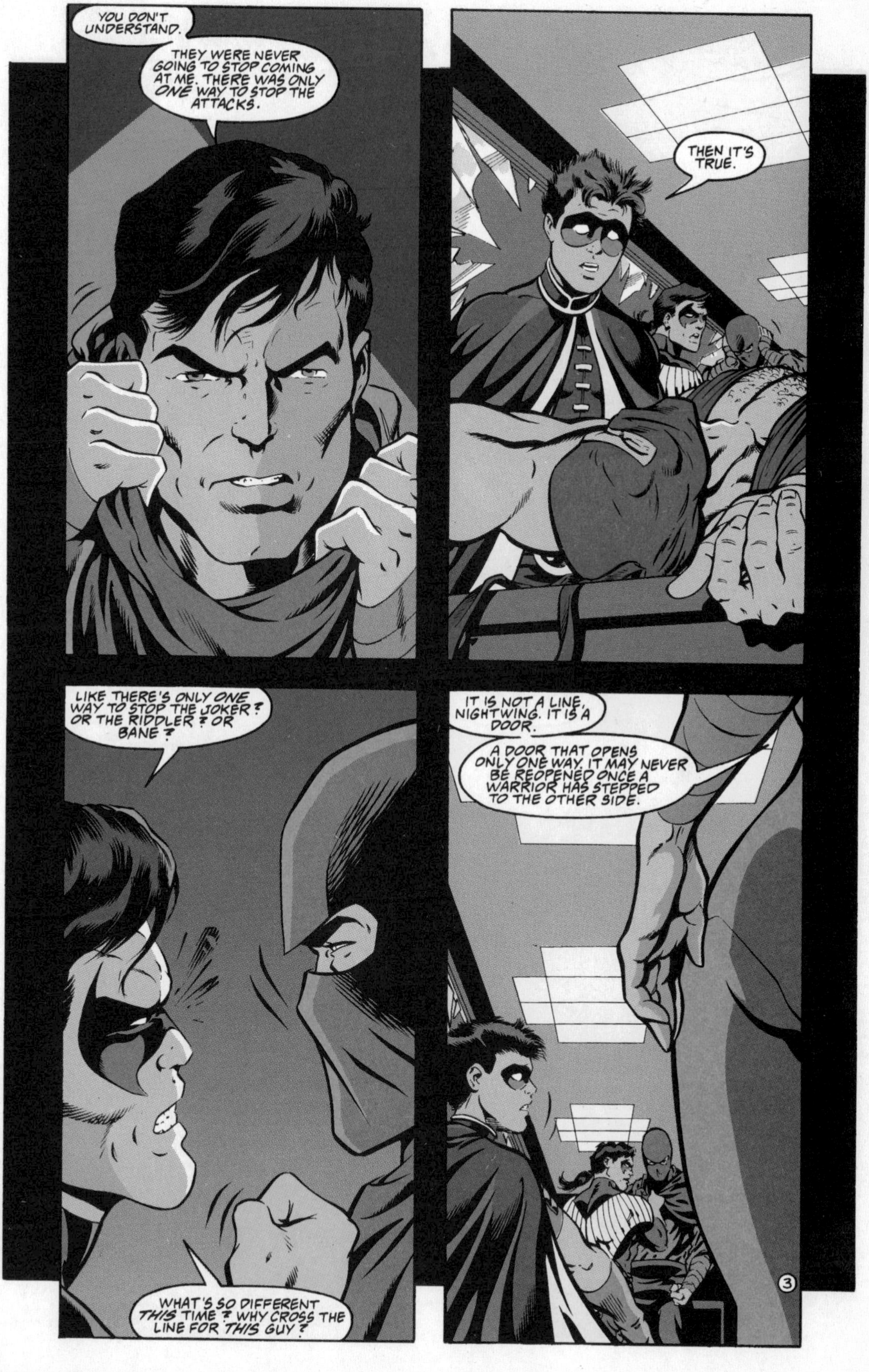
YOU DON'T UNDERSTAND.
THEY WERE NEVER GOING TO STOP COMING AT ME. THERE WAS ONLY ONE WAY TO STOP THE ATTACKS.
THEN IT'S TRUE.
LIKE THERE'S ONLY ONE WAY TO STOP THE JOKER? OR THE RIDDLER? OR BANE?
WHAT'S SO DIFFERENT THIS TIME? WHY CROSS THE LINE FOR THIS GUY?
IT IS NOT A LINE, NIGHTWING. IT IS A DOOR.
A DOOR THAT OPENS ONLY ONE WAY. IT MAY NEVER BE REOPENED ONCE A WARRIOR HAS STEPPED TO THE OTHER SIDE.
3

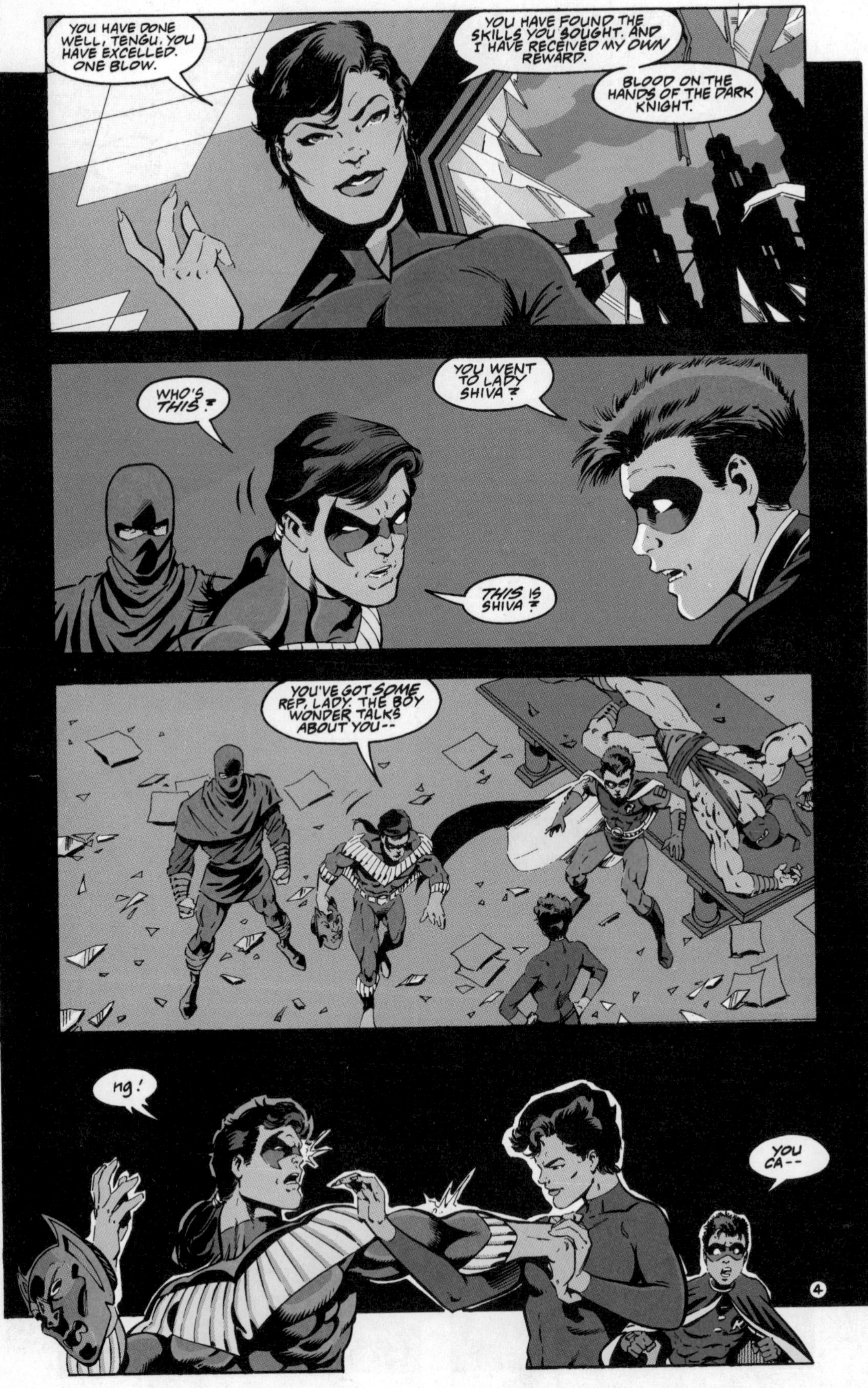
YOU HAVE DONE WELL, TENGU. YOU HAVE EXCELLED. ONE BLOW.
YOU HAVE FOUND THE SKILLS YOU SOUGHT. AND I HAVE RECEIVED MY OWN REWARD.
BLOOD ON THE HANDS OF THE DARK KNIGHT.
WHO'S THIS?
YOU WENT TO LADY SHIVA?
THIS IS SHIVA?
YOU'VE GOT SOME REP, LADY. THE BOY WONDER TALKS ABOUT YOU--
ng!
YOU CA--
4

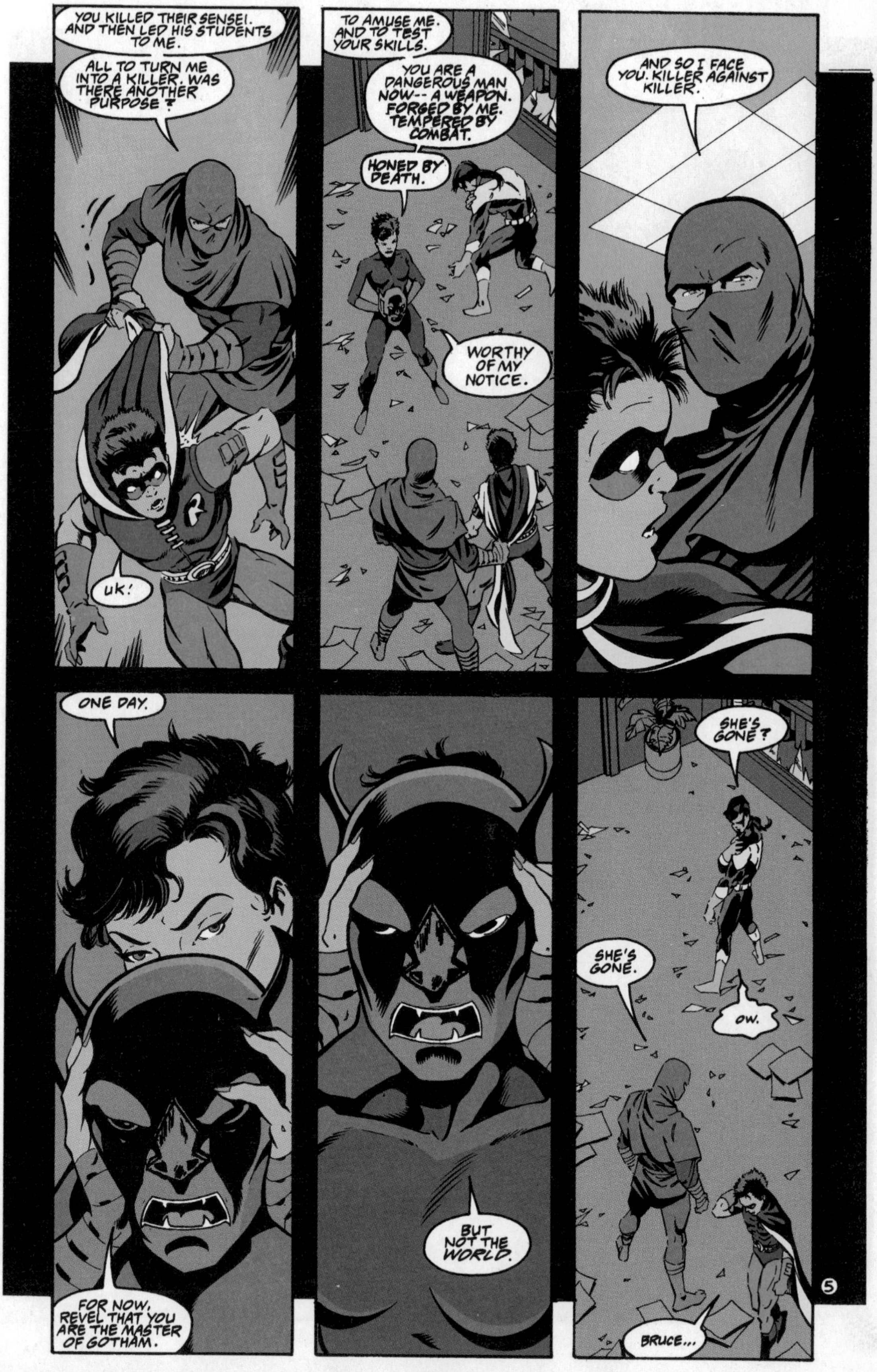
YOU KILLED THEIR SENSEI. AND THEN LED HIS STUDENTS TO ME.
ALL TO TURN ME INTO A KILLER. WAS THERE ANOTHER PURPOSE ?
UK!
TO AMUSE ME. AND TO TEST YOUR SKILLS.
YOU ARE A DANGEROUS MAN NOW-- A WEAPON. FORGED BY ME. TEMPERED BY COMBAT.
HONED BY DEATH.
WORTHY OF MY NOTICE.
AND SO I FACE YOU. KILLER AGAINST KILLER.
ONE DAY.
FOR NOW, REVEL THAT YOU ARE THE MASTER OF GOTHAM.
BUT NOT THE WORLD.
SHE'S GONE ?
SHE'S GONE.
OW.
BRUCE...
5

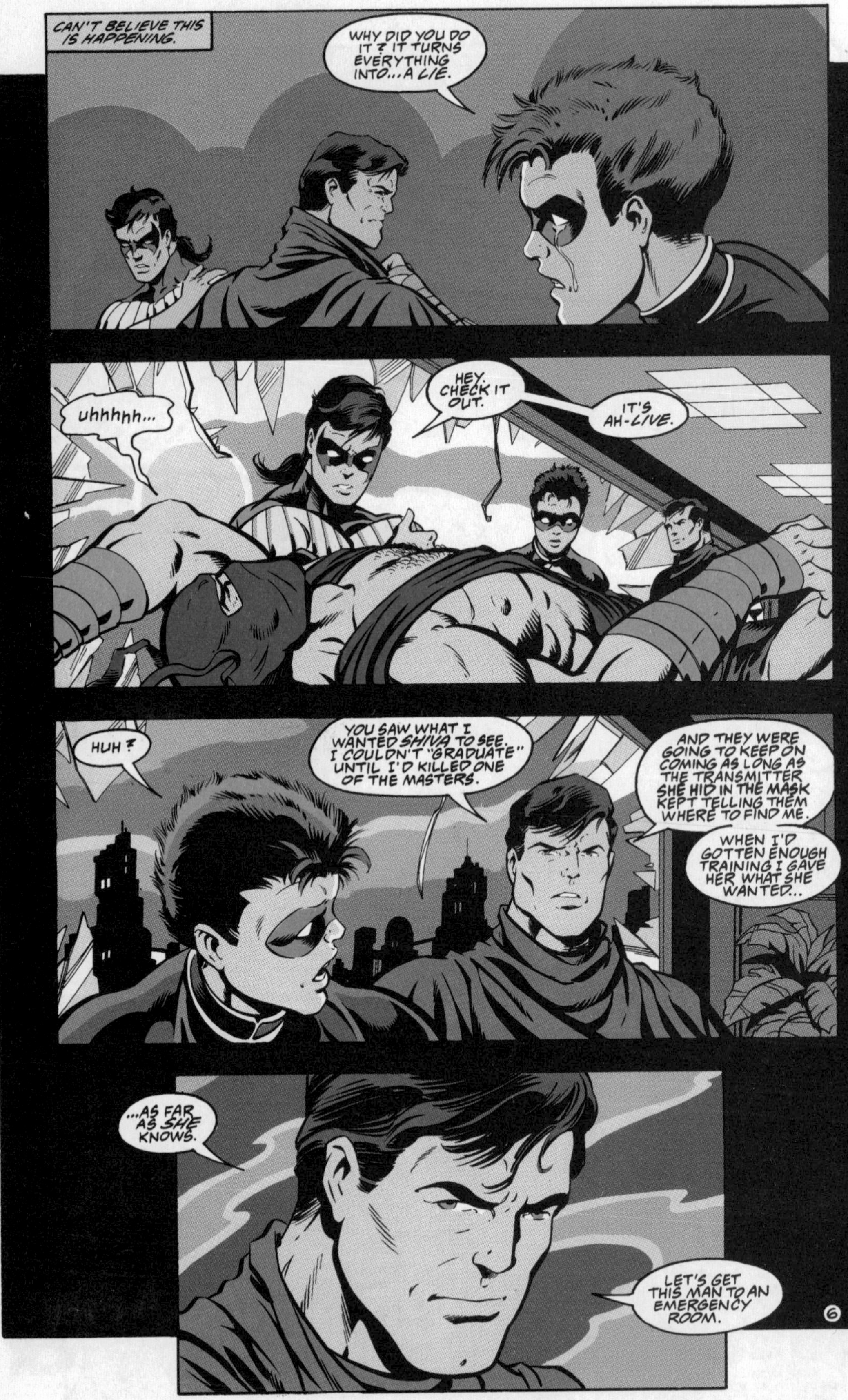

CAN'T BELIEVE THIS IS HAPPENING.
WHY DID YOU DO IT? IT TURNS EVERYTHING INTO... A LIE.
uhhhhh...
HEY. CHECK IT OUT.
IT'S AH-LIVE.
HUH?
YOU SAW WHAT I WANTED SHIVA TO SEE. I COULDN'T "GRADUATE" UNTIL I'D KILLED ONE OF THE MASTERS.
AND THEY WERE GOING TO KEEP ON COMING AS LONG AS THE TRANSMITTER SHE HID IN THE MASK KEPT TELLING THEM WHERE TO FIND ME.
WHEN I'D GOTTEN ENOUGH TRAINING I GAVE HER WHAT SHE WANTED...
...AS FAR AS SHE KNOWS.
LET'S GET THIS MAN TO AN EMERGENCY ROOM.
6

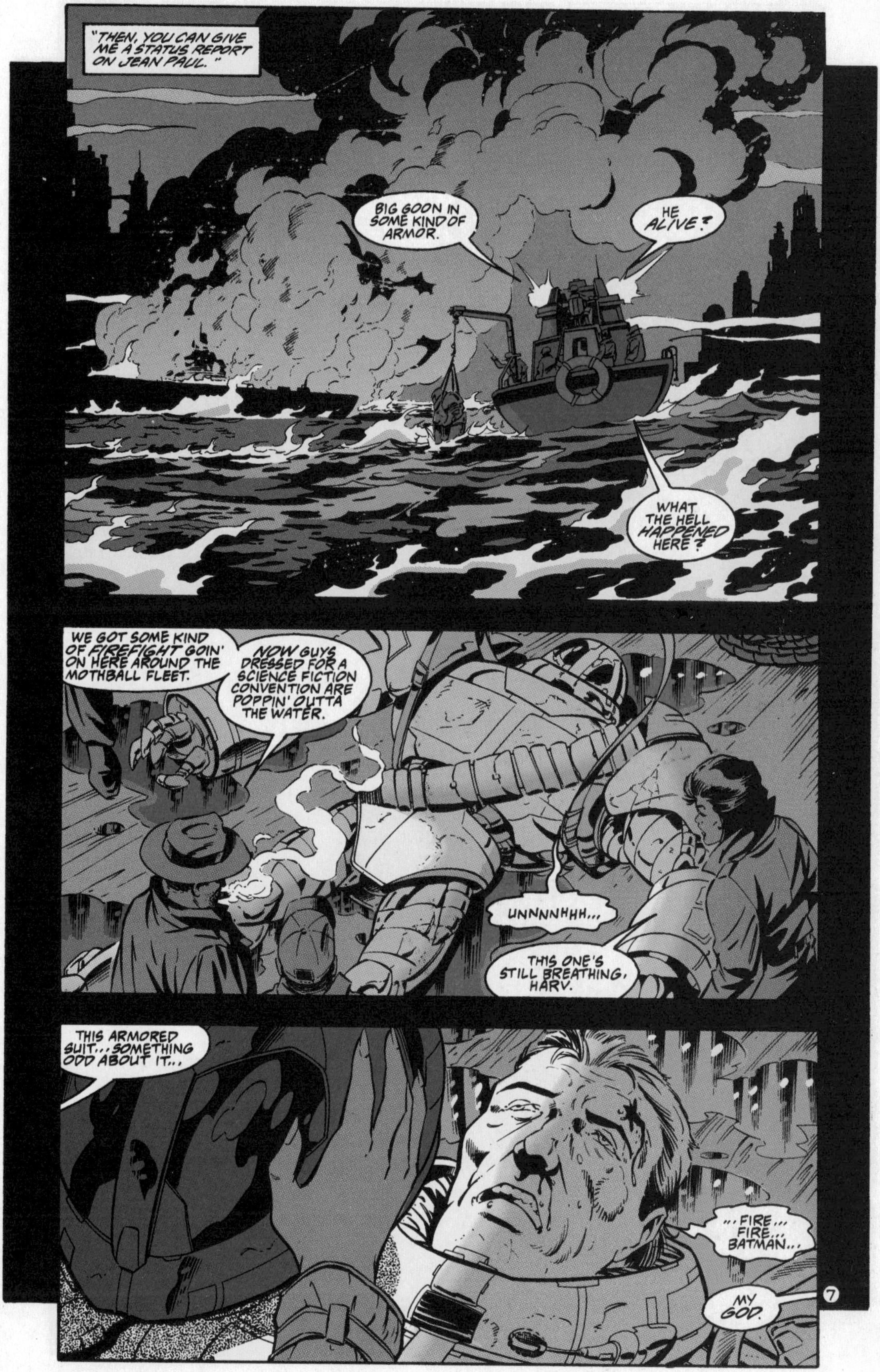
"THEN, YOU CAN GIVE ME A STATUS REPORT ON JEAN PAUL."
BIG GOON IN SOME KIND OF ARMOR.
HE ALIVE?
WHAT THE HELL HAPPENED HERE?
WE GOT SOME KIND OF FIREFIGHT GOIN' ON HERE AROUND THE MOTHBALL FLEET.
NOW GUYS DRESSED FOR A SCIENCE FICTION CONVENTION ARE POPPIN' OUTTA THE WATER.
UNNNNHHH...
THIS ONE'S STILL BREATHING, HARV.
THIS ARMORED SUIT... SOMETHING ODD ABOUT IT...
...FIRE... FIRE... BATMAN...
MY GOD.
7

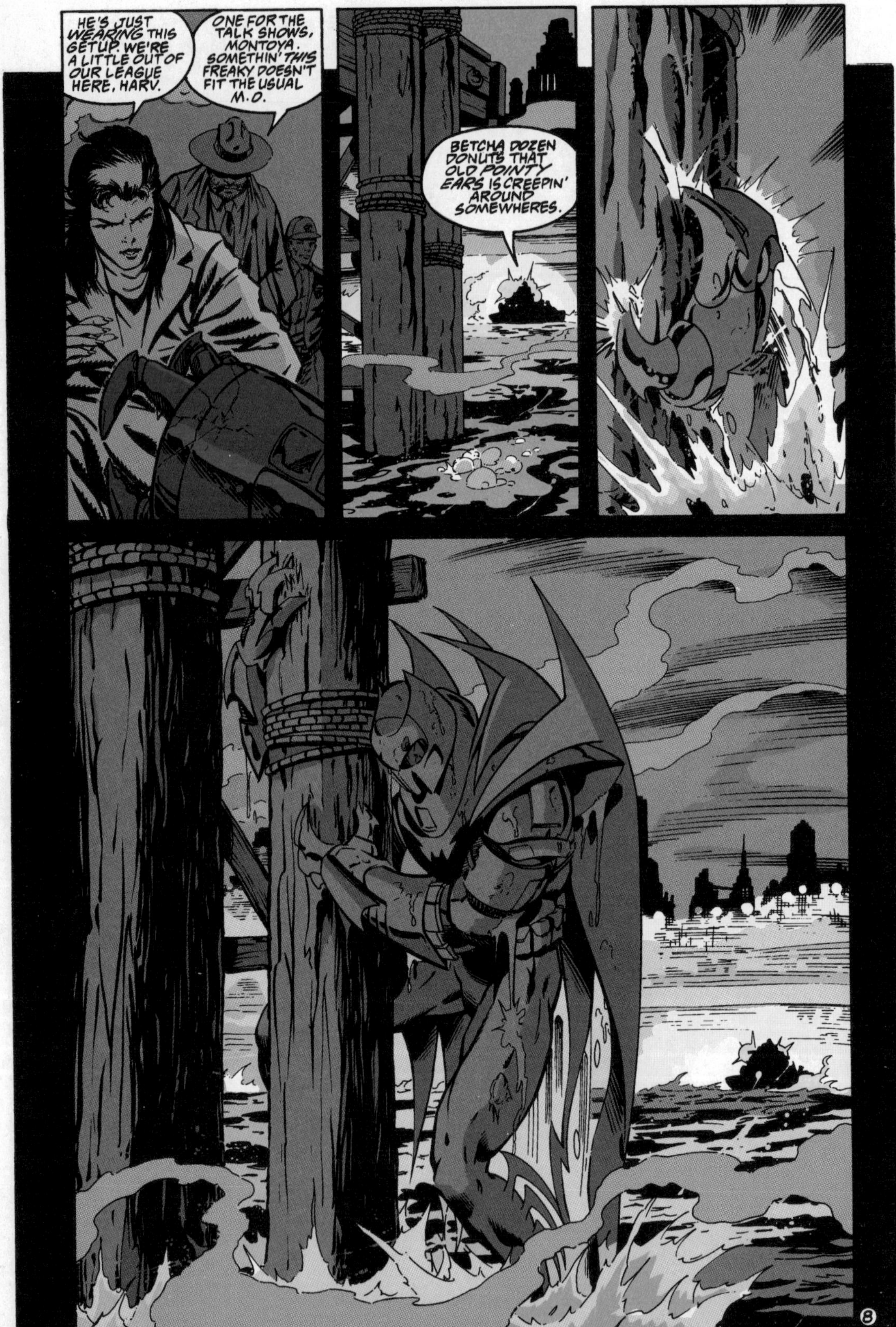
HE'S JUST WEARING THIS GETUP. WE'RE A LITTLE OUT OF OUR LEAGUE HERE, HARV.
ONE FOR THE TALK SHOWS, MONTOYA. SOMETHIN' THIS FREAKY DOESN'T FIT THE USUAL M.O.
BETCHA DOZEN DONUTS THAT OLD POINTY EARS IS CREEPIN' AROUND SOMEWHERES.
8

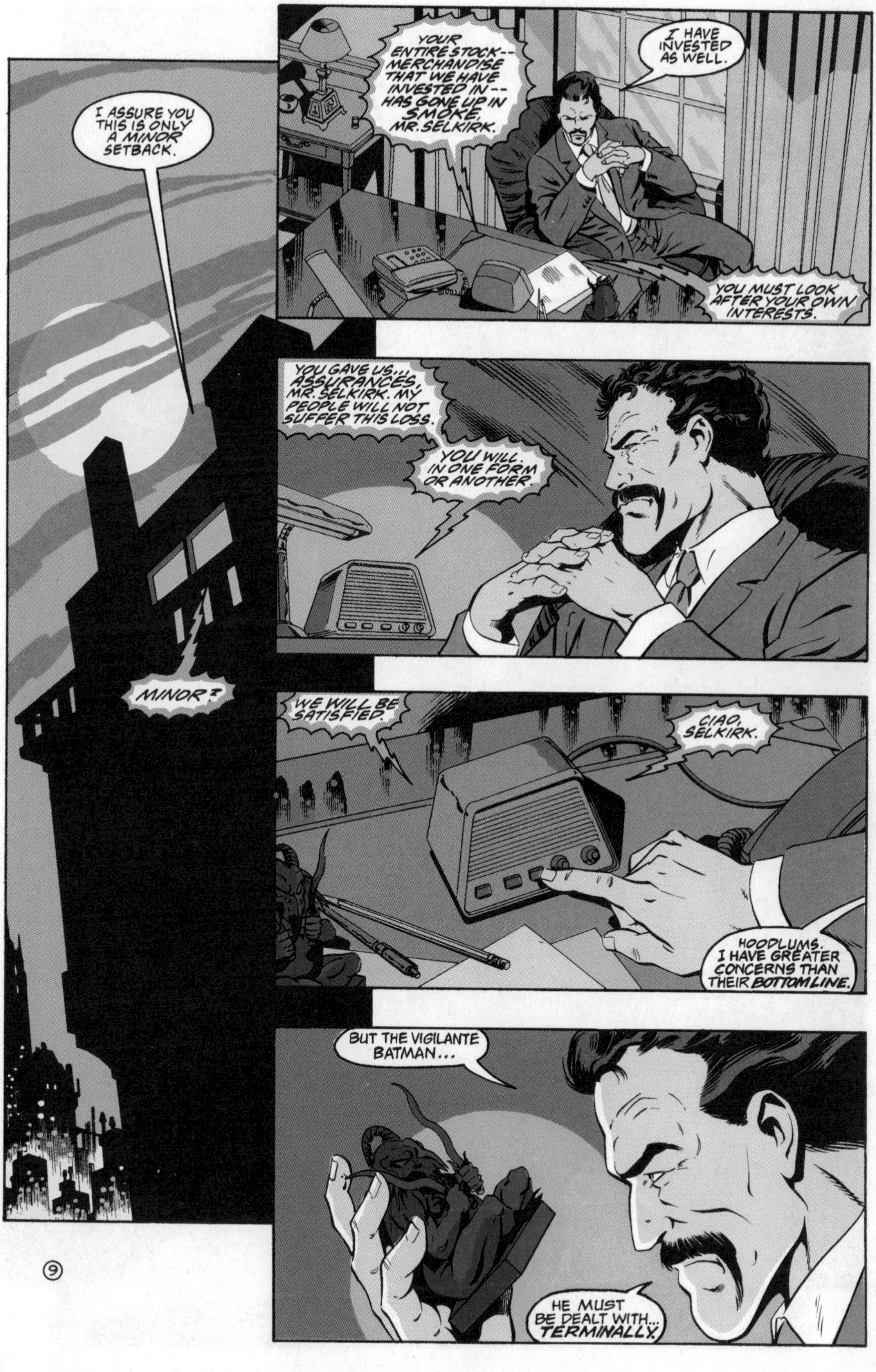
YOUR ENTIRE STOCK-- MERCHANDISE THAT WE HAVE INVESTED IN-- HAS GONE UP IN SMOKE, MR. SELKIRK.
I HAVE INVESTED AS WELL.
YOU MUST LOOK AFTER YOUR OWN INTERESTS.
I ASSURE YOU THIS IS ONLY A MINOR SETBACK.
MINOR?
YOU GAVE US... ASSURANCES, MR. SELKIRK. MY PEOPLE WILL NOT SUFFER THIS LOSS.
YOU WILL. IN ONE FORM OR ANOTHER.
WE WILL BE SATISFIED.
CIAO, SELKIRK.
HOODLUMS. I HAVE GREATER CONCERNS THAN THEIR BOTTOM LINE.
BUT THE VIGILANTE BATMAN...
HE MUST BE DEALT WITH... TERMINALLY.
9

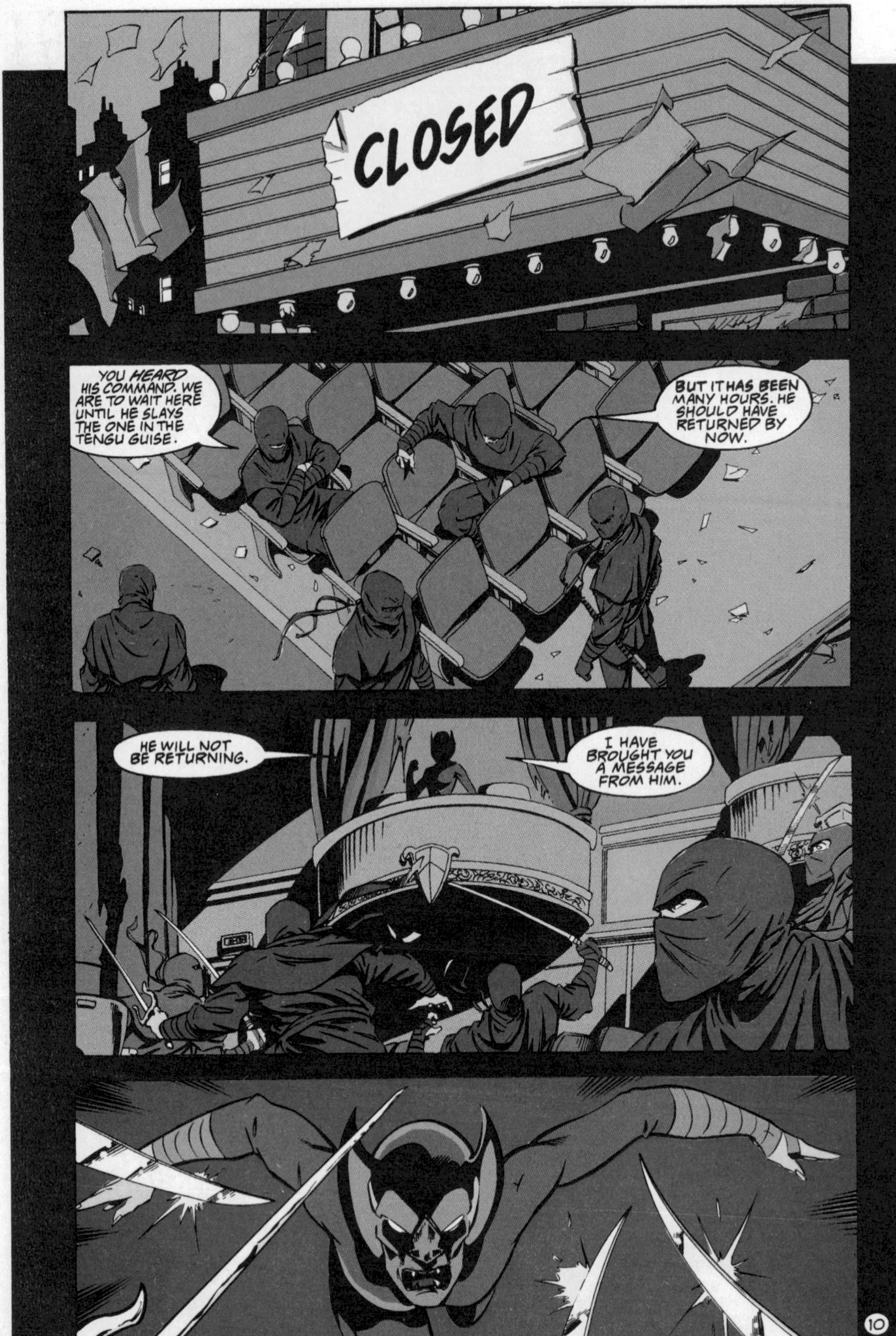
CLOSED
YOU HEARD HIS COMMAND. WE ARE TO WAIT HERE UNTIL HE SLAYS THE ONE IN THE TENGU GUISE.
BUT IT HAS BEEN MANY HOURS. HE SHOULD HAVE RETURNED BY NOW.
HE WILL NOT BE RETURNING.
I HAVE BROUGHT YOU A MESSAGE FROM HIM.
10

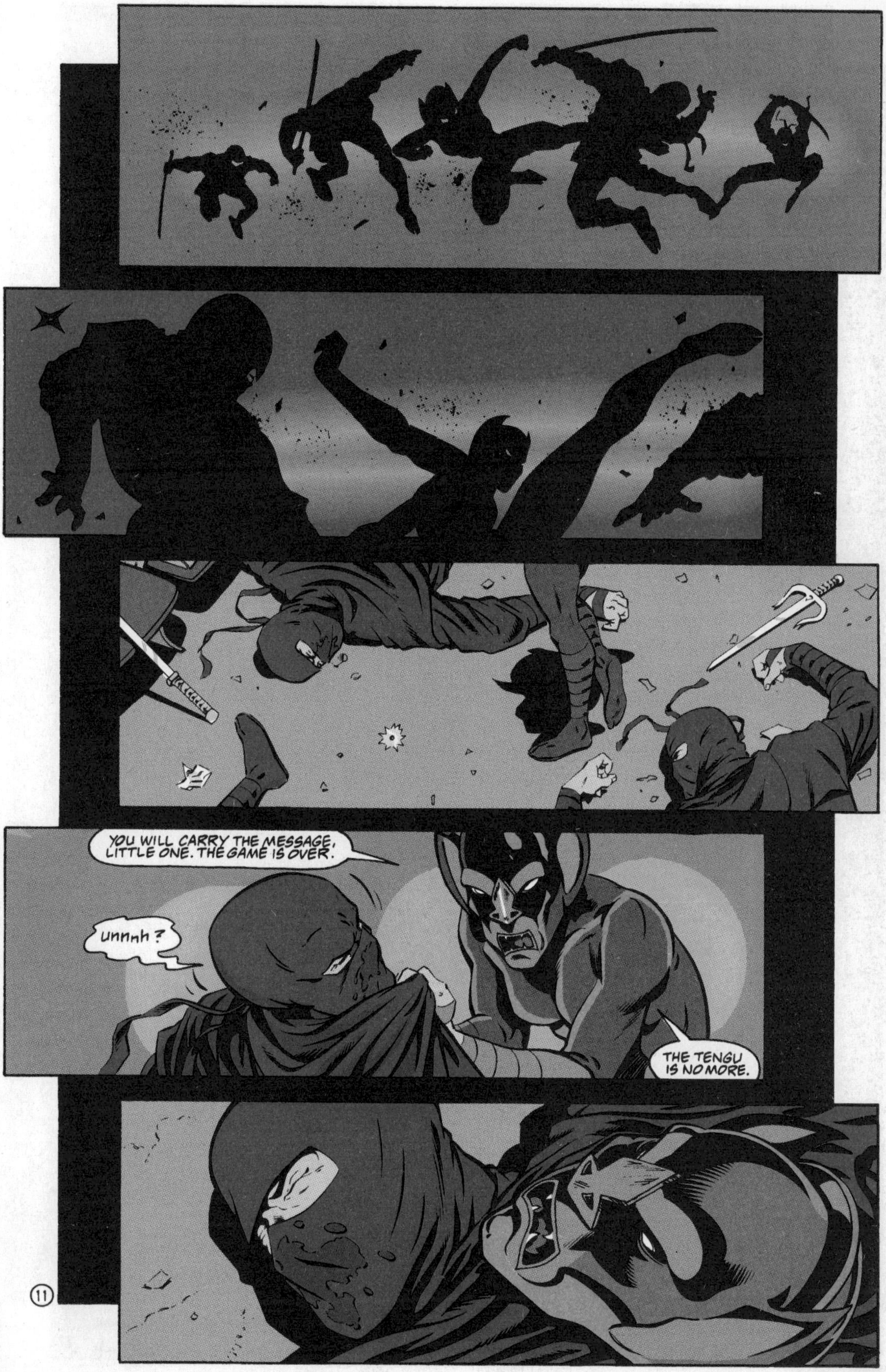
YOU WILL CARRY THE MESSAGE, LITTLE ONE. THE GAME IS OVER.
unnnh?
THE TENGU IS NO MORE.
11

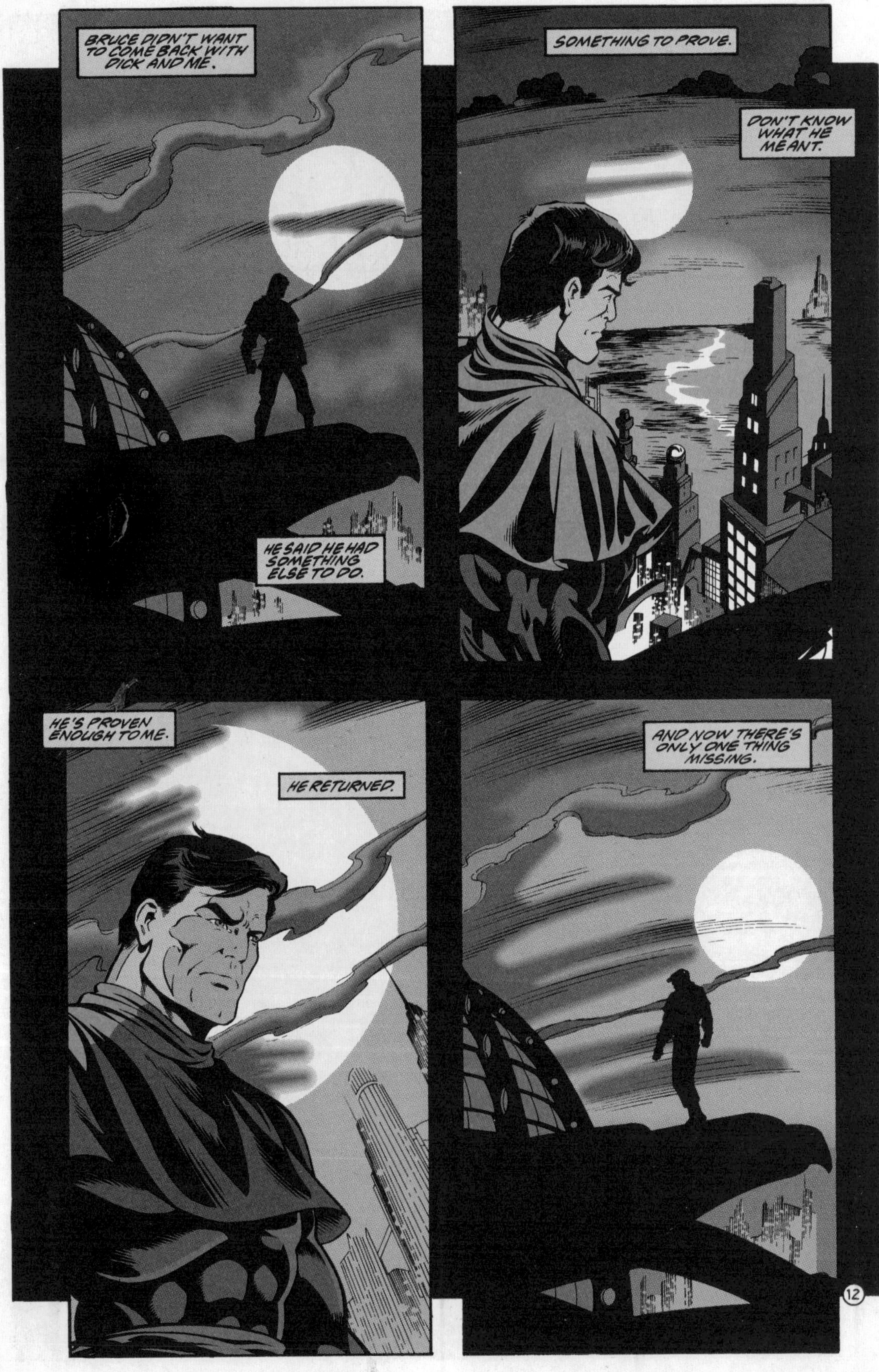
BRUCE DIDN'T WANT TO COME BACK WITH DICK AND ME.
HE SAID HE HAD SOMETHING ELSE TO DO.
SOMETHING TO PROVE.
DON'T KNOW WHAT HE MEANT.
HE'S PROVEN ENOUGH TO ME.
HE RETURNED.
AND NOW THERE'S ONLY ONE THING MISSING.
12

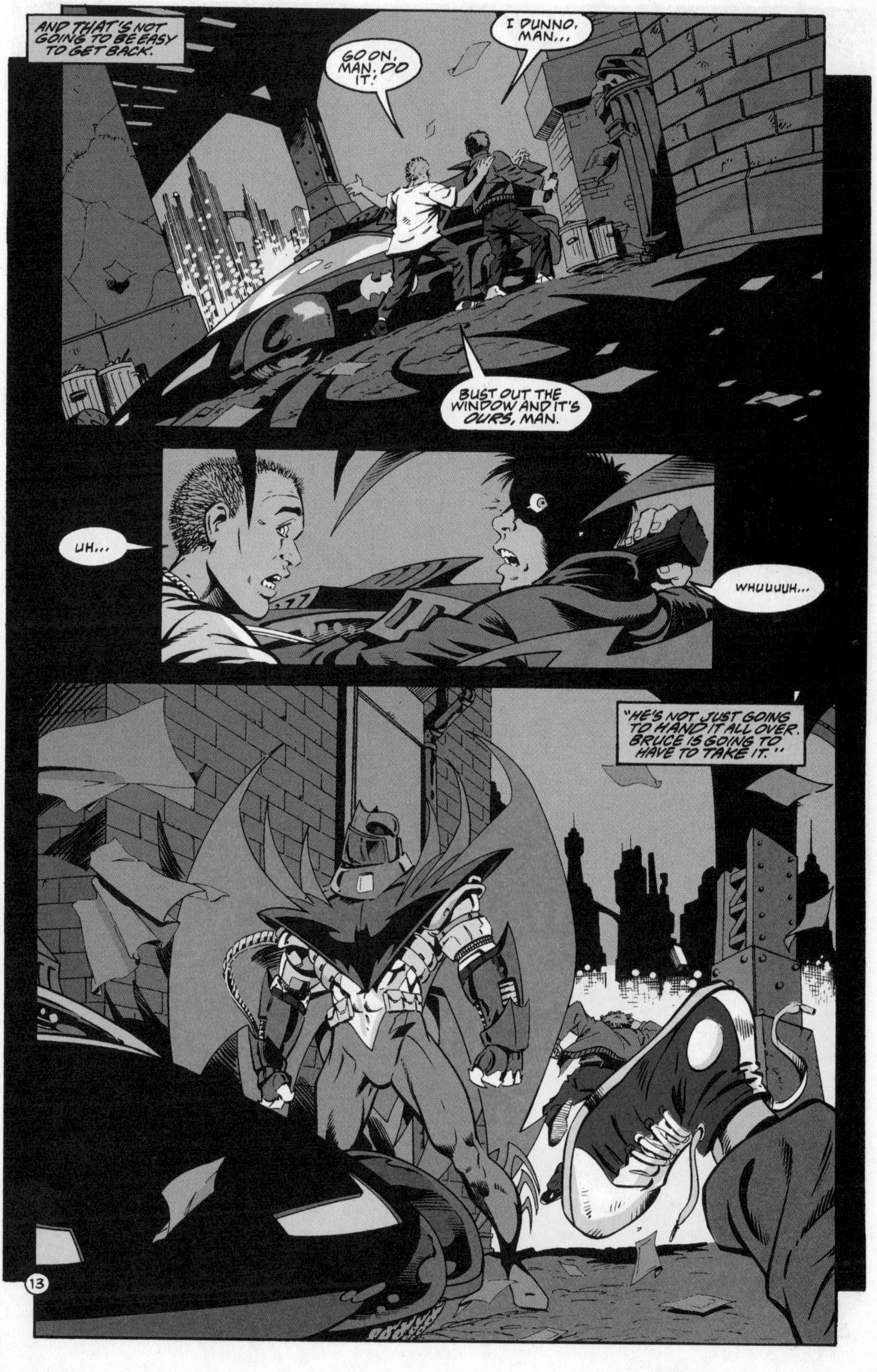
AND THAT'S NOT GOING TO BE EASY TO GET BACK.
GO ON, MAN. DO IT!
I DUNNO, MAN...
BUST OUT THE WINDOW AND IT'S OURS, MAN.
UH...
WHUUUUH...
"HE'S NOT JUST GOING TO HAND IT ALL OVER. BRUCE IS GOING TO HAVE TO TAKE IT."
13

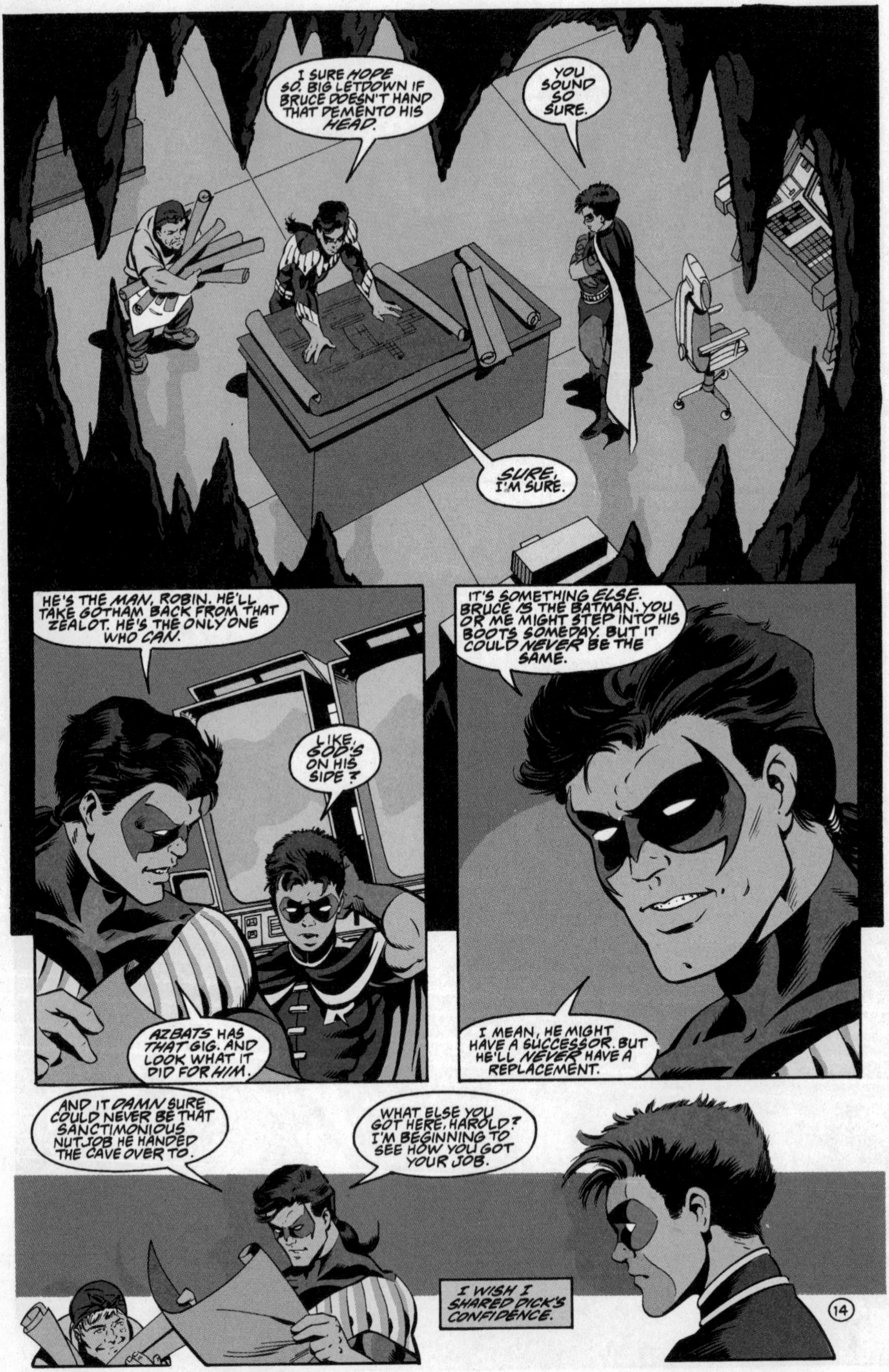
I SURE HOPE SO. BIG LETDOWN IF BRUCE DOESN'T HAND THAT DEMENTO HIS HEAD.
YOU SOUND SO SURE.
SURE, I'M SURE.
HE'S THE MAN, ROBIN. HE'LL TAKE GOTHAM BACK FROM THAT ZEALOT. HE'S THE ONLY ONE WHO CAN.
LIKE, GOD'S ON HIS SIDE?
AZBATS HAS THAT GIG. AND LOOK WHAT IT DID FOR HIM.
IT'S SOMETHING ELSE. BRUCE IS THE BATMAN. YOU OR ME MIGHT STEP INTO HIS BOOTS SOMEDAY. BUT IT COULD NEVER BE THE SAME.
I MEAN, HE MIGHT HAVE A SUCCESSOR. BUT HE'LL NEVER HAVE A REPLACEMENT.
AND IT DAMN SURE COULD NEVER BE THAT SANCTIMONIOUS NUTJOB HE HANDED THE CAVE OVER TO.
WHAT ELSE YOU GOT HERE, HAROLD? I'M BEGINNING TO SEE HOW YOU GOT YOUR JOB.
I WISH I SHARED DICK'S CONFIDENCE.
14

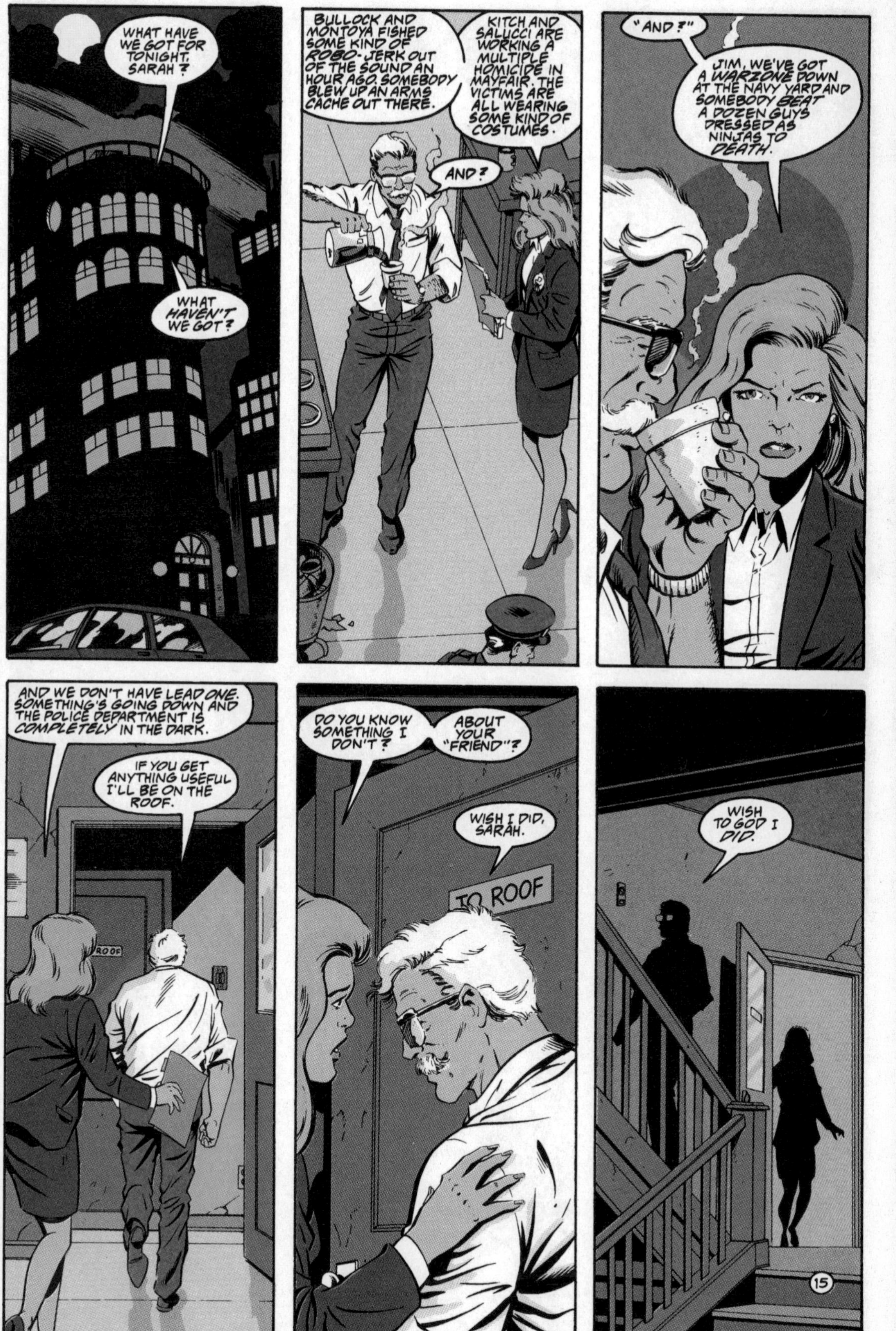
WHAT HAVE WE GOT FOR TONIGHT, SARAH?
WHAT HAVEN'T WE GOT?
BULLOCK AND MONTOYA FISHED SOME KIND OF ROBO-JERK OUT OF THE SOUND AN HOUR AGO. SOMEBODY BLEW UP AN ARMS CACHE OUT THERE.
KITCH AND SALUCCI ARE WORKING A MULTIPLE HOMICIDE IN MAYFAIR. THE VICTIMS ARE ALL WEARING SOME KIND OF COSTUMES.
AND?
"AND?"
JIM, WE'VE GOT A WARZONE DOWN AT THE NAVY YARD AND SOMEBODY BEAT A DOZEN GUYS DRESSED AS NINJAS TO DEATH.
AND WE DON'T HAVE LEAD ONE. SOMETHING'S GOING DOWN AND THE POLICE DEPARTMENT IS COMPLETELY IN THE DARK.
IF YOU GET ANYTHING USEFUL I'LL BE ON THE ROOF.
ROOF
DO YOU KNOW SOMETHING I DON'T?
ABOUT YOUR "FRIEND"?
WISH I DID, SARAH.
TO ROOF
WISH TO GOD I DID.
15

RRRING!

I CAN GET THAT, MRS. MCILVAINE.

DAD?

TIM, DO YOU KNOW WHAT TIME IT IS?

SORRY. ME AND SOME OF THE GUYS DECIDED TO STAY FOR ANOTHER MOVIE. I WON'T BE LONG. I HAVE TO WAIT FOR A RIDE.

I WANT YOU BACK HERE AS SOON AS POSSIBLE. WE'LL SEE ABOUT A CAR FOR YOU TOMORROW AND THEN THERE'LL BE NO MORE EXCUSES.

OKAY, DAD. I'M SORRY.

JUST SO IT DOESN'T HAPPEN AGAIN.

THIS IS THE ONLY DOWNSIDE TO BEING ROBIN. I HAVE TO LIE TO MY DAD.

I HATE IT.

WELL, LOOK AT THE BRIGHT SIDE...

...YOU HAVE SOMEONE TO LIE TO.

LET'S GET TO WORK.

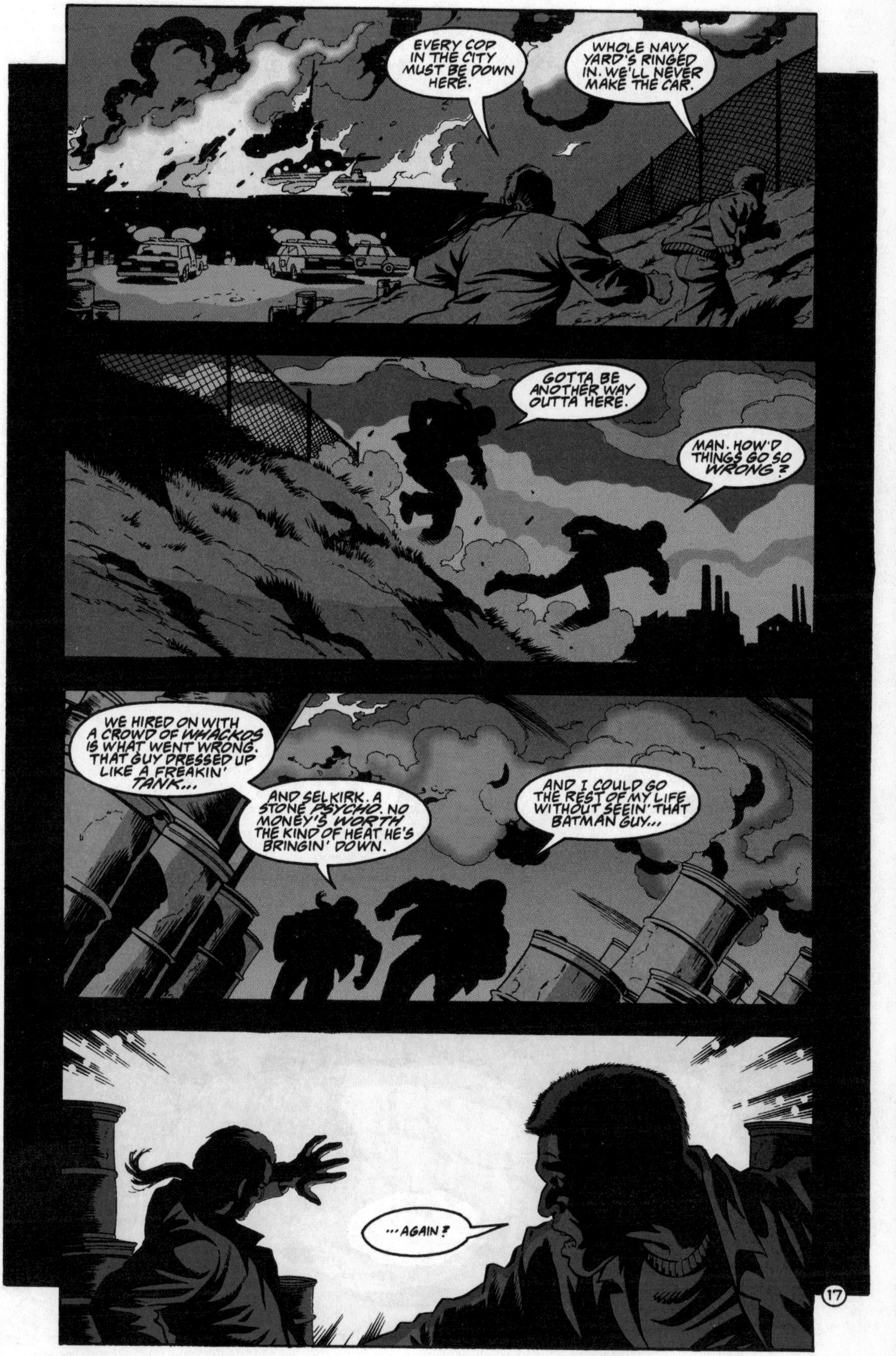
EVERY COP IN THE CITY MUST BE DOWN HERE.
WHOLE NAVY YARD'S RINGED IN. WE'LL NEVER MAKE THE CAR.
GOTTA BE ANOTHER WAY OUTTA HERE.
MAN. HOW'D THINGS GO SO WRONG?
WE HIRED ON WITH A CROWD OF WHACKOS IS WHAT WENT WRONG. THAT GUY DRESSED UP LIKE A FREAKIN' TANK...
AND SELKIRK. A STONE PSYCHO. NO MONEY'S WORTH THE KIND OF HEAT HE'S BRINGIN' DOWN.
AND I COULD GO THE REST OF MY LIFE WITHOUT SEEIN' THAT BATMAN GUY...
...AGAIN?
17

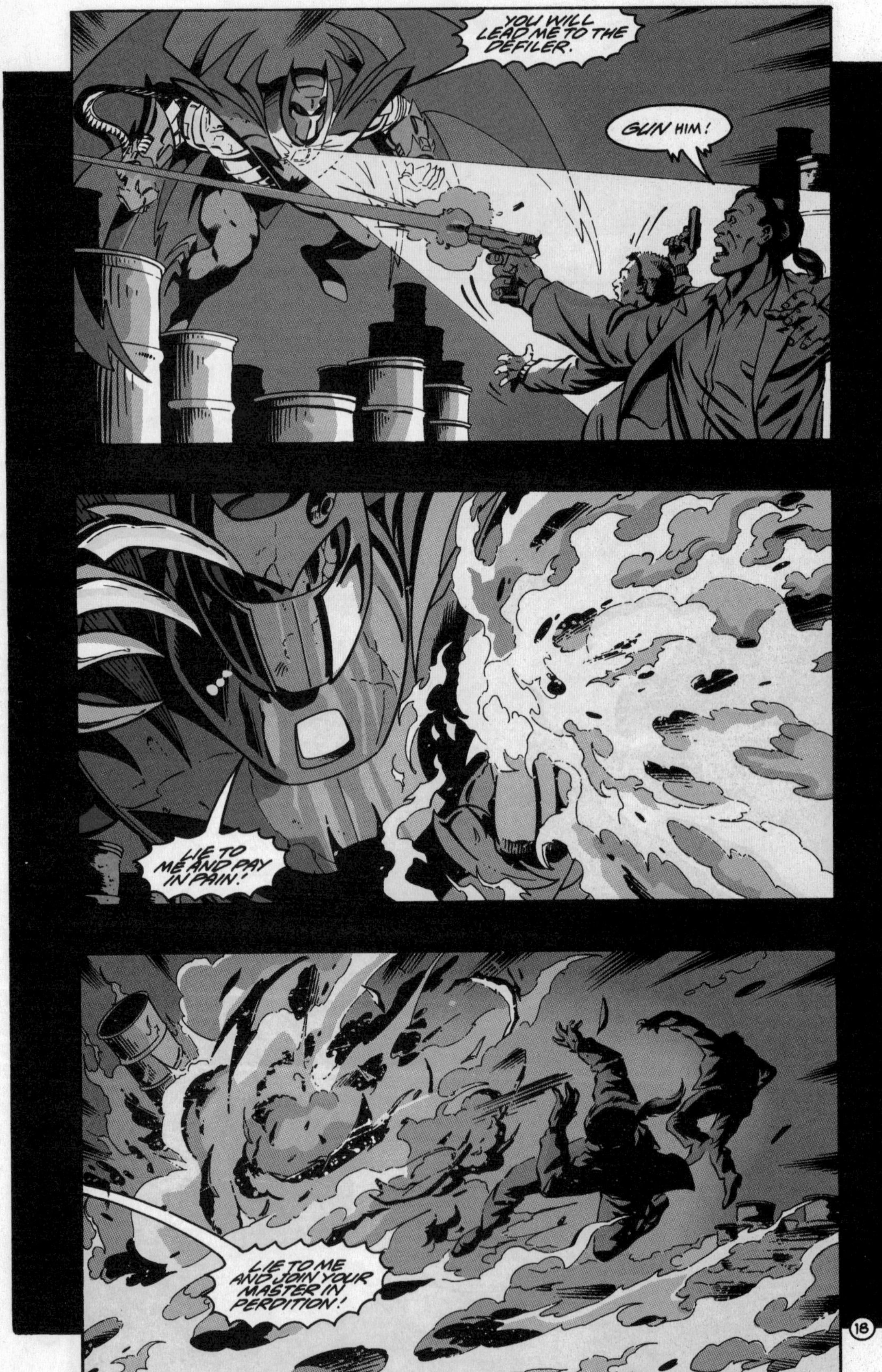
YOU WILL LEAD ME TO THE DEFILER.
GUN HIM!
LIE TO ME AND PAY IN PAIN!
LIE TO ME AND JOIN YOUR MASTER IN PERDITION!
18

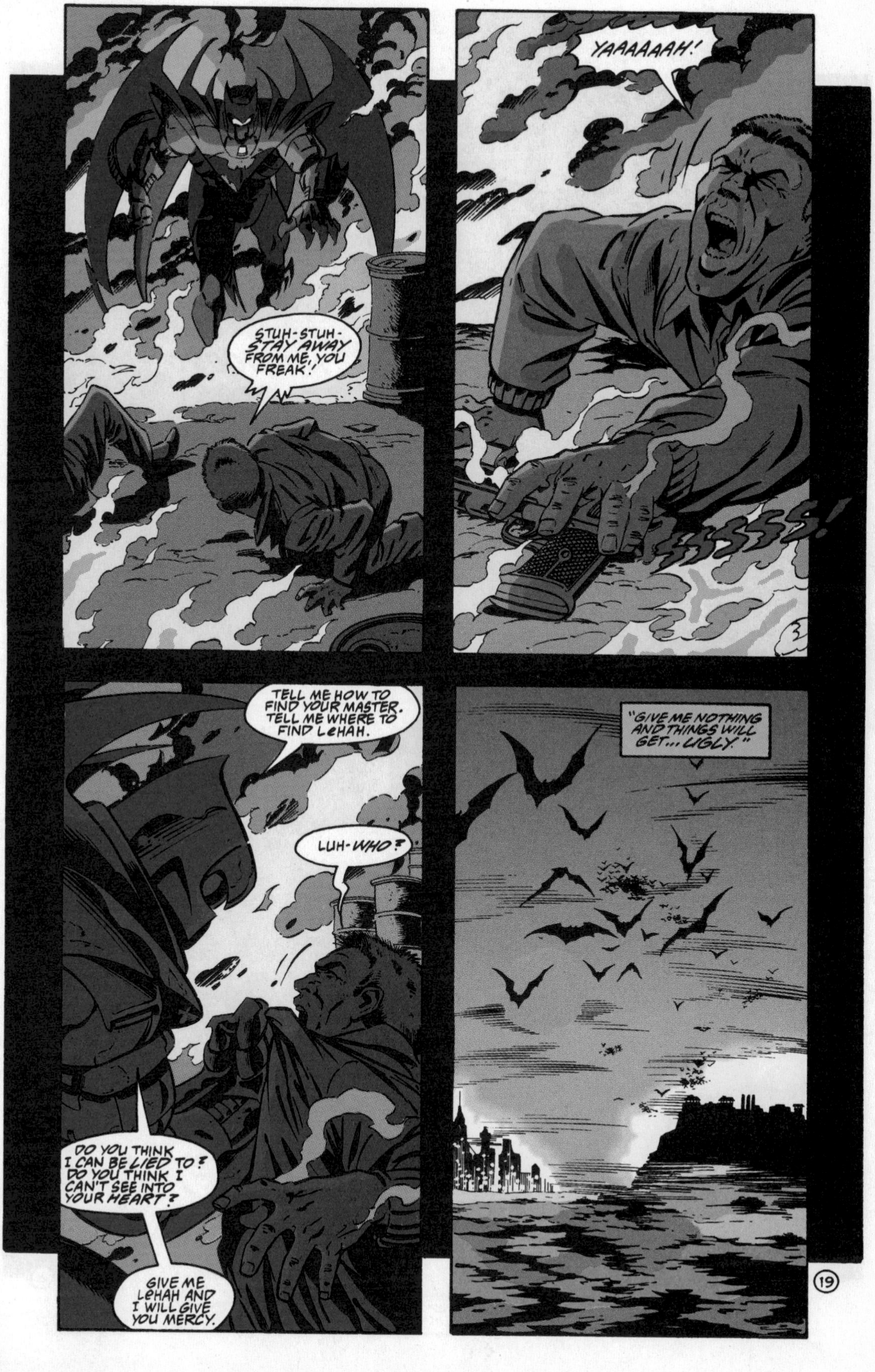
STUH-STUH-STAY AWAY FROM ME, YOU FREAK!
YAAAAAAH!
SSSSSS!
TELL ME HOW TO FIND YOUR MASTER. TELL ME WHERE TO FIND LEHAH.
LUH-WHO?
DO YOU THINK I CAN BE LIED TO? DO YOU THINK I CAN'T SEE INTO YOUR HEART?
GIVE ME LEHAH AND I WILL GIVE YOU MERCY.
"GIVE ME NOTHING AND THINGS WILL GET... UGLY."
19

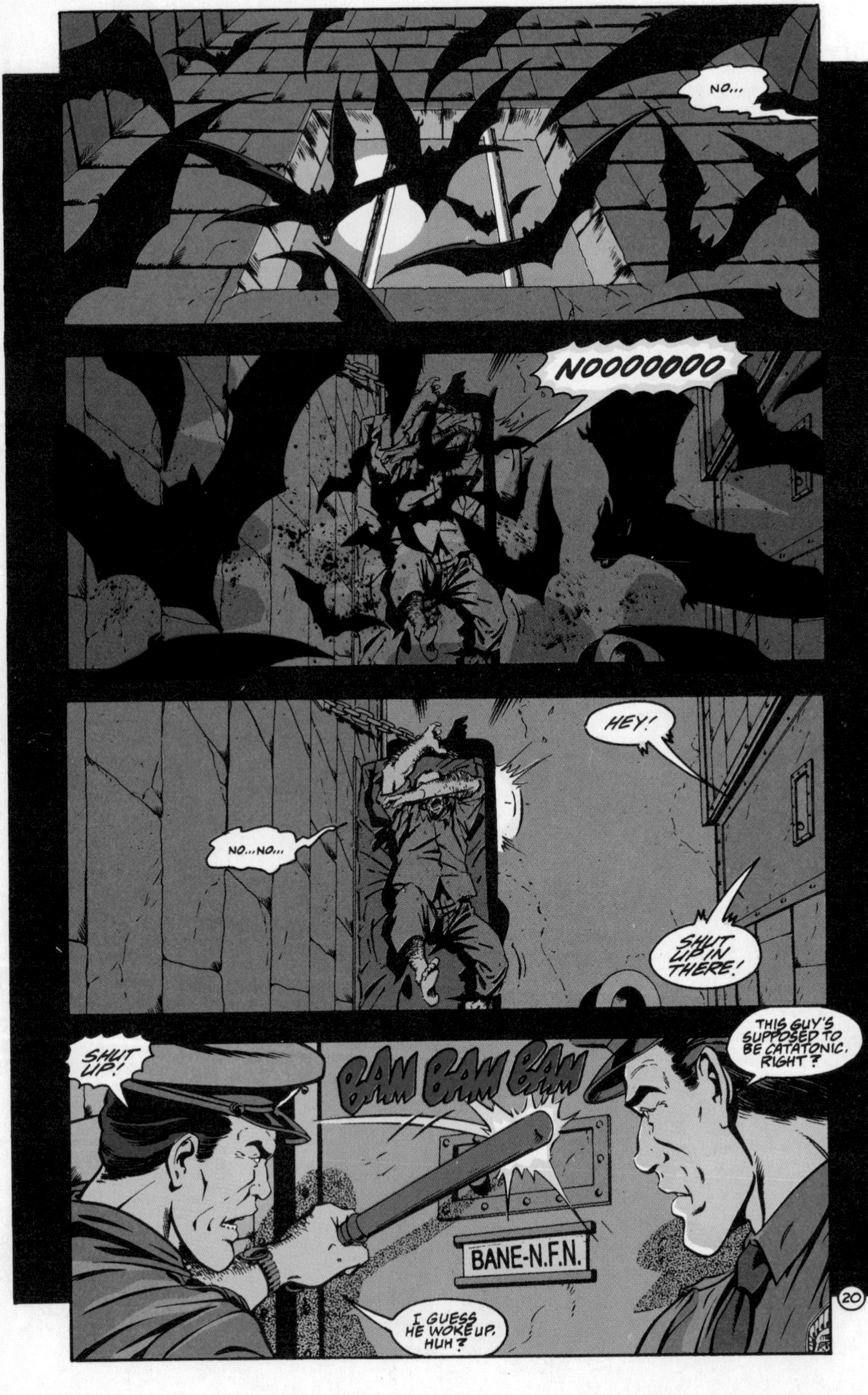
NO...
NOOOOOOO
HEY!
NO...NO...
SHUT UP IN THERE!
SHUT UP!
BAM BAM BAM
THIS GUY'S SUPPOSED TO BE CATATONIC, RIGHT?
BANE-N.F.N.
I GUESS HE WOKE UP, HUH?
20

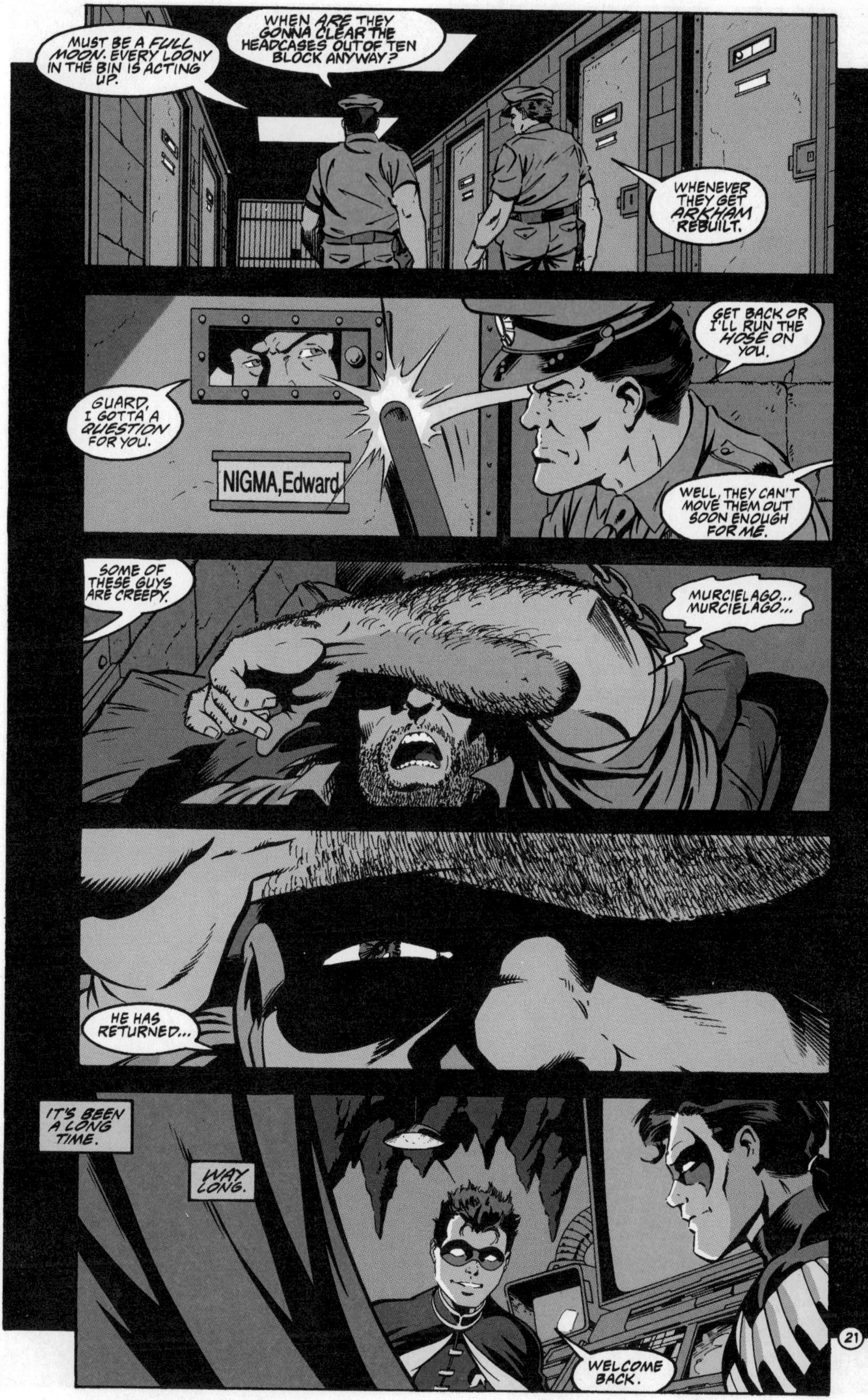
MUST BE A FULL MOON. EVERY LOONY IN THE BIN IS ACTING UP.
WHEN ARE THEY GONNA CLEAR THE HEADCASES OUT OF TEN BLOCK ANYWAY?
WHENEVER THEY GET ARKHAM REBUILT.
GUARD, I GOTTA' A QUESTION FOR YOU.
NIGMA, Edward
GET BACK OR I'LL RUN THE HOSE ON YOU.
WELL, THEY CAN'T MOVE THEM OUT SOON ENOUGH FOR ME.
SOME OF THESE GUYS ARE CREEPY.
MURCIELAGO... MURCIELAGO...
HE HAS RETURNED...
IT'S BEEN A LONG TIME.
WAY LONG.
WELCOME BACK.
21

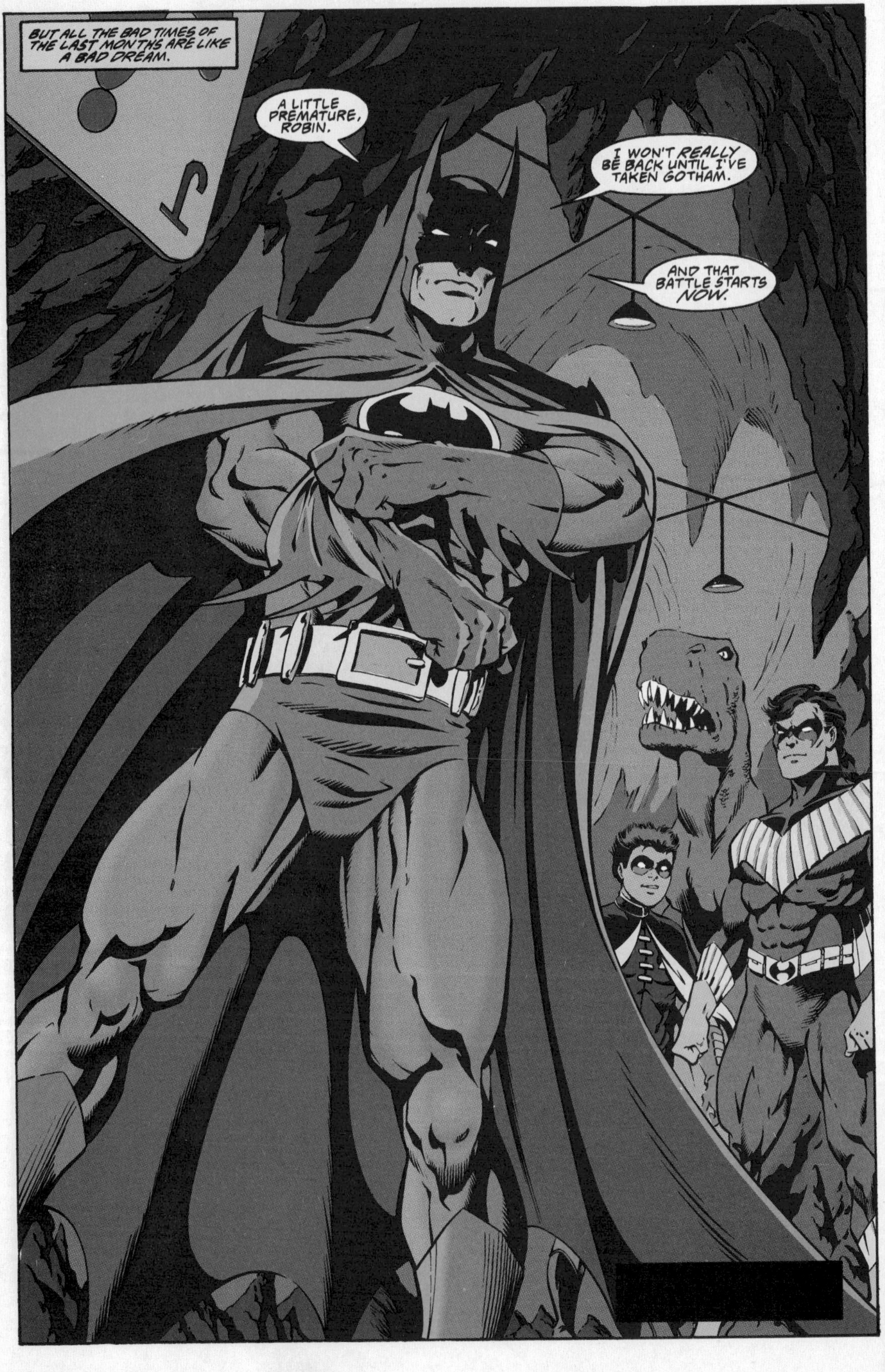
BUT ALL THE BAD TIMES OF THE LAST MONTHS ARE LIKE A BAD DREAM.
A LITTLE PREMATURE, ROBIN.
I WON'T REALLY BE BACK UNTIL I'VE TAKEN GOTHAM.
AND THAT BATTLE STARTS NOW.
[redacted]

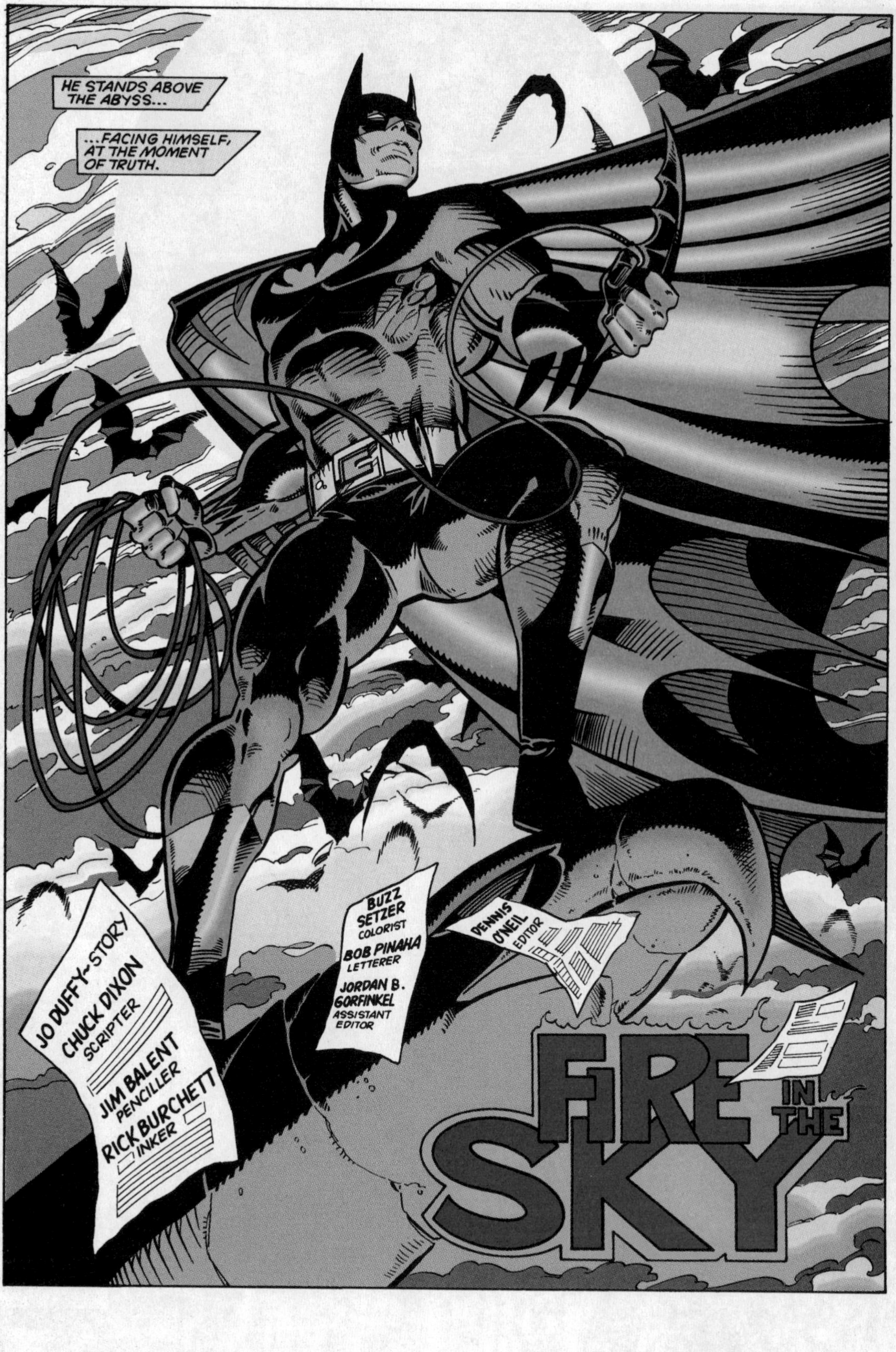

HE STANDS ABOVE THE ABYSS...
...FACING HIMSELF, AT THE MOMENT OF TRUTH.
JO DUFFY-STORY
CHUCK DIXON SCRIPTER
JIM BALENT PENCILLER
RICK BURCHETT INKER
BUZZ SETZER COLORIST
BOB PINAHA LETTERER
JORDAN B. GORFINKEL ASSISTANT EDITOR
DENNIS O'NEIL EDITOR
FIRE IN THE SKY

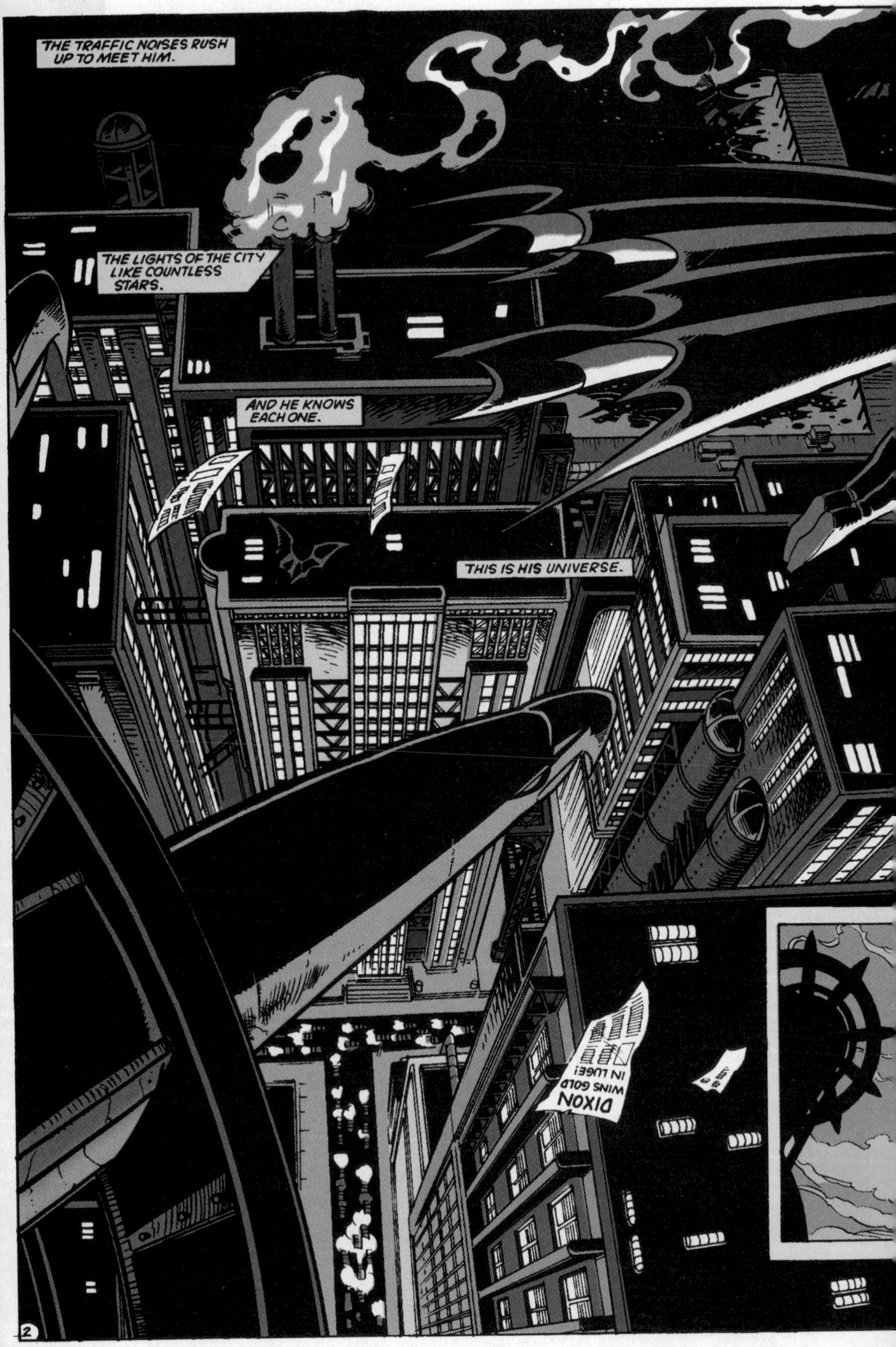
THE TRAFFIC NOISES RUSH UP TO MEET HIM.
THE LIGHTS OF THE CITY LIKE COUNTLESS STARS.
AND HE KNOWS EACH ONE.
THIS IS HIS UNIVERSE.
DIXON WINS GOLD IN LUGE!

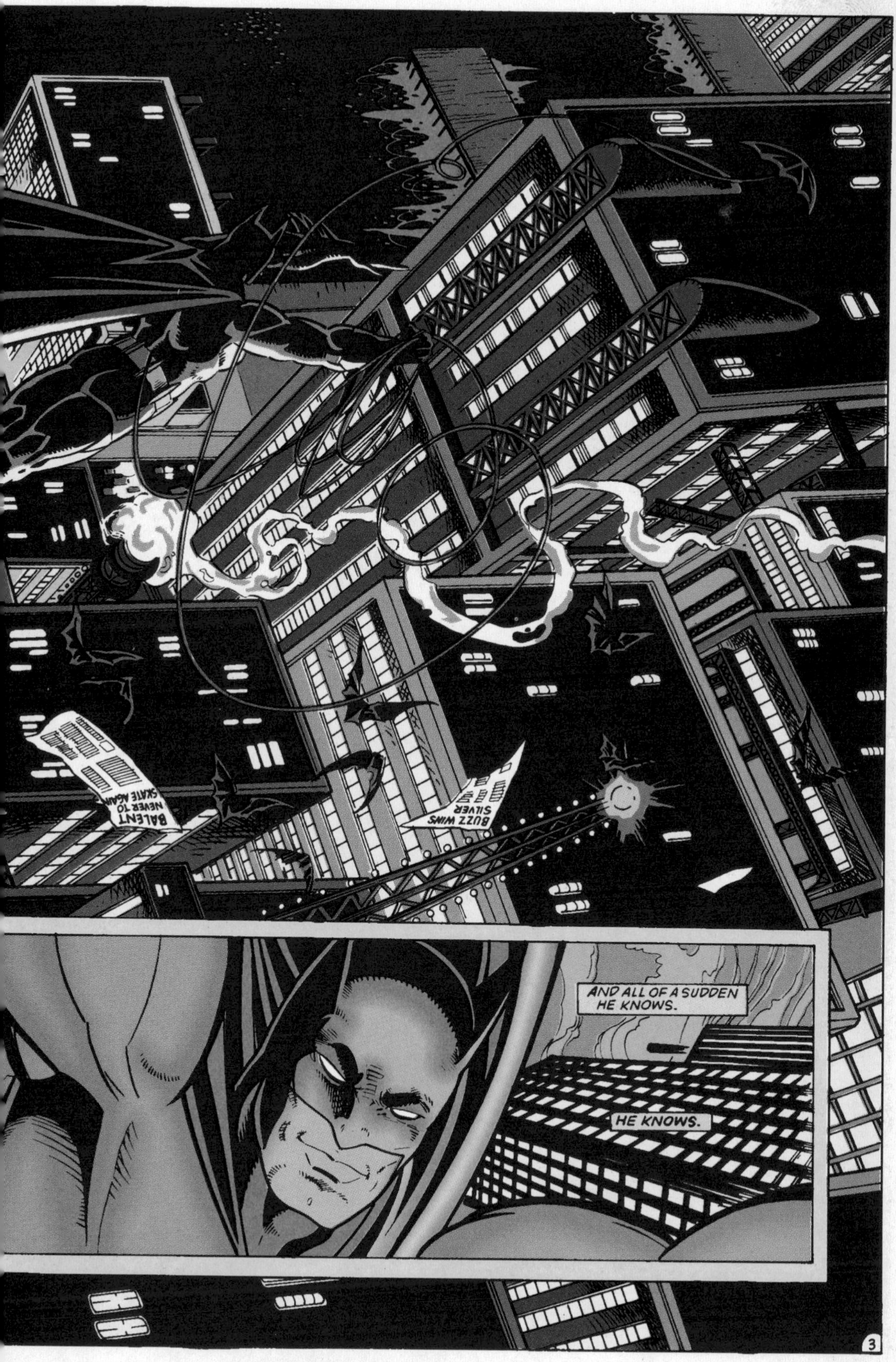
BALENT NEVER TO SKATE AGAIN
BUZZ WINS SILVER
AND ALL OF A SUDDEN HE KNOWS.
HE KNOWS.
3

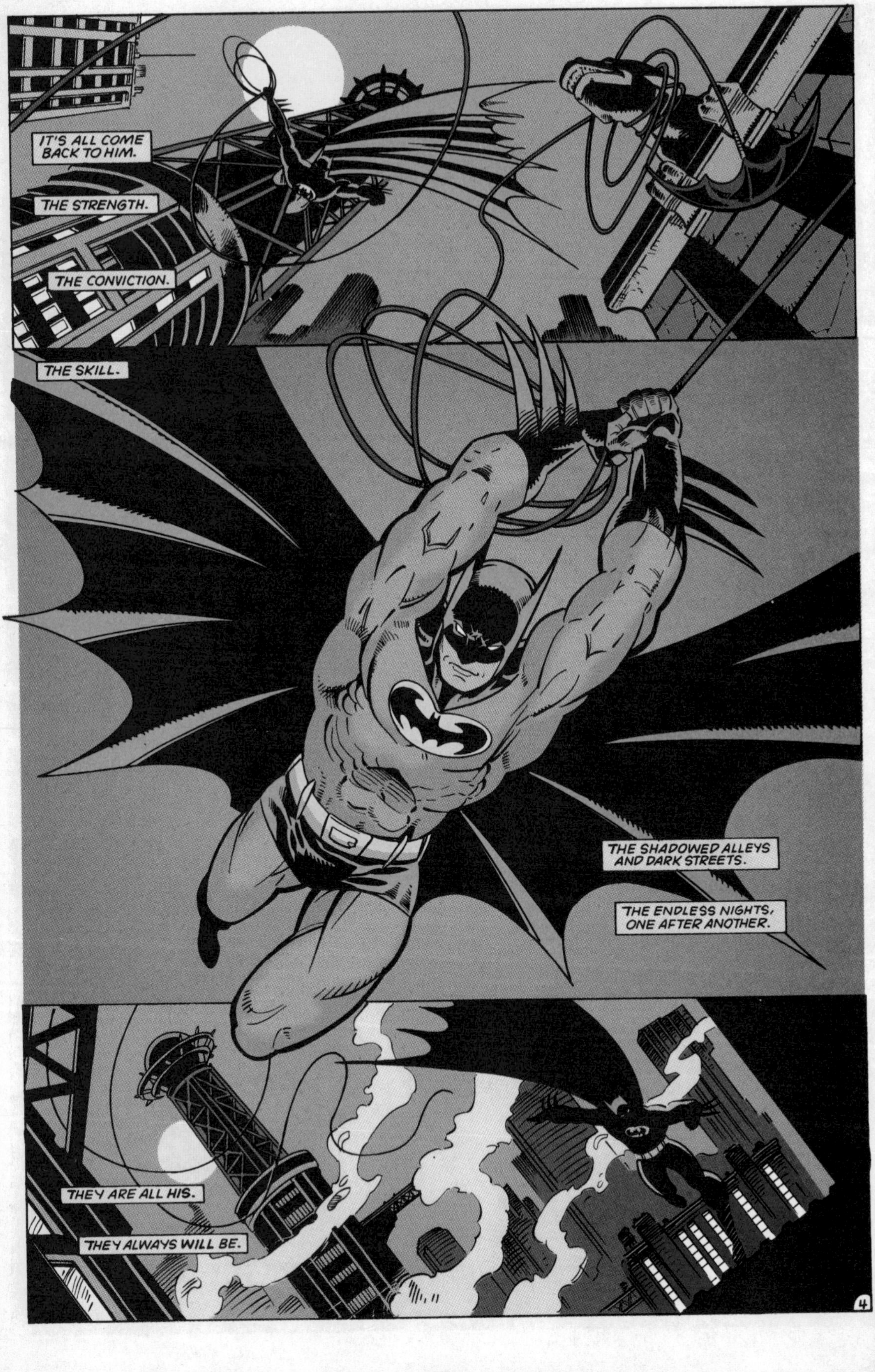
IT'S ALL COME BACK TO HIM.
THE STRENGTH.
THE CONVICTION.
THE SKILL.
THE SHADOWED ALLEYS AND DARK STREETS.
THE ENDLESS NIGHTS, ONE AFTER ANOTHER.
THEY ARE ALL HIS.
THEY ALWAYS WILL BE.
4

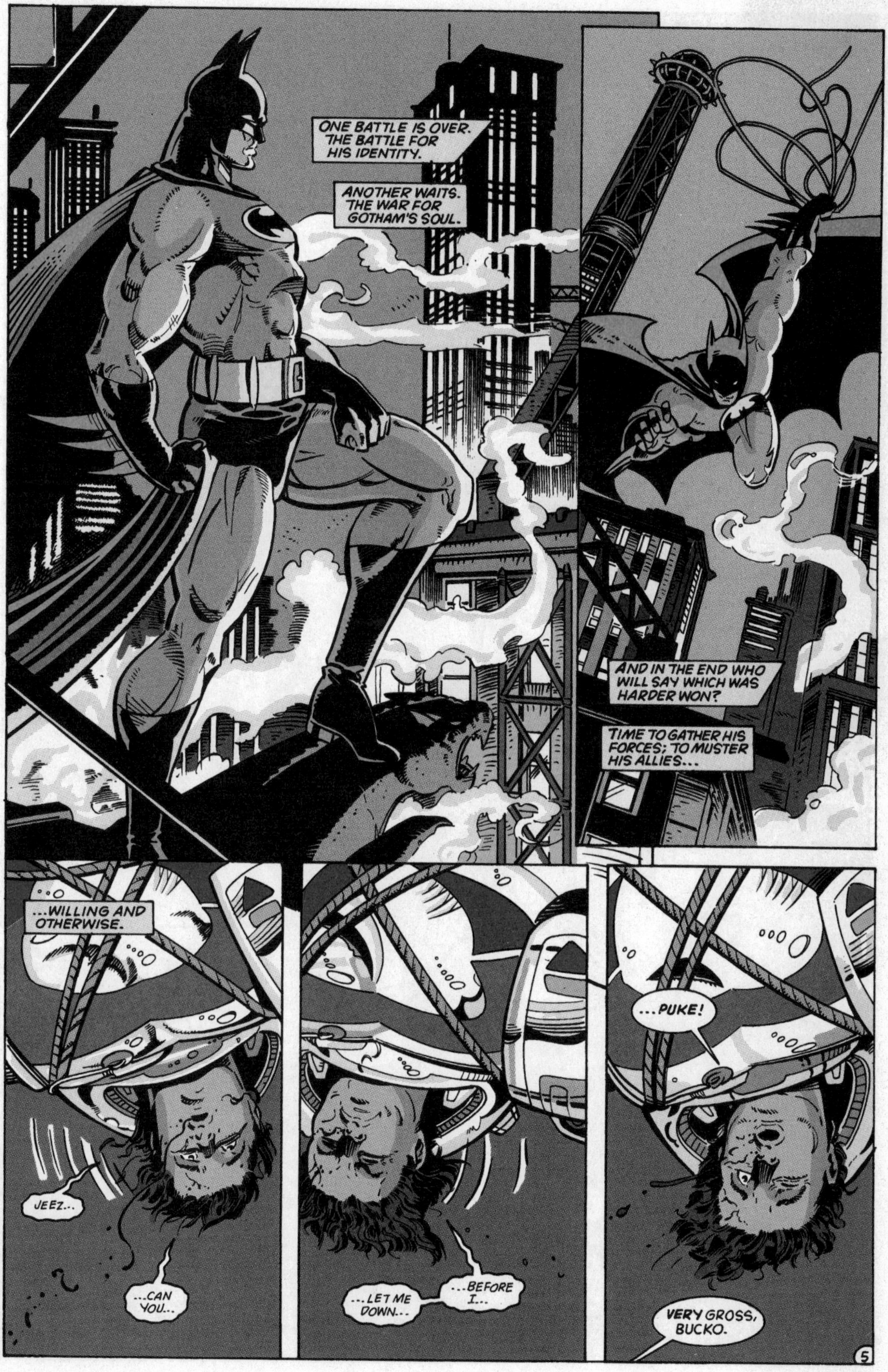
ONE BATTLE IS OVER. THE BATTLE FOR HIS IDENTITY.
ANOTHER WAITS. THE WAR FOR GOTHAM'S SOUL.
AND IN THE END WHO WILL SAY WHICH WAS HARDER WON?
TIME TO GATHER HIS FORCES; TO MUSTER HIS ALLIES...
...WILLING AND OTHERWISE.
JEEZ...
...CAN YOU...
...LET ME DOWN...
...BEFORE I...
...PUKE!
VERY GROSS, BUCKO.
5

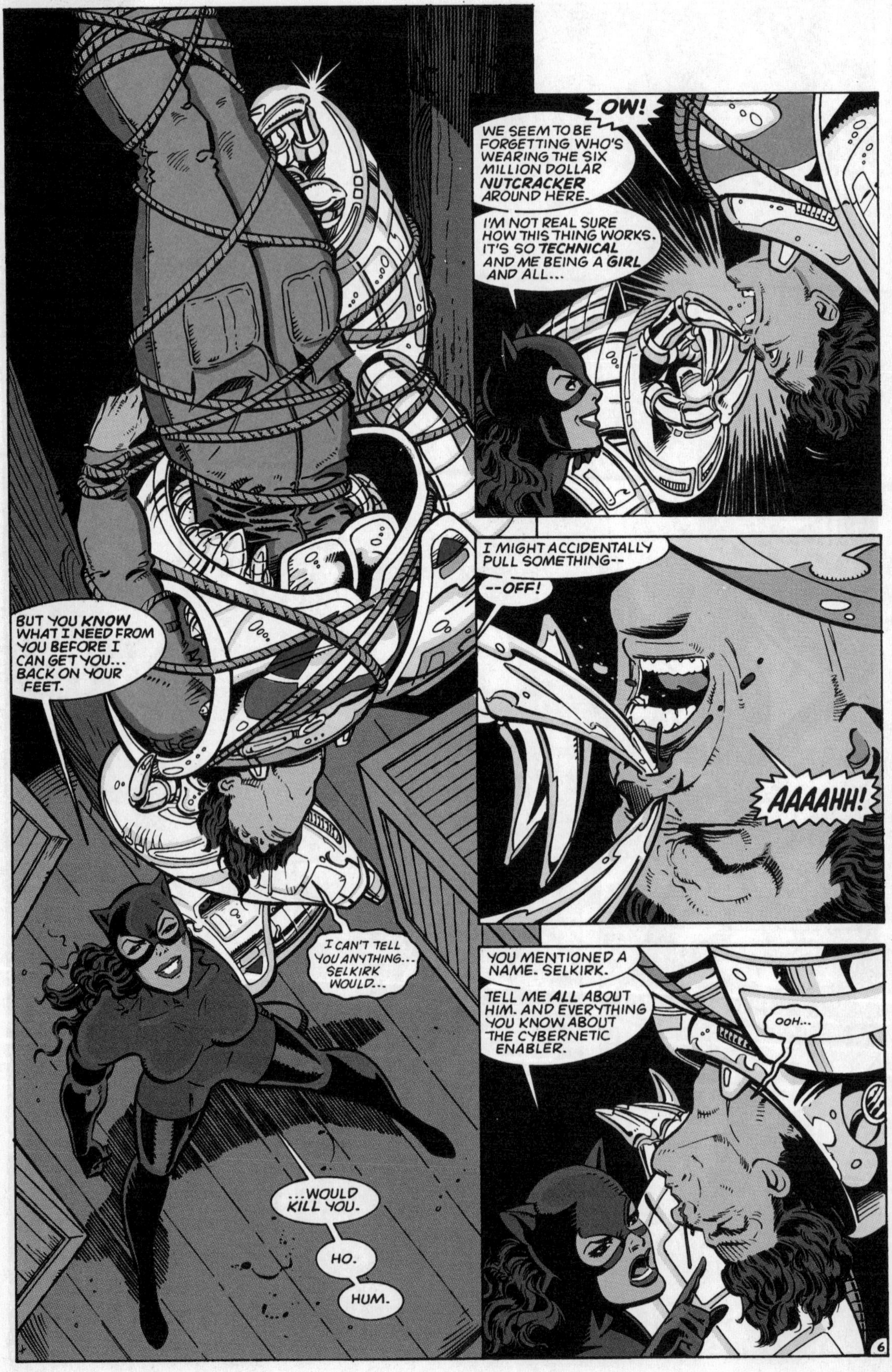
BUT YOU KNOW WHAT I NEED FROM YOU BEFORE I CAN GET YOU... BACK ON YOUR FEET.
I CAN'T TELL YOU ANYTHING... SELKIRK WOULD...
...WOULD KILL YOU.
HO.
HUM.
OW!
WE SEEM TO BE FORGETTING WHO'S WEARING THE SIX MILLION DOLLAR NUTCRACKER AROUND HERE.
I'M NOT REAL SURE HOW THIS THING WORKS. IT'S SO TECHNICAL AND ME BEING A GIRL AND ALL...
I MIGHT ACCIDENTALLY PULL SOMETHING--
--OFF!
AAAAHH!
YOU MENTIONED A NAME. SELKIRK.
TELL ME ALL ABOUT HIM. AND EVERYTHING YOU KNOW ABOUT THE CYBERNETIC ENABLER.
OOH...

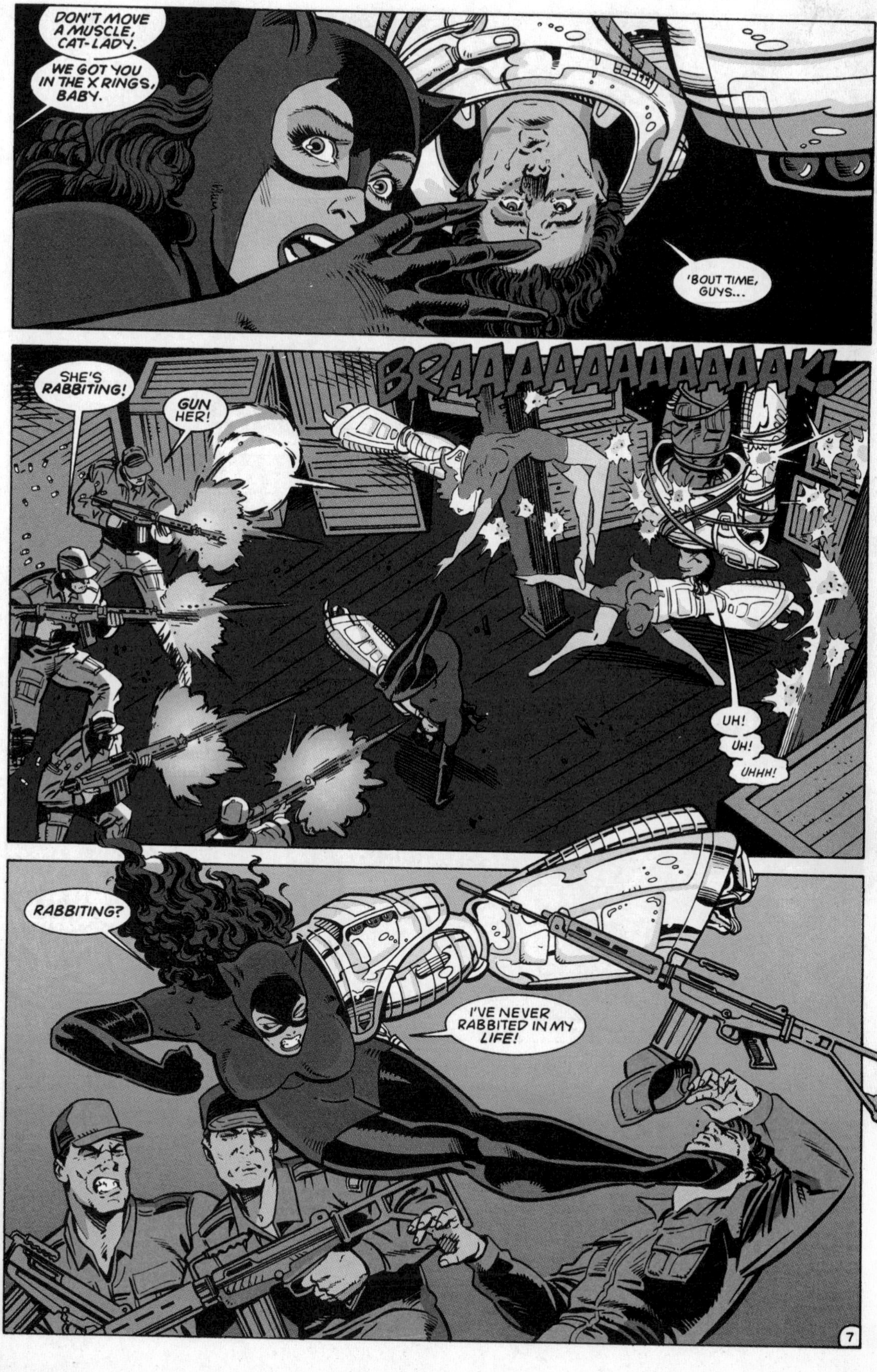
DON'T MOVE A MUSCLE, CAT-LADY.
WE GOT YOU IN THE X RINGS, BABY.
'BOUT TIME, GUYS...
BRAAAAAAAAAAAK!
SHE'S RABBITING!
GUN HER!
UH! UH! UHHH!
RABBITING?
I'VE NEVER RABBITED IN MY LIFE!
7

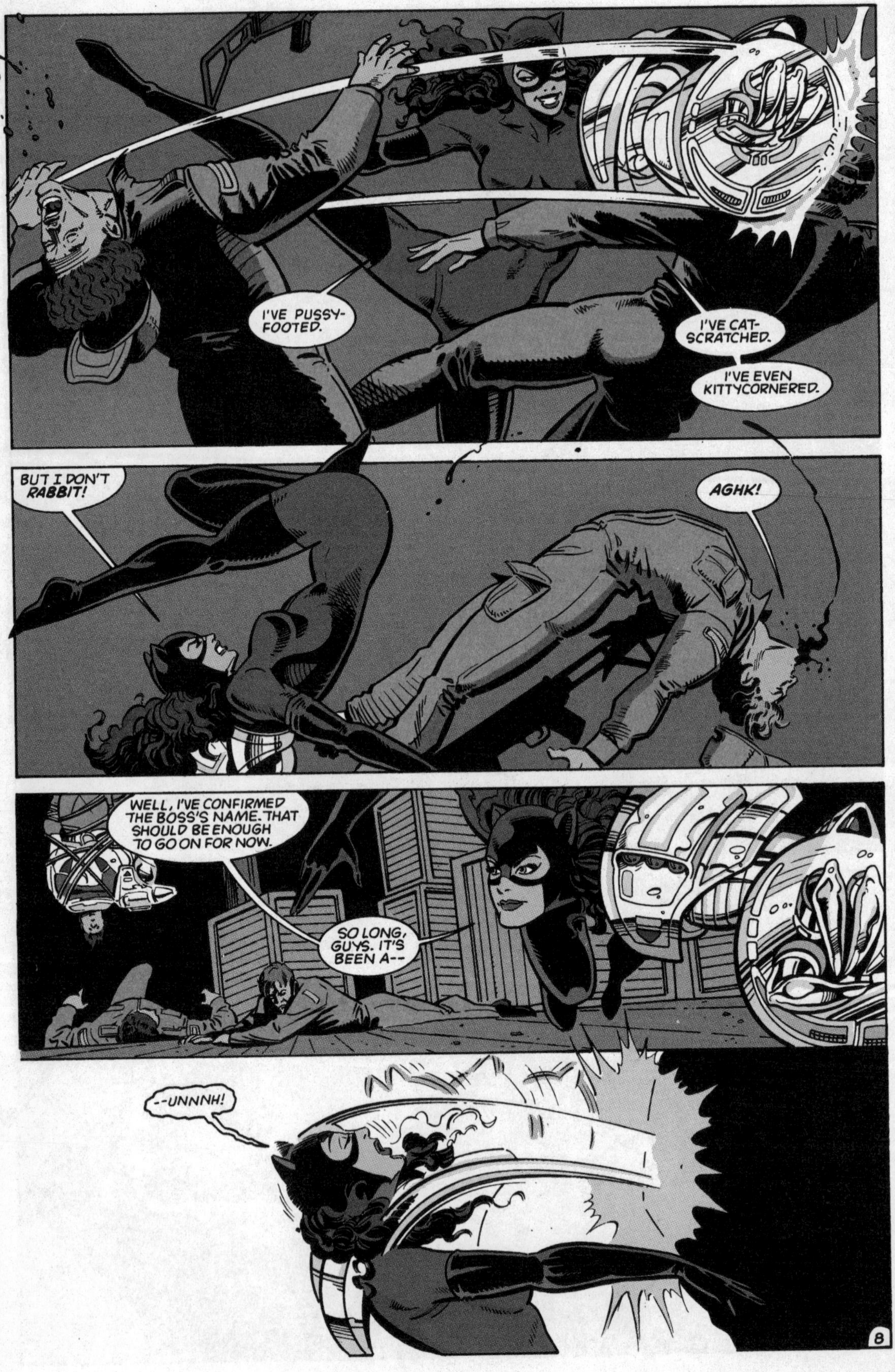
I'VE PUSSY-FOOTED.
I'VE CAT-SCRATCHED.
I'VE EVEN KITTYCORNERED.
BUT I DON'T RABBIT!
AGHK!
WELL, I'VE CONFIRMED THE BOSS'S NAME. THAT SHOULD BE ENOUGH TO GO ON FOR NOW.
SO LONG, GUYS. IT'S BEEN A--
--UNNNH!
8

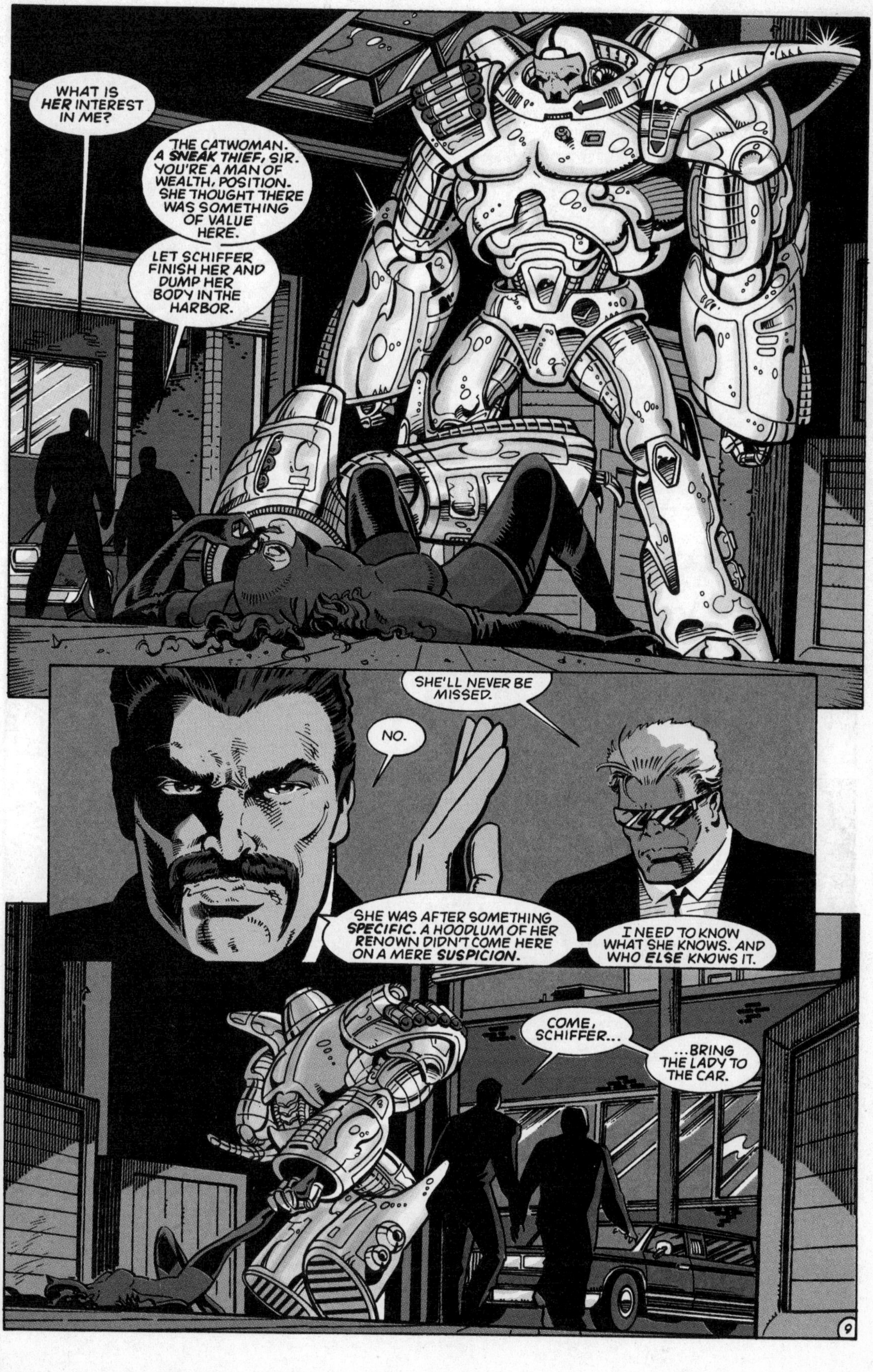
WHAT IS HER INTEREST IN ME?
THE CATWOMAN. A SNEAK THIEF, SIR. YOU'RE A MAN OF WEALTH, POSITION. SHE THOUGHT THERE WAS SOMETHING OF VALUE HERE.
LET SCHIFFER FINISH HER AND DUMP HER BODY IN THE HARBOR.
SHE'LL NEVER BE MISSED.
NO.
SHE WAS AFTER SOMETHING SPECIFIC. A HOODLUM OF HER RENOWN DIDN'T COME HERE ON A MERE SUSPICION.
I NEED TO KNOW WHAT SHE KNOWS. AND WHO ELSE KNOWS IT.
COME, SCHIFFER...
...BRING THE LADY TO THE CAR.
9

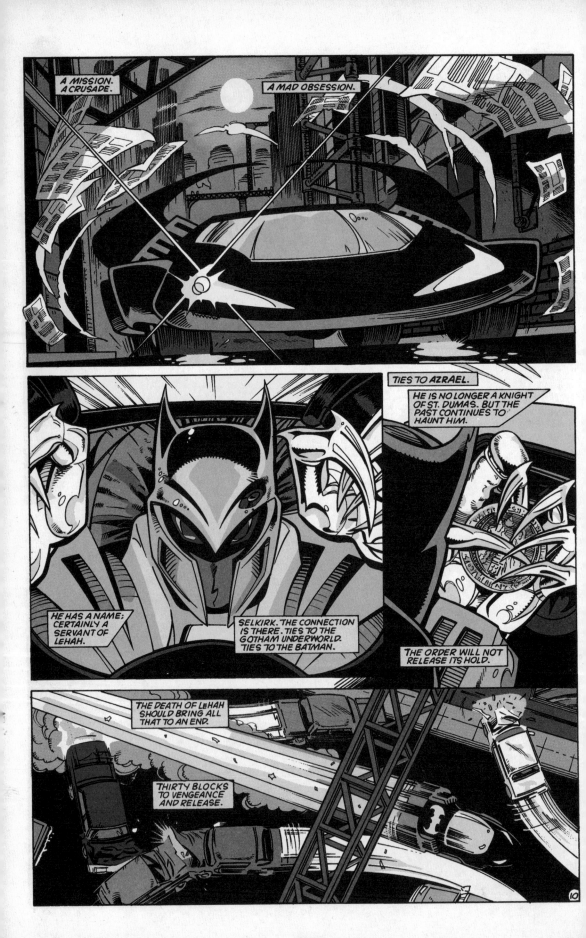

A MISSION. A CRUSADE.

A MAD OBSESSION.

TIES TO AZRAEL.

HE IS NO LONGER A KNIGHT OF ST. DUMAS. BUT THE PAST CONTINUES TO HAUNT HIM.

HE HAS A NAME: CERTAINLY A SERVANT OF LEHAH.

SELKIRK. THE CONNECTION IS THERE. TIES TO THE GOTHAM UNDERWORLD. TIES TO THE BATMAN.

THE ORDER WILL NOT RELEASE ITS HOLD.

THE DEATH OF LEHAH SHOULD BRING ALL THAT TO AN END.

THIRTY BLOCKS TO VENGEANCE AND RELEASE.

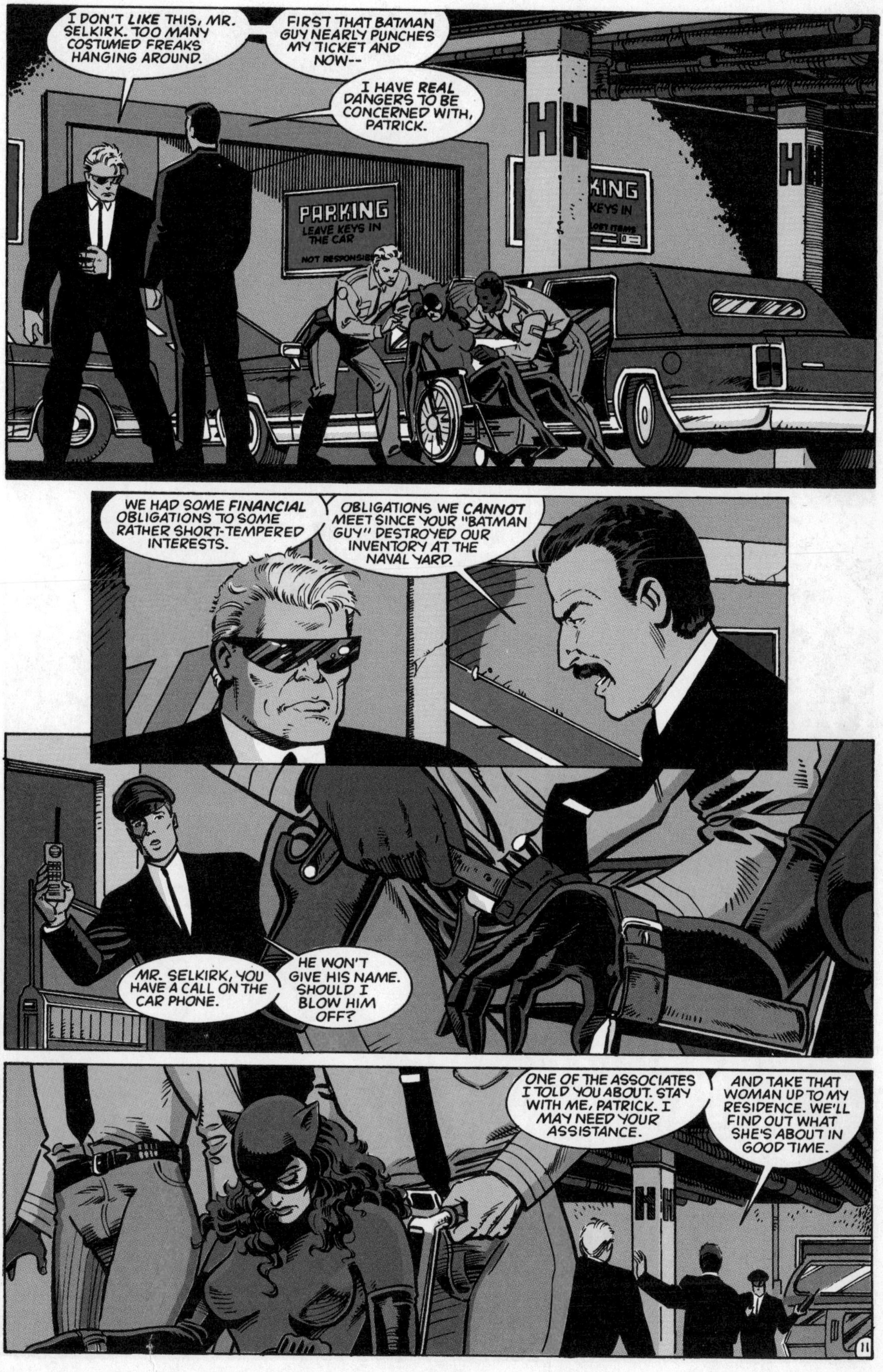
I DON'T LIKE THIS, MR. SELKIRK. TOO MANY COSTUMED FREAKS HANGING AROUND.
FIRST THAT BATMAN GUY NEARLY PUNCHES MY TICKET AND NOW--
I HAVE REAL DANGERS TO BE CONCERNED WITH, PATRICK.
PARKING
LEAVE KEYS IN THE CAR
NOT RESPONSIBL
KING
KEYS IN
WE HAD SOME FINANCIAL OBLIGATIONS TO SOME RATHER SHORT-TEMPERED INTERESTS.
OBLIGATIONS WE CANNOT MEET SINCE YOUR "BATMAN GUY" DESTROYED OUR INVENTORY AT THE NAVAL YARD.
MR. SELKIRK, YOU HAVE A CALL ON THE CAR PHONE.
HE WON'T GIVE HIS NAME. SHOULD I BLOW HIM OFF?
ONE OF THE ASSOCIATES I TOLD YOU ABOUT. STAY WITH ME, PATRICK. I MAY NEED YOUR ASSISTANCE.
AND TAKE THAT WOMAN UP TO MY RESIDENCE. WE'LL FIND OUT WHAT SHE'S ABOUT IN GOOD TIME.
11

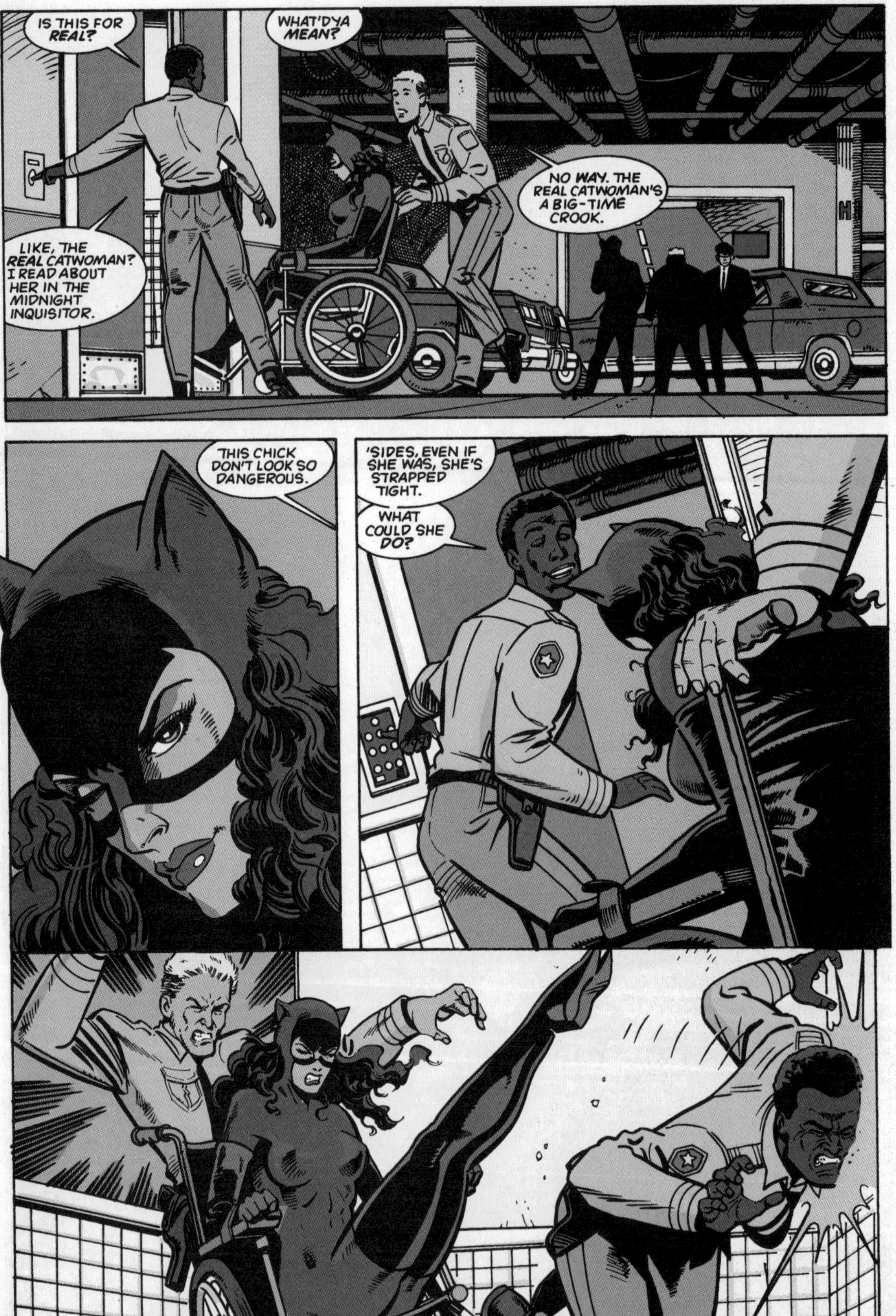
IS THIS FOR REAL?
WHAT'D'YA MEAN?
LIKE, THE REAL CATWOMAN? I READ ABOUT HER IN THE MIDNIGHT INQUISITOR.
NO WAY. THE REAL CATWOMAN'S A BIG-TIME CROOK.
THIS CHICK DON'T LOOK SO DANGEROUS.
'SIDES, EVEN IF SHE WAS, SHE'S STRAPPED TIGHT.
WHAT COULD SHE DO?
12

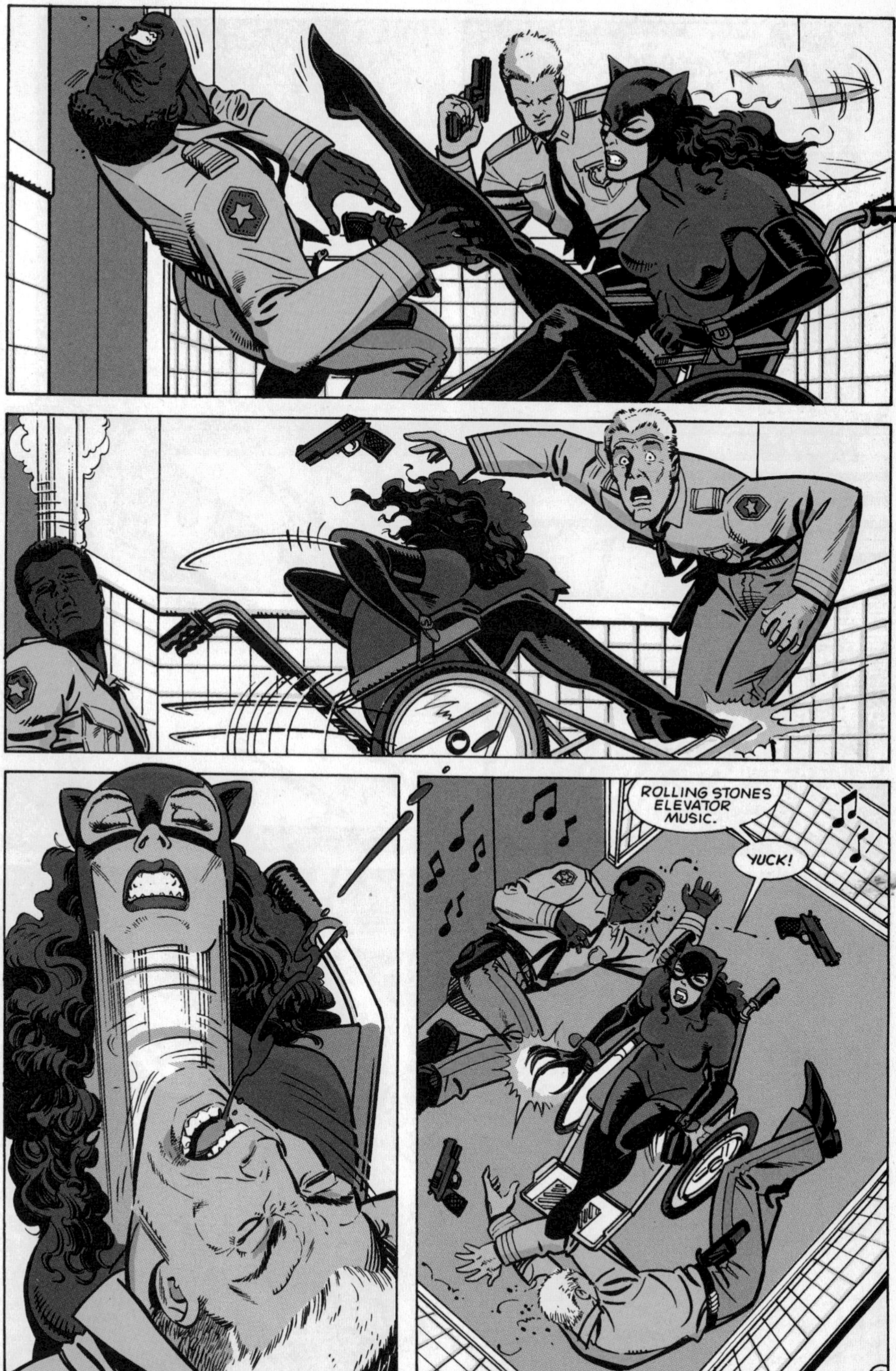
ROLLING STONES ELEVATOR MUSIC.
YUCK!
13

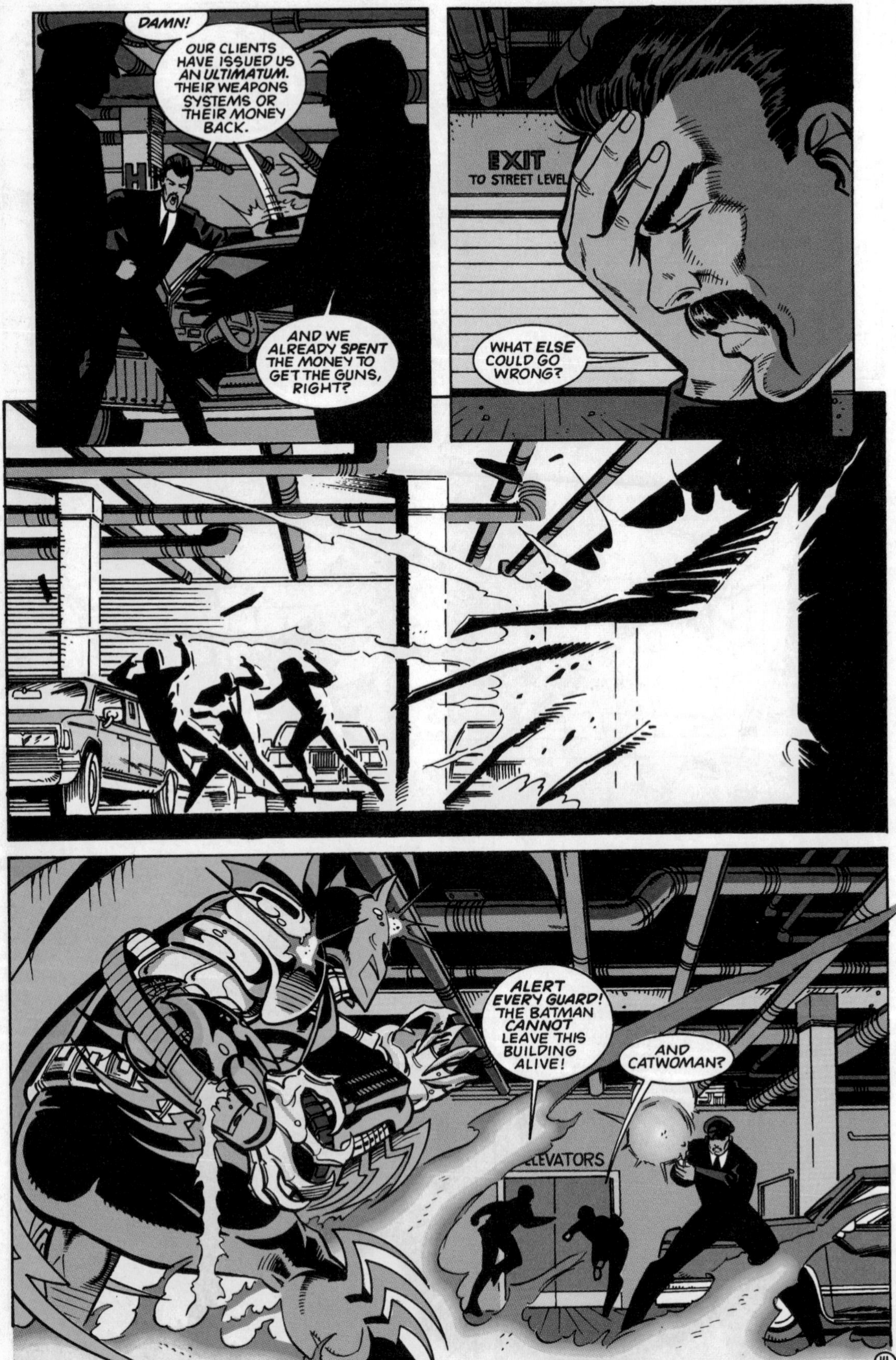
DAMN!
OUR CLIENTS HAVE ISSUED US AN ULTIMATUM. THEIR WEAPONS SYSTEMS OR THEIR MONEY BACK.
AND WE ALREADY SPENT THE MONEY TO GET THE GUNS, RIGHT?
EXIT TO STREET LEVEL
WHAT ELSE COULD GO WRONG?
ALERT EVERY GUARD! THE BATMAN CANNOT LEAVE THIS BUILDING ALIVE!
AND CATWOMAN?
ELEVATORS
14

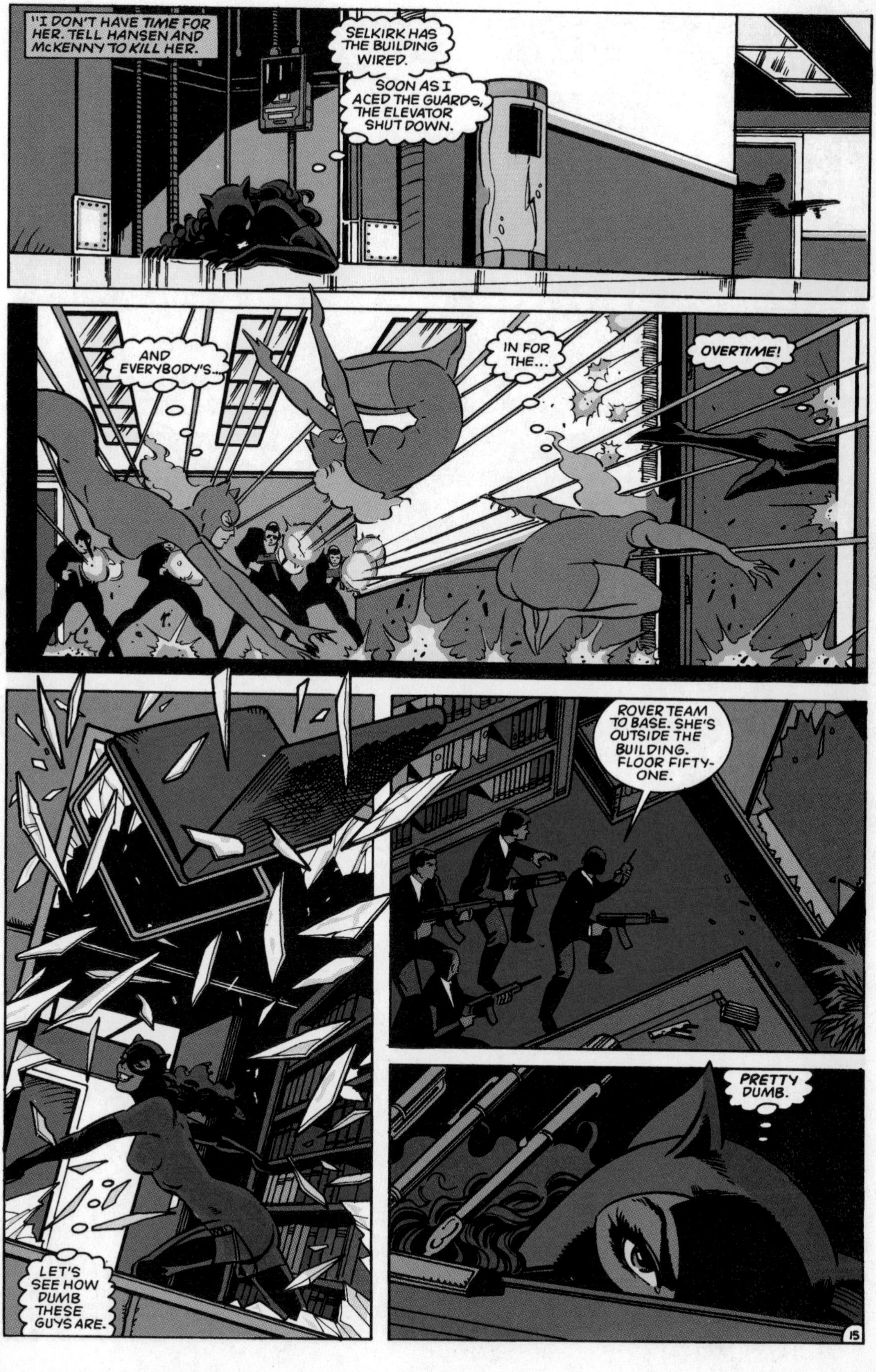
"I DON'T HAVE TIME FOR HER. TELL HANSEN AND McKENNY TO KILL HER.
SELKIRK HAS THE BUILDING WIRED.
SOON AS I ACED THE GUARDS, THE ELEVATOR SHUT DOWN.
AND EVERYBODY'S...
IN FOR THE...
OVERTIME!
LET'S SEE HOW DUMB THESE GUYS ARE.
ROVER TEAM TO BASE. SHE'S OUTSIDE THE BUILDING. FLOOR FIFTY-ONE.
PRETTY DUMB.
15

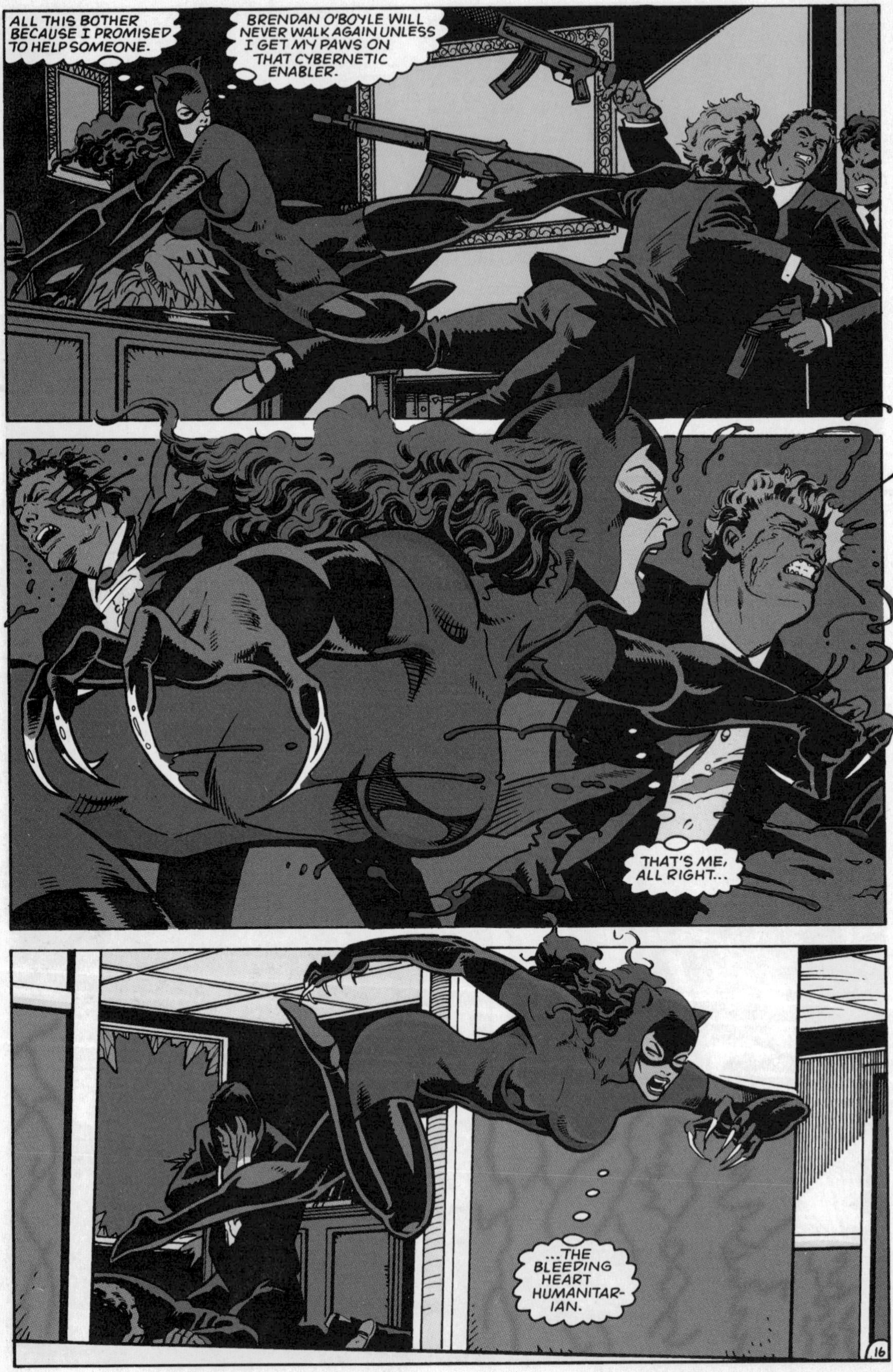
ALL THIS BOTHER BECAUSE I PROMISED TO HELP SOMEONE.
BRENDAN O'BOYLE WILL NEVER WALK AGAIN UNLESS I GET MY PAWS ON THAT CYBERNETIC ENABLER.
THAT'S ME, ALL RIGHT...
...THE BLEEDING HEART HUMANITAR-IAN.
16

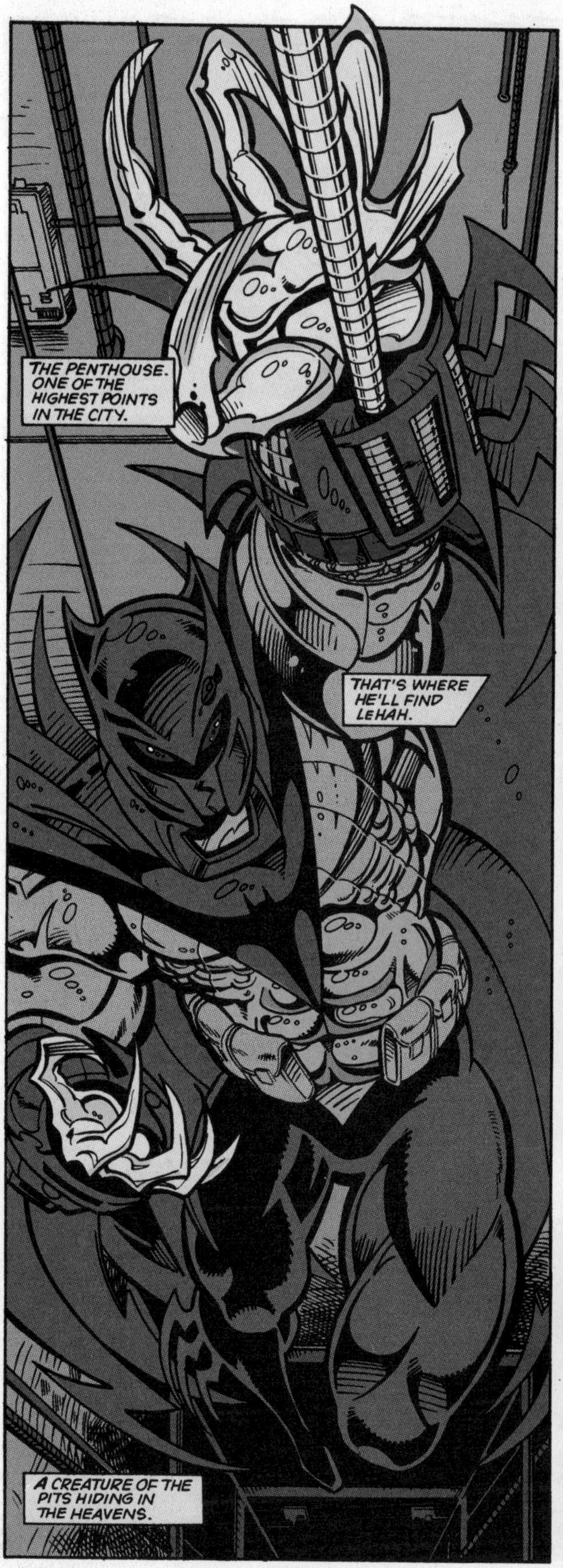
THE PENTHOUSE. ONE OF THE HIGHEST POINTS IN THE CITY.
THAT'S WHERE HE'LL FIND LEHAH.
A CREATURE OF THE PITS HIDING IN THE HEAVENS.

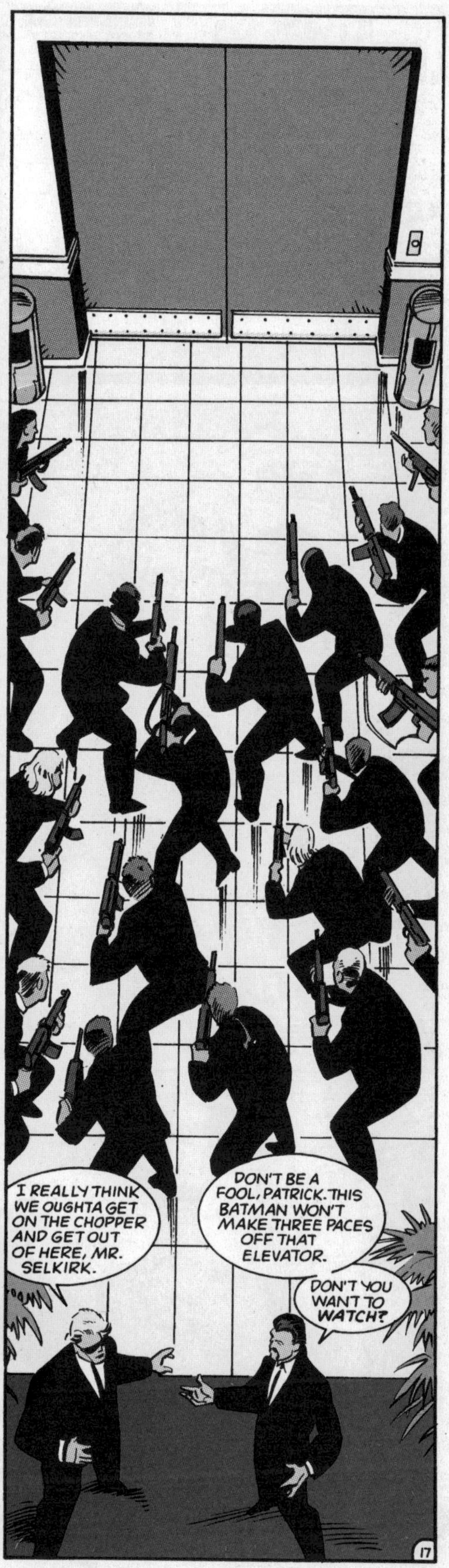
I REALLY THINK WE OUGHTA GET ON THE CHOPPER AND GET OUT OF HERE, MR. SELKIRK.
DON'T BE A FOOL, PATRICK. THIS BATMAN WON'T MAKE THREE PACES OFF THAT ELEVATOR.
DON'T YOU WANT TO WATCH?
17

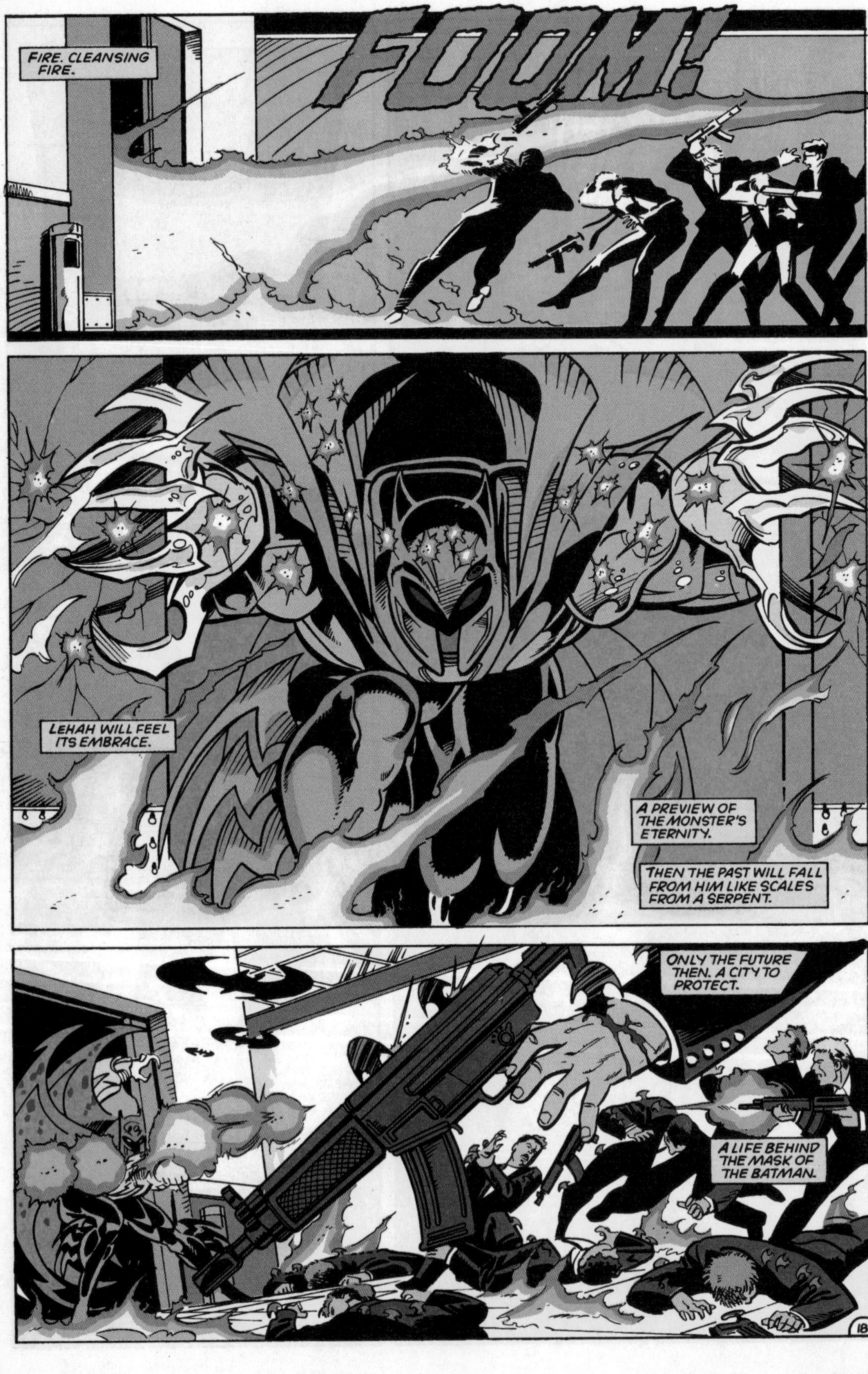
FIRE. CLEANSING FIRE.
FOOM!
LEHAH WILL FEEL ITS EMBRACE.
A PREVIEW OF THE MONSTER'S ETERNITY.
THEN THE PAST WILL FALL FROM HIM LIKE SCALES FROM A SERPENT.
ONLY THE FUTURE THEN. A CITY TO PROTECT.
A LIFE BEHIND THE MASK OF THE BATMAN.
18

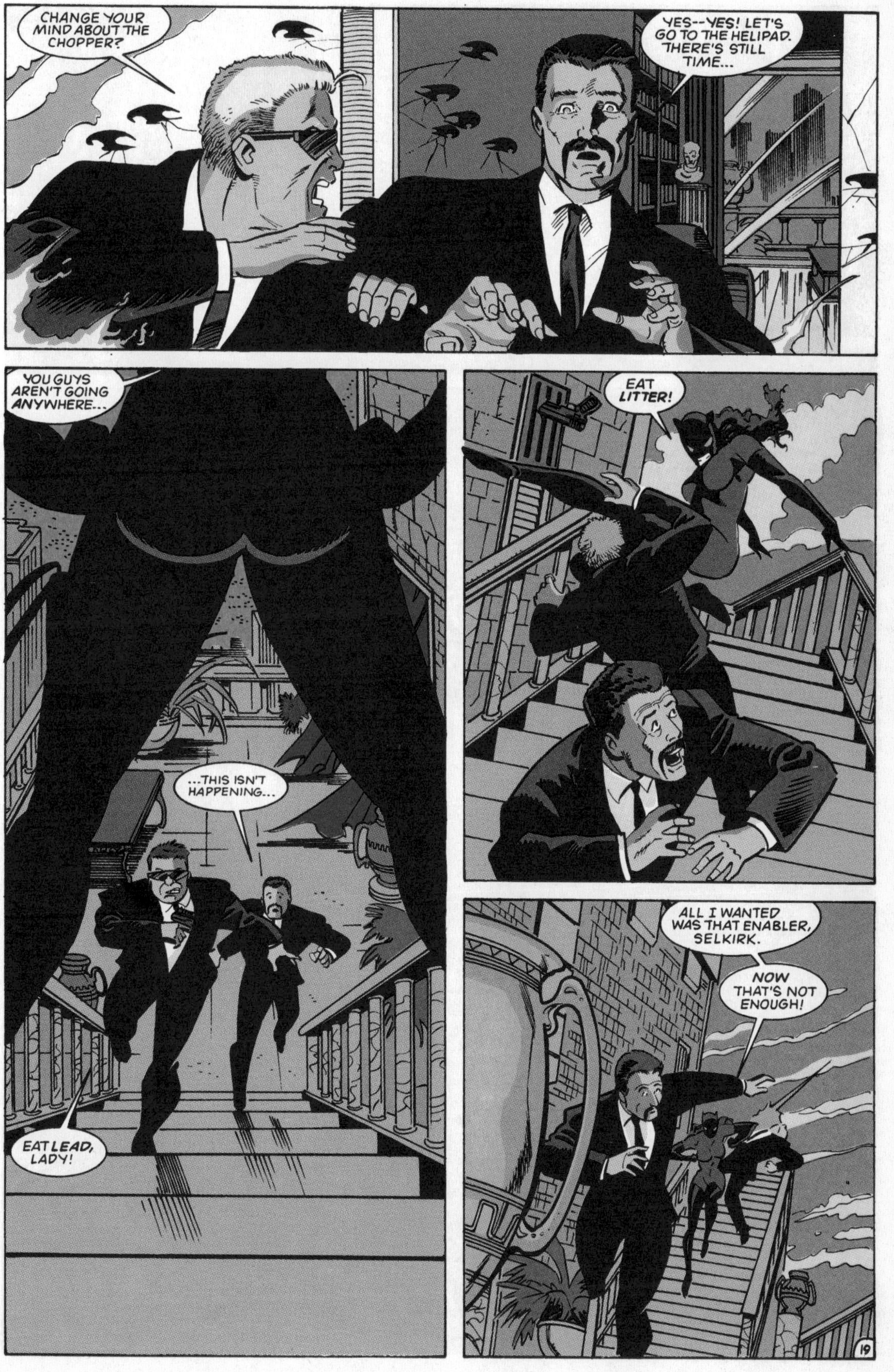
CHANGE YOUR MIND ABOUT THE CHOPPER?
YES--YES! LET'S GO TO THE HELIPAD. THERE'S STILL TIME...
YOU GUYS AREN'T GOING ANYWHERE...
...THIS ISN'T HAPPENING...
EAT LEAD, LADY!
EAT LITTER!
ALL I WANTED WAS THAT ENABLER, SELKIRK.
NOW THAT'S NOT ENOUGH!
19

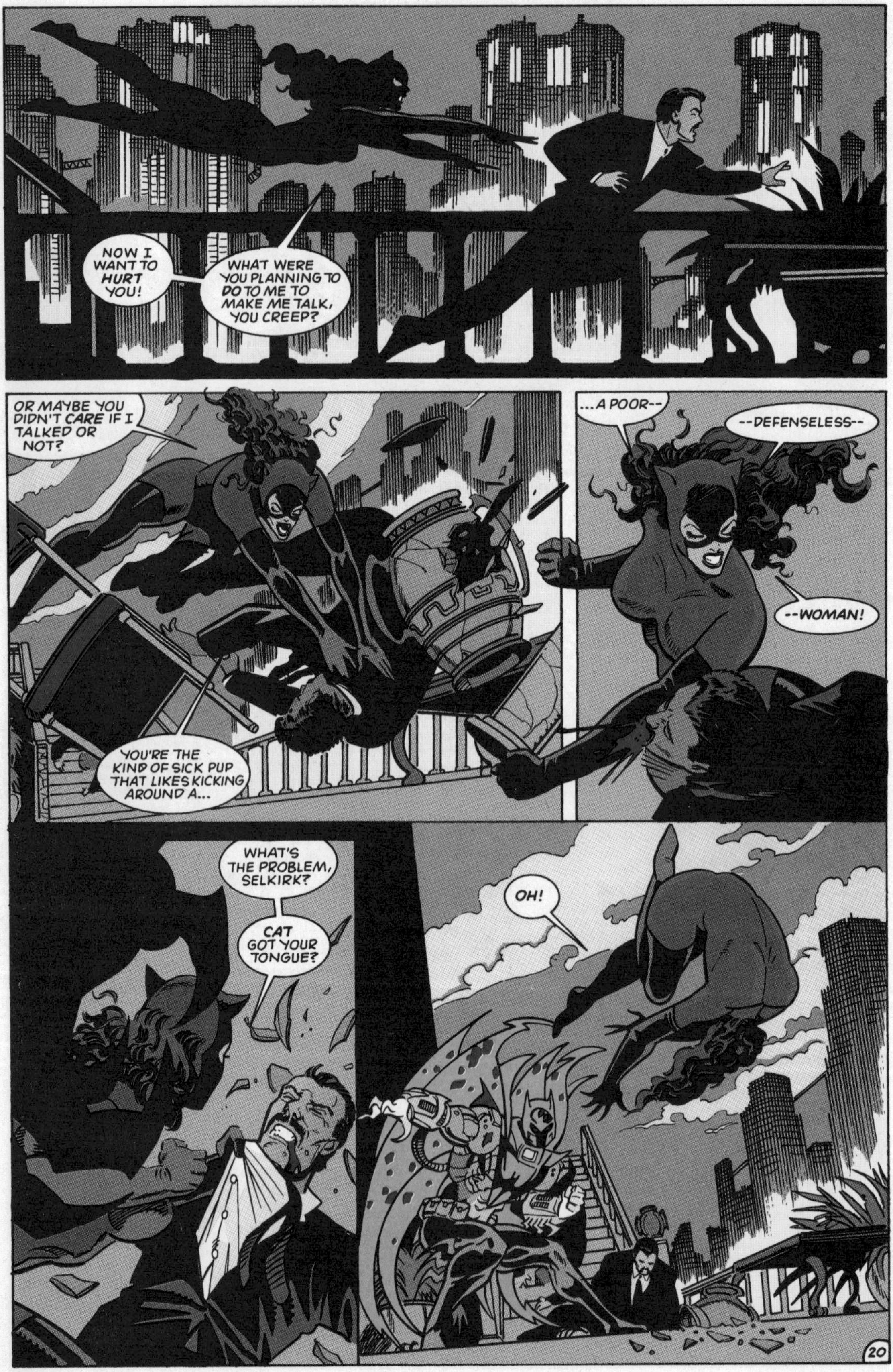
NOW I WANT TO HURT YOU!
WHAT WERE YOU PLANNING TO DO TO ME TO MAKE ME TALK, YOU CREEP?
OR MAYBE YOU DIDN'T CARE IF I TALKED OR NOT?
YOU'RE THE KIND OF SICK PUP THAT LIKES KICKING AROUND A...
...A POOR--
--DEFENSELESS--
--WOMAN!
WHAT'S THE PROBLEM, SELKIRK?
CAT GOT YOUR TONGUE?
OH!
20

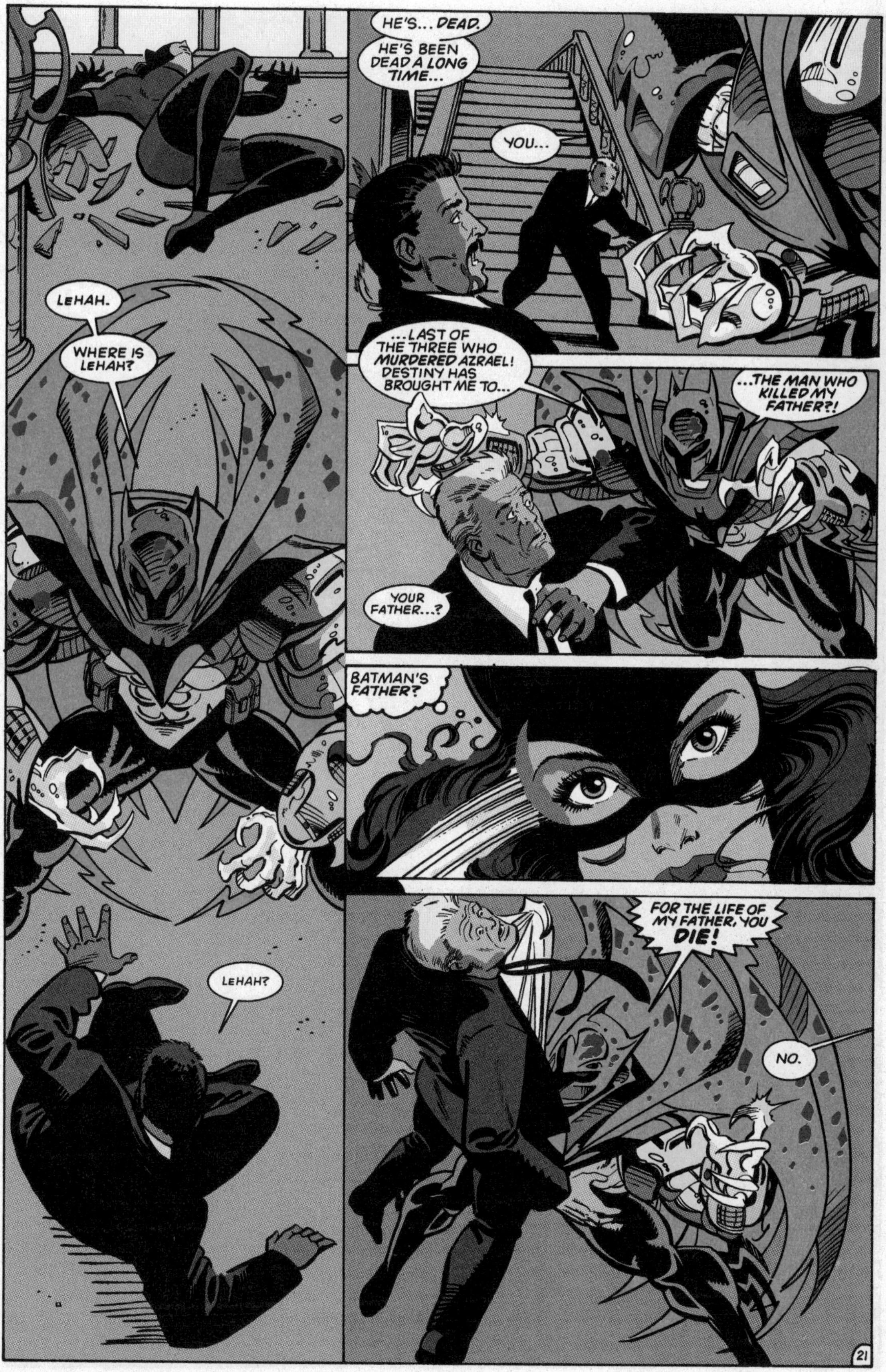

LEHAH.
WHERE IS LEHAH?
LEHAH?
HE'S... DEAD.
HE'S BEEN DEAD A LONG TIME...
YOU...
...LAST OF THE THREE WHO MURDERED AZRAEL! DESTINY HAS BROUGHT ME TO...
...THE MAN WHO KILLED MY FATHER?!
YOUR FATHER...?
BATMAN'S FATHER?
FOR THE LIFE OF MY FATHER, YOU DIE!
NO.
21

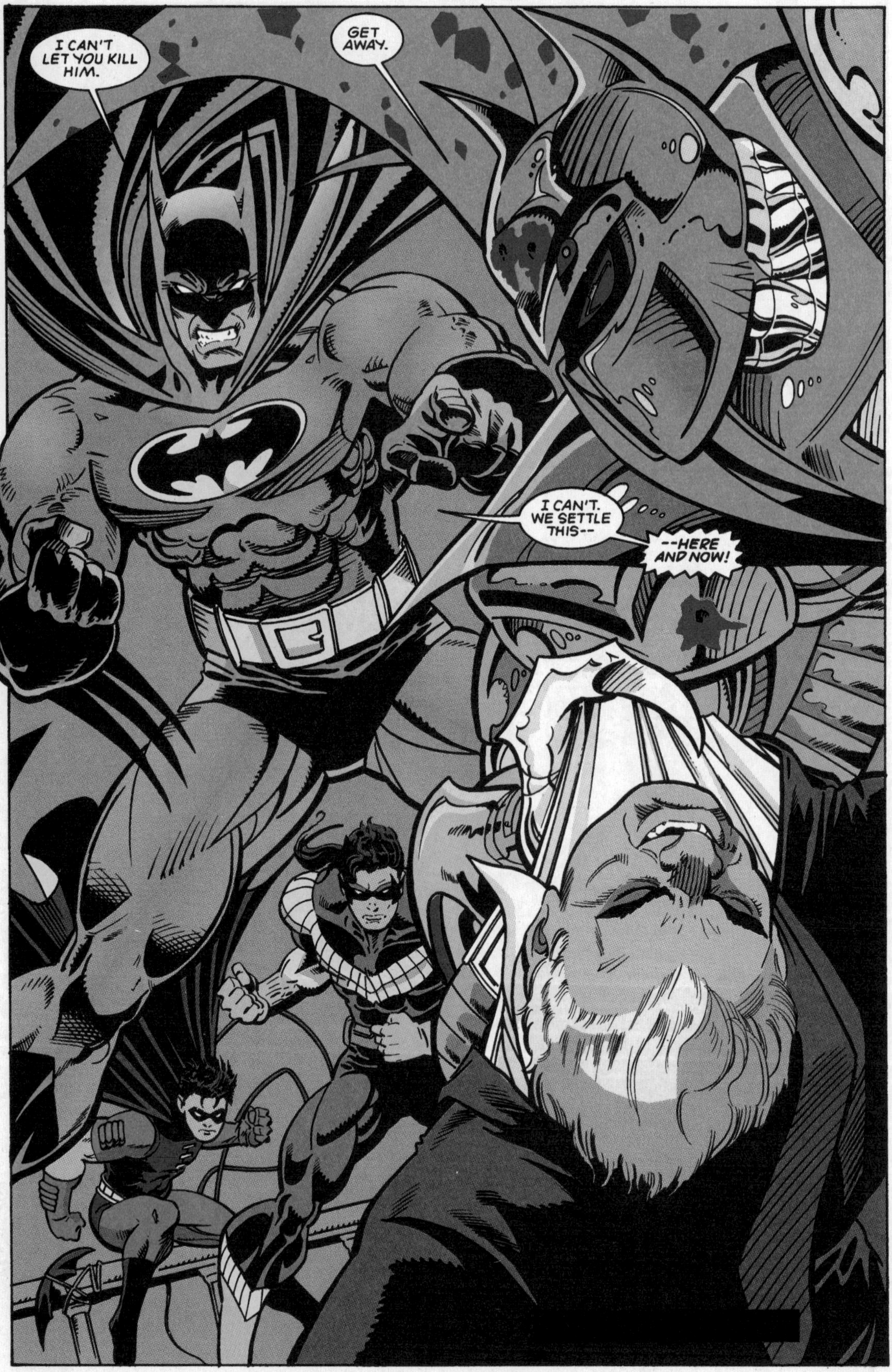
I CAN'T LET YOU KILL HIM.
GET AWAY.
I CAN'T. WE SETTLE THIS--
--HERE AND NOW!
[redacted]

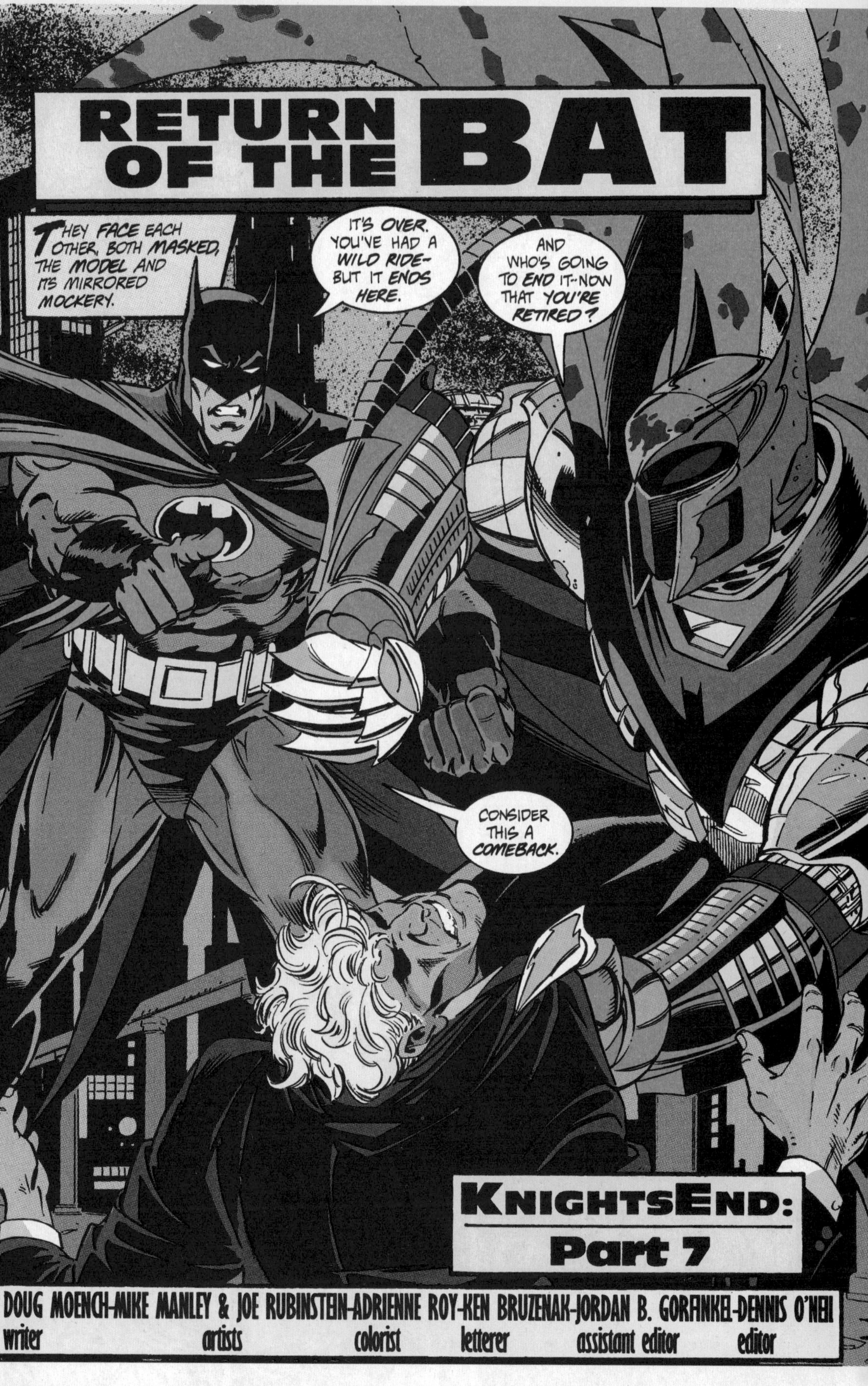

RETURN OF THE BAT
THEY FACE EACH OTHER, BOTH MASKED, THE MODEL AND ITS MIRRORED MOCKERY.
IT'S OVER. YOU'VE HAD A WILD RIDE-- BUT IT ENDS HERE.
AND WHO'S GOING TO END IT--NOW THAT YOU'RE RETIRED?
CONSIDER THIS A COMEBACK.
KNIGHTSEND: Part 7
DOUG MOENCH-MIKE MANLEY & JOE RUBINSTEIN-ADRIENNE ROY-KEN BRUZENAK-JORDAN B. GORFINKEL-DENNIS O'NEIL
writer artists colorist letterer assistant editor editor

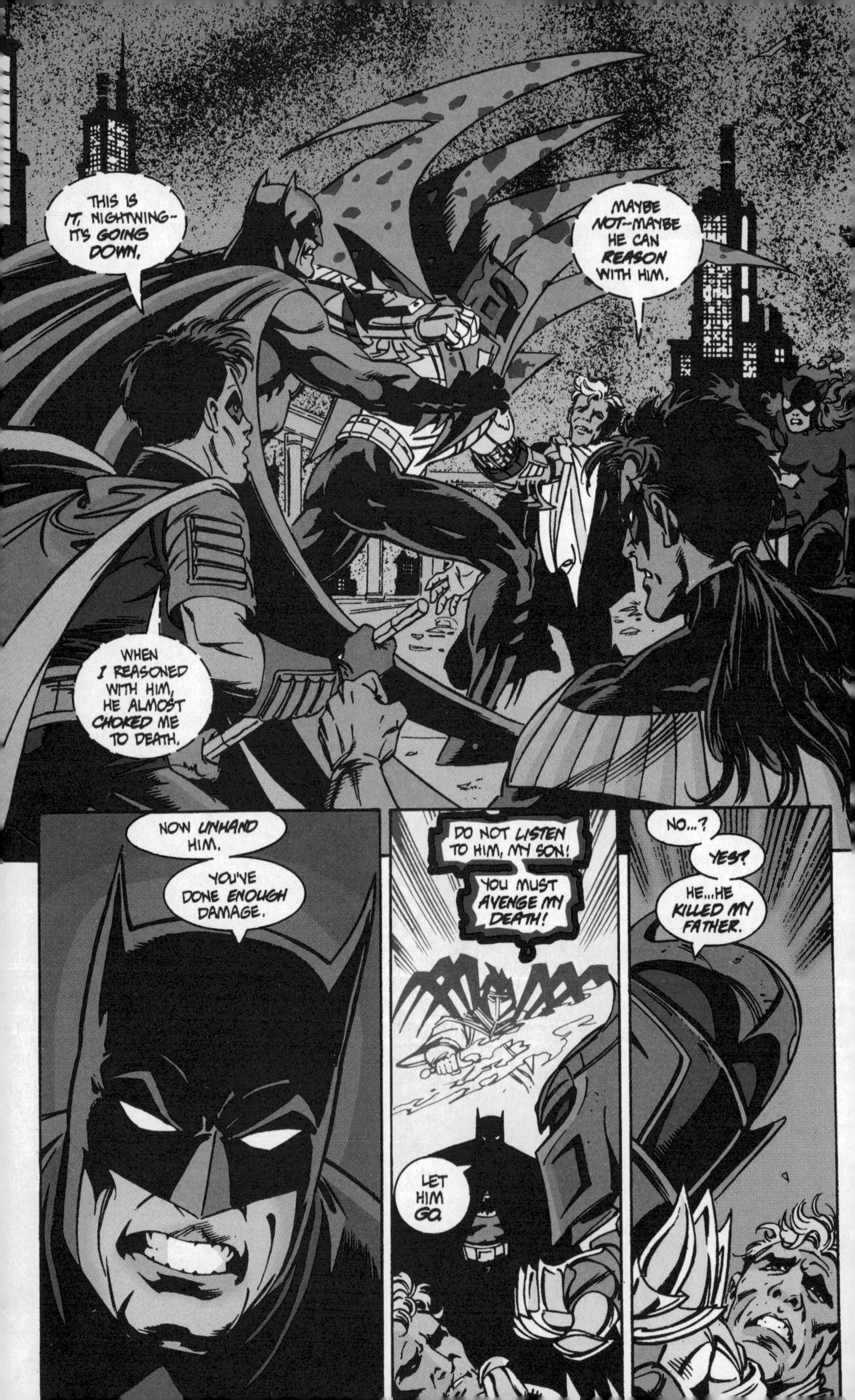
THIS IS IT, NIGHTWING-- IT'S GOING DOWN.
MAYBE NOT--MAYBE HE CAN REASON WITH HIM.
WHEN I REASONED WITH HIM, HE ALMOST CHOKED ME TO DEATH.
NOW UNHAND HIM.
YOU'VE DONE ENOUGH DAMAGE.
DO NOT LISTEN TO HIM, MY SON!
YOU MUST AVENGE MY DEATH!
LET HIM GO.
NO...?
YES?
HE...HE KILLED MY FATHER.

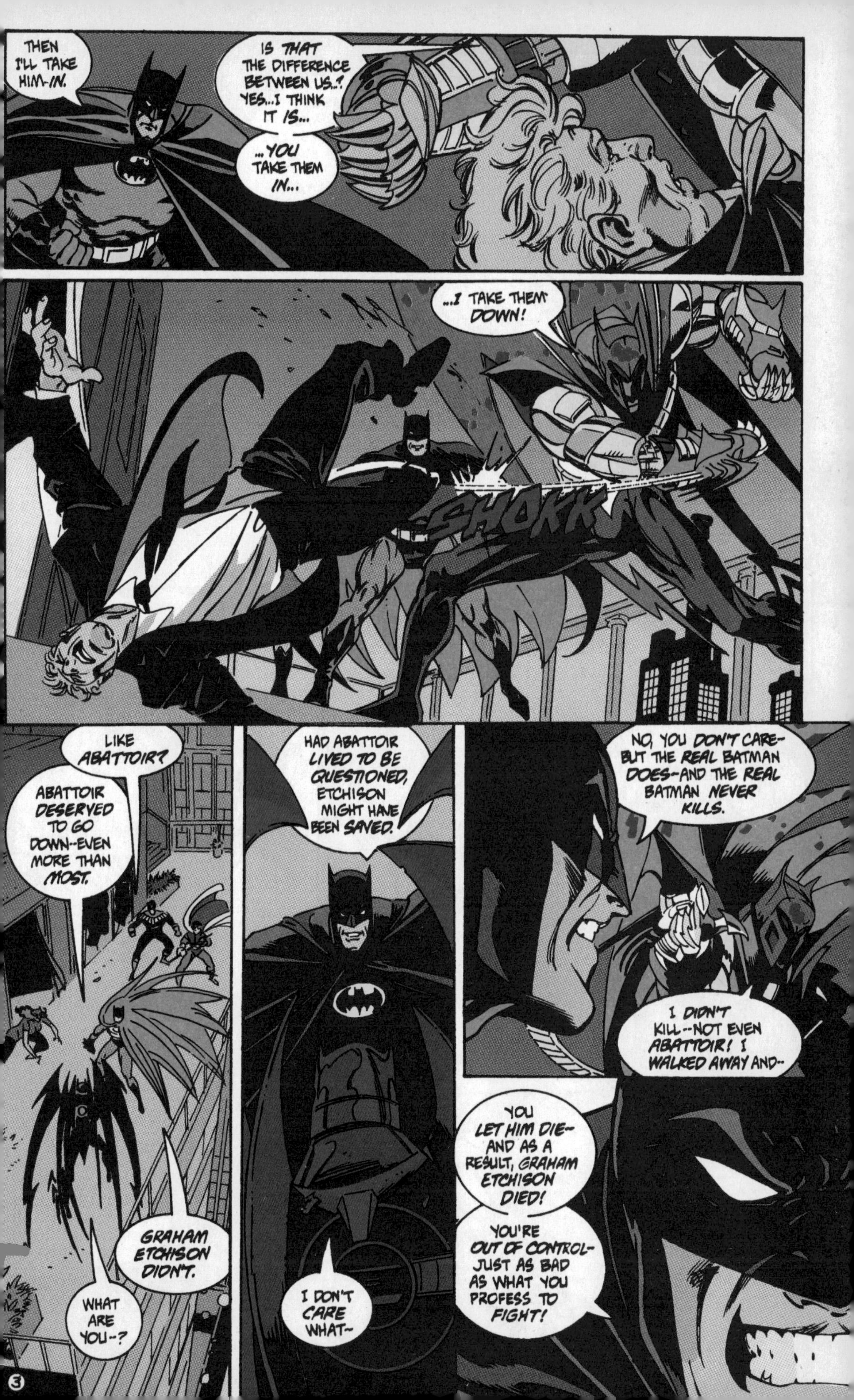
THEN I'LL TAKE HIM--IN.
IS THAT THE DIFFERENCE BETWEEN US..? YES...I THINK IT IS...
...YOU TAKE THEM IN...
...I TAKE THEM DOWN!
SHOKK
LIKE ABATTOIR?
ABATTOIR DESERVED TO GO DOWN--EVEN MORE THAN MOST.
GRAHAM ETCHISON DIDN'T.
WHAT ARE YOU--?
HAD ABATTOIR LIVED TO BE QUESTIONED, ETCHISON MIGHT HAVE BEEN SAVED.
I DON'T CARE WHAT-
NO, YOU DON'T CARE-BUT THE REAL BATMAN DOES--AND THE REAL BATMAN NEVER KILLS.
I DIDN'T KILL--NOT EVEN ABATTOIR! I WALKED AWAY AND--
YOU LET HIM DIE-AND AS A RESULT, GRAHAM ETCHISON DIED!
YOU'RE OUT OF CONTROL-JUST AS BAD AS WHAT YOU PROFESS TO FIGHT!
3

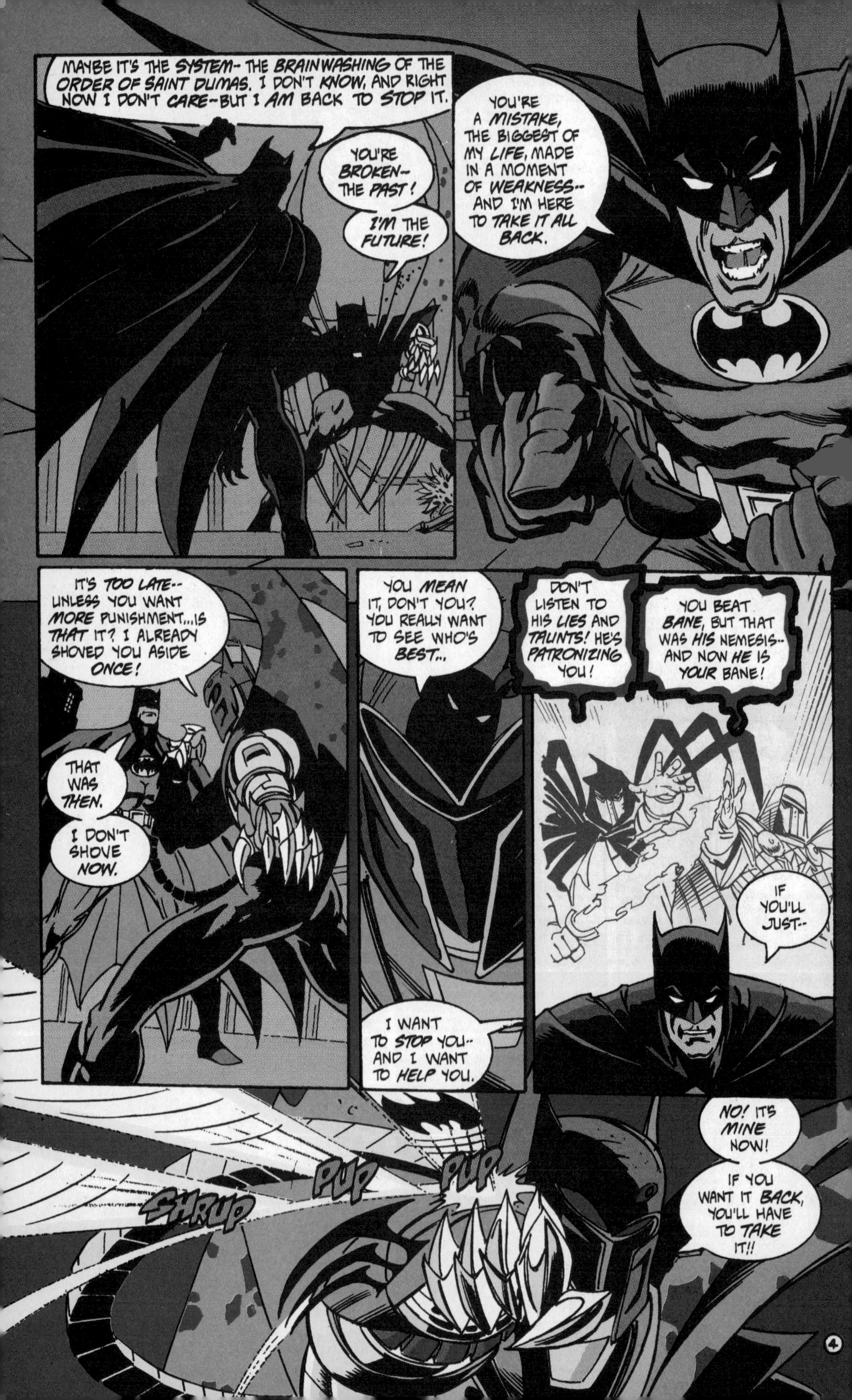
MAYBE IT'S THE SYSTEM-- THE BRAINWASHING OF THE ORDER OF SAINT DUMAS. I DON'T KNOW, AND RIGHT NOW I DON'T CARE--BUT I AM BACK TO STOP IT.
YOU'RE BROKEN-- THE PAST!
I'M THE FUTURE!
YOU'RE A MISTAKE, THE BIGGEST OF MY LIFE, MADE IN A MOMENT OF WEAKNESS-- AND I'M HERE TO TAKE IT ALL BACK.
IT'S TOO LATE-- UNLESS YOU WANT MORE PUNISHMENT...IS THAT IT? I ALREADY SHOVED YOU ASIDE ONCE!
THAT WAS THEN.
I DON'T SHOVE NOW.
YOU MEAN IT, DON'T YOU? YOU REALLY WANT TO SEE WHO'S BEST...
I WANT TO STOP YOU-- AND I WANT TO HELP YOU.
DON'T LISTEN TO HIS LIES AND TAUNTS! HE'S PATRONIZING YOU!
YOU BEAT BANE, BUT THAT WAS HIS NEMESIS-- AND NOW HE IS YOUR BANE!
IF YOU'LL JUST--
SHRUP
PUP
PUP
NO! IT'S MINE NOW!
IF YOU WANT IT BACK, YOU'LL HAVE TO TAKE IT!!

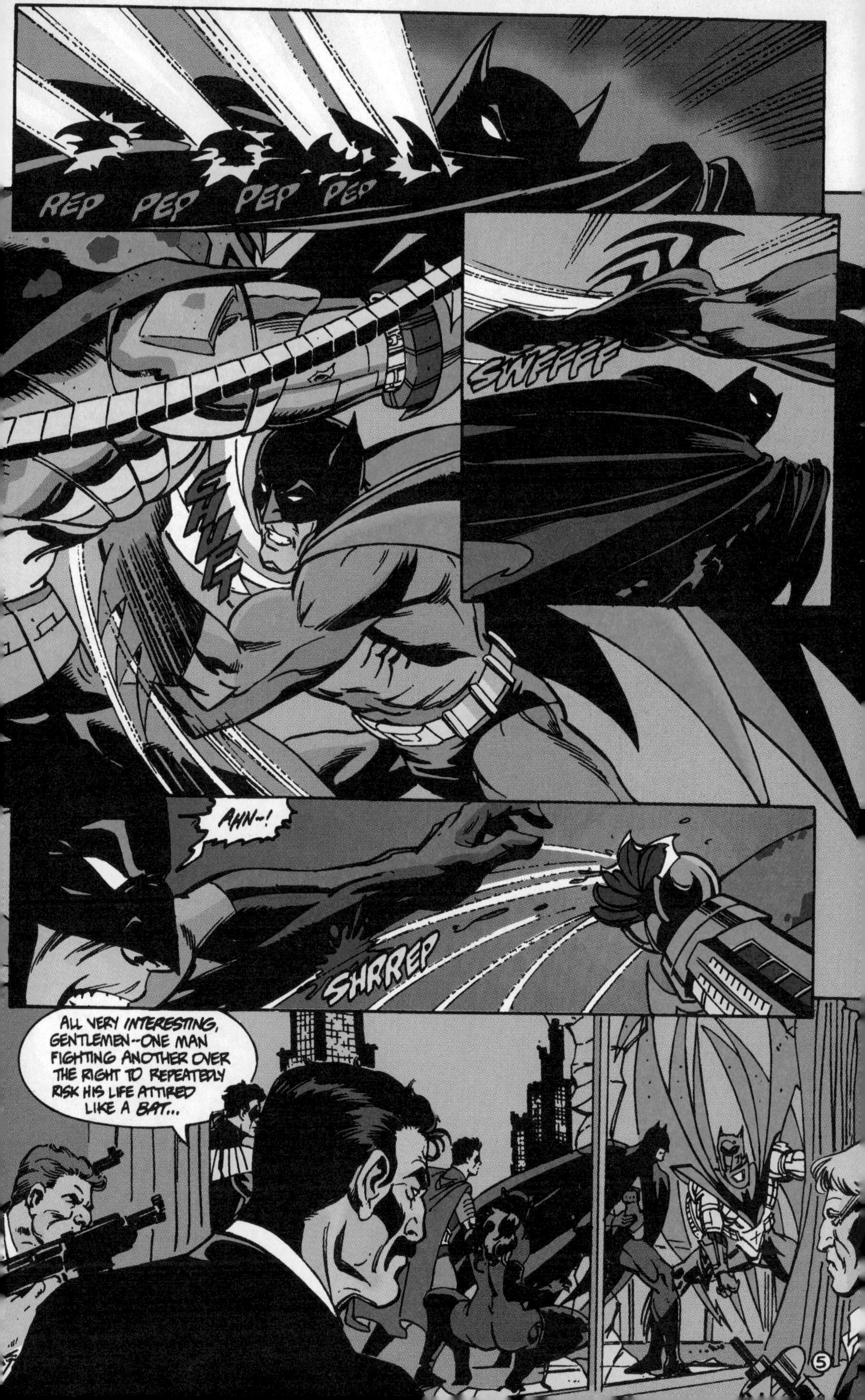
REP PEP PEP PEP
SWFFFF
CHUCK
AHN--!
SHRREP
ALL VERY INTERESTING, GENTLEMEN--ONE MAN FIGHTING ANOTHER OVER THE RIGHT TO REPEATEDLY RISK HIS LIFE ATTIRED LIKE A BAT...
5

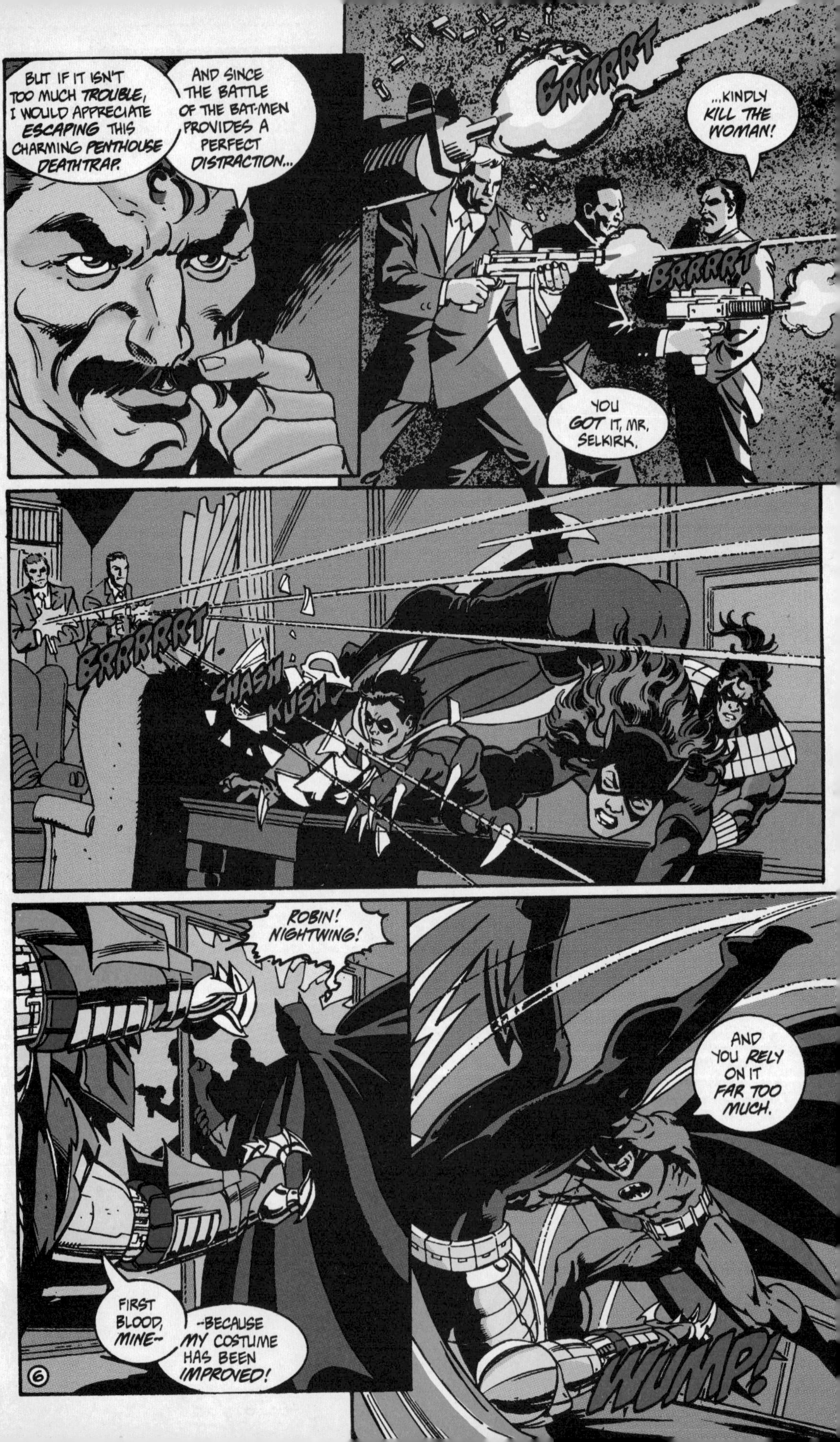
BUT IF IT ISN'T TOO MUCH TROUBLE, I WOULD APPRECIATE ESCAPING THIS CHARMING PENTHOUSE DEATHTRAP.
AND SINCE THE BATTLE OF THE BAT-MEN PROVIDES A PERFECT DISTRACTION...
BRRRRT
...KINDLY KILL THE WOMAN!
BRRRRT
YOU GOT IT, MR. SELKIRK.
BRRRRRT
CHASH
KUSH
ROBIN! NIGHTWING!
FIRST BLOOD, MINE--
--BECAUSE MY COSTUME HAS BEEN IMPROVED!
6
AND YOU RELY ON IT FAR TOO MUCH.
WUMP!

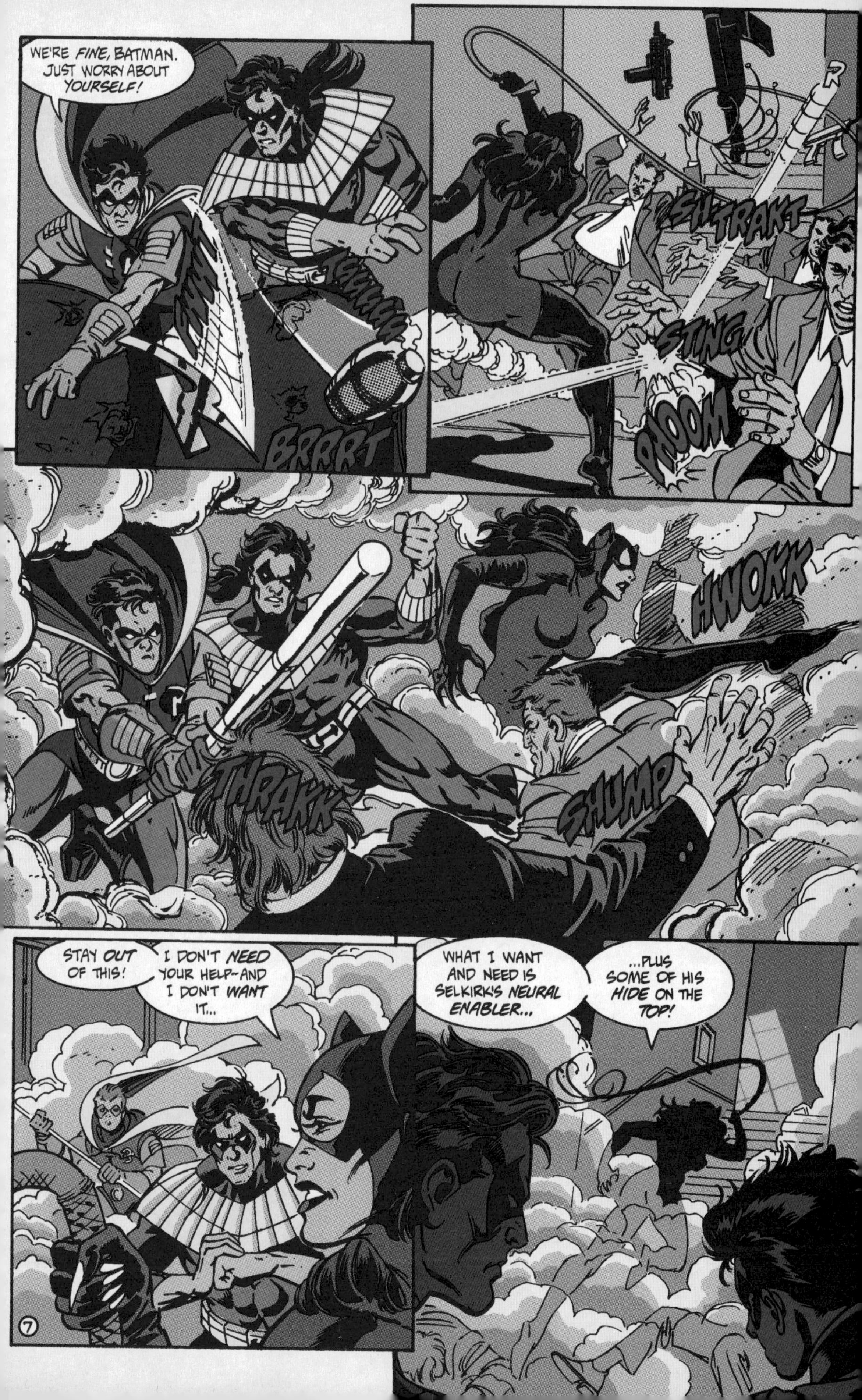
WE'RE FINE, BATMAN. JUST WORRY ABOUT YOURSELF!
BRRRT
SHTRAKT
STING
PHOOM
HWOKK
THRAKK
SHUMP
STAY OUT OF THIS!
I DON'T NEED YOUR HELP--AND I DON'T WANT IT...
WHAT I WANT AND NEED IS SELKIRK'S NEURAL ENABLER...
...PLUS SOME OF HIS HIDE ON THE TOP!

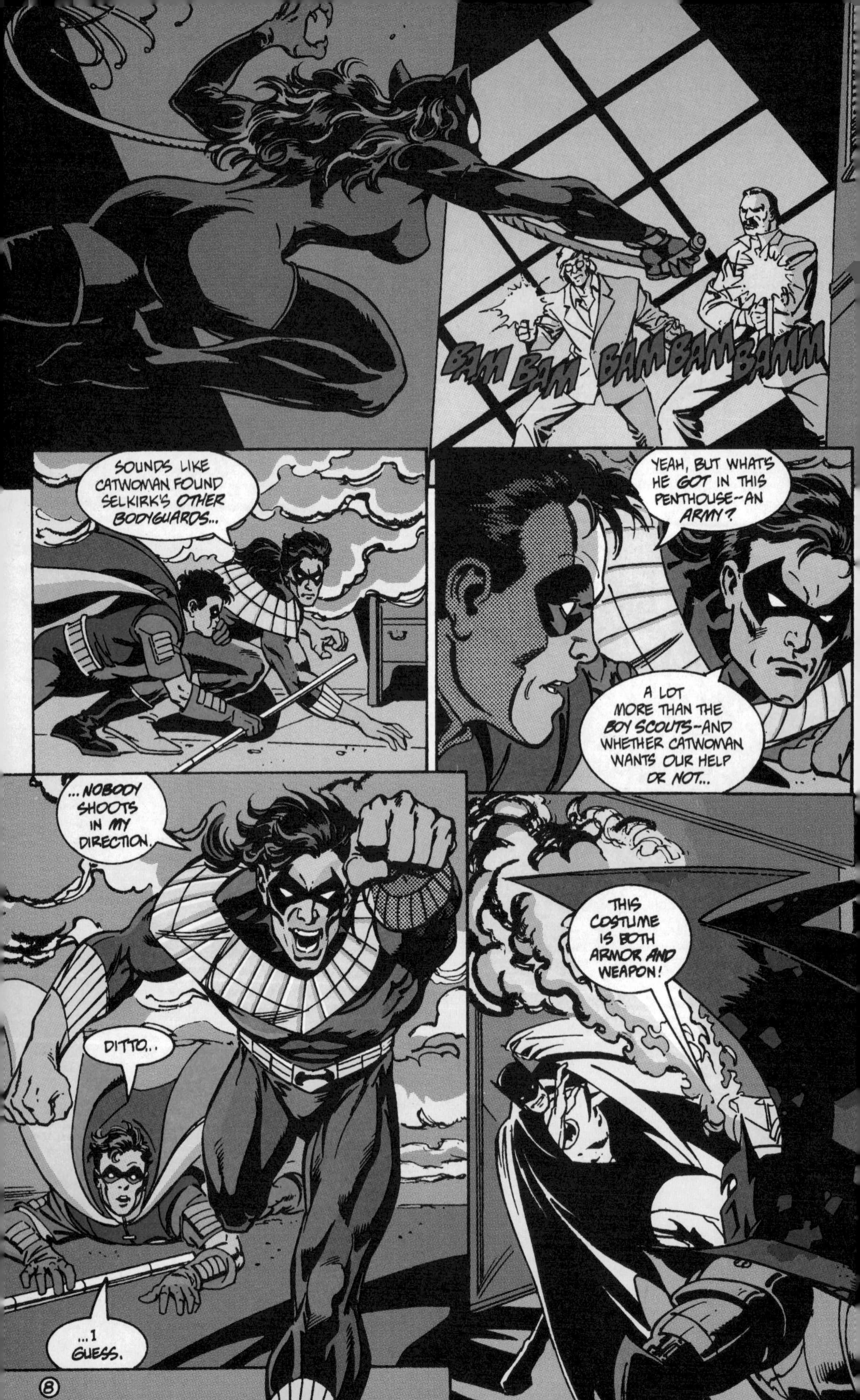
BAM BAM BAM BAM BAMM
SOUNDS LIKE CATWOMAN FOUND SELKIRK'S OTHER BODYGUARDS...
YEAH, BUT WHAT'S HE GOT IN THIS PENTHOUSE--AN ARMY?
A LOT MORE THAN THE BOY SCOUTS--AND WHETHER CATWOMAN WANTS OUR HELP OR NOT...
...NOBODY SHOOTS IN MY DIRECTION.
DITTO...
...I GUESS.
THIS COSTUME IS BOTH ARMOR AND WEAPON!

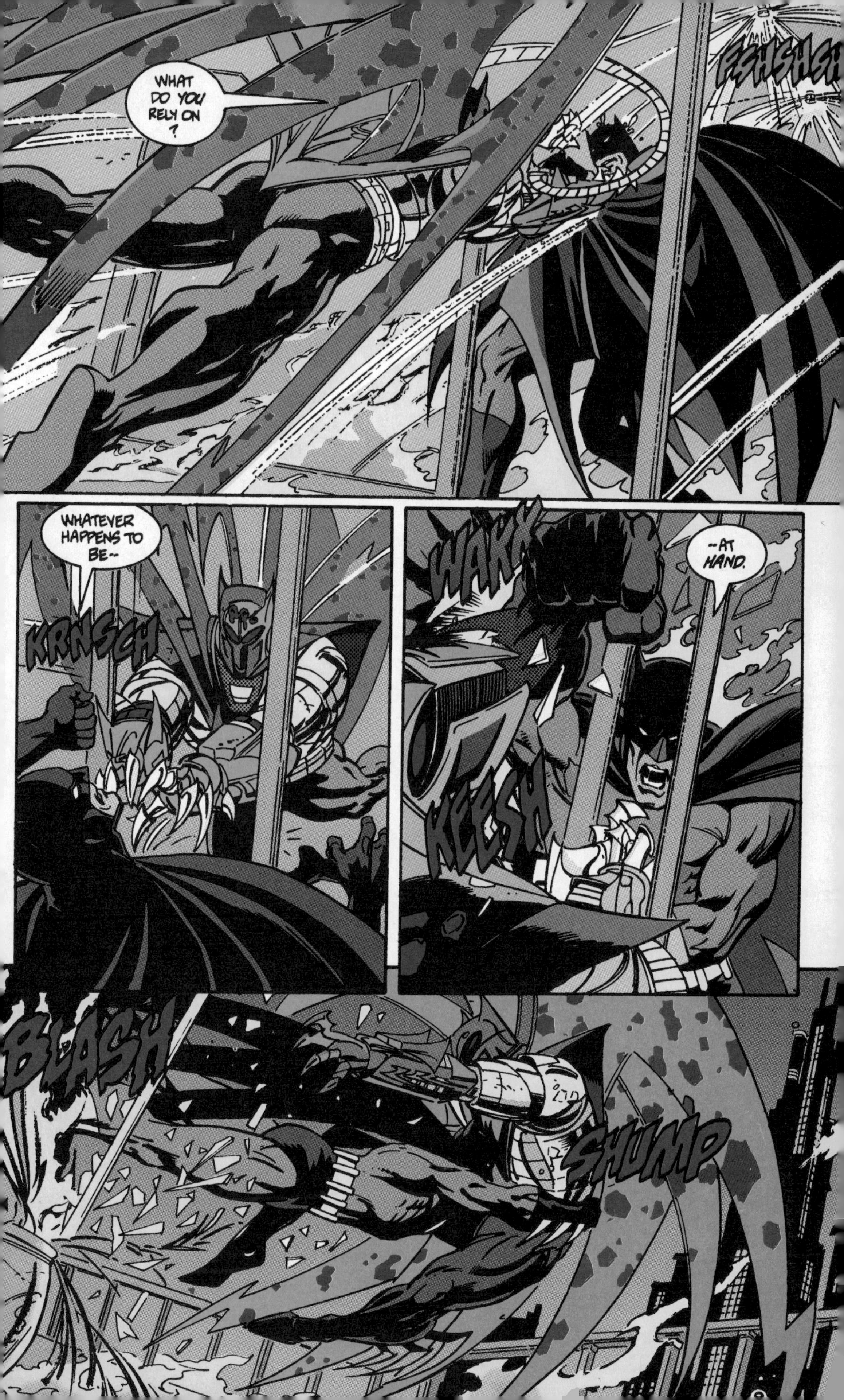
WHAT DO YOU RELY ON ?
FSHSHGH
WHATEVER HAPPENS TO BE--
KRNSCH
WAKK
--AT HAND.
KEESH
BLASH
SHUMP

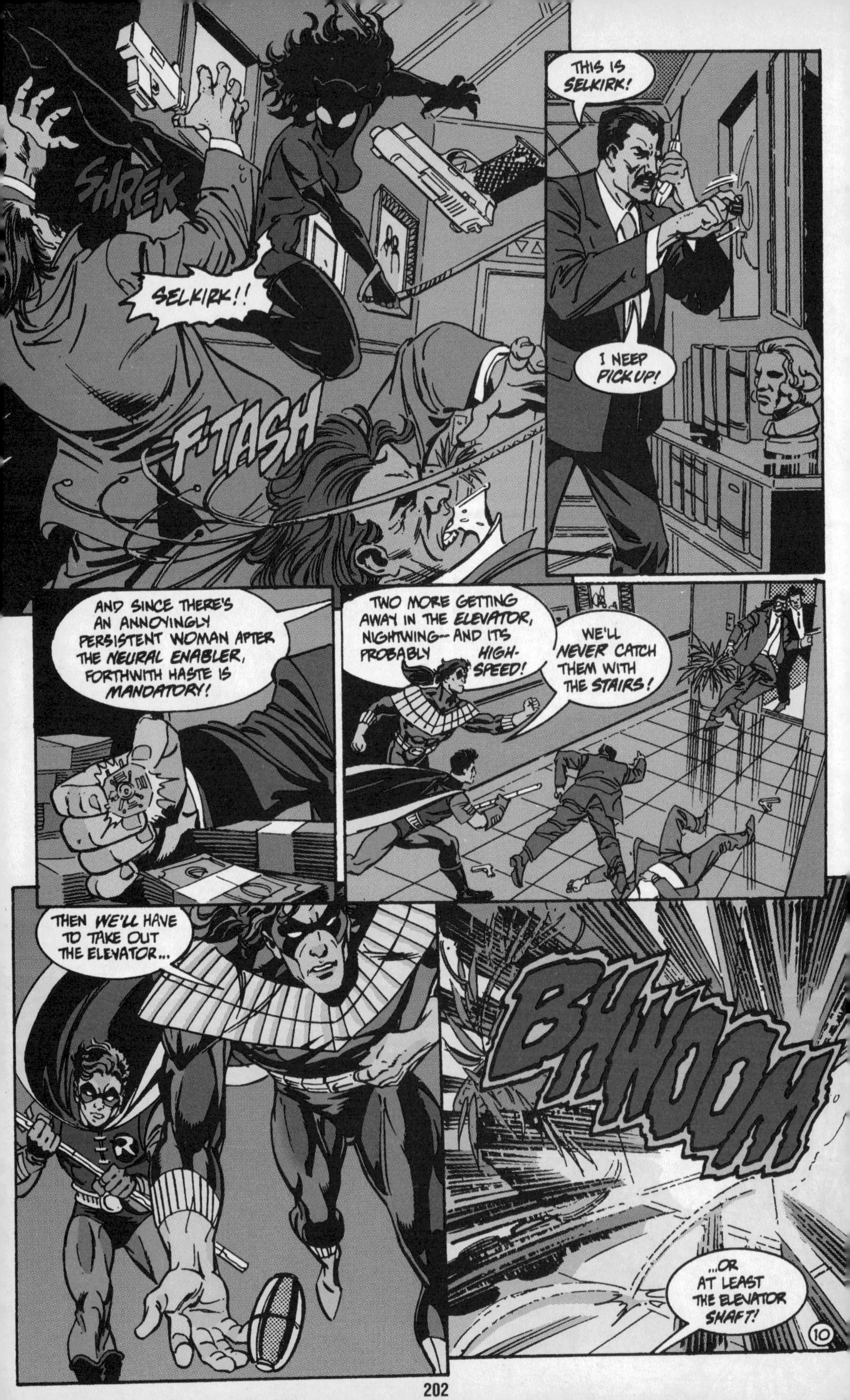
SHREK
SELKIRK!!
F-TASH
THIS IS SELKIRK!
I NEED PICKUP!
AND SINCE THERE'S AN ANNOYINGLY PERSISTENT WOMAN AFTER THE NEURAL ENABLER, FORTHWITH HASTE IS MANDATORY!
TWO MORE GETTING AWAY IN THE ELEVATOR, NIGHTWING-- AND ITS PROBABLY HIGH-SPEED!
WE'LL NEVER CATCH THEM WITH THE STAIRS!
THEN WE'LL HAVE TO TAKE OUT THE ELEVATOR...
BHWOOM
...OR AT LEAST THE ELEVATOR SHAFT!
10

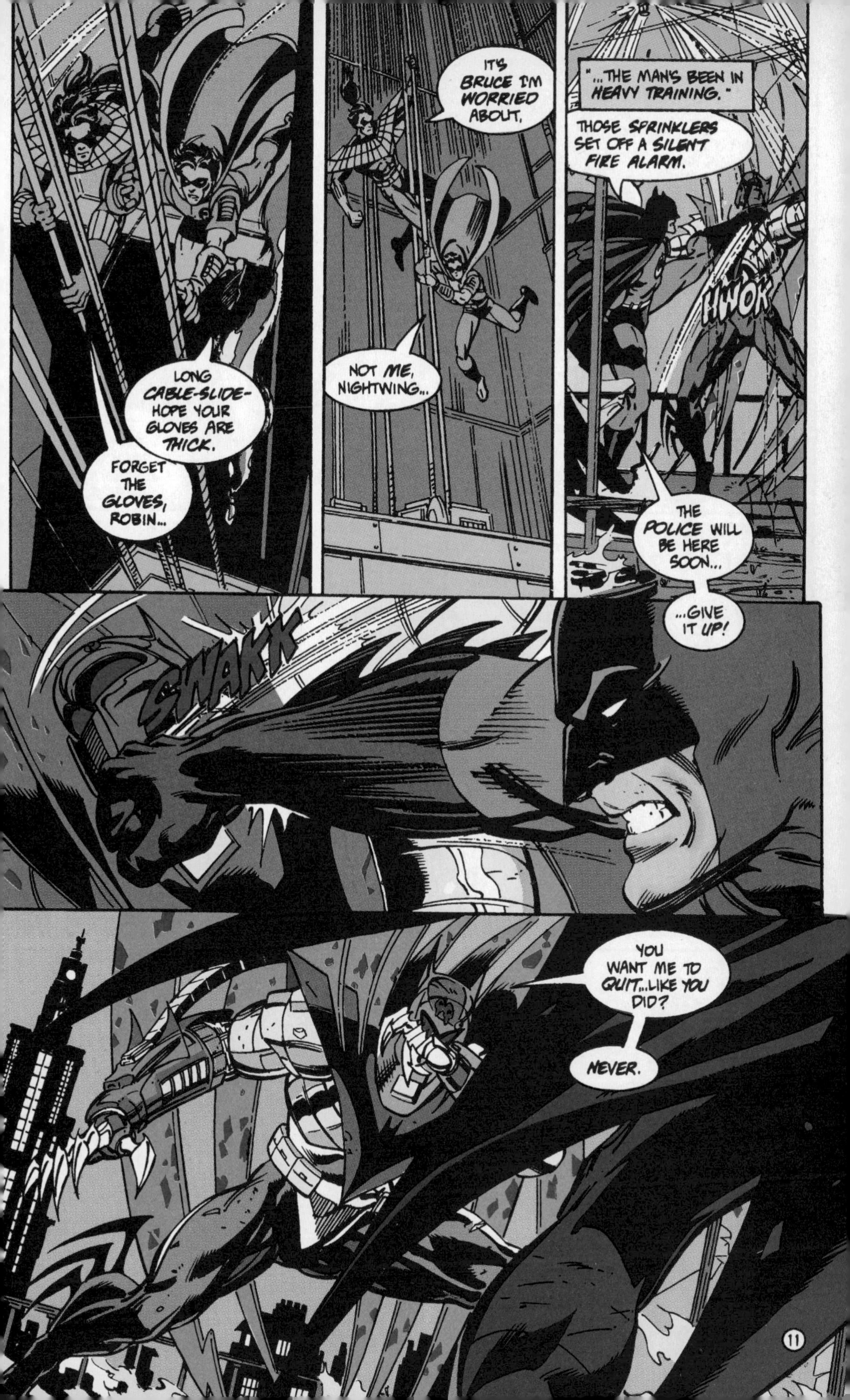
LONG CABLE-SLIDE- HOPE YOUR GLOVES ARE THICK.
FORGET THE GLOVES, ROBIN...
IT'S BRUCE I'M WORRIED ABOUT.
NOT ME, NIGHTWING...
"...THE MAN'S BEEN IN HEAVY TRAINING."
THOSE SPRINKLERS SET OFF A SILENT FIRE ALARM.
HWOK
THE POLICE WILL BE HERE SOON...
...GIVE IT UP!
SWAKK
YOU WANT ME TO QUIT...LIKE YOU DID?
NEVER.

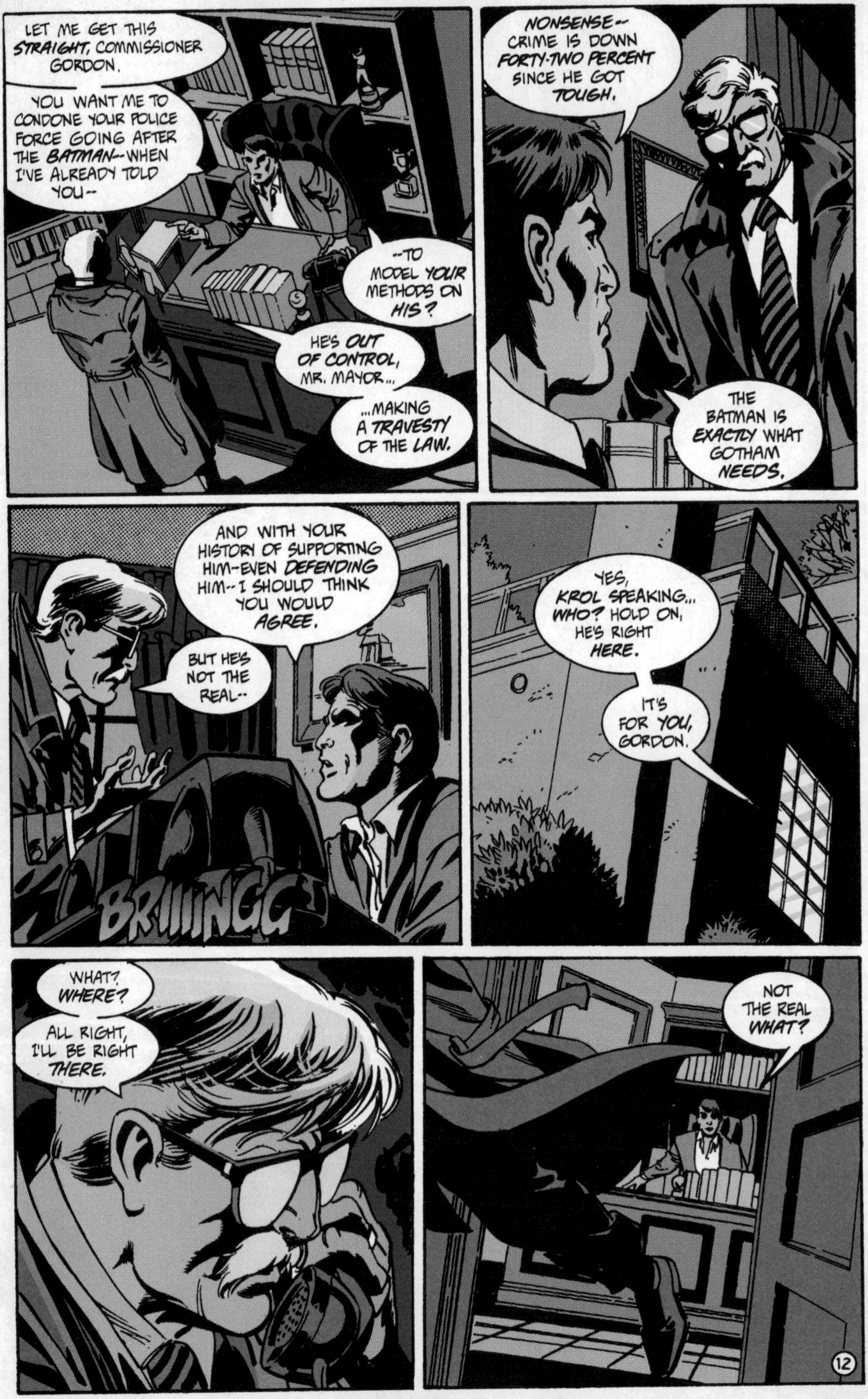
LET ME GET THIS STRAIGHT, COMMISSIONER GORDON.
YOU WANT ME TO CONDONE YOUR POLICE FORCE GOING AFTER THE BATMAN--WHEN I'VE ALREADY TOLD YOU--
--TO MODEL YOUR METHODS ON HIS?
HE'S OUT OF CONTROL, MR. MAYOR...
...MAKING A TRAVESTY OF THE LAW.
NONSENSE-- CRIME IS DOWN FORTY-TWO PERCENT SINCE HE GOT TOUGH.
THE BATMAN IS EXACTLY WHAT GOTHAM NEEDS.
AND WITH YOUR HISTORY OF SUPPORTING HIM--EVEN DEFENDING HIM--I SHOULD THINK YOU WOULD AGREE.
BUT HE'S NOT THE REAL--
BRIIINGG
YES, KROL SPEAKING... WHO? HOLD ON, HE'S RIGHT HERE.
IT'S FOR YOU, GORDON.
WHAT? WHERE?
ALL RIGHT, I'LL BE RIGHT THERE.
NOT THE REAL WHAT?
12

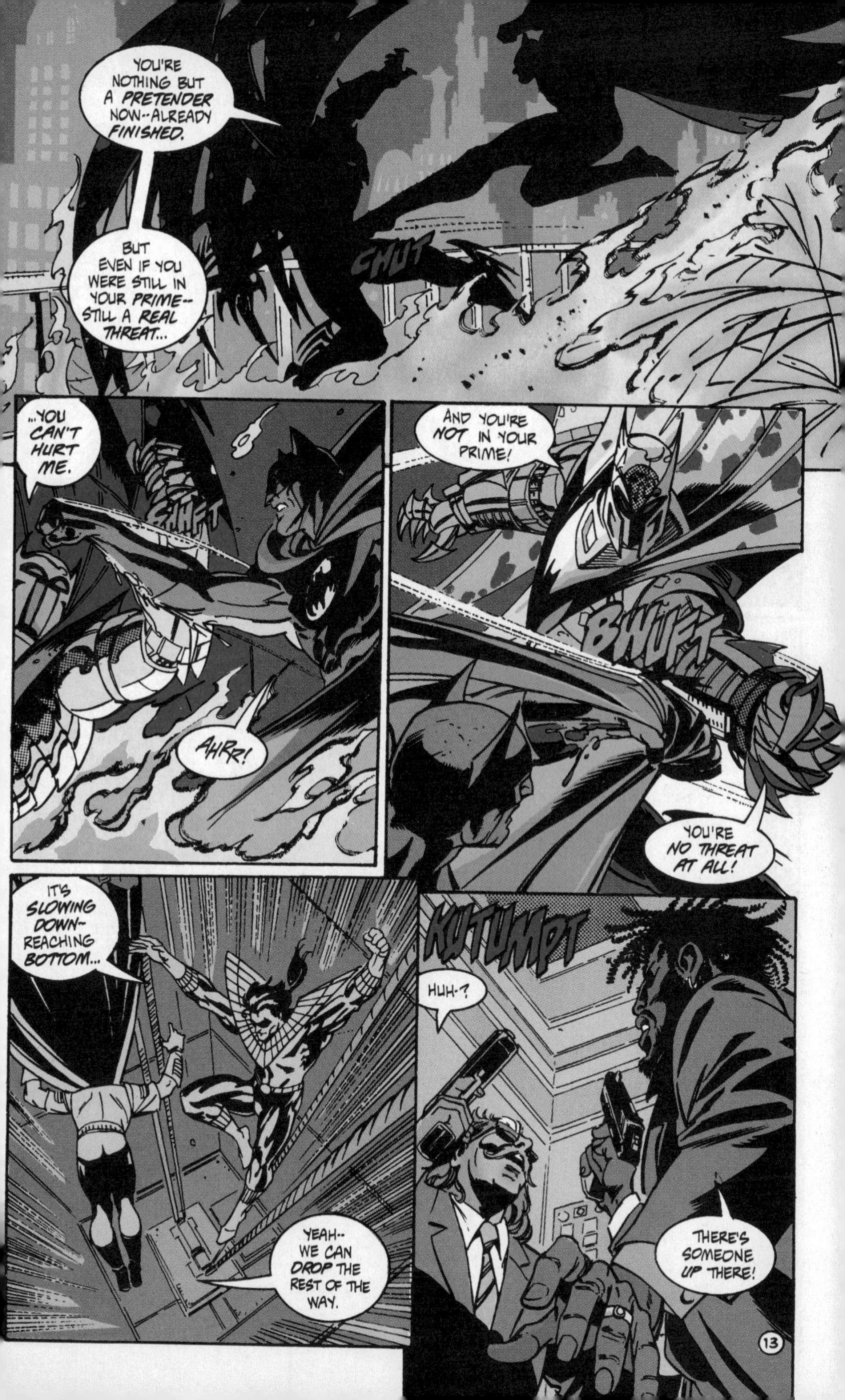
YOU'RE NOTHING BUT A PRETENDER NOW--ALREADY FINISHED.
BUT EVEN IF YOU WERE STILL IN YOUR PRIME-- STILL A REAL THREAT...
CHUT
...YOU CAN'T HURT ME.
SHHFT
AHRR!
AND YOU'RE NOT IN YOUR PRIME!
BWUFF
YOU'RE NO THREAT AT ALL!
IT'S SLOWING DOWN-- REACHING BOTTOM...
YEAH-- WE CAN DROP THE REST OF THE WAY.
KUTUMPT
HUH-?
THERE'S SOMEONE UP THERE!
13

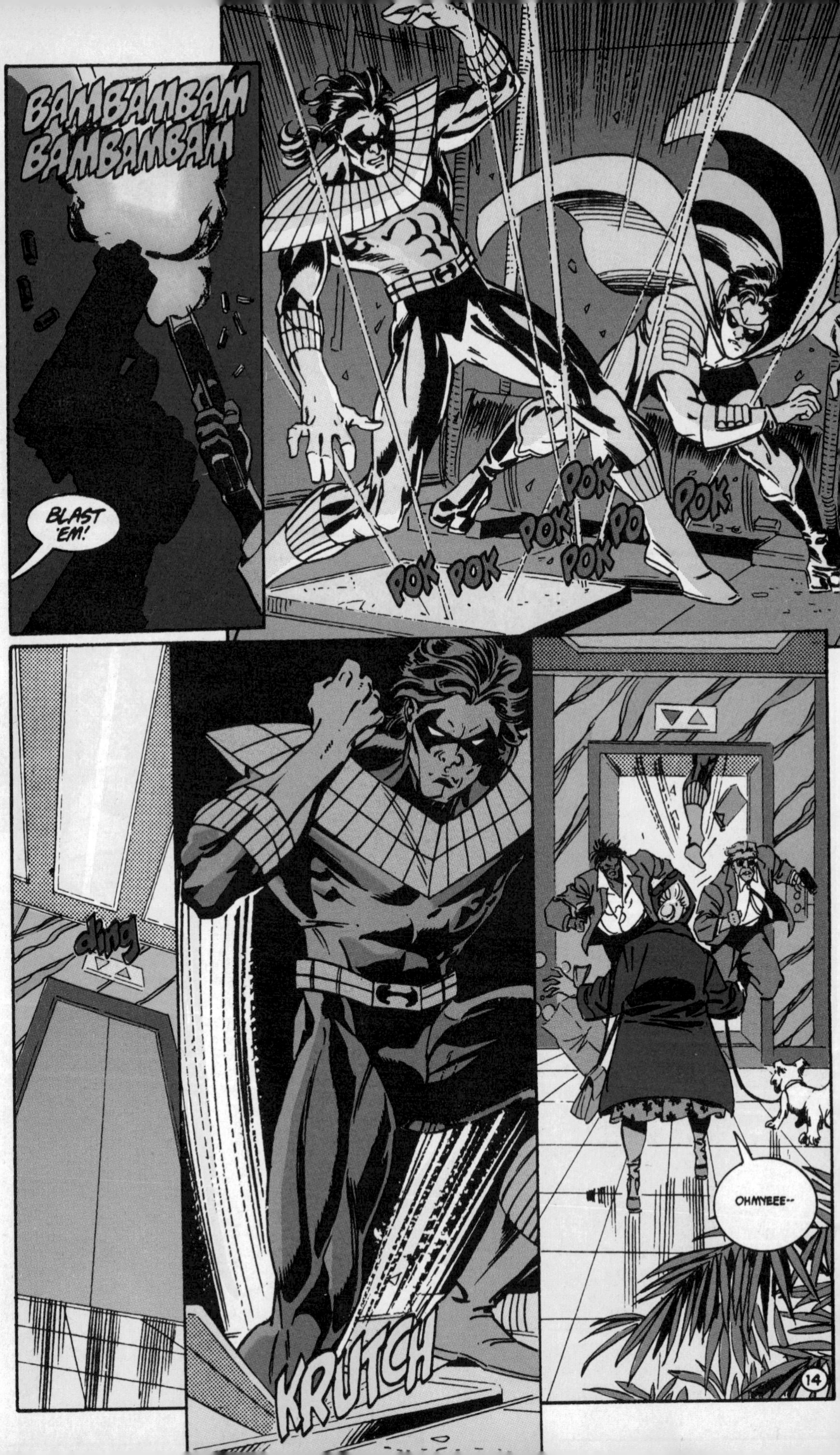
BAMBAMBAM
BAMBAMBAM
BLAST 'EM!
POK POK POK POK POK POK POK
ding
KRUTCH
OHMYEEE--
14

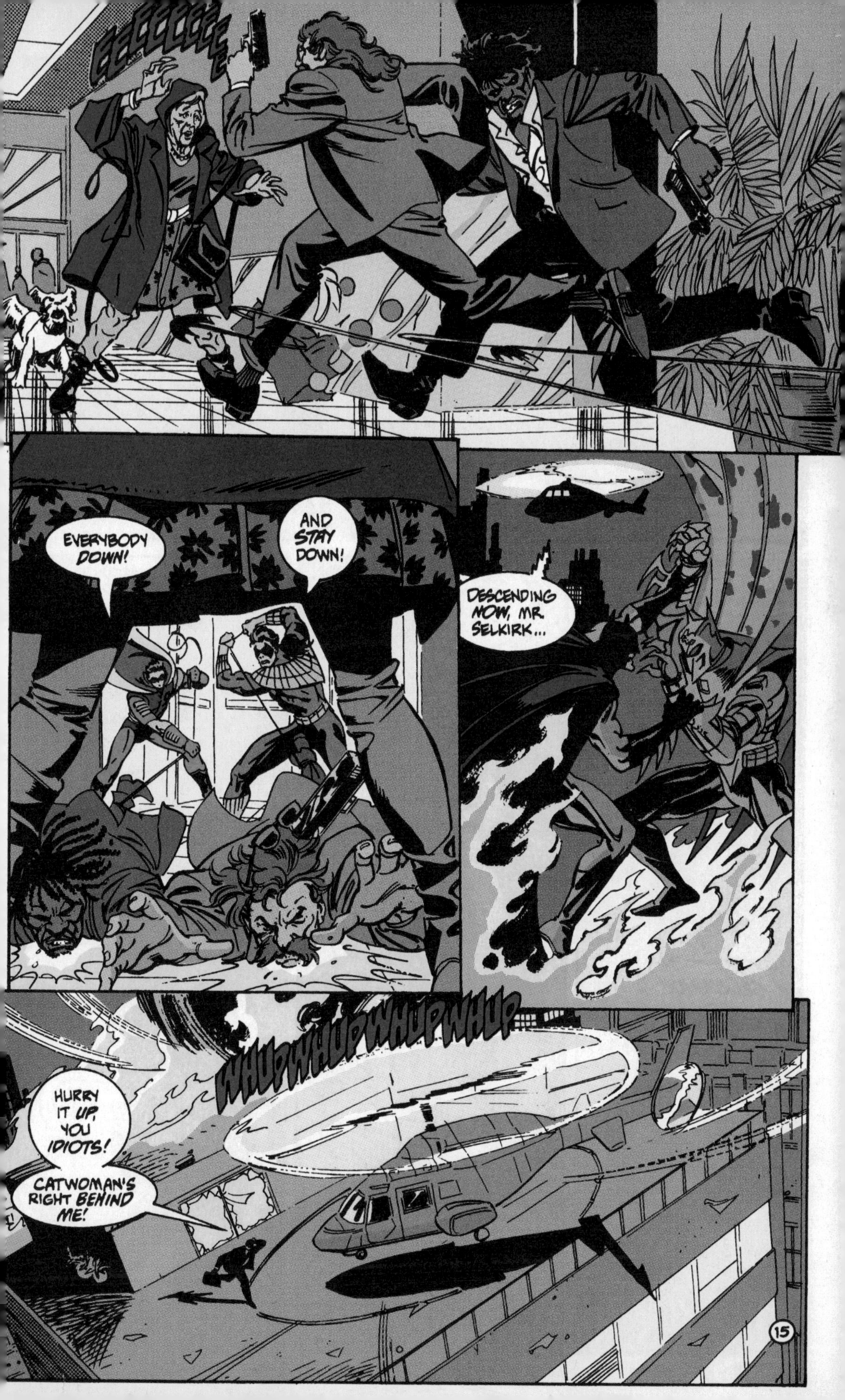
EEEEEEEEE
EVERYBODY DOWN!
AND STAY DOWN!
DESCENDING NOW, MR. SELKIRK...
WHUPWHUPWHUPWHUP
HURRY IT UP, YOU IDIOTS!
CATWOMAN'S RIGHT BEHIND ME!

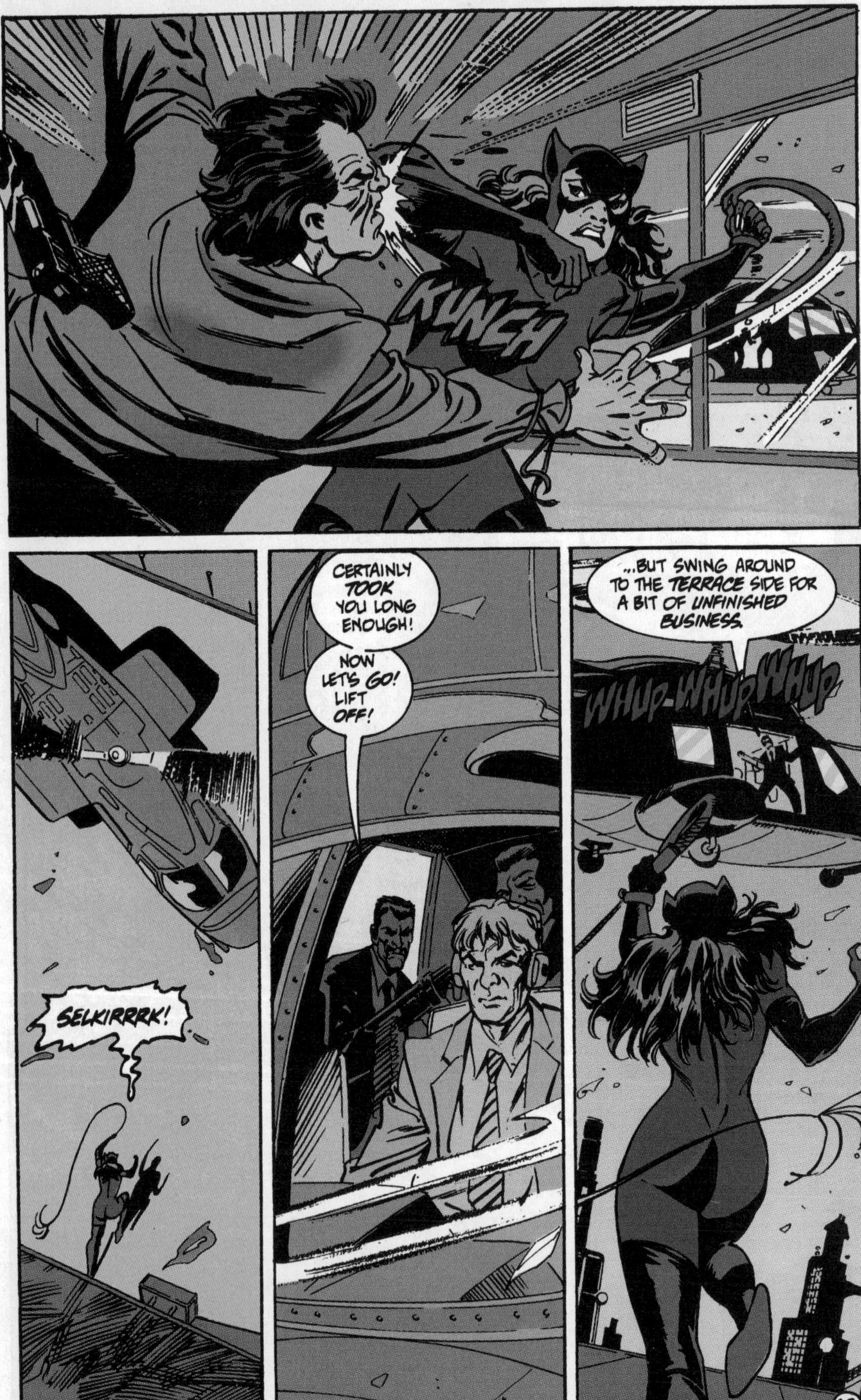
SELKIRRRK!
CERTAINLY TOOK YOU LONG ENOUGH!
NOW LET'S GO! LIFT OFF!
...BUT SWING AROUND TO THE TERRACE SIDE FOR A BIT OF UNFINISHED BUSINESS.
WHUP WHUP WHUP
16

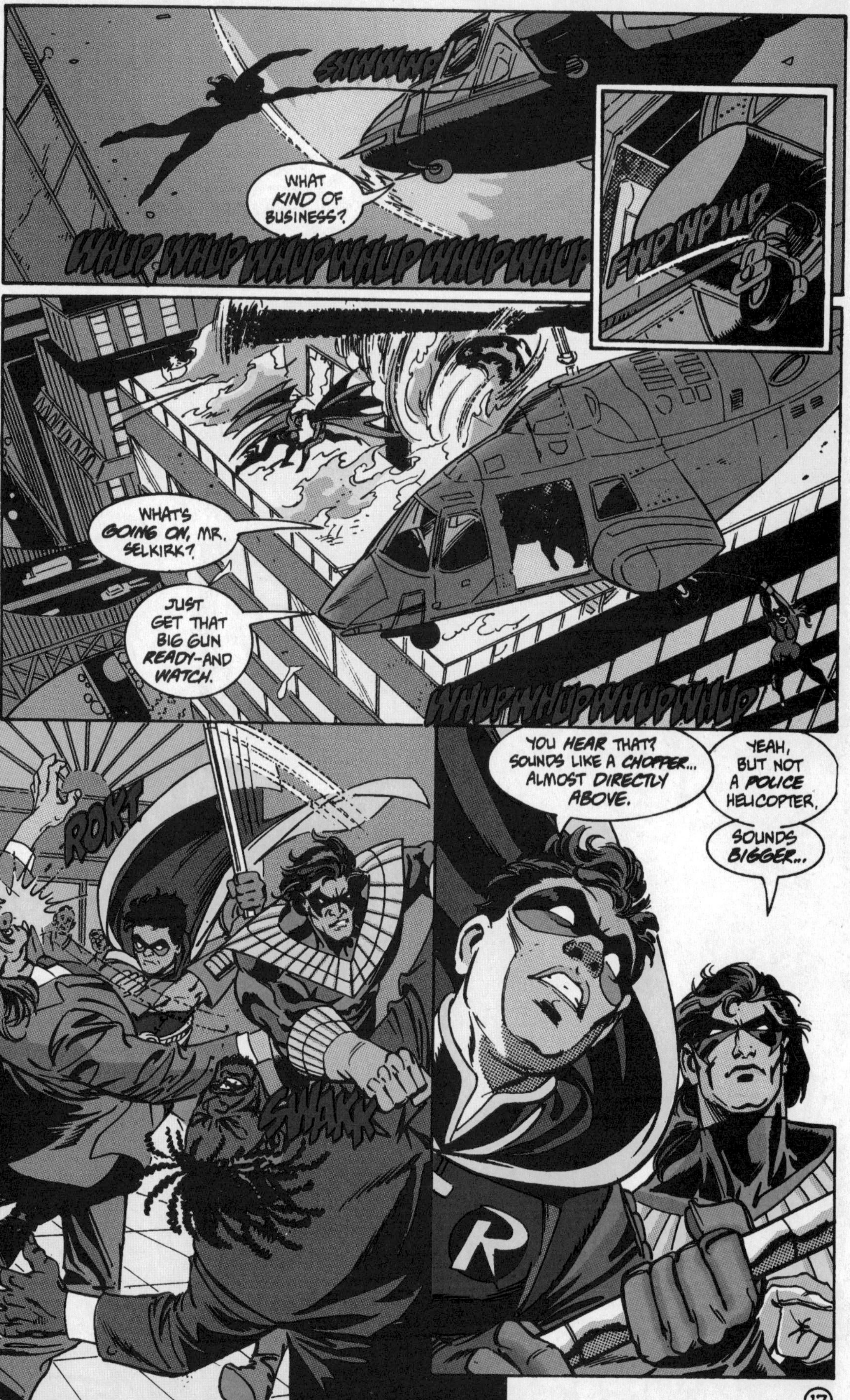
SHWWWP
WHAT KIND OF BUSINESS?
WHUP WHUP WHUP WHUP WHUP WHUP
FWP WP WP
WHAT'S GOING ON, MR. SELKIRK?
JUST GET THAT BIG GUN READY--AND WATCH.
WHUPWHUPWHUPWHUP
ROKT
SHAKK
YOU HEAR THAT? SOUNDS LIKE A CHOPPER... ALMOST DIRECTLY ABOVE.
YEAH, BUT NOT A POLICE HELICOPTER.
SOUNDS BIGGER...

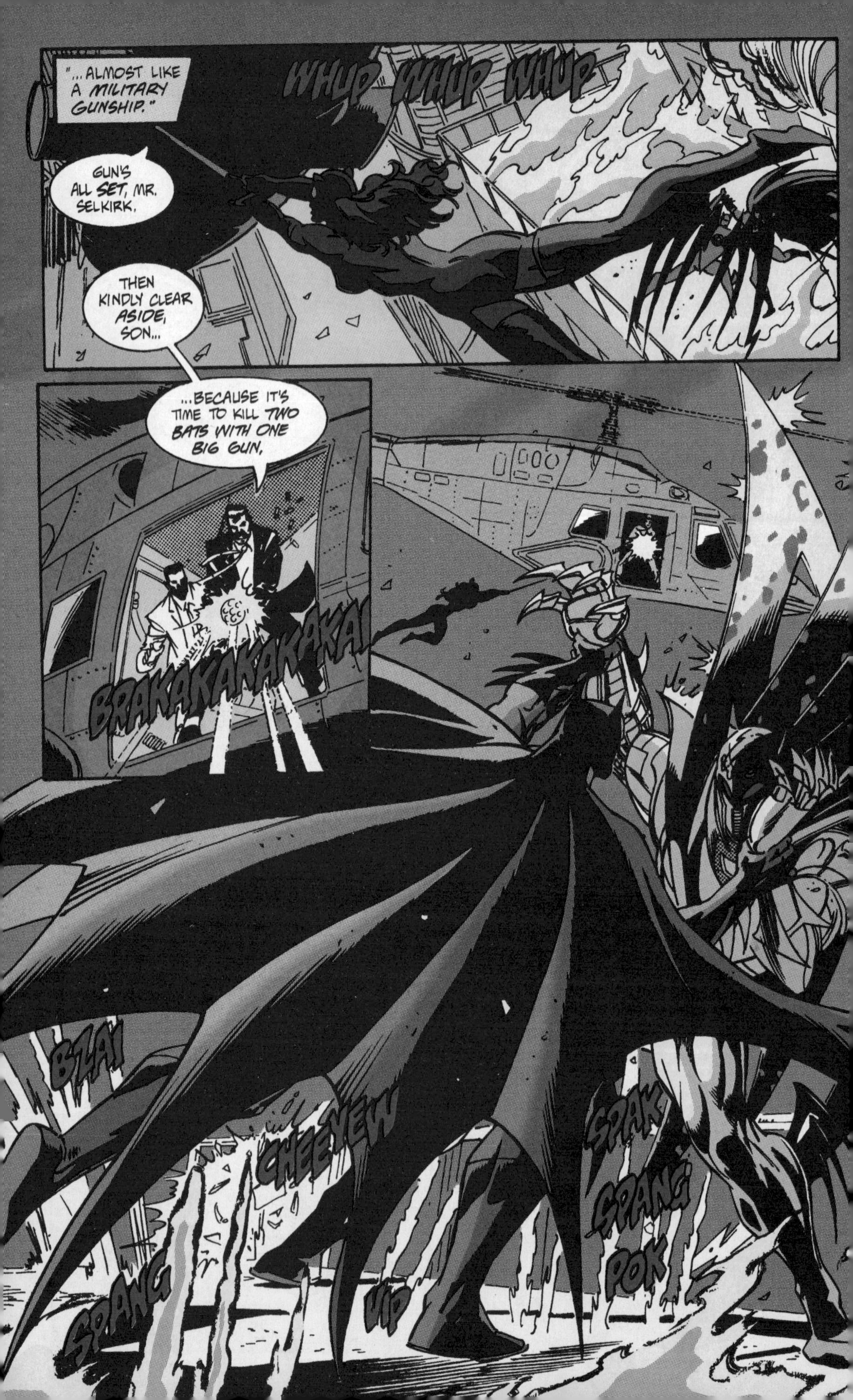
"...ALMOST LIKE A MILITARY GUNSHIP."
WHUP WHUP WHUP
GUN'S ALL SET, MR. SELKIRK.
THEN KINDLY CLEAR ASIDE, SON...
...BECAUSE IT'S TIME TO KILL TWO BATS WITH ONE BIG GUN.
BRAKAKAKAKAKAKA
BZAI
CHEEYEW
SPAK
SPANG
POK
SPANG
UP

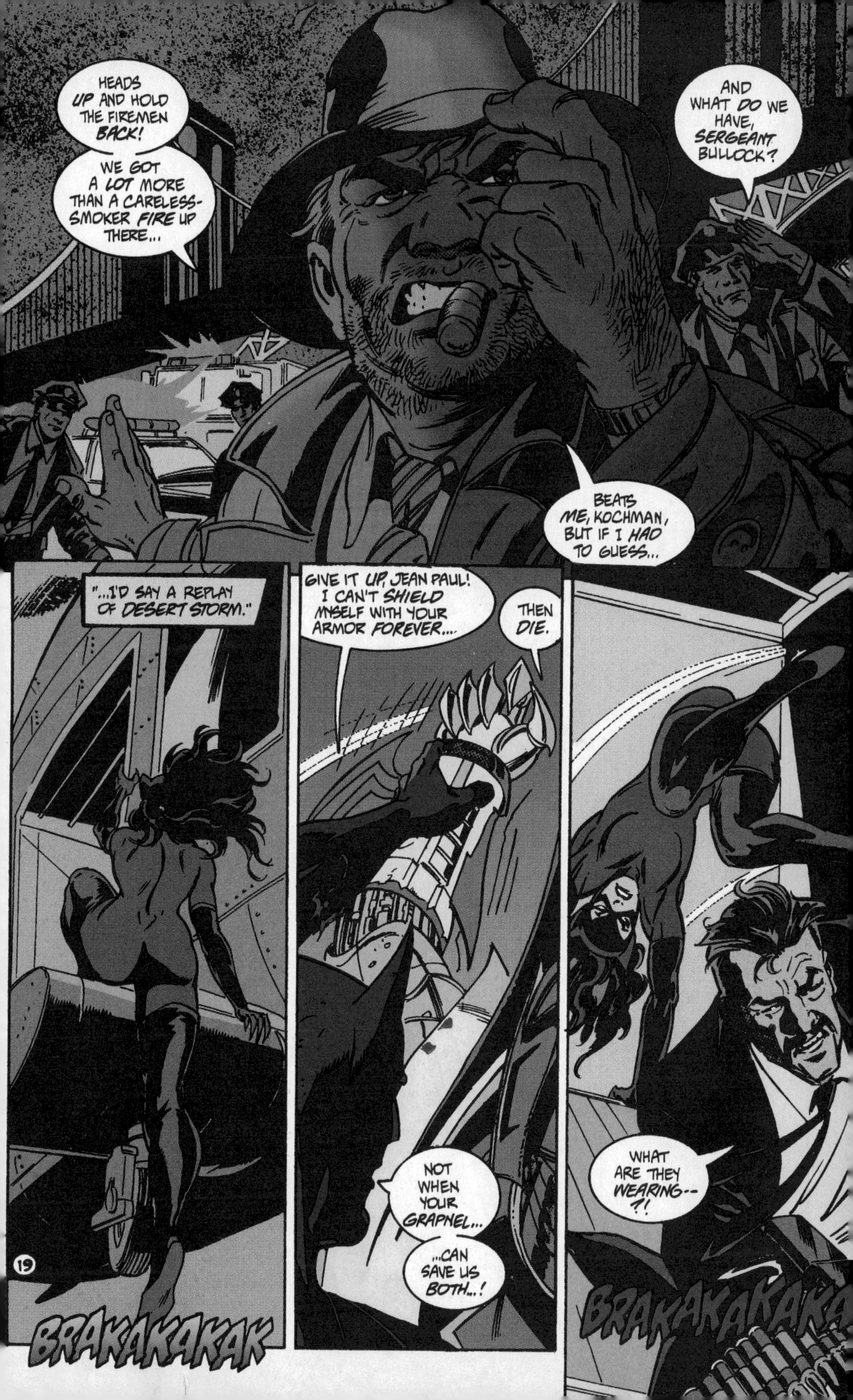
HEADS UP AND HOLD THE FIREMEN BACK!
WE GOT A LOT MORE THAN A CARELESS-SMOKER FIRE UP THERE...
AND WHAT DO WE HAVE, SERGEANT BULLOCK?
BEATS ME, KOCHMAN, BUT IF I HAD TO GUESS...
"...I'D SAY A REPLAY OF DESERT STORM."
19
BRAKAKAKAK
GIVE IT UP, JEAN PAUL! I CAN'T SHIELD MYSELF WITH YOUR ARMOR FOREVER....
THEN DIE.
NOT WHEN YOUR GRAPNEL...
...CAN SAVE US BOTH...!
WHAT ARE THEY WEARING--?!
BRAKAKAKAKA

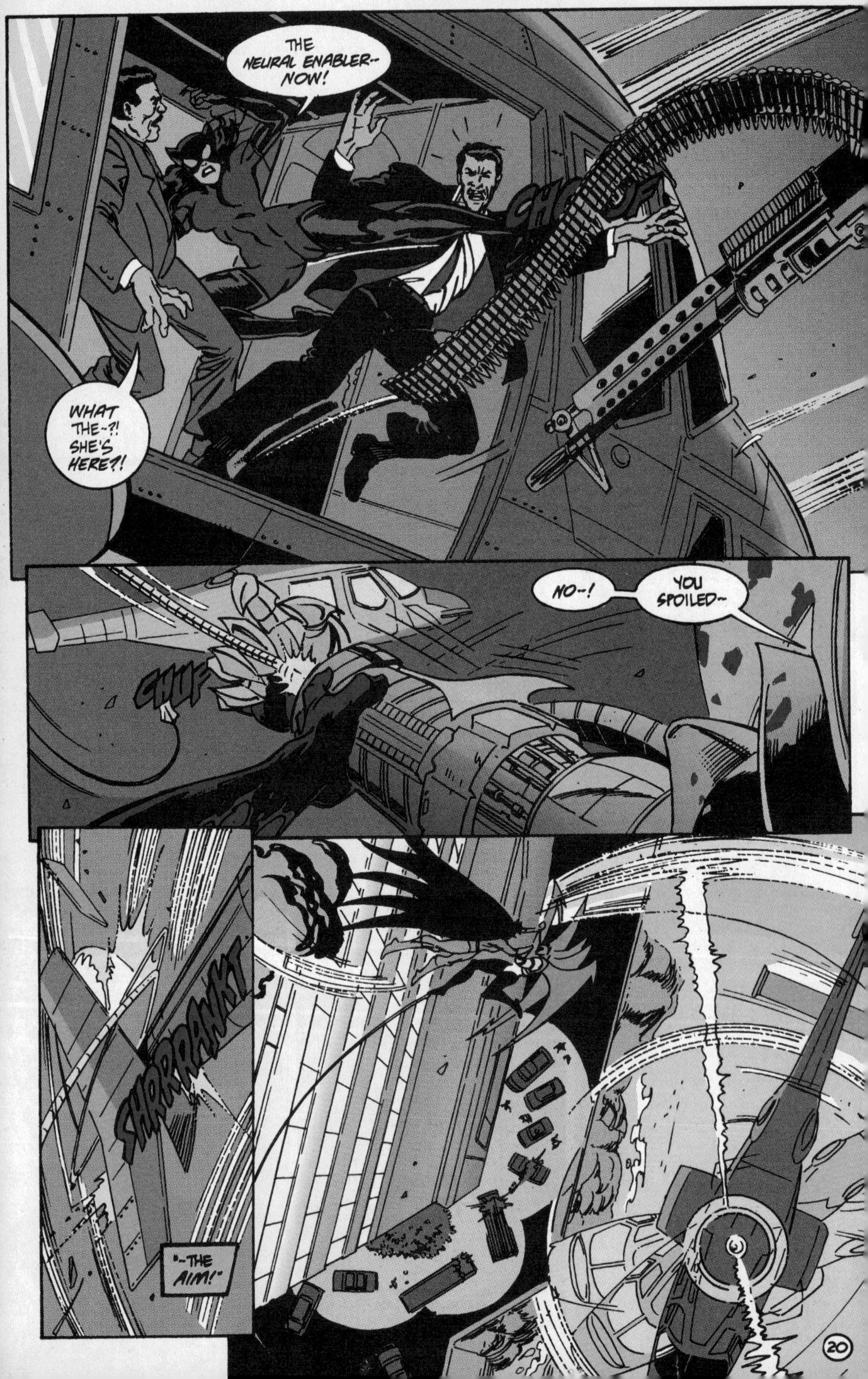
THE NEURAL ENABLER-- NOW!
CHOOF
WHAT THE--?! SHE'S HERE?!
NO--!
YOU SPOILED--
CHUF
SHRRAANKT
"--THE AIM!"

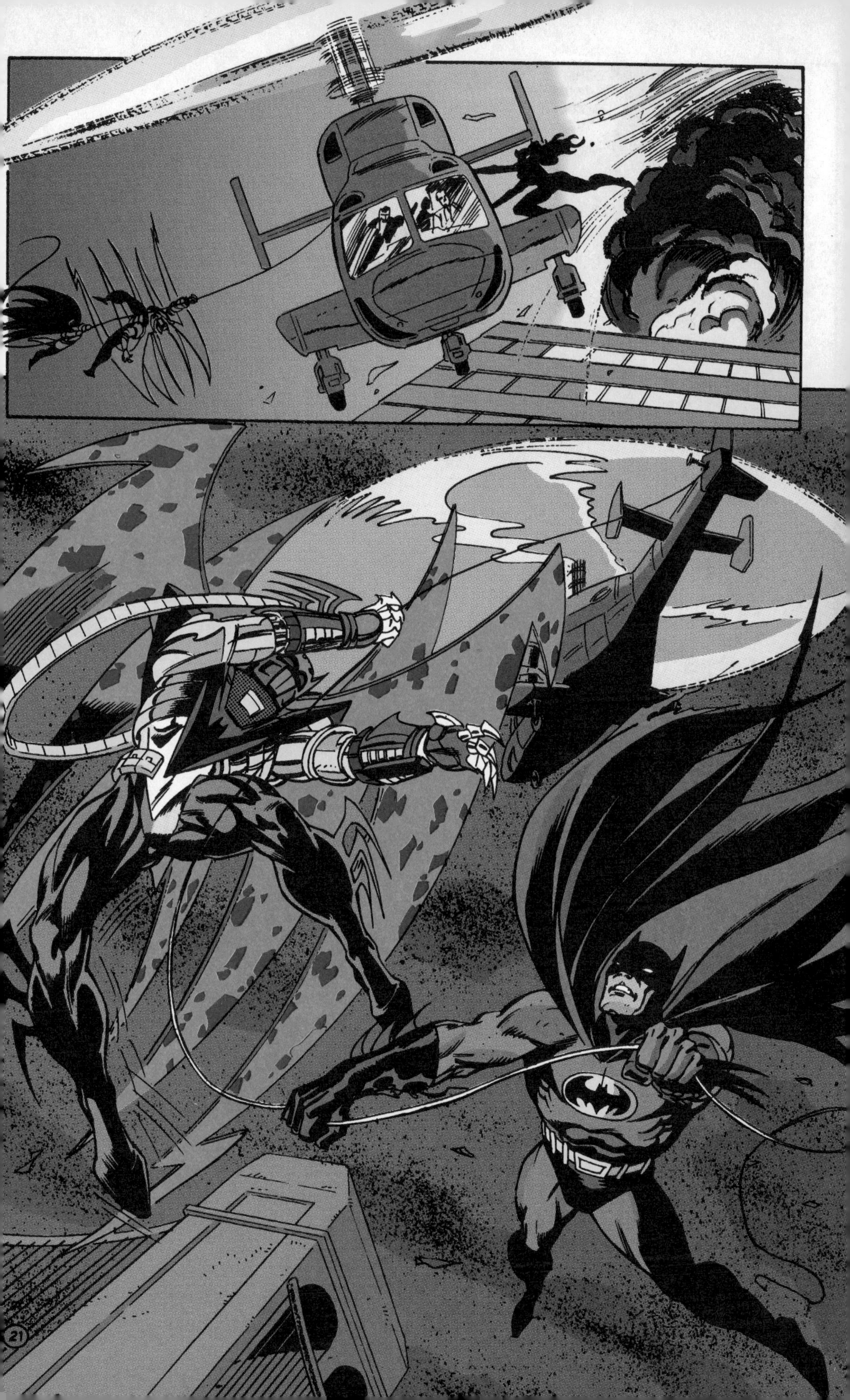

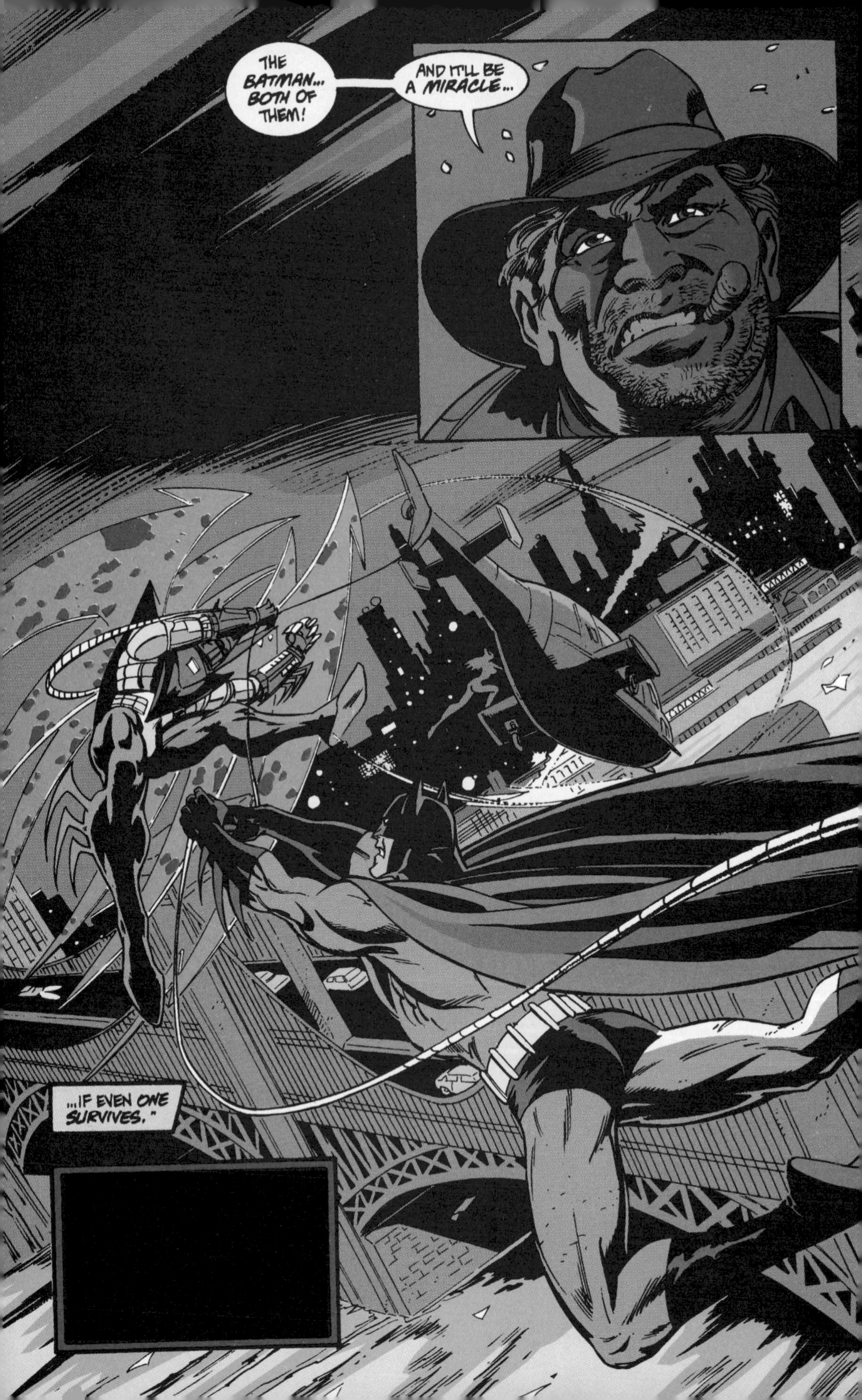
THE BATMAN... BOTH OF THEM!
AND IT'LL BE A MIRACLE...
...IF EVEN ONE SURVIVES."

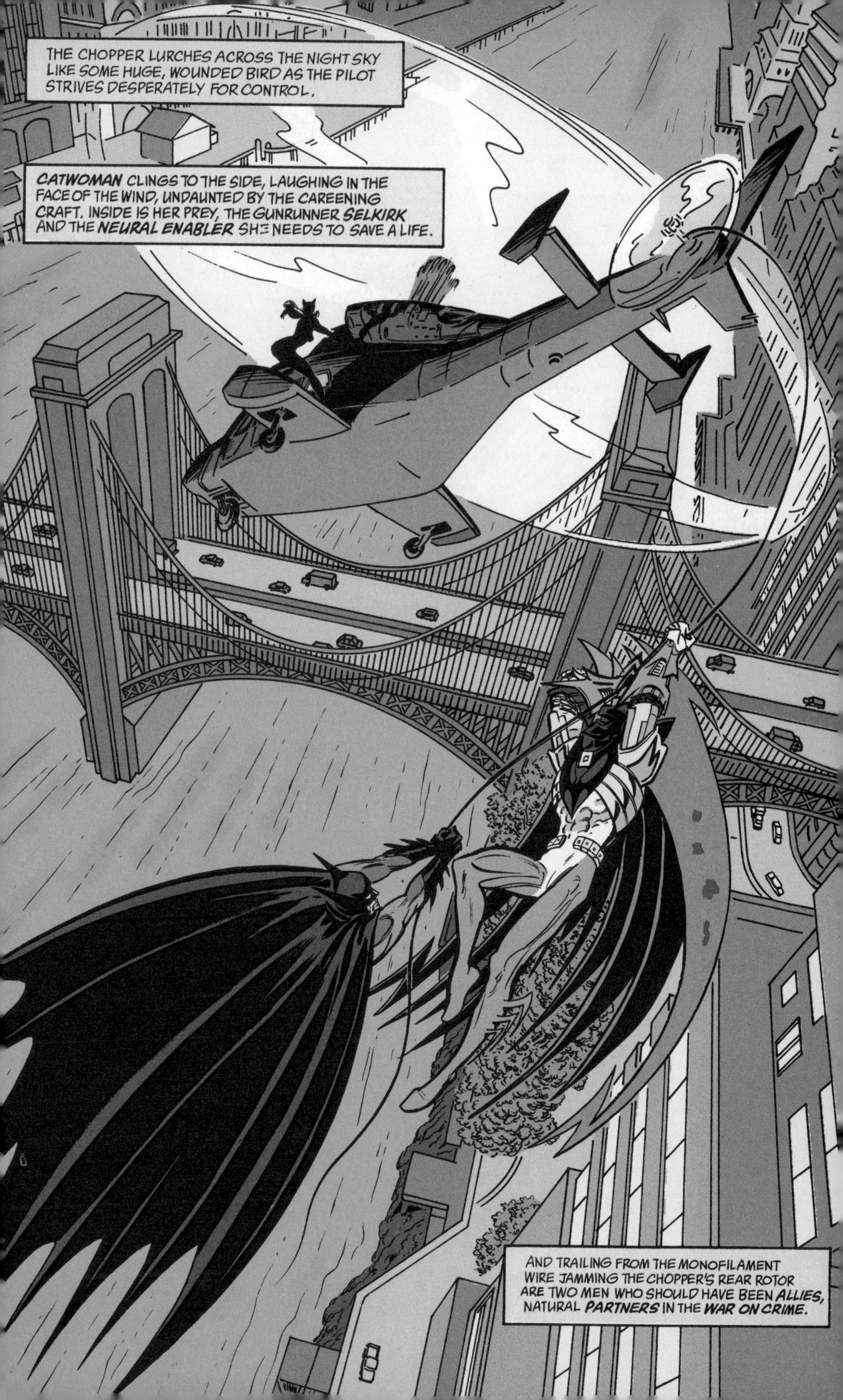
THE CHOPPER LURCHES ACROSS THE NIGHT SKY LIKE SOME HUGE, WOUNDED BIRD AS THE PILOT STRIVES DESPERATELY FOR CONTROL.
CATWOMAN CLINGS TO THE SIDE, LAUGHING IN THE FACE OF THE WIND, UNDAUNTED BY THE CAREENING CRAFT. INSIDE IS HER PREY, THE GUNRUNNER SELKIRK AND THE NEURAL ENABLER SHE NEEDS TO SAVE A LIFE.
AND TRAILING FROM THE MONOFILAMENT WIRE JAMMING THE CHOPPER'S REAR ROTOR ARE TWO MEN WHO SHOULD HAVE BEEN ALLIES, NATURAL PARTNERS IN THE WAR ON CRIME.

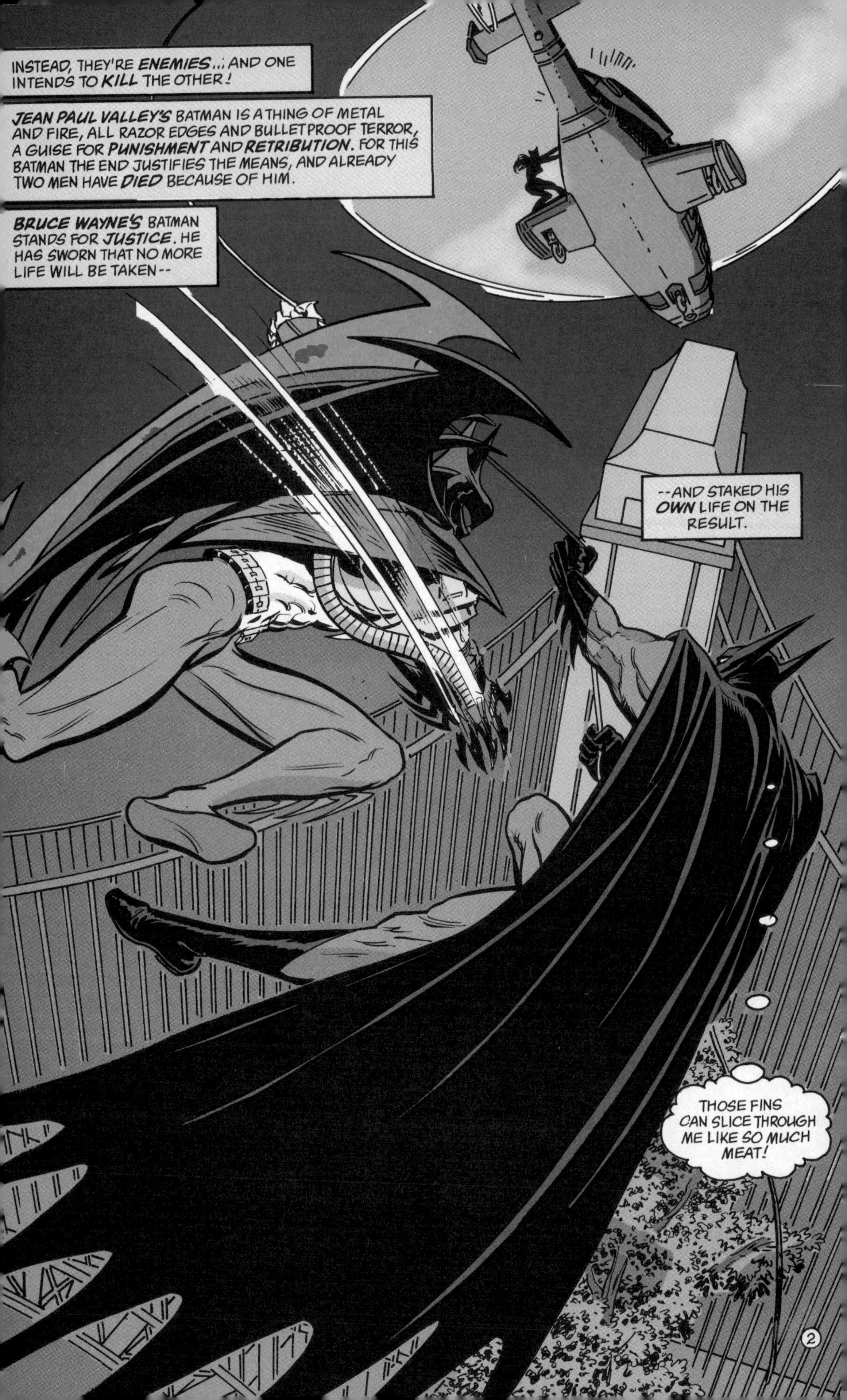
INSTEAD, THEY'RE ENEMIES...; AND ONE INTENDS TO KILL THE OTHER!
JEAN PAUL VALLEY'S BATMAN IS A THING OF METAL AND FIRE, ALL RAZOR EDGES AND BULLETPROOF TERROR, A GUISE FOR PUNISHMENT AND RETRIBUTION. FOR THIS BATMAN THE END JUSTIFIES THE MEANS, AND ALREADY TWO MEN HAVE DIED BECAUSE OF HIM.
BRUCE WAYNE'S BATMAN STANDS FOR JUSTICE. HE HAS SWORN THAT NO MORE LIFE WILL BE TAKEN--
--AND STAKED HIS OWN LIFE ON THE RESULT.
THOSE FINS CAN SLICE THROUGH ME LIKE SO MUCH MEAT!
2

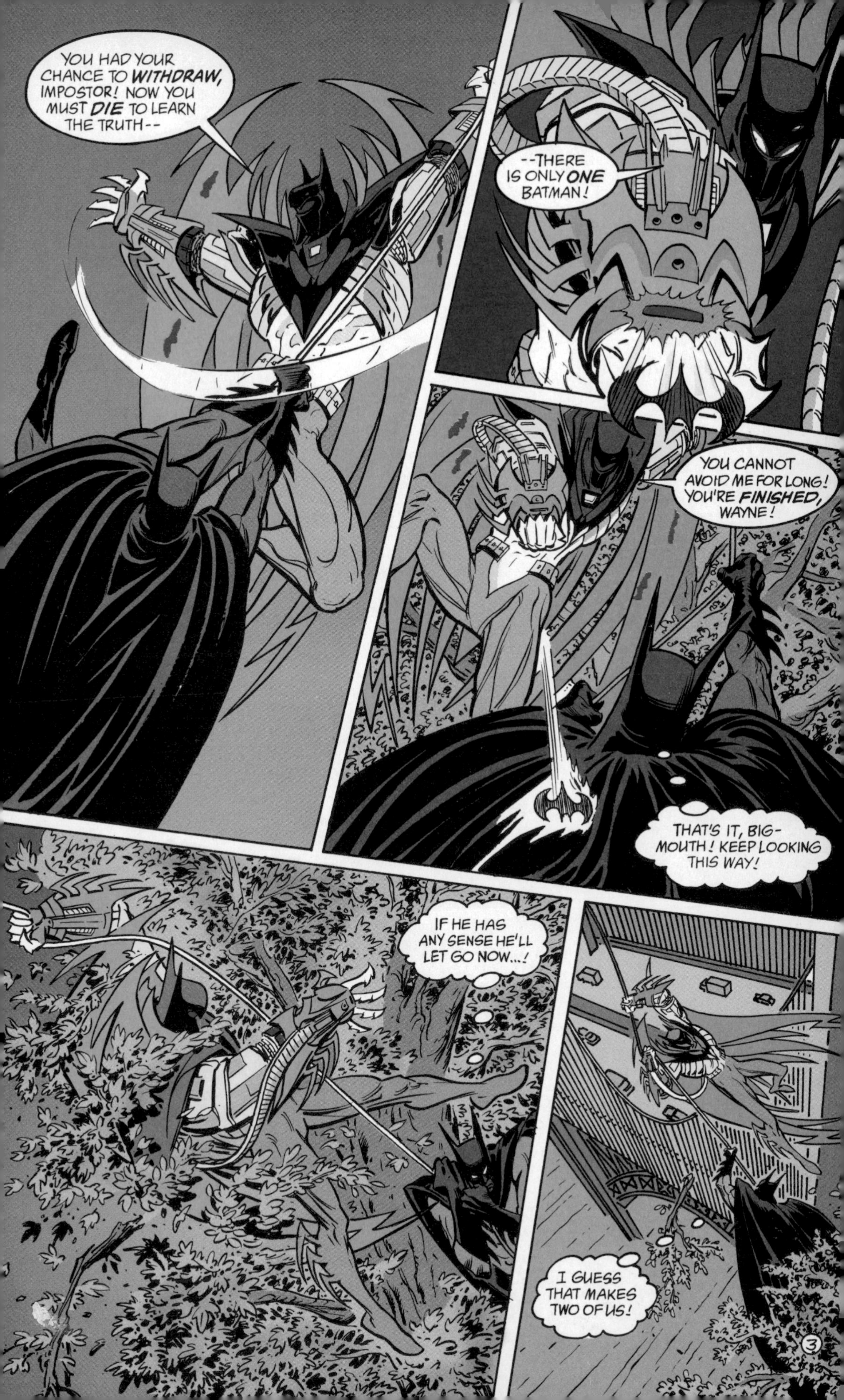
YOU HAD YOUR CHANCE TO WITHDRAW, IMPOSTOR! NOW YOU MUST DIE TO LEARN THE TRUTH--
--THERE IS ONLY ONE BATMAN!
YOU CANNOT AVOID ME FOR LONG! YOU'RE FINISHED, WAYNE!
THAT'S IT, BIG-MOUTH! KEEP LOOKING THIS WAY!
IF HE HAS ANY SENSE HE'LL LET GO NOW...!
I GUESS THAT MAKES TWO OF US!

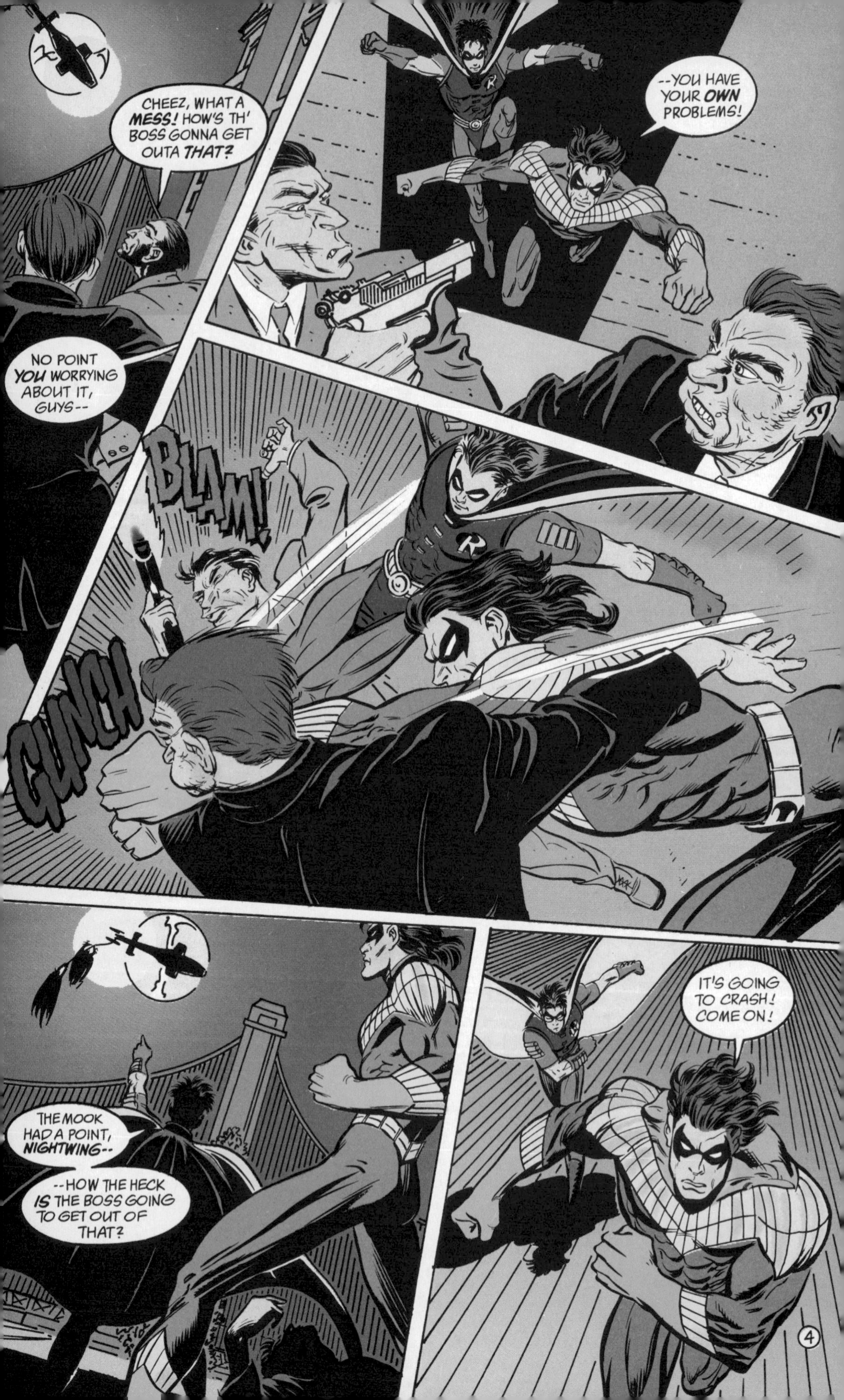
CHEEZ, WHAT A MESS! HOW'S TH' BOSS GONNA GET OUTA THAT?
NO POINT YOU WORRYING ABOUT IT, GUYS--
--YOU HAVE YOUR OWN PROBLEMS!
BLAM!
GUNCH
THE MOOK HAD A POINT, NIGHTWING--
--HOW THE HECK IS THE BOSS GOING TO GET OUT OF THAT?
IT'S GOING TO CRASH! COME ON!

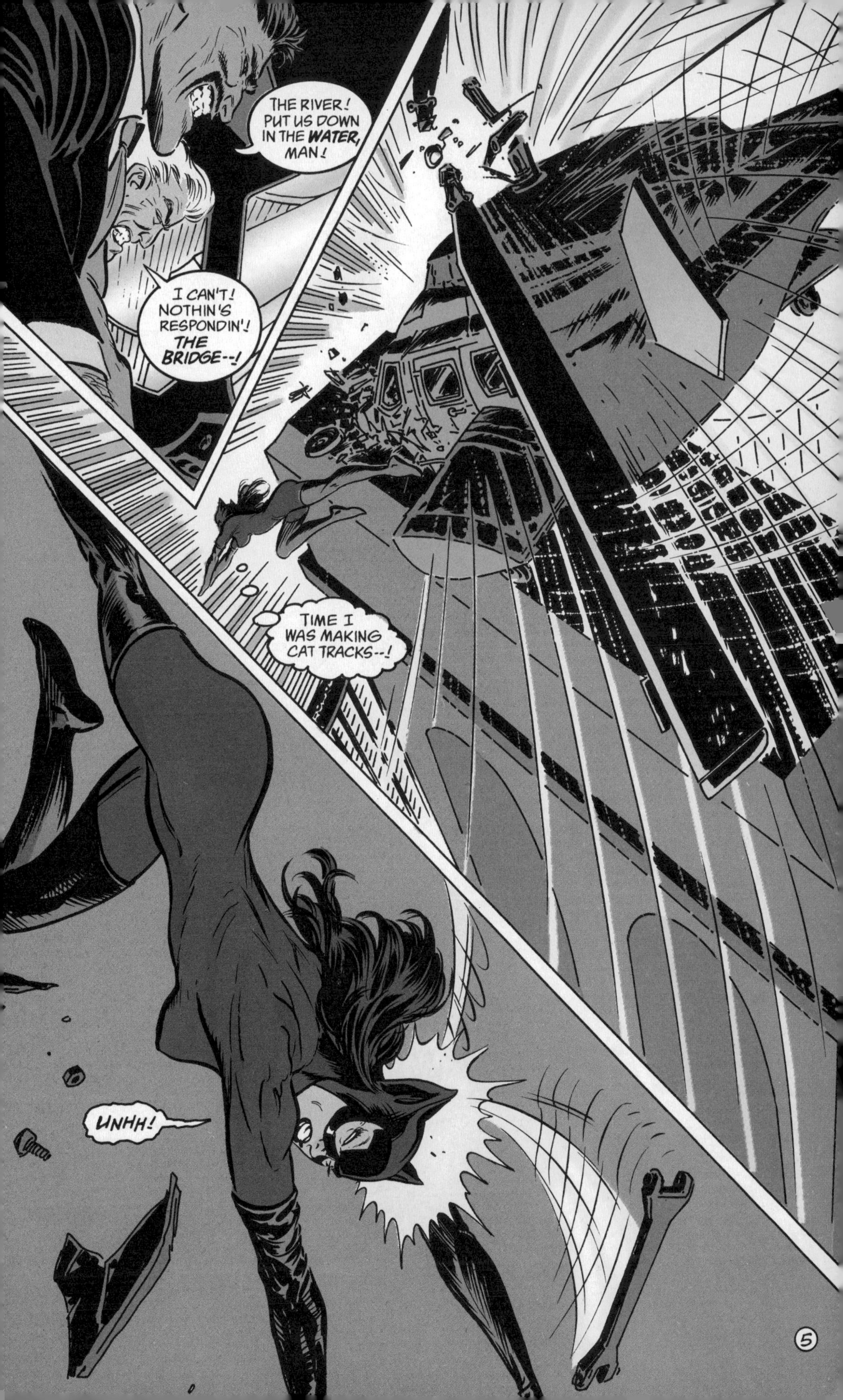
THE RIVER! PUT US DOWN IN THE WATER, MAN!
I CAN'T! NOTHIN'S RESPONDIN'! THE BRIDGE--!
TIME I WAS MAKING CAT TRACKS--!
UNHH!
5

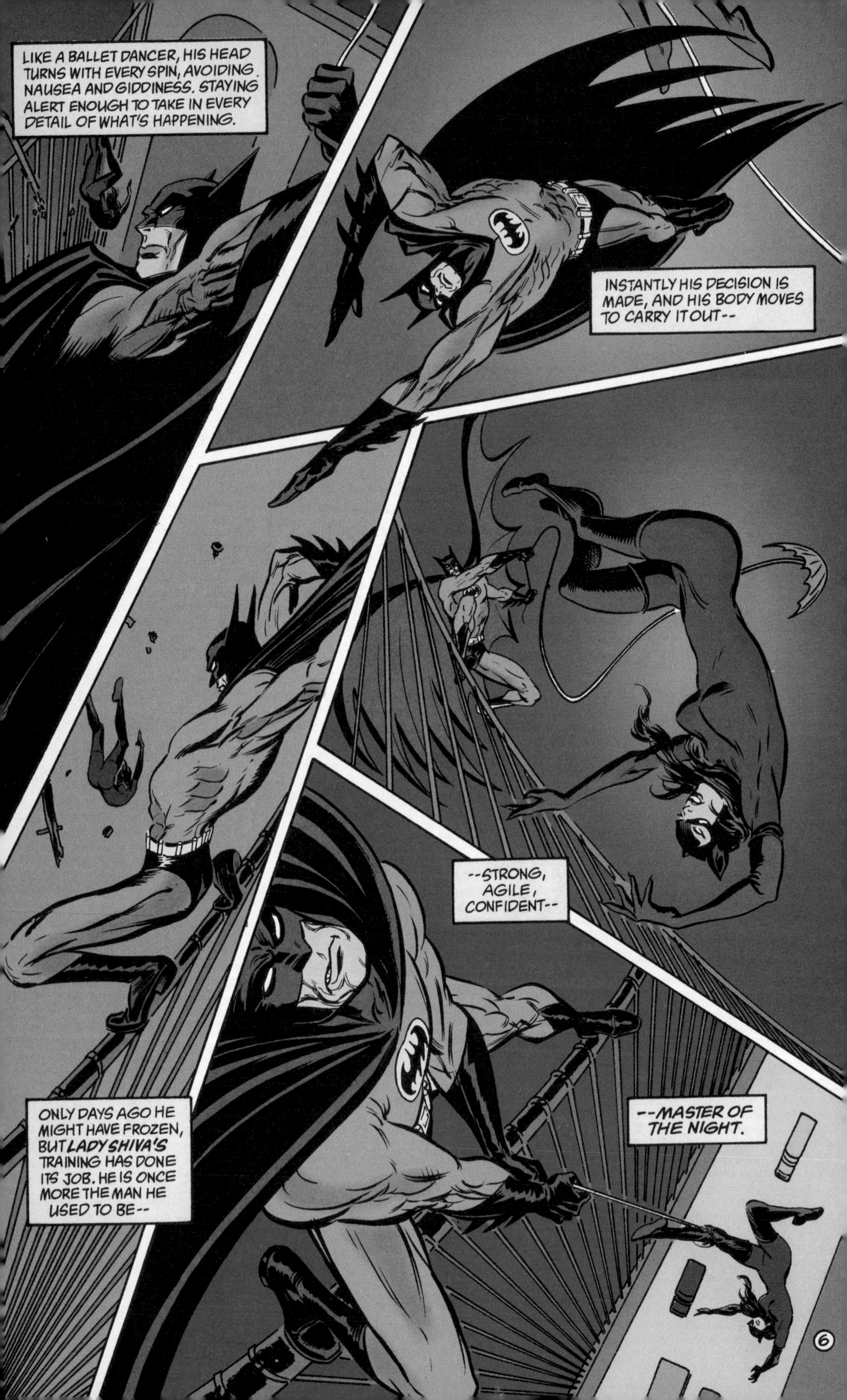
LIKE A BALLET DANCER, HIS HEAD TURNS WITH EVERY SPIN, AVOIDING NAUSEA AND GIDDINESS. STAYING ALERT ENOUGH TO TAKE IN EVERY DETAIL OF WHAT'S HAPPENING.
INSTANTLY HIS DECISION IS MADE, AND HIS BODY MOVES TO CARRY IT OUT--
--STRONG, AGILE, CONFIDENT--
ONLY DAYS AGO HE MIGHT HAVE FROZEN, BUT LADY SHIVA'S TRAINING HAS DONE ITS JOB. HE IS ONCE MORE THE MAN HE USED TO BE--
--MASTER OF THE NIGHT.

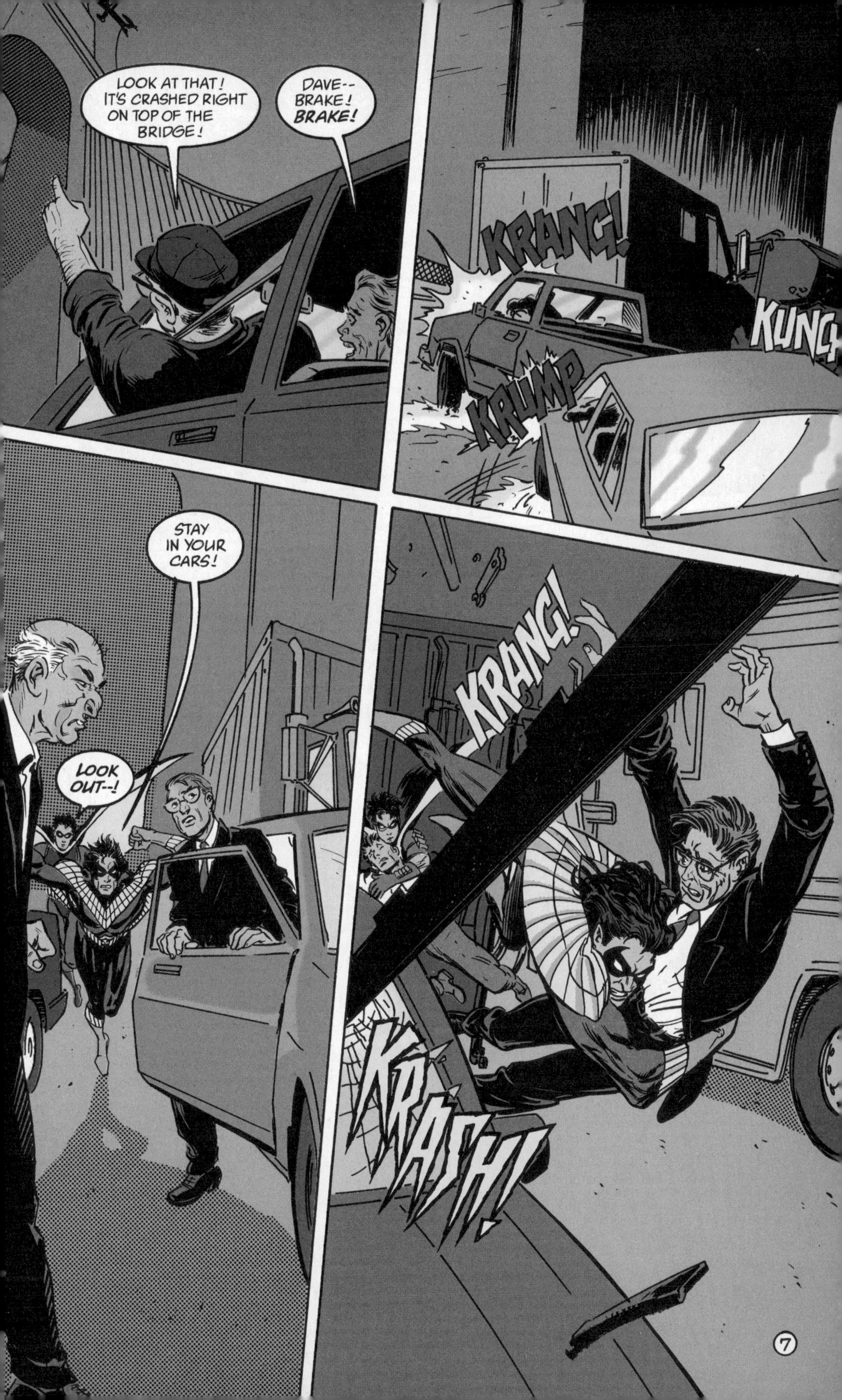
LOOK AT THAT! IT'S CRASHED RIGHT ON TOP OF THE BRIDGE!
DAVE-- BRAKE! BRAKE!
KRANG!
KUNCH
KRUMP
STAY IN YOUR CARS!
LOOK OUT--!
KRANG!
KRASH!

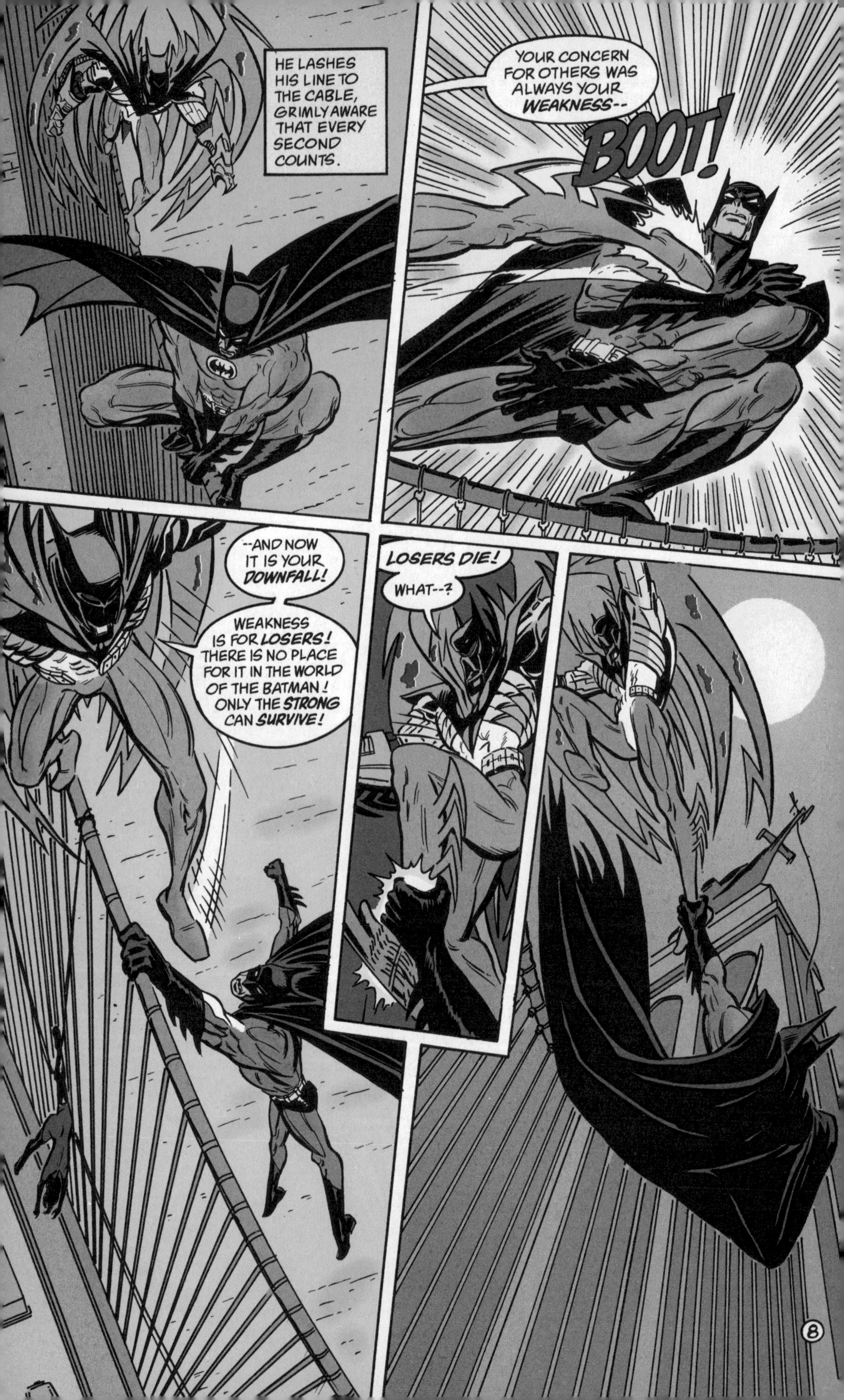
HE LASHES HIS LINE TO THE CABLE, GRIMLY AWARE THAT EVERY SECOND COUNTS.
YOUR CONCERN FOR OTHERS WAS ALWAYS YOUR WEAKNESS--
BOOT!
--AND NOW IT IS YOUR DOWNFALL!
WEAKNESS IS FOR LOSERS! THERE IS NO PLACE FOR IT IN THE WORLD OF THE BATMAN! ONLY THE STRONG CAN SURVIVE!
LOSERS DIE!
WHAT--?
8

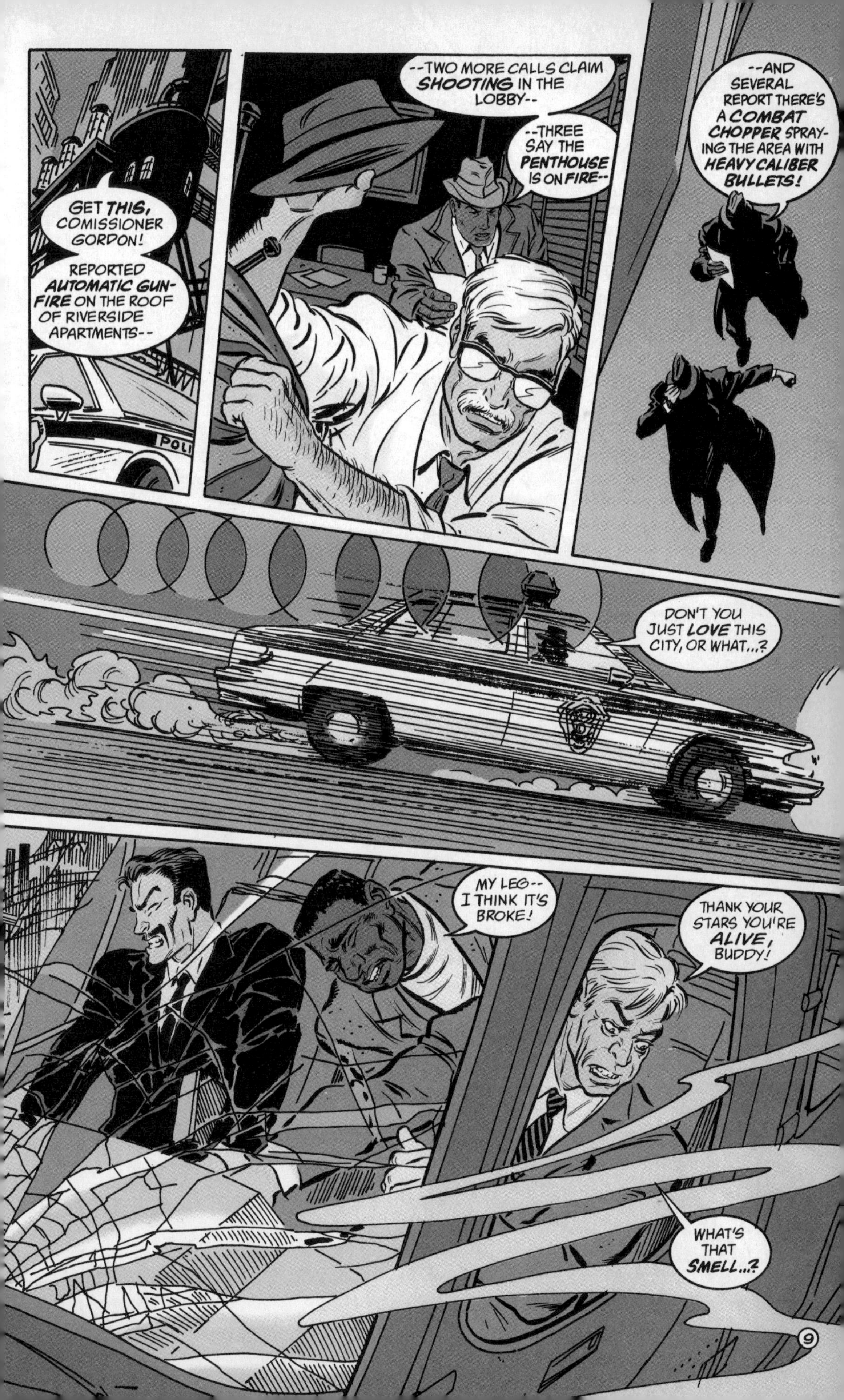
GET THIS, COMISSIONER GORDON!
REPORTED AUTOMATIC GUN-FIRE ON THE ROOF OF RIVERSIDE APARTMENTS--
--TWO MORE CALLS CLAIM SHOOTING IN THE LOBBY--
--THREE SAY THE PENTHOUSE IS ON FIRE--
--AND SEVERAL REPORT THERE'S A COMBAT CHOPPER SPRAY-ING THE AREA WITH HEAVY CALIBER BULLETS!
DON'T YOU JUST LOVE THIS CITY, OR WHAT...?
MY LEG-- I THINK IT'S BROKE!
THANK YOUR STARS YOU'RE ALIVE, BUDDY!
WHAT'S THAT SMELL...?

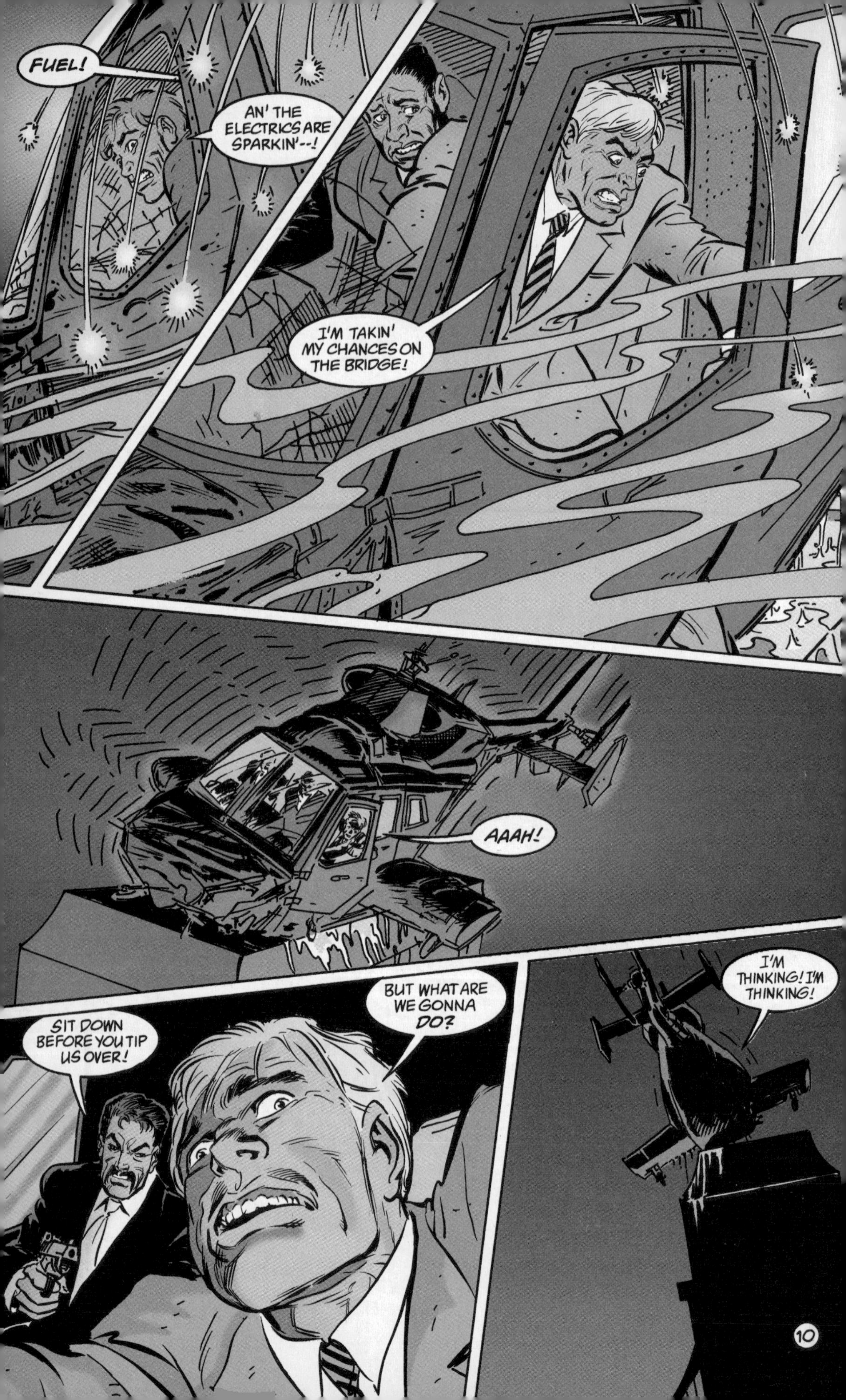
FUEL!
AN' THE ELECTRICS ARE SPARKIN'--!
I'M TAKIN' MY CHANCES ON THE BRIDGE!
AAAH!
SIT DOWN BEFORE YOU TIP US OVER!
BUT WHAT ARE WE GONNA DO?
I'M THINKING! I'M THINKING!

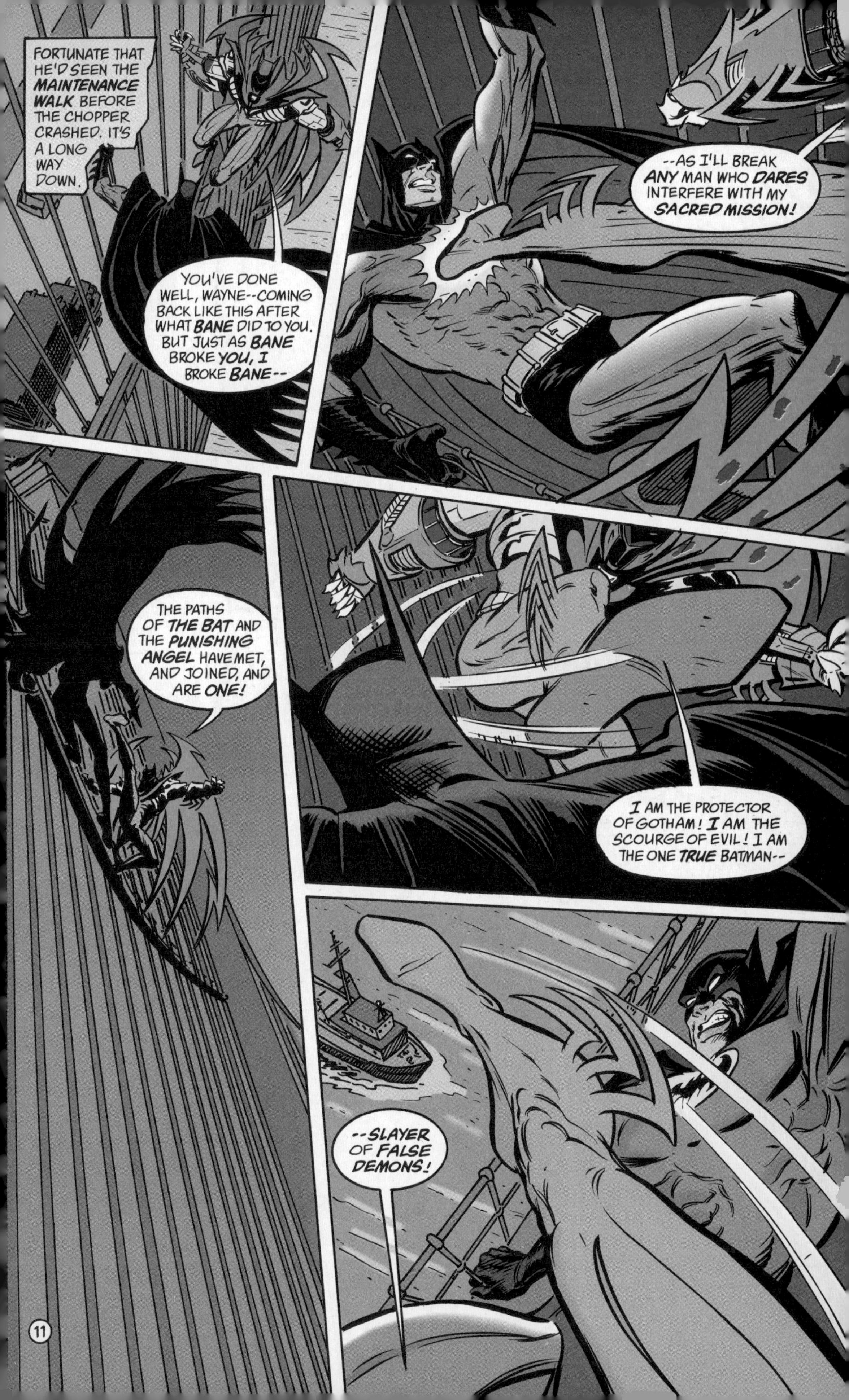
FORTUNATE THAT HE'D SEEN THE MAINTENANCE WALK BEFORE THE CHOPPER CRASHED. IT'S A LONG WAY DOWN.
YOU'VE DONE WELL, WAYNE--COMING BACK LIKE THIS AFTER WHAT BANE DID TO YOU. BUT JUST AS BANE BROKE YOU, I BROKE BANE--
--AS I'LL BREAK ANY MAN WHO DARES INTERFERE WITH MY SACRED MISSION!
THE PATHS OF THE BAT AND THE PUNISHING ANGEL HAVE MET, AND JOINED, AND ARE ONE!
I AM THE PROTECTOR OF GOTHAM! I AM THE SCOURGE OF EVIL! I AM THE ONE TRUE BATMAN--
--SLAYER OF FALSE DEMONS!

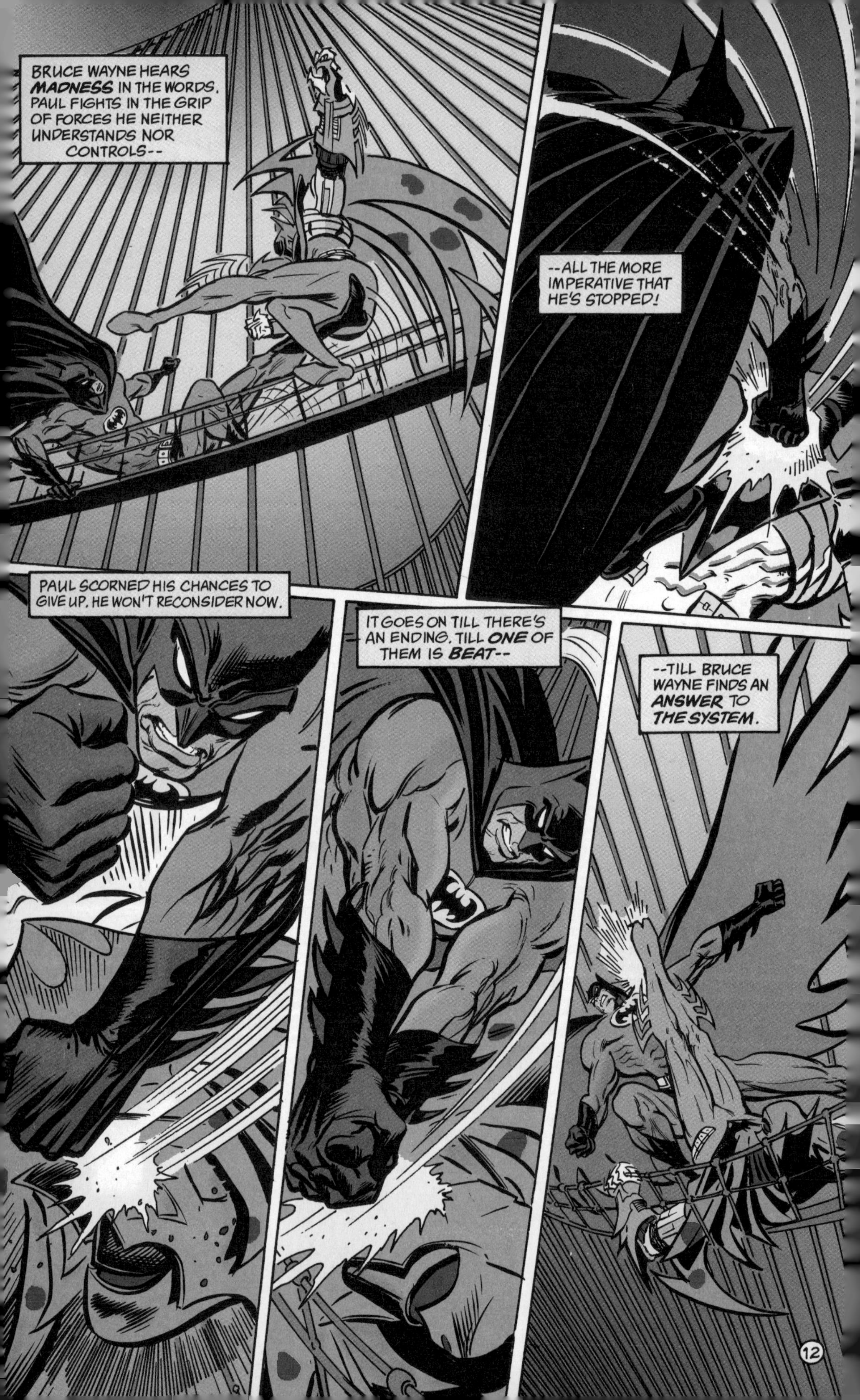

BRUCE WAYNE HEARS MADNESS IN THE WORDS. PAUL FIGHTS IN THE GRIP OF FORCES HE NEITHER UNDERSTANDS NOR CONTROLS--
--ALL THE MORE IMPERATIVE THAT HE'S STOPPED!
PAUL SCORNED HIS CHANCES TO GIVE UP. HE WON'T RECONSIDER NOW.
IT GOES ON TILL THERE'S AN ENDING. TILL ONE OF THEM IS BEAT--
--TILL BRUCE WAYNE FINDS AN ANSWER TO THE SYSTEM.
12

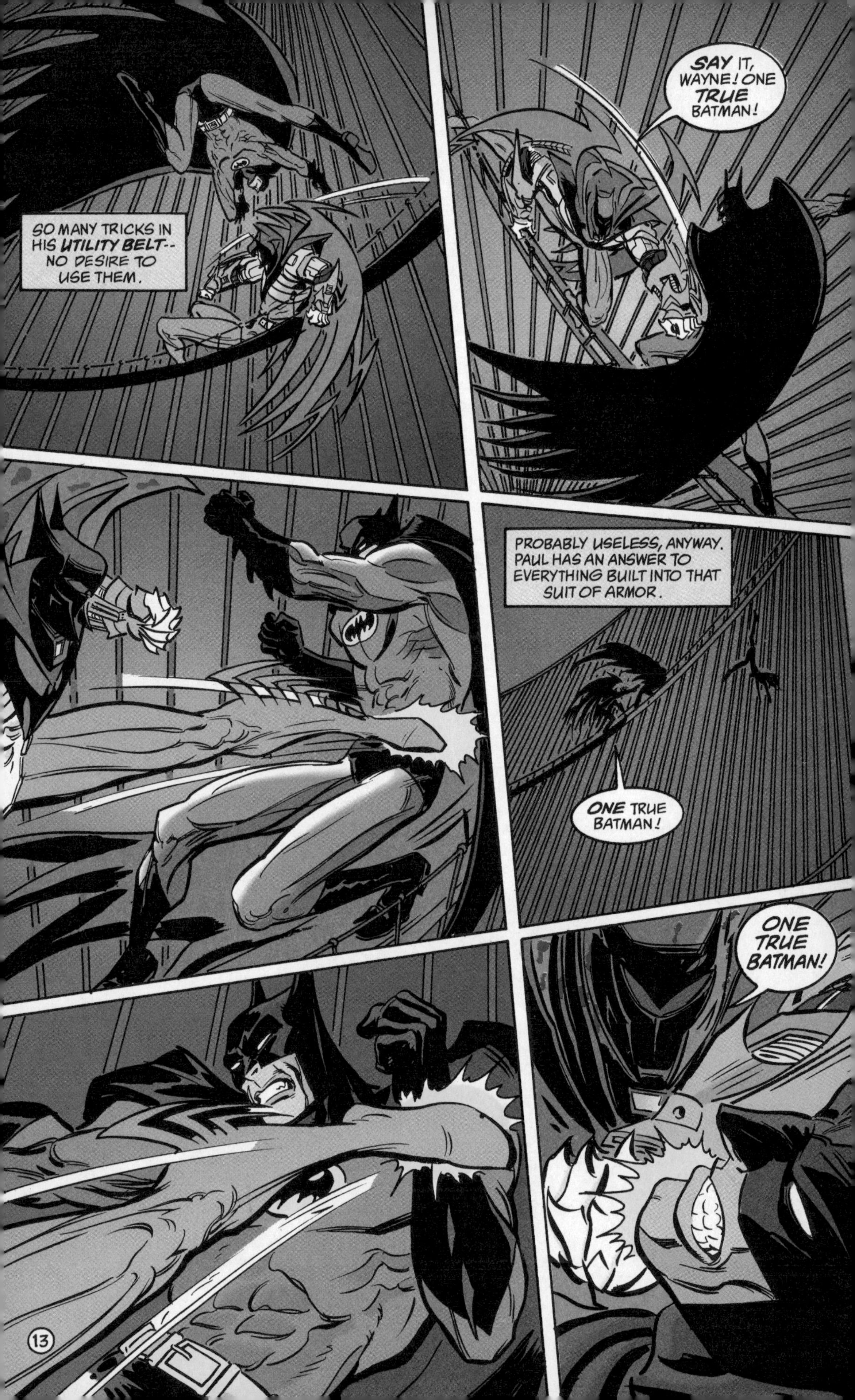
SO MANY TRICKS IN HIS UTILITY BELT-- NO DESIRE TO USE THEM.
SAY IT, WAYNE! ONE TRUE BATMAN!
PROBABLY USELESS, ANYWAY. PAUL HAS AN ANSWER TO EVERYTHING BUILT INTO THAT SUIT OF ARMOR.
ONE TRUE BATMAN!
ONE TRUE BATMAN!

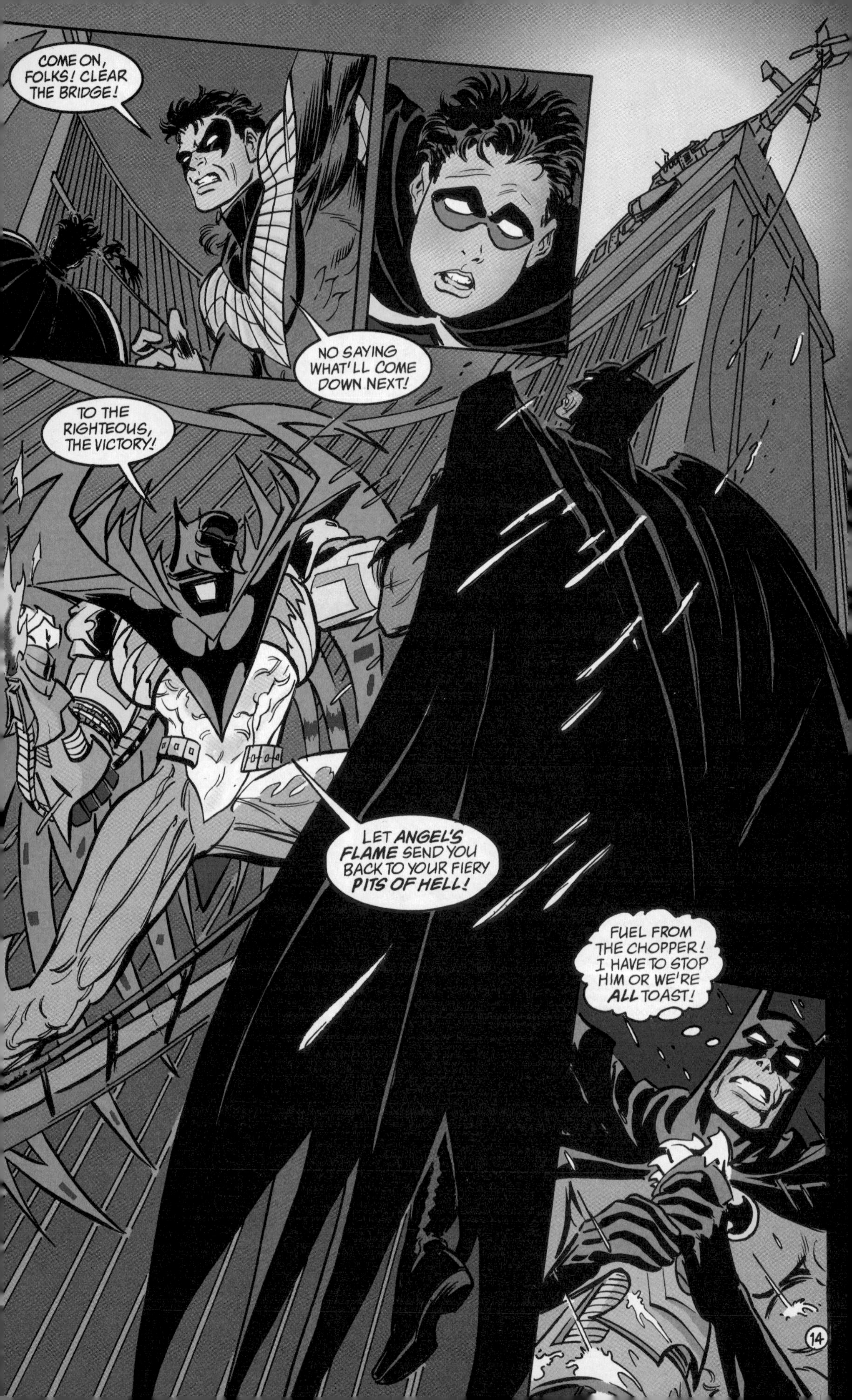

COME ON, FOLKS! CLEAR THE BRIDGE!
NO SAYING WHAT'LL COME DOWN NEXT!
TO THE RIGHTEOUS, THE VICTORY!
LET ANGEL'S FLAME SEND YOU BACK TO YOUR FIERY PITS OF HELL!
FUEL FROM THE CHOPPER! I HAVE TO STOP HIM OR WE'RE ALL TOAST!
14

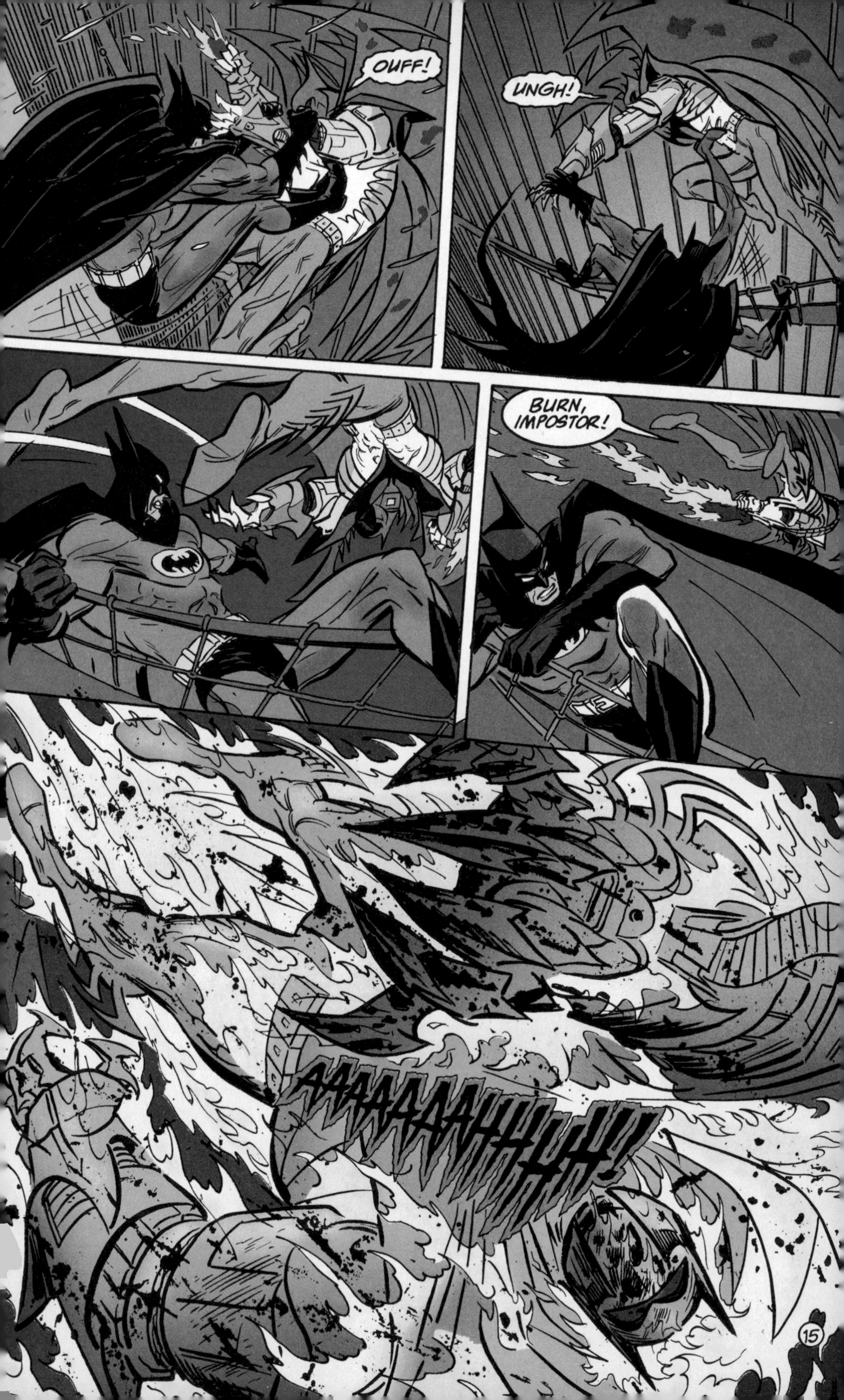
OUFF!
UNGH!
BURN, IMPOSTOR!
AAAAAAAHHHHH!
15

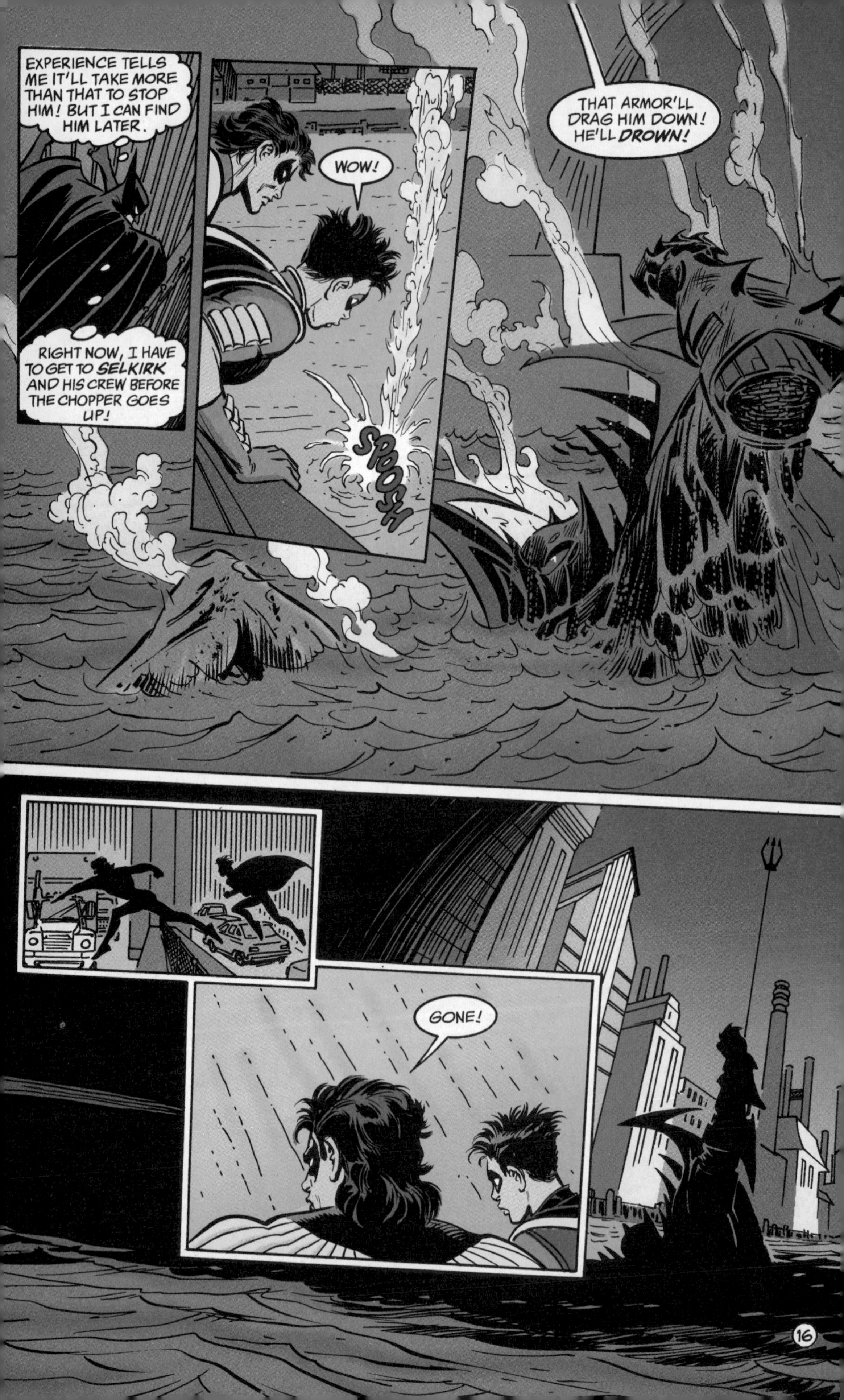
EXPERIENCE TELLS ME IT'LL TAKE MORE THAN THAT TO STOP HIM! BUT I CAN FIND HIM LATER.
RIGHT NOW, I HAVE TO GET TO SELKIRK AND HIS CREW BEFORE THE CHOPPER GOES UP!
WOW!
SPOOSH
THAT ARMOR'LL DRAG HIM DOWN! HE'LL DROWN!
GONE!

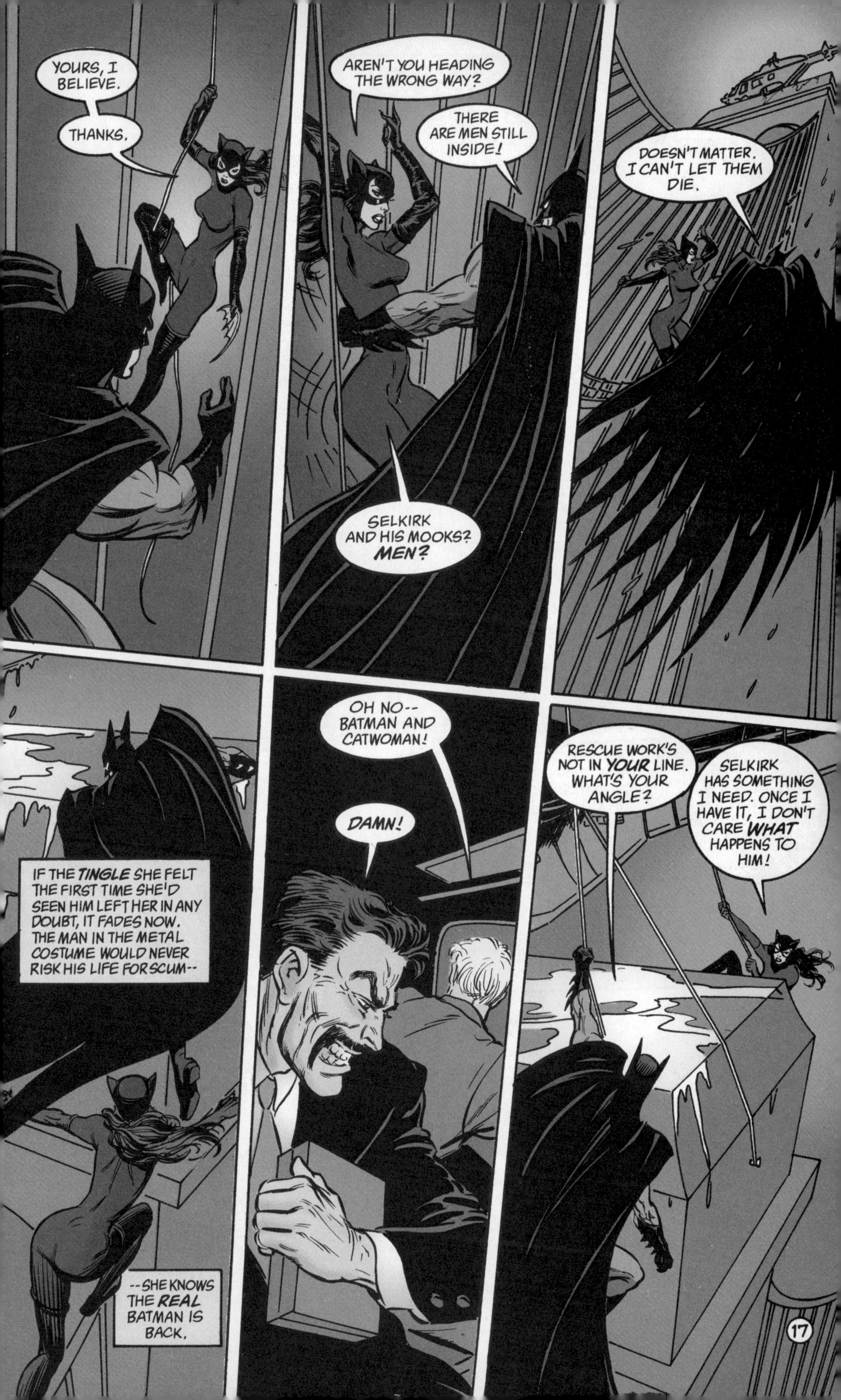
YOURS, I BELIEVE.
THANKS.
AREN'T YOU HEADING THE WRONG WAY?
THERE ARE MEN STILL INSIDE!
SELKIRK AND HIS MOOKS? MEN?
DOESN'T MATTER. I CAN'T LET THEM DIE.
IF THE TINGLE SHE FELT THE FIRST TIME SHE'D SEEN HIM LEFT HER IN ANY DOUBT, IT FADES NOW. THE MAN IN THE METAL COSTUME WOULD NEVER RISK HIS LIFE FOR SCUM--
--SHE KNOWS THE REAL BATMAN IS BACK.
OH NO-- BATMAN AND CATWOMAN!
DAMN!
RESCUE WORK'S NOT IN YOUR LINE. WHAT'S YOUR ANGLE?
SELKIRK HAS SOMETHING I NEED. ONCE I HAVE IT, I DON'T CARE WHAT HAPPENS TO HIM!

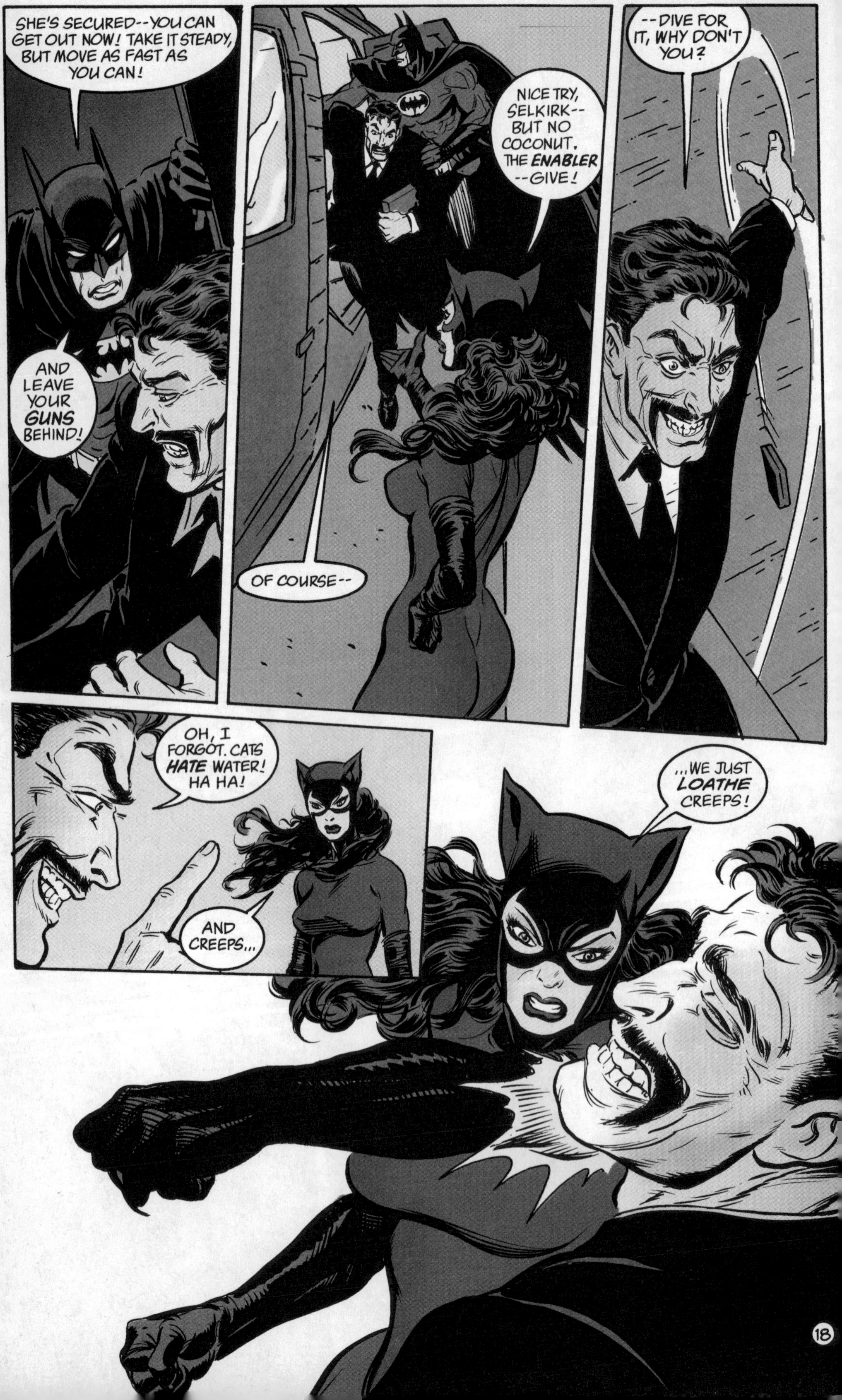
SHE'S SECURED--YOU CAN GET OUT NOW! TAKE IT STEADY, BUT MOVE AS FAST AS YOU CAN!
AND LEAVE YOUR GUNS BEHIND!
NICE TRY, SELKIRK-- BUT NO COCONUT. THE ENABLER --GIVE!
OF COURSE--
--DIVE FOR IT, WHY DON'T YOU?
OH, I FORGOT. CATS HATE WATER! HA HA!
AND CREEPS,...
...WE JUST LOATHE CREEPS!

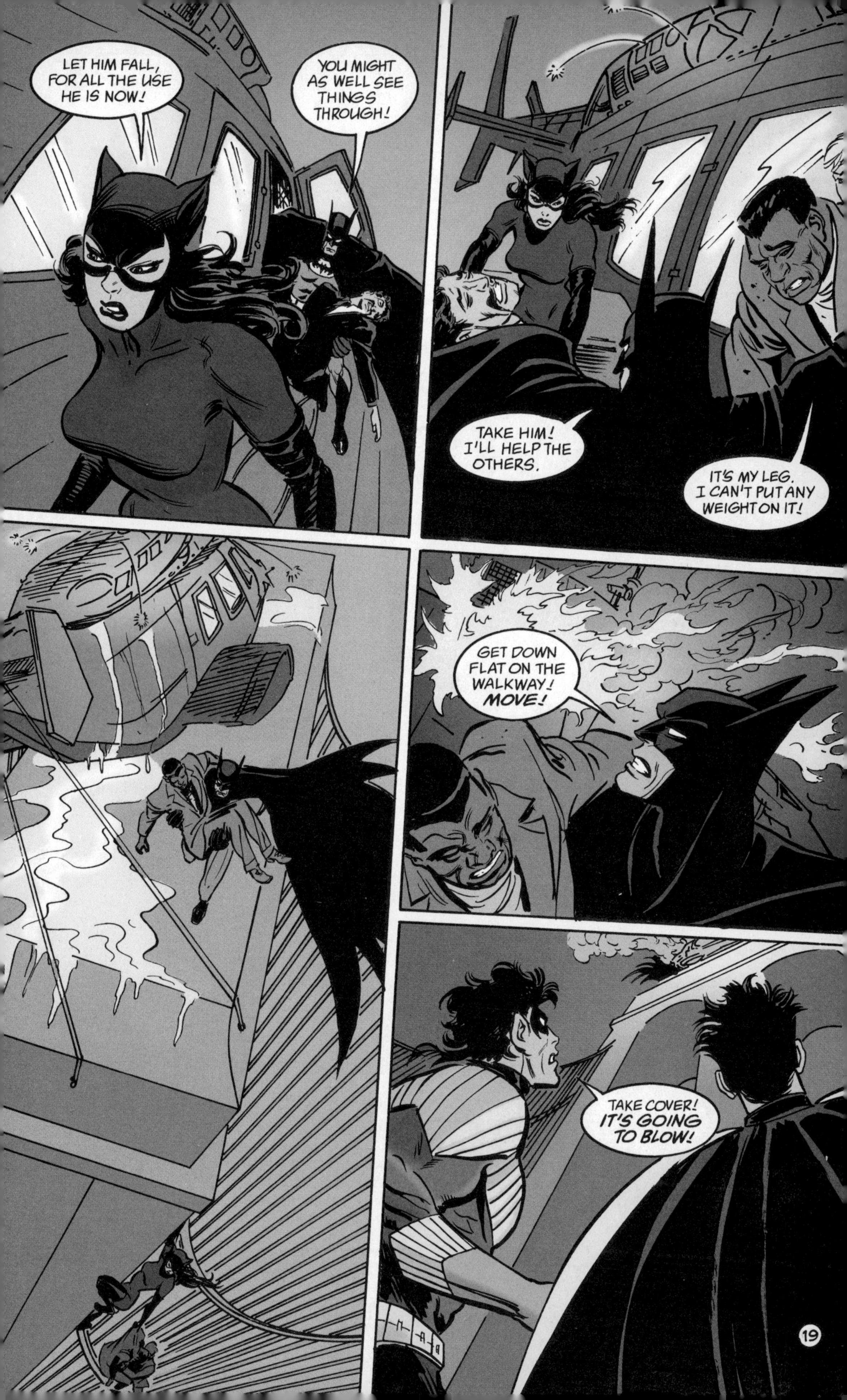
LET HIM FALL, FOR ALL THE USE HE IS NOW!
YOU MIGHT AS WELL SEE THINGS THROUGH!
TAKE HIM! I'LL HELP THE OTHERS.
IT'S MY LEG. I CAN'T PUT ANY WEIGHT ON IT!
GET DOWN FLAT ON THE WALKWAY! MOVE!
TAKE COVER! IT'S GOING TO BLOW!

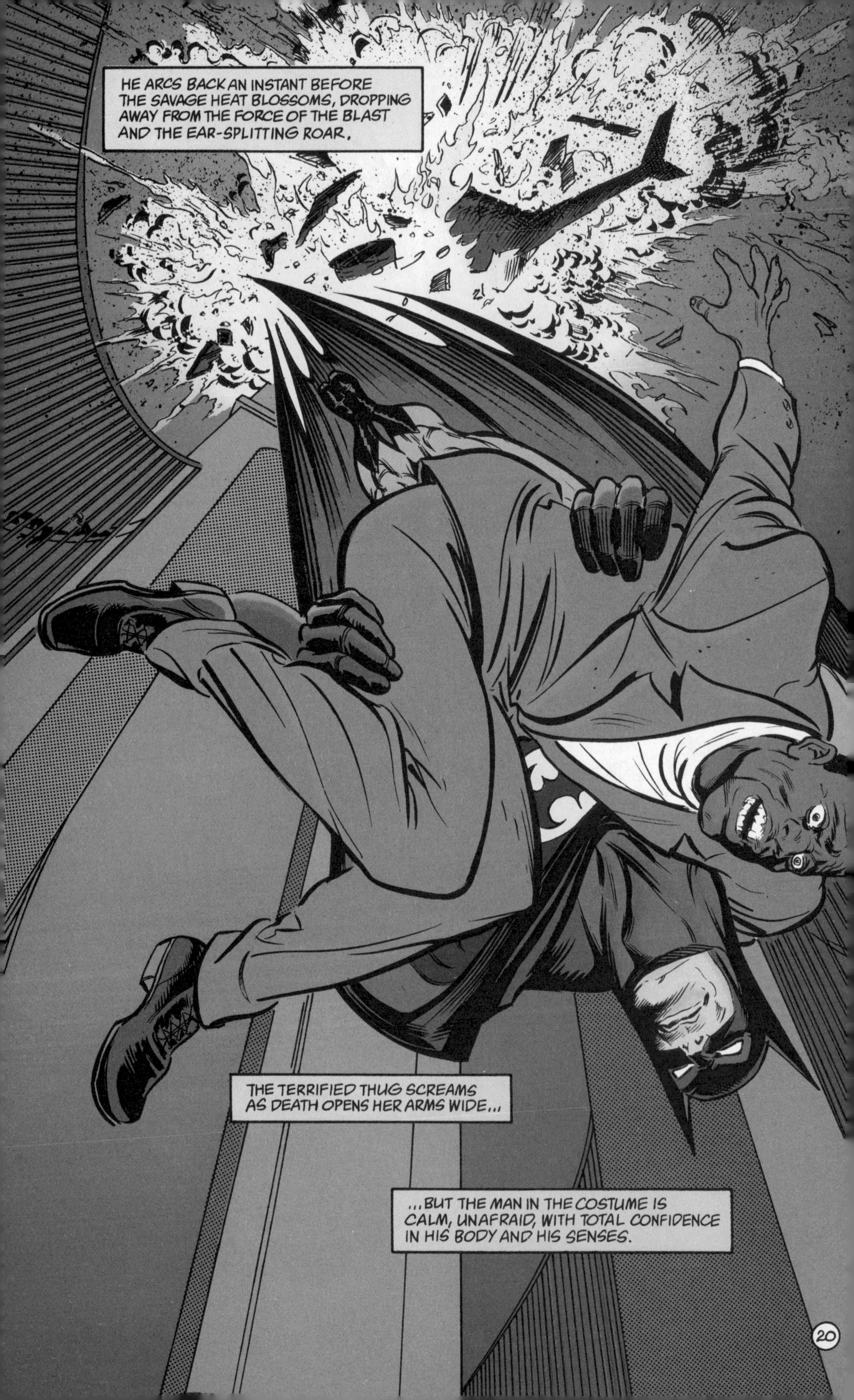
HE ARCS BACK AN INSTANT BEFORE THE SAVAGE HEAT BLOSSOMS, DROPPING AWAY FROM THE FORCE OF THE BLAST AND THE EAR-SPLITTING ROAR.
THE TERRIFIED THUG SCREAMS AS DEATH OPENS HER ARMS WIDE...
...BUT THE MAN IN THE COSTUME IS CALM, UNAFRAID, WITH TOTAL CONFIDENCE IN HIS BODY AND HIS SENSES.

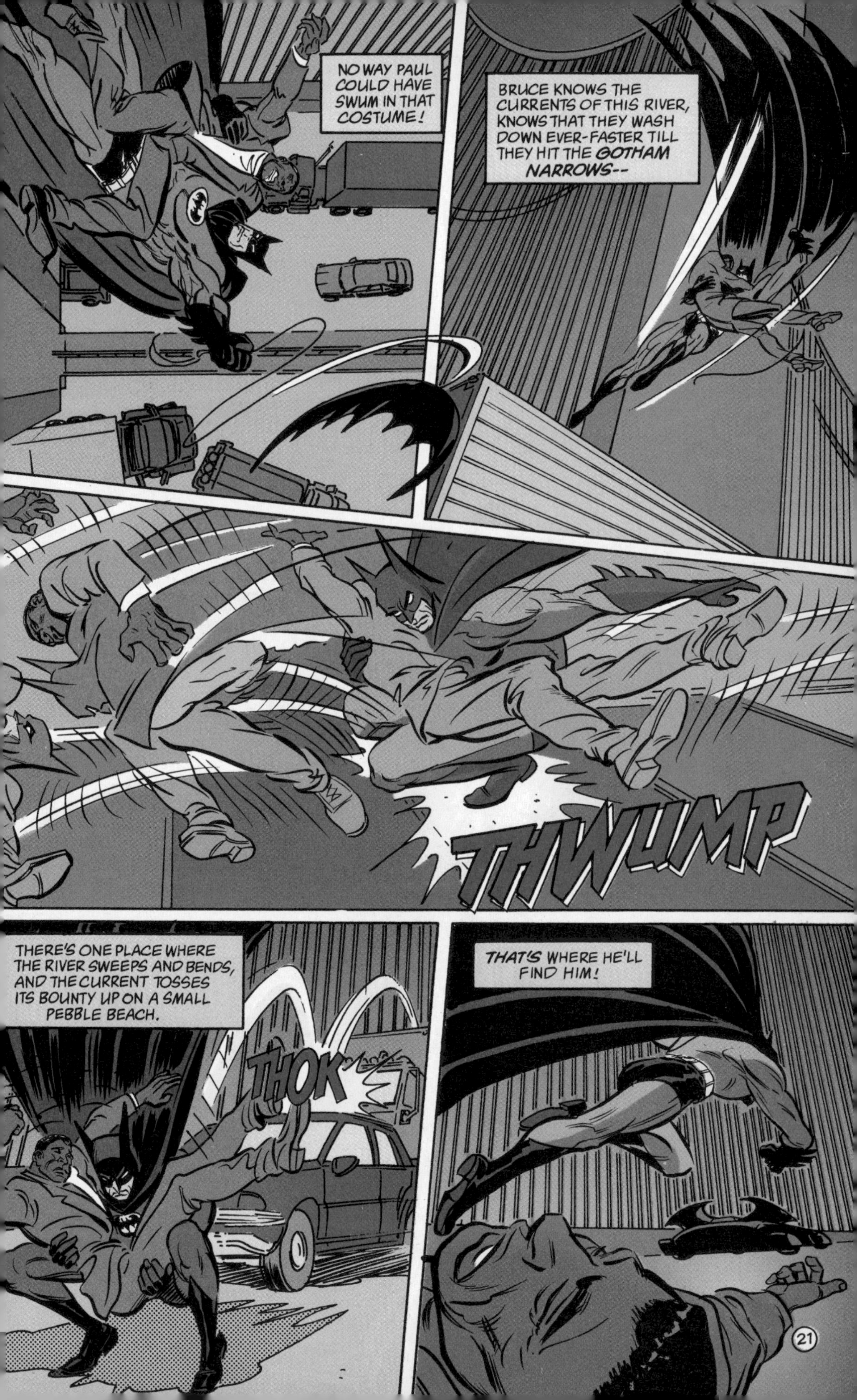
NO WAY PAUL COULD HAVE SWUM IN THAT COSTUME!
BRUCE KNOWS THE CURRENTS OF THIS RIVER, KNOWS THAT THEY WASH DOWN EVER-FASTER TILL THEY HIT THE *GOTHAM NARROWS*--
THWUMP
THERE'S ONE PLACE WHERE THE RIVER SWEEPS AND BENDS, AND THE CURRENT TOSSES ITS BOUNTY UP ON A SMALL PEBBLE BEACH.
THOK
THAT'S WHERE HE'LL FIND HIM!

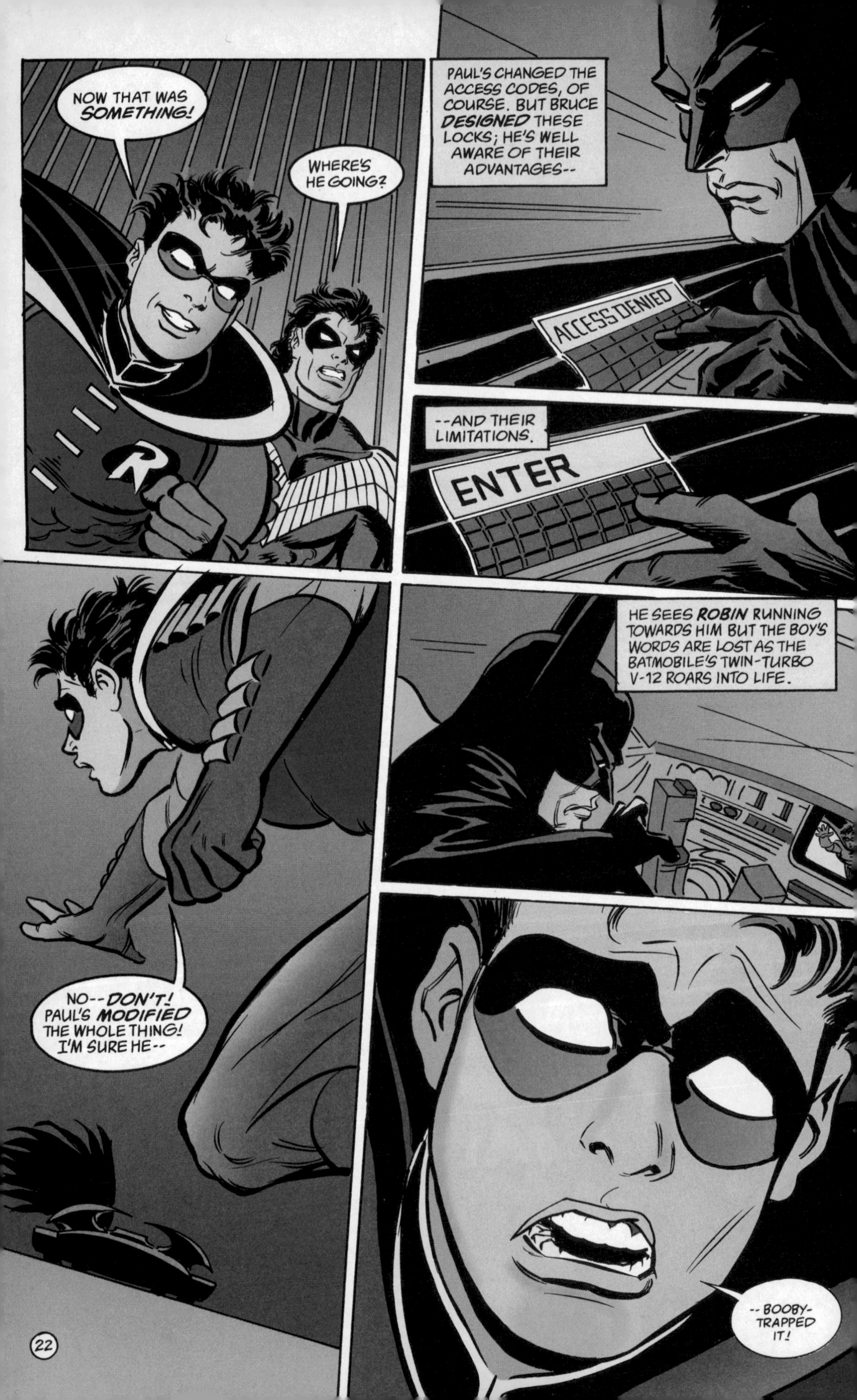

NOW THAT WAS SOMETHING!
WHERE'S HE GOING?
PAUL'S CHANGED THE ACCESS CODES, OF COURSE. BUT BRUCE DESIGNED THESE LOCKS; HE'S WELL AWARE OF THEIR ADVANTAGES--
ACCESS DENIED
--AND THEIR LIMITATIONS.
ENTER
NO--DON'T! PAUL'S MODIFIED THE WHOLE THING! I'M SURE HE--
HE SEES ROBIN RUNNING TOWARDS HIM BUT THE BOY'S WORDS ARE LOST AS THE BATMOBILE'S TWIN-TURBO V-12 ROARS INTO LIFE.
--BOOBY-TRAPPED IT!

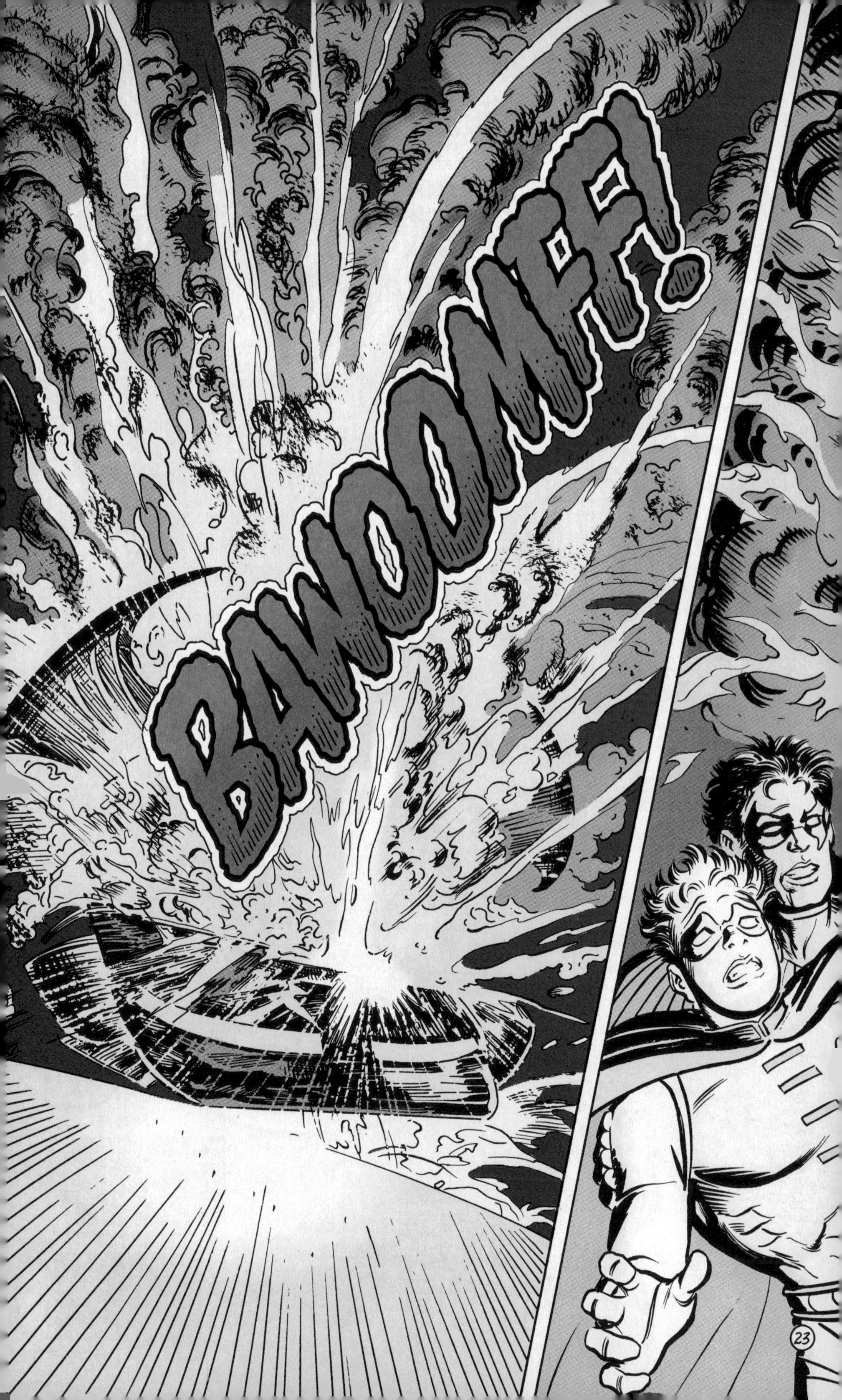
BAWOOMFF!

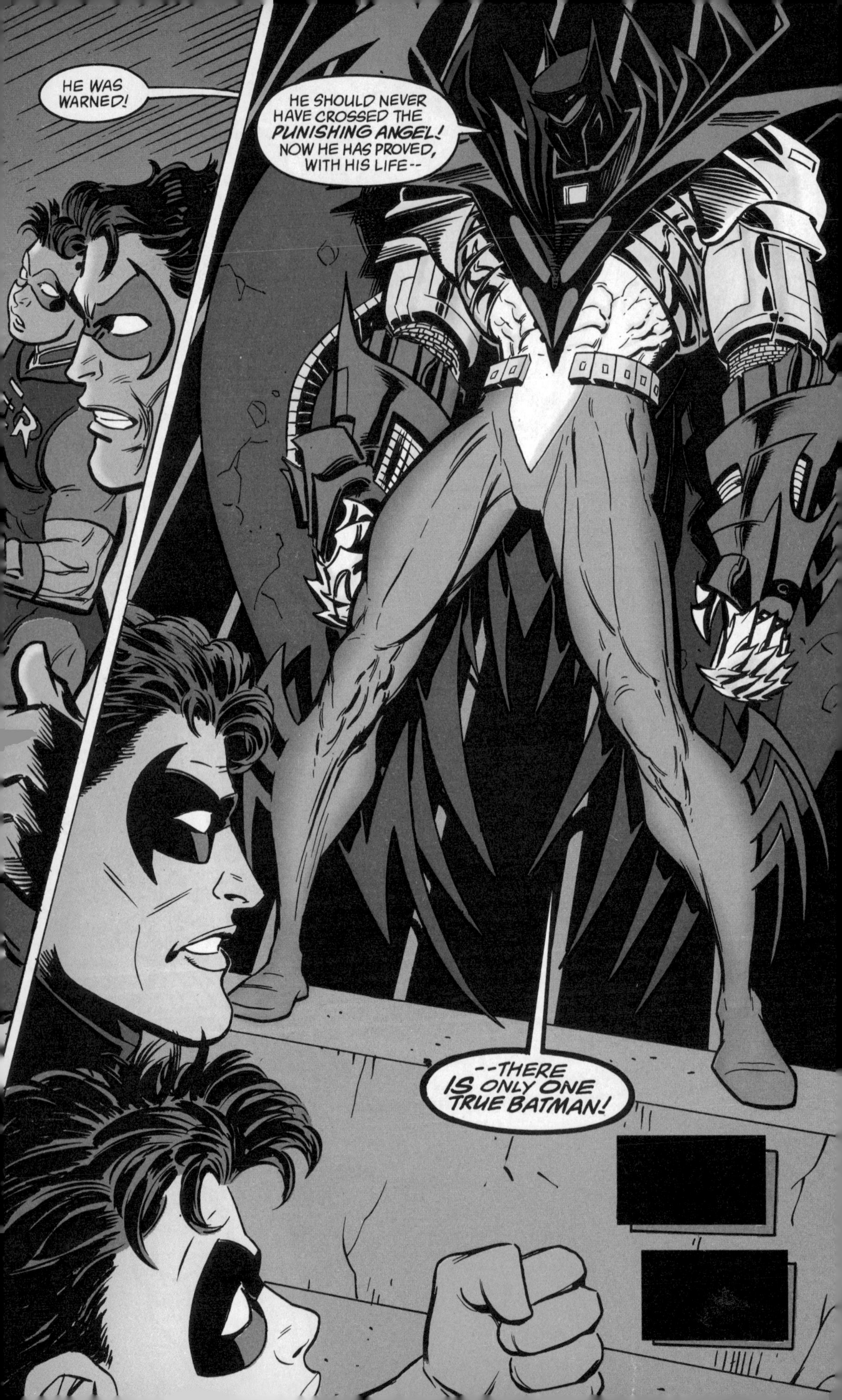
HE WAS WARNED!
HE SHOULD NEVER HAVE CROSSED THE PUNISHING ANGEL! NOW HE HAS PROVED, WITH HIS LIFE--
--THERE IS ONLY ONE TRUE BATMAN!
[redacted]
[redacted]

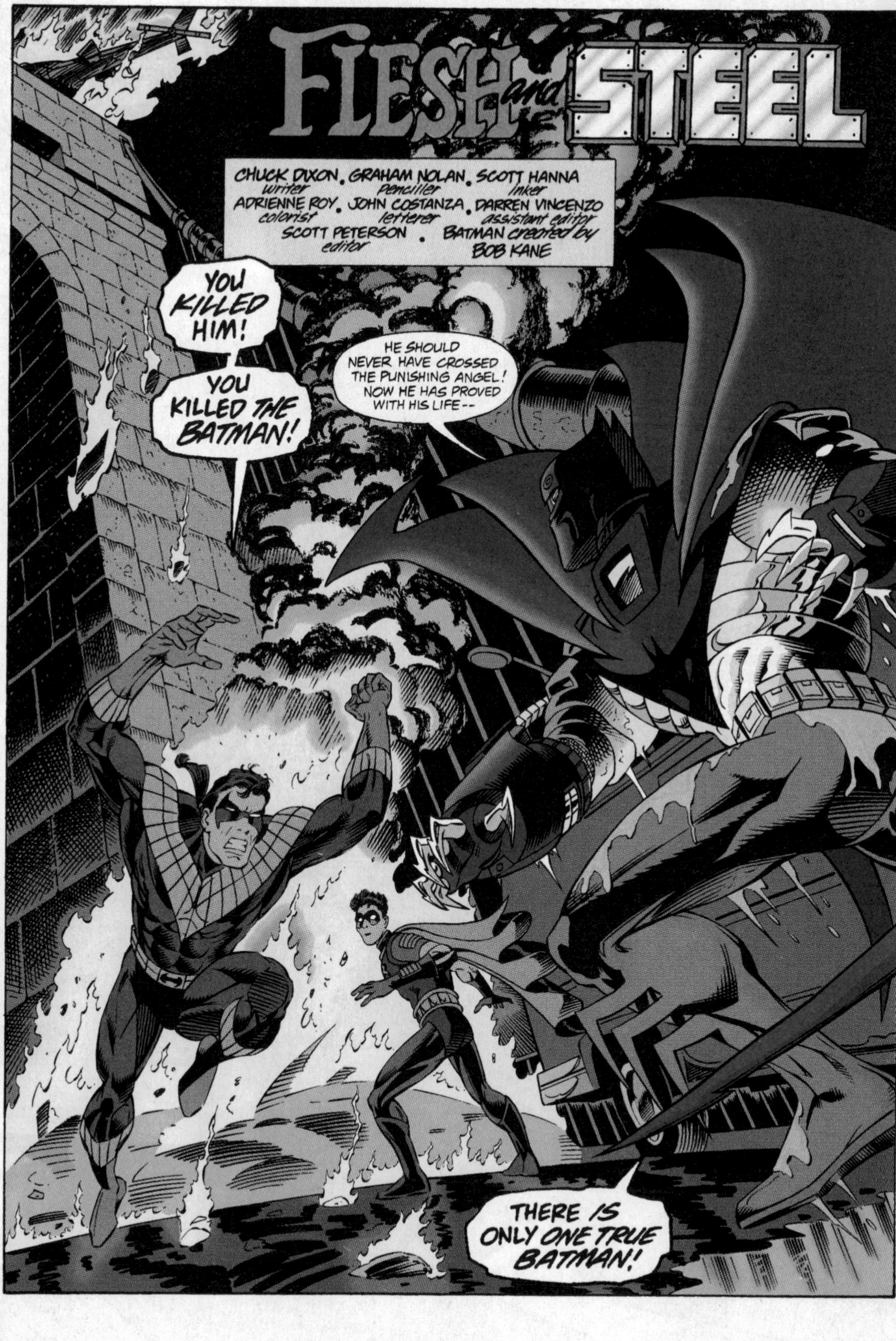
FLESH and STEEL
CHUCK DIXON writer • GRAHAM NOLAN penciller • SCOTT HANNA inker
ADRIENNE ROY colorist • JOHN COSTANZA letterer • DARREN VINCENZO assistant editor
SCOTT PETERSON editor • BATMAN created by BOB KANE
YOU KILLED HIM!
YOU KILLED THE BATMAN!
HE SHOULD NEVER HAVE CROSSED THE PUNISHING ANGEL! NOW HE HAS PROVED WITH HIS LIFE--
THERE IS ONLY ONE TRUE BATMAN!

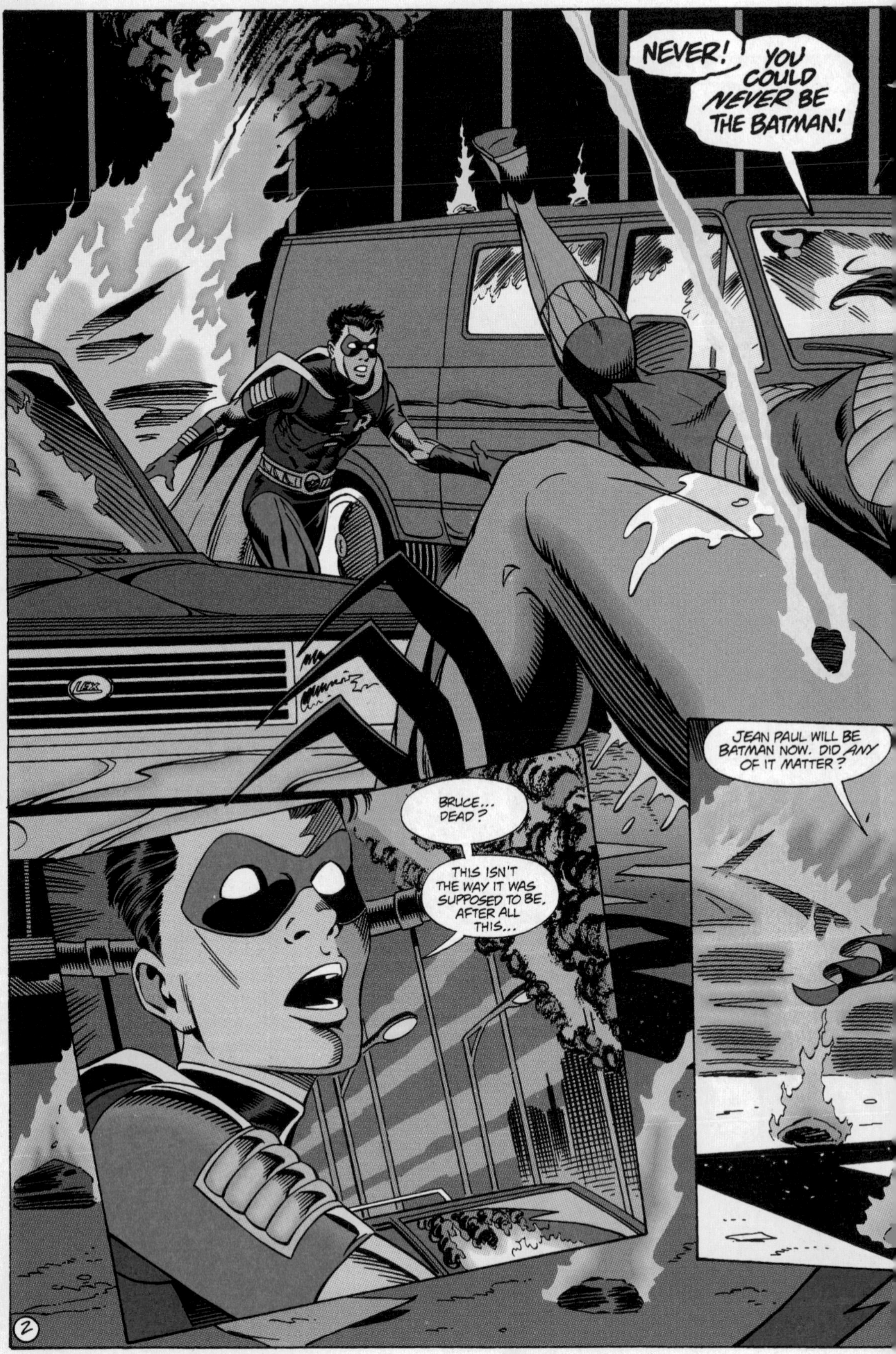
NEVER!
YOU COULD NEVER BE THE BATMAN!
BRUCE... DEAD?
THIS ISN'T THE WAY IT WAS SUPPOSED TO BE. AFTER ALL THIS...
JEAN PAUL WILL BE BATMAN NOW. DID ANY OF IT MATTER?
2

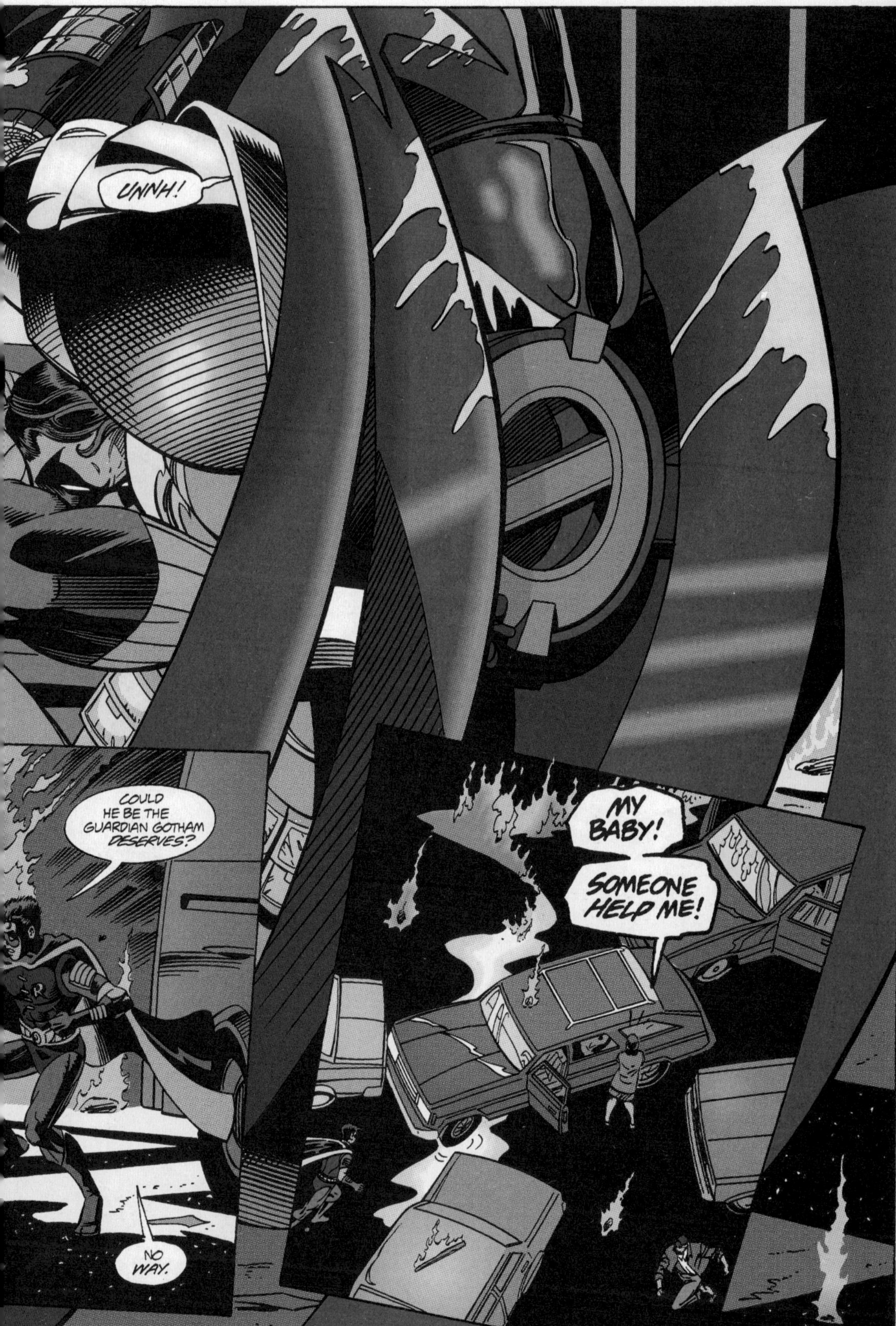
UNNH!
COULD HE BE THE GUARDIAN GOTHAM DESERVES?
NO WAY.
MY BABY!
SOMEONE HELP ME!
3

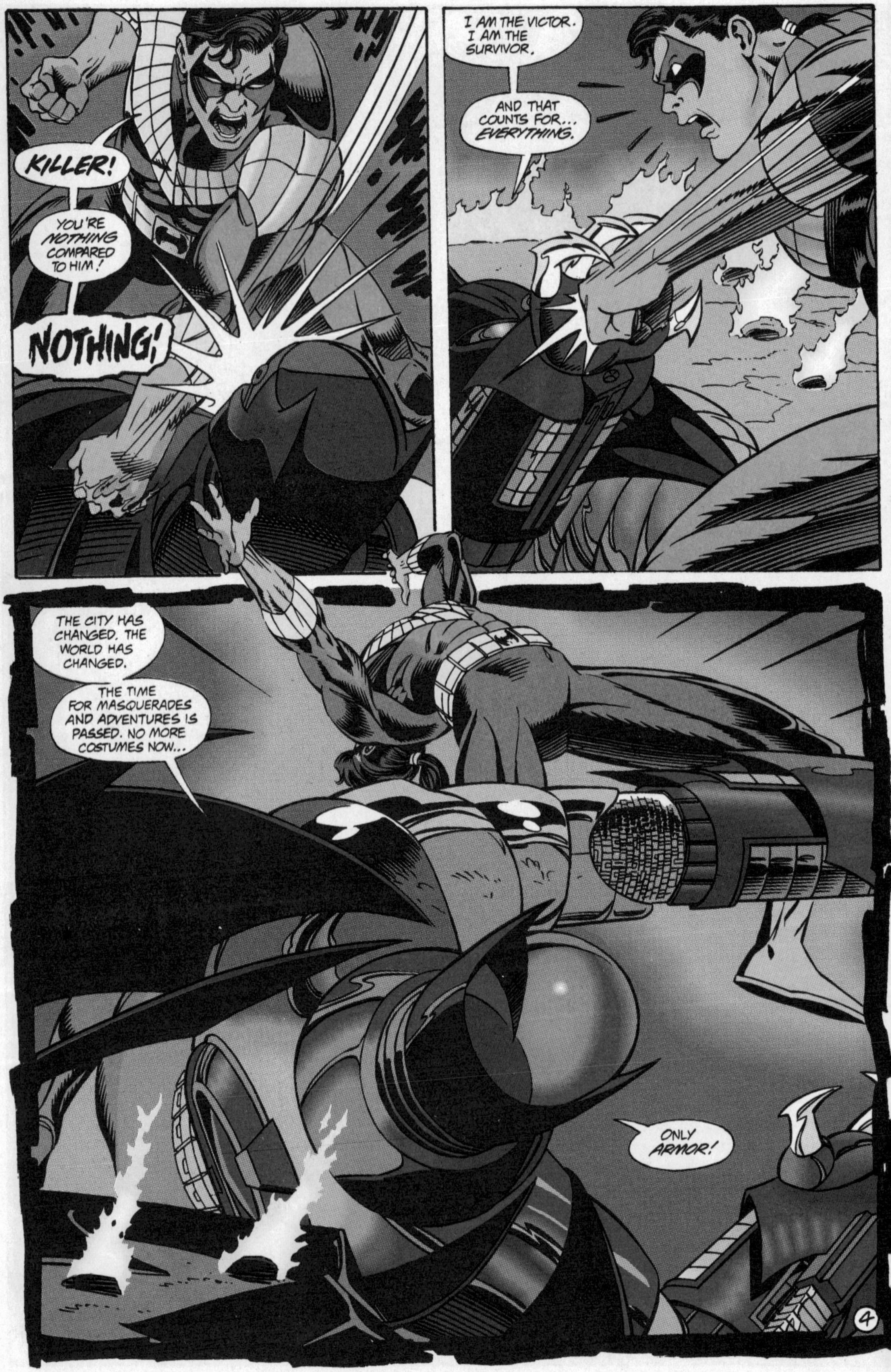
KILLER!
YOU'RE NOTHING COMPARED TO HIM!
NOTHING!
I AM THE VICTOR. I AM THE SURVIVOR.
AND THAT COUNTS FOR... EVERYTHING.
THE CITY HAS CHANGED. THE WORLD HAS CHANGED.
THE TIME FOR MASQUERADES AND ADVENTURES IS PASSED. NO MORE COSTUMES NOW...
ONLY ARMOR!
4

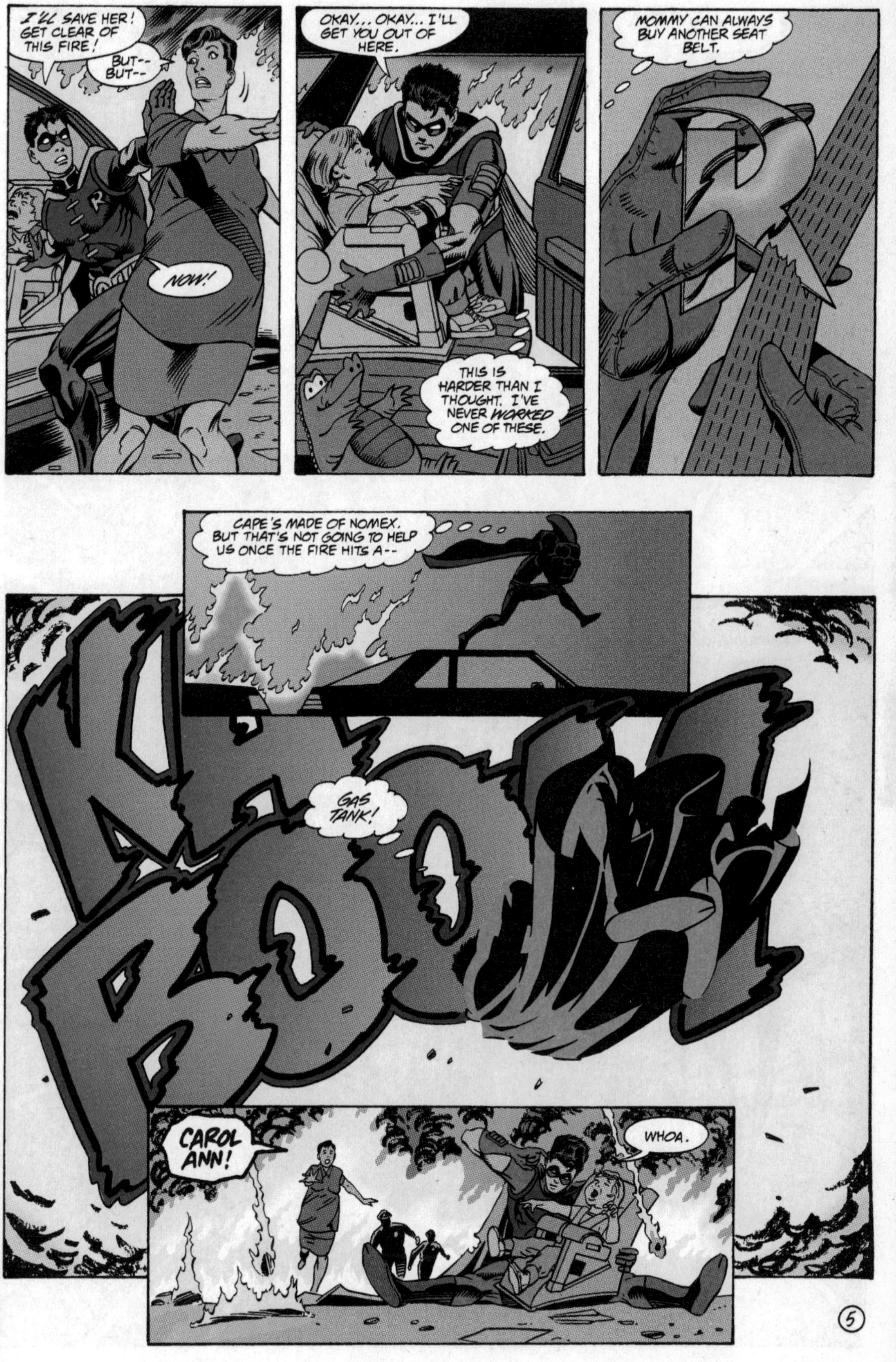

I'LL SAVE HER! GET CLEAR OF THIS FIRE!
BUT-- BUT--
NOW!
OKAY... OKAY... I'LL GET YOU OUT OF HERE.
THIS IS HARDER THAN I THOUGHT. I'VE NEVER WORKED ONE OF THESE.
MOMMY CAN ALWAYS BUY ANOTHER SEAT BELT.
CAPE'S MADE OF NOMEX. BUT THAT'S NOT GOING TO HELP US ONCE THE FIRE HITS A--
GAS TANK!
CAROL ANN!
WHOA.
5

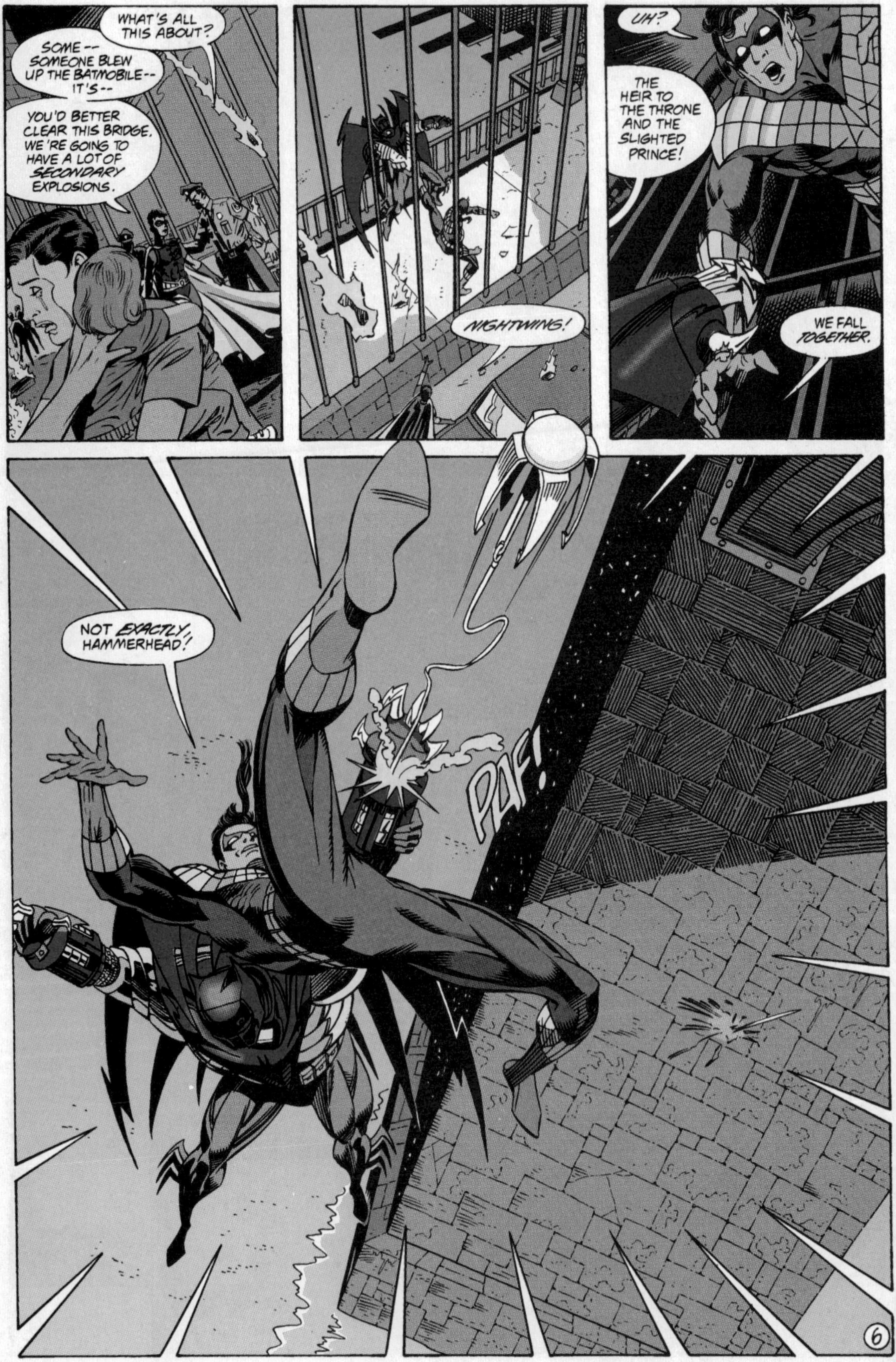
WHAT'S ALL THIS ABOUT?
SOME-- SOMEONE BLEW UP THE BATMOBILE-- IT'S--
YOU'D BETTER CLEAR THIS BRIDGE. WE'RE GOING TO HAVE A LOT OF SECONDARY EXPLOSIONS.
NIGHTWING!
UH?
THE HEIR TO THE THRONE AND THE SLIGHTED PRINCE!
WE FALL TOGETHER.
NOT EXACTLY, HAMMERHEAD!
PAF!
6

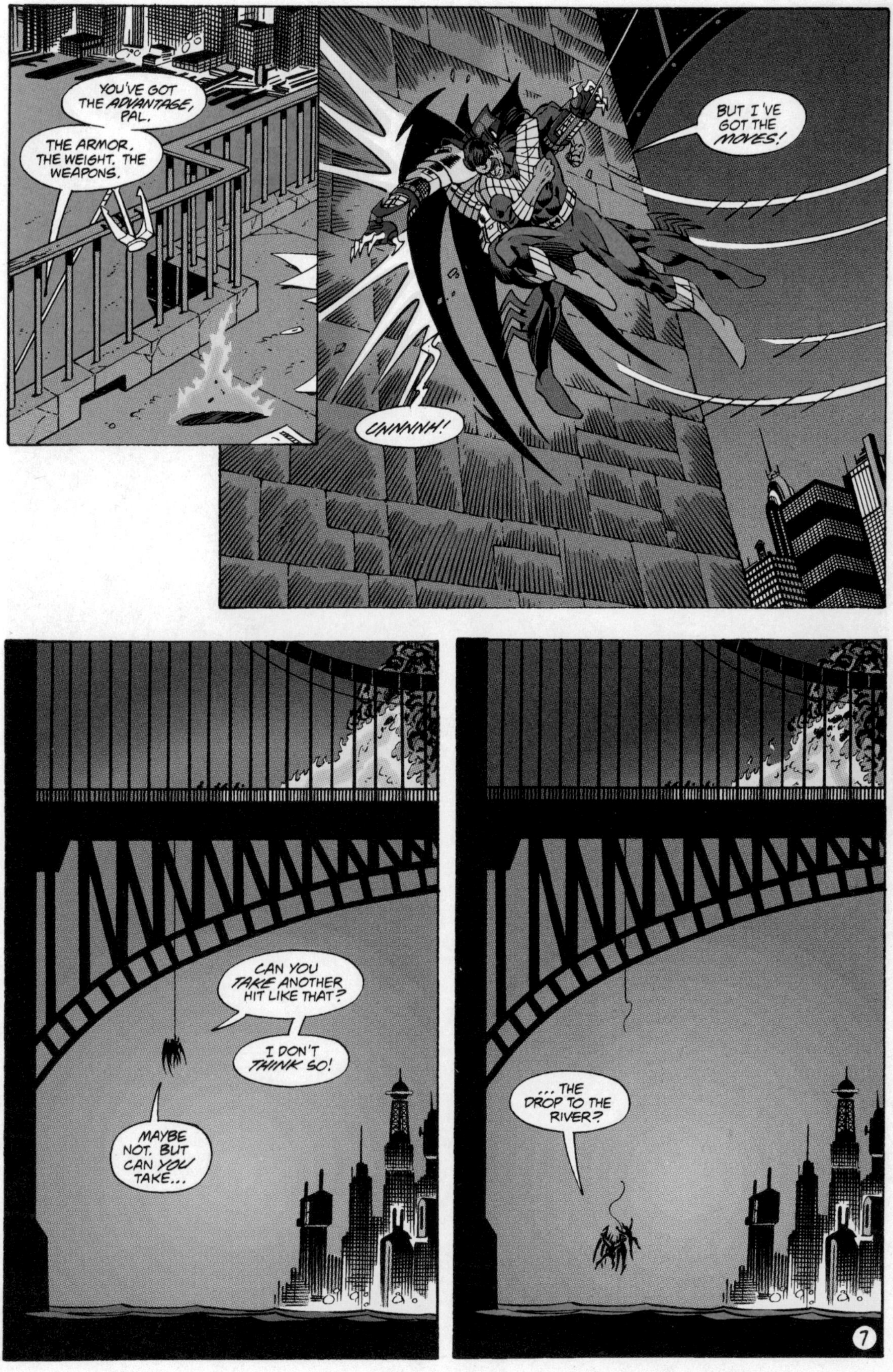
YOU'VE GOT THE ADVANTAGE, PAL.
THE ARMOR, THE WEIGHT. THE WEAPONS.
BUT I'VE GOT THE MOVES!
UNNNNH!
CAN YOU TAKE ANOTHER HIT LIKE THAT?
I DON'T THINK SO!
MAYBE NOT. BUT CAN YOU TAKE...
...THE DROP TO THE RIVER?
7

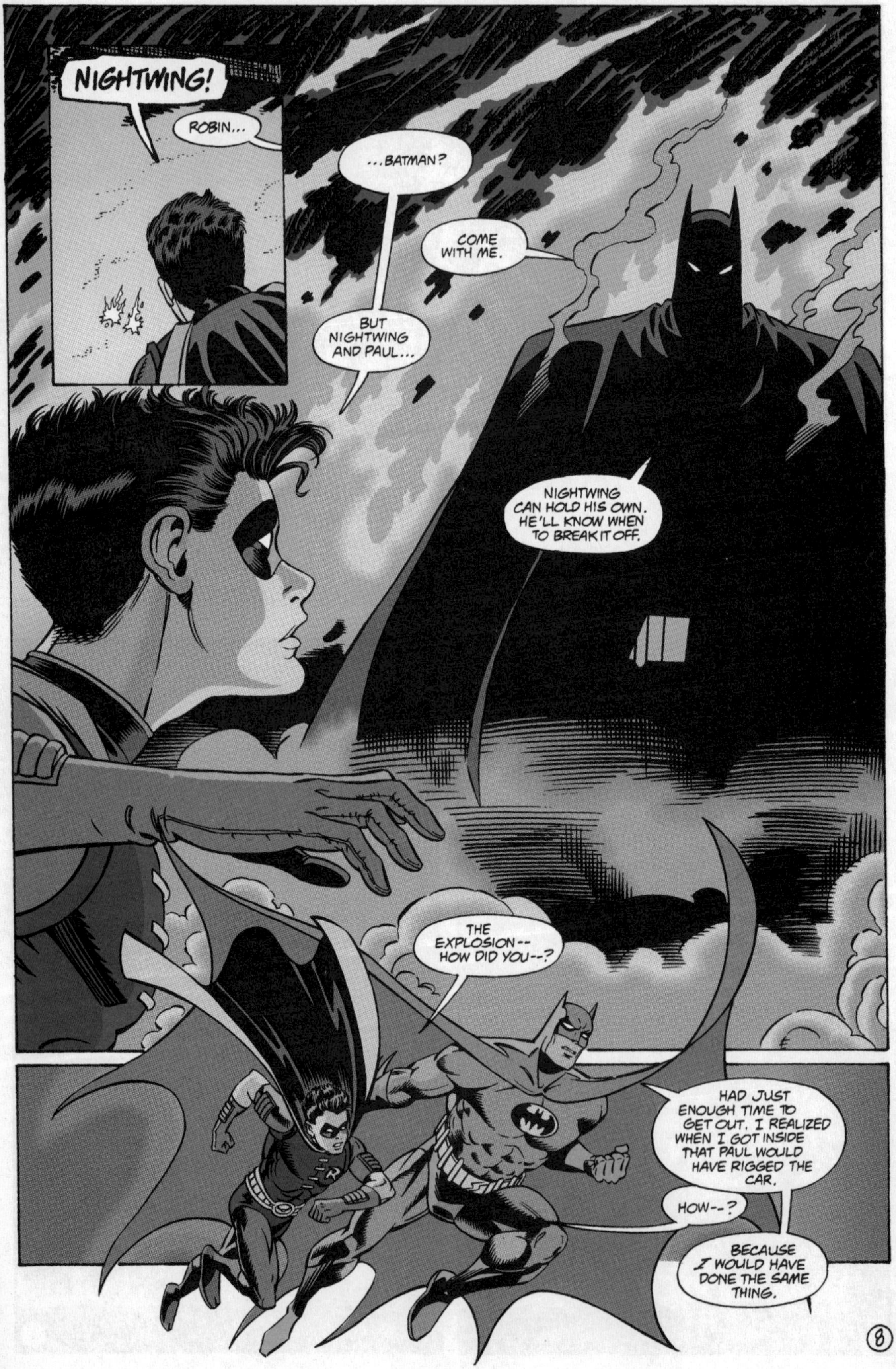
NIGHTWING!
ROBIN...
...BATMAN?
COME WITH ME.
BUT NIGHTWING AND PAUL...
NIGHTWING CAN HOLD HIS OWN. HE'LL KNOW WHEN TO BREAK IT OFF.
THE EXPLOSION-- HOW DID YOU--?
HAD JUST ENOUGH TIME TO GET OUT. I REALIZED WHEN I GOT INSIDE THAT PAUL WOULD HAVE RIGGED THE CAR.
HOW--?
BECAUSE I WOULD HAVE DONE THE SAME THING.
8

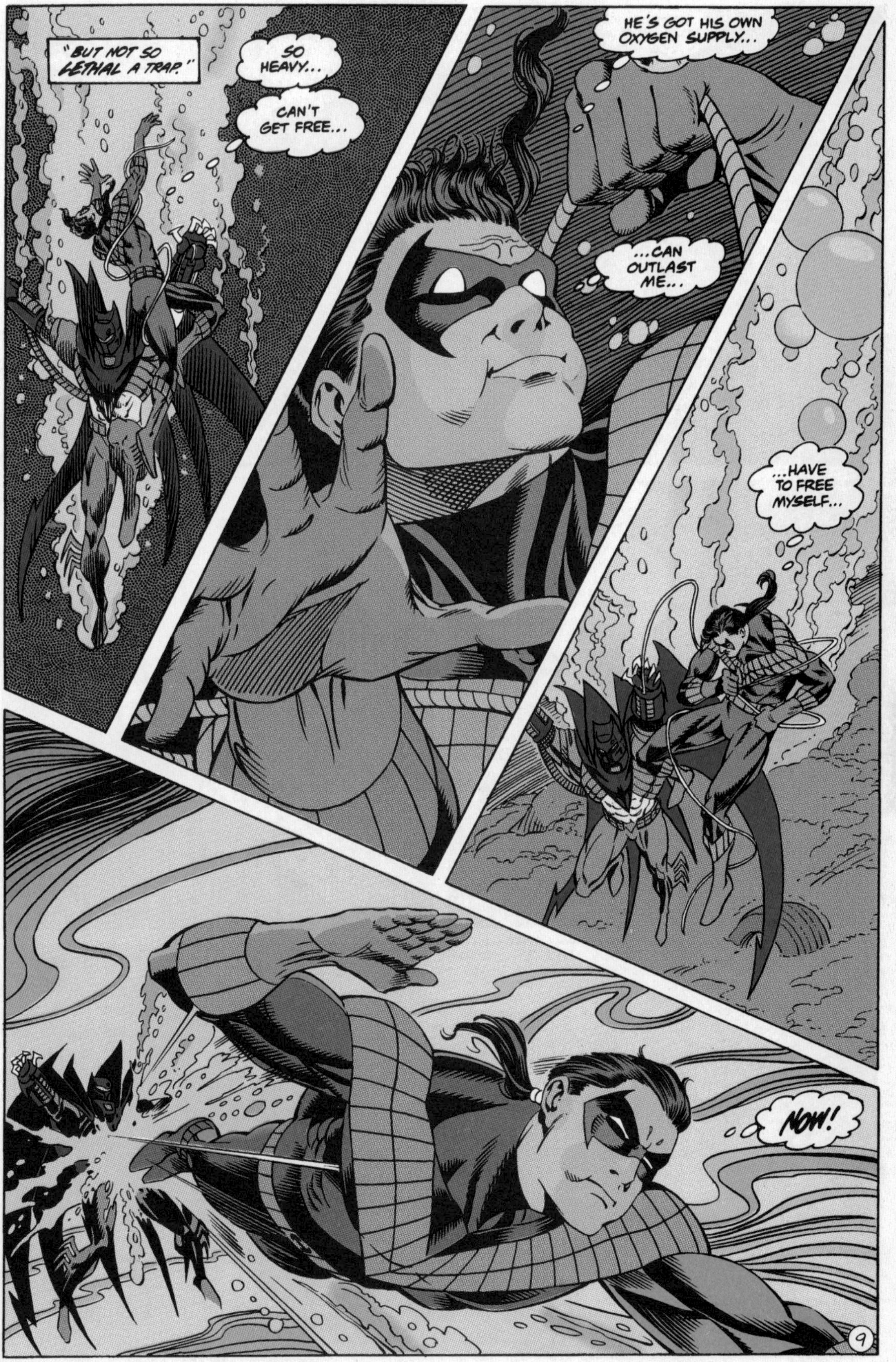
"BUT NOT SO LETHAL A TRAP."
SO HEAVY...
CAN'T GET FREE...
HE'S GOT HIS OWN OXYGEN SUPPLY...
...CAN OUTLAST ME...
...HAVE TO FREE MYSELF...
NOW!
9

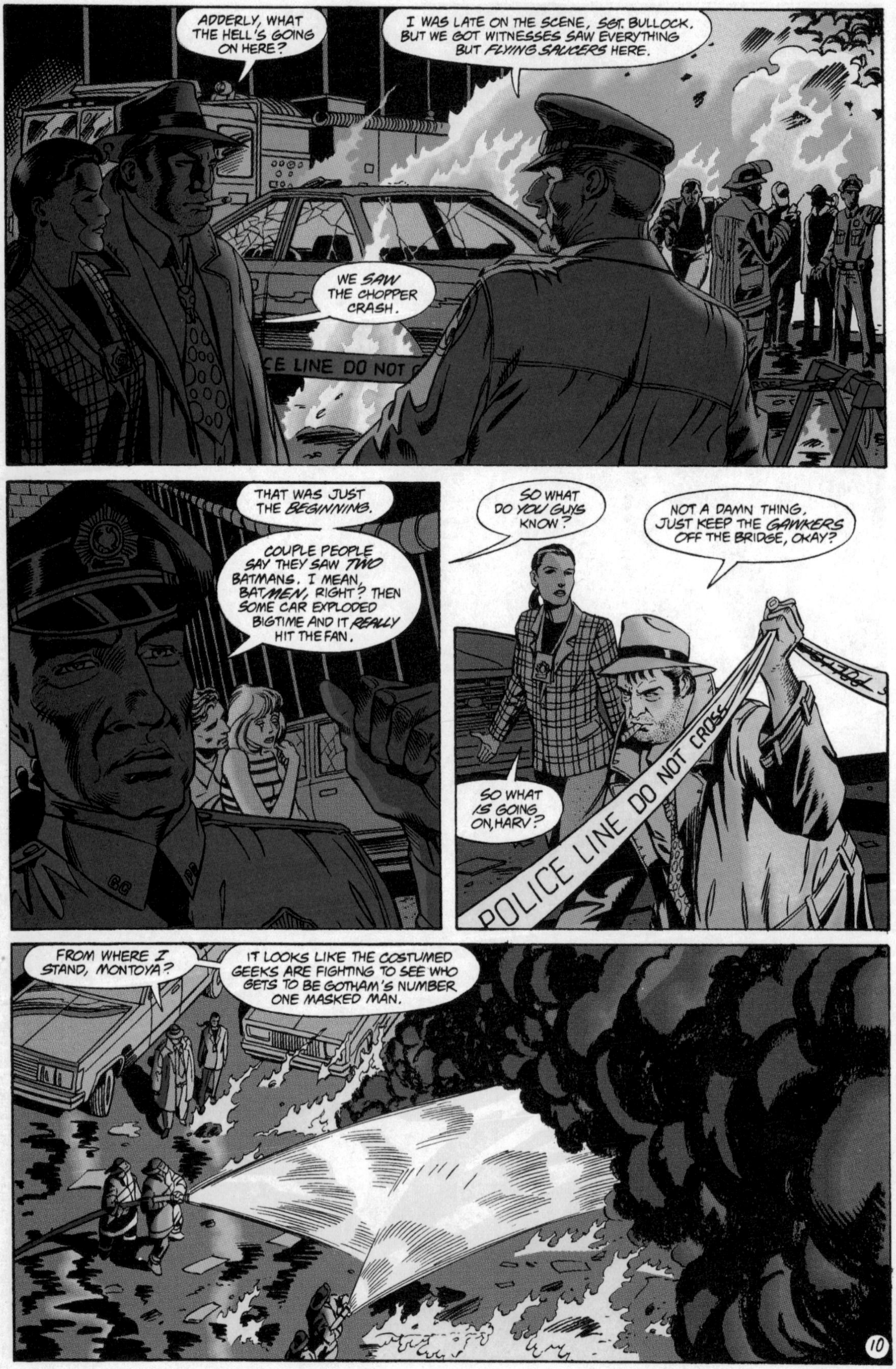
ADDERLY, WHAT THE HELL'S GOING ON HERE?
I WAS LATE ON THE SCENE, SGT. BULLOCK. BUT WE GOT WITNESSES SAW EVERYTHING BUT FLYING SAUCERS HERE.
WE SAW THE CHOPPER CRASH.
CE LINE DO NOT C
THAT WAS JUST THE BEGINNING.
COUPLE PEOPLE SAY THEY SAW TWO BATMANS. I MEAN, BATMEN, RIGHT? THEN SOME CAR EXPLODED BIGTIME AND IT REALLY HIT THE FAN.
SO WHAT DO YOU GUYS KNOW?
NOT A DAMN THING. JUST KEEP THE GAWKERS OFF THE BRIDGE, OKAY?
SO WHAT IS GOING ON, HARV?
POLICE LINE DO NOT CROSS
FROM WHERE I STAND, MONTOYA?
IT LOOKS LIKE THE COSTUMED GEEKS ARE FIGHTING TO SEE WHO GETS TO BE GOTHAM'S NUMBER ONE MASKED MAN.
10

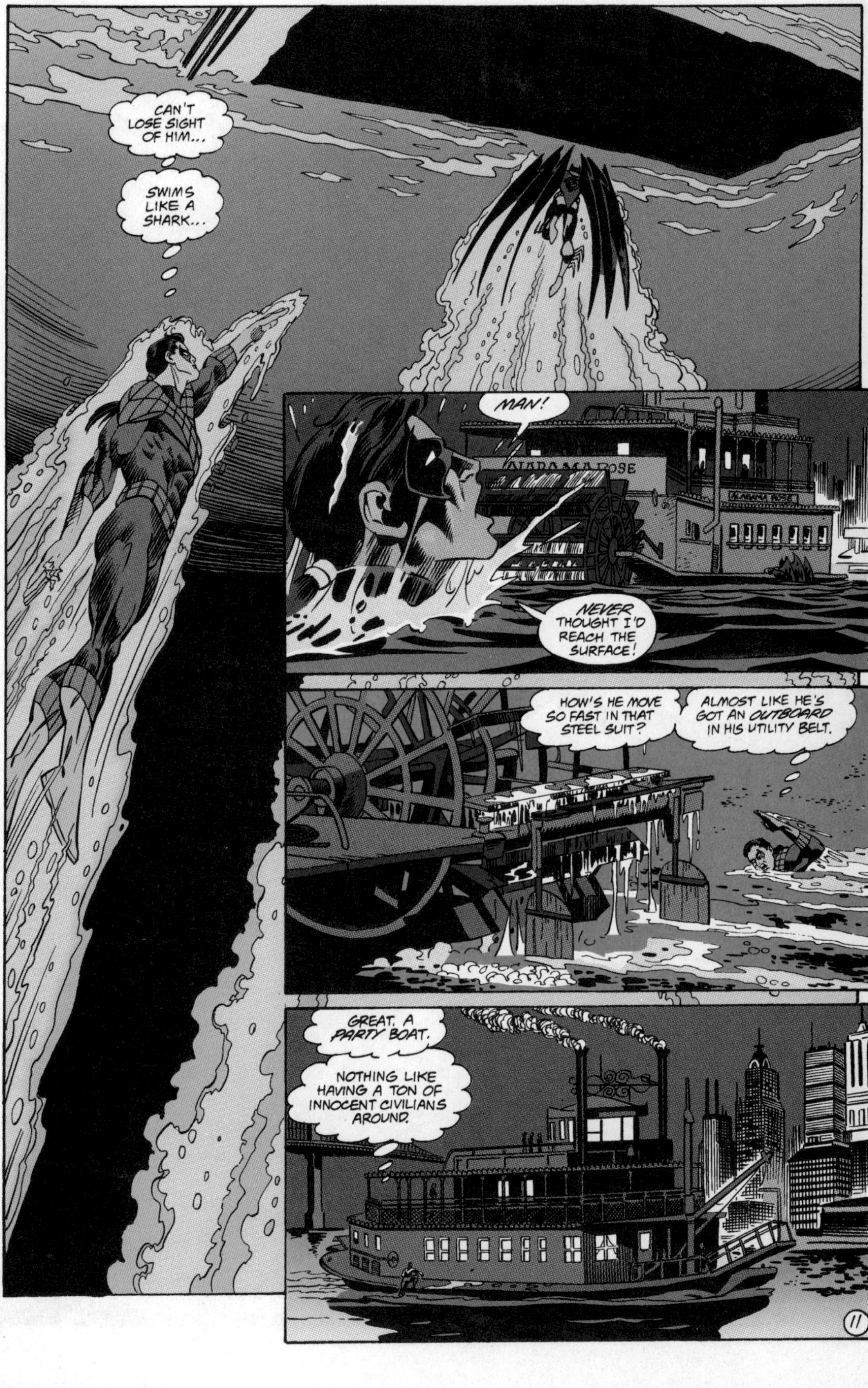
CAN'T LOSE SIGHT OF HIM...
SWIMS LIKE A SHARK...
MAN!
ALABAMA ROSE
NEVER THOUGHT I'D REACH THE SURFACE!
HOW'S HE MOVE SO FAST IN THAT STEEL SUIT?
ALMOST LIKE HE'S GOT AN OUTBOARD IN HIS UTILITY BELT.
GREAT, A PARTY BOAT.
NOTHING LIKE HAVING A TON OF INNOCENT CIVILIANS AROUND.
11

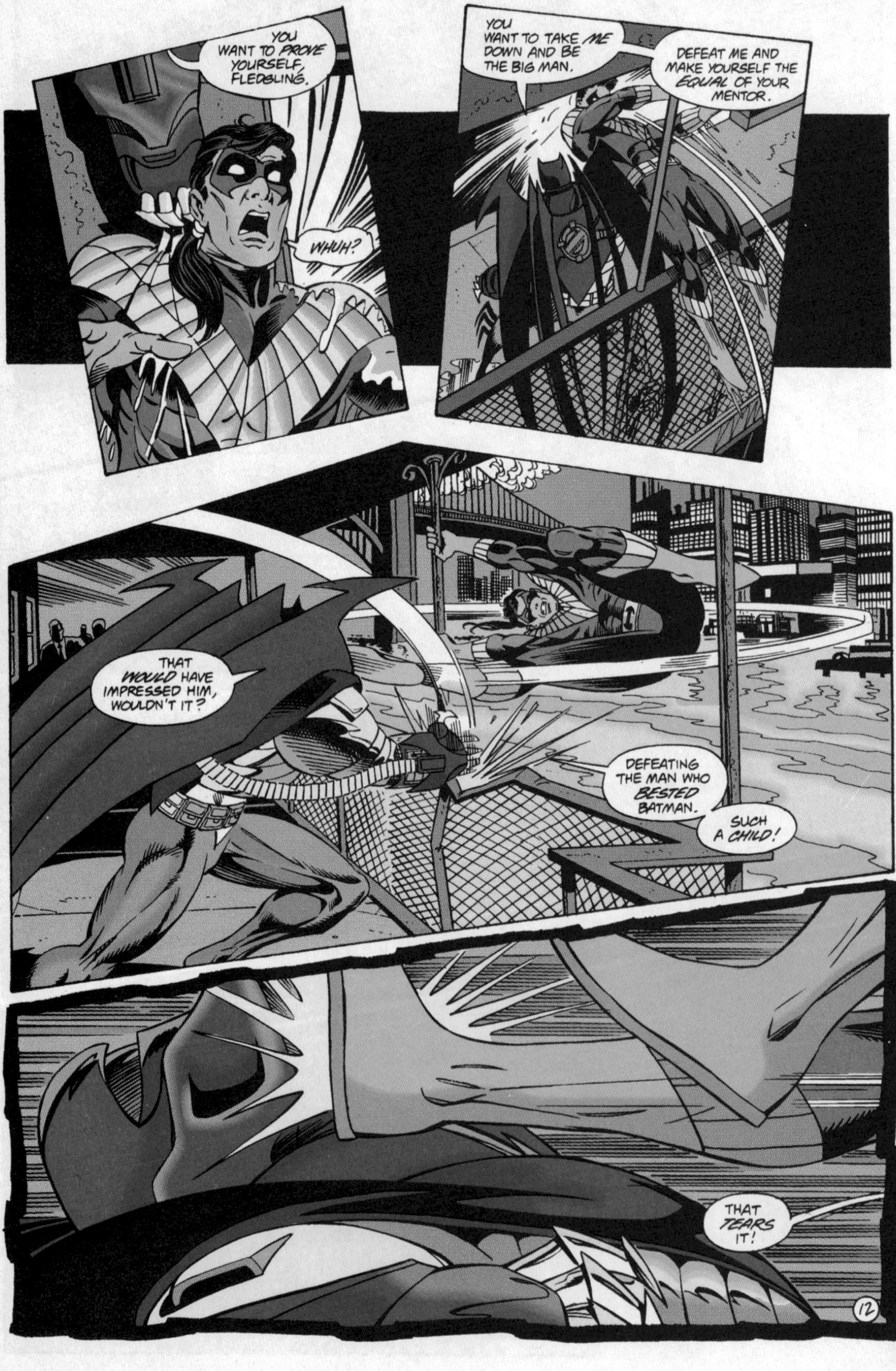
YOU WANT TO PROVE YOURSELF, FLEDGLING.
WHUH?
YOU WANT TO TAKE ME DOWN AND BE THE BIG MAN.
DEFEAT ME AND MAKE YOURSELF THE EQUAL OF YOUR MENTOR.
THAT WOULD HAVE IMPRESSED HIM, WOULDN'T IT?
DEFEATING THE MAN WHO BESTED BATMAN.
SUCH A CHILD!
THAT TEARS IT!
12

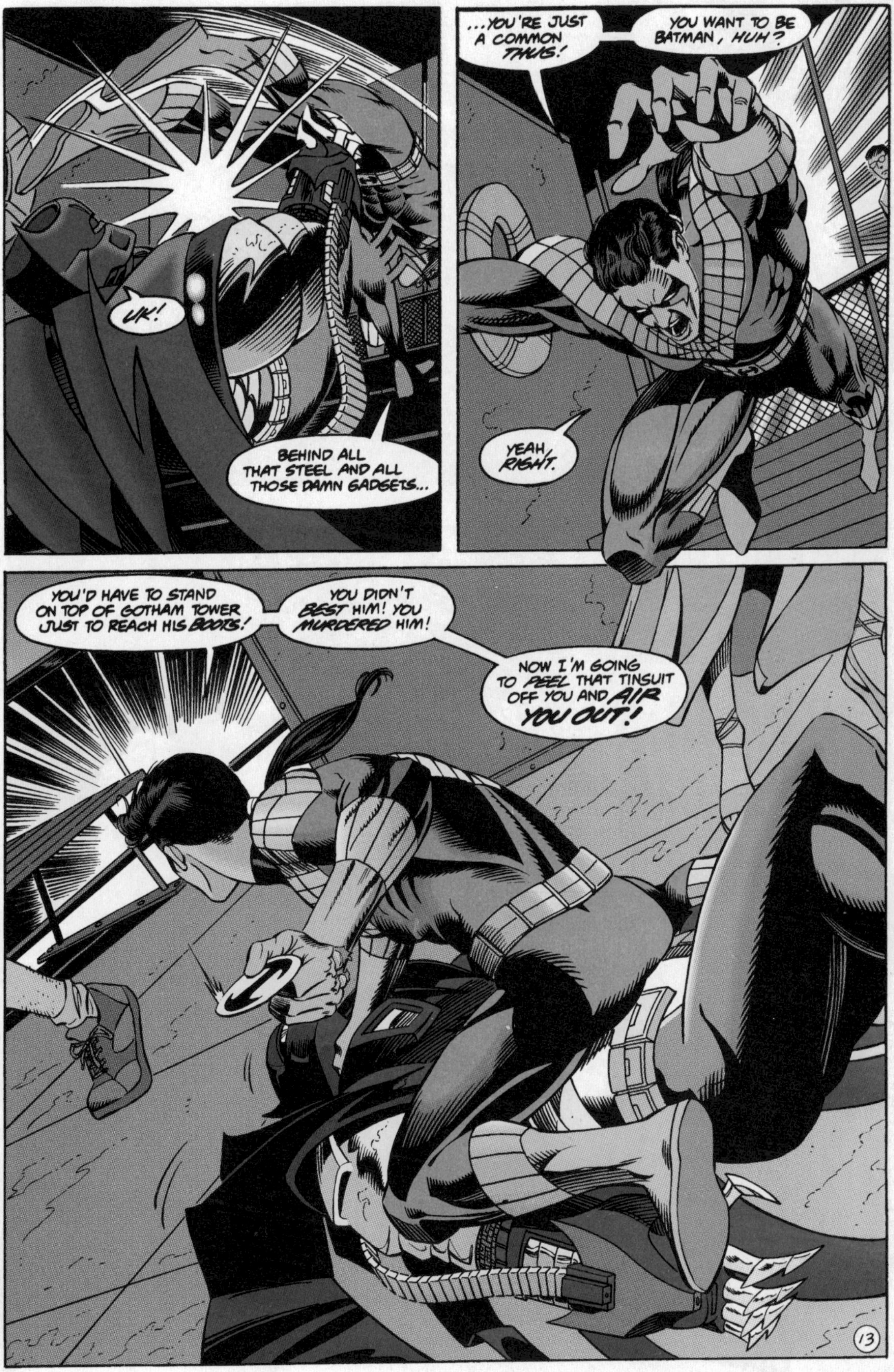
UK!
BEHIND ALL THAT STEEL AND ALL THOSE DAMN GADGETS...
...YOU'RE JUST A COMMON THUG!
YOU WANT TO BE BATMAN, HUH?
YEAH, RIGHT.
YOU'D HAVE TO STAND ON TOP OF GOTHAM TOWER JUST TO REACH HIS BOOTS!
YOU DIDN'T BEST HIM! YOU MURDERED HIM!
NOW I'M GOING TO PEEL THAT TINSUIT OFF YOU AND AIR YOU OUT!
13

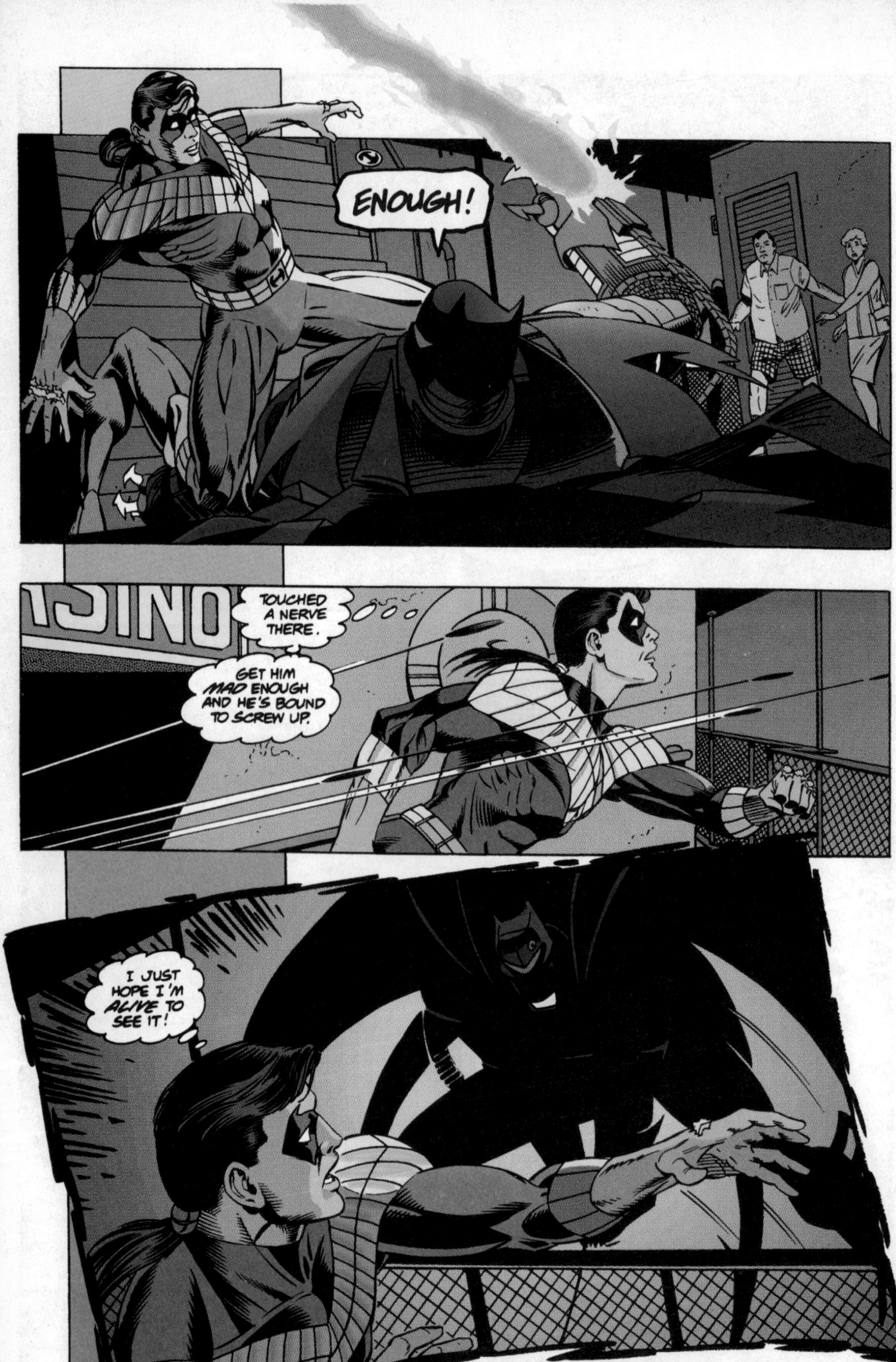
ENOUGH!
TOUCHED A NERVE THERE.
GET HIM MAD ENOUGH AND HE'S BOUND TO SCREW UP.
I JUST HOPE I'M ALIVE TO SEE IT!
14

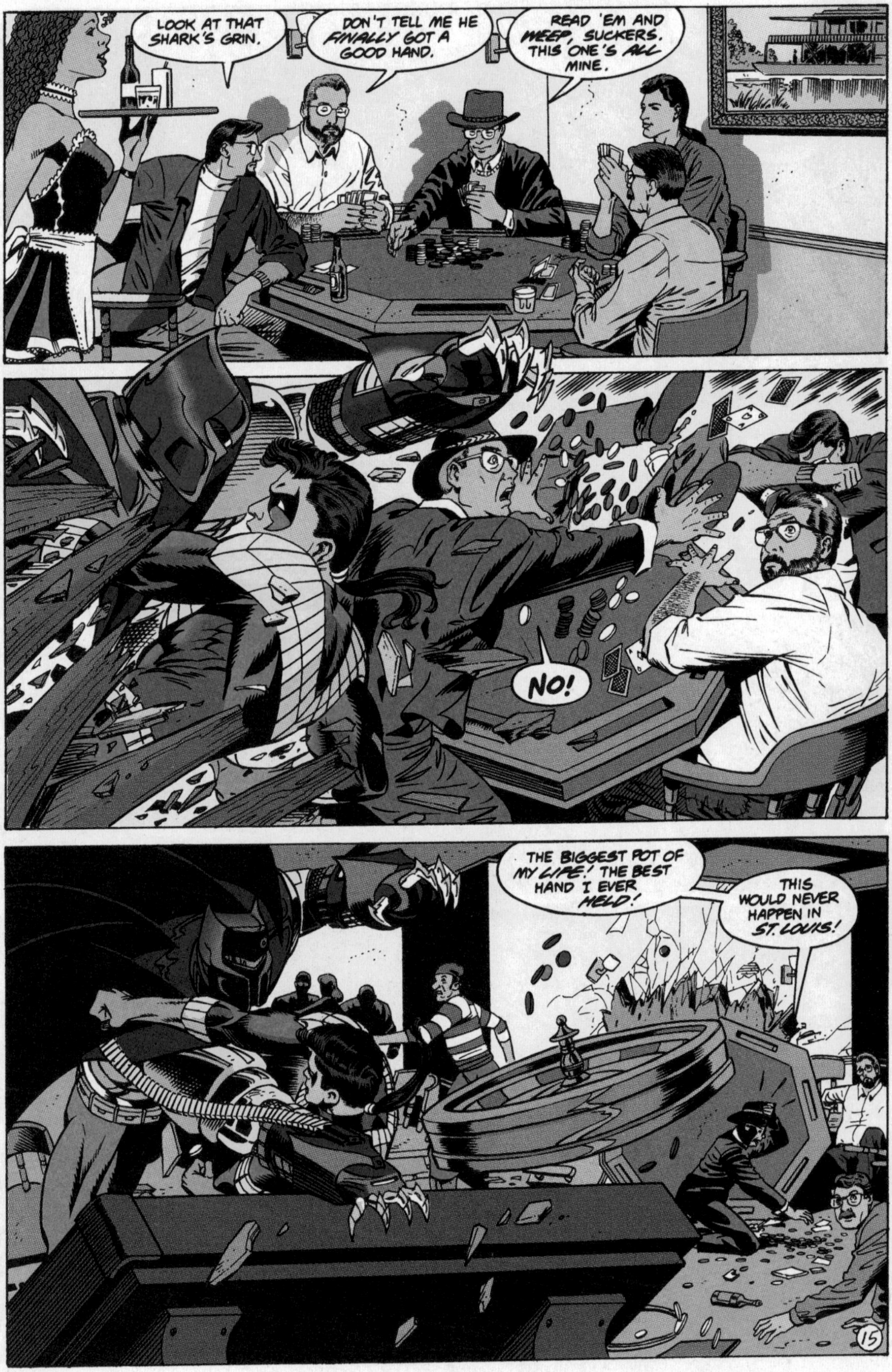
LOOK AT THAT SHARK'S GRIN.
DON'T TELL ME HE FINALLY GOT A GOOD HAND.
READ 'EM AND WEEP, SUCKERS. THIS ONE'S ALL MINE.
NO!
THE BIGGEST POT OF MY LIFE! THE BEST HAND I EVER HELD!
THIS WOULD NEVER HAPPEN IN ST. LOUIS!
15

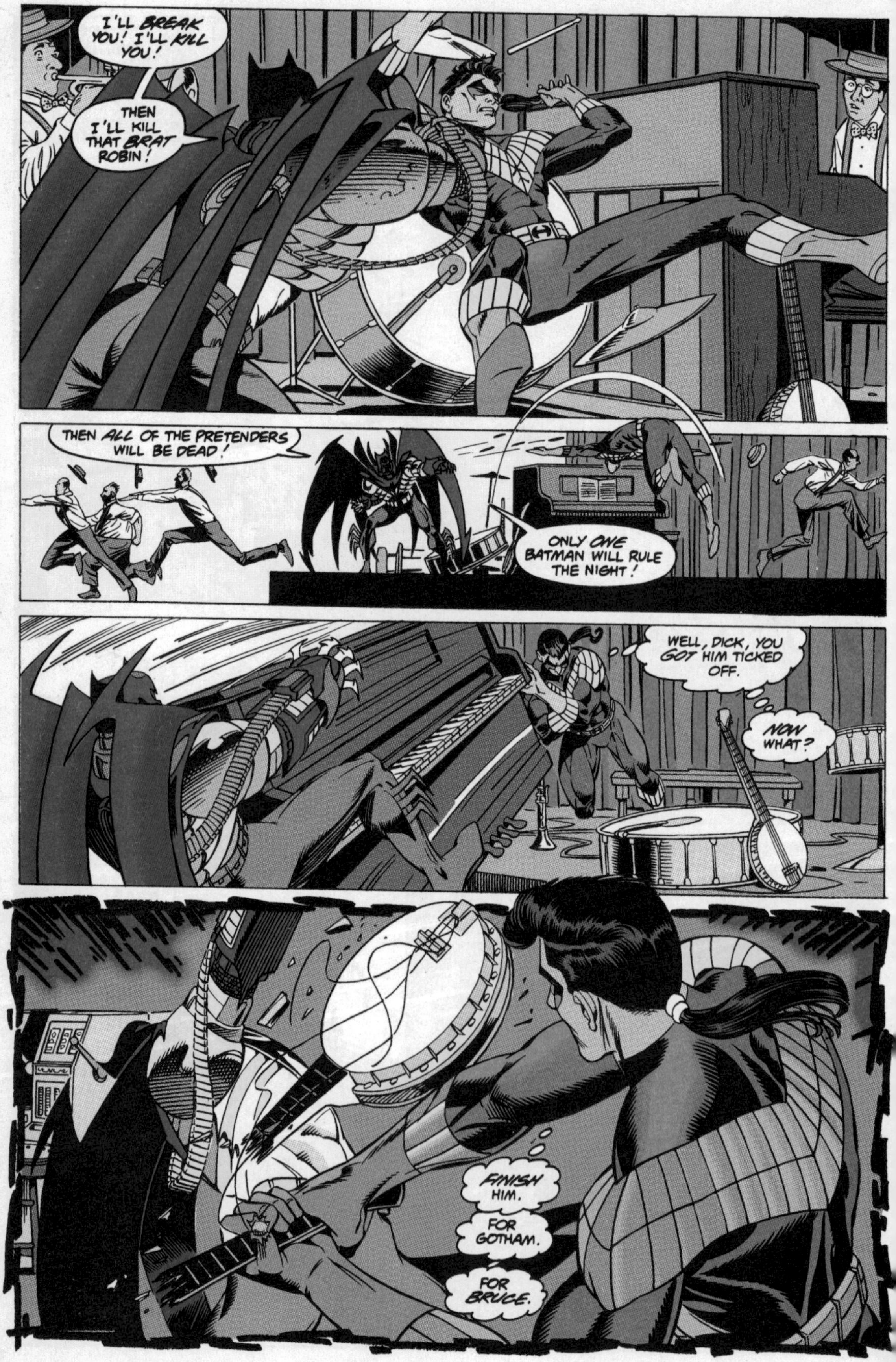
I'LL BREAK YOU! I'LL KILL YOU!
THEN I'LL KILL THAT BRAT ROBIN!
THEN ALL OF THE PRETENDERS WILL BE DEAD!
ONLY ONE BATMAN WILL RULE THE NIGHT!
WELL, DICK, YOU GOT HIM TICKED OFF.
NOW WHAT?
FINISH HIM.
FOR GOTHAM.
FOR BRUCE.

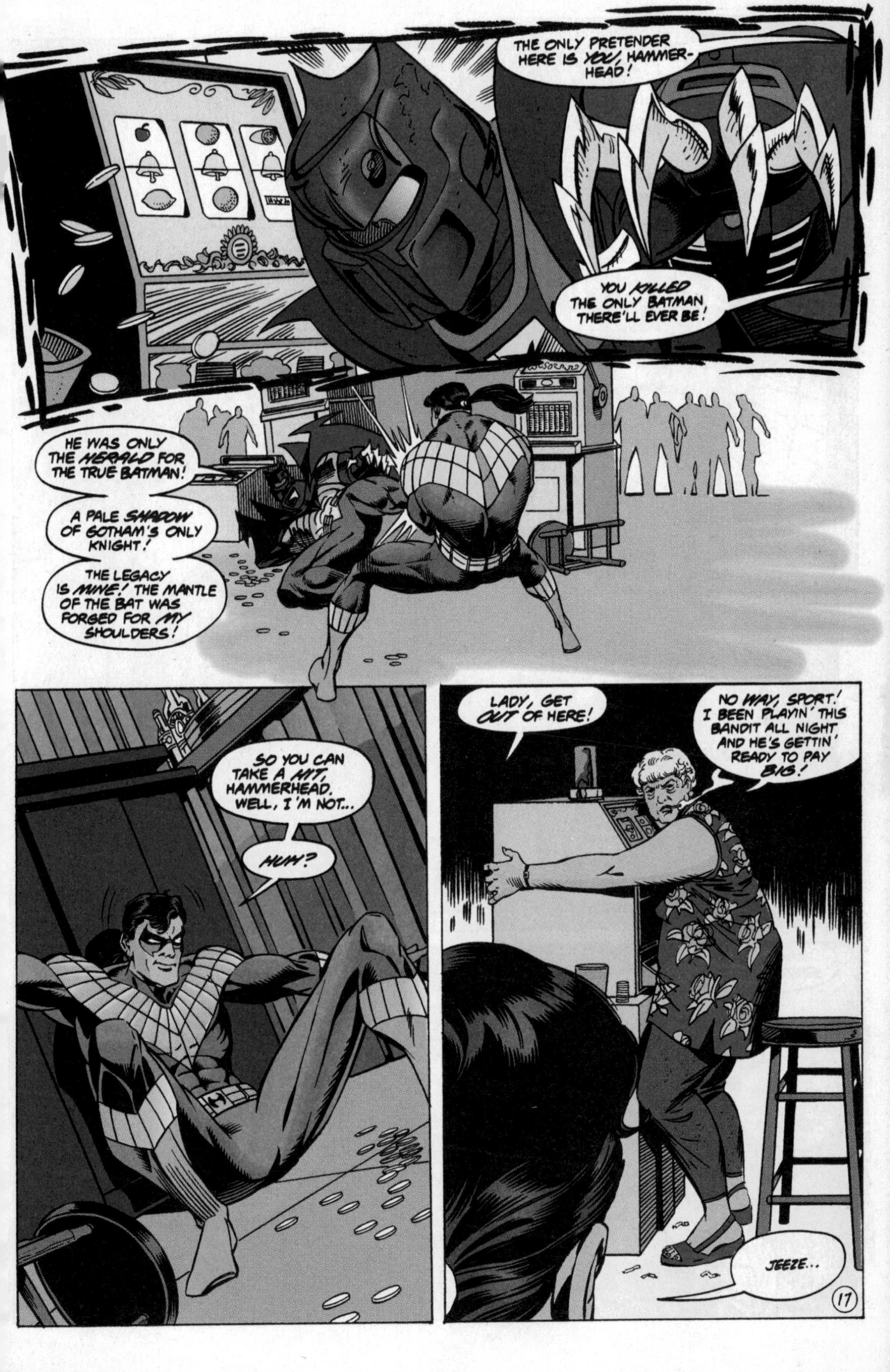
THE ONLY PRETENDER HERE IS YOU, HAMMER-HEAD!
YOU KILLED THE ONLY BATMAN THERE'LL EVER BE!
HE WAS ONLY THE HERALD FOR THE TRUE BATMAN!
A PALE SHADOW OF GOTHAM'S ONLY KNIGHT!
THE LEGACY IS MINE! THE MANTLE OF THE BAT WAS FORGED FOR MY SHOULDERS!
SO YOU CAN TAKE A HIT, HAMMERHEAD. WELL, I'M NOT...
HUH?
LADY, GET OUT OF HERE!
NO WAY, SPORT! I BEEN PLAYIN' THIS BANDIT ALL NIGHT AND HE'S GETTIN' READY TO PAY BIG!
JEEZE...
17

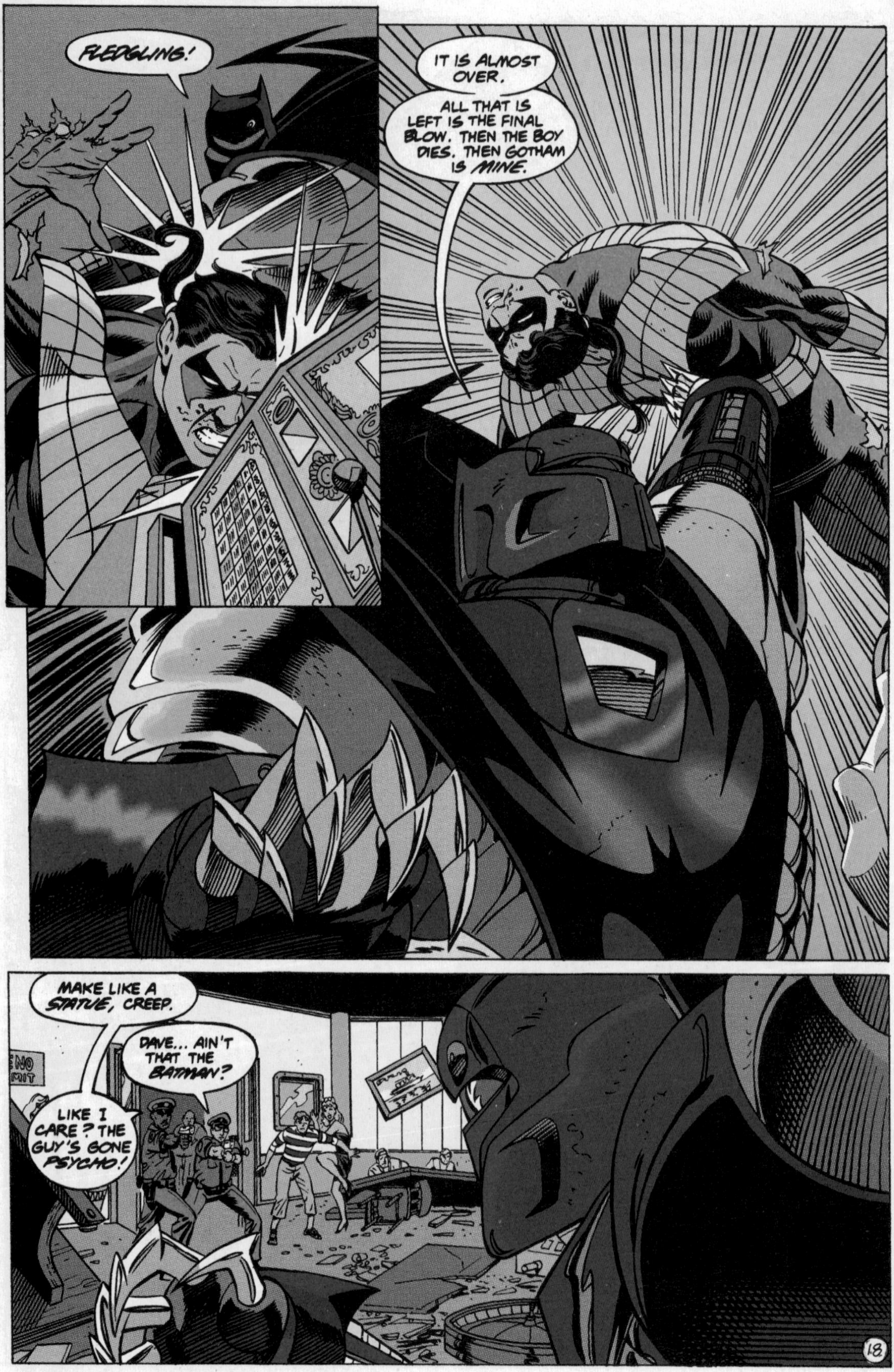
FLEDGLING!
IT IS ALMOST OVER.
ALL THAT IS LEFT IS THE FINAL BLOW. THEN THE BOY DIES. THEN GOTHAM IS MINE.
MAKE LIKE A STATUE, CREEP.
DAVE... AIN'T THAT THE BATMAN?
LIKE I CARE? THE GUY'S GONE PSYCHO!
18

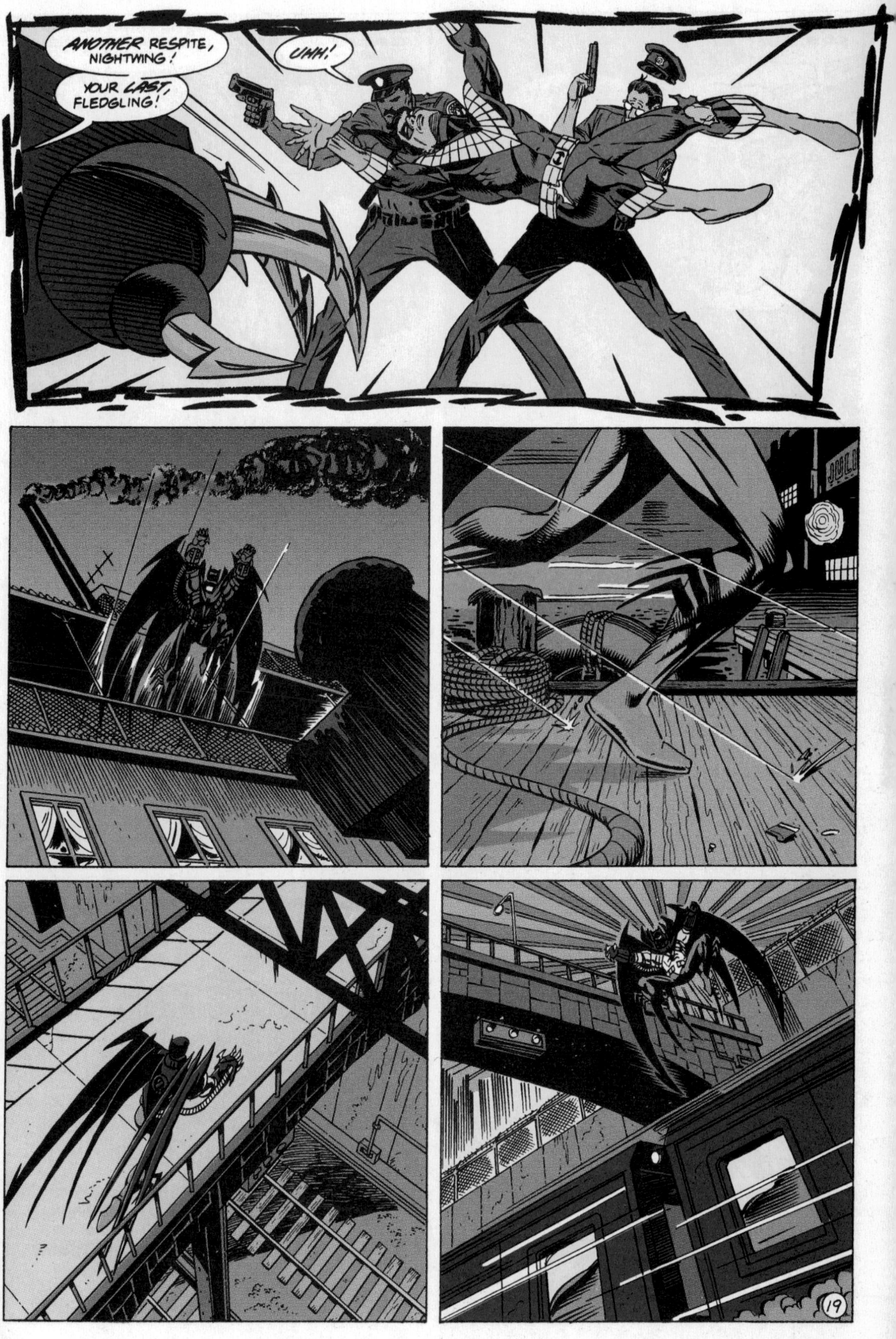
ANOTHER RESPITE, NIGHTWING!
YOUR LAST, FLEDGLING!
UHH!
19

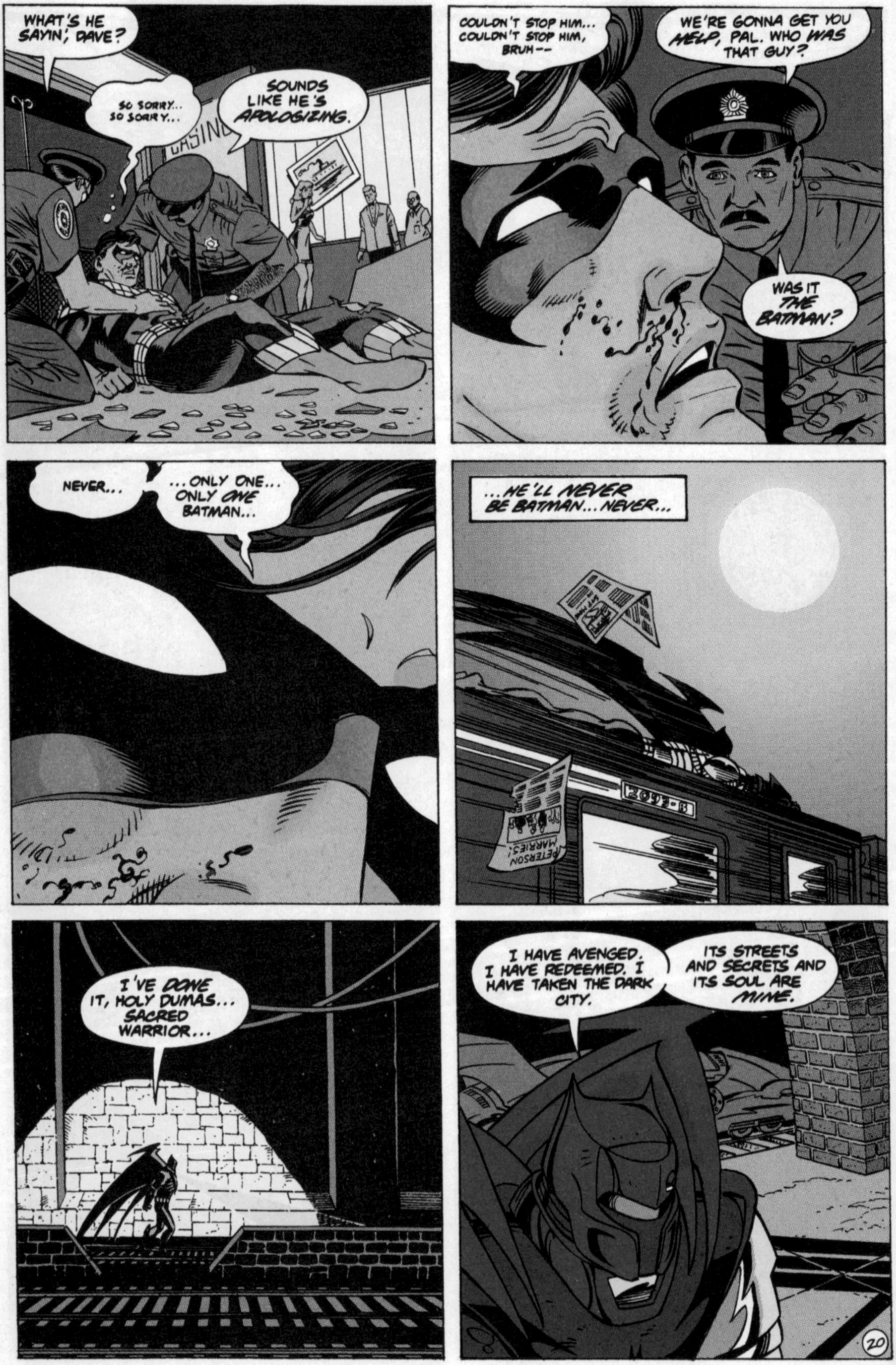
WHAT'S HE SAYIN', DAVE?
SO SORRY... SO SORRY...
SOUNDS LIKE HE'S APOLOGIZING.
CASINO
COULDN'T STOP HIM... COULDN'T STOP HIM, BRUH--
WE'RE GONNA GET YOU HELP, PAL. WHO WAS THAT GUY?
WAS IT THE BATMAN?
NEVER...
...ONLY ONE... ONLY ONE BATMAN...
...HE'LL NEVER BE BATMAN... NEVER...
2093-B
PETERSON MARRIES!
I'VE DONE IT, HOLY DUMAS... SACRED WARRIOR...
I HAVE AVENGED. I HAVE REDEEMED. I HAVE TAKEN THE DARK CITY.
ITS STREETS AND SECRETS AND ITS SOUL ARE MINE.
20

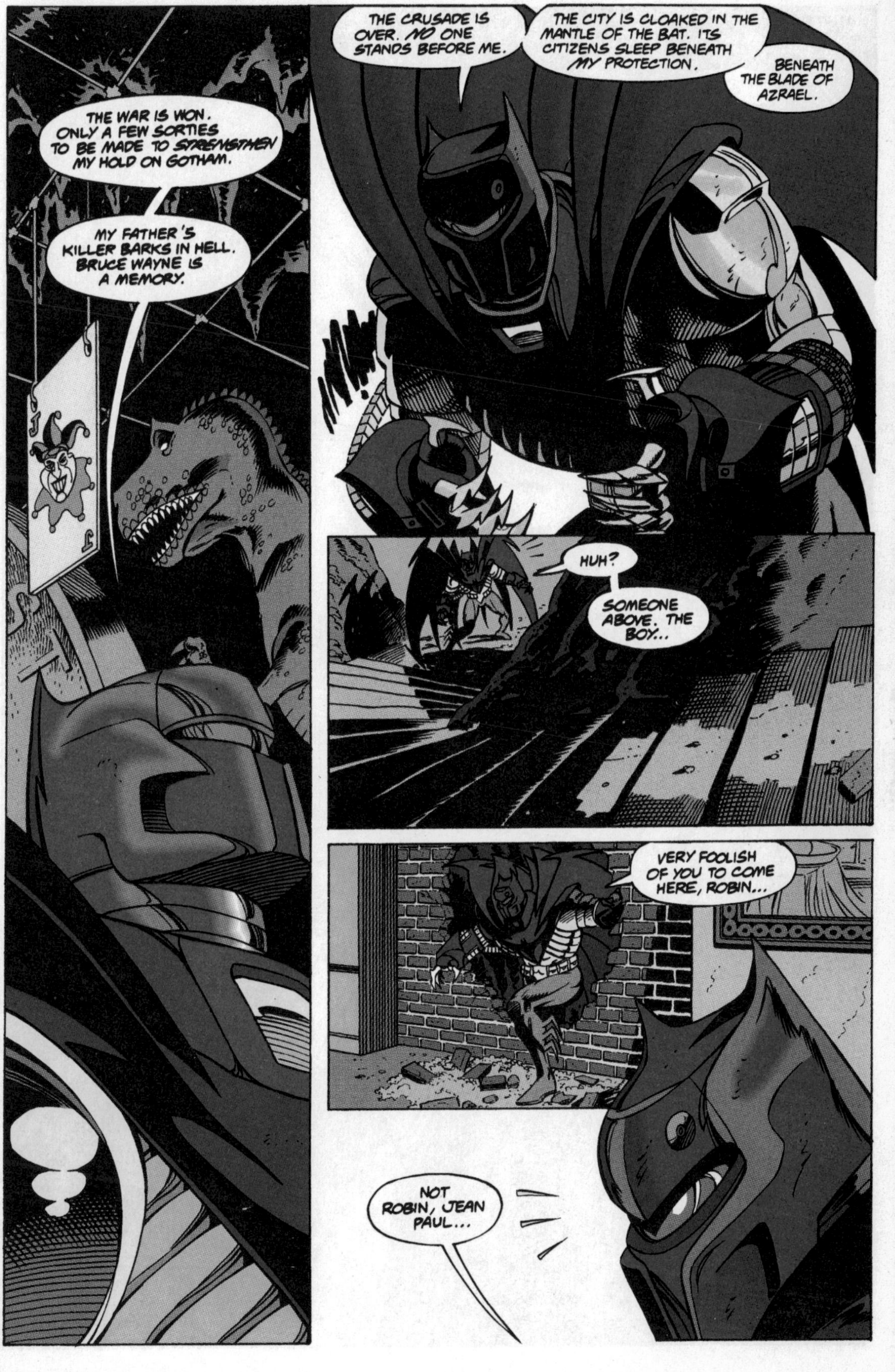
THE WAR IS WON. ONLY A FEW SORTIES TO BE MADE TO STRENGTHEN MY HOLD ON GOTHAM.
MY FATHER'S KILLER BARKS IN HELL. BRUCE WAYNE IS A MEMORY.
THE CRUSADE IS OVER. NO ONE STANDS BEFORE ME.
THE CITY IS CLOAKED IN THE MANTLE OF THE BAT. ITS CITIZENS SLEEP BENEATH MY PROTECTION.
BENEATH THE BLADE OF AZRAEL.
HUH?
SOMEONE ABOVE. THE BOY...
VERY FOOLISH OF YOU TO COME HERE, ROBIN...
NOT ROBIN, JEAN PAUL...

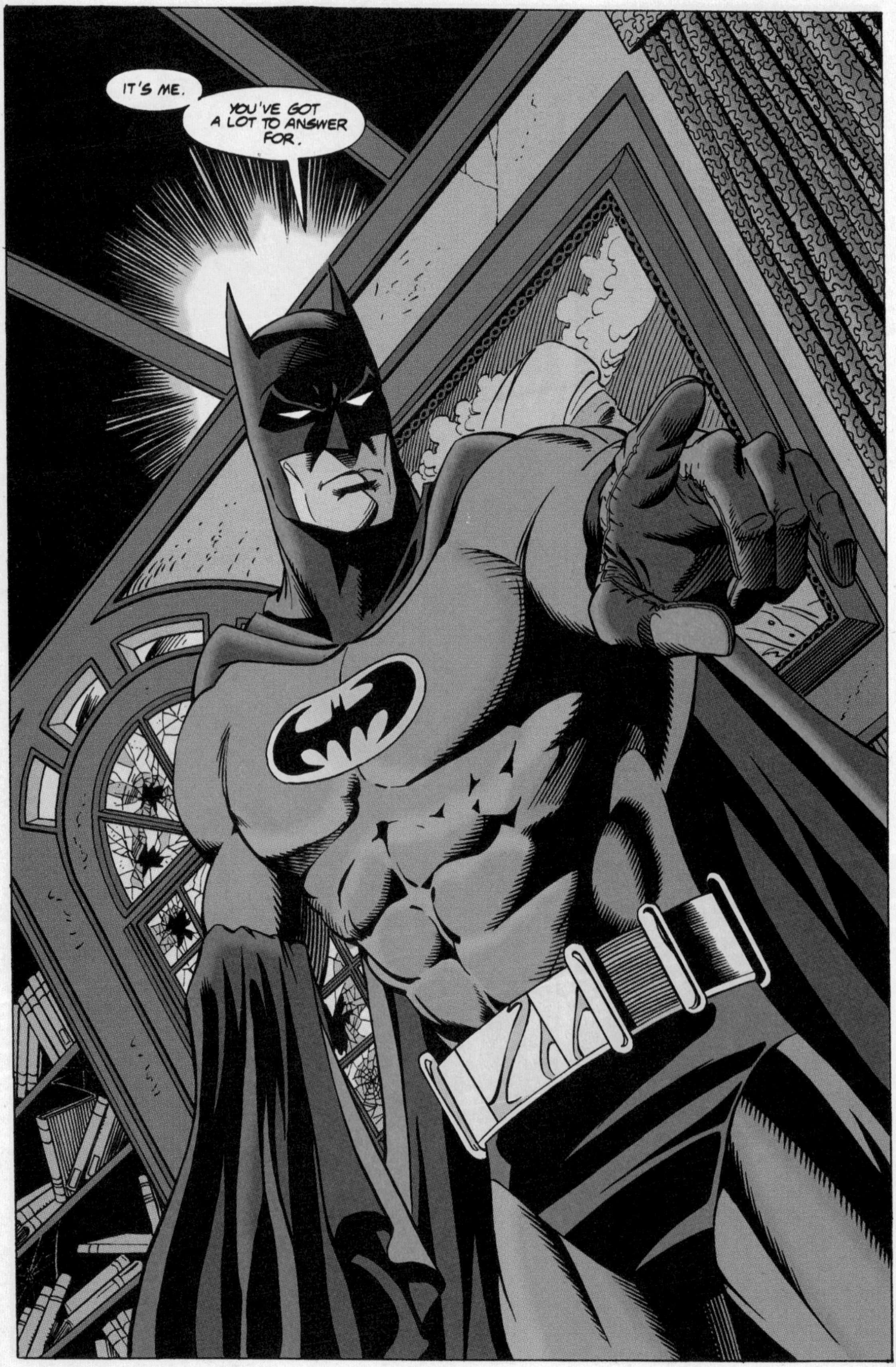
IT'S ME.
YOU'VE GOT A LOT TO ANSWER FOR.

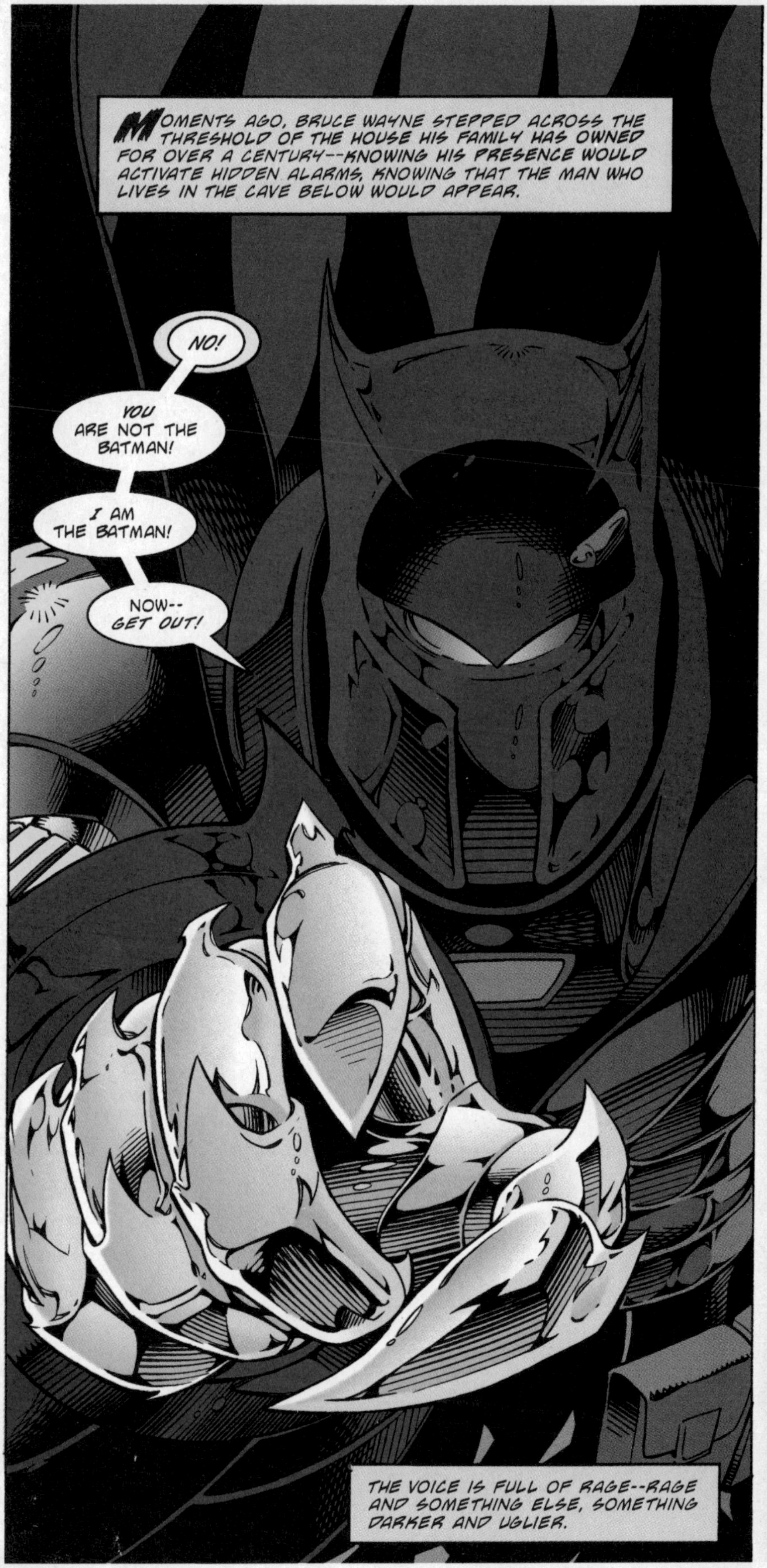
MOMENTS AGO, BRUCE WAYNE STEPPED ACROSS THE THRESHOLD OF THE HOUSE HIS FAMILY HAS OWNED FOR OVER A CENTURY--KNOWING HIS PRESENCE WOULD ACTIVATE HIDDEN ALARMS, KNOWING THAT THE MAN WHO LIVES IN THE CAVE BELOW WOULD APPEAR.
NO!
YOU ARE NOT THE BATMAN!
I AM THE BATMAN!
NOW-- GET OUT!
THE VOICE IS FULL OF RAGE--RAGE AND SOMETHING ELSE, SOMETHING DARKER AND UGLIER.

CLIMAX

writer
DENNY O'NEIL

penciller
BARRY KITSON

inker
SCOTT HANNA

letterer
WILLIE SCHUBERT

colorist
DIGITAL CHAMELEON

assistant editor
CHUCK KIM

associate editor
JIM SPIVEY

editor
ARCHIE GOODWIN

BATMAN created
by **BOB KANE**

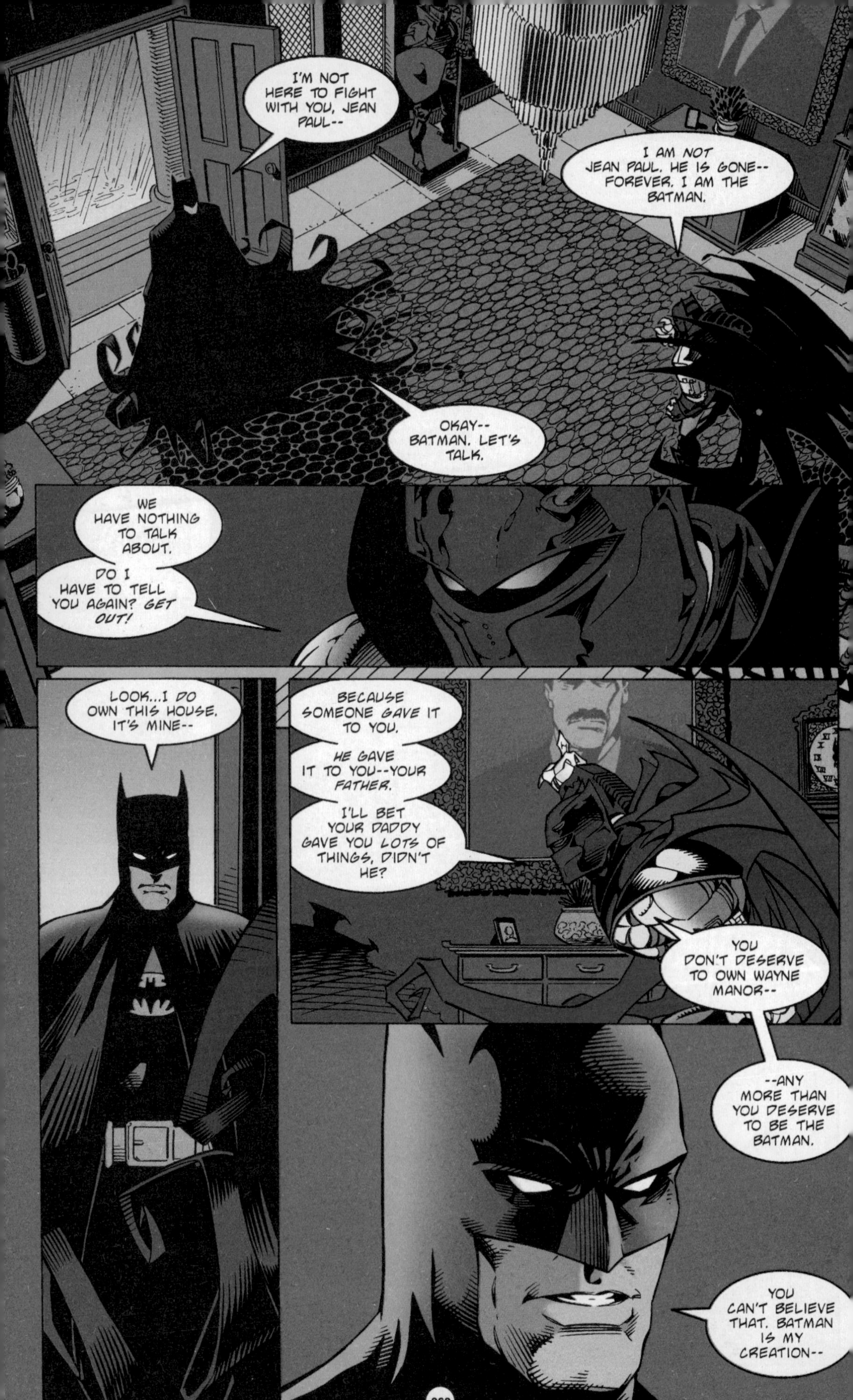

I'M NOT HERE TO FIGHT WITH YOU, JEAN PAUL--
I AM NOT JEAN PAUL. HE IS GONE-- FOREVER. I AM THE BATMAN.
OKAY-- BATMAN. LET'S TALK.
WE HAVE NOTHING TO TALK ABOUT.
DO I HAVE TO TELL YOU AGAIN? GET OUT!
LOOK...I DO OWN THIS HOUSE. IT'S MINE--
BECAUSE SOMEONE GAVE IT TO YOU.
HE GAVE IT TO YOU--YOUR FATHER.
I'LL BET YOUR DADDY GAVE YOU LOTS OF THINGS, DIDN'T HE?
YOU DON'T DESERVE TO OWN WAYNE MANOR--
--ANY MORE THAN YOU DESERVE TO BE THE BATMAN.
YOU CAN'T BELIEVE THAT. BATMAN IS MY CREATION--

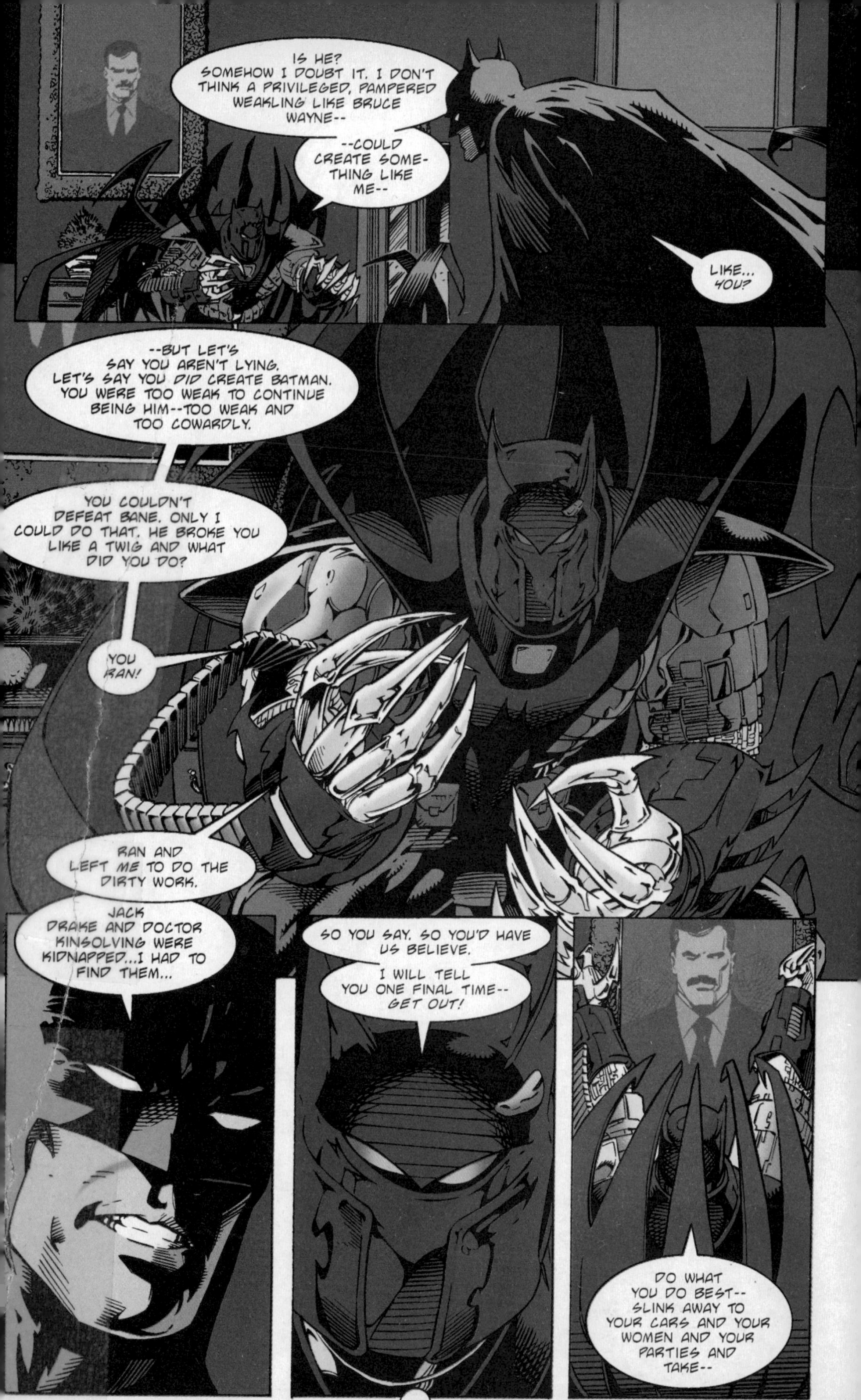
IS HE? SOMEHOW I DOUBT IT. I DON'T THINK A PRIVILEGED, PAMPERED WEAKLING LIKE BRUCE WAYNE--
--COULD CREATE SOMETHING LIKE ME--
LIKE... YOU?
--BUT LET'S SAY YOU AREN'T LYING. LET'S SAY YOU *DID* CREATE BATMAN. YOU WERE TOO WEAK TO CONTINUE BEING HIM--TOO WEAK AND TOO COWARDLY.
YOU COULDN'T DEFEAT BANE. ONLY I COULD DO THAT. HE BROKE YOU LIKE A TWIG AND WHAT DID YOU DO?
YOU *RAN!*
RAN AND LEFT *ME* TO DO THE DIRTY WORK.
JACK DRAKE AND DOCTOR KINSOLVING WERE KIDNAPPED...I HAD TO FIND THEM...
SO YOU SAY. SO YOU'D HAVE US BELIEVE.
I WILL TELL YOU ONE FINAL TIME-- *GET OUT!*
DO WHAT YOU DO BEST-- SLINK AWAY TO YOUR CARS AND YOUR WOMEN AND YOUR PARTIES AND TAKE--

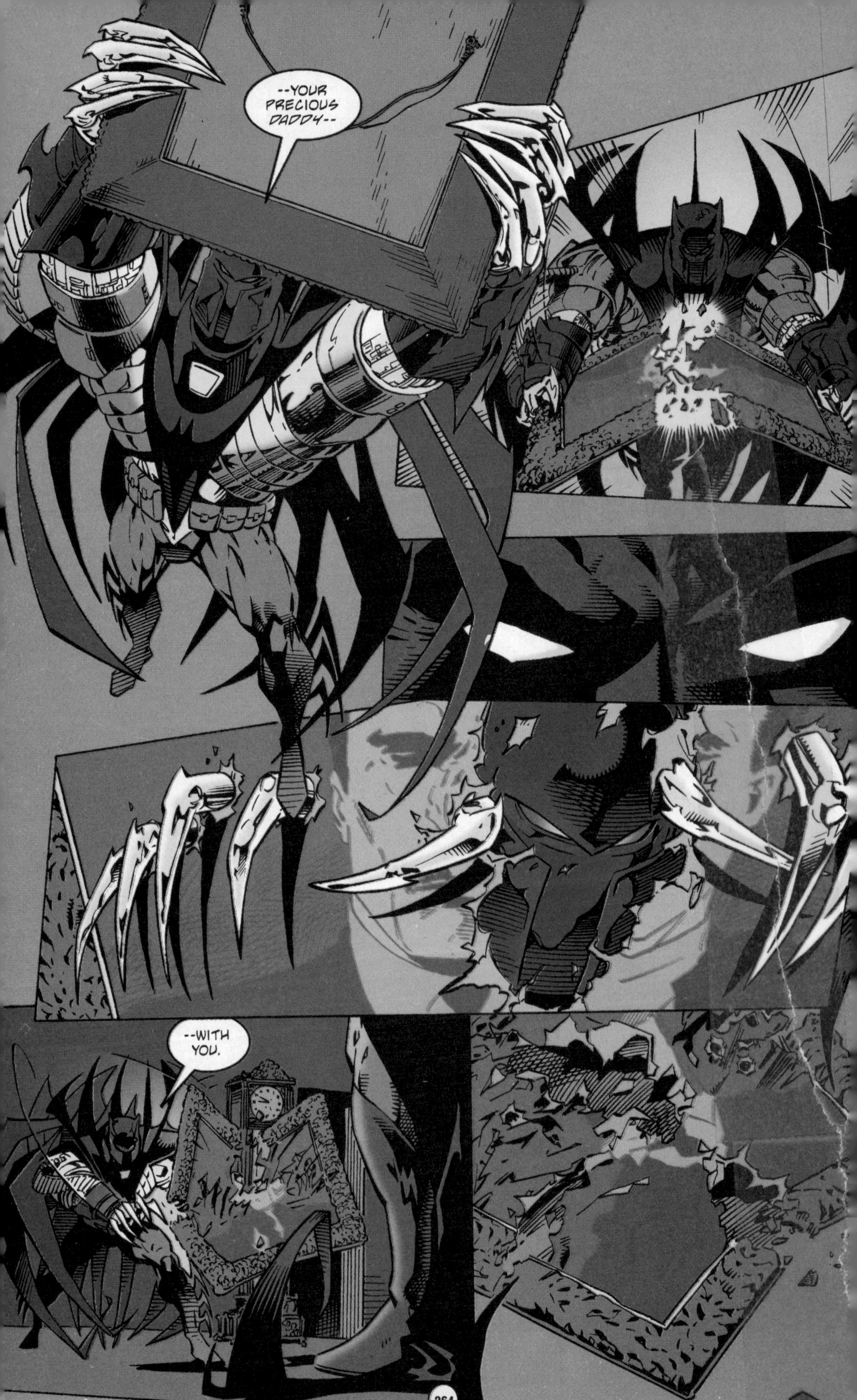
--YOUR PRECIOUS DADDY--
--WITH YOU.

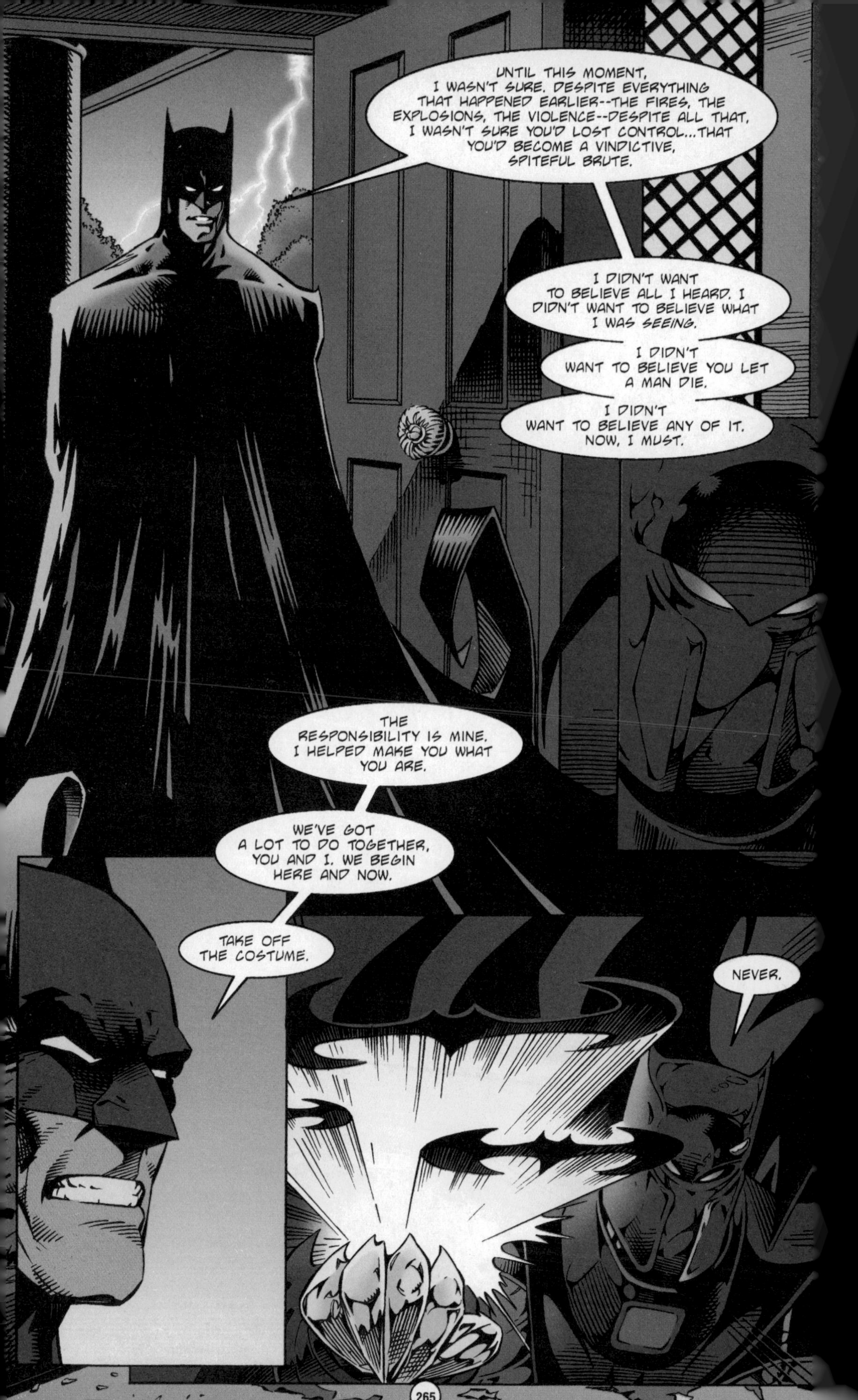

UNTIL THIS MOMENT, I WASN'T SURE. DESPITE EVERYTHING THAT HAPPENED EARLIER--THE FIRES, THE EXPLOSIONS, THE VIOLENCE--DESPITE ALL THAT, I WASN'T SURE YOU'D LOST CONTROL...THAT YOU'D BECOME A VINDICTIVE, SPITEFUL BRUTE.
I DIDN'T WANT TO BELIEVE ALL I HEARD. I DIDN'T WANT TO BELIEVE WHAT I WAS SEEING.
I DIDN'T WANT TO BELIEVE YOU LET A MAN DIE.
I DIDN'T WANT TO BELIEVE ANY OF IT. NOW, I MUST.
THE RESPONSIBILITY IS MINE. I HELPED MAKE YOU WHAT YOU ARE.
WE'VE GOT A LOT TO DO TOGETHER, YOU AND I. WE BEGIN HERE AND NOW.
TAKE OFF THE COSTUME.
NEVER.

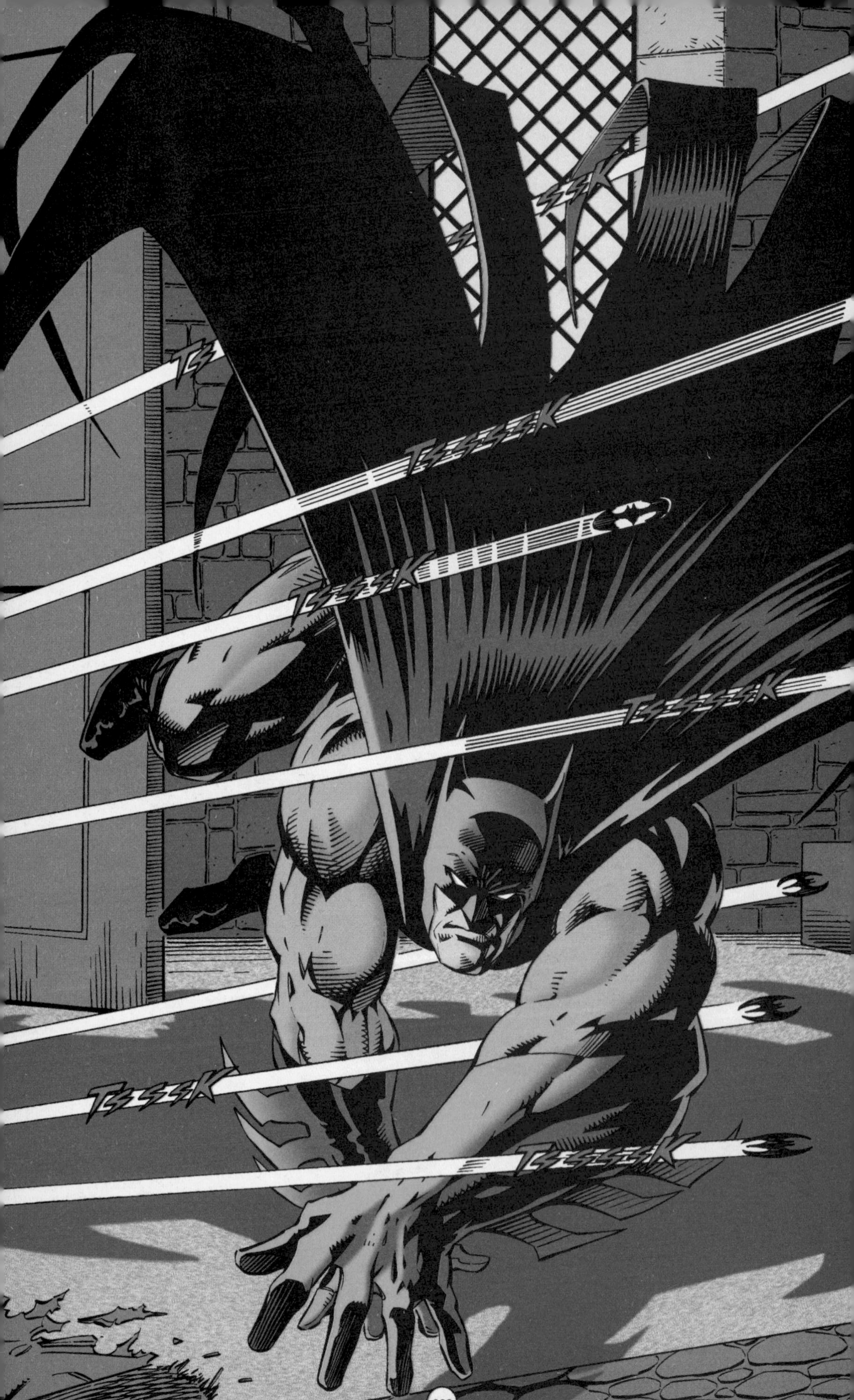
TSSSSK
TSSSSK
TSSSSSK
TSSSSK
TSSSSSSK

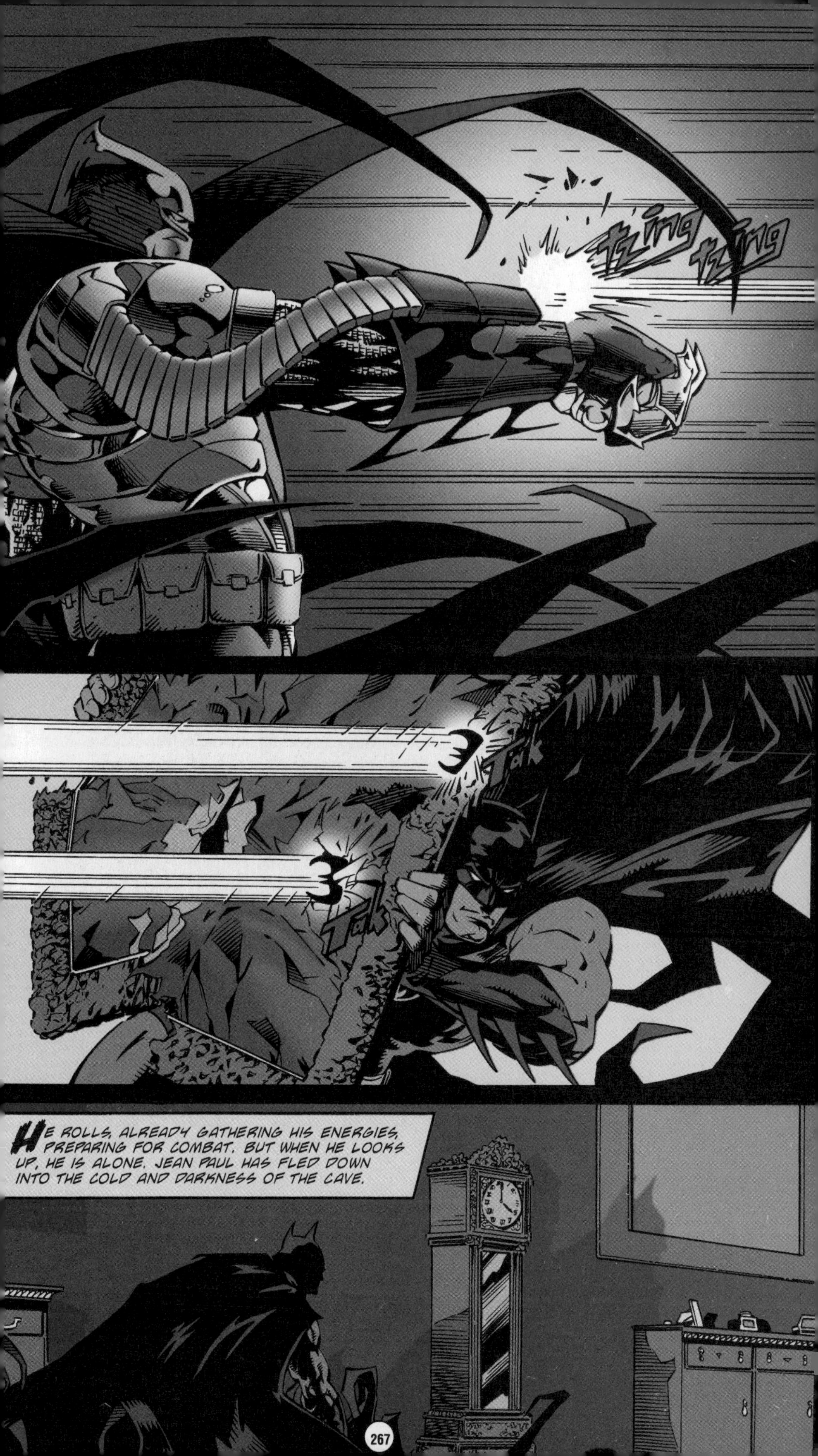

tzing tzing
HE ROLLS, ALREADY GATHERING HIS ENERGIES, PREPARING FOR COMBAT. BUT WHEN HE LOOKS UP, HE IS ALONE. JEAN PAUL HAS FLED DOWN INTO THE COLD AND DARKNESS OF THE CAVE.

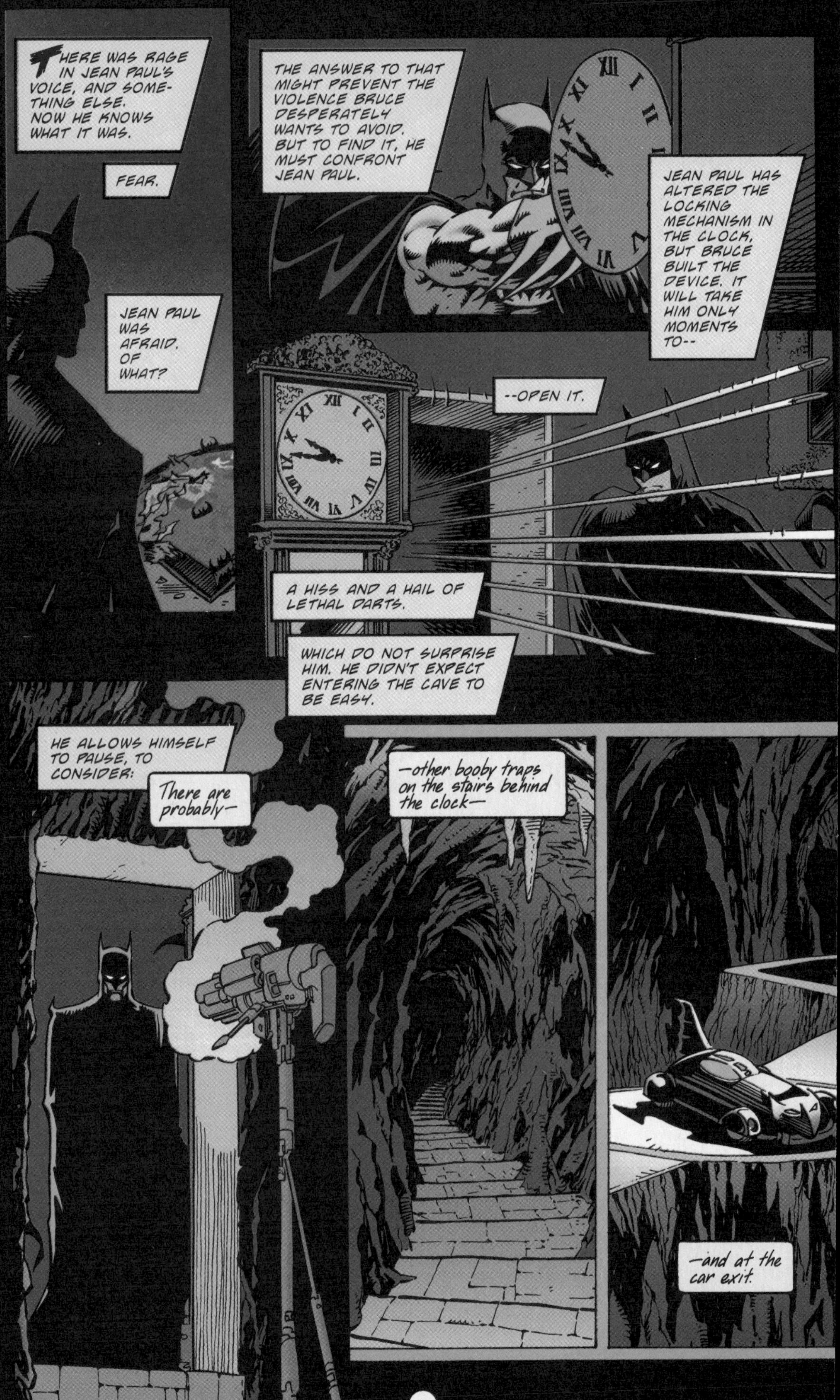

THERE WAS RAGE IN JEAN PAUL'S VOICE, AND SOMETHING ELSE. NOW HE KNOWS WHAT IT WAS.
FEAR.
JEAN PAUL WAS AFRAID. OF WHAT?
THE ANSWER TO THAT MIGHT PREVENT THE VIOLENCE BRUCE DESPERATELY WANTS TO AVOID. BUT TO FIND IT, HE MUST CONFRONT JEAN PAUL.
JEAN PAUL HAS ALTERED THE LOCKING MECHANISM IN THE CLOCK, BUT BRUCE BUILT THE DEVICE. IT WILL TAKE HIM ONLY MOMENTS TO--
--OPEN IT.
A HISS AND A HAIL OF LETHAL DARTS.
WHICH DO NOT SURPRISE HIM. HE DIDN'T EXPECT ENTERING THE CAVE TO BE EASY.
HE ALLOWS HIMSELF TO PAUSE, TO CONSIDER:
There are probably—
—other booby traps on the stairs behind the clock—
—and at the car exit.

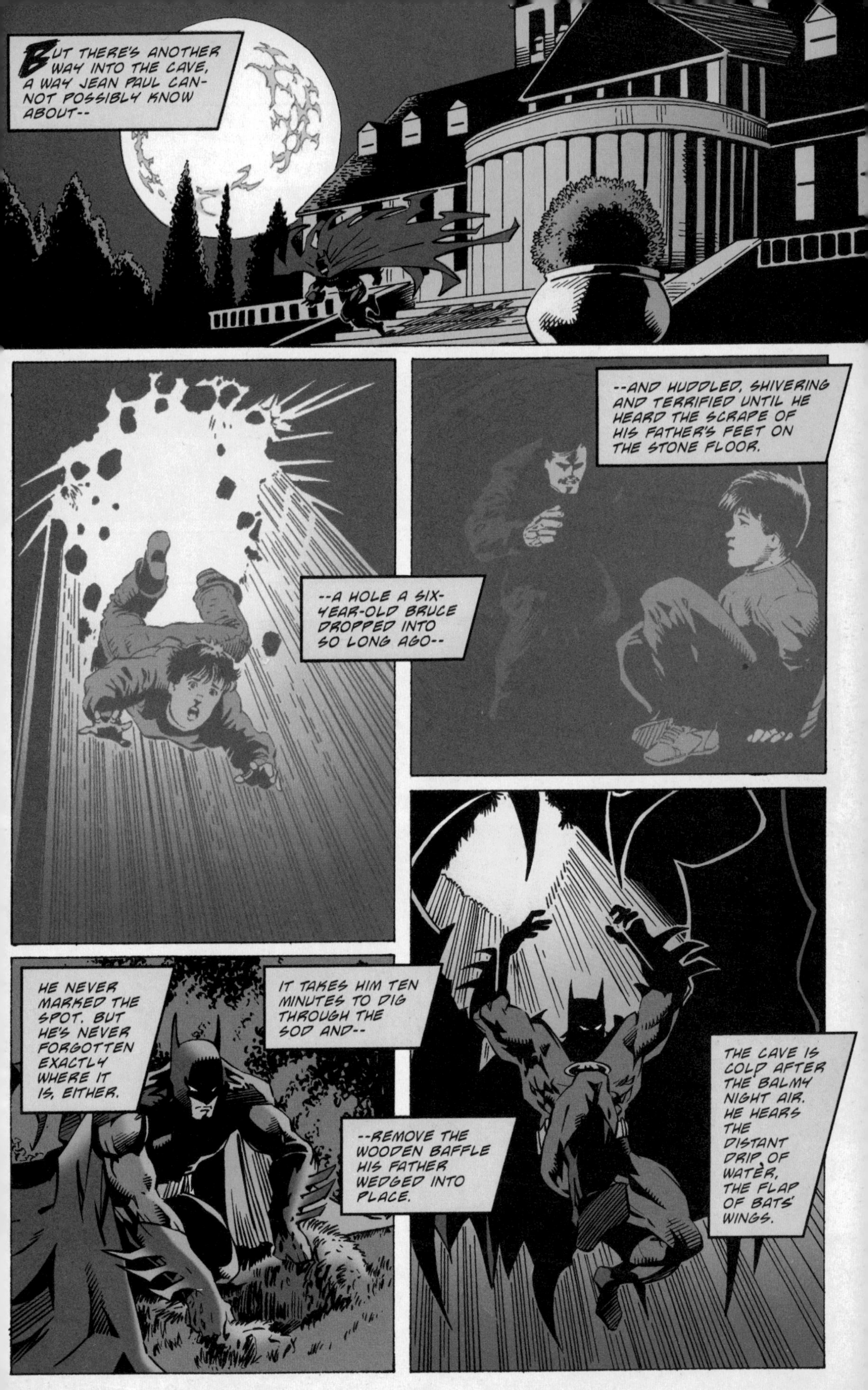
BUT THERE'S ANOTHER WAY INTO THE CAVE, A WAY JEAN PAUL CANNOT POSSIBLY KNOW ABOUT--
--A HOLE A SIX-YEAR-OLD BRUCE DROPPED INTO SO LONG AGO--
--AND HUDDLED, SHIVERING AND TERRIFIED UNTIL HE HEARD THE SCRAPE OF HIS FATHER'S FEET ON THE STONE FLOOR.
HE NEVER MARKED THE SPOT. BUT HE'S NEVER FORGOTTEN EXACTLY WHERE IT IS, EITHER.
IT TAKES HIM TEN MINUTES TO DIG THROUGH THE SOD AND--
--REMOVE THE WOODEN BAFFLE HIS FATHER WEDGED INTO PLACE.
THE CAVE IS COLD AFTER THE BALMY NIGHT AIR. HE HEARS THE DISTANT DRIP OF WATER, THE FLAP OF BATS' WINGS.

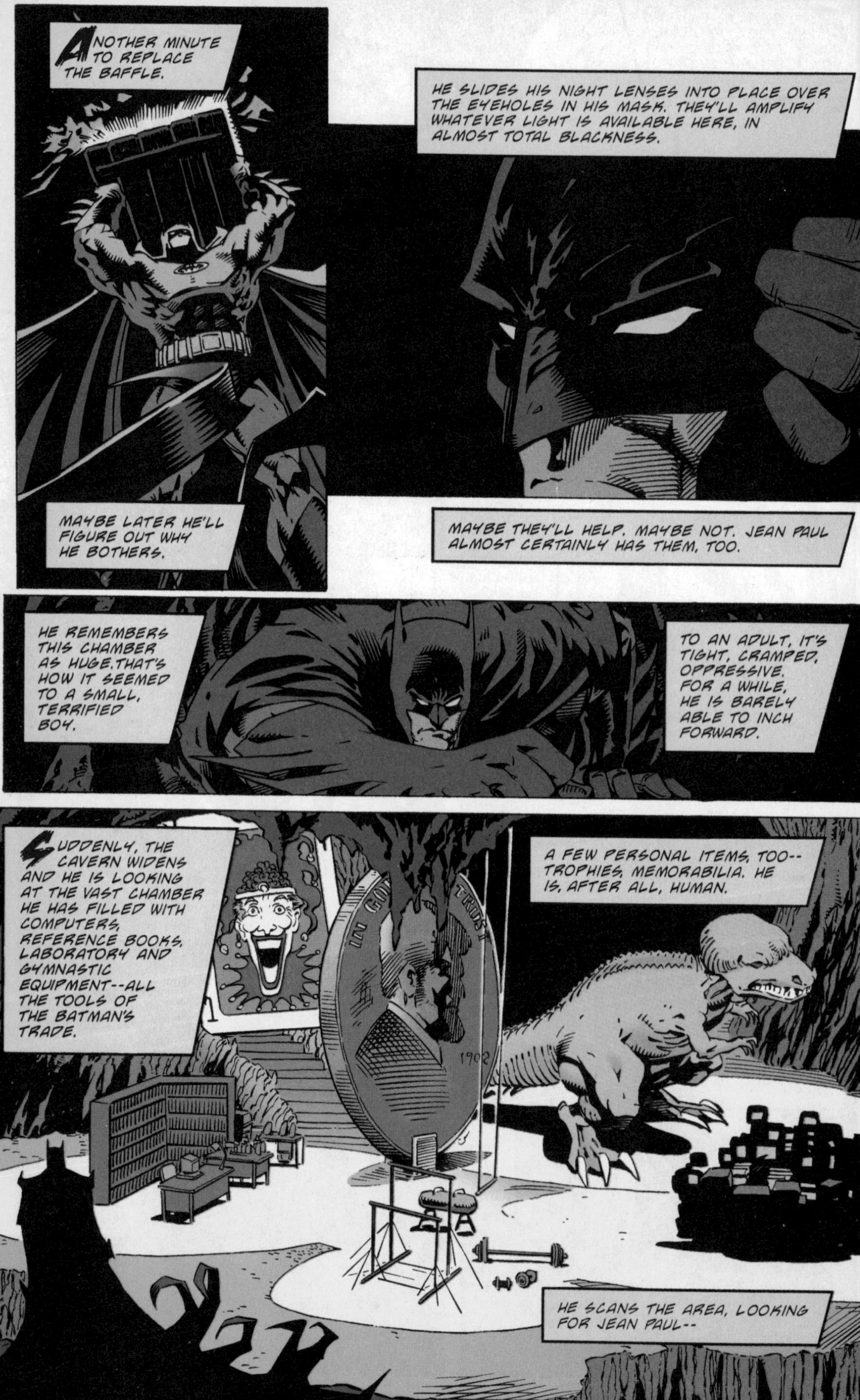
ANOTHER MINUTE TO REPLACE THE BAFFLE.
MAYBE LATER HE'LL FIGURE OUT WHY HE BOTHERS.
HE SLIDES HIS NIGHT LENSES INTO PLACE OVER THE EYEHOLES IN HIS MASK. THEY'LL AMPLIFY WHATEVER LIGHT IS AVAILABLE HERE, IN ALMOST TOTAL BLACKNESS.
MAYBE THEY'LL HELP. MAYBE NOT. JEAN PAUL ALMOST CERTAINLY HAS THEM, TOO.
HE REMEMBERS THIS CHAMBER AS HUGE.THAT'S HOW IT SEEMED TO A SMALL, TERRIFIED BOY.
TO AN ADULT, IT'S TIGHT, CRAMPED, OPPRESSIVE. FOR A WHILE, HE IS BARELY ABLE TO INCH FORWARD.
SUDDENLY, THE CAVERN WIDENS AND HE IS LOOKING AT THE VAST CHAMBER HE HAS FILLED WITH COMPUTERS, REFERENCE BOOKS, LABORATORY AND GYMNASTIC EQUIPMENT--ALL THE TOOLS OF THE BATMAN'S TRADE.
A FEW PERSONAL ITEMS, TOO--TROPHIES, MEMORABILIA. HE IS, AFTER ALL, HUMAN.
HE SCANS THE AREA, LOOKING FOR JEAN PAUL--

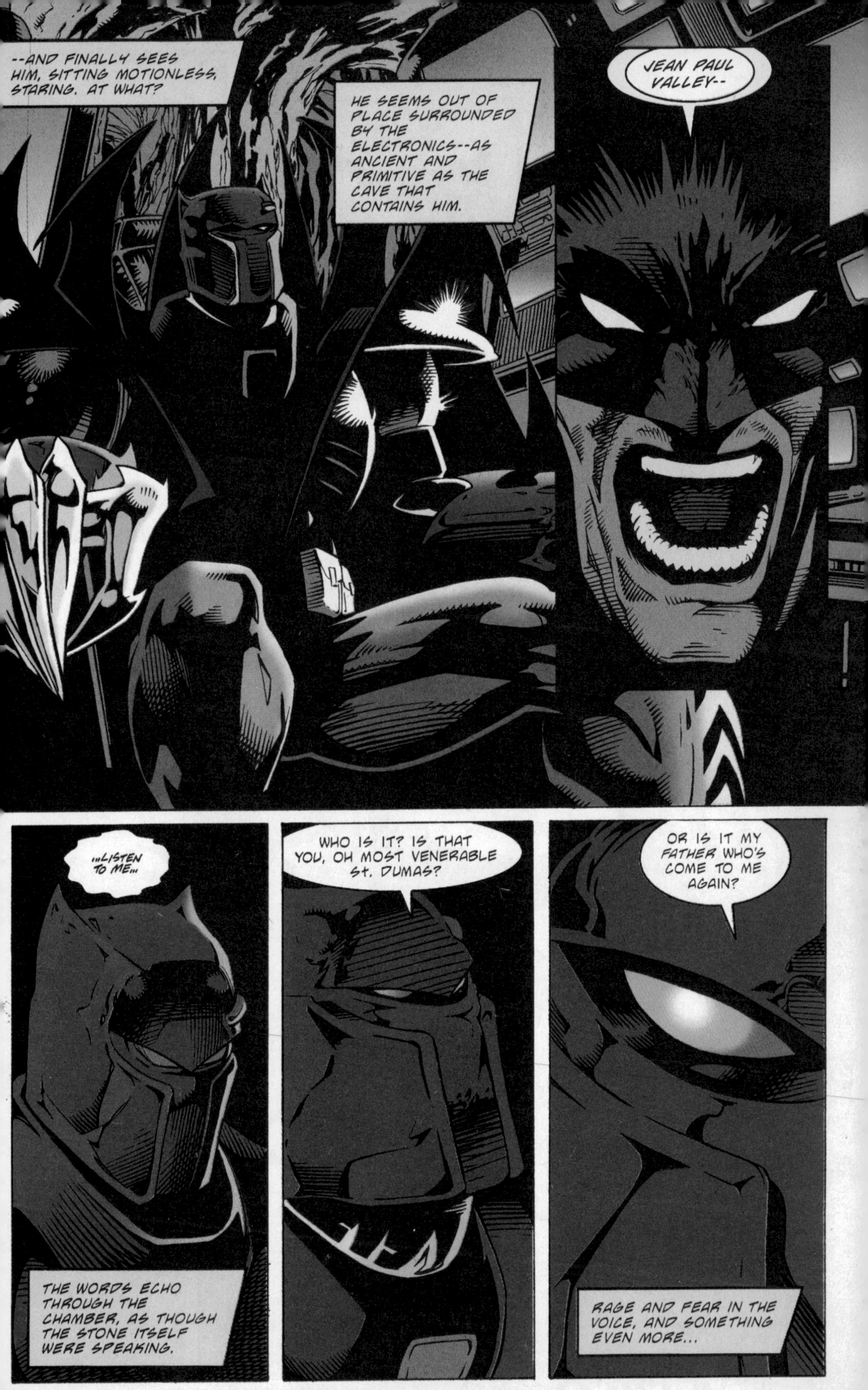
--AND FINALLY SEES HIM, SITTING MOTIONLESS, STARING. AT WHAT?
HE SEEMS OUT OF PLACE SURROUNDED BY THE ELECTRONICS--AS ANCIENT AND PRIMITIVE AS THE CAVE THAT CONTAINS HIM.
JEAN PAUL VALLEY--
...LISTEN TO ME...
THE WORDS ECHO THROUGH THE CHAMBER, AS THOUGH THE STONE ITSELF WERE SPEAKING.
WHO IS IT? IS THAT YOU, OH MOST VENERABLE St. DUMAS?
OR IS IT MY FATHER WHO'S COME TO ME AGAIN?
RAGE AND FEAR IN THE VOICE, AND SOMETHING EVEN MORE...

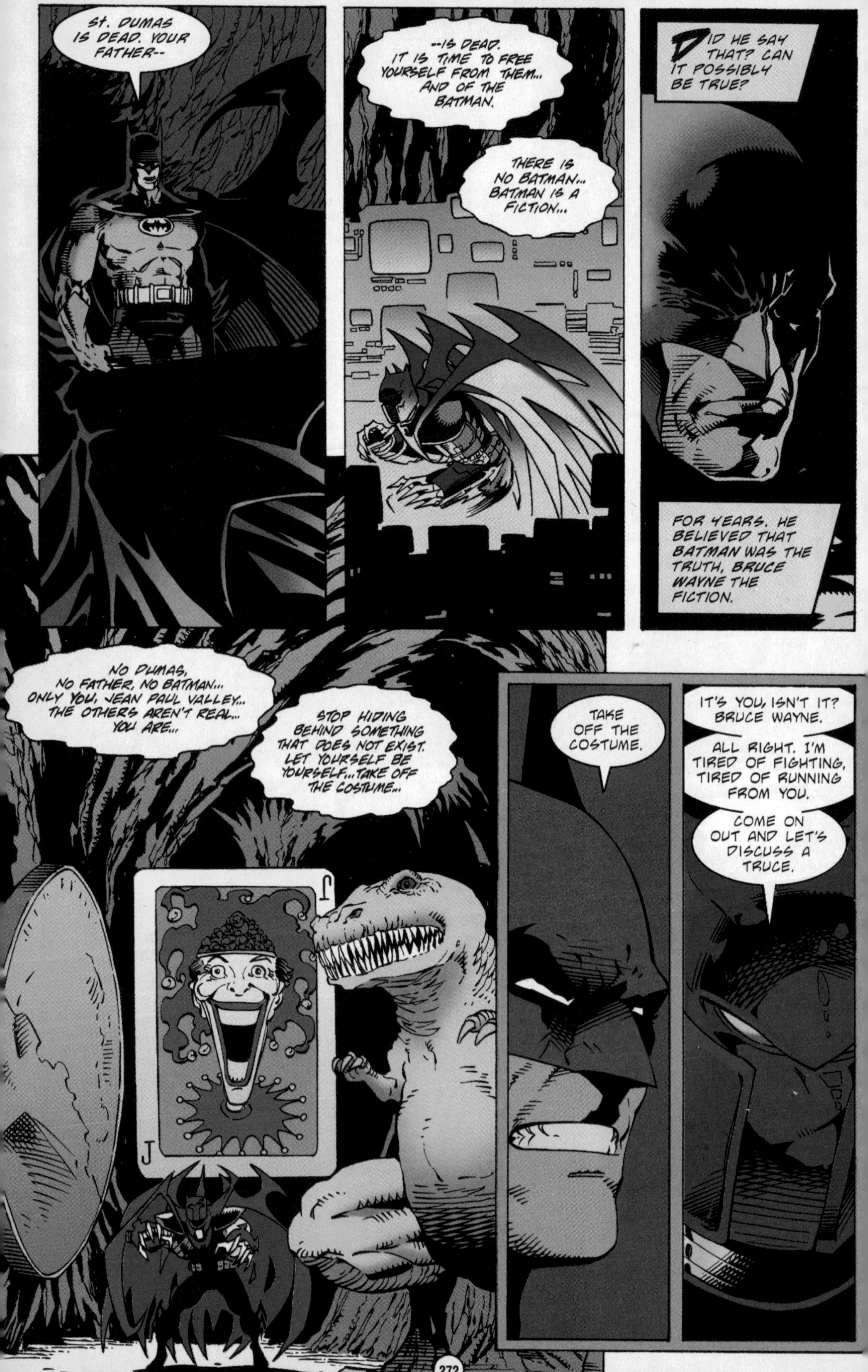
ST. DUMAS IS DEAD. YOUR FATHER--
--IS DEAD. IT IS TIME TO FREE YOURSELF FROM THEM... AND OF THE BATMAN.
THERE IS NO BATMAN... BATMAN IS A FICTION...
DID HE SAY THAT? CAN IT POSSIBLY BE TRUE?
FOR YEARS. HE BELIEVED THAT BATMAN WAS THE TRUTH, BRUCE WAYNE THE FICTION.
NO DUMAS, NO FATHER, NO BATMAN... ONLY YOU, JEAN PAUL VALLEY... THE OTHERS AREN'T REAL... YOU ARE...
STOP HIDING BEHIND SOMETHING THAT DOES NOT EXIST. LET YOURSELF BE YOURSELF...TAKE OFF THE COSTUME...
TAKE OFF THE COSTUME.
IT'S YOU, ISN'T IT? BRUCE WAYNE.
ALL RIGHT. I'M TIRED OF FIGHTING, TIRED OF RUNNING FROM YOU.
COME ON OUT AND LET'S DISCUSS A TRUCE.

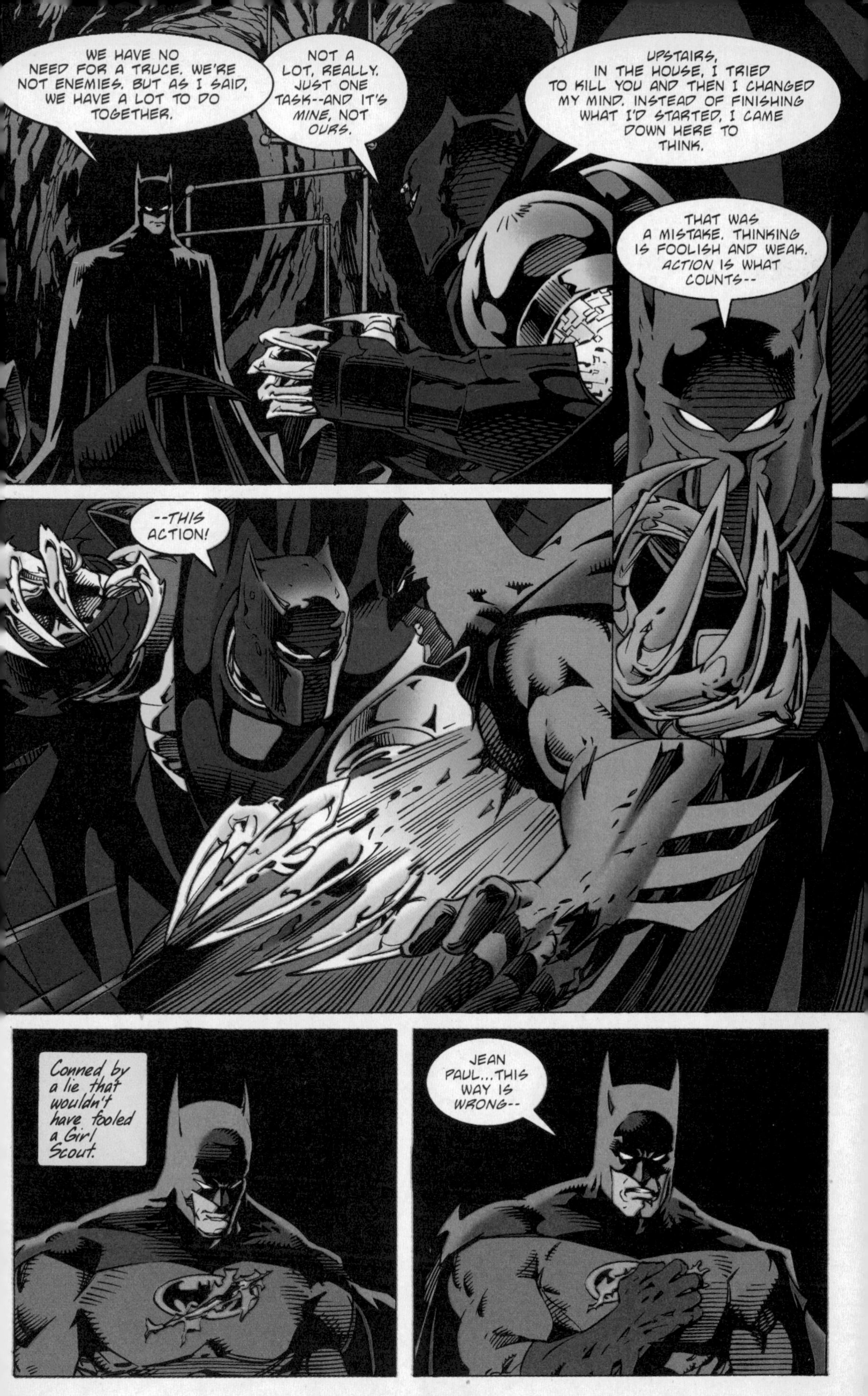
WE HAVE NO NEED FOR A TRUCE. WE'RE NOT ENEMIES. BUT AS I SAID, WE HAVE A LOT TO DO TOGETHER.
NOT A LOT, REALLY. JUST ONE TASK--AND IT'S MINE, NOT OURS.
UPSTAIRS, IN THE HOUSE, I TRIED TO KILL YOU AND THEN I CHANGED MY MIND. INSTEAD OF FINISHING WHAT I'D STARTED, I CAME DOWN HERE TO THINK.
THAT WAS A MISTAKE. THINKING IS FOOLISH AND WEAK. ACTION IS WHAT COUNTS--
--THIS ACTION!
Conned by a lie that wouldn't have fooled a Girl Scout.
JEAN PAUL...THIS WAY IS WRONG--

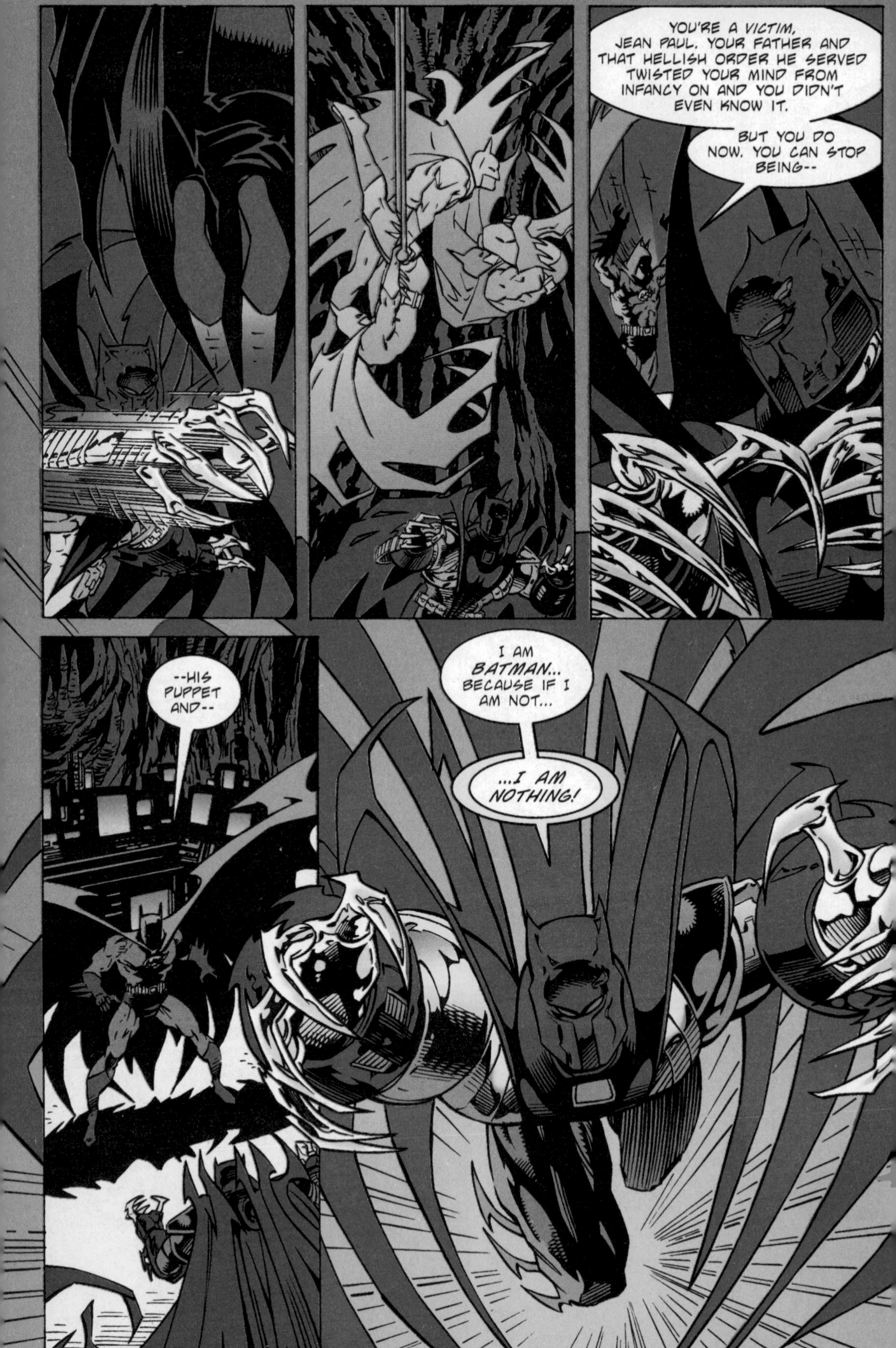
YOU'RE A *VICTIM*, JEAN PAUL. YOUR FATHER AND THAT HELLISH ORDER HE SERVED TWISTED YOUR MIND FROM INFANCY ON AND YOU DIDN'T EVEN KNOW IT.
BUT YOU DO NOW. YOU CAN STOP BEING--
--HIS PUPPET AND--
I AM *BATMAN*... BECAUSE IF I AM NOT...
...*I AM NOTHING!*

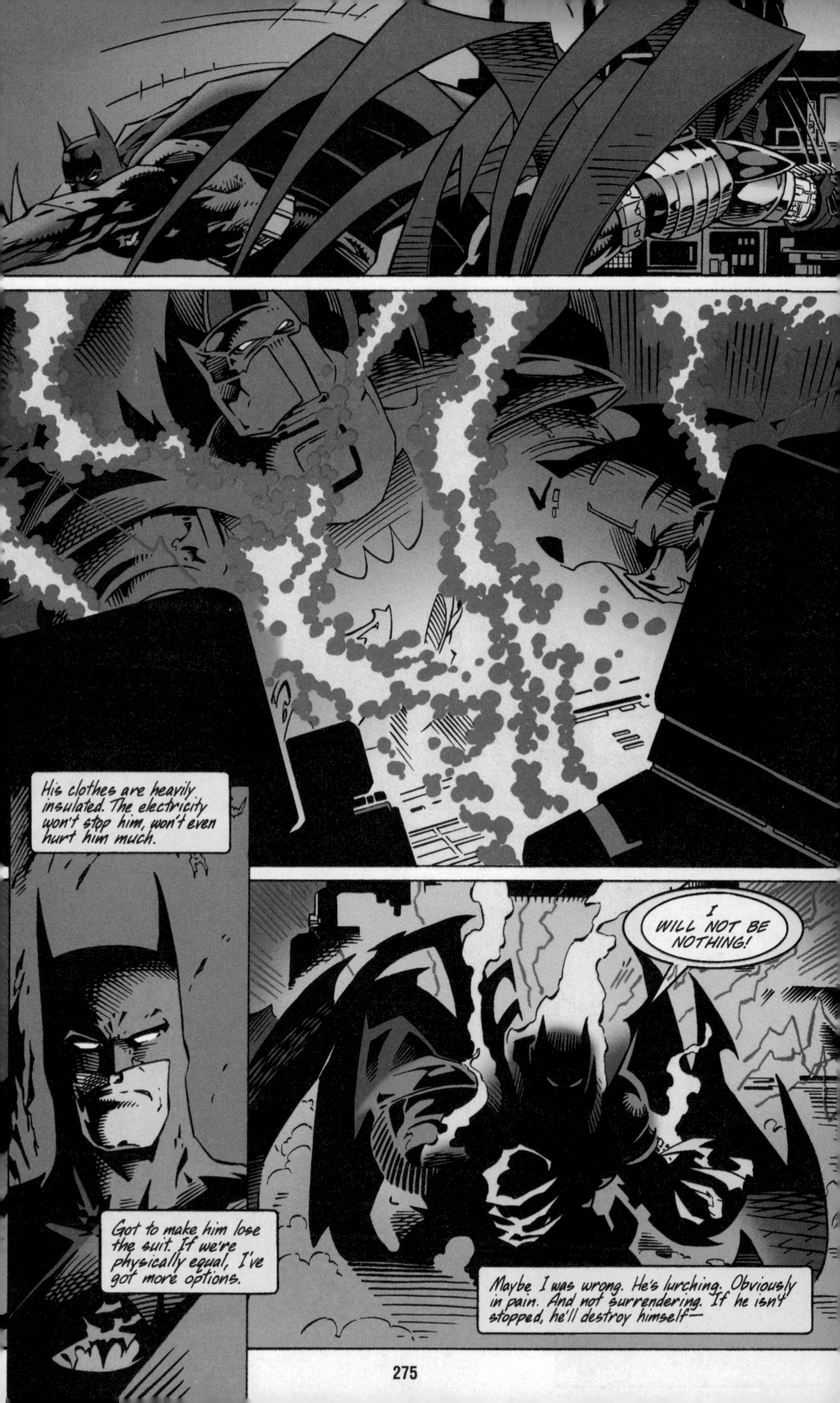

His clothes are heavily insulated. The electricity won't stop him, won't even hurt him much.
I WILL NOT BE NOTHING!
Got to make him lose the suit. If we're physically equal, I've got more options.
Maybe I was wrong. He's lurching. Obviously in pain. And not surrendering. If he isn't stopped, he'll destroy himself—

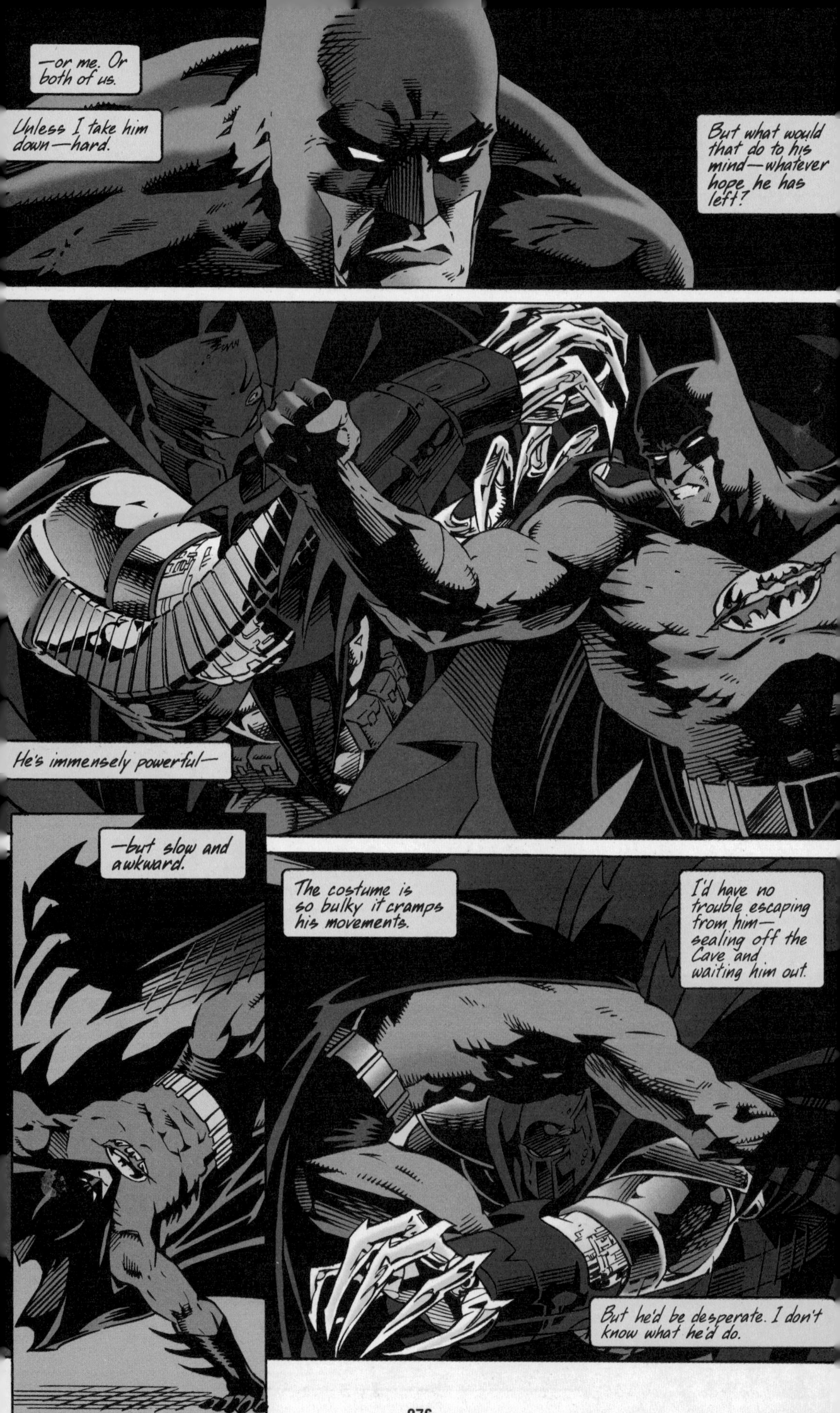
—or me. Or both of us.
Unless I take him down—hard.
But what would that do to his mind—whatever hope he has left?
He's immensely powerful—
—but slow and awkward.
The costume is so bulky it cramps his movements.
I'd have no trouble escaping from him—sealing off the Cave and waiting him out.
But he'd be desperate. I don't know what he'd do.

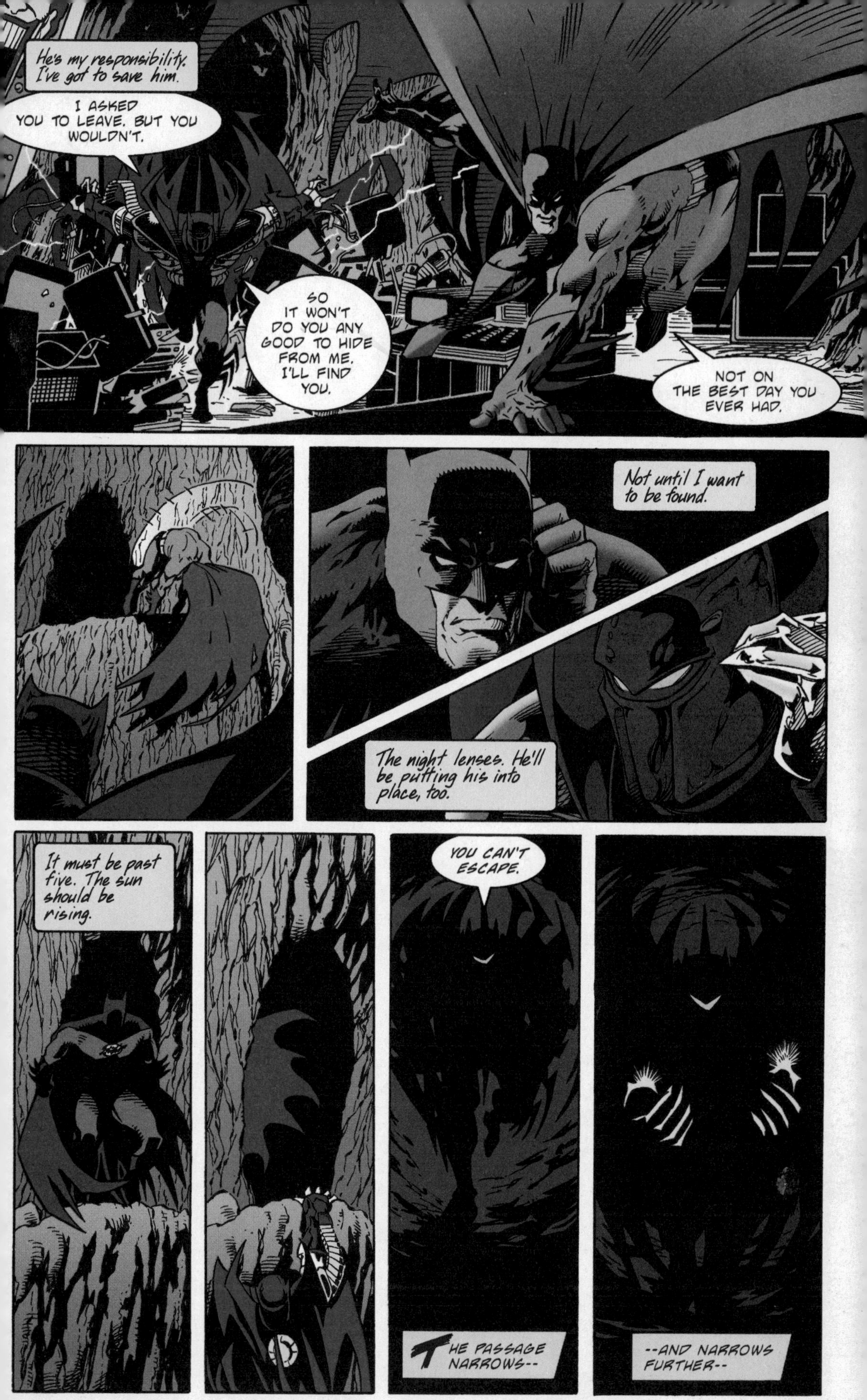
He's my responsibility. I've got to save him.
I ASKED YOU TO LEAVE. BUT YOU WOULDN'T.
SO IT WON'T DO YOU ANY GOOD TO HIDE FROM ME. I'LL FIND YOU.
NOT ON THE BEST DAY YOU EVER HAD.
Not until I want to be found.
The night lenses. He'll be putting his into place, too.
It must be past five. The sun should be rising.
YOU CAN'T ESCAPE.
THE PASSAGE NARROWS--
--AND NARROWS FURTHER--

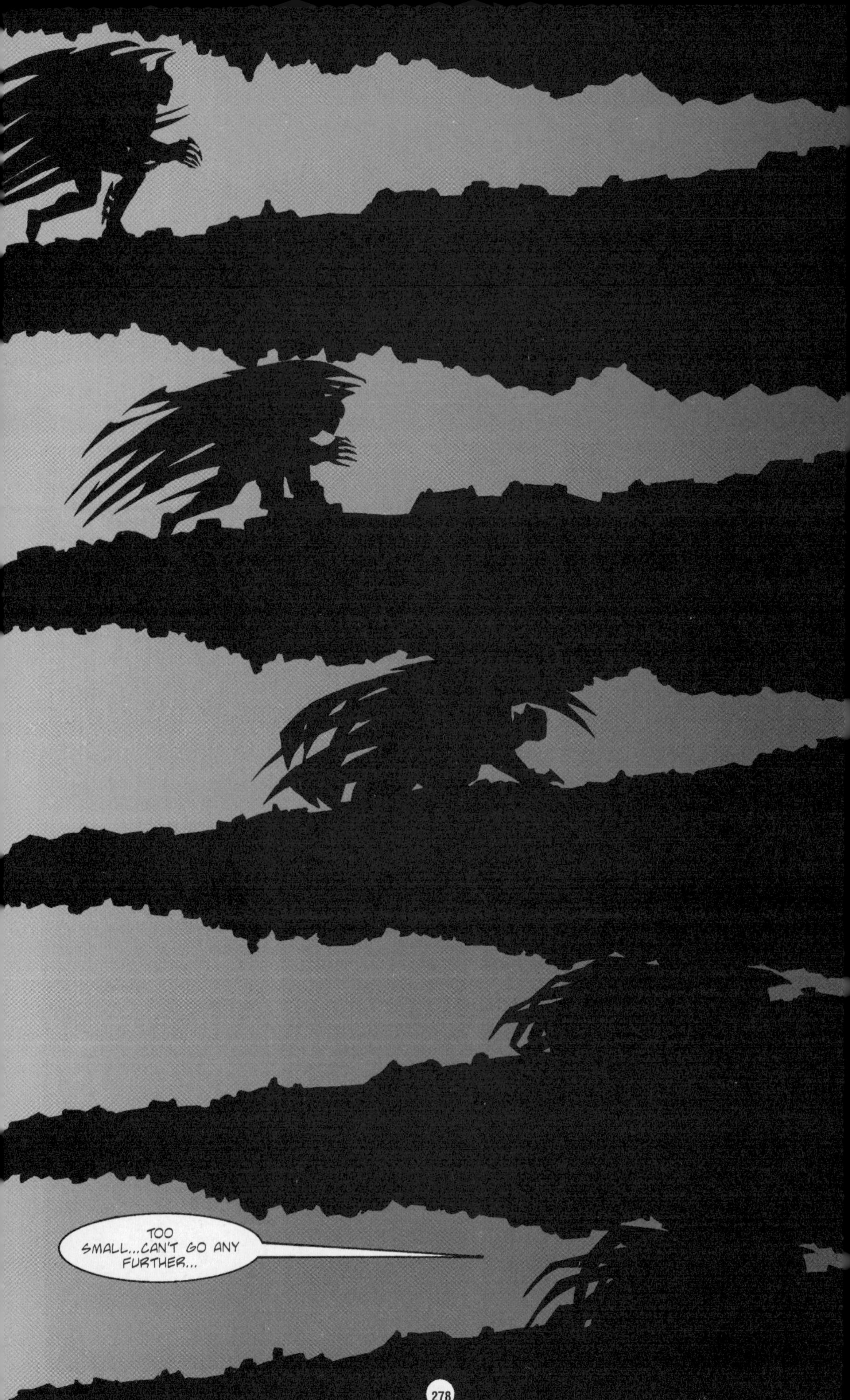
TOO SMALL...CAN'T GO ANY FURTHER...

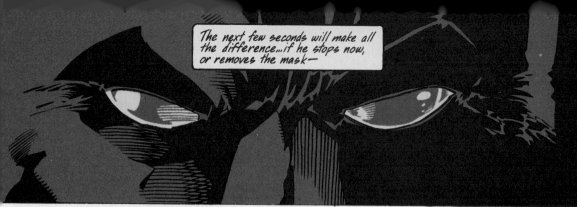

The next few seconds will make all the difference...if he stops now, or removes the mask—

NOT GIVING UP, ARE YOU?

Perfect. He's lost the suit but he's leaving the mask on...

...coming ahead...

THE TUNNEL ENDS. BRUCE RISES, FEELING HIS MUSCLES LOOSEN, HIS BREATHING RETURN TO NORMAL--RISES AND WAITS.

HE LISTENS TO THE DISTANT DRIP OF WATER, THE FLAP OF BATS' WINGS--

--AND THE GRUNTS OF THE APPROACHING MAN WHO IS BOTH HIS PURSUER AND HIS QUARRY...

THEN--

SO. YOU'VE GOT NO MORE ROOM TO RUN.

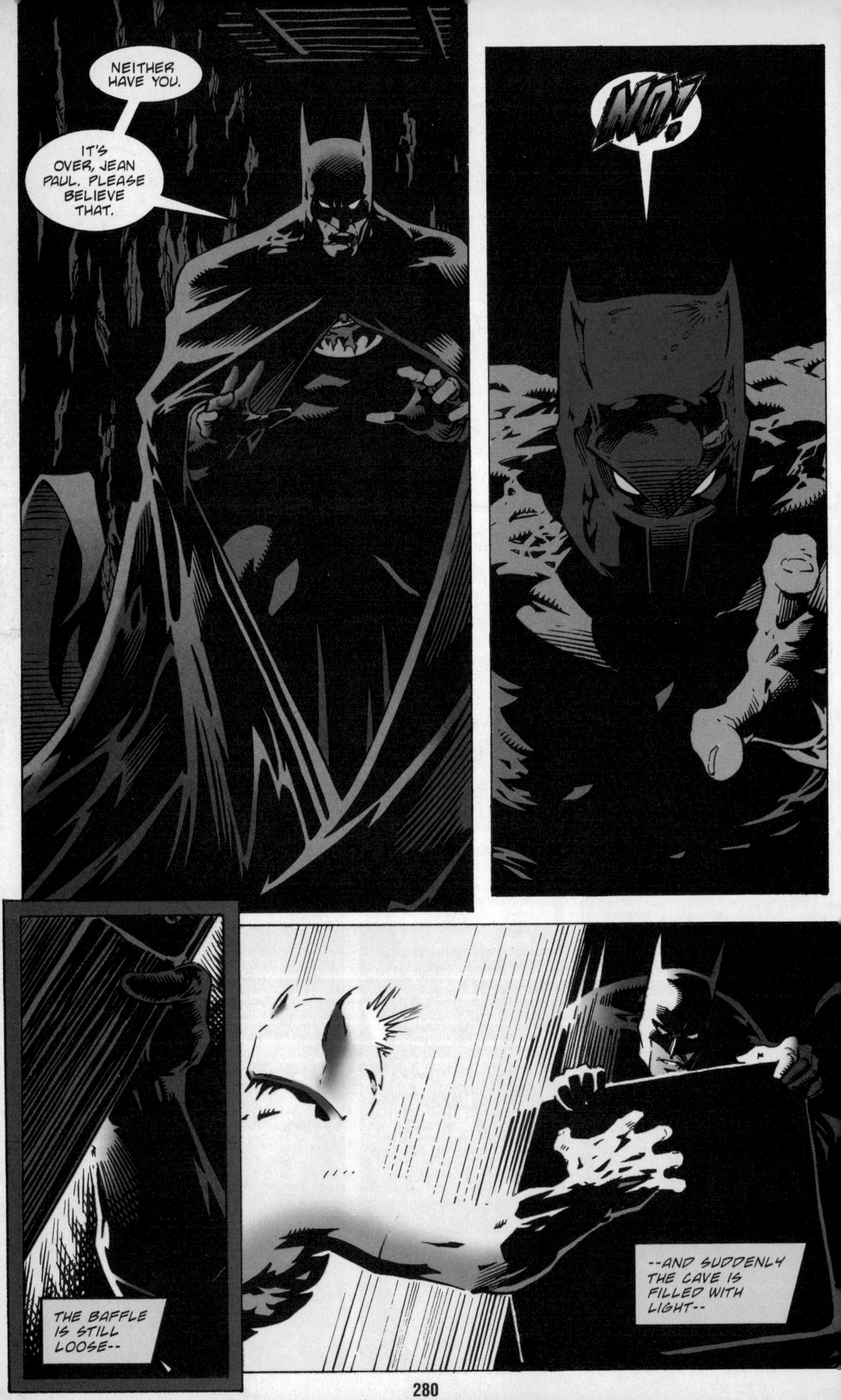
NEITHER HAVE YOU.
IT'S OVER, JEAN PAUL. PLEASE BELIEVE THAT.
NO!
THE BAFFLE IS STILL LOOSE--
--AND SUDDENLY THE CAVE IS FILLED WITH LIGHT--

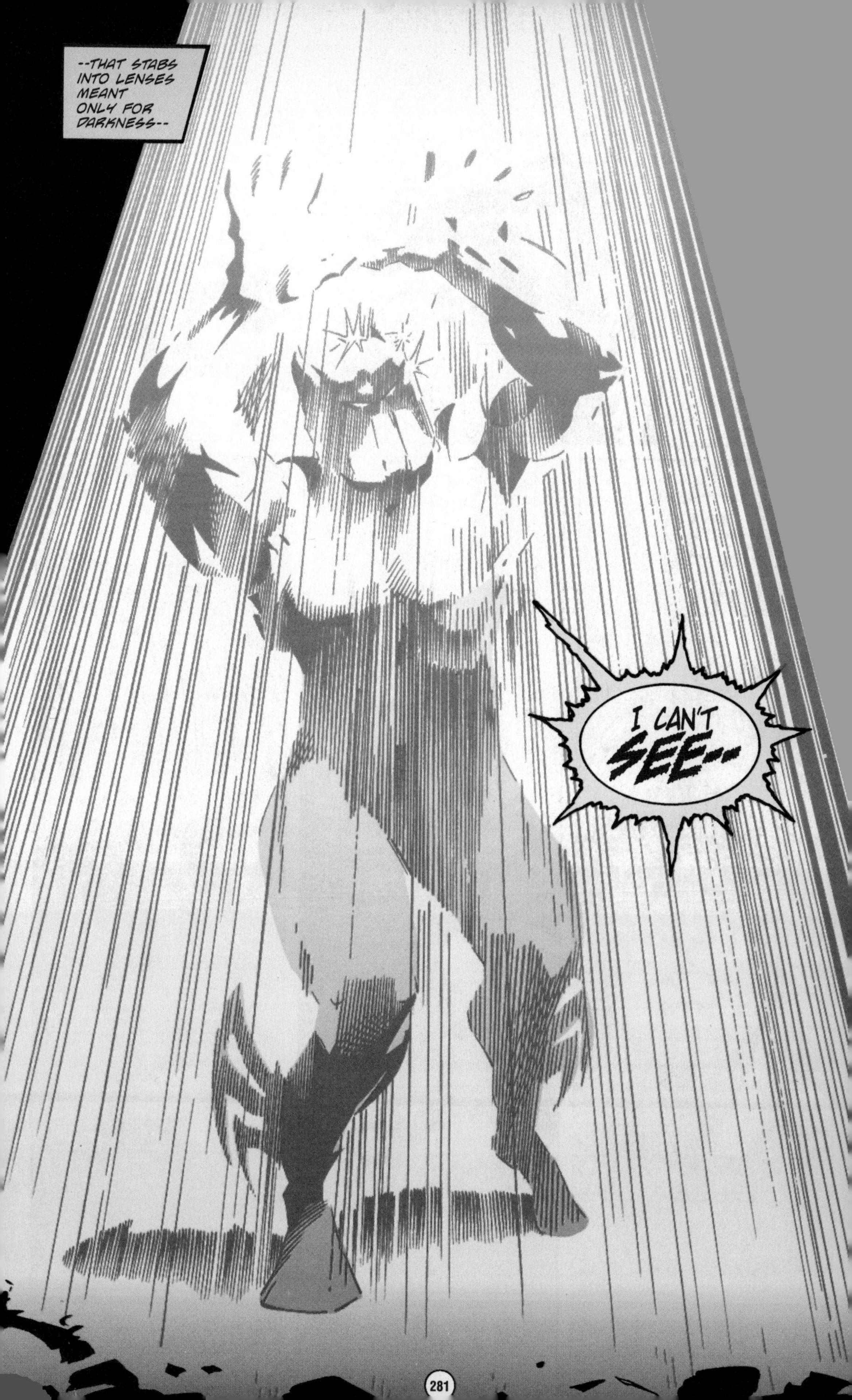
--THAT STABS INTO LENSES MEANT ONLY FOR DARKNESS--
I CAN'T SEE--

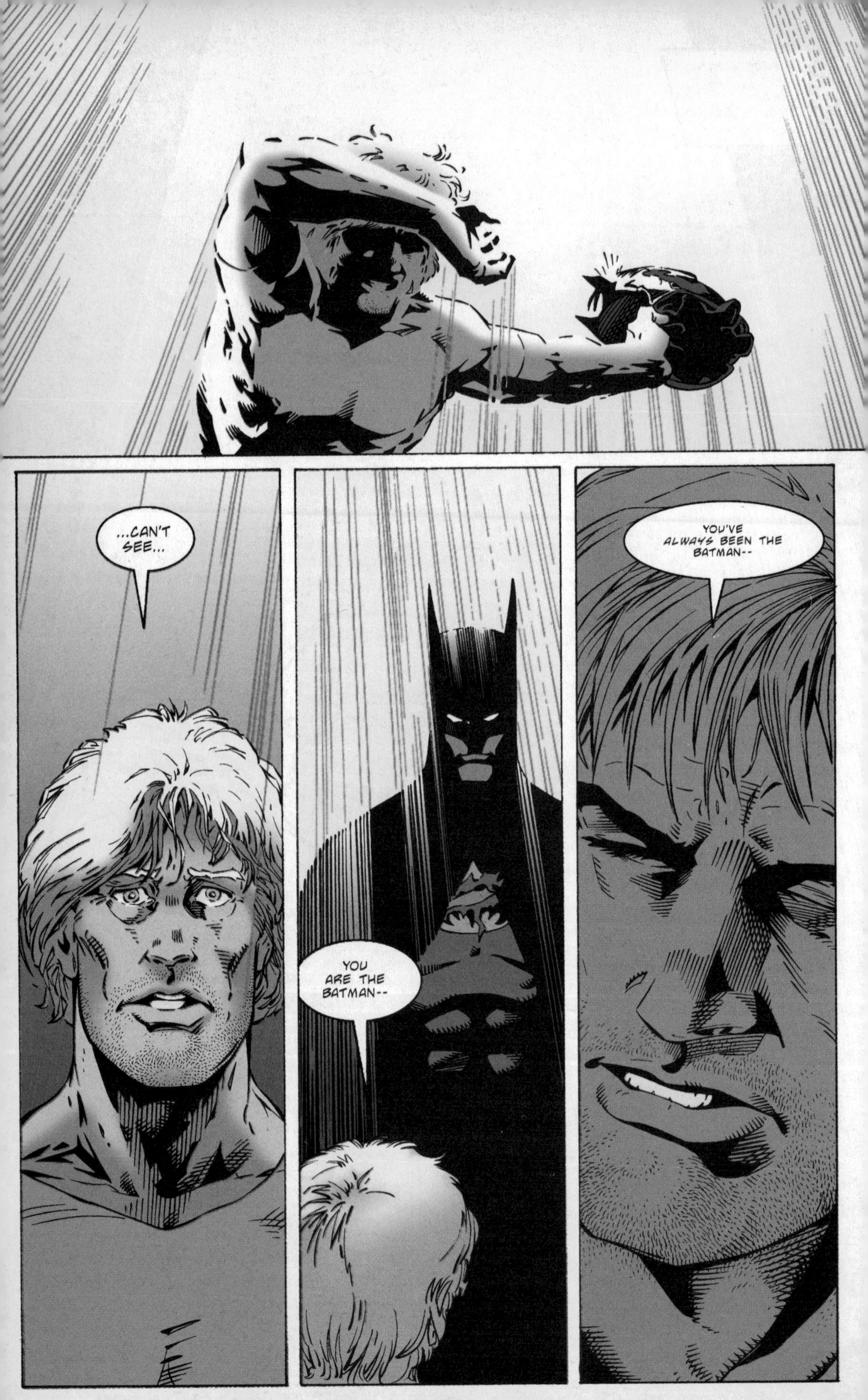
...CAN'T SEE...
YOU ARE THE BATMAN--
YOU'VE ALWAYS BEEN THE BATMAN--

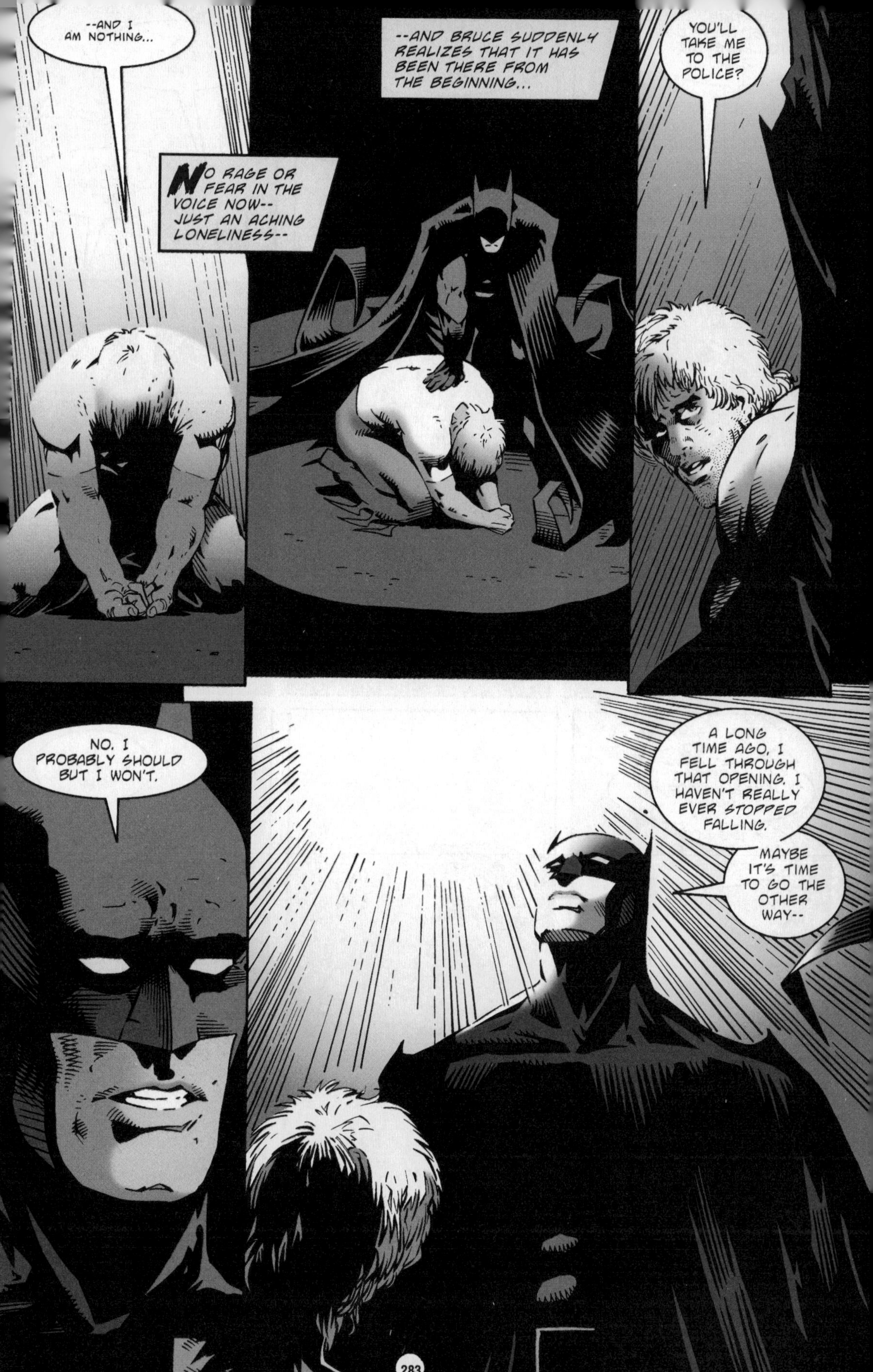
--AND I AM NOTHING...
NO RAGE OR FEAR IN THE VOICE NOW-- JUST AN ACHING LONELINESS--
--AND BRUCE SUDDENLY REALIZES THAT IT HAS BEEN THERE FROM THE BEGINNING...
YOU'LL TAKE ME TO THE POLICE?
NO. I PROBABLY SHOULD BUT I WON'T.
A LONG TIME AGO, I FELL THROUGH THAT OPENING. I HAVEN'T REALLY EVER STOPPED FALLING.
MAYBE IT'S TIME TO GO THE OTHER WAY--

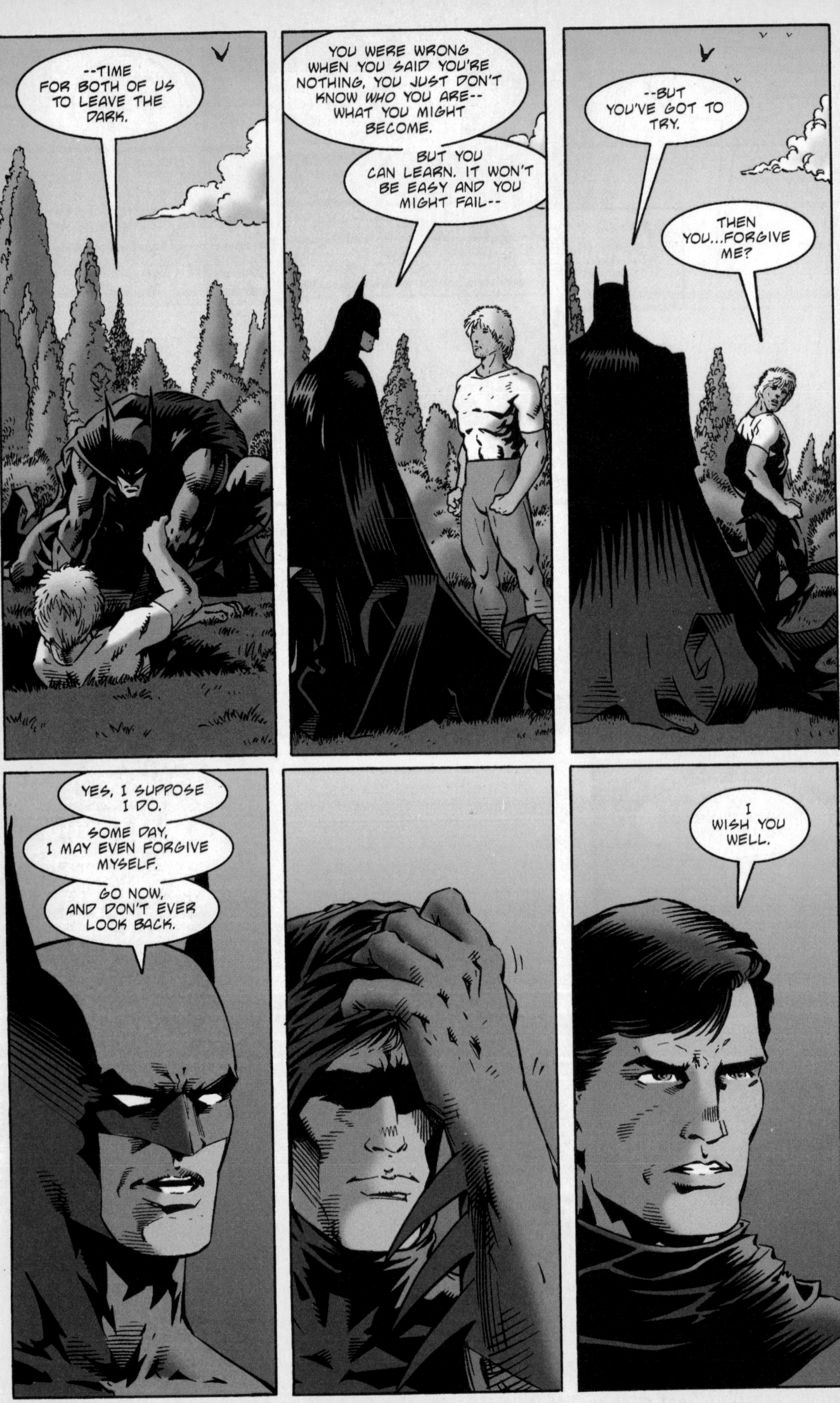
--TIME FOR BOTH OF US TO LEAVE THE DARK.
YOU WERE WRONG WHEN YOU SAID YOU'RE NOTHING. YOU JUST DON'T KNOW WHO YOU ARE-- WHAT YOU MIGHT BECOME.
BUT YOU CAN LEARN. IT WON'T BE EASY AND YOU MIGHT FAIL--
--BUT YOU'VE GOT TO TRY.
THEN YOU...FORGIVE ME?
YES, I SUPPOSE I DO.
SOME DAY, I MAY EVEN FORGIVE MYSELF.
GO NOW, AND DON'T EVER LOOK BACK.
I WISH YOU WELL.

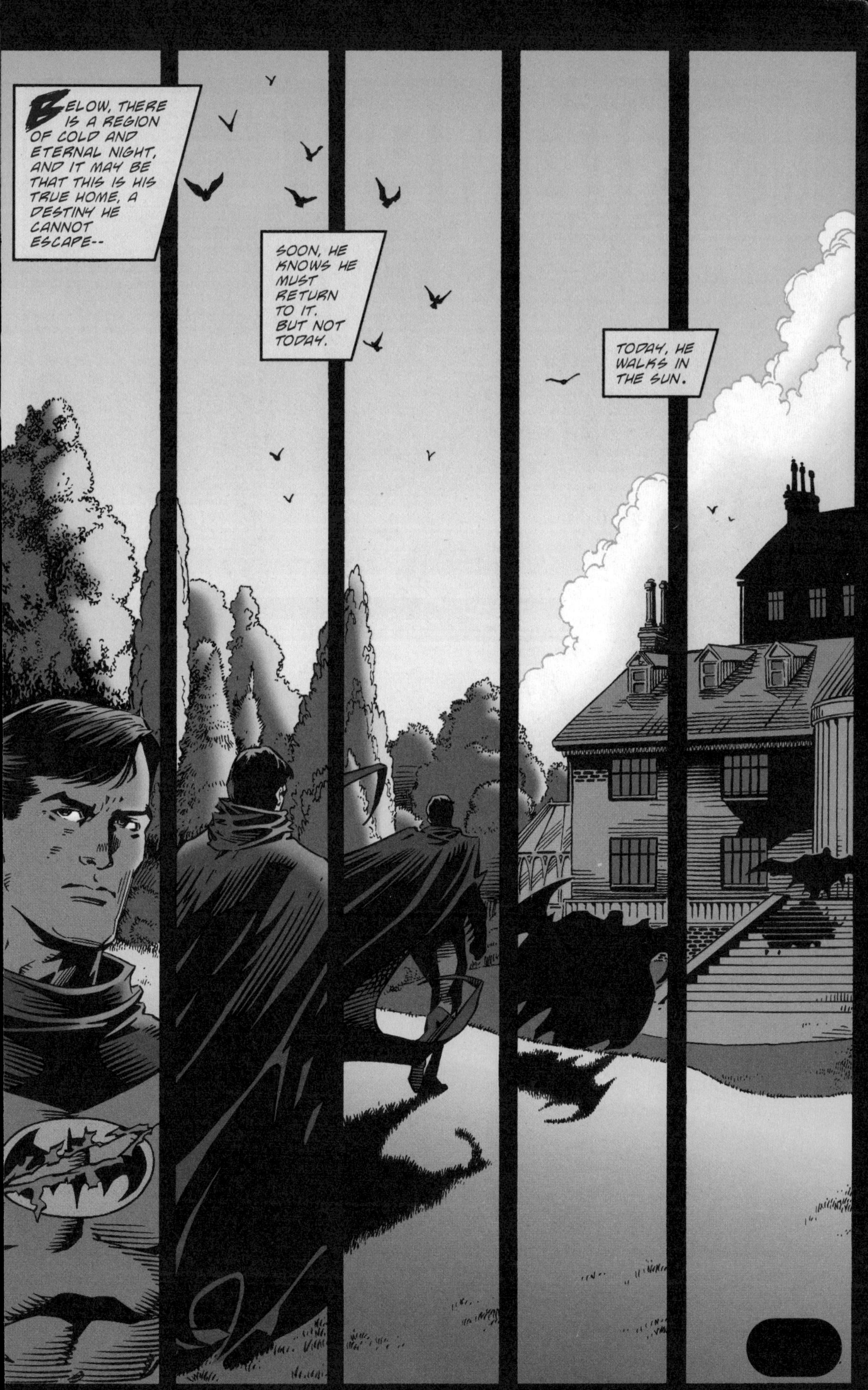
BELOW, THERE IS A REGION OF COLD AND ETERNAL NIGHT, AND IT MAY BE THAT THIS IS HIS TRUE HOME, A DESTINY HE CANNOT ESCAPE--
SOON, HE KNOWS HE MUST RETURN TO IT. BUT NOT TODAY.
TODAY, HE WALKS IN THE SUN.

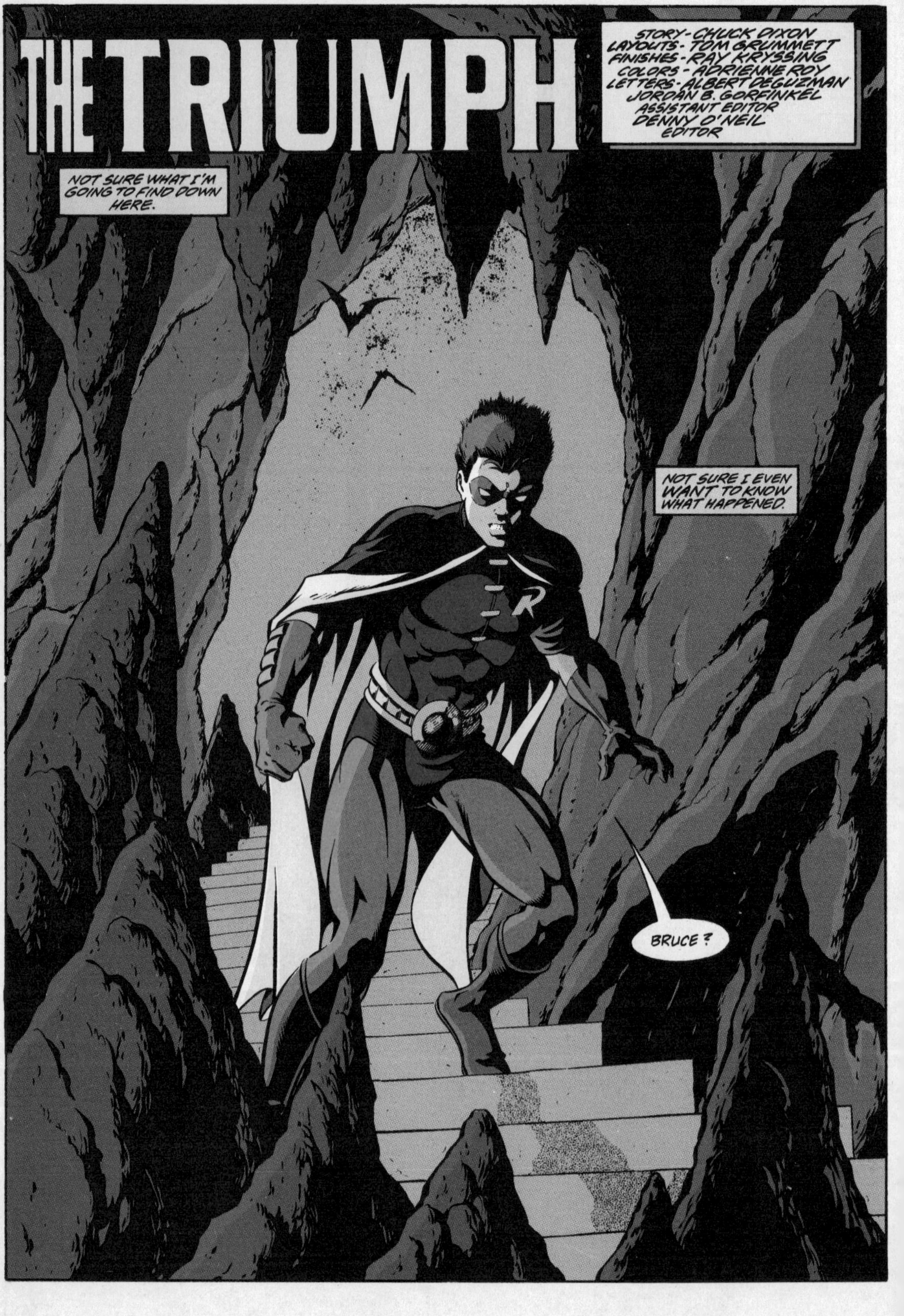
THE TRIUMPH
STORY - CHUCK DIXON
LAYOUTS - TOM GRUMMETT
FINISHES - RAY KRYSSING
COLORS - ADRIENNE ROY
LETTERS - ALBERT DEGUZMAN
JORDAN B. GORFINKEL
ASSISTANT EDITOR
DENNY O'NEIL
EDITOR
NOT SURE WHAT I'M GOING TO FIND DOWN HERE.
NOT SURE I EVEN WANT TO KNOW WHAT HAPPENED.
BRUCE?

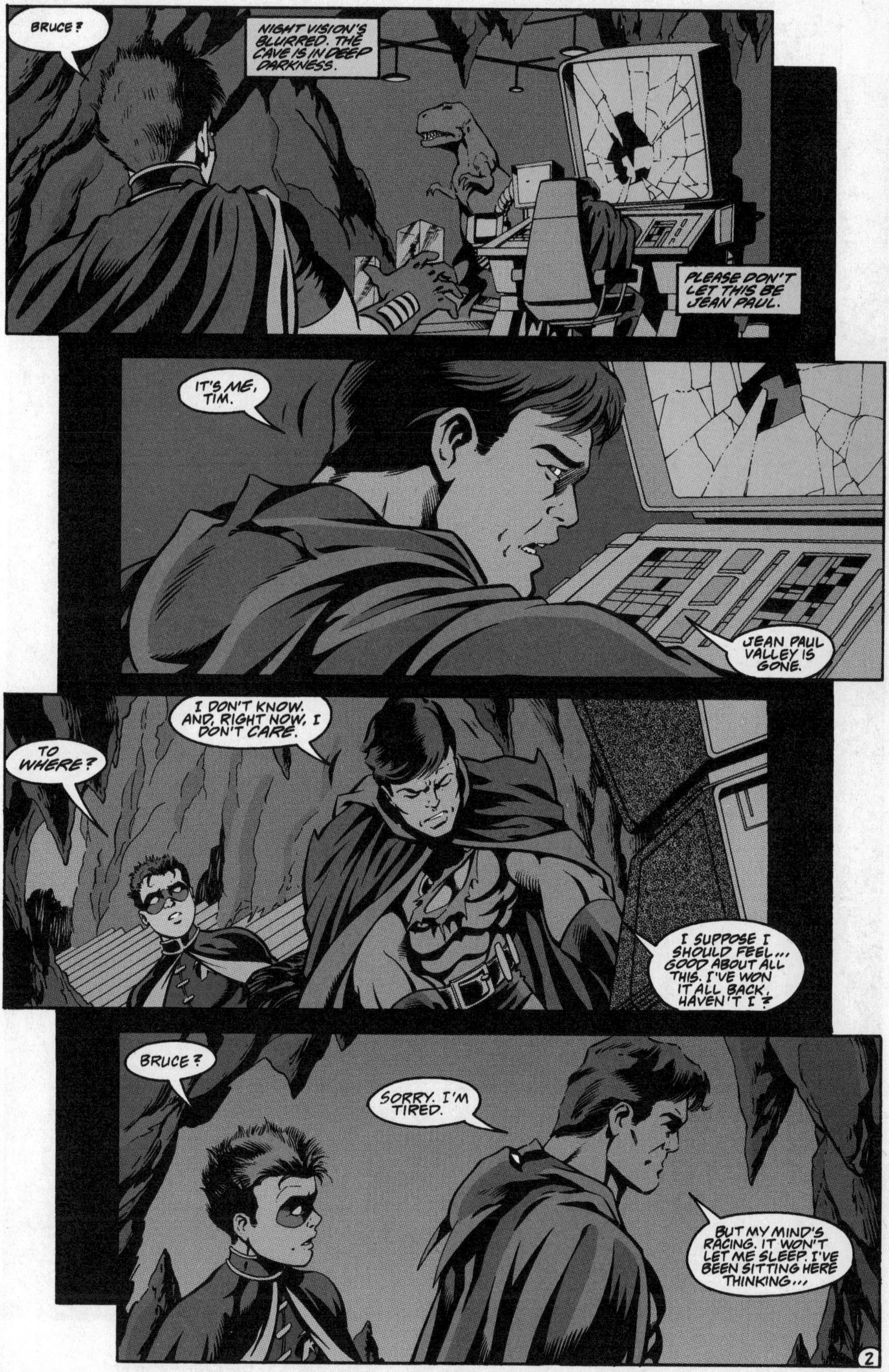
BRUCE?
NIGHT VISION'S BLURRED. THE CAVE IS IN DEEP DARKNESS.
PLEASE DON'T LET THIS BE JEAN PAUL.
IT'S ME, TIM.
JEAN PAUL VALLEY IS GONE.
TO WHERE?
I DON'T KNOW. AND, RIGHT NOW, I DON'T CARE.
I SUPPOSE I SHOULD FEEL... GOOD ABOUT ALL THIS. I'VE WON IT ALL BACK, HAVEN'T I?
BRUCE?
SORRY. I'M TIRED.
BUT MY MIND'S RACING. IT WON'T LET ME SLEEP. I'VE BEEN SITTING HERE THINKING...
2

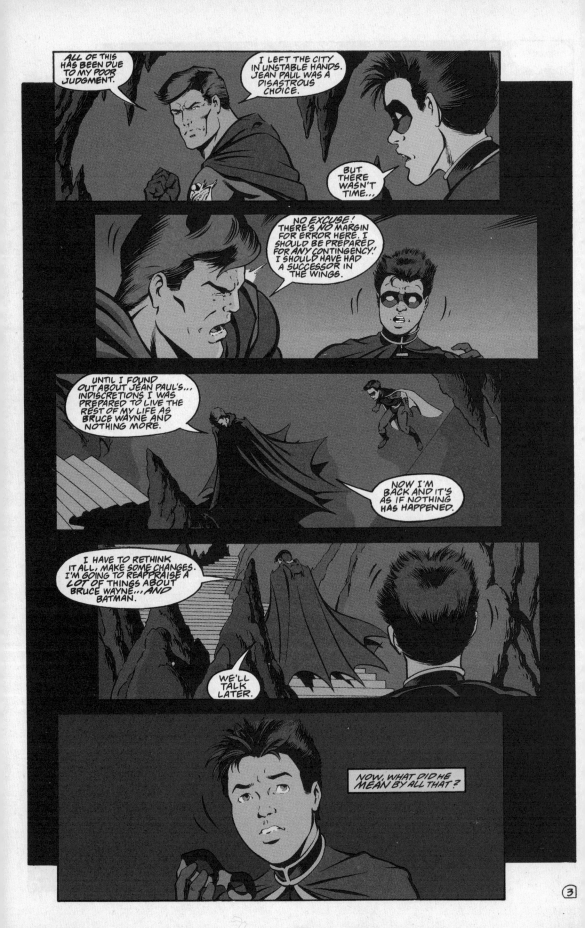

ALL OF THIS HAS BEEN DUE TO MY POOR JUDGMENT.

I LEFT THE CITY IN UNSTABLE HANDS. JEAN PAUL WAS A DISASTROUS CHOICE.

BUT THERE WASN'T TIME...

NO EXCUSE! THERE'S *NO* MARGIN FOR ERROR HERE. I SHOULD BE PREPARED FOR *ANY* CONTINGENCY! I SHOULD HAVE HAD A SUCCESSOR IN THE WINGS.

UNTIL I FOUND OUT ABOUT JEAN PAUL'S... INDISCRETIONS I WAS PREPARED TO LIVE THE REST OF MY LIFE AS BRUCE WAYNE AND NOTHING MORE.

NOW I'M BACK AND IT'S AS IF NOTHING HAS HAPPENED.

I HAVE TO RETHINK IT ALL, MAKE SOME CHANGES. I'M GOING TO REAPPRAISE A *LOT* OF THINGS ABOUT BRUCE WAYNE..., *AND* BATMAN.

WE'LL TALK LATER.

NOW, WHAT DID HE MEAN BY ALL THAT?

③

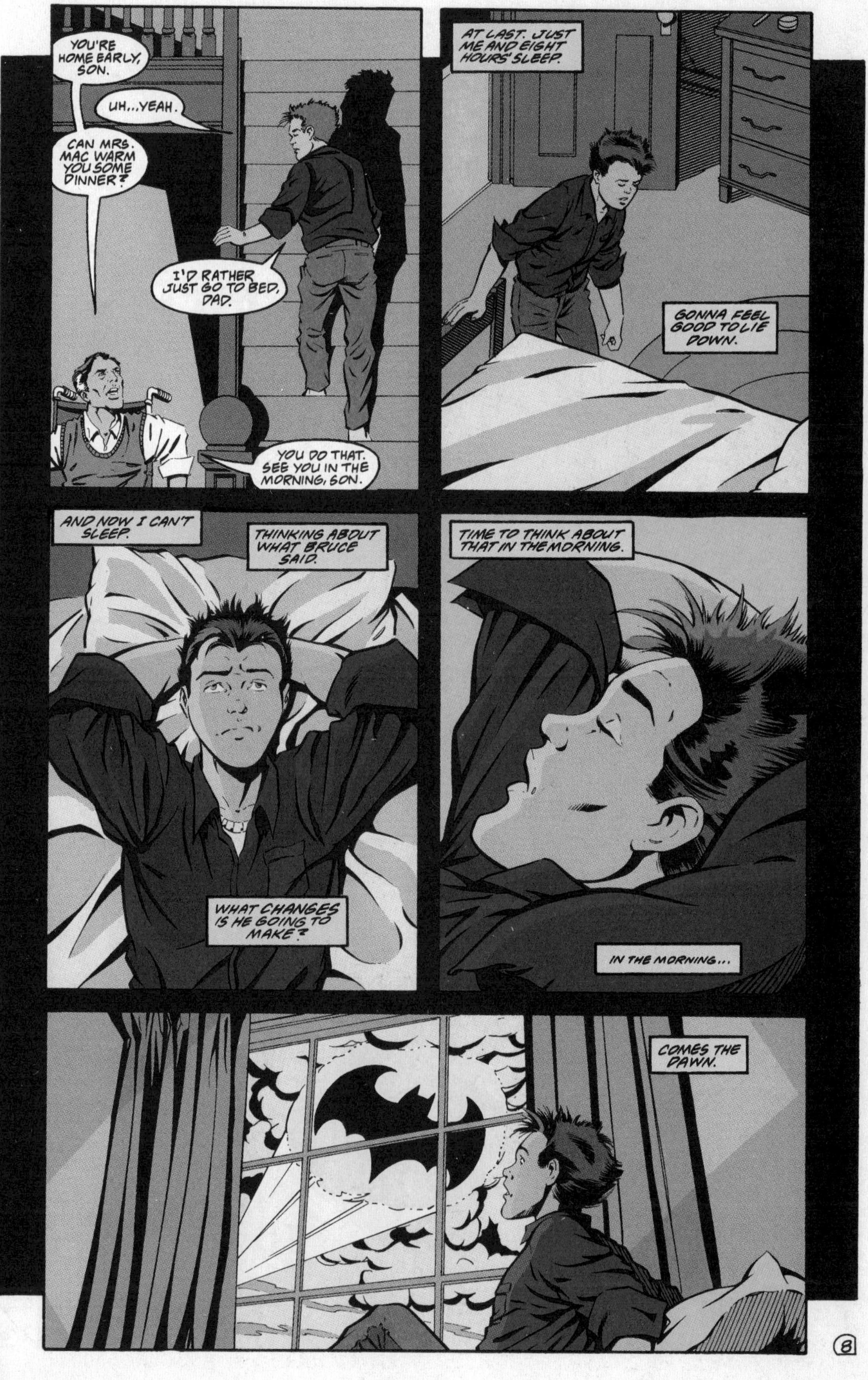

YOU'RE HOME EARLY, SON.
UH...YEAH.
CAN MRS. MAC WARM YOU SOME DINNER?
I'D RATHER JUST GO TO BED, DAD.
YOU DO THAT. SEE YOU IN THE MORNING, SON.
AT LAST. JUST ME AND EIGHT HOURS' SLEEP.
GONNA FEEL GOOD TO LIE DOWN.
AND NOW I CAN'T SLEEP.
THINKING ABOUT WHAT BRUCE SAID.
WHAT CHANGES IS HE GOING TO MAKE?
TIME TO THINK ABOUT THAT IN THE MORNING.
IN THE MORNING...
COMES THE DAWN.
8

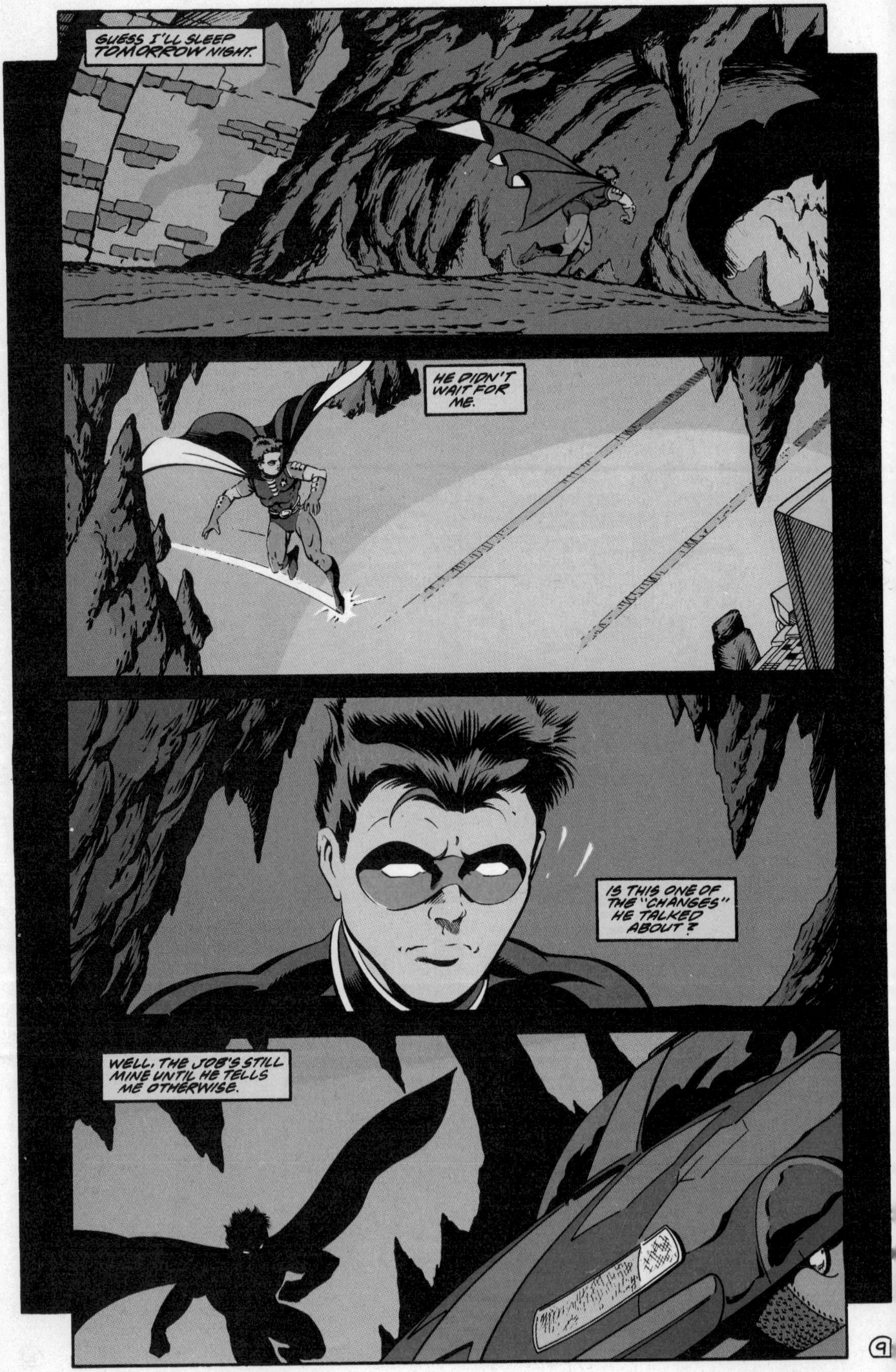
GUESS I'LL SLEEP TOMORROW NIGHT.
HE DIDN'T WAIT FOR ME.
IS THIS ONE OF THE "CHANGES" HE TALKED ABOUT?
WELL, THE JOB'S STILL MINE UNTIL HE TELLS ME OTHERWISE.
9

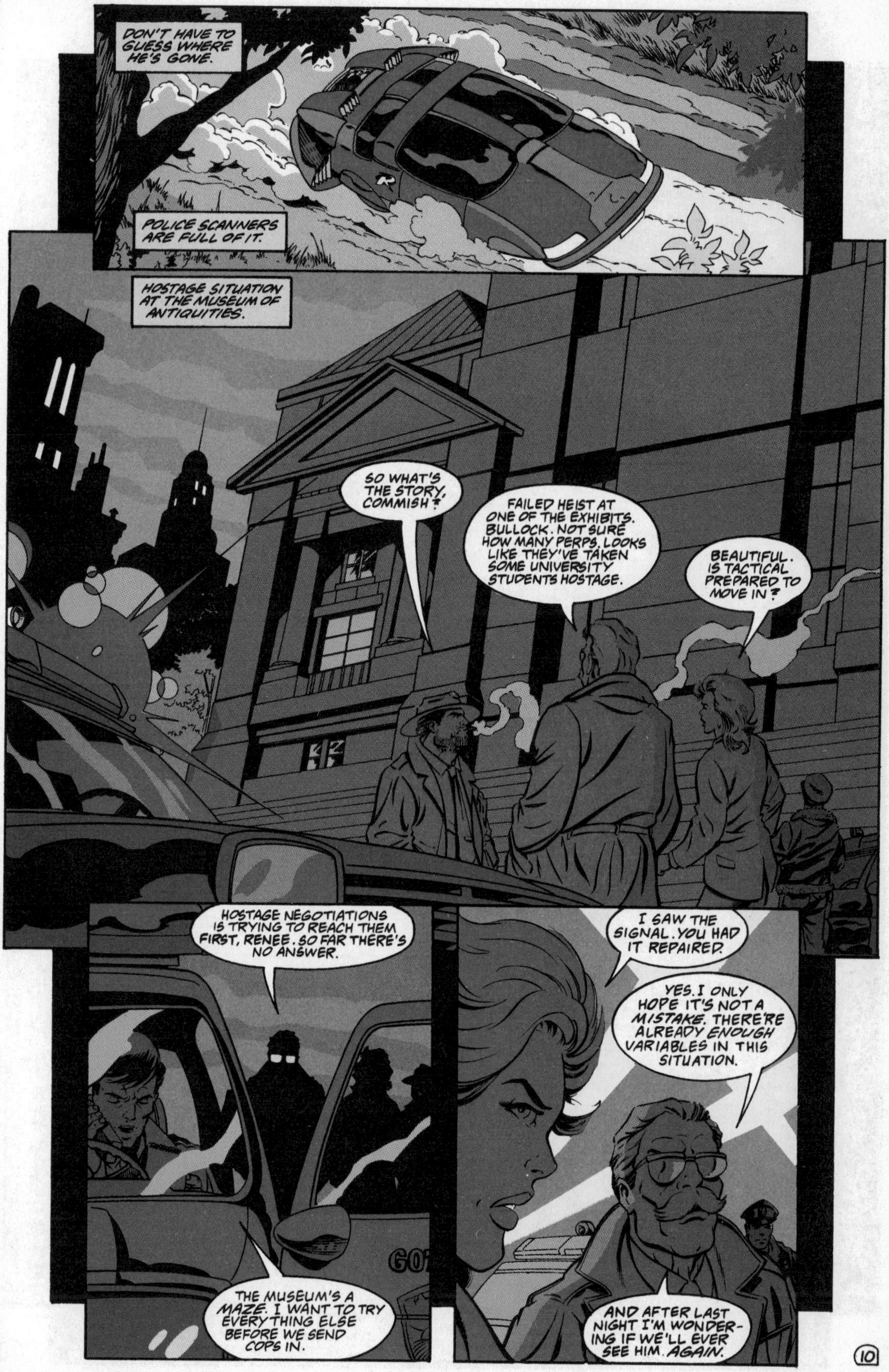
DON'T HAVE TO GUESS WHERE HE'S GONE.
POLICE SCANNERS ARE FULL OF IT.
HOSTAGE SITUATION AT THE MUSEUM OF ANTIQUITIES.
SO WHAT'S THE STORY, COMMISH?
FAILED HEIST AT ONE OF THE EXHIBITS. BULLOCK. NOT SURE HOW MANY PERPS, LOOKS LIKE THEY'VE TAKEN SOME UNIVERSITY STUDENTS HOSTAGE.
BEAUTIFUL. IS TACTICAL PREPARED TO MOVE IN?
HOSTAGE NEGOTIATIONS IS TRYING TO REACH THEM FIRST, RENEE. SO FAR THERE'S NO ANSWER.
THE MUSEUM'S A MAZE. I WANT TO TRY EVERYTHING ELSE BEFORE WE SEND COPS IN.
I SAW THE SIGNAL. YOU HAD IT REPAIRED.
YES. I ONLY HOPE IT'S NOT A MISTAKE. THERE'RE ALREADY ENOUGH VARIABLES IN THIS SITUATION.
AND AFTER LAST NIGHT I'M WONDERING IF WE'LL EVER SEE HIM. AGAIN.
10

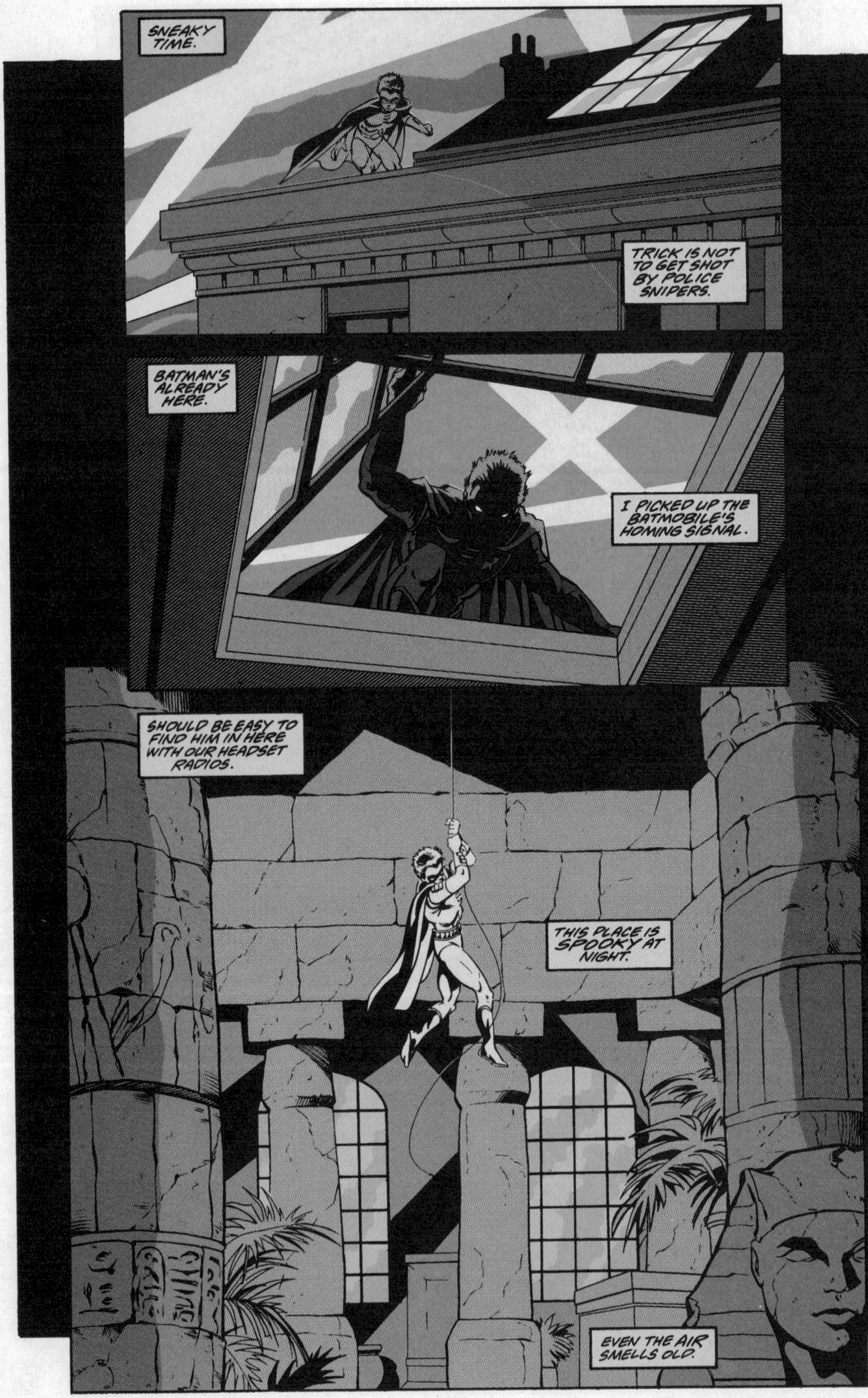
SNEAKY TIME.
TRICK IS NOT TO GET SHOT BY POLICE SNIPERS.
BATMAN'S ALREADY HERE.
I PICKED UP THE BATMOBILE'S HOMING SIGNAL.
SHOULD BE EASY TO FIND HIM IN HERE WITH OUR HEADSET RADIOS.
THIS PLACE IS SPOOKY AT NIGHT.
EVEN THE AIR SMELLS OLD.
11

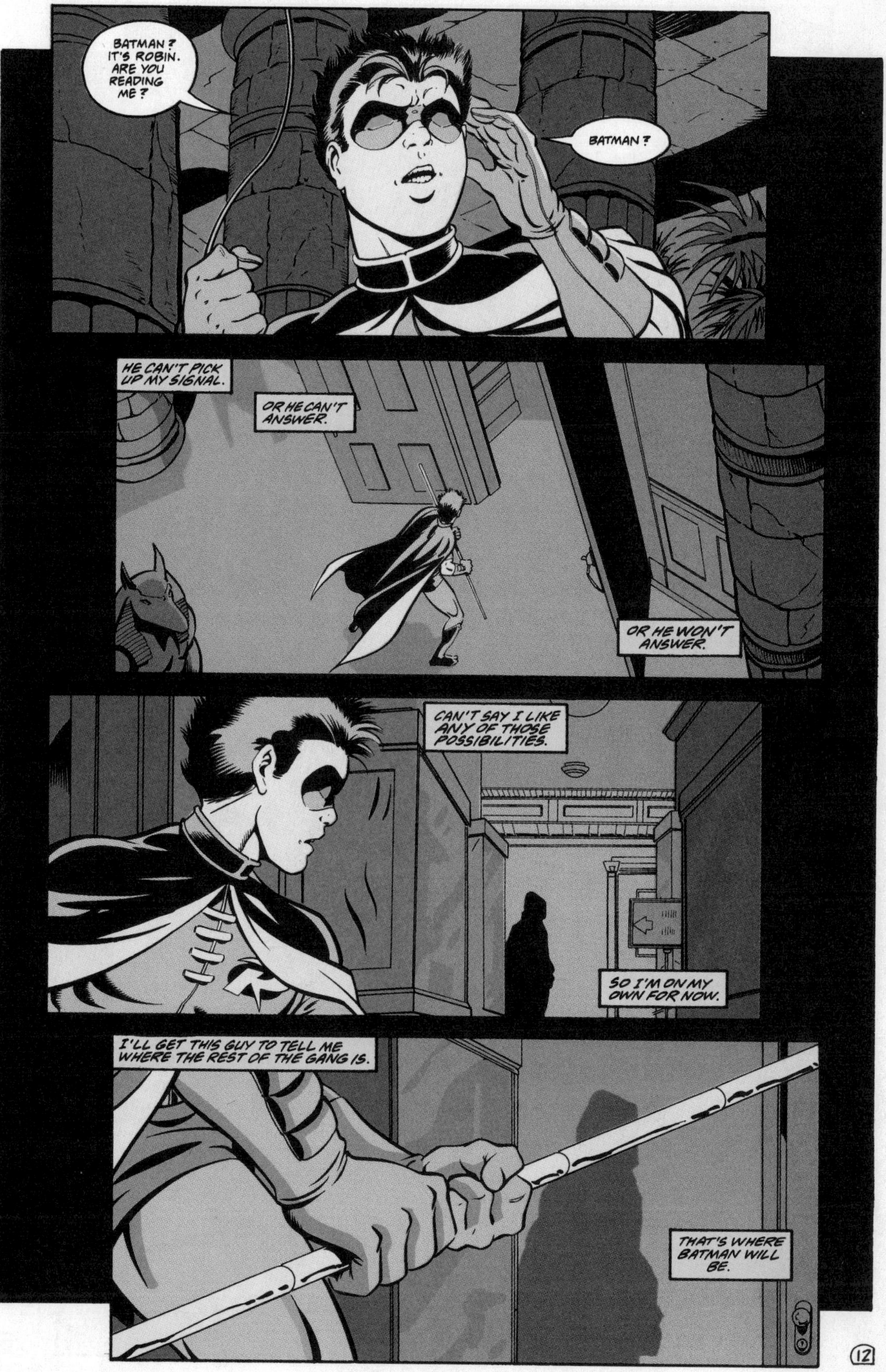
BATMAN? IT'S ROBIN. ARE YOU READING ME?
BATMAN?
HE CAN'T PICK UP MY SIGNAL.
OR HE CAN'T ANSWER.
OR HE WON'T ANSWER.
CAN'T SAY I LIKE ANY OF THOSE POSSIBILITIES.
SO I'M ON MY OWN FOR NOW.
I'LL GET THIS GUY TO TELL ME WHERE THE REST OF THE GANG IS.
THAT'S WHERE BATMAN WILL BE.
12

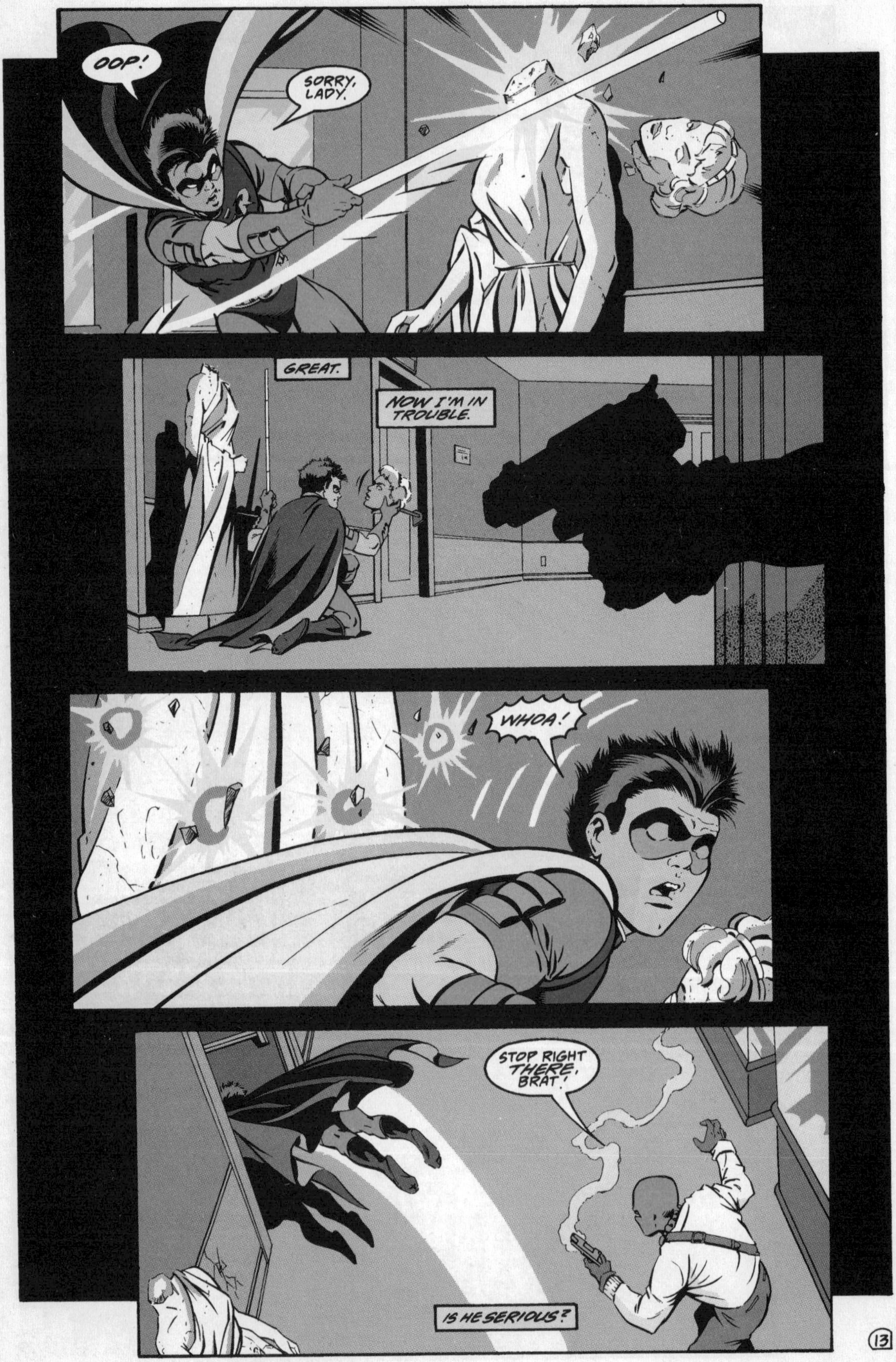
OOP!
SORRY, LADY.
GREAT.
NOW I'M IN TROUBLE.
WHOA!
STOP RIGHT THERE, BRAT!
IS HE SERIOUS?
13

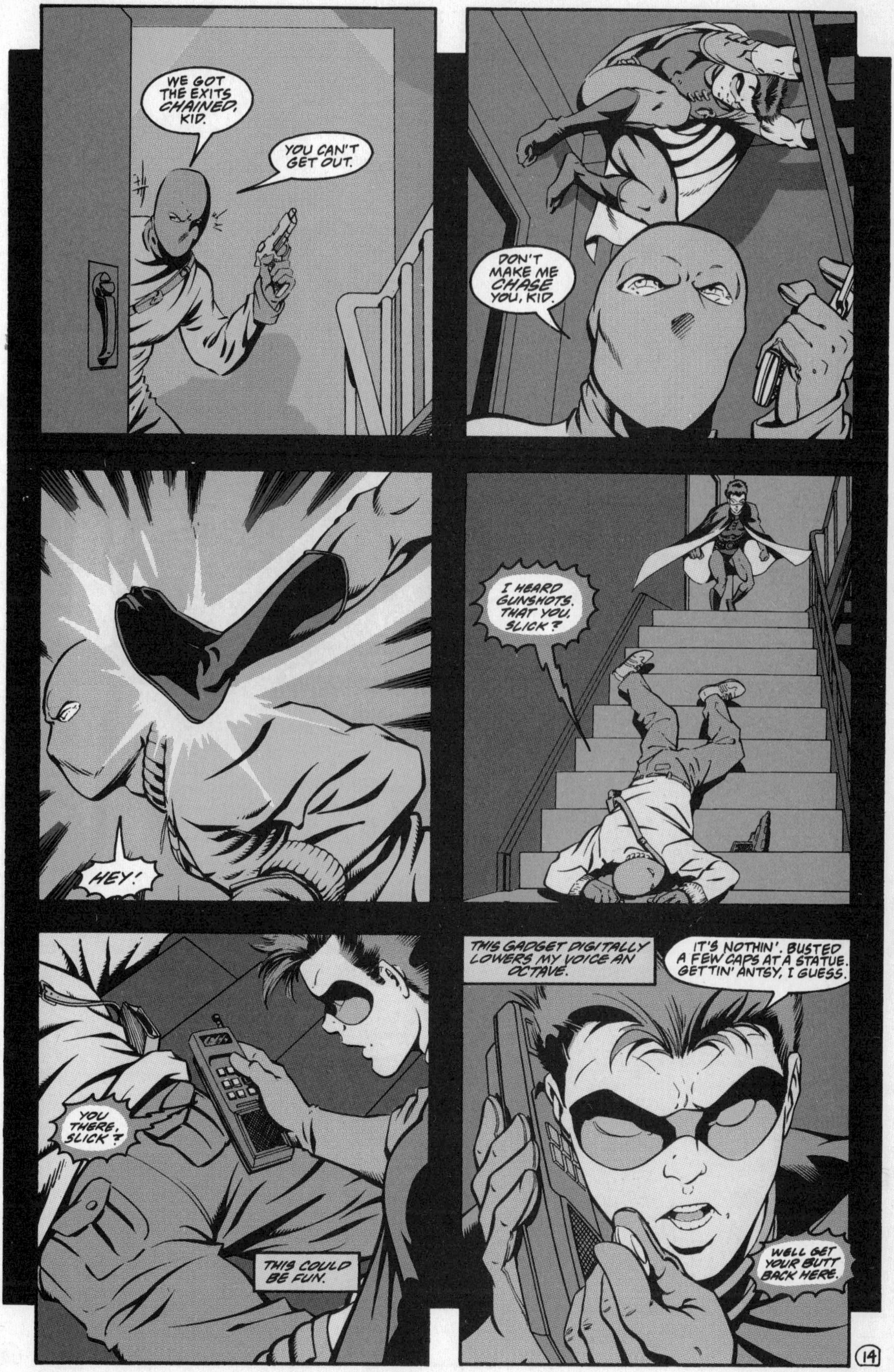
WE GOT THE EXITS CHAINED, KID.
YOU CAN'T GET OUT.
DON'T MAKE ME CHASE YOU, KID.
HEY!
I HEARD GUNSHOTS. THAT YOU, SLICK?
YOU THERE, SLICK?
THIS COULD BE FUN.
THIS GADGET DIGITALLY LOWERS MY VOICE AN OCTAVE.
IT'S NOTHIN'. BUSTED A FEW CAPS AT A STATUE. GETTIN' ANTSY, I GUESS.
WELL GET YOUR BUTT BACK HERE.
14

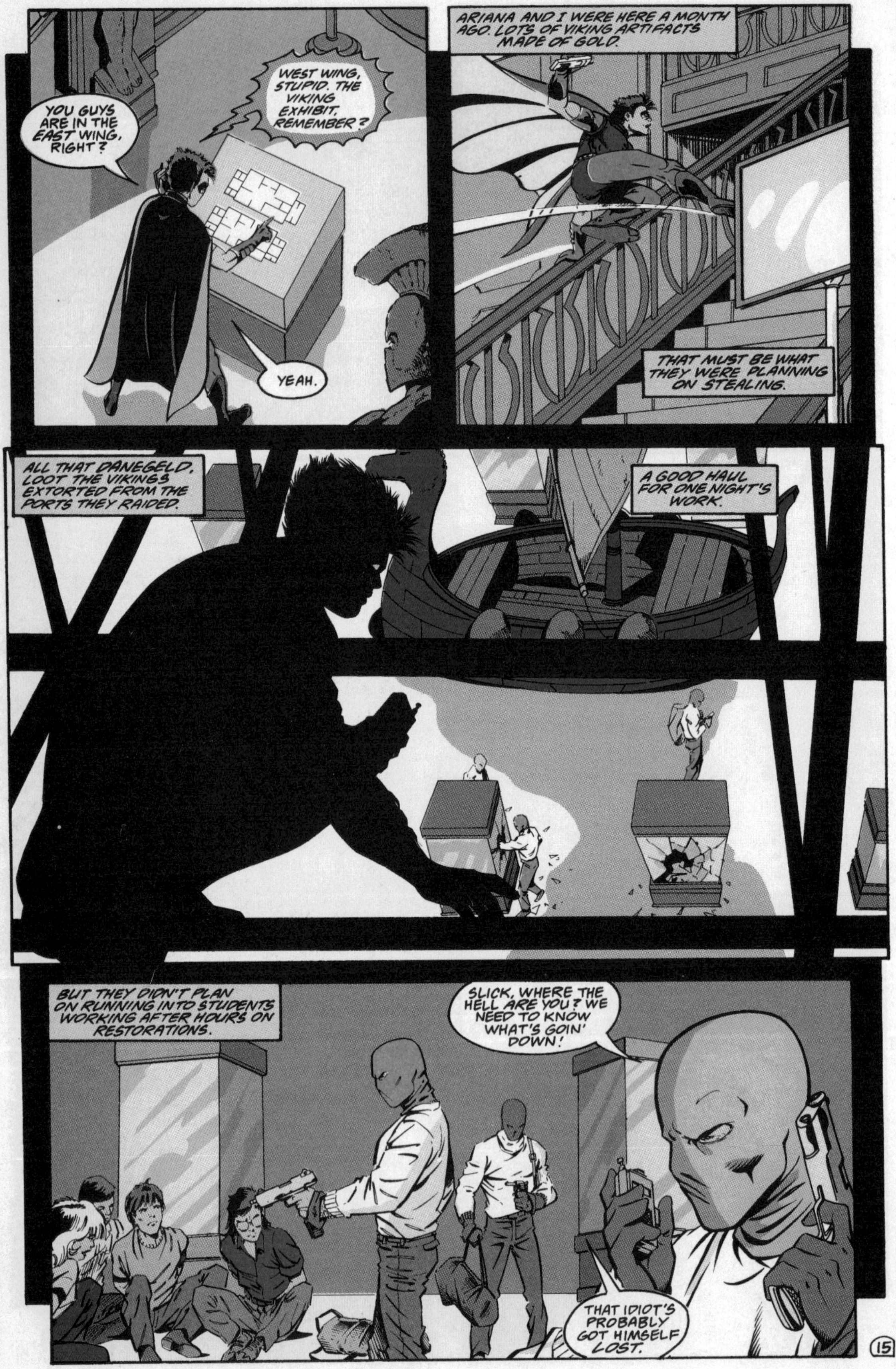
YOU GUYS ARE IN THE EAST WING, RIGHT?
WEST WING, STUPID. THE VIKING EXHIBIT, REMEMBER?
YEAH.
ARIANA AND I WERE HERE A MONTH AGO. LOTS OF VIKING ARTIFACTS MADE OF GOLD.
THAT MUST BE WHAT THEY WERE PLANNING ON STEALING.
ALL THAT DANEGELD, LOOT THE VIKINGS EXTORTED FROM THE PORTS THEY RAIDED.
A GOOD HAUL FOR ONE NIGHT'S WORK.
BUT THEY DIDN'T PLAN ON RUNNING INTO STUDENTS WORKING AFTER HOURS ON RESTORATIONS.
SLICK, WHERE THE HELL ARE YOU? WE NEED TO KNOW WHAT'S GOIN' DOWN!
THAT IDIOT'S PROBABLY GOT HIMSELF LOST.
15

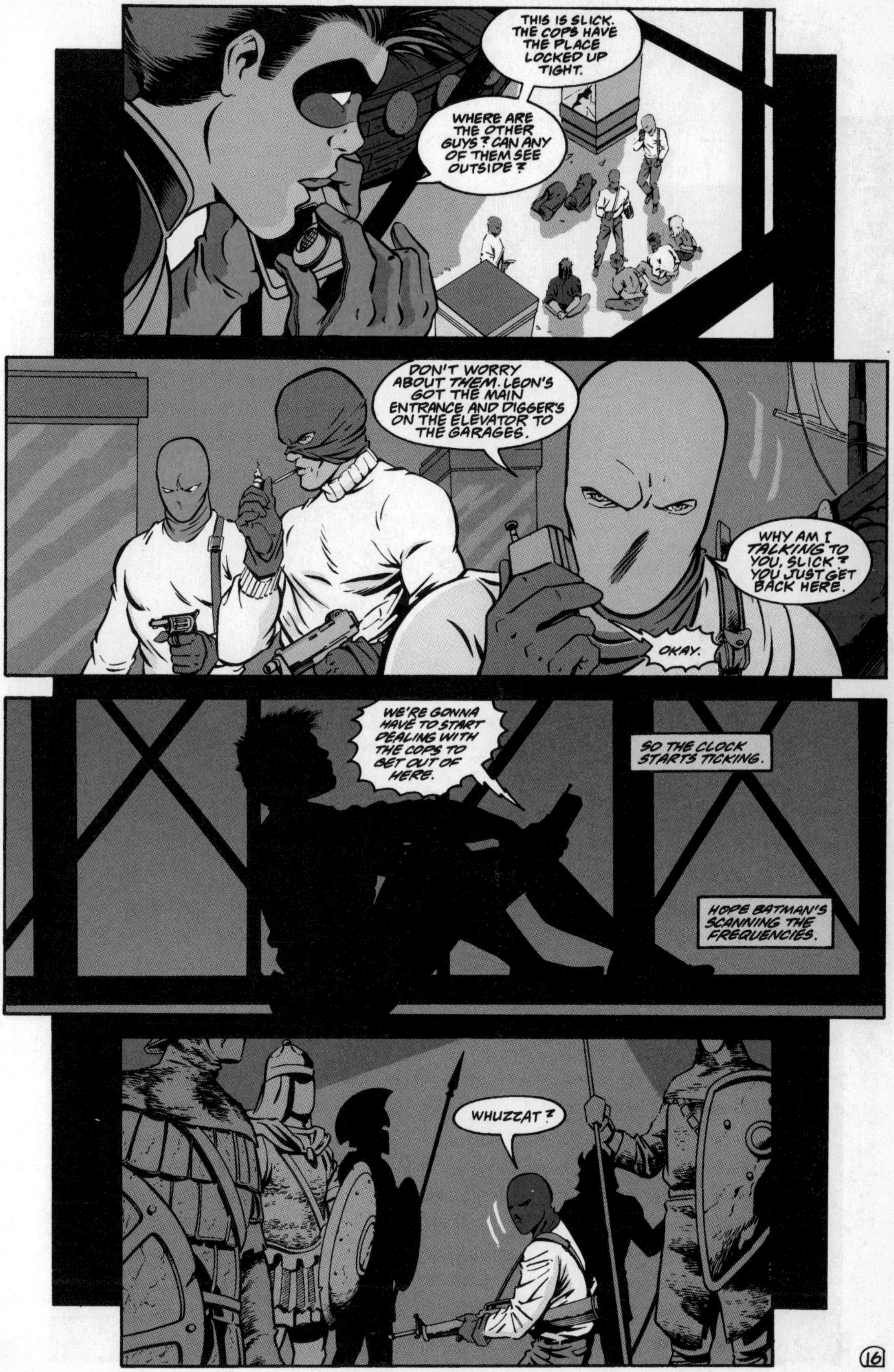
THIS IS SLICK. THE COPS HAVE THE PLACE LOCKED UP TIGHT.
WHERE ARE THE OTHER GUYS? CAN ANY OF THEM SEE OUTSIDE?
DON'T WORRY ABOUT THEM. LEON'S GOT THE MAIN ENTRANCE AND DIGGER'S ON THE ELEVATOR TO THE GARAGES.
WHY AM I TALKING TO YOU, SLICK? YOU JUST GET BACK HERE.
OKAY.
WE'RE GONNA HAVE TO START DEALING WITH THE COPS TO GET OUT OF HERE.
SO THE CLOCK STARTS TICKING.
HOPE BATMAN'S SCANNING THE FREQUENCIES.
WHUZZAT?
16

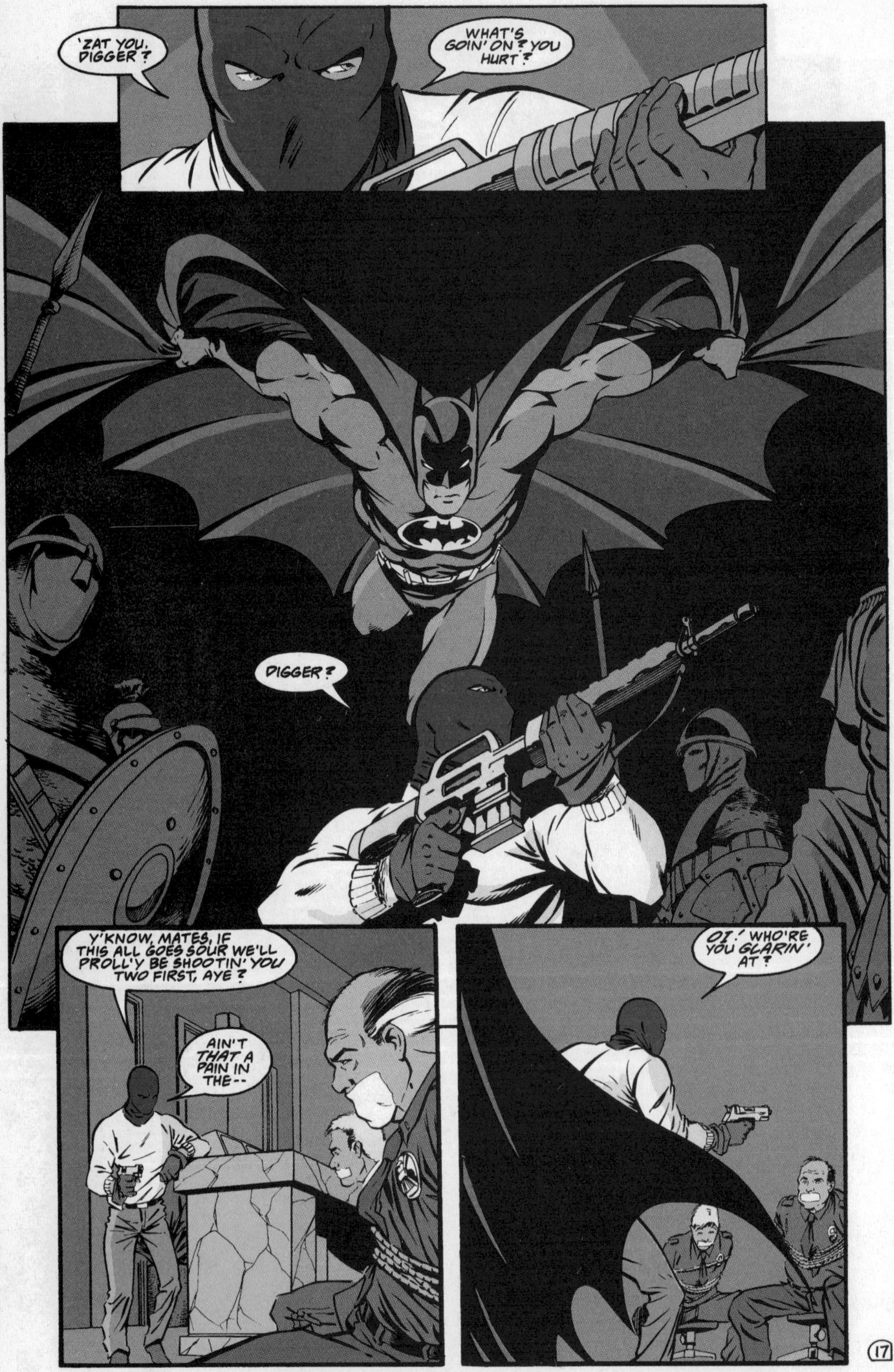
'ZAT YOU, DIGGER?
WHAT'S GOIN' ON? YOU HURT?
DIGGER?
Y'KNOW, MATES, IF THIS ALL GOES SOUR WE'LL PROLL'Y BE SHOOTIN' YOU TWO FIRST, AYE?
AIN'T THAT A PAIN IN THE--
OI! WHO'RE YOU GLARIN' AT?
17

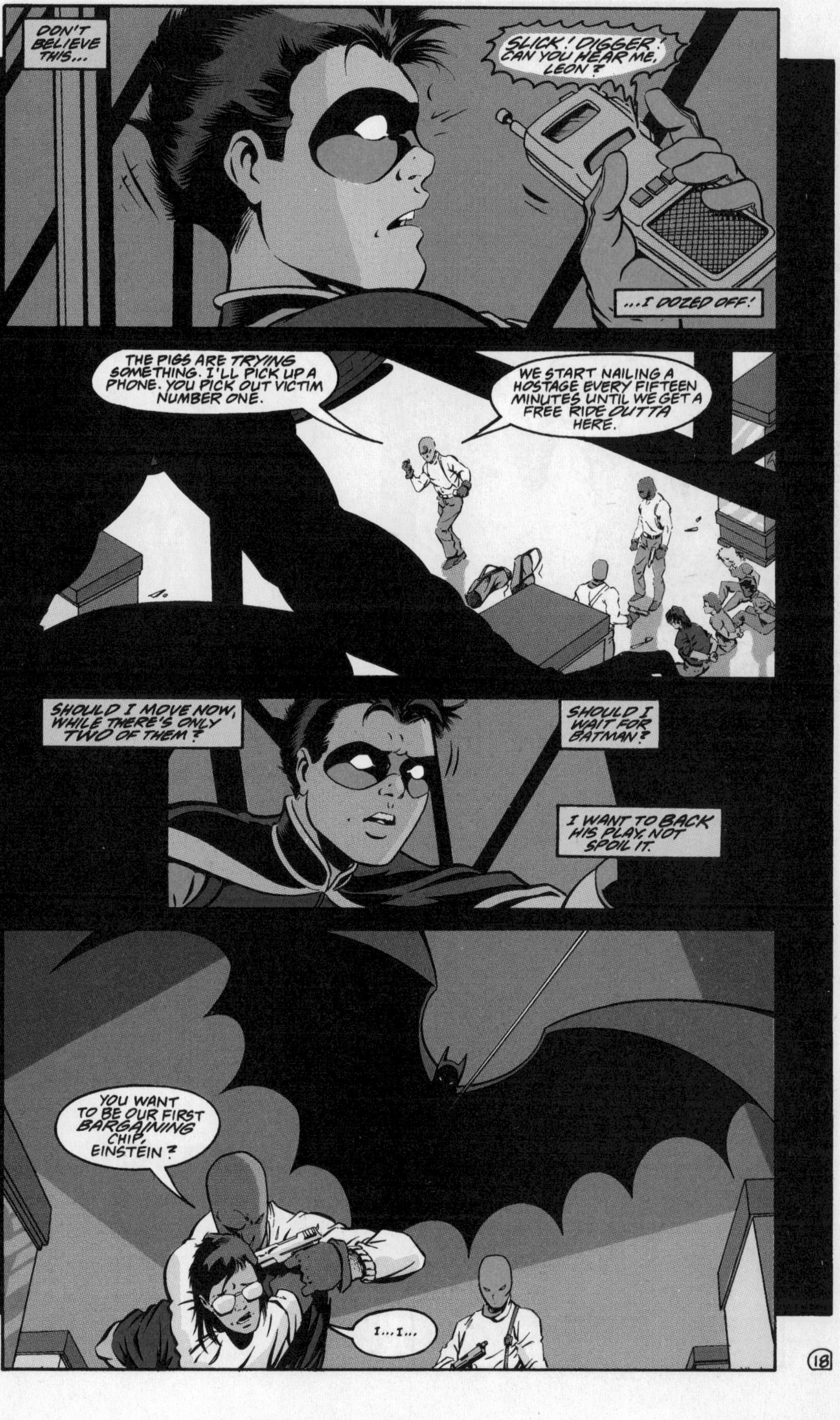
DON'T BELIEVE THIS...
SLICK! DIGGER! CAN YOU HEAR ME, LEON?
...I DOZED OFF!
THE PIGS ARE TRYING SOMETHING. I'LL PICK UP A PHONE. YOU PICK OUT VICTIM NUMBER ONE.
WE START NAILING A HOSTAGE EVERY FIFTEEN MINUTES UNTIL WE GET A FREE RIDE OUTTA HERE.
SHOULD I MOVE NOW, WHILE THERE'S ONLY TWO OF THEM?
SHOULD I WAIT FOR BATMAN?
I WANT TO BACK HIS PLAY, NOT SPOIL IT.
YOU WANT TO BE OUR FIRST BARGAINING CHIP, EINSTEIN?
I...I...
18

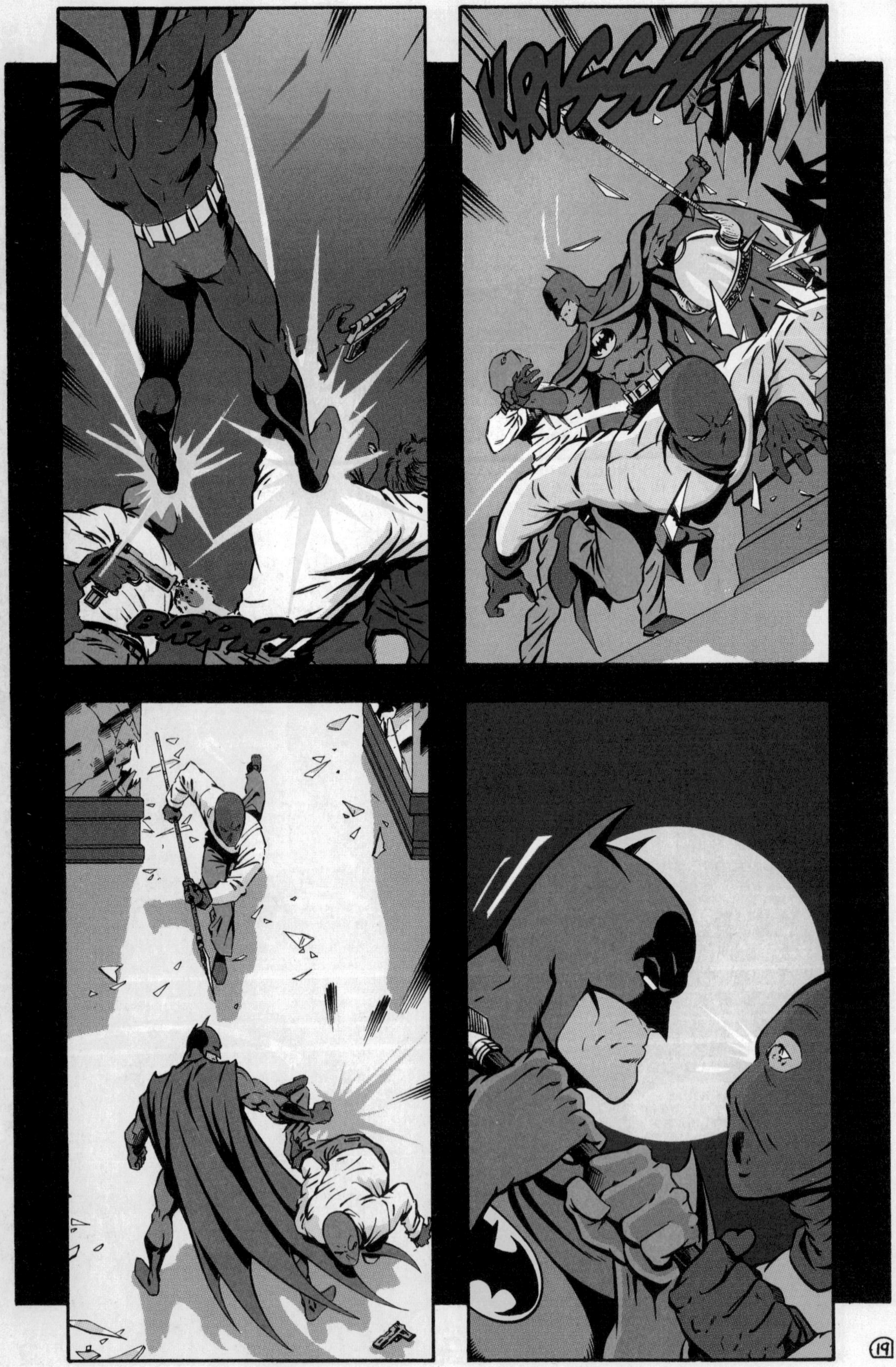
BRRRPT!

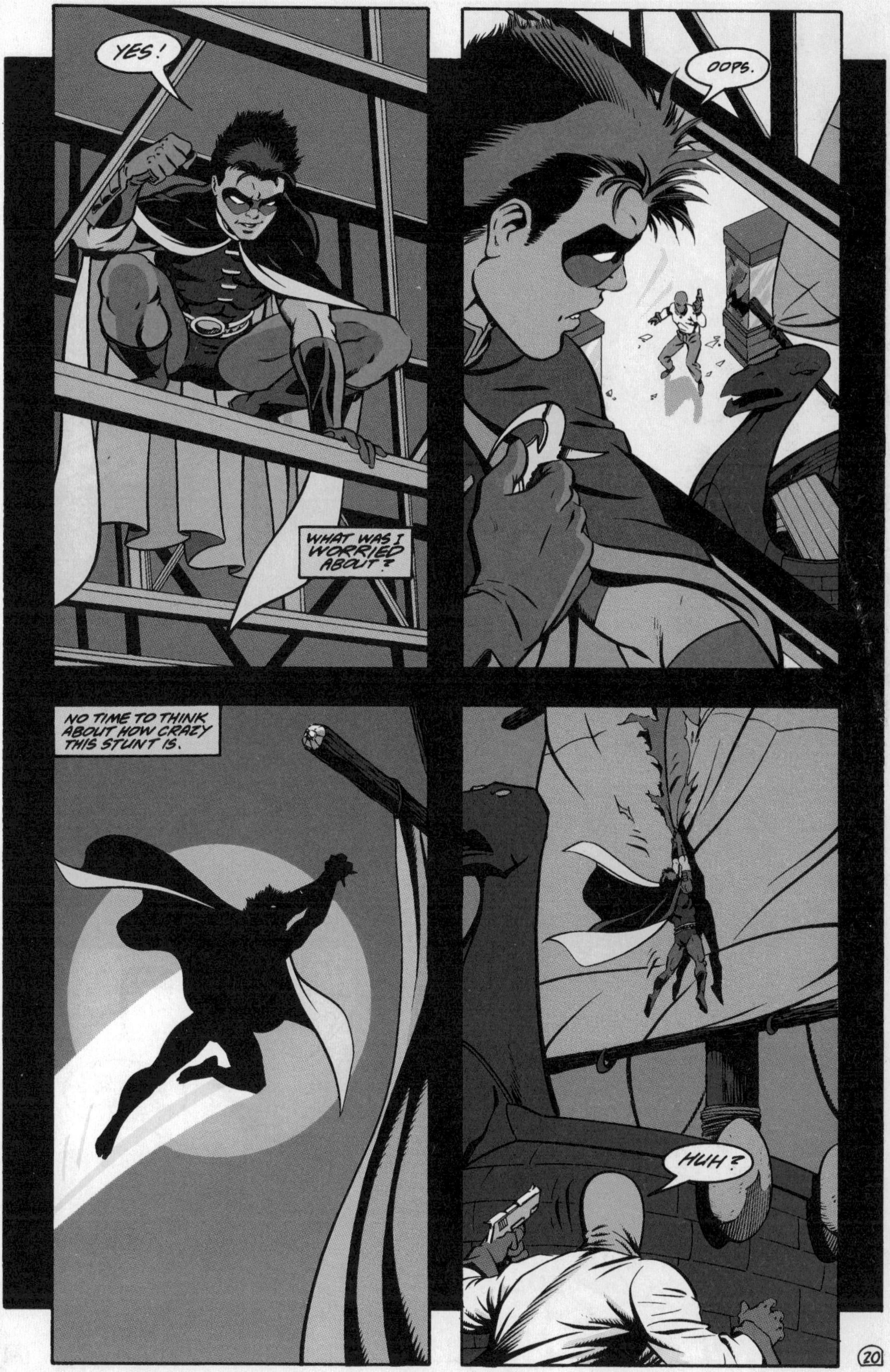
YES!
WHAT WAS I WORRIED ABOUT?
OOPS.
NO TIME TO THINK ABOUT HOW CRAZY THIS STUNT IS.
HUH?
20

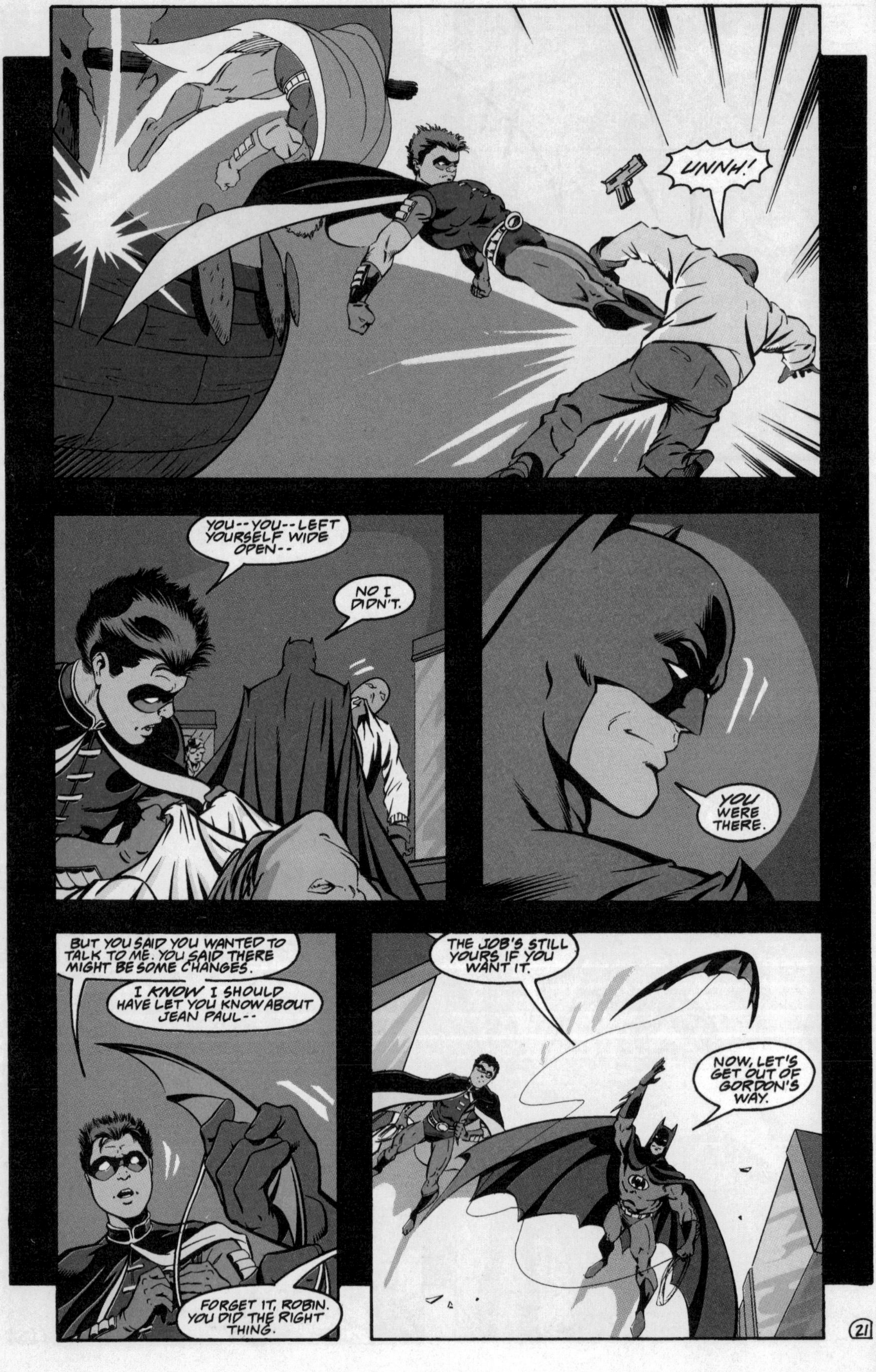
UNNH!
YOU--YOU--LEFT YOURSELF WIDE OPEN--
NO I DIDN'T.
YOU WERE THERE.
BUT YOU SAID YOU WANTED TO TALK TO ME. YOU SAID THERE MIGHT BE SOME CHANGES.
I KNOW I SHOULD HAVE LET YOU KNOW ABOUT JEAN PAUL--
FORGET IT, ROBIN. YOU DID THE RIGHT THING.
THE JOB'S STILL YOURS IF YOU WANT IT.
NOW, LET'S GET OUT OF GORDON'S WAY.
21

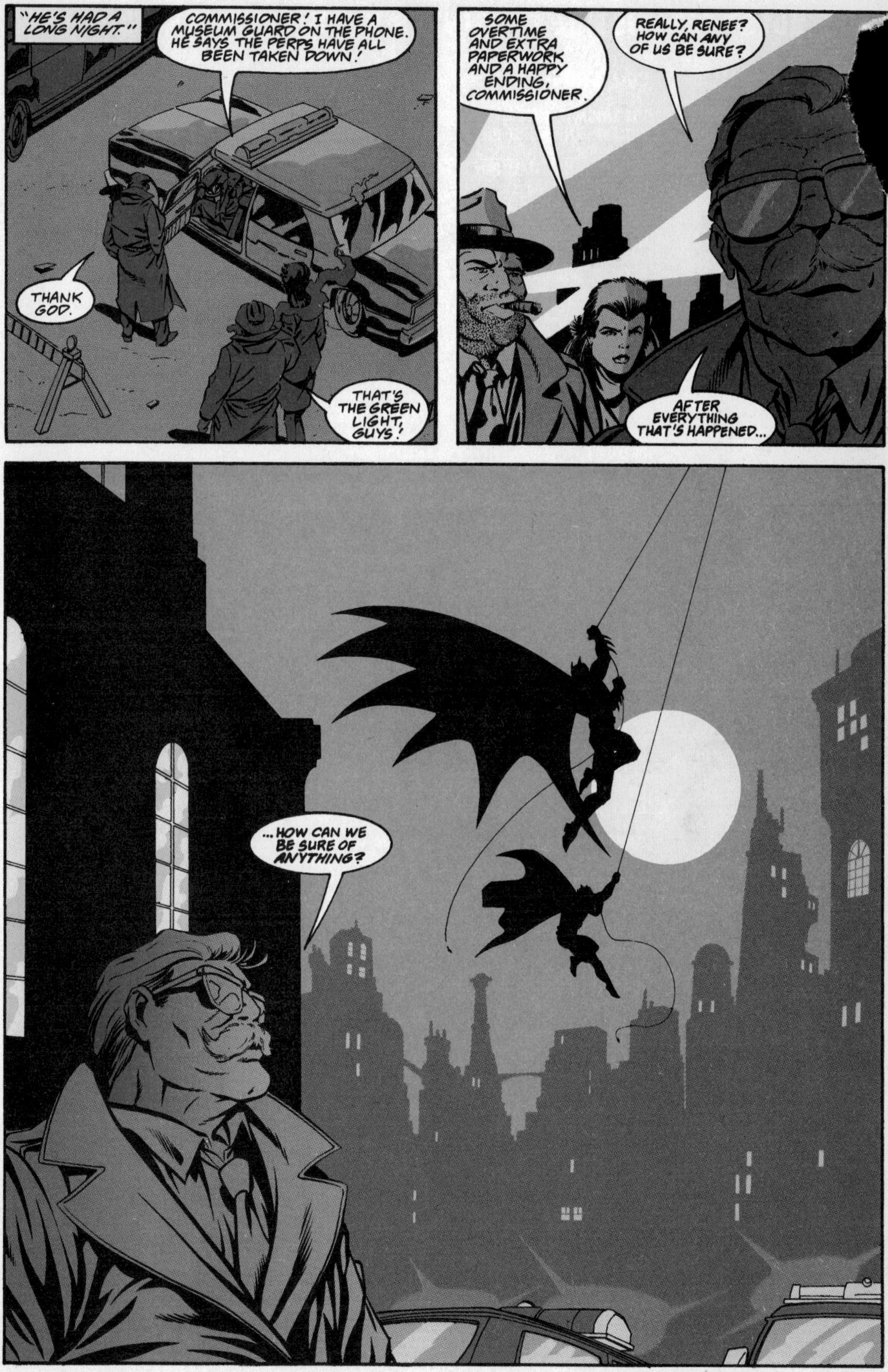
"HE'S HAD A LONG NIGHT."
COMMISSIONER! I HAVE A MUSEUM GUARD ON THE PHONE. HE SAYS THE PERPS HAVE ALL BEEN TAKEN DOWN!
THANK GOD.
THAT'S THE GREEN LIGHT, GUYS!
SOME OVERTIME AND EXTRA PAPERWORK AND A HAPPY ENDING, COMMISSIONER.
REALLY, RENEE? HOW CAN ANY OF US BE SURE?
AFTER EVERYTHING THAT'S HAPPENED...
...HOW CAN WE BE SURE OF ANYTHING?

HE QUEST FOR JUSTICE CONTINUES IN THESE BOOKS FROM DC:

)R READERS OF ALL AGES

HE BATMAN ADVENTURES:
HE LOST YEARS
ilary Bader/Bo Hampton/
erry Beatty

HE BATMAN ADVENTURES
. Puckett/T. Templeton/
. Burchett/various

3ATMAN & SUPERMAN
ADVENTURES: World's Finest
Paul Dini/Joe Staton/
erry Beatty

3ATMAN BEYOND
ilary Bader/Rick Burchett/
arious

3ATMAN: THE DARK KNIGHT
ADVENTURES
Kelley Puckett/Mike Parobeck/
Rick Burchett

3ATMAN: WAR ON CRIME
Paul Dini/Alex Ross

GRAPHIC NOVELS

3ATMAN: ARKHAM ASYLUM
Suggested for mature readers
Grant Morrison/Dave McKean

3ATMAN: FORTUNATE SON
Gerard Jones/Gene Ha

3ATMAN: THE KILLING JOKE
Suggested for mature readers
Alan Moore/Brian Bolland/
John Higgins

HE BATMAN ADVENTURES:
MAD LOVE
Paul Dini/Bruce Timm

3ATMAN: NIGHT CRIES
Archie Goodwin/Scott Hampton

3ATMAN: BLOODSTORM
Doug Moench/Kelley Jones/
John Beatty

3ATMAN: CRIMSON MIST
Doug Moench/Kelley Jones/
John Beatty

3ATMAN: THE CHALICE
Chuck Dixon/John Van Fleet

3ATMAN/DEADMAN:
DEATH AND GLORY
James Robinson/John Estes

3ATMAN/DRACULA: RED RAIN
Doug Moench/Kelley Jones/
Malcolm Jones III

3ATMAN: SON OF THE DEMON
Mike Barr/Jerry Bingham

COLLECTIONS

THE KNIGHTFALL Trilogy
BATMAN: KNIGHTFALL Part 1:
Broken Bat
BATMAN: KNIGHTFALL Part 2:
Who Rules the Night
BATMAN: KNIGHTFALL Part 3:
KnightsEnd
Various writers and artists

BATMAN: ANARKY
Alan Grant/Norm Breyfogle/
various

BATMAN: A DEATH IN
THE FAMILY
Jim Starlin/Jim Aparo/
Mike DeCarlo

BATMAN: A LONELY PLACE
OF DYING
Marv Wolfman/George Pérez/
various

BATMAN BLACK AND WHITE
Various writers and artists

BATMAN: CATACLYSM
Various writers and artists

BATMAN: COLLECTED LEGENDS
OF THE DARK KNIGHT
J. Robinson/J.F. Moore/
A. Grant/T. Sale/C. Russell/
K. O'Neill

BATMAN: THE DARK KNIGHT
RETURNS
10TH ANNIVERSARY EDITION
Frank Miller/Klaus Janson/
Lynn Varley

BATMAN: DARK KNIGHT
DYNASTY
M. Barr/S. Hampton/G. Frank/
S. McDaniels/various

BATMAN: DARK LEGENDS
Various writers and artists

BATMAN: FACES
Matt Wagner

BATMAN: FEATURING
TWO-FACE AND THE RIDDLER
Various writers and artists

BATMAN: FOUR OF A KIND
Various writers and artists

BATMAN: GOTHIC
Grant Morrison/Klaus Janson

BATMAN: HAUNTED KNIGHT
Jeph Loeb/Tim Sale

BATMAN IN THE SIXTIES
Various writers and artists

BATMAN IN THE SEVENTIES
Various writers and artists

BATMAN: THE LONG HALLOWEEN
Jeph Loeb/Tim Sale

BATMAN: MANBAT
Jamie Delano/John Bolton

BATMAN: NO MAN'S LAND
VOL. 1
B. Gale/D. Grayson/
A. Maleev/D. Eaglesham/
W. Faucher

BATMAN: NO MAN'S LAND
VOL. 2
Various writers and artists

BATMAN: OTHER REALMS
Mark Kneece/Bo Hampton/
Scott Hampton

BATMAN: PRODIGAL
Various writers and artists

BATMAN: SHAMAN
Dennis O'Neil/Ed Hannigan/
John Beatty

BATMAN: STRANGE
APPARITIONS
S. Englehart/M. Rogers/
T. Austin/various

BATMAN: SWORD OF AZRAEL
Dennis O'Neil/Joe Quesada/
Kevin Nowlan

BATMAN: TALES OF THE DEMON
Dennis O'Neil/Neal Adams/
various

BATMAN: THE MOVIES
Dennis O'Neil/various

BATMAN: THRILLKILLER
Howard Chaykin/Dan Brereton

BATMAN: VENOM
Dennis O'Neil/Trevor Von Eeden/
various

BATMAN VS. PREDATOR:
THE COLLECTED EDITION
Dave Gibbons/Andy Kubert/
Adam Kubert

BATMAN VS. PREDATOR II:
BLOODMATCH
Doug Moench/Paul Gulacy/
Terry Austin

BATMAN VS. PREDATOR III:
BLOOD TIES
Chuck Dixon/Rodolfo Damaggio/
Robert Campanella

BATMAN: YEAR ONE
Frank Miller/David Mazzucchelli

THE GREATEST BATMAN
STORIES EVER TOLD Vol. 1
Various writers and artists

THE GREATEST JOKER
STORIES EVER TOLD
Various writers and artists

CATWOMAN: THE CATFILE
Chuck Dixon/Jim Balent/
Bob Smith

NIGHTWING: ROUGH JUSTICE
Chuck Dixon/Scott McDaniels/
Karl Story

NIGHTWING: TIES THAT BIND
Dennis O'Neil/Alan Grant/
various

NIGHTWING: A KNIGHT
IN BLÜDHAVEN
Chuck Dixon/Scott McDaniel/
Karl Story

ROBIN: A HERO REBORN
Chuck Dixon/Tom Lyle/
Bob Smith

ARCHIVE EDITIONS

BATMAN ARCHIVES Vol. 1
(DETECTIVE COMICS 27-50)
BATMAN ARCHIVES Vol. 2
(DETECTIVE COMICS 51-70)
BATMAN ARCHIVES Vol. 3
(DETECTIVE COMICS 71-86)
BATMAN ARCHIVES Vol. 4
(DETECTIVE COMICS 87-102)
All by B. Kane/B. Finger/D. Sprang/
various

BATMAN: THE DARK KNIGHT
ARCHIVES Vol. 1
(BATMAN 1-4)
BATMAN: THE DARK KNIGHT
ARCHIVES Vol. 2
(BATMAN 5-8)
All by Bob Kane/Bill Finger/various

WORLD'S FINEST COMICS
ARCHIVES Vol. 1
(SUPERMAN 76,
WORLD'S FINEST 71-85)
B. Finger/E. Hamilton/C. Swan/
various

TO FIND MORE COLLECTED EDITIONS AND MONTHLY COMIC BOOKS FROM DC COMICS,
CALL 1-888-COMIC BOOK FOR THE NEAREST COMICS SHOP OR GO TO YOUR LOCAL BOOK STORE